CORINNE FENNESSY

READING for LIFE

SECOND EDITION

PEARSON

Boston Columbus Indianapolis New York San Francisco Upper Saddle River
Amsterdam Cape Town Dubai London Madrid Milan Munich Paris Montréal Toronto
Delhi Mexico City São Paulo Sydney Hong Kong Seoul Singapore Taipei Tokyo

PEARSON

Editor in Chief: Eric Stano
Editorial Assistant: Jamie Fortner
Senior Development Editor: David Kear
Director of Marketing: Roxanne McCarley
Senior Supplements Editor: Donna Campion
Executive Digital Producer: Stefanie A. Snajder
Digital Editor: Sara Gordus
Digital Content Specialist: Julia Pomann
Production Manager: Ellen MacElree
Project Coordination and Electronic Page Makeup: Integra
Cover Designer/Manager: Wendy Ann Fredericks
Cover Photo: © Nugene Chiang/AsiaPix/Corbis
Senior Manufacturing Buyer: Roy L. Pickering, Jr.
Printer/Binder: Courier/Kendallville
Cover Printer: Lehigh-Phoenix Color/Hagerstown

Design Development and Art Direction: Anthony Limerick
Design Director: Stuart Jackman
Publisher: Sophie Mitchell

Credits and acknowledgments borrowed from other sources, and reproduced, with permission, in this textbook appear on pages 495–497.

Library of Congress Cataloging-in-Publication Data
Fennessy, Corinne.
Reading for life/Corinne Fennessy.—Second edition.
pages cm
Includes bibliographical references and index.
ISBN 978-0-205-91036-6
1. Reading (Higher education) 2. College readers. 3. College students—Books and reading. 4. Study skills. I. Title.
LB1050.F39 2014
428.4—dc23

2013039279

10 9 8 7 6 5—V0UD—19 18 17 16 15

www.pearsonhighered.com

Student ISBN-13: 978-0-205-91036-6
Student ISBN-10: 0-205-91036-X
A la Carte ISBN-13: 978-0-321-96671-1
A la Carte ISBN-10: 0-321-96671-6

CHAPTER

1 PLAN TO SUCCEED

LEARNING STRATEGIES

Teamwork: Getting to Know Your Classmates 3

Setting Goals 3

Time Management: Building a Study Schedule 6

"Something's Gotta Give" 6

Daily Planners 7

MyReadingLab 10

What Is in MyReadingLab? 10

Organizing Your Notebook 11

U-Review 14

CHAPTER REVIEW

Study Skill Review 15

Reading Lab Assignments 16

Learning Reflection 16

Self-Evaluation Checklist 17

CHAPTER 2 THE FOUR-STEP READING PROCESS

FOCUS ON: Health Sciences 18

LEARNING STRATEGIES

The Four-Step Reading Process 19
Step 1: Preview Before You Read 20
Practice Previewing 21
Step 2: Read Actively 22
Step 3: Highlight and Annotate 22
Chunking Information 23
Step 4: Review 25
Practices 26
Textbook Selection 30
U-Review 32

READING SELECTIONS

READING 1
Vocabulary Preview 33
Preview 34
"FLIGHT NURSE HERO"
Corinne Fennessy 35
Review 38
Comprehension Questions 38
Vocabulary Practice 40
Questions for Writing and Discussion 41
Vocabulary Practice— Crossword 42

READING 2
Vocabulary Preview 43
Preview 44
"FROM ILLEGAL IMMIGRANT TO BRAIN SURGEON: DR. ALFREDO QUIÑONES"
C.F. Hopkins 45
Review 48
Comprehension Questions 48
Vocabulary Practice 50
Questions for Writing and Discussion 51
Vocabulary Practice— Word Maze 52

READING FOR LIFE

On the Job Interview
Arethea Moise, Registered Nurse 53
Watch the Video: "Twitter-ITIS: Online Medical Advice" 53
Real-Life Reading
Living Will 54
Textbook Graphic Aids 56
Building Vocabulary 57

CHAPTER REVIEW

Chapter Practices 57
Textbook Practice 62
Study Skill Review 64
Reading Lab Assignments 64
Learning Reflection 65
Self-Evaluation Checklist 65

CHAPTER 3

VOCABULARY SKILLS

FOCUS ON: Law Enforcement, Corrections, Fire Science, and EMT Services 66

LEARNING STRATEGIES

Using Context Clues to Determine Word Meanings 67
- Studying Vocabulary 69
- Practices 70
- Textbook Selection 73
- U-Review 74

Word Parts: Prefixes, Roots, and Suffixes 75
- Tips to Keep in Mind 75
- Tables of Prefixes, Roots, and Suffixes 76
- Practices 79
- U-Review 80

READING SELECTIONS

READING 1
- Vocabulary Preview 80
- Preview 81

"DANGEROUS DUTY" Corinne Fennessy 82
- Review 84
- Comprehension Questions 84
- Vocabulary Practice 86
- Questions for Writing and Discussion 87
- Vocabulary Practice 88

READING 2
- Vocabulary Preview 89
- Preview 90

"LEAP OF FAITH" Mike Santangelo, Mara Bovsun, and Allan Zullo 91
- Review 94
- Comprehension Questions 94
- Vocabulary Practice 96
- Questions for Writing and Discussion 97
- Vocabulary Practice 98
- Vocabulary Practice—Puzzle Grid 99

READING FOR LIFE

Real-Life Reading
- Drug Testing Consent Form 100

On the Job Interview
- Lieutenant David Scott, Pepperell (Massachusetts) Police Department 102
- Watch the Video: Controversial Sting Operation to Stop Apple iPhone Thieves 102

Textbook Graphic Aids 103

Building Vocabulary 104

CHAPTER REVIEW

Chapter Practices 105

Textbook Practice 108

Study Skill Review 110

Reading Lab Assignments 111

Learning Reflection 111

Staying on Track 112

Self-Evaluation Checklist 113

CHAPTER 4 TOPICS AND STATED MAIN IDEAS

FOCUS ON: **Business and Personal Finance** 114

LEARNING STRATEGIES

Topics, Stated Main Ideas, and Topic Sentences 115
How to Find the Topic 115
Getting the Specific Topic 116
Specific versus General Topics 116
Practices 118
Textbook Selection 119
U-Review 119
Stated Main Ideas 120
The Main Idea Is a Key 121
Main Idea Styles 121
Main Ideas and Inferences 122
Stated Main Idea: Checking Your Answer 123
Practices 123
Where to Find the Topic Sentence 124
Topic Sentence at the Beginning 124
Topic Sentence at the End 124
Topic Sentence in the Middle 124
Topic Sentences in the First and Last Sentences 125
Practices 125
Textbook Selection 130
U-Review 131

READING SELECTIONS

READING 1
Vocabulary Preview 132
Preview 133
"ESCAPING THE DEBT TRAP"
Corinne Fennessy 134
Review 136
Comprehension Questions 137
Vocabulary Practice 139
Questions for Writing and Discussion 140
Vocabulary Practice—Matching 141

READING 2
Vocabulary Preview 142
Preview 143
"GETTING THE JOB OF YOUR DREAMS"
Corinne Fennessy 144
Review 146
Comprehension Questions 147
Vocabulary Practice 148
Questions for Writing and Discussion 149
Vocabulary Practice—Team Password 150

READING FOR LIFE

On the Job Interview
Adam Metzinger, Trust Administrator 151
Watch the Video: College Students and Credit Cards 151
Real-Life Reading
Credit Card Agreement 152
Building Vocabulary 154
Textbook Graphic Aids 155

CHAPTER REVIEW

Chapter Practices 156
Textbook Practice 159
Study Skill Review 160
Reading Lab Assignments 162
Learning Reflection 162
Self-Evaluation Checklist 163

CHAPTER

5 SUPPORTING DETAILS

FOCUS ON: **Hospitality and Tourism** 164

LEARNING STRATEGIES

Major and Minor Details and Transitions 165
When Details Do Not Support 166
Practices 167
Major and Minor Details 168
Major Supporting Details 168
Minor Supporting Details 169
How Supporting Details Work 169
Transitions 170
Practices 171
Textbook Selection 175
U-Review 176

Concept Mapping 177
Practices 179
Textbook Selection 182
U-Review 183

READING SELECTIONS

READING 1
Vocabulary Preview 184
Preview 185
"LET'S TALK ABOUT YOUR LIFE, SON"
Bobby Flay 186
Review 189
Comprehension Questions 190
Vocabulary Practice 192
Questions for Writing and Discssion 193
Vocabulary Practice—Speed Quiz 194
Supporting Deatils Chart 195

READING 2
Vocabulary Preview 196
Preview 197
"STUDENT TRAVEL—SEE THE WORLD!"
Corinne Fennessy 198
Review 200
Comprehension Questions 200
Vocabulary Practice 202
Questions for Writing and Discussion 203
Vocabulary Practice—Crossword 204

READING FOR LIFE

On the Job Interview
Chef Nora Galdiano 205
Watch the Video: Chef Bobby Flay 205
Real-Life Reading
Health Insurance Policy 206
Textbook Graphic Aids 208
Building Vocabulary 209

CHAPTER REVIEW

Chapter Practices 210
Textbook Practice 214
Study Skill Review 215
Reading Lab Assignments 216
Learning Reflection 216
Self-Evaluation Checklist 217

CHAPTER 6 DRAWING CONCLUSIONS

FOCUS ON: **Sociology and Education** 218

LEARNING STRATEGIES

Drawing Conclusions 219
Drawing Conclusions from a Photo 220
How to Draw Logical Conclusions 220
Sweeping Generalizations or Absolute Statements 221
Practices 222
Textbook Selection 225
U-Review 227

READING SELECTIONS

READING 1
Vocabulary Preview 228
Preview 229
"COLLEGE DRINKING: HARMLESS FUN?" Corinne Fennessy 230
Review 232
Comprehension Questions 233
Vocabulary Practice 235
Questions for Writing and Discssion 236
Team Activity —Speed Quiz 237

READING 2
Vocabulary Preview 238
Preview 240
"WHERE WISHES COME TRUE" Corinne Fennessy 240
Review 243
Comprehension Questions 244
Vocabulary Practice 246
Questions for Writing and Discussion 247
Vocabulary Practice—Crossword 248

READING FOR LIFE

On the Job Interview
Kim Walter, High School Chemistry Teacher 249
Watch the Video: High Fashion, Deadly Factories 249
Real-Life Reading
Applying for Student Financial Aid 250
Building Vocabulary 252
Textbook Graphic Aids 253

CHAPTER REVIEW

Chapter Practices 254
Textbook Practice 257
Study Skill Review 259
Reading Lab Assignments 260
Learning Reflection 260
Self-Evaluation Checklist 261

CHAPTER 7

IMPLIED MAIN IDEAS AND CENTRAL POINT

FOCUS ON: The Arts and Related Fields 262

LEARNING STRATEGIES

Implied Main Ideas 263
- Practices 264
- Textbook Selection 267
- U-Review 268

Recognizing Stated Main Ideas and Implied Main Ideas 268
- Practices 270
- Textbook Selection 273

The Central Point 274
- Practices 275
- Textbook Selection 279
- U-Review 280

READING SELECTIONS

READING 1
- Vocabulary Preview 281
- Preview 282

"MY BEST ROLE EVER!"
Marcia Gay Harden 282
- Review 285
- Comprehension Questions 285
- Vocabulary Practice 287
- Questions for Writing and Discussion 288
- Vocabulary Practice—Drawing Word Game 289

READING 2
- Vocabulary Preview 290
- Preview 291

"FROM SKETCH TO SCREEN: TIM BURTON" 292
- Review 295
- Comprehension Questions 295
- Vocabulary Practice 297
- Questions for Writing and Discussion 298
- Vocabulary Practice—Crossword 299

READING FOR LIFE

On the Job Interview
- Meaghan Girouard, Graphic Artist 300
- Watch the Video: African Orphan Now Ballerina 300

Building Vocabulary 301

Real-Life Reading
- Car Leasing Agreements 302

Textbook Graphic Aids 304

CHAPTER REVIEW

Chapter Practices 306

Textbook Practice 309

Study Skill Review 311

Reading Lab Assignments 312

Learning Reflection 312

Self-Evaluation Checklist 313

CHAPTER

8 PATTERNS OF ORGANIZATION

FOCUS ON: **Sports and Fitness** 314

LEARNING STRATEGIES

Patterns of Organization 315

Transition Words and Phrases 316

Relationships within and Between Sentences 316

Definition Pattern 317

Listing Pattern 318

Cause-and-Effect Pattern 319

Compare-and-Contrast Pattern 320

Time Order (Chronological Order) Pattern 321

Practices 322

Textbook Selection 325

U-Review 327

Recognizing Overall Patterns of Organization 328

Practices 329

Textbook Selection 332

U-Review 333

READING SELECTIONS

READING 1

Vocabulary Preview 334

Preview 335

"DANGEROUSLY STRONG"
Elizabeth Foy Larsen 335

Review 339

Comprehension Questions 340

Vocabulary Practice 342

Questions for Writing and Discussion 343

Vocabulary Practice—Concentration Game 344

READING 2

Vocabulary Preview 345

Preview 346

"TRUE GRIT: BETHANY HAMILTON'S STORY"
Margy Rochlin 347

Review 349

Comprehension Questions 350

Vocabulary Practice 352

Questions for Writing and Discussion 353

Vocabulary Practice 354

READING FOR LIFE

On the Job Interview

Rick Muhr, Coach and Consultant 355

Watch the Video: Five Power Foods 355

Real-Life Reading

Refund and Repayment Policy 356

Building Vocabulary 358

Textbook Graphic Aids 359

CHAPTER REVIEW

Chapter Practices 360

Textbook Practice 364

Study Skill Review 366

Reading Lab Assignments 368

Learning Reflection 368

Self-Evaluation Checklist 369

CHAPTER

9 CRITICAL READING AND THINKING

FOCUS ON: Science 370

LEARNING STRATEGIES

Critical Reading and Thinking 371
Fact and Opinion 371
- Words That Signal Opinion 372
- Judgment Words in Opinions 372
- Sentences with Both Fact and Opinion 373
- Is It Wrong to Use Opinions in Writing? 373
- Can It Be Proved? 374
- Practices 374
- Textbook Selection 376
- U-Review 376

Author's Purpose 376
Author's Tone 378
- Tone Words 379

Author's Intended Audience 380
- Practices 381
- Textbook Selection 384
- U-Review 385

READING SELECTIONS

READING 1
- Vocabulary Preview 386
- Preview 388

"OPERATION SEAL RESCUE" Monica Rozenfeld 388
- Review 391
- Comprehension Questions 391
- Vocabulary Practice 393
- Questions for Writing and Discussion 394
- Vocabulary Practice—Concentration Game 395

READING 2
- Vocabulary Preview 396
- Preview 398

"A GREENER EARTH: ENERGY ALTERNATIVES" Corinne Fennessy 398
- Review 401
- Comprehension Questions 401
- Vocabulary Practice 403
- Questions for Writing and Discussion 404
- Vocabulary Practice—Guess the Phrase 405

READING FOR LIFE

On the Job Interview
- Dr. Scott Gearhart, Veterinarian at Sea World, Orlando, Florida 406
- Watch the Video: Bone Collector Solves Cold Cases 406

Building Vocabulary 407
Real-Life Reading
- Nutrition Labels 408

Textbook Graphic Aids 410

CHAPTER REVIEW

Chapter Practices 412
Textbook Practice 415
Study Skill Review 417
Reading Lab Assignments 418
Learning Reflection 418
Self-Evaluation Checklist 419

CHAPTER 10 STUDY SKILLS

FOCUS ON: Technology 420

LEARNING STRATEGIES

Paraphrasing and Summarizing 421
Paraphrasing 421
Summarizing 423
Taking Effective Notes 424
What to Write 426
Outlining 427
Outline of the Paragraph 428
Practice Outlining 429
Taking Tests 430
Important Tips for Test Taking 430
Prepare 430
Study Tips 430
Effective Learning 431
The Day Before the Test 431
The Day of the Test 431
At the Test 431
Using Metacognition 432
Metacognition Involves Several Steps 432
Practice 434
Textbook Selection 437
U-Review 439

READING SELECTIONS

READING 1
Vocabulary Preview 440
Preview 441
"BIONIC SOLDIERS" Corinne Fennessy 442
Review 444
Comprehension Questions 444
Vocabulary Practice 446
Vocabulary Practice—Crossword 447
Questions for Writing and Discussion 448

READING 2
Vocabulary Preview 449
Preview 450
"ATTACK OF THE CYBER-THIEVES" Karen Collins and Jackie Shemko 451
Review 454
Comprehension Questions 454
Vocabulary Practice 456
Questions for Writing and Discussion 457
Vocabulary Practice—Guess the Phrase 458

READING FOR LIFE

Real-Life Reading
Instructions 458
On the Job Interview
Kyle Williams, Show Systems Integrators in Orlando, Florida 461
Watch the Video: Robot Arm Gives Humans Strength 461
Textbook Graphic Aids 462
Building Vocabulary 464

CHAPTER REVIEW

Chapter Practices 465
Textbook Practice 468
Reading Lab Assignments 469
Study Skill Review 470
Learning Reflection 471
Self-Evaluation Checklist 471

COMBINED SKILLS TESTS

Test 1 474
Test 2 476
Test 3 478
Test 4 480
Test 5 483

APPENDIX

Using a Glossary or Dictionary 487
Using a Glossary 487
Using a Dictionary 487
Using a Published Dictionary 488
Figurative Speech 490
Denotation and Connotation 490
Improving Reading Rate and Endurance 491
Timed Readings 491
What Influences Your Rate? 492
Post-Test Survey: How Did You Learn? 493
Credits **495**
Index **499**

PREFACE

More than fifteen years ago, when I started teaching college preparatory reading, the textbooks available at that time required students to struggle through the reading selections and extensive multiple-choice practice exercises. My students did not understand how either their textbook or their college preparatory reading course related to their lives or future goals. I saw the need for a textbook that would relate what they learned in the classroom to real-life applications, including academic reading and real documents they will encounter outside of school.

Research has shown that students who are engaged in the learning process are more successful than passive learners. When students are motivated, they are more likely to participate in the learning process. To accomplish this, they need materials and activities that are related to their academic and personal needs. They also need interesting articles that will inspire them to succeed and opportunities to discuss and engage in critical thinking. *Reading for Life* engages students in reading through an activities-based learning approach to help them master key reading skills and strategies.

Learning Principles Incorporated into *Reading for Life*

Reading for Life is shaped by several pedagogical principles backed by research. First, students are most successful when they are active learners. Students learn best by participating, not by just listening or reading extensively about how to do something. Furthermore, this text teaches reading as a thinking process by taking students through the steps of reading actively. As you go through each chapter, you will find a multitude of instructive features that support the active learning approach. Furthermore, in order to support instructors, the Instructor's Manual includes complete instructions to enable instructors to easily incorporate active learning, collaborative learning, and closure activities.

Second, student motivation increases when the material students are reading is related to their lives and their goals. Each chapter in this text is focused on a different career domain. Moreover, I have carefully chosen highly motivating selections about real people who have overcome challenges and have succeeded. These selections lead students through the process of reading actively to help them master key reading skills and strategies. The selections also provide critical thinking questions for discussion or writing.

Third, research has shown that collaborative learning is one of the most effective ways that students learn. In response to this, many of the activities and assignments in *Reading for Life* are done in pairs or teams. This book provides ample opportunities for students to talk through their thinking processes and to learn from each other. This also benefits students who have an auditory learning style, who learn best by listening and speaking. In addition, it reinforces active learning by engaging more students in the learning process.

Chapter Features in *Reading for Life*

The multitude of features within every chapter of *Reading for Life* supports the book's goal to engage students in preparatory college reading through active learning and real-life connections.

What's New to This Edition

The second edition of *Reading for Life* has been enhanced to reflect effective current practices in developmental reading and to prepare students for the next level in the series, *Reading for College.* Beginning developmental readers need more time to assimilate the concepts of patterns of organization and critical thinking skills. Thus, the information on patterns has been modified to provide more practice in the five most common patterns in order to build a foundation that will enable them to broaden their knowledge of patterns in the next level text, *Reading for College.*

Beginning developmental readers also need study skills, so an entire chapter is devoted to these concepts. The study skills chapter can be introduced any time during the semester, or sections of this chapter can be interjected during the semester at various intervals. Vocabulary development is an essential part of reading instruction for developmental readers. Each chapter provides practice using words in context, vocabulary activities, and learning vocabulary parts. In addition, the "On the Job Interviews" with real people has been enhanced with videos relating to the chapter's career focus to engage students' interest and present new career ideas.

The overall organization of the text has been modified to reflect the scope and sequence of skills that build upon each other. For example, after the literal comprehension skills (topics, stated main ideas, and supporting details), inferential reading is introduced in drawing conclusions. Students must be able to draw conclusions before they can form implied main ideas and central points. Since determining an overall pattern of organization also requires inferential thinking, this skill has been placed after drawing conclusions and implied main ideas. Since both stated and implied main ideas are important clues to determining the overall pattern of organization, the order of these chapters follows this sequence.

Some other new additions to the second edition are:

- new articles for improving reading comprehension
- additional models and examples for skills
- links to chapter practices in the text to MyReadingLab so students can work online
- a new layout and improved organization in each chapter

The *Instructor's Manual and Test Bank,* by Karen Cowden, has many more new active learning strategies and activities, as well as formal and informal assessment tools.

HOW *Reading for Life* MAKES READING REAL

6

DRAWING CONCLUSIO' 'S

LEARNING STRATEGIES
Drawing Conclusions 219
READING SELECTIONS
READING 1: "College Drinking: Harmless Fun?" 230
READING 2: "Where Wishes Come True" 240
READING FOR LIFE
On the Job Interview 249
Real-Life Reading 250
Building Vocabulary 252
Textbook Graphic Aids 253
CHAPTER REVIEW
Chapter Practice 254
Textbook Practice 257
Study Skill Review 259
Reading Lab Assignments 260
Learning Reflection 260
Self-Evaluation Checklist 261

FOCUS ON: Sociology and Education

Peo… …no choose care… …soc… …y and education of… …fir… …ir greatest satisfaction by helping others improve their lives through better … …g conditions, improved health, and education. Some opportunities begin … two-year college degree, and others may require a bachelor's or m… …a degree. In education, you might enjoy teaching a specific subject, such… …orts, technology, or theater. People who work in sociology often he… …ers obtain housing, welfare, health care, and other social services. Some pe… …work directly with clients while others help set up programs and run th…

Drawing conclusions is an invaluable sk… …hese fields. Social services workers need to be able to evaluate conditi… …nd needs, and come to conclusions about what issues need to be … …ssed. Teachers need to be able to determine how their class is performing … whole and as individuals, so that they can tailor their instruction better. To … …ls, workers in these fields must be able to look at supporting details, us… …examine facts, and support their conclusions.

In this chapter, you will:

LEARNING OBJECTIV…

1 learn how to draw logical conclusions.

218 CHAPTER 6: Drawing Conclusions

Each chapter is organized around a **CAREER THEME** to inspire students about different career options.

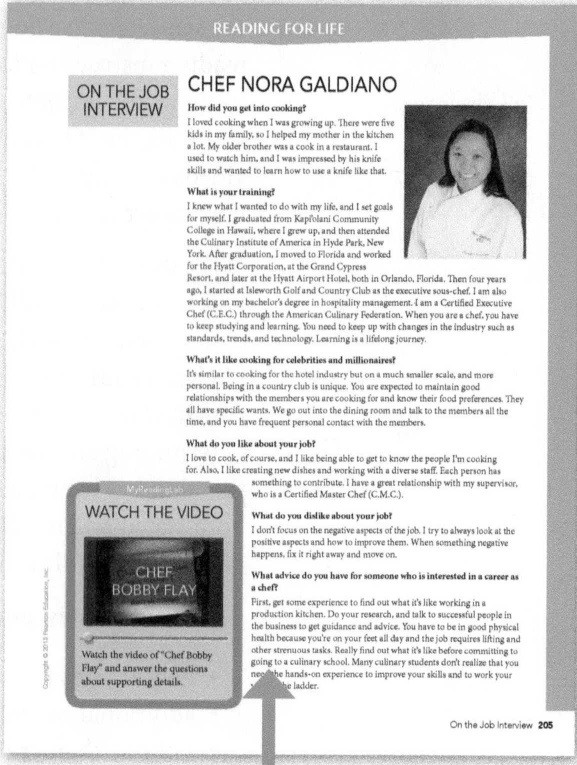

READING FOR LIFE

ON THE JOB INTERVIEW

CHEF NORA GALDIANO

How did you get into cooking?

I loved cooking when I was growing up. There were five kids in my family, so I helped my mother in the kitchen a lot. My older brother was a cook in a restaurant. I used to watch him, and I was impressed by his knife skills and wanted to learn how to use a knife like that.

What is your training?

I knew what I wanted to do with my life, and I set goals for myself. I graduated from Kapi'olani Community College in Hawaii, where I grew up, and then attended the Culinary Institute of America in Hyde Park, New York. After graduation, I moved to Florida and worked for the Hyatt Corporation, at the Grand Cypress Resort, and later at the Hyatt Airport Hotel, both in Orlando, Florida. Then four years ago, I started at Isleworth Golf and Country Club as the executive sous-chef. I am also working on my bachelor's degree in hospitality management. I am a Certified Executive Chef (C.E.C.) through the American Culinary Federation. When you are a chef, you have to keep studying and learning. You need to keep up with changes in the industry such as standards, trends, and technology. Learning is a lifelong journey.

What's it like cooking for celebrities and millionaires?

It's similar to cooking for the hotel industry but on a much smaller scale, and more personal. Being in a country club is unique. You are expected to maintain good relationships with the members you are cooking for and know their food preferences. They all have specific wants. We go out into the dining room and talk to the members all the time, and you have frequent personal contact with the members.

What do you like about your job?

I love to cook, of course, and I like being able to get to know the people I'm cooking for. Also, I like creating new dishes and working with a diverse staff. Each person has something to contribute. I have a great relationship with my supervisor, who is a Certified Master Chef (C.M.C.).

MyReadingLab

WATCH THE VIDEO

CHEF BOBBY FLAY

Watch the video of "Chef Bobby Flay" and answer the questions about supporting details.

What do you dislike about your job?

I don't focus on the negative aspects of the job. I try to always look at the positive aspects and how to improve them. When something negative happens, fix it right away and move on.

What advice do you have for someone who is interested in a career as a chef?

First, get some experience to find out what it's like working in a production kitchen. Do your research, and talk to successful people in the business to get guidance and advice. You have to be in good physical health because you're on your feet all day and the job requires lifting and other strenuous tasks. Really find out what it's like before committing to going to a culinary school. Many culinary students don't realize that you ne… …he hands-on experience to improve your skills and to work your … …he ladder.

On the Job Interview 205

ON THE JOB INTERVIEW boxed features show real people who are presently working in careers related to that chapter's theme and who share personal experience and advice.

READING FOR LIFE

REAL-LIFE READING

CREDIT CARD AGREEMENT

If you apply for a credit card with a bank or other financial institution, you should read the terms of the credit card agreement carefully. The following is an excerpt (part) of a credit card agreement. Use the four-step reading process as you read, and then answer the questions that follow to check your comprehension. Preview the selection first, and then read it and answer the questions that follow with your team.

TERMS AND CONDITIONS

FEES: We may charge your account for the following fees. The application and payment of a fee will not release you from responsibility of the action which caused the fees.

LATE PAYMENT: We may charge a $25.00 late fee to your account if you do not pay at least the minimum payment by the stated due date. In addition to the late fee, we will cancel any temporary low rate offers if your payment is late more than one billing cycle during the promotion. We will charge an additional late fee of 10% of your balance for each billing cycle that your account is past due.

OVER THE LIMIT: If you go over your credit limit or cash advance limit by $50.00 or more, we will add an additional $30.00 Over the Limit fee to your account for each billing cycle that you remain over your credit limit.

RETURNED PAYMENT: If you make a payment on your account with a check from some other financial institution and that check is not honored by the financial institution on which it is drawn, you will be charged a fee of $35.00.

RETURNED CHECK: If you write a check from your account and that check is not honored because your account is in default or over the limit, we will charge you a fee of $35.00.

CASH ADVANCE FEE: An additional finance charge will be added to your account each time you obtain a cash advance. This additional finance charge will be 8% of the amount of the cash advance with a maximum of $30.00. Internet transactions are exempt from the cash advance fee.

ENTIRE BALANCE DUE: If you fail to make a required payment when due or default on any other term in this agreement, we can declare the entire balance of your account due and payable at once without notice. We can also demand complete immediate payment if you make any false or misleading statement on your application or if you die or file for bankruptcy.

COLLECTION COSTS: To the extent permitted by applicable law, you agree to pay all costs and disbursements, including reasonable attorney fees, incurred by us in legal proceedings to collect or enforce your indebtedness.

152 CHAPTER 4: Topics and Stated Main Ideas

REAL-LIFE READING selections show students the value of reading skills to situations in everyday life.

HOW *Reading for Life* ENGAGES STUDENTS THROUGH ACTIVITIES

PREVIEW questions begin each reading selection so that students can connect their prior knowledge with the reading topic.

The **READING SELECTIONS** are accompanied by questions designed to keep the reading process active so students can monitor their comprehension.

READING SELECTIONS

MyReadingLab

Reading 1
PREVIEW

1. Describe an animal rescue that you have seen or heard about.
2. If an animal is injured and needs first aid, what would you do?

After you preview the article, write one or two preview questions on the lines below:

MyReadingLab

Reading 1

As you read, answer the questions in the margins to check your comprehension.

"Operation Seal Rescue"

by Monica Rozenfled

Volunteers from around the world team up to save hundreds of baby seals stranded during a storm.

1 Last winter, a seal rescue center in the Netherlands received an urgent call. A person had spotted dozens of seal pups washed ashore on several nearby islands. The baby seals, less than a year old, had been resting on sandbanks between the islands when high storm tides swept them into the water.

2 Many of the pups drowned in the high tides. Others were stranded on local beaches and didn't have the energy to hunt for fish. With their strength waning, they were vulnerable to deadly illness and starvation.

3 A rescue squad from the Seal Rehabilitation and Research Centre in Pieterburen, Netherlands, sprang into action. In the next few weeks, the squad rounded up 385 stranded grey and harbor seals.

4 The center usually takes in about 300 to 400 seals a year, nursing them back to health and returning them to the wild. But the numbers have been growing recently. Last year, the facility rescued more than 800 seals. Why? One reason is climate change, which can lead to more intense storms. In addition, pollution, disease, and fewer fish to eat have left pups fighting harder than ever before to survive.

Why have seal pup rescues been increasing over recent years?

388 **CHAPTER 9:** Critical Reading and Thinking

READING SELECTIONS

Pup Rescue

5 Pulling off a rescue effort as large as the one last winter was a challenge. About 70 volunteers from the Netherlands and around the world lent a hand to save the seals. People everywhere donated necessities like towels, bowls, and even small backyard pools for the pups to rest in. "When you have a rescue station, you have to be very creative," says Lenie 't Hart, the center's founder.

6 Getting the pups to the center was another issue. They had to be transported by ferries, rescue boats, and vans. One van held 20 seals at once! The logistics were very complex. "It was like a military operation," says 't Hart.

7 Once the pups were on the mainland, they were driven to the rehabilitation center, where they could get medical treatment, food, and some much-needed rest.

Health Checkup

8 At the center, the first thing on the agenda was to weigh and measure the seals. Workers drew blood samples to check for diseases, and gave them vaccinations to ward off infections.

9 One of the biggest threats to stranded seal pups is the disease lungworm. This respiratory infection is caused by worm-like parasites from the fish the seals eat. The parasites grow inside the seal's lungs, making it difficult for the animal to breathe.

10 Healthy seals can usually fight off lungworm infections. But 't Hart has noticed more seals dying from it in recent years. Infected seals that are too exhausted to hunt stay onshore instead of returning to the water. If they're not rescued, they become emaciated and die in a matter of days or weeks.

11 Pollution and overfishing may be partly to blame for seals becoming more vulnerable to infections like lungworm. Pollution can weaken a seal's disease-fighting immune system. The same is true for overfishing. If there aren't enough fish for the pups to eat, they will be underweight and have a harder time fighting off illness.

What medical attention must the seal pups get, and why?

Road to Recovery

12 The goal of the rescue is to help the seals recover so they can return to the ocean and survive on their own. At the center, the seal pups are put on a diet consisting of a soupy mixture of ground-up **herring** and water. Then they're moved to an isolated area so they can rest undisturbed in pools until they're healthy.

herring: a type of fish eaten by seals

13 After the pups have had time to recuperate, the rescue team begins to train the young animals to catch their own food. Once the pups reach a healthy weight—roughly 50 kilograms (110 pounds) for grey seals and 35 to 40 kg (77 to 88 lbs) for harbor seals—the rescue center releases them into the wild.

14 About 60 to 70 percent of the seals that come to the Seal Rehabilitation and Research Centre survive. None of them spends longer than six months and the center. "These are independent animals," says 't Hart. "They do not belong in captivity."

What happens to the seal pups after six months in the rehabilitation center?

Continued...

Reading 1: "Operation Seal Rescue" **389**

U-REVIEW sections appear immediately after students practice key reading skills to bring closure to the reading skills.

LEARNING STRATEGIES

MyReadingLab

U-REVIEW

With your team, answer the following questions. You may go back to review the information in the chapter if needed.

1. What is a conclusion?
   a. a guess about something
   b. a guess based on what you think about something
   c. an idea that is determined by looking at facts
   d. an assumption
2. What does CLUES stand for?
   a. comprehend, look at the details, use the facts at hand, explain your main idea, and support your conclusion with facts
   b. comprehend, look at the main idea, use the facts at hand, examine the details, and support your conclusion with facts
   c. check comprehension, look at the supporting details, use only the facts at hand, examine the facts, and support your conclusion with facts
   d. comprehending, logical thinking, understanding, explaining, and simplifying
3. What is an assumption?
   a. something you know to be true
   b. something you guess is probably true, but there are no facts in the passage to prove it
   c. something you do when you use all the facts in the passage
   d. making a conclusion based on the facts in the passage
4. What should you do after you make your conclusion?
   a. State the main idea.
   b. Support your conclusion by looking for the facts in the passage that prove it.
   c. Examine the details.
   d. Look for absolutes.
5. Which of the following statements is accurate regarding the words *all, none, no one, everyone, always,* and *never*?
   a. Never draw a conclusion using one of those terms.
   b. You should not assume a conclusion using those terms is true unless the passage specifically states it.
   c. Those terms are always acceptable in logical conclusions.
   d. Never believe anything that uses these terms.

Drawing Conclusions **227**

CHAPTER REVIEW

CHAPTER PRACTICE 1

Read the following paragraph. Circle the topic, and underline the topic sentence. Then, complete the exercises that follow.

When you invest your money, you should know which investments are insured and which ones are not. An *insured investment* will guarantee that what you invested will be paid back, plus some interest. An *uninsured investment* is a risk, meaning that you may get less money back than what you invested. Examples of insured investments are savings accounts, money market accounts, and certificates of deposit (CDs). Investments that are not insured are stocks, mutual funds, and annuities. A mutual fund is an account to purchase stocks, bonds, and other investments. An annuity is a long-term savings contract that invests your money for a certain period of time at a specific interest rate.

Label each of the following: T = topic, TS = topic sentence, or SD = supporting detail. One will be a topic, one will be a topic sentence, and two will be supporting details.

1. ______ When you invest your money, you should know which investments are insured and which ones are not.
2. ______ Investments that are not insured are mutual funds and annuities.
3. ______ An annuity is a long-term savings contract that invests your money for a certain period of time at a specific interest rate.
4. ______ Insured and uninsured investments
5. Identify the meaning of the underlined word in the following sentence: An uninsured investment is a risk, meaning that you may get less money back than what you invested.
   a. underinsured
   b. not insured
   c. all insured
   d. not sure

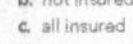

156 CHAPTER 4: Topics and Stated Main Ideas

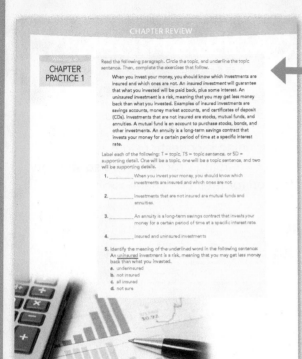

End-of-chapter review sections review key concepts using a variety of study skills such as note cards, diagrams, charts, and concept maps.

A variety of **GAMES AND ACTIVITIES** is included to further engage students in active and collaborative learning.

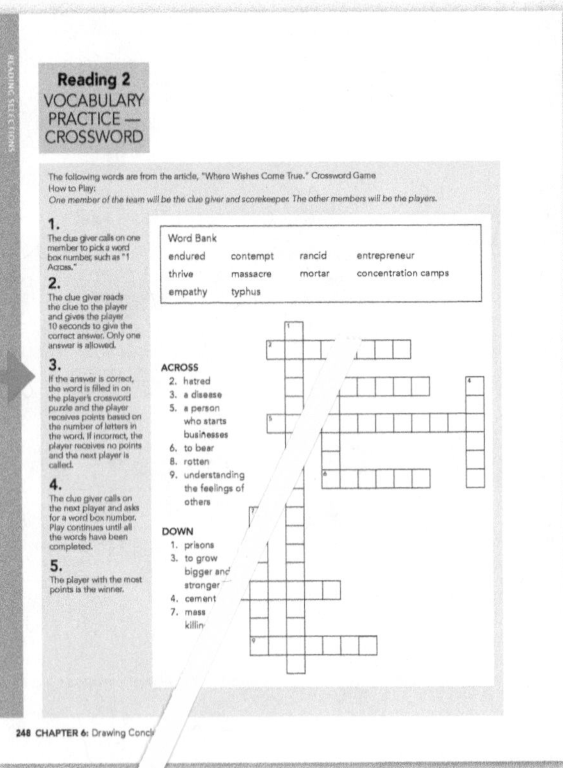

READING SELECTIONS

Reading 2
VOCABULARY PRACTICE — CROSSWORD

The following words are from the article, "Where Wishes Come True." Crossword Game
How to Play:
One member of the team will be the clue giver and scorekeeper. The other members will be the players.

1. The clue giver calls on one member to pick a word box number, such as "1 Across."

2. The clue giver reads the clue to the player and gives the player 10 seconds to give the correct answer. Only one answer is allowed.

3. If the answer is correct, the word is filled in on the player's crossword puzzle and the player receives points based on the number of letters in the word. If incorrect, the player receives no points and the next player is called.

4. The clue giver calls on the next player and asks for a word box number. Play continues until all the words have been completed.

5. The player with the most points is the winner.

Word Bank			
endured	contempt	rancid	entrepreneur
thrive	massacre	mortar	concentration camps
empathy	typhus		

ACROSS
2. hatred
3. a disease
5. a person who starts businesses
6. to bear
8. rotten
9. understanding the feelings of others

DOWN
1. prisons
3. to grow bigger and stronger
4. cement
7. mass killin

248 CHAPTER 6: Drawing Concl

TEXTBOOK SELECTION

LEARNING STRATEGIES

Census 2000: Minorities Now a Majority in the Largest U.S. Cities

The 2000 U.S. census reported that minorities—Hispanics, African Americans, and Asians—are now a majority of the population in 48 of the 100 largest U.S. cities, up from 30 in 1990. What accounts for the change? The reason is that large cities have been losing their non-Hispanic white populations. For example, by 2000, Santa Ana, California, had lost 38 percent of the white population it had in 1990; the drop was 40 percent in Birmingham, Alabama, and a whopping 53 percent in Detroit, Michigan. The white share of the population of the 100 largest cities fell from 52.1 percent in 1990 to 43.8 percent in 2000.

But perhaps the biggest reason for the minority–majority trend is the increase in immigration. Immigration, coupled with higher birth rates among new immigrants, resulted in a 43 percent gain in the Hispanic population (almost 4 million people) of the largest 100 cities between 1990 and 2000. The Asian population also surged by 40 percent (more than 1.1 million people). The African American population remained steady over the course of the 1990s.

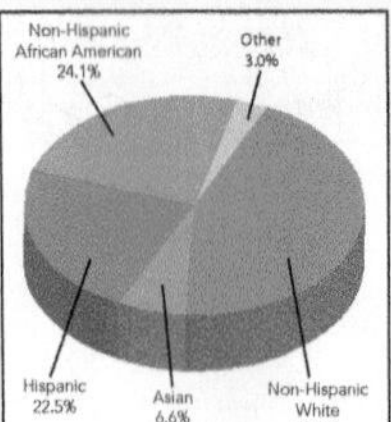

Population Profile for the 100 Largest U.S. Cities, 2000
Racial and ethnic minorities make up a majority of the population of this country's 100 largest cities.
Source: Based on U.S. Census Bureau (2001).

Drawing Conclusions 225

Every chapter includes **TEXTBOOK SELECTIONS** to help students learn to read academic material, including how to read **TEXTBOOK GRAPHIC AIDS.**

Abundant **PRACTICES** and **SKILL-BUILDING EXERCISES** are included so students can apply the key reading and study skills.

MyReadingLab

PRACTICE 3

Read the following paragraph. Underline and label the topic sentence with "TS," and underline the major details. Then, answer the questions that follow.

People who enjoy playing games like lotteries, card games, and other games of chance can find employment in the casino industry. Most gaming-service employees work in casinos, and their work can vary from management to surveillance and investigation. One career opportunity is as a gaming supervisor. This is someone who oversees the games and the personnel in a specific area. Gaming supervisors make sure that players and workers are following the rules and will explain them clearly if needed. *Another* career opportunity is as a gaming manager. Gaming managers prepare work schedules and are responsible for hiring and training new personnel. *Finally,* gaming dealers are also employed to operate games such as blackjack, roulette, and craps. To become qualified for one of these positions, you will need a degree in hospitality or special training to become licensed by your state's casino control board or commission.

1. What is the topic?
   - **a.** gaming supervisors
   - **b.** casinos
   - **c.** gambling
   - **d.** gaming careers
2. What is the topic sentence?
   - **a.** People who enjoy playing games like lotteries, card games, and other games of chance can find employment in the casino industry.
   - **b.** Most gaming-service employees work in casinos, and their work can vary from management to surveillance and investigation.
   - **c.** One career opportunity is as a gaming supervisor.
   - **d.** To become qualified for one of these positions, you will need a degree in hospitality or special training to become licensed by your state's casino control board or commission.
3. Which of the following is not a major supporting detail?
   - **a.** One career opportunity is as a gaming supervisor.
   - **b.** Another career opportunity is as a gaming manager.
   - **c.** Gaming supervisors make sure that players and workers are following the rules and will explain them clearly if needed.
   - **d.** Finally, gaming dealers are also employed to operate games such as blackjack, roulette, and craps.
4. Identify the minor detail that supports the following major detail: "Another career opportunity is as a gaming manager."
   - **a.** To become qualified for one of these positions, you will need a degree in hospitality or special training to become licensed by your state's casino control board or commission.
   - **b.** Gaming managers prepare work schedules and are responsible for hiring and training new personnel.
   - **c.** Most gaming-service employees work in casinos, and their work can vary from management to surveillance and investigation.
   - **d.** This is someone who oversees the games and the personnel in a specific area.

Continued...

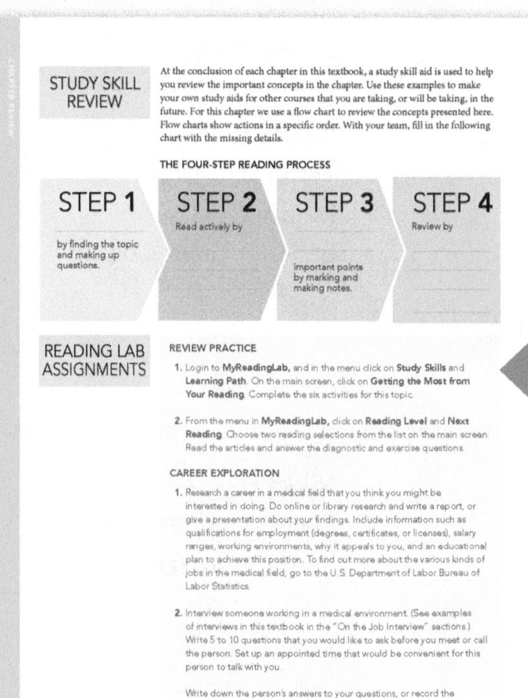

STUDY SKILL REVIEW

At the conclusion of each chapter in this textbook, a study skill aid is used to help you review the important concepts in the chapter. Use these examples to make your own study aids for other courses that you are taking, or will be taking, in the future. For this chapter we use a flow chart to review the concepts presented here. Flow charts show actions in a specific order. With your team, fill in the following chart with the missing details.

THE FOUR-STEP READING PROCESS

READING LAB ASSIGNMENTS

REVIEW PRACTICE

1. Login to **MyReadingLab**, and in the menu click on **Study Skills** and **Learning Path**. On the main screen, click on **Getting the Most from Your Reading**. Complete the six activities for this topic.
2. From the menu in **MyReadingLab**, click on **Reading Level** and **Next Reading**. Choose two reading selections from the list on the main screen. Read the articles and answer the diagnostic and exercise questions.

CAREER EXPLORATION

1. Research a career in a medical field that you think you might be interested in doing. Do online or library research and write a report, or give a presentation about your findings. Include information such as qualifications for employment (degrees, certificates, or licenses), salary ranges, working environments, why it appeals to you, and an educational plan to achieve this position. To find out more about the various kinds of jobs in the medical field, go to the U.S. Department of Labor Bureau of Labor Statistics.
2. Interview someone working in a medical environment. (See examples of interviews in this textbook in the "On the Job Interview" sections.) Write 5 to 10 questions that you would like to ask before you meet or call the person. Set up an appointed time that would be convenient for this person to talk with you.

   Write down the person's answers to your questions, or record the interview.

64 CHAPTER 2: The Four-Step Reading Process

READING LAB ASSIGNMENTS direct students to MyReadingLab for additional practice of skills, reading comprehension, and research opportunities.

ACKNOWLEDGMENTS

I would like to thank David Kear, my Senior Development Editor, for his guidance and support in writing this second edition of Reading for Life. He has been my rudder and the wind in my sail. I would also like to acknowledge my editor, Eric Stano, for providing me the opportunity to publish this book with Pearson. My sincere gratitude goes to Anthony Limerick at DK in London, and Amanda Zagnoli at Integra for their conscientious attention to every detail in the beautiful design of this text. I wish to thank Karen Cowden, a colleague and friend, for revising and improving the Instructor's Manual and Test Bank to the second edition. There are also many other people who worked behind the scenes to publish this book, and I am indebted to all of them. It may take a village to raise a child, but it takes an international coalition to publish a book!

I have been blessed to work with many dedicated colleagues at Valencia College in Orlando, FL, who have supported and encouraged me throughout this process. Their feedback has been a tremendous help in refining this second edition and helping to shape the first edition of Reading for College.

Last, but never least, I would like to acknowledge my husband, Craig, for his patience and his support of my career as a writer and instructor. Writing demands long hours at the computer, and he has understood my passion for expressing my ideas with the hope that others may benefit from them.

Finally, I would like to gratefully recognize the following reviewers whose invaluable insights on the first edition informed this revision:

Janet Anthon
Mott Community College

Rachel Hoover
Frostburg State University

Judy Covington
Trident Technical College

Tracie Varitek
Henry Ford Community College

Teresa Carrillo
Joliet Junior College

Richard Gair
Valencia College

Deidre Rowley
Imperial Valley College

Their contributions have built upon the guidance provided by previous reviewers:

Taddese Addo
Community College of Denver

Dale Boyle
Community College of Rhode Island

Kathleen Carlson
Brevard Community College

Judy Covington
Trident Technical College

Nikka Harris
Rochester Community College

Cathy Hunsicker
Dalton State College

Kimberly Jones
College of Southern Idaho

Susie Khirallah-Johnston
Tyler Junior College

Mary Nielsen
Dalton State College

Elizabeth O'Scanlon
Santa Barbara City College

Christine Proctor
St. Louis Community College at Meramac

Regina Ray
Dalton State College

Linda Saumell
Miami Dade–Homestead Campus

Dawn Sedik
Valencia Community College

Alan Shuttleworth
Sierra College

Dr. Phebe Simmons
Blinn College

TC Stuwe
Salt Lake Community College

1 PLAN TO SUCCEED

LEARNING STRATEGIES

Teamwork: Getting to Know Your Classmates 3
Setting Goals 3
Time Management: Building a Study Schedule 6
Organizing Your Notebook 11

CHAPTER REVIEW

Study Skill Review 15
Reading Lab Assignments 16
Learning Reflection 16
Self-Evaluation Checklist 17

In this chapter, you will:

LEARNINGS OBJECTIVES

1 understand why teamwork is an effective way to learn.
2 set short-term, mid-term, and long-term goals.
3 identify how to manage your time more effectively.
4 understand how to organize a notebook.

OBJECTIVE 1

Understand why teamwork is an effective way to learn.

TEAMWORK: GETTING TO KNOW YOUR CLASSMATES

One of the most important qualities that employers look for in potential employees is that of a "team player." Employers know that good ideas, products, and services become even better when more people are involved in the creative process.

Some people do not warm up to the idea of working in teams. They prefer to work alone, and this is understandable. But in the real world, you also have to be able to work with other people. Getting along with others, sharing ideas, supporting each other, and helping each other are key skills in teamwork.

Get into groups of two or three, and take turns interviewing each other. Try to find out something unique about the other person. Think about what you would like to know about someone who is sitting across the aisle or across the room. Questions should include his or her first and last name (spelled correctly), why he or she is in college, careers the student finds interesting, hobbies, what the student does in his or her spare time, part-time jobs, and so on. Jot down the information you gathered in the space provided below. Next, introduce the student you interviewed to the class. When you introduce this person, be sure to speak loudly and clearly enough so that everyone can hear you.

Today I met:

....

....

....

OBJECTIVE 2

Set short-term, mid-term, and long-term goals.

SETTING GOALS

To succeed at anything in life, you must have plans and goals. Setting goals and mapping out a plan to reach those goals will greatly help you achieve them.

Goals should be set high, but they should also be realistic. Do not settle for second best when planning your future. Don't stop at becoming the manager or the supervisor. Aim for the top position—the president of the company—if that's what you want. Have faith in your ability to do the things you want to do, and then go out and do them.

If you fail along the way, as you sometimes will, learn from your mistakes. Do not be discouraged by setbacks or failure, for failure is how we learn to succeed. Successful people do not let failure defeat them. Every great invention and every new process that has been developed has come by trial and error. As the famous animal psychologist Cesar Millan says, "Mistakes don't bother me because that's how I learn."

MyReadingLab

WRITE DOWN YOUR GOALS

Write your own goals in the spaces provided below. They can be about anything, not just school. Aim high, but be realistic. Try to be as specific as you can when writing goals, and describe how you will accomplish them. (Use notebook paper if you require more space.)

EXAMPLE:

"By the end of this semester, I will get As in all of my classes. (How?) I will stick to my study schedule, do all of my homework, study for tests, and attend all of my classes on time."

In the next month, I will:

....

....

By the end of this semester, I will:

....

....

By the end of next semester, I will:

....

....

In a year, I will:

....

....

In two years, I will:

....

....

In five years, I will:

....

....

Keep this list in your book or in your notebook. If you change your goals, make changes to your list. At the end of the month, check to see if you accomplished your "one month" goals. Continue to check this list at least once a month to see if you are on track for your longer-term goals. If you find that you are wandering off track, set new goals that will help you get back on track.

EXAMPLE:

Old goal:

"By the end of the semester, I will get As in all of my classes."

New goal:

"My new goal is to get an A in reading class and a B+ in math class."

(How will you accomplish this?)

"I will get extra tutoring in math, see my instructor for help, go to the math center or lab, spend more time (an extra three hours each week) practicing math skills, and study more for tests and quizzes."

After you have filled in your goals, share them with a small group. Listen for specific strategies on how each person intends to accomplish his or her goals. Remember to encourage one another and tell each other, "You can do it! Just don't give up!"

At the end of this semester, keep this list of goals in a safe place at home. Every once in a while, take it out and read it. Ask yourself if you have accomplished any of your goals. Then look into the mirror and tell yourself what you will do to make them happen.

The old adage, "Quitters never win and winners never quit!" holds especially true in college. Start over if you must, but don't become discouraged and drop out. No matter what job you will have in life, you will always benefit from having a college education. Just keep on going to college, and you will earn that degree.

OBJECTIVE 3

Identify how to manage your time more effectively.

TIME MANAGEMENT: BUILDING A STUDY SCHEDULE

To succeed at anything, you must start with a good plan. Putting ideas down on paper or on the computer helps to make them real, giving them shape and form. It is also a good way of thinking through problems. Seeing something visually helps you see things you didn't think of when you just went over it in your mind. Your first plan for success in college should be to make a study schedule. Simply telling yourself, "I'll do my homework when I have time between classes and my job," is not going to work once the semester gets going and your life becomes busier than you ever believed it could possibly be.

Take a few minutes now to plot out time each day for review, to study for tests, and to do homework. A good general rule is to plan one hour of study time each week for each hour of class time. For example, each course that meets three hours a week, you need to set aside a minimum of three hours of study time. The more difficult the course is for you, the more time you will need to spend on studying.

Even if you don't have a written homework assignment to complete for the next class, you still have homework: studying and reviewing. In future chapters, you will learn why it's important to study even when you don't have an assignment or a test coming up.

Decide now when you will study. Choose a time when you know you will be awake and not sleepy or tired, and not interrupted by distractions. Make it known to all of your family and friends that you need to study and would appreciate it if they would not interrupt you, call you, text you, or chat online with you at those times. Turn off your phone during study time. You need to concentrate when you study, or you will find yourself forgetting what you learned. That's a waste of time you will not be able to afford.

HERE'S WHAT YOU SHOULD PUT ON THE STUDY SCHEDULE:

- When you are in class and traveling to or from school
- When you are at a job or other regular commitments
- When you can study, do homework, and review
- When you'll eat three meals a day and sleep at least seven hours a night
- When you can relax with friends and family
- When you worship or volunteer

"Something's Gotta Give"

There are only 24 hours in a day, and like the old song says, "Something's Gotta Give," meaning you can't do it all. If you find that you don't have the time to study that you need, you must cut down on something else, such as watching TV, playing video games, talking on the phone, or even working too many hours. Give up some of life's frills, or take fewer trips to the mall. You might find that your new schedule actually helps you to concentrate on the important things in life instead of on the things that eat up your time and money but offer no long-term benefits.

Once you have completed your schedule, stick to it! Hang it on your wall. Make an extra copy for your notebook or your car. The important thing is not to let any distractions invade your study time. If a true emergency comes up, then reschedule your study time, but don't neglect it.

Success is all about making the right choices and following through. If you get off track on your schedule, make every effort to get back on track as soon as possible. Make adjustments when needed, but don't cheat yourself out of your study time. When the grades arrive, you don't want to feel disappointed because you didn't give it your best effort.

Daily Planners

Take advantage of any free planning calendars that your college or local businesses might offer. You can also use an appointment calendar on your cell phone or computer. Get into the habit of writing something down every day, even if it's a simple reminder, such as, "Buy a notebook." Write down homework assignments, long-term assignments, project due dates, reminders about tests or papers the week before they are due, and anything else that you want to remember. Also, record information about your study partners in each class, such as their e-mail addresses or phone numbers. Developing habits takes time. Practice good habits daily and they will become a part of your normal routine.

STUDY PLAN						
Sunday	Monday	Tuesday	Wednesday	Thursday	Friday	Saturday
7:00 a.m.	7:00 a.m.	7:00 a.m.	7:00 a.m.	7:00 a.m.	7:00 a.m.	7:00 a.m.
8:00	8:00	8:00	8:00	8:00	8:00	8:00
9:00	9:00	9:00	9:00	9:00—	9:00	9:00
10:00	10:00	10:00	10:00	10:00	10:00	10:00
11:00	11:00	11:00	11:00	11:00	11:00	11:00
12:00 p.m.	12:00 p.m.	12:00 p.m.	12:00 p.m.	12:00 p.m.	12:00 p.m.	12:00 p.m.
1:00	1:00	1:00	1:00	1:00	1:00	1:00
2:00	2:00	2:00	2:00	2:00	2:00	2:00
3:00	3:00	3:00	3:00	3:00	3:00	3:00
4:00	4:00	4:00	4:00	4:00	4:00	4:00
5:00	5:00	5:00	5:00	5:00	5:00	5:00
6:00	6:00	6:00	6:00	6:00	6:00	6:00
7:00	7:00	7:00	7:00	7:00	7:00	7:00
8:00	8:00	8:00	8:00	8:00	8:00	8:00
9:00	9:00	9:00	9:00	9:00	9:00	9:00
10:00	10:00	10:00	10:00	10:00	10:00	10:00
11:00	11:00	11:00	11:00	11:00	11:00	11:00
12:00 a.m.	12:00 a.m.	12:00 a.m.	12:00 a.m.	12:00 a.m.	12:00 a.m.	12:00 a.m.

MyReadingLab

COLLEGE READINESS CHECKLIST

Are you ready for college? Put a check mark next to the following tasks that you have already completed, and circle the ones that you still need to do.

- ☐ 1. Purchase all required texts and materials for each course.
- ☐ 2. Keep a copy of your schedule in your notebook.
- ☐ 3. Read the syllabus for each course so you will know what your professors expect of you.
- ☐ 4. Make a study schedule of when you will study and do homework each day.
- ☐ 5. Know where to go to get extra help if needed.
- ☐ 6. Keep an assignment notebook or appointment program in your cell phone to record dates for short-term assignments, long-term assignments, and tests.
- ☐ 7. Have a place set up for doing homework, complete with supplies and away from distractions.
- ☐ 8. Inform your friends and supervisor at work that you are in college and will have to arrange your work schedule and free time around your study time.
- ☐ 9. Get your student I.D. card.
- ☐ 10. Make arrangements for travel to and from classes, for babysitters, or for other responsibilities outside of school.
- ☐ 11. Pay for classes by the date payment is due (or you'll be dropped from the classes).

Add any other tasks not included on this list that you still have to do:

....

....

....

....

....

....

....

....

MyReadingLab

MyReadingLab™

MyReadingLab is a Web site published by Pearson Education. The lab assignments in this text will coordinate with the skills that are taught in this course.

Once you are registered to use MyReadingLab, your name and all of your scores will be recorded and saved. Only you and your instructor will be able to see your results. You will have a secure password to access your scores.

One of the benefits of an online reading lab is that you can work on it at any time and from anywhere you have Internet access.

What Is in MyReadingLab?

In MyReadingLab, you can complete all the assignments in this book identified with the MyReadingLab logo. Simply log into MyReadingLab and answer the questions online. Your answers to practices and writing prompts will be recorded in the gradebook, and you'll get immediate feedback on your answers. There are also passages to read and questions to answer for skills practice, much like the exercises in this book. These exercises will give you additional independent practice and immediate feedback on your answers. The site will also give you explanations for incorrect answers. The questions are mostly multiple choice, with a few questions where you must type in an answer.

Besides the skills practices, there are also vocabulary exercises, study skills resources, and Lexile readings. A Lexile is a type of score that tells you your overall comprehension, based on how many multiple-choice questions you answered correctly. The Lexile readings are on a variety of topics, and you can select the ones you want to read.

As you improve in your reading comprehension, you will be given stories at higher reading levels. At each level, you choose which stories interest you. The more questions you answer correctly, the higher your Lexile score will go. By the end of the course, you will see an improvement in your Lexile score if you read carefully and answer the questions to the best of your ability.

MyReadingLab is designed to be user friendly and interesting. Remember that the purpose of the lab is to help you to improve your reading comprehension. If you take shortcuts and don't put in your best effort, you will not see much improvement. Make a commitment to do the work seriously. Plan enough time in your study schedule to complete the lab assignments without rushing through them. Do them to the best of your ability, and you will see improvement over the duration of the course.

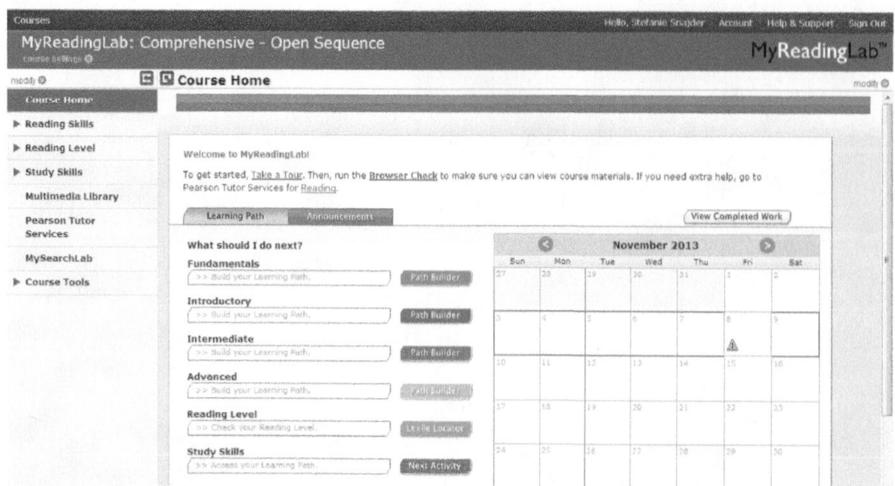

OBJECTIVE 4

Understand how to organize a notebook.

ORGANIZING YOUR NOTEBOOK

Keeping your papers organized is one of the most important keys to success in college. In a very short time, you will have more papers than you'll know what to do with. Throwing them into your book bag or shoving them anywhere into your notebook will only lead to frustration and wasted time when you need them later. Get into the habit of taking the time to put things away in their proper places. Once you see how much it improves your learning experience, you'll want to apply it to all of your other courses as well.

Staying organized requires self-discipline. Most students will say, "I don't have time to use a notebook!" Yet they are the ones who waste the most time trying to find papers. Putting papers in a notebook will actually save you time. You won't be frustrated or feel that things are out of control, and you may even see higher grades.

Here's what to do:

1. Buy a big three-ring binder with pockets inside, a pack of notebook paper, and dividers. Also, buy a small hole-puncher that will fit into your book bag. Don't waste money on binders or notebooks that are too thin to hold all of your class papers. Buy a set of dividers for each course you are taking. It's okay to use the same notebook for two or three classes, but if you are taking more than that, you may wish to use two notebooks of different colors. For example, Mindy has reading and math on Mondays and Wednesdays, so she has one notebook for those subjects. She also takes speech and humanities on Tuesdays and Thursdays, so she us[illegible] a different-colored notebook for thos[illegible] classes. Using two different-colored notebooks will help you avoid the mistake of bringing the wrong notebook to class.

3-RING BINDER

[illegible]TEBOOK PAPER

PLA[illegible]C POCKETS

DIVIDERS

2. Make labels for your reading course dividers. Your instructor will suggest the best way to label your dividers, but for a start, you can label them:

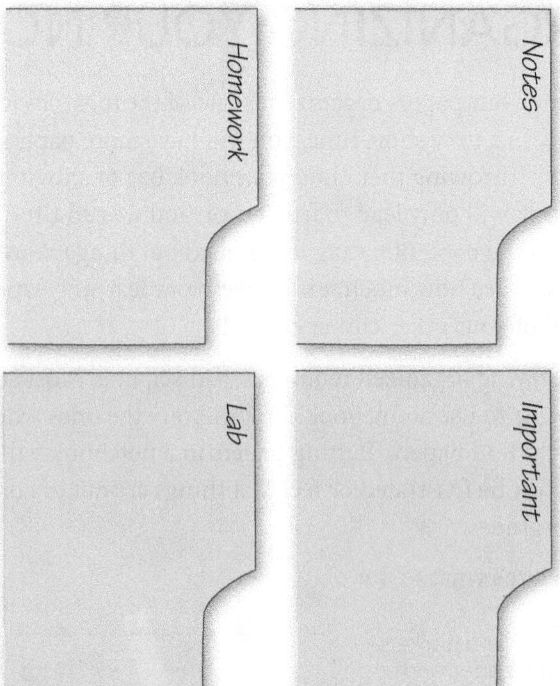

Quizzes/Test

Lab

Important

3. Put the dividers together in the front of your notebook.

4. Put 10 sheets of notebook paper into the "Homework" section. At the top of each page, create column headings such as the following:

At the end of class, write down the homework assignment that your instructor announces. If there is a printed description or schedule of your assignment, punch holes in it and put it into the "Homework" section. If your instructor announces a quiz or a lab assignment, also write it in this section. Don't forget to check your assignment list the day *before* class to make sure that you will be prepared!

	DATE	ASSIGNMENT	DUE
	06.01.2014	Read Chapter 4 and answer review questions.	06.07.2014

5. Punch holes in the instructor's syllabus and put this after the tab labeled "Important." The syllabus contains all of the most important information about the course. The "Important" tab is where you will keep all the course-related handouts that you are given by your instructor, such as the syllabus, the course schedule, information about labs, and other important papers that you will need.

6. Put about 25 sheets of notebook paper into the "Notes" section. This is where you will write down things like vocabulary definitions, class notes, and anything else you need to learn in this course. Don't mix other courses' notes in this section, such as math notes. This section is strictly for reading notes only.

7. When you complete a homework assignment, put it into the notebook at the *front* of the "Homework" section so it will be ready to hand in at the beginning of class. Remember to include your name, the date, and the title of the assignment at the top. Add page numbers if necessary. Don't use class time to get your papers ready to hand in. Instructors generally do not appreciate watching students tear out sheets of paper, write their names on them, ask for a stapler, or do other similar tasks that should be done outside of class.

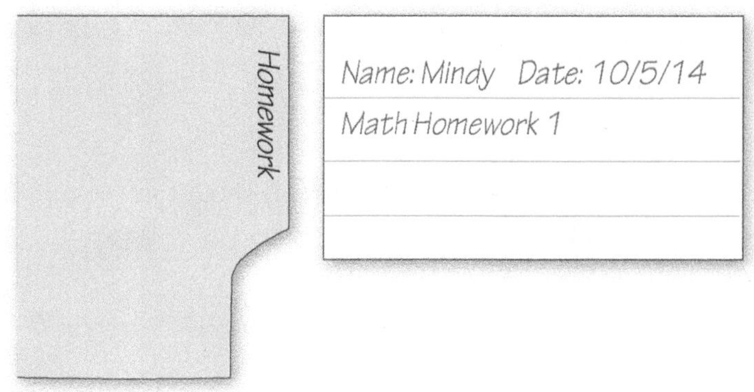

8. When papers are returned to you, take a minute to put them back into the "Homework" section of your notebook. Don't stuff them just anywhere! Each time you add a new paper, add it to the back so that the papers will be in chronological order. That way, when you need to go back to find an assignment to verify a grade or to study, it will be easier to find.

Name: Mindy Date: 10/5/14
Math Homework 1
A: well done!

9. Save all of your papers and tests until you have your final grade at the end of the semester. Rarely, but occasionally, you may want to ask an instructor how he or she arrived at your final grade. Your papers are important evidence of your work.

10. Use stick-on notes, colored stick-on tabs, or highlighters to mark important pages in your notebook. For example, if you have made a chart of transitions that you want to refer back to, add a colorful tab that will help you find it more easily.

Transitions

Keeping a notebook can actually give you a sense of satisfaction and accomplishment. Take a minute at the end of every class and study session to put things in the right place in your notebook. The next time you look for that homework assignment, you'll know exactly where it is.

Follow the same procedure for your other courses. If you use spiral notebooks for taking notes, buy the ones with three holes so they will fit into your large notebook in the "Notes" section. You can still take them out when you want to write in them, but put them back into the notebook for safe keeping.

U-REVIEW

Take a few minutes to think about the answers to the following questions. Then pair up with someone and take turns asking each other the questions. Allow your partner time to answer. When finished, if he or she leaves out any information, you should give it. Continue taking turns until all of the questions are answered.

1. Why is setting goals important?

2. Why should you set up a study schedule?

3. Why is it important to keep an organized notebook?

4. What is the syllabus, and what should you do with it?

5. What should you do after you have completed your homework?

MyReadingLab

SELF-EVALUATION CHECKLIST

Rate yourself on the following items, using the following scale:

1 = strongly disagree

2 = disagree

3 = neither agree nor disagree

4 = agree

5 = strongly agree

1. I completed all of the assigned work on time. ....

2. I understand all of the concepts in this chapter. ....

3. I contributed to teamwork and class discussions. ....

4. I completed all of the assigned lab work on time. ....

5. I came to class on time. ....

6. I attended class every day. ....

7. I studied for any quizzes or tests we had for this chapter. ....

8. I asked questions when I didn't understand something. ....

9. I checked my comprehension during reading. ....

10. I know what is expected of me in the coming week. ....

2

THE FOUR-STEP READING PROCESS

LEARNING STRATEGIES

The Four-Step Reading Process 19

READING SELECTIONS

READING 1: "Flight Nurse Hero" 33

READING 2: "From Illegal Immigrant to Brain Surgeon: Dr. Alfred Quiñones 43

READING FOR LIFE

On the Job Interview 53

Real-Life Reading 54

Textbook Graphic Aids 56

Building Vocabulary 57

CHAPTER REVIEW

Chapter Review 57

Textbook Practice 62

Study Skill Review 64

Reading Lab Assignments 64

Learning Reflection 65

Self-Evaluation Checklist 65

FOCUS ON: Health Sciences

This chapter focuses on careers in the medical field and the academic preparation needed to specialize in this area. Most pre-med students need to take courses in math and science, including biology, microbiology, and chemistry. As you explore the readings and textbook selections in this chapter, think about how your own interests and skills might fit into a career in the medical field. If you are interested in technology, you may like to work as a radiologist, a cardiovascular technician, or a sonographer. People with a love for the arts or music can use art and music therapy to help children, disabled adults, and patients with psychological disorders. Or perhaps you'd like to go into physical and occupational therapy, where you can help rehabilitate others after a serious illness or injury.

The health sciences is a career field where the need for skilled professionals will always exceed the supply. The four-step reading process will help you excel in these fields. Applying this process to reading medical charts, the latest research on occupational therapy, or technical guidelines for medical equipment will allow you to better understand and serve patients.

In this chapter, you will:

LEARNING OBJECTIVE

1 identify how to improve reading comprehension using the four-step reading process.

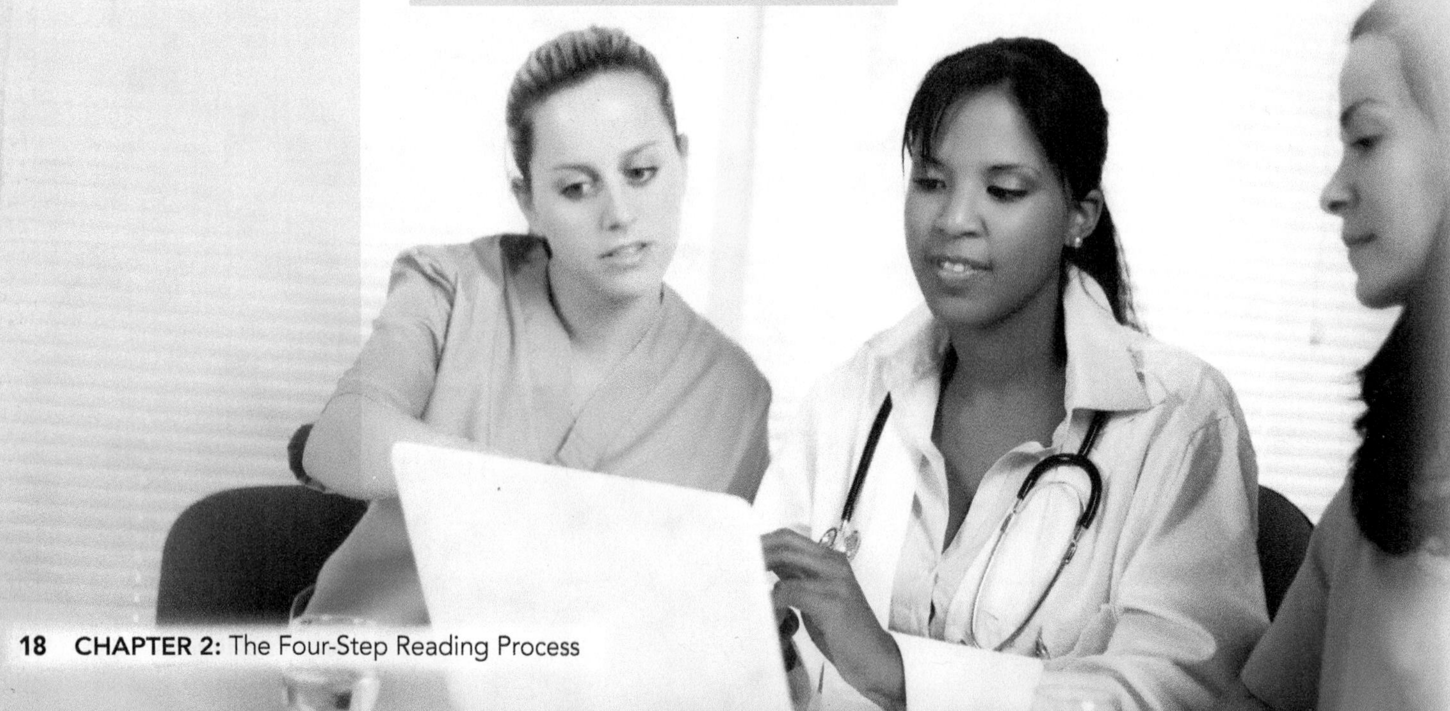

OBJECTIVE 1

Identify how to improve reading comprehension using the four-step reading process.

THE FOUR-STEP READING PROCESS

Has this ever happened to you? After reading an article or a chapter in a book, you closed the book and said, "I have no idea what I just read!" This type of "forgetting" what we just read is a common occurrence and usually happens because we weren't thinking about what we were reading. Our eyes were engaged, but our brains were not. This happens because we are not reading actively. We start on page one and continue until we finish the book or the chapter, and then close the book and think about something else. The result is that we cannot remember what we have read a day, an hour, or even minutes later.

In college, you will be given reading assignments on a regular basis for nearly all of your courses. You will be expected to understand the concepts that you read about and be ready to explain them in class or on a quiz. Some of the reading assignments will be more challenging than any you were given in high school. You might find yourself saying, "There's no way I can read all that and remember it!" But you can recall information for all of your college reading assignments if you develop the good habits described here. Reading actively will also help you to be successful in your career because you will remember and understand any materials that you will be expected to read.

STEP 1 Preview Before You Read

STEP 2 Read Actively

STEP 3 Highlight and Annotate

STEP 4 Review

STEP 1
Preview Before You Read

Previewing is important because it gets your brain thinking about the topic that you will be reading about. It gives your brain time to recall information you already know about the topic. It also helps you to understand the new information more easily. Your brain creates pathways for recalling information. Each time you recall information about a topic and learn new information, it will strengthen your understanding and improve your recall.

Previewing also allows you to decide how you will approach the material. Some things should be "skimmed" over, and other things should be read more slowly for better comprehension and recall. While previewing, you can decide what's important to remember and what is not.

Much of your reading in college will be in textbooks. Always read with a pencil in your hand and a highlighter. This habit will help you to read faster and more efficiently. Begin by looking over the reading selection:

- Read the title and bold headings.
- Look at pictures, graphs, diagrams, charts, or any other visual aids.
- Read the chapter introduction.
- Read the chapter summary.
- Read questions at the end of the chapter.
- Read words in bold print, such as key terms.
- Read the first sentence of each section.

As you preview, think of some questions you hope will be answered in the reading. For example, here are some headings from the textbook *Introduction to Biology*: "Chemistry and Cells," "Genetics," and "Animal Physiology." Each of these should be turned into a question. For instance, for "Genetics" you might ask, "What is genetics?" As you read that section, you will look for the answer to that question. This gives you a purpose for reading. You will be searching for the answer to the question, and you will be more focused on what you are reading and less likely to forget what you just read.

Also, previewing helps you call to mind your prior knowledge about a topic (what you already know). This is an important step for comprehension. If you find that you don't know anything about the topic, conduct some research to gain some background knowledge before you read. Go online and research some of the key terms you found during your preview of the reading selection. Check additional resources in the library, or ask your professor to provide some background information. Use your textbook glossary or the index for more background information. Next, as you read the selection, check your comprehension to make sure the information makes sense and has meaning for you. If it doesn't, you may need to find out more about the topic first, and then read the selection again.

Turn the following headings into questions. Begin with words such as who, what, when, where, why, or how.

"Blood Types"

?

"The Effects of Smoking"

?

"Sports Injuries"

?

Practice Previewing

Read the underlined text in the following passage. These are the parts you should read while previewing the material.

Sample preview questions:

- What is this passage about?
- What is dizziness, and what are some common causes of it?
- How should a person with dizziness be treated?

Read the title and introduction.

DIZZINESS

Dizziness is a feeling of being unbalanced or spinning, and it is a common symptom that can be caused by any number of conditions. Most commonly, it occurs when someone has not eaten or has an inner ear infection. Other causes of common dizziness are stress and viral infections.

Read the heading and first sentence of the paragraph.

Treatment

Most causes of dizziness are not serious, and the symptom can be treated by having the patient sit or lie down. Give the patient something to drink, and find out when he or she last ate. Often a few slow deep breaths will help restore oxygen to the brain. If the dizziness does not go away, or happens frequently, a physician should be consulted. If dizziness is accompanied by chest pain, difficulty in breathing, sudden weakness, numbness or tingling, or severe bleeding, call emergency services immediately. This could be the sign of a stroke or heart attack.

Read the last paragraph or summary.

As in any medical emergency, it is best to keep the patient calm, comfortable, and relaxed until the problem goes away or until medical assistance arrives. When the patient feels the dizziness has passed, advise him or her to stand up slowly and to get plenty of rest and fluids over the next 24 hours.

STEP 2
Read Actively

Reading actively means that you are reading to find answers to your preview questions. As you read, look for important points that the author is making about the topic. Usually there is a main idea and several major details to explain or prove the main idea. Ask yourself, "What is this selection about?" and then, "What's the most important point about this topic?" Read to find the answers, and you will be able to stay focused on what you are reading. If you find yourself getting distracted, stop and repeat the preview questions you are trying to answer.

Read one section at a time, such as the paragraphs under one heading. If you find the answers to your preview questions, underline them so you can find them later. Read the whole paragraph before you underline, or you might find yourself underlining the whole thing. By underlining the most important ideas only, you are chunking information and making it easier to remember. Your memory can fill in the details once you focus on the big idea. Try to limit your highlighting and underlining of a section to about 25 percent or less. You will underline more in some paragraphs than others, depending on how many major points are made.

STEP 3
Highlight and Annotate

Make sure you have underlined the author's main point, if it is stated. Then, make notes in the margins of your text; this is called "annotating." Doing this will help you to remember what you read. It will also help you to review and summarize the information into a "word byte"—a single word or phrase that describes what the section is about. Furthermore, it will help you find information quickly when you need to go back to look up answers to questions or take notes.

When you need to review, you will save time by reading just the notes in the margins and highlighted information. If you do not have room in your margins for short notes, or if you are planning to sell your book at the end of the semester, buy some small sticky notes, such as Post-it® notes, and write on them instead.

Example

The main idea—notice how the topic is underlined in the title and its definition is underlined in the first sentence. All definitions to key terms are important, so always underline them.

Make note of sentences that begin with transition words like "first," "second," or "third." These are often important points.

Getting Down to Business — *Types of Business*

A business is any activity that provides goods or services to consumers for the purpose of making a profit. When Phil Knight and Bill Bowerman, his running coach at the University of Oregon, created Blue Ribbon Sports (the predecessor of Nike), they started a business. The product was athletic shoes, and the company's founders hoped to sell shoes to runners for more than it cost to make and market them. If they were successful (which they were), they'd make a profit. — *Def. Business*

Before we go on, let's make a couple of important distinctions concerning the terms in our definitions. First, whereas Nike produces and sells goods (athletic shoes, — *For-profit businesses*

Use abbreviations, like "Def" for "definition" and "Ex" for "example."

Numbering major details will help you remember them. In this case, the two types of businesses are numbered: for-profit and nonprofit.

apparel, and equipment), many businesses provide services. Your bank is a service company, as is your Internet provider. Airlines, law firms, movie theaters, and hospitals are also service companies. Many companies provide both goods and services. For example, your local car dealership sells goods (cars) and also provides a service (automobile repairs).

1st: For-profit
Goods vs. Services
Ex: Nike: Goods
Ex: Bank: Service

Goods AND services companies
Ex: Car dealership

2nd: Nonprofit org.
Ex: Post office, Red Cross

Second, some organizations are not set up to make profits. Many are established to provide social or educational services. Such not-for-profit (or nonprofit) organizations include the U.S. post office, museums, almost all colleges and universities, the Sierra Club, and the American Red Cross. Most of these organizations, however, function in much the same way as a business. They establish goals and work to meet them in an effective and efficient manner. Thus, most of the business principles introduced in this course also apply to nonprofits.

Nonprofits: function like for-profit businesses

You can also use sticky notes over the edge of a page to mark the page or describe it for easy reference later. Often students are hesitant to write in their textbooks, but annotating is such a powerful learning tool that you can't afford to skip it. It is well worth the investment in your textbook if you earn good grades by highlighting and annotating.

Chunking Information

Your brain is wired to store information in different stages. It first stores it in your immediate memory, which only lasts about 30 seconds. If you want to remember this information for a class or a quiz, you'll need to move it to your working memory. And, like a moving truck that can only move one truckload at a time, your brain will only be able to handle a limited amount of material at once. That's why you need to learn material in chunks. Stopping at the end of a section and reviewing what you just read helps your brain to remember and understand it better. Begin by asking yourself questions about what you just read, like:

"What did I just read about?"

"What was the most important idea the author tried to explain?"

"What other important points explain the main point?"

Try answering these three questions about the textbook selection "Getting Down to Business" in the example on the preceding page. You can look at the notes in the margins to help you.

If you want to learn this material, you will need to move it into your long-term memory. To do this, you must make sure that the material makes sense and has meaning for you.* The more you can meet these two requirements, the better you will remember what you just read. One way to do this is to try to think of your own examples and how the concepts apply to them. This helps you to connect what you learn to what you already know.

CHUNKING INFORMATION

Look at the definition for a business in the textbook selection "Getting Down to Business" on page 22. Can you think of other examples (besides the ones mentioned in the text) that fit this description? In the following spaces, jot down a couple of examples of businesses that you know. According to the definition, they must be in business to make a profit.

Businesses:

....

Next, the author discussed businesses that produce goods and those that provide services. Write your own examples of these types of businesses:

Goods:

....

Services:

....

Then, the author discussed businesses that provide both goods and services. Give your own examples of this:

Goods and Services:

....

Finally, the author discussed nonprofit businesses. Write two of your own examples:

Nonprofit:

....

Next, check your recall of the textbook selection by answering these questions. Try to answer the questions without looking back. Check when you are done to see if you answered the questions correctly.

1. What is the definition of a business?
2. What are two different types of businesses, and what is one example of each type?

The important thing to remember about active reading is that you are active, not just passing your eyes over the page. You are looking for answers to questions, making decisions about what is important and should be underlined, summarizing and making notes in the margins, and then making sense and meaning of what you just read. You go back over it again and think about what you read and how it relates to what you already know. You reread parts of it to highlight or annotate. And by providing the extra examples of your own, your brain makes connections between what you already know and what you are learning. The more that you practice this process, the more quickly and efficiently you'll be able to do it.

STEP **4**
Review

You should review new material every day. That's why it's important to set aside time to study even when you don't have a quiz or specific assignment that is due. During your study time, read through your class notes and test yourself. One easy way is to read the notes you made in the margins or in your notebook. As you are reading, try to explain what they mean. Imagine that *you* are the instructor trying to teach it to the class. If you have forgotten the information, this means it is not in your long-term memory yet. You need to review it again by going back and reading the sentences you underlined or highlighted. Try making up questions and writing the answers down. You can use note cards to write the questions on one side and the answers on the back. Practice answering them with a friend, or read them aloud. Try making a computer aid or graphic aid, such as a table, chart, concept map, or diagram to help you study.

If you spend 15 or 20 minutes reviewing material every night for each class you are taking, you will have a much stronger understanding and recall for what you are learning in class. You can earn those top grades and qualify for scholarship money, too.

This is why sticking to a study schedule is so important in college. Don't shortchange yourself by skimming through the text or not reading it at all. By doing that, you will be wasting your time and the money you spent on tuition. One thing is true: Students who take shortcuts in their learning fail faster than everybody else. Is that what you want? Or do you want to pass your courses with good grades? Investing time is as important as investing money in your education.

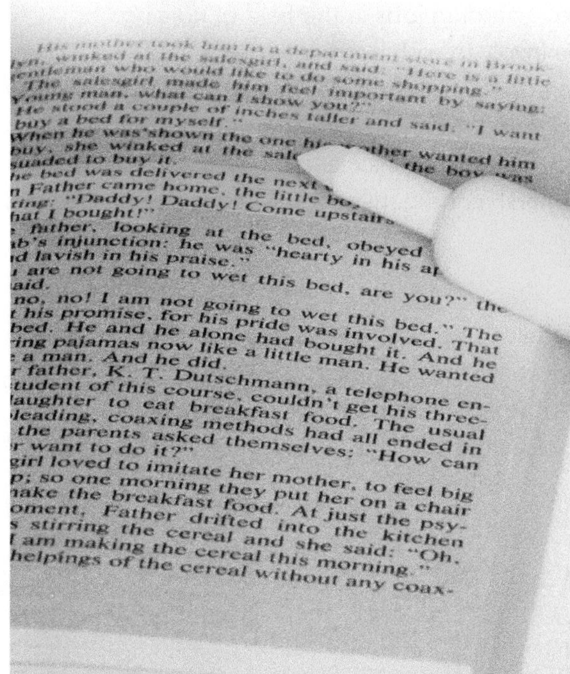

MyReadingLab

PRACTICE 1

1. Preview the article "Flight Nursing" with your team. Share any information you know about the topic with your learning partners before you start.
2. Underline the parts of the article that you read during your preview.
3. Write two questions you expect to have answered in this article. When writing preview questions, let your curiosity guide you. What information would *you* like to learn about this subject? Also, notice clues in the photos and bold print to help you think of questions.

Write your preview questions here:

1. ....

....

....

2. ....

....

....

4. Share what you wrote with your team.
5. Read silently to find the answers to your questions. Don't be concerned if your questions are not answered. Simply looking for the answers will help you to stay focused as you read. After you complete each of the four sections, underline or highlight anything that you think is important or that you would like to bring to someone else's attention later. If you find answers to your questions, underline them. Remember not to underline more than about a quarter of what you have read.

"FLIGHT NURSING"

If you are considering a career as a flight nurse, you have chosen one of the most challenging and rewarding jobs in the field of nursing. As a flight nurse, you will be involved with both emergency and non-emergency air transportation of injured or critically ill patients. You will provide care to trauma victims and monitor their vital signs as they are flown to hospitals. It is a job that demands excellent physical condition and a willingness to work in harsh conditions, often with long hours around the clock.

Requirements

Flight nursing requires a bachelor's degree in registered nursing with Advanced Cardiac Life Support (ACLS) certification. Also, it usually requires certification in Pediatric Advanced Life Support (PALS). Some jobs may require additional certification.

Continued...

Employment

Flight nurses are employed by trauma centers in hospitals, the military, and public and private transport companies. Employers look for nurses with three to five years of nursing experience and someone who is willing to perform physically demanding work. When not on flight duty, these nurses have to also be willing to perform routine tasks. Flight nurses can make anywhere from $50,000 to $85,000 a year, depending on where they work.

Resources

For more information on what it is like to be a flight nurse, go to the Discover Nursing website and read articles about real flight nurses. You can also request more information from the National Flight Nurses Association (NFNA) in Denver.

AFTER READING

6. When you have finished reading, summarize what the passage was about in one or two sentences. How would you describe this selection to someone who hasn't read it? Be brief and very general in your description.

My summary of "Flight Nursing":

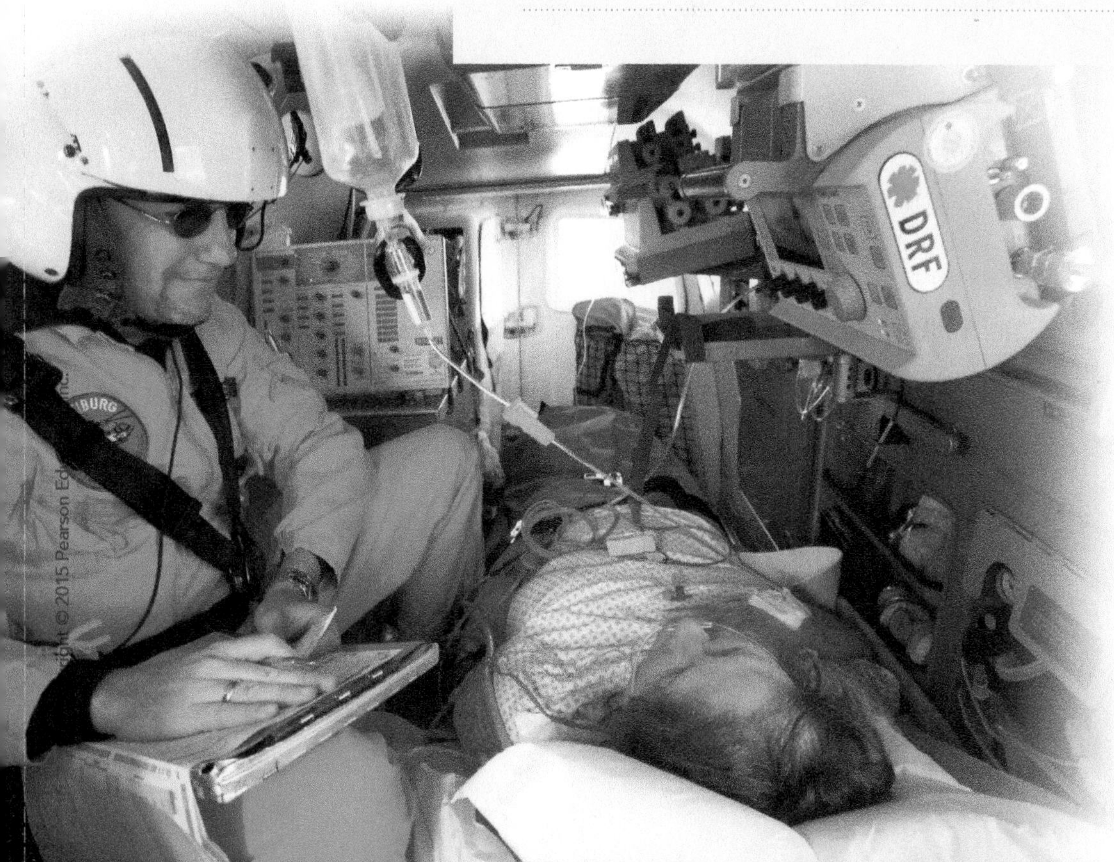

MyReadingLab

PRACTICE 2

For short articles, preview by reading the title, the headings, and the first sentence of each paragraph. Preview the following selection, and then answer the questions that follow. Underline everything that you previewed.

1. What is the topic? ....

2. What is one question you hope to have answered in this selection?

....

THE BUSINESS OF HEALTH CARE

[1] Medical fields urgently need people who are able to manage the business of health care. [2] Health administration is a growing field needing trained supervisors, managers, and directors. [3] They are responsible for managing large or small health care facilities such as hospitals, clinics, doctors' offices, veterinarians' offices, and health insurance companies. [4] These professionals help to improve the quality of patient care while keeping costs under control. [5] Health administrators need good computer skills, as well as good communication skills. [6] People with strong business skills are needed to help patients receive the best possible care available to them.

Requirements

[7] To become a health administrator, you will need to have a bachelor's degree in business or health administration. [8] Besides general education courses, you will need to take courses in business, law, and health care. [9] To find out more, search the Internet or see a college counselor.

Now, go back and read the article. Finally, review by answering the following questions.

1. What do health administrators do?

....

2. What kinds of skills do health administrators need?

....

3. What is the main requirement for health administration?

....

MyReadingLab

PRACTICE 3

Practice the four-step reading process with the following article by previewing, reading actively, highlighting and annotating, and reviewing. First, preview the article by reading the titles and first sentence of each paragraph, then highlight what you previewed. Based on what you previewed, answer the first two questions.

1. What is the topic (subject) of this article?

   Cholesterol

2. What are two questions that you expect this article will answer?

   1.) How does it effect you?
   2.) what is cholesterol?

CHOLESTEROL

Are your cholesterol levels within a healthy range? Do you know your LDL? Your HDL? When cholesterol (a fatty substance found in animal cell membranes) clogs up the blood vessels, it can lead to heart attack or stroke. Because cholesterol doesn't dissolve in water, it is carried throughout the body attached to proteins called lipoproteins. Low-density lipoproteins are high in cholesterol and low in protein. LDLs distribute cholesterol throughout the body. High-density lipoproteins (HDL) contain more protein than cholesterol. Your cholesterol level is measured by a blood test which determines the amount of LDL and HDL in your blood. If your total cholesterol is higher than 200, or your LDL is above 100, your doctor will recommend cutting back on saturated fat with high cholesterol levels in your diet, which is found in foods such as meat, oils, butter, or fried foods. Eating more fruits, vegetables, and grains instead will help to lower your cholesterol. In some cases, medications may be prescribed to lower LDL levels.

The Effects of Too Much Cholesterol

When your blood flow is restricted by deposits of cholesterol in your blood vessels, diminished blood flow to the heart can cause chest pain, or angina, to occur. A completely blocked artery can lead to a heart attack, which causes the oxygen-starved heart tissue to die. This results in permanent heart damage and may eventually lead to severe cardiac disease and death.

Besides restricting blood flow to the heart, fatty deposits in the arteries can also restrict blood flow to the brain. This can lead to a stroke, which can cause irreversible damage to the brain tissue. Although some cholesterol is needed to help your body's cells maintain fluidity and to build hormones such as estrogen and testosterone, too much cholesterol can have damaging and fatal effects.

Continued...

MyReadingLab

PRACTICE 3

...continued

Now read actively, looking for answers to your preview questions. Mark the answers if you find them, reading one section at a time. Next, highlight and annotate by underlining the answers to your preview questions, plus any important points that interested you. Make brief notes in the margins to describe what each paragraph is about. Finally, review by answering the following questions.

1. What is cholesterol?

2. Explain what HDL and LDL levels are.

3. What are some of the effects of high LDL levels of cholesterol?

MyReadingLab

TEXTBOOK SELECTION

Preview the textbook selection as a team. Each member of the team chooses one or two of the questions below. If there are more questions than people on your team, the whole team can work on the leftover questions. When you find the answer, underline it in the textbook. When your team has finished all five questions, take turns sharing your answers.

QUESTIONS

1. What is the topic (subject) of the information in this selection?

2. What are some specific subjects that will be discussed?

3. What do the diagrams and photograph show?

4. Based on what you previewed, write one question you can use to ask another team.

....

....

5. What are some terms that will be defined in this textbook selection?

....

....

....

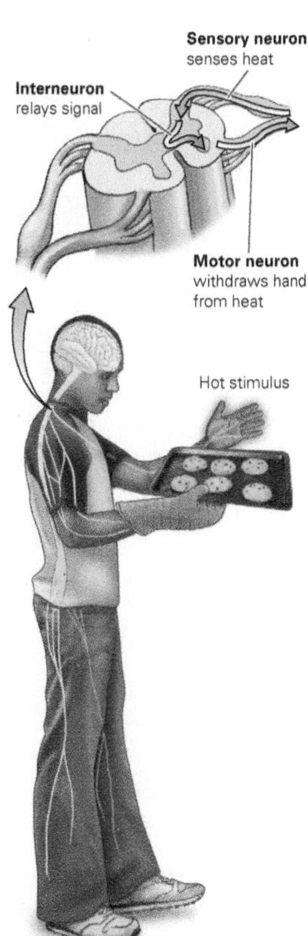

Figure 21.4 **A reflex arc.** A reflex arc can consist of a sensory receptor, a sensory neuron, an interneuron, a motor neuron, and an effector. Touching a hot baking sheet evokes the withdrawal reflex.

21.2 The Brain

The brain is the region of the body where decisions are reached and where bodily activities are directed and coordinated. The human brain is about the size of a small cantaloupe. Brains of the evolutionary ancestors to humans tend to be smaller and less complex *(Figure 21.5)*. The brain is housed inside the skull, where it sits in a liquid bath, called **cerebrospinal fluid,** that protects and cushions it.

In addition to housing 100–200 billion neurons, the brain is composed of other cells called **glial cells.** There are 10 times as many glial cells in the brain as there are neurons. In contrast to neurons, glial cells do not carry messages. Instead, they support the neurons by supplying nutrients, helping to repair the brain after injury, and attacking invading bacteria. Structurally, the brain is subdivided into many important anatomical regions, including the cerebrum, thalamus, hypothalamus, cerebellum, and brain stem *(Figure 21.6)*.

Cerebrum

The **cerebrum** fills the whole upper part of the skull. This part of the brain controls language, memory, sensations, and decision making. The cerebrum has two hemispheres, each divided into four lobes *(Figure 21.7)*:

1. The **temporal lobe** is involved in processing auditory and olfactory information and is important in memory and emotion.
2. The **occipital lobe** processes visual information from the eyes.
3. The **parietal lobe** processes information about touch and is involved in self-awareness.
4. The **frontal lobe** processes voluntary muscle movements and is involved in planning and organizing future expressive behavior.

The deeply wrinkled outer surface of the cerebrum is called the **cerebral cortex.** In humans, the cerebral cortex, if unfolded, would be the size of a 16-inch pizza. The folding of the cortex increases the surface area and allows this structure to fit inside the skull. The cortex contains areas for understanding and generating speech, areas that receive input from the eyes, and areas that receive other sensory information from the body. It also contains areas that allow planning.

The cerebrum and its cortex are divided from front to back into two halves—the right and left cerebral hemispheres—by a deep groove or fissure. At the base of this fissure lies a thick bundle of nerve fibers, the **corpus callosum,** which functions as a communication link between the hemispheres. The **caudate nuclei** are paired structures found deep within each cerebral hemisphere. These structures function as part of the pathway that coordinates movement.

Thalamus and Hypothalamus

Deep inside the brain, lying between the two cerebral hemispheres, are the thalamus and the hypothalamus. The **thalamus** relays information between the spinal cord and the cerebrum. The thalamus is the first region of the brain to receive messages signaling such sensations as pain, pressure, and temperature. The thalamus suppresses some signals and enhances others, which are then relayed to the cerebrum. The cerebrum processes these messages and sends signals to the spinal cord and to neurons in muscles when action is necessary. The **hypothalamus,** located just under the thalamus and about the size of a kidney bean, is the control center for sex drive, pleasure, pain, hunger, thirst, blood pressure, and body temperature. The hypothalamus also releases hormones, including those that regulate the production of sperm and egg cells as well as the menstrual cycle.

U-REVIEW

THINK, PAIR, AND SHARE

First, answer the following questions about the chapter by yourself. If you need to, go back and look up the correct answers. After you have completed your answers, pair up with another person. Take turns asking each other the questions. Give your partner enough time to answer, and wait until he or she is done answering before making any corrections or additions to the answer.

1. What is the first step in the four-step reading process, how is it done, and why should you do it?

2. What is the second step in the reading process, how is it done, and why should you do it?

3. What is the third step in the reading process, how is it done, and why should you do it?

4. What is the fourth step in the reading process, how is it done, and why should you do it?

MyReadingLab
Reading 1
VOCABULARY PREVIEW

"Flight Nurse Hero" by Corinne Fennessy

The following vocabulary words are from the article "Flight Nurse Hero." With a partner or in a team, choose the correct meanings of the underlined words in the following sentences. Use context clues (LEADS), word part clues, and parts of speech to help you figure out the meanings.

1. The baby was born with a congenital (kon-JEN-i-tl) heart defect, which needed surgery.
   a. having had since birth
   b. heart
   c. friendly
   d. necessary
2. When someone is unconscious, the first thing you should check is the person's respiration (res-pur-A-shun). If he or she is not breathing, it could be due to a blocked airway.
   a. sweat
   b. hope
   c. breathing
   d. heartbeat
3. Karen works as a respiratory therapist (RES-pur-a-tor-ee THER-a-pist) to help people with breathing problems.
   a. someone who helps people with emotional problems
   b. someone who helps people with breathing problems
   c. someone who helps people with heart problems
   d. a machine to assist breathing
4. The baby was lying inside an Isolette (eye-so-LET) when the nurse came to give her medicine.
   a. crib
   b. box
   c. machine
   d. a type of incubator for babies
5. The tall mangroves (MAN-grovz) that grow in swampy areas provide shelter and food for wildlife.
   a. a type of tropical tree or shrub that grows in swamps
   b. a swamp
   c. a place where animals and fish live
   d. shelters
6. You should note the locations of egress (EE-gress) on a plane in case of an emergency evacuation.
   a. parachutes
   b. wings
   c. exit
   d. food preparation

Continued...

MyReadingLab

Reading 1

...continued

7. Even though I called him to the dinner table three times, Robbie was oblivious (ob-LIV-ee-us) to my calls because he was so interested in the TV show.
   a. angry
   b. unaware of
   c. listening for
   d. ignoring
8. She wants to be a neonatal (nee-o-NATE-al) nurse because she loves taking care of babies.
   a. nursing home
   b. physical therapy
   c. full-time
   d. having to do with young babies
9. We drove on the causeway (KOZ-way) over the bay to get to the city.
   a. a type of bridge
   b. ferry
   c. tunnel
   d. street
10. The spinning rotors (RO-terz) of the helicopter caused my hat to blow off.
   a. motors
   b. fans
   c. blades
   d. engines

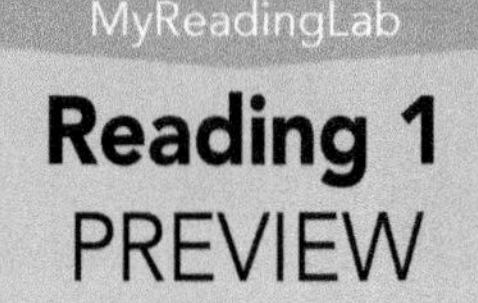

1. Have you ever experienced a medical emergency yourself or with someone you know? Describe what happened.
2. What do you know about medical transportation using helicopters?

Directions: As you read this article, practice the four-step reading process. Preview the article, and then write on the following lines one or two questions that you would hope to have answered.

....

....

....

MyReadingLab

Reading 1

As you read, answer the questions in the margins to check your comprehension.

"Flight Nurse Hero"

by Corinne Fennessy

1 It was July 2000, and Diane Muhl-Ludes expected a busy day. As a flight nurse for All Children's Hospital in Tampa, FL, she knew that anything could happen. She and her husband Scott, an intensive-care nurse, both knew that nurses were on the front line during any emergencies.

2 Just two years ago, Diane was driving past a golf course and saw cars pulled off the side of the road.

3 "I had the strangest feeling come over me, like, 'Diane, you have to stop, *right now*,'" she told reporter Dave Sheiber of the St. Petersburg Times. She parked her car and ran across a busy highway to find a truck lying upside down deep in a sewer retention pond. She rushed into the water to help find the truck driver.

4 "I had this really bizarre, gut feeling that the body was right there below where the door of the cab would have been," she said.

What did Diane do at the golf course that day?

5 Her instincts proved right, and after flipping the truck with the help of several more people, they found him. She held the driver's neck to protect it from spinal injury. When they reached the shore, she began mouth-to-mouth resuscitation. He choked, coughed, and began to breathe. She later learned that he was one of her neighbors' sons who had moved away a few years ago. The doctors and paramedics credited Diane with saving his life.

6 Almost two years later, Diane's husband took a message from the American Red Cross. Diane would be recognized as a national "Nursing Hero" for saving the truck driver. Scott tried calling her, but Diane was busy loading a stretcher with a critically ill baby girl into a helicopter. The child suffered from a congenital heart condition and had to be rushed to the hospital in Tampa.

7 The baby was strapped into an Isolette and hooked up to medical equipment for measuring her heartbeat and respiration. Her partner was Kevin Lockwood, a respiratory therapist, who would help monitor the baby's oxygen levels.

stabilized: kept at a steady level

8 The helicopter pilot finished his routine checks before taking off. Diane and Kevin plugged in their intercom headphones and checked the baby's levels. Luckily, her oxygen level had **stabilized** because the baby had to breathe on her own during the flight.

mangling: twisting

9 As the chopper flew over Tampa Bay, the sky grew darker. Diane had an uneasy feeling. She always hated flying over water because she knew that if the helicopter crashed, it would flip over and sink like a rock. If there were mangroves below, the helicopter rotors could get tangled in the branches, **mangling** them and crashing.

Continued...

MyReadingLab

Reading 1

...continued

10 She soon spotted the Skyway Bridge spanning Tampa Bay and knew it would not be long before they landed on the Bayfront Medical Center helipad.

11 Then it came-- a deafening explosion that jolted the helicopter. KA-BOOM!

12 "What's that?" she yelled.

What happened as they flew over Tampa Bay?

"Hang on!" the pilot cried, and called into his radio, "Mayday! Mayday! Bayflite 3 is going down!"

13 The helicopter began spinning as it fell from the sky toward the open water below. Diane grabbed onto Kevin with one hand and onto the baby's stretcher with the other. She knew that they were about to crash and she braced herself for it.

horrific: horrible

14 Suddenly there was a **horrific** grinding noise and another explosion. BOOM! The helicopter crashed violently, and then skidded across the pavement. Diane felt herself flung sideways and her face collided painfully with something hard.

15 The pilot had made an emergency landing on a causeway in Tampa Bay. Headlights approached in the distance from both directions as he called for help on the radio. Suddenly, the chopper burst into flames.

intercom: the on-board communication system

16 "Egress! Egress!" he shouted over the **intercom**.

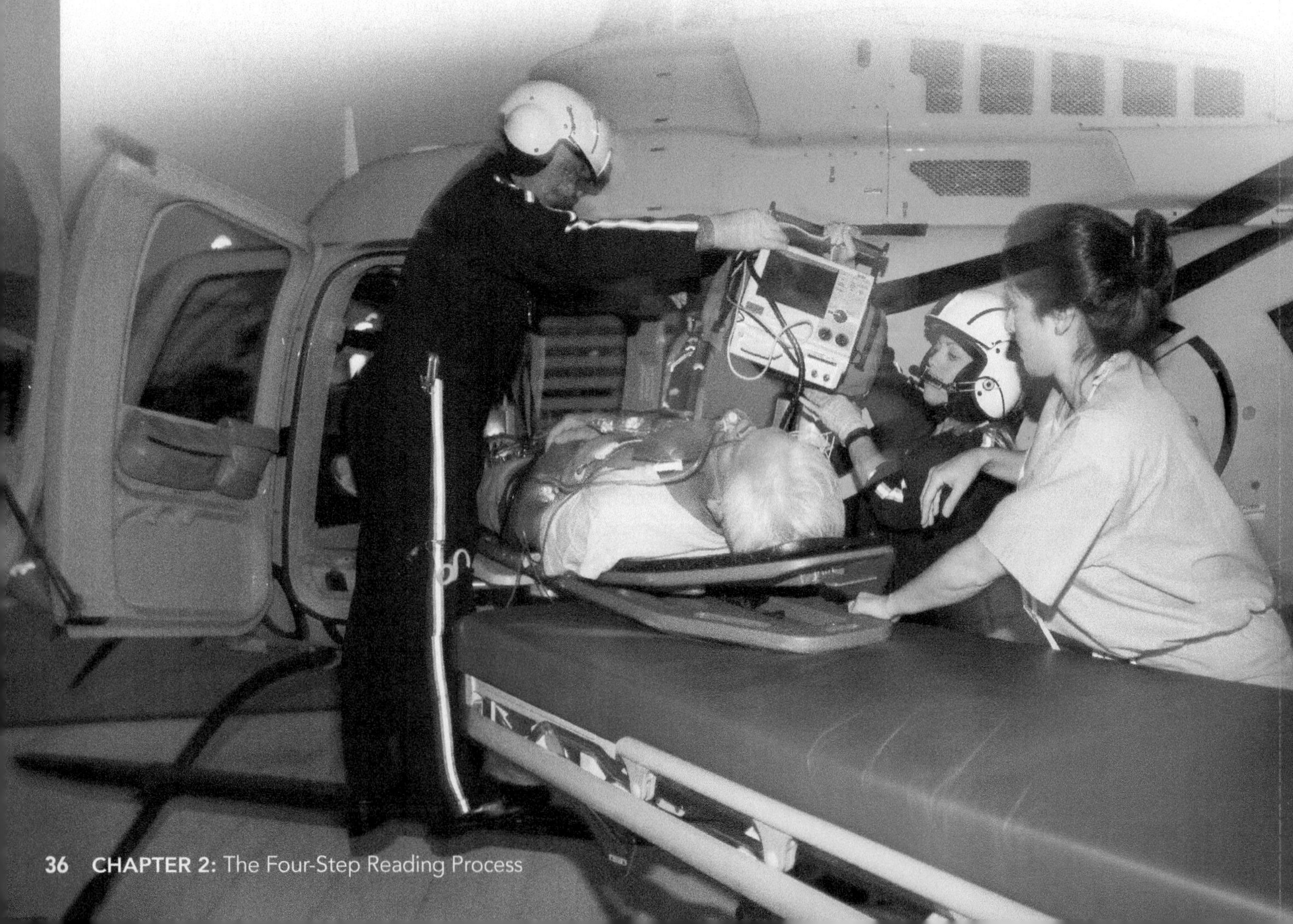

17 Kevin shoved the door open with all of his weight and jumped onto the pavement. Diane and Kevin grabbed the stretcher and swiftly lifted it out from the burning chopper. Running toward the traffic, they rushed the stretcher away from the burning helicopter that could explode at any moment.

18 Oblivious to the danger, Diane began waving her arms madly at the traffic speeding toward them. Tires screeched and horns blared as the flames of the burning chopper soared 20 feet into the air.

19 Without medical equipment and monitors, the baby could die. Diane sprinted to one of the cars and borrowed a cell phone. She called the hospital and told them about the crash, asking them to send another helicopter. Then she asked them to call her husband and tell him that she was all right.

What did Diane and Kevin do to save their patient's life?

20 Diane and Kevin checked the baby's vital signs. The baby was unharmed and still stable. Within minutes, they heard sirens in the distance and the thudding of a rescue helicopter approaching the scene. As soon as it landed, Kevin and Diane loaded the stretcher inside and took off for Bayfront Medical Center.

21 On their arrival, they rushed the baby into the neonatal intensive care unit where doctors and nurses took her into their care. Diane and Kevin soon learned that baby was going to be all right. Heaving sighs of relief, they sank down into chairs.

22 Scott had received Diane's message and said, "I had a weird feeling that something was going to happen. Usually Diane leaves me a message whenever she goes on a flight, and I just say, 'Fly safe.' But this time, she said she was heading down to Naples for a sick baby, and she left me a message that said, 'Say a prayer for me.' That was different—she'd never said that."

23 Ironically, the next day while at work Diane learned that she had been chosen as a National Nursing Hero for saving the 17 year-old truck driver nearly two years before. She would be honored at the Red Cross headquarters in Washington, D.C.

What do you think made Diane respond to each of the emergencies she had faced?

24 Perhaps Diane had a premonition about stopping that day she saved the teenager's life, and perhaps something had told her to ask her husband for a prayer before her flight to Tampa. Whatever the reason, she had listened to her inner voice and did what all good nurses do—she saved lives.

1,002 words divided by ________ minutes = ________ words per minute

MyReadingLab

Reading 1 REVIEW

It is a good habit to summarize everything you read to strengthen your comprehension.

Complete the following summary of "Flight Nurse Hero" by filling in the missing information in the paragraph below.

Flight Nurse Diane Muhl-Ludes made two heroic rescues. In July 2000, she saved a .... from drowning after he crashed his truck into a .... Two years later, she rescued a .... from a burning .... The patient was on a medical flight when the helicopter .... on .... Diane delivered her patient safely to Bayfront Medical Center. She received an award from the Red Cross as a National Nursing Hero.

MyReadingLab

Reading 1 COMPREHENSION QUESTIONS

The following questions will help you to recall the main idea and the details of "Flight Nurse Hero." Review any parts of the article that you need to in order to find the correct answers.

1. What is the topic (subject) of this article? (Who or what is this article about?)

a. flight nursing
b. Diane Muhl-Ludes' heroic rescues
c. neonatals
d. Diane's career as a flight nurse

MAIN IDEA

2. What is the main idea of the article? (What is the most general statement that tells the most important point of the article?)

a. A sick baby was transported to another hospital by helicopter.
b. Diane Muhl-Ludes made two heroic rescues during her career as a nurse.
c. A helicopter caused a crash.
d. Flight nursing can be dangerous.

SUPPORTING DETAILS

3. What happened to Diane in July 2000?

a. She saved a baby during a helicopter crash.
b. She rescued a teen from a burning helicopter.
c. She saved the life of a teenage truck driver.
d. She stopped cars when a helicopter crashed on the Tampa Bay causeway.

4. Why was Diane afraid of flying over water or swamps?

a. She thought they may have alligators in them.
b. She knew that if the helicopter crashed, it would sink.
c. She didn't have much confidence in the pilot's ability to navigate over water.
d. She couldn't swim.

5. **What did Diane and Kevin do as soon as they landed on the bridge?**
   a. They moved the baby's stretcher away from the burning chopper.
   b. They began giving the patient mouth-to-mouth resuscitation.
   c. They both ran out of the helicopter and away from the burning chopper.
   d. They called for help and requested another helicopter.

6. **What did Diane do once she was on the highway?**
   a. She waved her arms to flag down a car to ask for a ride to the hospital.
   b. She called her husband to tell him she was all right.
   c. She borrowed a cell phone and called the hospital for help.

7. **What happened after they landed on the causeway?**
   a. An ambulance came and took the baby to the hospital.
   b. Another helicopter came and took the crew and the baby to the hospital.
   c. A driver on the causeway offered to take them to the nearest hospital.
   d. The fire department's emergency rescue team took the baby to the hospital.

VOCABULARY IN CONTEXT

Using context clues and word part clues, determine the best meaning for the underlined word in each of these sentences. If necessary, use a dictionary.

8. **Suddenly there was a horrific grinding noise and another explosion.**
   a. ugly
   b. strong
   c. horrifying
   d. likely

9. **"Mayday, Mayday! Bayflite 3 is going down!" the pilot called into the radio (paragraph 15).**
   a. the day of the month
   b. emergency
   c. a command to jump
   d. a person's name

10. **It was probably right beneath us now, spanning Tampa Bay (paragraph 10).**
   a. turning
   b. swimming
   c. circling
   d. crossing

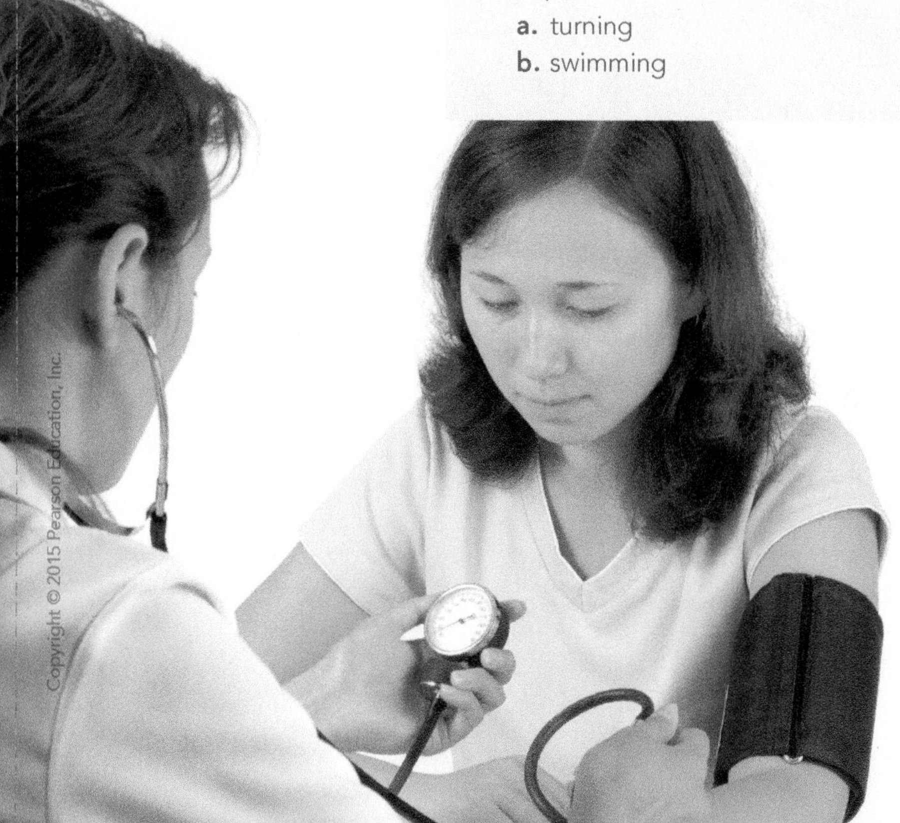

MyReadingLab

Reading 1 VOCABULARY PRACTICE

Use the vocabulary words from the following Word Bank to complete the sentences. Write the words into the blanks provided.

WORD BANK			
congenital	respiration	respiratory therapist	Isolette
mangroves	egress	oblivious	neonatal
causeway	rotors		

1. The pediatric nurse placed the newborn infant into a(n) ....

2. Damian was not allowed to play on his high school football team because the doctor found that he had a(n) .... heart defect.

3. We paddled our canoes around the .... looking for rare birds and wildlife in the swamp.

4. The emergency medical technician checked the patient's pulse and ....

5. José is .... to Maria's flirting with him. He hasn't a clue how she feels about him.

6. The .... of the helicopter collided with the signal tower and crashed.

7. Janeka wanted to be a(n) .... so she could treat people with breathing problems.

8. Working in the .... unit of the hospital, Cassandra got used to the sound of crying babies.

9. A crash on the .... caused a huge traffic jam for nearly two hours.

10. In case of an emergency, it is a good idea to note the best route of .... from your office building.

MyReadingLab

Reading 1 QUESTIONS FOR WRITING AND DISCUSSION

Review any parts of the article you need to answer the following questions.

1. What personal characteristics would a good flight nurse need to have?

2. Why do you think Diane risks her own life to rescue others?

3. What actions in the article showed that Diane is well suited for her profession?

4. What feelings did Diane display during the article that showed her "human side"?

5. Do you feel that Diane should be regarded as a hero? Why or why not?

Reading 1
VOCABULARY PRACTICE—CROSSWORD

Read the clues at the bottom. Fill in the crossword with the words in the Word Bank.

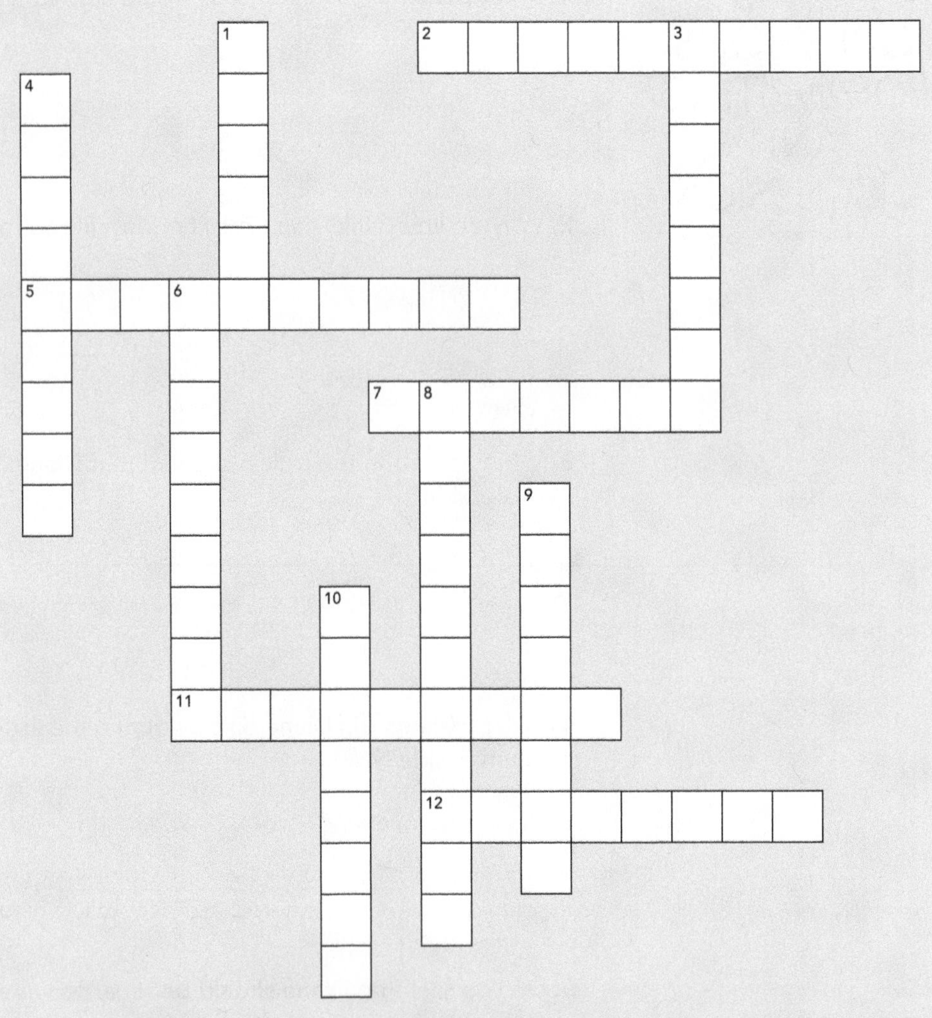

WORD BANK

CAUSEWAY	CONGENITAL	CRUCIAL	EGRESS
INTERCOM	ISOLETTE	MANGROVES	NEONATAL
OBLIVIOUS	REPOSITION	RESPIRATION	SATURATED

ACROSS

2. having this since birth
5. to put in position again
7. extremely important
11. filled with
12. communication system

DOWN

1. exit
3. newborn (adj.)
4. tropical trees or shrubs
6. not aware
8. breathing
9. a type of baby incubator
10. a bridge

MyReadingLab

Reading 2
VOCABULARY PREVIEW

From Illegal Immigrant to Brain Surgeon: Dr. Alfredo Quiñones

by C. F. Hopkins

The following vocabulary words are from the article, "From Illegal Immigrant to Brain Surgeon: Dr. Alfredo Quiñones." With a partner or in a team, choose the correct meanings of the underlined words in the following sentences. Use context clues (LEADS), word part clues, and parts of speech to help you figure out the meanings.

1. At age 14, Quiñones qualified for an accelerated (ak-SELL-er-ate-ed) program that prepared students for jobs as elementary school teachers. (paragraph 8)
   a. faster than regular
   b. shorter than regular
   c. financially assisted
   d. popular
2. In the spring of 1993, his mentor (MEN-tor) looked over his transcripts and told Alfredo that he stood a good chance of getting into Harvard Medical School.
   a. supervisor
   b. friend
   c. someone who watches another
   d. someone who gives advice to another
3. Alfredo soon became known as Dr. Q, an affectionate and conscientious (kon-shee-EN-shus) person who is sensitive to the needs of his patients.
   a. popular
   b. responsible
   c. joyful
   d. careful
4. Dr. Quiñones studied the brain at medical school because he was interested in neurosurgery (NUR-oh-sur-jer-ee).
   a. surgery on the nerves
   b. surgery on the heart
   c. brain surgery
   d. bone surgery
5. Our camp was in such a remote (re-MOTE) location that we had to hike two hours from the nearest road to reach it.
   a. easy to find
   b. far from civilization
   c. unbelievable
   d. unreachable
6. Many people living in poor countries are so destitute (DES-ti-toot) that they break laws to survive.
   a. poverty-stricken
   b. unhappy
   c. untrustworthy
   d. illegal

Continued...

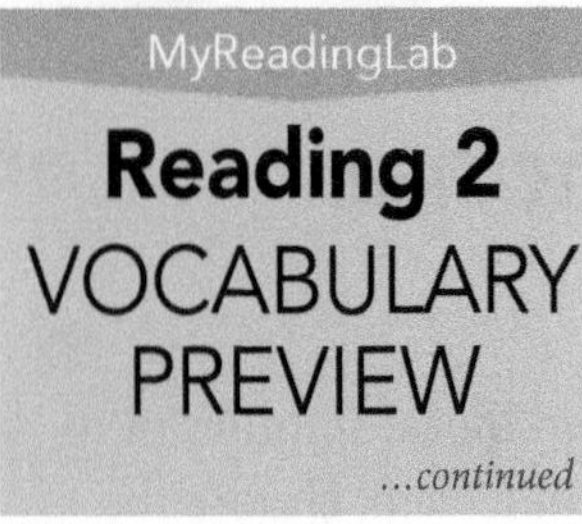

7. During college, my roommate and I lived very frugally (FROO-gal-lee) by cooking our own meals and sharing things.
   a. simply
   b. satisfactorily
   c. in comfort
   d. in a thrifty manner

8. Even though college was difficult for Su Ling, she persevered (per-se-VEER'd) and earned her degree.
   a. studied hard
   b. persuaded
   c. put up with
   d. kept on trying

9. The brain is an organ with such complexity (kom-PLEX-it-ee) that it has taken researchers decades to understand its operation.
   a. difficulty
   b. determination
   c. being very complicated
   d. simplicity

10. Jonathan didn't have all the parts he needed for his computer, so he had to scrounge (skrownj) around to find them.
    a. to lead
    b. to seek out
    c. to pay for
    d. to scrub

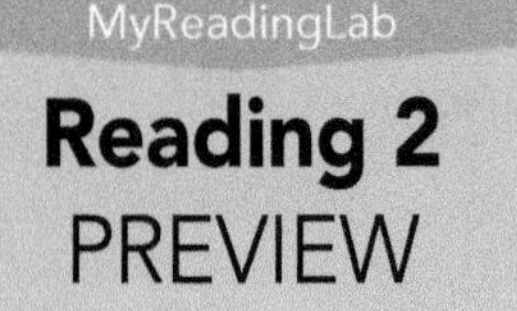

1. Do you know anyone who has come from another country? Why did he or she come, and what was their experience like?
2. Have you ever traveled to a country where you didn't know the language? Describe your experiences.

Directions: As you read this article, practice the four-step reading process. Preview the article, and then write on the following lines one or two questions that you would hope to have answered.

....

....

....

....

MyReadingLab

Reading 2

As you read, answer the questions in the margins to check your comprehension.

"From Illegal Immigrant to Brain Surgeon: Dr. Alfredo Quiñones"

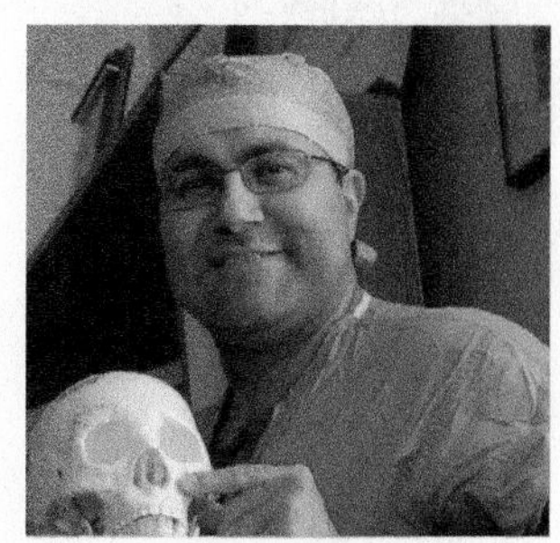

by C.F. Hopkins © 2013

Dr. Alfredo Quiñones wasn't always a top brain surgeon in the U.S. His life is literally a rags-to-riches story about a hungry teenager who hopped the fence from Mexico in search of a better life.

1 Alfredo Quiñones-Hinojosa's adventure began in Mexico, 1968, when he was born. His father owned a gas station in a small town where his wife and their five children, who also lived there. Although they were poor, the family was loving and happy. From age five, Alfredo pumped gas and attended school. One day, he found his father crying behind the gas station. He told his son that the country was in an economic depression, and that he had lost everything. His father encouraged him to stay in school and get an education so he wouldn't end up destitute like him.

2 At age 14, Alfredo entered an accelerated training program for elementary school teachers. This meant getting up at 4:30 a.m. to get the bus and hitchhiking home in the scorching heat. Alfredo graduated near the top of his class, and he was offered a teaching job at a remote school. Because he had no political connections, this was his only opportunity.

3 Because Alfredo had worked summer jobs in the U.S., he knew he could find work there picking crops. He decided to cross the border and meet his cousin who was working in the U.S. On his first attempt, Alfredo was captured by border police and taken back to Mexico. But he tried again that same night. The police were nowhere in sight, and his cousin picked him up. It was the night of his 19th birthday.

How did Alfredo get his start in America?

4 Alfredo went to work on a California farm picking tomatoes for $155 a week. He slept in a camper trailer in a field, wearing the same old clothes every day. He sent some money home to his parents and saved the rest by eating whatever crops he could scrounge, and by living frugally. He kept a dictionary in his pocket and taught himself English. Eventually, he began driving farm equipment and learning how to service the engines. His thirst for knowledge and determination drove him to succeed so that he could help others, and because, "I had that hunger in my gut."

5 In Stockton, California, Alfredo attended night classes at San Joaquin Delta College, and worked loading sulfur and fish lard during the day. It was back-breaking and smelly work, but he persisted because he had a goal.

"I realized that the only way to move up in society was through hard work and education . . . I knew the opportunities were there, that all I had to

Continued...

MyReadingLab

Reading 2

...continued

do was knock on the door, but it was difficult. I couldn't stop working, which meant having to go to classes at night smelling like sulfur, but I persevered," he said.

6 Within a year, he was promoted to a foreman at work and took the night shift so he could attend college full-time during the day. Using a combination of scholarships, loans, a small grant, and tutoring other students, he paid his way through the University of California at Berkeley. His grades were good, and his mentor told him that he had a good chance at attending Harvard Medical School—one of the top med schools in the country.

7 In 1994, Alfredo was accepted at Harvard in Boston. He became a U.S. citizen a year later. Med school was an ordeal, but Alfredo was used to challenges and not one to give up easily.

"The challenges weren't physical or intellectual, although I was still learning English at the time, but more emotional. I had classmates who committed suicide because of the pressure, which added a level of complexity. Finding my own path was the biggest challenge."

8 In his usual fashion, Alfredo applied himself to med school working extremely hard. At Harvard he decided to become a brain surgeon. "One day, I was walking through Brigham and Women's Hospital and I saw Dr. Peter Black, the chairman of neurosurgery. I introduced myself, and he invited me that day to come to watch him do an operation. As it happened, he was doing an "awake" surgery, where the patient's brain is exposed and the patient is awake so that the surgeon can ask questions. As I watched that, I fell in love with brain surgery."

How did Alfredo get his education and medical training?

9 Alfredo returned to California to continue his medical training at the University of California at San Francisco. His hard-work **ethic** continued to see him through one of the most difficult periods of his life. He often worked up to 130 hours a week for $30,000 a year. He also married and began a family. Despite the intense pressure, he didn't give up.

"I felt what my father felt, not being able to put food on the table for my family. But I had a dream," he said. But it was during this time that Alfredo realized he was doing the work that he was intended to do. His first surgery was a patient with **brain trauma**. It was a life-and-death situation. Although the patient died, Alfredo felt that he had been given a gift.

brain trauma: a brain injury causing damage

10 "I realized I could work with my hands and touch this incredible organ, which is what I do now. I cannot conceive of a much more intimate relationship than that. A patient grants you the gift of trusting you with his life, and there is no room for mistakes," Alfredo told a NY Times reporter, Claudia Dreifus. Alfredo soon became known as Dr. Q, an affectionate and conscientious person who is sensitive to the needs of his patients. Dr. Q is now a professor of neurosurgery and **oncology** at Johns Hopkins Hospital in New York City where he performs about 250 surgeries a year and continues his education through research. "I am a surgeon and a teacher, but I always let people teach me. I am always learning."

oncology: the study of cancer

11 After a long day at the hospital, he heads for his research laboratory in Baltimore, MD, to conduct research on brain tumors. So far, Dr. Q has earned more than 20 awards for his work, and has published 113 scientific articles with his team. In 2011, he published his autobiography, *Becoming*

Dr Q: My Journey from Migrant Farm Worker to Brain Surgeon, and he is the lead editor on a forthcoming edition of a neurosurgery textbook. Dr. Q says, "Awards, fame, and glory mean nothing if you don't use them properly... No one award is more important than another. I'm always thinking about how I can use what I've achieved to do more, to make the world a better place."

12 Despite his long hours, Dr. Q still manages to find time for his wife and their three children. Dr. Q also helps to raise money for cancer research and makes time to visit his patients. He meets with all his patients and their families several times to help them face an uncertain future. Getting to know patients is sometimes the most painful part if the surgery doesn't work. "When they're scared, I'm one of them. I'm just lucky that patients allow me to touch their brains, their lives."

13 Now 40 years old, he has no plans of slowing down. Dr. Q continues working to make the world a better place. When asked about what other career he would consider, Dr. Q says, "I believe I was born to do what I do. I'm sure I would have been successful if I had chosen another path, but would anything make me happier? No."

1,220 words divided by ________ minutes = ________ words per minute

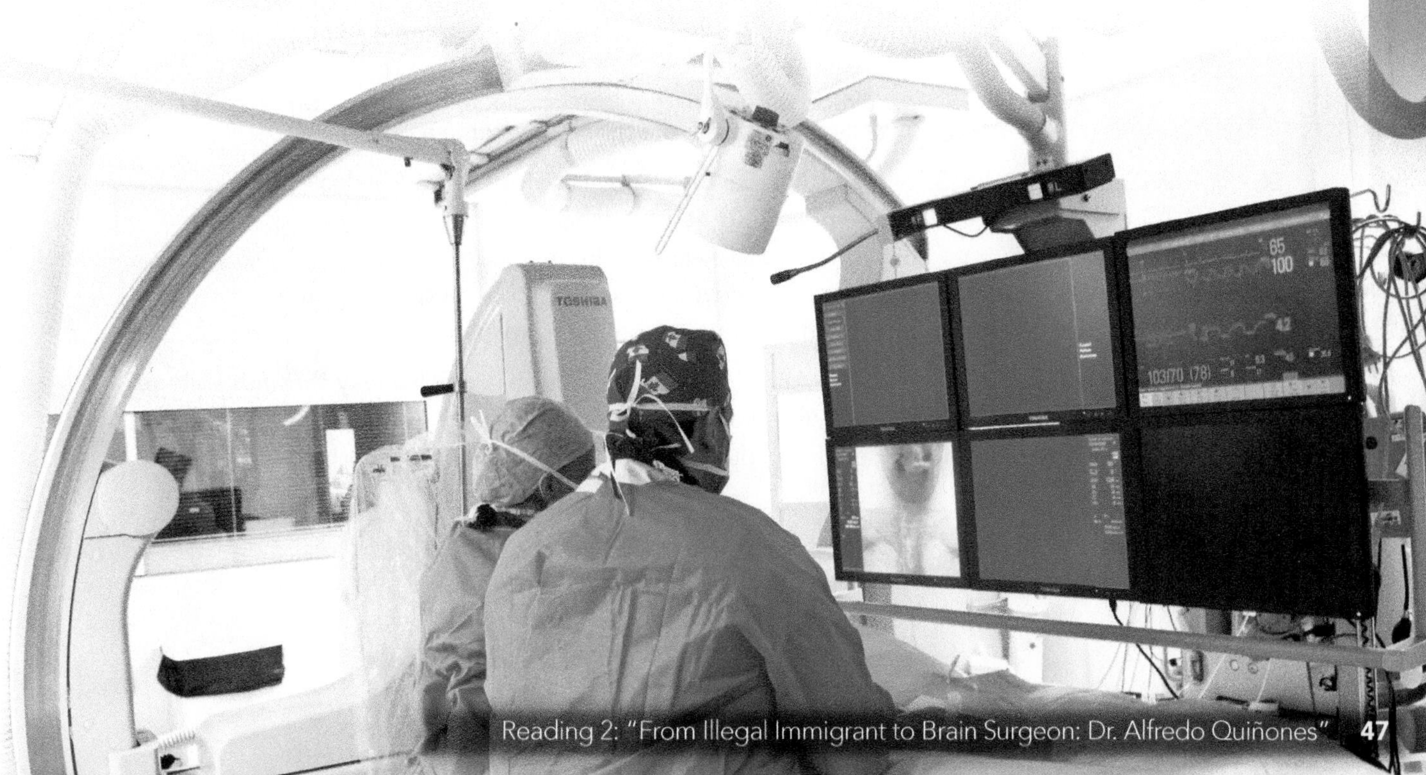

MyReadingLab

Reading 2 REVIEW

It's a good habit to summarize everything you read to strengthen your comprehension.

Directions: Complete the following summary of "From Illegal Immigrant to Brain Surgeon: Dr. Alfredo Quiñones" by filling in the blanks.

(Who?) ...., an illegal immigrant from ...., worked in ...., where he (did what?) .... He put himself through .... and .... to become a doctor. He is now a successful .... at Johns Hopkins Hospital.

MyReadingLab

Reading 2 COMPREHENSION QUESTIONS

The following questions will help you to recall the main idea and the details of "From Illegal Immigrant to Brain Surgeon: Dr. Alfredo Quiñones." Review any parts of the article you need in order to find the correct answers.

FINDING THE TOPIC

1. What is the topic (subject) of this article? (Who or what was this story about?)

a. illegal immigrants
b. neurosurgery
c. Alfredo Quiñones-Hinojosa
d. Mexican doctors

MAIN IDEA

2. What is the main idea of the story? (What is the most general idea that tells the most important point about the whole story?)

a. Alfredo Quiñones-Hinojosa entered the United States as an illegal immigrant and went to Harvard University.
b. Alfredo Quiñones-Hinojosa faced hardship in the United States.
c. Alfredo Quiñones-Hinojosa overcame prejudice and hatred to succeed.
d. Alfredo Quiñones-Hinojosa, an illegal immigrant, put himself through college and medical school to become a neurosurgeon.

SUPPORTING DETAILS (REREAD TO FIND THE ANSWERS TO THESE)

3. Why did Alfredo Quiñones-Hinojosa leave Mexico?

a. He wanted to get a good paying job in teaching.
b. He wanted to pick crops in America.
c. His parents moved to the U.S. and brought him with them.
d. He wanted to get a better paying job.

4. How did Alfredo Quiñones-Hinojosa pay his way through college?

a. He received a scholarship from Mexico.
b. He worked during the day, saved his money, and attended night classes.
c. He asked his cousins to help him pay for his tuition.
d. He took online classes to save money.

5. At Harvard Medical School, some students committed suicide because
   a. they knew they couldn't pass their courses.
   b. the pressure to succeed was so intense.
   c. heir studies were too difficult.
   d. they were afraid to quit school and disappoint their parents.

DRAWING CONCLUSIONS

6. **One of the main reasons Quiñones is so successful is that**
   a. he had the determination to succeed, and was willing to work hard for it.
   b. he had a family to help him get through college and medical school.
   c. he had people around him who encouraged him to become a doctor.
   d. he was satisfied with what he had.

7. **When Dr. Quiñones said, "I had that hunger in my gut," what did he mean?**
   a. He was hungry and wanted to make more money to buy food.
   b. The reason he worked hard was to become famous.
   c. He wanted to accomplish great things and to achieve his goals.
   d. He was hungry from working all day.

VOCABULARY IN CONTEXT

Using context clues and word part clues, determine the best meaning for the underlined word in each of these sentences. If necessary, use a dictionary to check your answers.

8. **His hard-work ethic continued to see him through one of the most difficult periods of his life. (paragraph 9)**
   a. rule of conduct
   b. morals
   c. relating to race
   d. employment

9. **"The challenges weren't physical or intellectual, although I was still learning English at the time, but more emotional."**
   a. relating to feelings
   b. relating to knowledge
   c. interesting
   d. smart

10. **Using a combination of scholarships, loans, a small grant, and tutoring other students, he paid his way through the University of California at Berkeley.**
    a. money donated by an organization
    b. a loan
    c. an inheritance
    d. a fee

MyReadingLab

Reading 2 VOCABULARY PRACTICE

Use the vocabulary words from the following Word Bank to complete the sentences. Write the words into the blanks provided.

WORD BANK

destitute	remote	scrounge	accelerated
frugally	persevered	mentor	neurosurgery
complexity	conscientious		

1. Jamal is a very .... student. He always completes his assignments and studies for every test.

2. After losing their jobs and homes during the recession of 2007–2008, many families were so .... that they had to move into homeless shelters.

3. Brianna's boyfriend likes to live very ...., but she often gets tired of his penny-pinching when they go on dates.

4. Lina and Sam registered for a(n) .... math course so they could complete two semesters of math in one.

5. Due to the .... of this physics problem, the class was divided into teams and each team worked on one part of the problem.

6. Although Enrico had to work full-time to pay his rent and college expenses, he .... until he completed his studies and graduated.

7. Eleana decided to specialize in .... after she graduated from medical school because she was fascinated by her research on the brain.

8. If you don't have enough food for dinner, I'm certain we can .... around in my kitchen to find some.

9. Travon chose to attend college in a very .... part of New Mexico so he could study the geological formations in that area.

10. Chen-Li was fortunate to have a .... at the university who helped her get accepted into nursing school.

MyReadingLab

Reading 2 QUESTIONS FOR WRITING AND DISCUSSION

Review any parts of the article you need to answer the following questions.

1. Dr. Quiñones has medical degrees and numerous awards, yet he feels that he must keep on learning. Why do you think he feels this way?

2. The U.S. has many immigrants who have achieved success. Some of them have come illegally, like Dr. Quiñones. What is your opinion regarding immigration?

3. In the article, Dr. Quiñones says, "Awards, fame, and glory mean nothing if you don't use them properly." What do you think he means by this?

4. What difficulties did Dr. Quiñones face when he was in college and medical school?

5. Dr. Quiñones achieves his goals because he puts forth tremendous effort. What goals would you be willing to achieve making the same sacrifices that he made?

Reading 2
VOCABULARY PRACTICE—WORD MAZE

In the word maze below, find the following words and their closest meanings in the surrounding boxes. The meaning of a vocabulary word must touch the box where the vocabulary word is found. Circle or shade in the boxes containing the words and their meanings to find the path through the maze. The first one is done for you.

WORD BANK

destitute	accelerated	remote	frugally
scrounge	persevered	mentor	complexity
neurosurgery	conscientious		

START

(complexity)	old	impossible	thoughtful
small	(very complicated)	injustice	fight
smile	aware of	mentor	boss
unpleasant	manager	friend	advisor
torrid	vehicles	accelerated	causeway
harmful	quickly	went faster	speeding
political	persevered	prejudice	location
kept on trying	judicial	criminal	believable
painfully	scrounge	carelessly	studying
to seek out	without effort	causing pain	interesting
remote	controller	obvious	attention
unlikely	faraway	online action	play a part
very hot	between acts	frugally	associate
saturated	actions	play	thrifty
a disease	faraway	conscientious	aware of
mortar	like another	imitate	responsible
unlike	electric plug	destitute	interesting
emergency	very poor	nerve doctor	specialist
nursing	new surgeon	neurosurgery	type of fish
internet website	nerve surgeon	nervous doctor	brain surgery

FINISH

ON THE JOB INTERVIEW

ARETHEA MOISE,

REGISTERED NURSE

1. How did you become interested in being a nurse?

I was born to become a nurse. As a child, I played nurse with my dolls and helped care for my younger brother and sister. I had midwives and nurses in my family back in Jamaica.

2. When you were in college, what were some of the obstacles that you had to overcome?

I was a single mom, and I was able to live at home with my parents while I went to college. I had to get up at 5 a.m. to go to clinicals. I had to take care of my son after classes and study hard to keep up my grades.

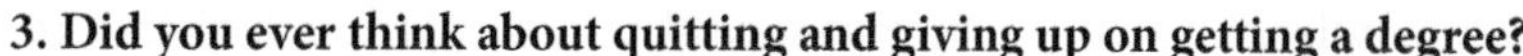

3. Did you ever think about quitting and giving up on getting a degree?

There were many times I wanted to quit. The hardest times were when my son cried when I had to leave him to go to classes. I also became so exhausted that at one point I had to drop a class and retake it because I was overworked and became ill. But I came back stronger and took the class again successfully.

4. Where do you work now, and what do you like about your job?

I am working as a nurse at Dr. Philips Hospital in Orlando, Florida. I love my job there because, as a preceptor, I monitor the new nurses who are just starting out. I am also finishing up my master's degree and teaching part-time. What I like most about my job is being able to help people through difficult times. It is so rewarding, and I love what I do.

5. What do you dislike about your job?

The long shifts are hard. Sometimes I have to work 12 to 14 hours in one shift. And sometimes it's hard working with nurses who are not team players. Everyone is on teams, and we help each other out. My unit works great together, but once in a while there is someone who is not cooperative, and she or he will make things more difficult than they need to be.

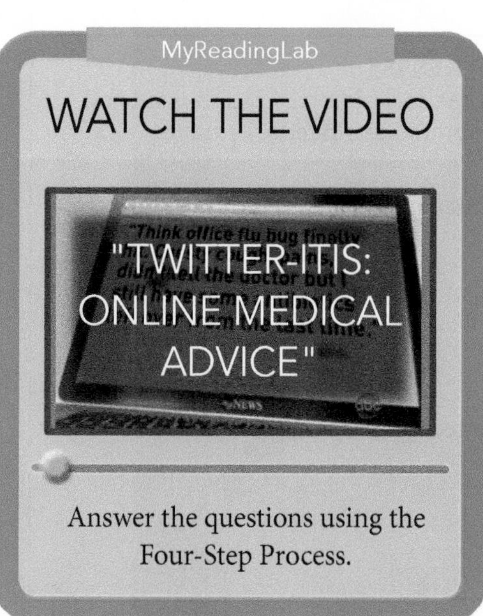

MyReadingLab
WATCH THE VIDEO
"TWITTER-ITIS: ONLINE MEDICAL ADVICE"
Answer the questions using the Four-Step Process.

6. If you could give college students one piece of advice, what would it be?

First, stay focused on your goal. Discouraging things will happen in your life, and you have to be determined to succeed. Having a degree has changed my whole life. I was able to buy a home and have the security of knowing I will always have a good job. Second, talk to an academic counselor at your school to make sure you are taking the right courses. Without the right courses, you won't get accepted into the nursing program.

7. What are your plans for the future?

I am completing my master's degree, and I teach part-time now at the community college. I may decide to do it full-time some day. I love the enthusiasm of the students who are so excited about becoming nurses. I am married now and my husband is in medical school. But I know I will be able to find a good job wherever I go because of the demand for nurses. I love this career, and I can't imagine doing anything else.

MyReadingLab

REAL-LIFE READING

LIVING WILL

In life you will have to read and understand many important documents. Read the following Living Will document, and then answer the questions that follow. Use the four-step reading process as you read, and then answer the questions that follow to check your comprehension.

LIVING WILL

I, ..., intend that this document states my wishes regarding my medical care if I am unable to communicate them otherwise. I declare that I am of sound mind and body and that I have not been influenced by anyone in regard to these statements. This declaration must be honored as my legal right to accept or refuse medical treatment.

For this declaration to be valid, my doctor and another doctor must review my condition. They must both agree that I am not able to regain consciousness, and that I am incapable of living without a life support system. If I am unable to participate in decisions regarding my medical care, the declarations in this living will must be followed.

I wish that my medical treatment will be as follows: ....

....

My family, my medical caregivers, and my medical facility shall not be held for any criminal liability as a result of following the wishes expressed in this document.

If I change my mind regarding these wishes, I may communicate it in any way at any time to my family or health care providers.

Signed copies of this declaration are to be regarded as legal as the original.

After careful consideration, I declare that I understand and I accept the consequences of my expressed wishes in this document.

Signed,

....

(Declarant's signature) (Declarant's name printed)

....

(date)

STATEMENT OF WITNESSES

We the witnesses of this document declare that the declarant is of sound mind and body and has made this declaration without undue influence or fraud.

....

Signature of witness 1 Printed name of witness 1

Address ....

....

....

Signature of witness 2 Printed name of witness 2

Address ....

....

Note: This is an example of a living will and is not a legal document.

1. **What does this document do?**
   - **a.** It gives the doctor the right to decide what kind of medical treatment to give the person named in the document.
   - **b.** It gives the family the right to decide what kind of medical treatment to give the person named in the document.
   - **c.** It states that the person will give up all of his or her rights to decide upon what medical treatment to get.
   - **d.** It describes the declarant's (the patient's) wishes regarding his or her medical treatment if he or she cannot communicate them later.
2. **What does the word "declarant" mean?**
   - **a.** The person who witnesses the document.
   - **b.** The person who is completing the document and is named in the document.
   - **c.** The person who will give the medical care.
   - **d.** Someone who is a family member of the patient.
3. **According to the document, which of these statements is not true?**
   - **a.** Two doctors must agree that the person is unable to continue life without life support.
   - **b.** If the patient should die as a result of respecting this living will, the family and the doctors will be held responsible.
   - **c.** The person named in the document declares to have normal mental abilities.
   - **d.** The person filling out this form can change his or her mind about what is on this document.
4. **True or false: All signed copies of this document are as legal as the original.**
   - **a.** True
   - **b.** False
5. **True or false: The document must be signed before two witnesses.**
   - **a.** True
   - **b.** False

MyReadingLab

TEXTBOOK GRAPHIC AIDS

incompatible: not able to be combined with

Read the following chart, and then answer the questions that follow.

BLOOD TRANSFUSION COMPATIBILITY AND INCOMPATIBILITY		
Recipient	Compatible donors	**Incompatible** donors
Type 0	Type 0	Type A Type B Type AB
Type A	Type 0 Type A	Type B Type AB
Type B	Type 0 Type B	Type A Type AB
Type AB	Type 0 Type A Type B Type AB	None

1. What does the chart show?
   a. blood types
   b. blood types that are common
   c. blood transfusion compatibility and incompatibility
   d. rare blood types
2. What blood types are described as recipients (who receive the blood transfusion)?
   a. types A and B
   b. types A, B, and AB
   c. types A, O, and B
   d. types A, B, AB, and O
3. What kind of blood is compatible for type O recipients?
   a. type O only
   b. types A and B
   c. types A, B, and AB
   d. none
4. For recipients with type A blood, which are incompatible donors?
   a. types B and AB
   b. types O and A
   c. types A and AB
   d. types O and B
5. For recipients with type AB blood, which donors are compatible?
   a. types A and B only
   b. all types
   c. types A, B, and O
   d. none

MyReadingLab

BUILDING VOCABULARY

Throughout this course, you will be introduced to word parts that make up many words in the English language. Study the following word parts, and then answer the questions that follow.

Prefixes	Roots	Suffixes
sub- *under*	-mit-, -mis- *to send*	-tion, -sion- *action, state of*
pre- *before*	-script-, -scribe- *to write*	

1. What English words can you create from the lists of word parts above?

2. Using a dictionary, look up the meanings of any of the words you wrote that you can't define. Use one of the words you wrote in a sentence that reveals its meaning with a context clue:

CHAPTER REVIEW

MyReadingLab

CHAPTER PRACTICE 1

Use the four-step reading process to read the passage and answer the questions.

STEP 1: Preview

1. What is the topic of the following passage?

   Dietionist and Nutrrtionists

2. What is one question you expect to have answered in this article?

   what are they?

STEP 2: Read actively to find answers to your questions.

Continued...

MyReadingLab

CHAPTER PRACTICE 1

...continued

STEP 3: Highlight (or underline) and annotate key points and answers to your questions.

DIETITIANS AND NUTRITIONISTS

1 If you love food and cooking, you may want to consider a career in the medical field. Dietitians and nutritionists are people who plan meals, manage food service systems, conduct research, and help patients learn how to follow special diets. There are several different types of careers in nutrition.

2 Clinical dietitians work in hospitals, nursing care homes, or other large institutions to plan meals and special nutrition programs for patients. They work with doctors and nurses to decide on the best diets for patients with special dietary needs. They may also work directly with patients to help them understand how their diets will help them to improve their health.

3 Community dietitians talk to people about nutrition in clinics, health agencies, and other health care organizations. They may also work in the food industry to analyze foods and provide nutritional information. Their job is to help professionals understand the benefits of good nutrition.

4 Management dietitians work in large institutions and act as managers and supervisors. They work in large health care facilities, companies, schools, and prisons. They manage the food services and plan meals as well as prepare records and reports.

5 Consultant dietitians work in businesses, such as supermarkets, sports teams, or companies. They do menu planning, budgeting, and nutritional counseling. They advise their clients on the best diets to follow, how foods should be stored and prepared, and what the costs of foods will be.

6 Whatever type of job dietitians and nutritionists have, they all need good people skills, good communication skills, and a love of food and good nutrition.

STEP 4: Review Questions

1. What are the four different types of dietitians' jobs described here?

....

....

....

Continued...

2. What skills do all of these jobs require?

3. Which is the correct meaning of the word "analyze" as it is used in paragraph 3?
   a. to define
   b. to separate into parts
   c. to examine in detail
   d. to figure out how to do something

MyReadingLab

CHAPTER PRACTICE 2

Use the four-step reading process to read the passage and answer the questions.

STEP 1: Preview

1. What is the topic of the following passage? Medicine

2. What is one question you expect to have answered in this article?
   What is sports medicine

STEP 2: Read actively to find answers to your questions.

STEP 3: Highlight (or underline) and annotate key points and answers to your questions.

SPORTS MEDICINE

[1]Sports medicine is a field where job opportunities are expected to grow much faster than the supply. [2]As long as there are athletes, there will always be a need to prevent and treat injuries.

[3]Athletic trainers are often on the sidelines of many sports events, ready to jump in to attend to an injured player or competitor and to provide immediate care. [4]Besides treatment, athletic trainers help prevent injuries by teaching players how to use injury-preventing equipment, as well as how to avoid becoming injured on the playing field.

[5]Athletic trainers work with doctors and other health care providers in colleges, high schools, hospitals, clinics, and professional sports teams. [6]They may spend a lot of time outdoors on the sidelines of playing fields, or indoors in hospitals and clinics, depending on the job.

Continued...

MyReadingLab

CHAPTER PRACTICE 2

...continued

[7]Those who are with professional sports teams may do a great deal of traveling and work long hours. [8]They are responsible for the safety and health of their players, which can be stressful when the team's success depends on an injured player. [9]Despite the challenges of being a professional team's trainer, many athletic trainers are in stiff competition for these positions. [10]Other trainers work in private training organizations for athletes who wish to prepare themselves for national and international competitions, such as marathons or the Olympics.

[11]Athletic trainers will continue to be in careers that offer a variety of opportunities for working in a sports environment. [12]For more information on how to become an athletic trainer, use the Internet or see a career counselor at your college.

STEP 4: Review Questions

1. What are some of the different places where athletic trainers may work?

   Highschool, College, Hospitals

2. What are the responsibilities of an athletic trainer on professional sports teams?

   To make sure they are safe

3. Why is the job of professional sports team athletic trainers more demanding than other athletic trainers' jobs?

MyReadingLab

CHAPTER PRACTICE 3

Use the four-step reading process to read the passage and answer the questions.

STEP 1: Preview the selection and answer the questions.

1. What is the topic of the following selection? ....

2. What is one question you expect to have answered in this selection?

....

STEP 2: Read actively to find answers to your questions.

STEP 3: Highlight (or underline) and annotate key points and answers to your questions.

WHAT IS CANCER?

replicates: copies

[1] Cancer is a disease that begins when a single cell **replicates** itself when it should not. [2] Cell division is the process a cell undergoes in order to make copies of itself. [3]This process is normally regulated so that a cell divides only when more cells are required and when conditions are favorable. [4] A cancerous cell is a rebellious cell that divides without being given the go-ahead.

[5]Cells that divide continually cause a pileup of cells that form a lump or tumor. [6] A tumor is a mass of cells that has no apparent function in the body. [7] Tumors that stay in one place and do not affect surrounding structures are said to be **benign** (be-NINE). [8] Some benign tumors remain harmless; others become cancerous. [9] Tumors that invade surrounding tissues are malignant, or cancerous. [10] The cells of a malignant tumor can break away and start new cancers at distant locations through a process called **metastasis**.

STEP 4: Review Questions

1. What is cancer?

   what types are there

   ....

2. How is a tumor formed?

   ....

3. What is the difference between a malignant tumor and a benign one?

   ....

MyReadingLab

TEXTBOOK PRACTICE

Preview the following paragraphs, then read actively and answer the questions.

STEP 1: Preview the textbook selection and answer the questions.

1. What is the topic of this selection?

....

....

2. What is one question you expect to have answered in this selection?

....

....

STEP 2: Read actively to find answers to your questions.

STEP 3: Highlight (or underline) and annotate key points and answers to your questions.

GENES AND CHROMOSOMES

(jeans & KROME-a-soams)

traits: characteristics

[1]Each normal sperm and egg contains information about "how to build an organism." [2]A large portion of that information is in the form of genes—segments of DNA that contain specific pieces of information about the **traits** of a living being.

Genes Are Instructions for Making Proteins

[3]Genes carry instructions about how to make proteins. [4]These proteins may be either structural (like the protein that makes up hair) or functional (like the protein lactase, which breaks down sugar). [5]Proteins give cells—and, by extension, organs and individuals—nearly all of their characteristics.

Genes in Combination

[6]Imagine genes as being roughly like the words in an instruction manual. [7]Words can have one meaning when they are alone (for instance, saw) and another meaning when used in combination with other words (see-saw). [8]Words can even change meaning in different contexts ("saw the wood" versus "sharpen the saw"). [9]Some words are repeated frequently in any set of directions, but other words are not. [10]It is the presence of certain words and their combination with other words that determines which instruction is given.

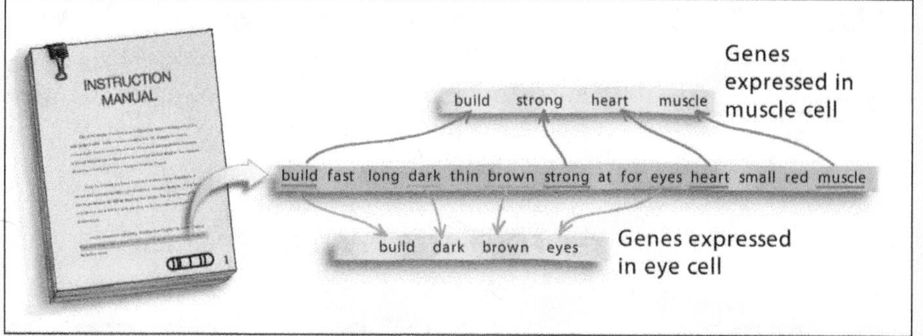

Figure 6.2 Genes as words in an instruction manual. Different words from the manual are used in different parts of the body, and even when the same words are used, they are often used in special combinations. In this way, the manual can provide instructions for making and operating the variety of body parts we possess.

STEP 4: Review Questions

1. What does DNA contain?

2. What are two types of proteins found in genes?

3. How are genes like words in an instruction manual?

STUDY SKILL REVIEW

At the conclusion of each chapter in this textbook, a study skill aid is used to help you review the important concepts in the chapter. Use these examples to make your own study aids for other courses that you are taking, or will be taking, in the future. For this chapter we use a flow chart to review the concepts presented here. Flow charts show actions in a specific order. With your team, fill in the following chart with the missing details.

THE FOUR-STEP READING PROCESS

STEP 1	STEP 2	STEP 3	STEP 4
.... by finding the topic and making up questions.	Read actively by	.... important points by marking and making notes.	Review by ....

READING LAB ASSIGNMENTS

REVIEW PRACTICE

1. Login to **MyReadingLab,** and in the menu click on **Study Skills** and **Learning Path**. On the main screen, click on **Getting the Most from Your Reading**. Complete the six activities for this topic.

2. From the menu in **MyReadingLab,** click on **Reading Level** and **Next Reading**. Choose two reading selections from the list on the main screen. Read the articles and answer the diagnostic and exercise questions.

CAREER EXPLORATION

1. Research a career in a medical field that you think you might be interested in doing. Do online or library research and write a report, or give a presentation about your findings. Include information such as qualifications for employment (degrees, certificates, or licenses), salary ranges, working environments, why it appeals to you, and an educational plan to achieve this position. To find out more about the various kinds of jobs in the medical field, go to the U.S. Department of Labor Bureau of Labor Statistics.

2. Interview someone working in a medical environment. (See examples of interviews in this textbook in the "On the Job Interview" sections.) Write 5 to 10 questions that you would like to ask before you meet or call the person. Set up an appointed time that would be convenient for this person to talk with you.

   Write down the person's answers to your questions, or record the interview.

MyReadingLab

LEARNING REFLECTION

Think about the skills and concepts presented in this chapter. What have you learned in this chapter that will help your reading comprehension and enable you to do well in college? Which learning strategy helped you the most in your learning?

MyReadingLab

SELF-EVALUATION CHECKLIST

Rate yourself on the following items, using the following scale:

1 = strongly disagree

2 = disagree

3 = neither agree nor disagree

4 = agree

5 = strongly agree

1. I completed all of the assigned work on time.

2. I understand all of the concepts in this chapter.

3. I contributed to teamwork and class discussions.

4. I completed all of the assigned lab work on time.

5. I came to class on time.

6. I attended class every day.

7. I studied for any quizzes or tests we had for this chapter.

8. I asked questions when I didn't understand something.

9. I checked my comprehension during reading.

10. I know what is expected of me in the coming week.

3 VOCABULARY SKILLS

LEARNING STRATEGIES

Using Context Clues to Determine Word Meanings 67

Word Parts: Prefixes, Roots, and Suffixes 75

READING SELECTIONS

READING 1: "Dangerous Duty" 80

READING 2: "Leap of Faith" 89

READING FOR LIFE

Real-Life Reading 100

On the Job Interview 102

Textbook Graphic Aids 103

Building Vocabulary 104

CHAPTER REVIEW

Chapter Practice 105

Textbook Practice 108

Study Skill Review 110

Reading Lab Assignments 111

Learning Reflection 111

Staying on Track 112

Self-Evaluation Checklist 113

FOCUS ON: Law Enforcement, Corrections, Fire Science, and EMT Services

People who work in law enforcement, corrections, fire science, and EMT services must be dedicated to serving others, with a true desire to make a difference in the world. Their unique qualities include a highly developed sense of responsibility, specialized training, and courage. There are numerous opportunities in these fields for anyone interested in patrolling the streets, working in forensics labs, working in prisons, working in security, or working in technical fields. Fire investigators study the causes of fires. Rescue teams go into potentially dangerous situations to save lives, and emergency medical technicians (EMTs) deal with real-life emergencies on a daily basis.

Being able to communicate effectively, quickly, and concisely is an important skill for anyone in these fields. EMTs dealing with an accident victim need to be able to share vital information quickly to save a patient, and law enforcement officials need to be able to interpret and apply the written word of the law. Building their vocabulary skills allows these professionals to communicate with one another and with the people they serve.

In this chapter, you will build your vocabulary skills and learn to:

LEARNING OBJECTIVES

1 use context clues to determine the meanings of unfamiliar words.

2 use word part clues to determine the meaning of a word.

What do you do when you're reading and you come to a word you don't know? Skip over it? Sound it out? Look it up in a dictionary? Ask someone else?

If you could figure out the meanings of new words without having to ask someone else or look them up in a dictionary, you would save time, and you would learn many more new words. There simply isn't enough time to look up the thousands of new words you will be exposed to in college. Skipping over them isn't wise, either, because you will never learn new words that way. Many of the new words you encounter will be terms that you must know in order to understand the key concepts of the material you are studying. Knowing the meanings of more words will unlock the author's message. What tools do you already use for figuring out the meanings of unfamiliar words?

OBJECTIVE 1

Use context clues to determine the meanings of unfamiliar words.

USING CONTEXT CLUES TO DETERMINE WORD MEANINGS

Sometimes it is necessary to read the entire paragraph to figure out the meaning of a word, but in many cases you can find context clues within the same sentence. For instance, what is the meaning of the word in bold print in the following sentence?

> Students who are **encumbered** by huge loans and debts often have a difficult time paying them back once they graduate.

Context clues are the words surrounding an unfamiliar word that help you to determine its meaning.

The clues in this sentence are the "huge loans and debts," which are burdens to students. Therefore, *encumbered* means to be burdened by something. When you come across a word you don't recognize, look at the words around it that you do know to find some clue as to the meaning of the word. There are several different types of clues you should look for:

1. Look for **synonyms** (words that mean the same thing) in the sentence.

   > The cliff was stratified; each layer held several types of colorful rock.

   What word in this sentence gives you a clue for the meaning of *stratified*?

2. Look for **definitions** set off by transitions, commas, parentheses, brackets, or dashes.
   - Transitions: Words and phrases such as "means," "refers to," "defined," "is," and "are" can be helpful because they indicate a definition is to follow. Notice the transitions in bold in the following sentences. They signal that a definition is to follow.

     > Doo-wop **is** a style of jazz singing.
     >
     > Lampreys **are** a snake-like fish.

   - Commas: Definitions for a term are often included in a phrase set off by commas.

The pulmonary circuit, *a pathway for the oxygen-depleted blood to return to the heart*, is pumped by the right side of the heart.

- Parentheses: Often a term will be defined in parentheses.

  At the dinner party, we ate raclette *(a Swedish dish of potatoes and cheese)* and drank wine.

- Brackets: Terms may also be defined in brackets.

  The process of photosynthesis *[how plants convert sunlight to energy]* can be demonstrated with a simple experiment.

- Dashes: Sometimes dashes are used to set off the definition of a word.

  The student improved his retention—*his ability to remember what he learned*—by previewing before he read the chapter.

- Explanations: Sometimes words are explained in descriptive ways rather than in exact definitions.

  A platypus *has a bill like a duck, has webbed feet like a duck, has fur and a tail like a beaver, lays eggs like a bird, and has poisonous spurs on its ankles.*

3. Look for **examples** of what the term is describing and for transitions, like the following, that indicate an example will follow: "such as," "known as," "for example," "to illustrate," "like," "including."

   Some herbivores, **like** the elephant, giraffe, and tapir, will feed on low-hanging trees or plants.

   What are herbivores?

4. Look for **antonyms** (the opposite of what the unfamiliar word means). These words show contrast and are often signaled by transitions such as:

on the other hand	however	instead
but	unlike	on the contrary
yet	although	as opposed to
conversely	despite	in contrast

   Unlike the smooth rocks found in many streams and river beds, the rocks along the northeastern seacoast can be very craggy.

   Which word states the opposite of *craggy*? What does *craggy* mean?

5. General sense, or "**logic**": To get a general sense of the sentence, place a finger over the unfamiliar word in a sentence, and read it saying, "blank" for the hidden word. Then try to put a word in the sentence that makes sense, using the clues in the sentence and paragraph to help you. Use logic and reasoning skills to figure out the meaning of the unknown word.

   She spoke and acted with such animosity toward the man who hit her car that I was surprised he didn't get angry.

   What does *animosity* mean? What clues help you figure out the meaning of *animosity*?

Sometimes you may have to read several sentences or a complete paragraph to figure out the unknown word, as in the following paragraph:

> The morning sun sparkled on the ruffled surface of the lake. A steady breeze drifted from the south. The air was crisp and clear, and the sky a brilliant blue. Only wisps of feathery clouds chased the wind. It was propitious weather for sailing.

What does *propitious* mean? What clues in the paragraph help you to determine the meaning of the word *propitious*?

Think like a detective and figure out the meanings of unfamiliar words by looking for "LEADS": Logic of the passage, Examples, Antonyms, Definitions, and Synonyms.

Studying Vocabulary

There are several ways you can learn the meanings of new words and terms. Be creative, and use your strongest learning style to study. Make it fun and you will learn the terms easily.

- Make flash cards by writing a vocabulary word on one side of a note card and the definition on the other, and then use them to quiz yourself.
- Record vocabulary words on your cell phone. You can text them or record a voice message to yourself. Review them until you have memorized the meanings.
- Keep a study sheet in your notebook with definitions and examples of how the terms are used.
- Download free puzzle software and create a crossword or other type of puzzle using the terms and their definitions. Trade puzzles with a study partner to test each other.
- Draw small illustrations for new terms to help you visualize meanings.

MyReadingLab

PRACTICE 1

Use context clues (LEADS) to determine the meanings of the underlined words in the following sentences.

1. The college would not give Damien his transfer credits until it could verify (VER-i-fy) his grades from the last school he attended.
   a. test
   b. prove
   c. deny
   d. lessen

2. The data from the graph showed that there were more felonies (FEL-un-eez) committed in theft than in fraud.
   a. major crimes
   b. prisons
   c. fraud
   d. situations

3. The realtor tried to reach an agreement with the homebuyer and the seller, but they reached an impasse (IM-pass) on the price.
   a. impossible
   b. bargain
   c. a deadlock
   d. delay

4. Rakeisha is such an extrovert (EX-tro-vert) that she would never be too shy to ask for seconds at the dinner table.
   a. shy person
   b. overweight person
   c. funny person
   d. outgoing person

5. The newlyweds were very elated (ee-LAY-ted) at their wedding reception, but the bride's mother was depressed.
   a. sad
   b. direct
   c. happy
   d. angry

MyReadingLab

PRACTICE 2

Use context clues (LEADS) to determine the meanings of the underlined words in the following sentences.

1. Mr. Martinez gives us a five-minute quiz at the beginning of each class. We have learned to write very succinctly (sus-SINKT-lee) to finish on time.
   a. easily
   b. long
   c. briefly and to the point
   d. essay
2. The cataract (CAT-er-act) falls almost 200 feet, splashing into a deep lake, where tour boats pass this beautiful display of nature.
   a. eye disease
   b. waterfall
   c. bird
   d. enormous
3. Our cat is so inquisitive (in-QUIZ-i-tiv) that she will often get herself trapped in unlikely places.
   a. talented
   b. carefully
   c. sweet-tempered
   d. curious
4. As a teacher, Mr. Collins is quite a sage (SAYJ); he often sounds like an encyclopedia.
   a. a wise person
   b. a fool
   c. boring
   d. journey
5. The suspect succumbed (sa-KUM-d) to the stress of intense questioning and admitted to stealing the money from the victim.
   a. misunderstood
   b. took
   c. gave in to
   d. arrangement

MyReadingLab

PRACTICE 3

Use context clues (LEADS) to determine the meanings of the underlined words in the following sentences. Consider the parts of speech when deciding the best definition.

1. The customer was outraged (OUT-raj'd) that his dinner arrived cold.
   a. not impressed
   b. angry
   c. overcharged
   d. happy

2. The meeting convened (kon-VEEN'd) at 7:00 p.m. with the Pledge of Allegiance to the flag.
   a. began
   b. continued
   c. ended
   d. was postponed

3. She has aspirations (as-pir-AY-shuns) to become a doctor and help children in poor neighborhoods.
   a. dreams or ambitions
   b. efforts
   c. strongly
   d. hopeful

4. After his favorite team was defeated in the championship, Jamal was very morose (muh-ROSE).
   a. pleased
   b. relaxed
   c. rested
   d. depressed

5. The blue whale is a leviathan (lev-EYE-ah-then). In fact, it is the largest creature on earth.
   a. mammal
   b. something that is narrow
   c. something that is huge
   d. heavy

MyReadingLab

TEXTBOOK SELECTION 1

Read the following textbook selection. Try to determine the meanings of the underlined words using context clues.

External Examination of the Crime Scene

[1] A firearm has the potential of providing some excellent fingerprints and must be examined carefully. [2] It should be handled by the checkered portion of the *pistol grip* and similar areas on long arms. [3] You cannot get prints from these areas. [4] *Do not put anything into the muzzle of the firearm.* [5] There is entirely too much evidence you can ruin by doing this. [6] As just mentioned, in contact or near-contact wounds, blood and tissue is sometimes ingested into the muzzle. [7] Also of concern is that the striations found on the bullet are imparted, for the most part, one inch or less from the tip of the muzzle.

[8] TIP: After recovery of prints from the firearm, you can use your fingerprint brush to dust the ***serial number*** and other markings on the firearm and then place these lifts in your notes or notebook. [9] By following this procedure, it can never be insinuated that you might have recorded the number incorrectly, because you have the actual impression.

QUESTIONS

1. What is the meaning of the word potential (po-TEN-shal) as it is used in sentence 1?
   a. possibility
   b. characteristic
   c. advantage
   d. idea
2. What is the meaning of the word ingested (in-JES-ted) as it is used in sentence 6?
   a. eaten
   b. taken inside of
   c. disturbed
   d. digested
3. What is the meaning of the word striations (stry-AY-shuns) as it is used in sentence 7?
   a. gunpowder
   b. points
   c. dangers
   d. markings
4. What is the meaning of the word lifts as it is used in sentence 8?
   a. picking up
   b. fingerprints or other impressions that have been picked up
   c. something added into shoes
   d. machines that lift loads
5. What is the meaning of the word insinuated (in-SIN-you-ay-t'd) as it is used in sentence 9?
   a. inserted
   b. imprinted
   c. suggested
   d. helpful

U-REVIEW 1

Get together in teams. Pass around a copy of the table below. Every team member must fill in one of the empty boxes until the table is complete.

TYPE OF CONTEXT CLUE	EXPLANATION OF WHAT IT IS	EXAMPLE SENTENCE
1.	The general logic of the sentence or paragraph helps to determine the meaning of a word.	After winning the game, Ricky gloated, calling the other team "losers."
2. Examples		Context clues, such as synonyms and antonyms, can help you determine the meaning of a word.
3.		Instead of making a profit for the year, our business ended up with a deficit.
4. Definition		A pseudonym is a false name that authors often use when publishing books.
5.	A word that means the same as the unknown word can be found in the sentence.	The newspaper was sued for libel because it had written several lies about the mayor.

OBJECTIVE 2

Use word part clues to determine the meaning of a word.

WORD PARTS: PREFIXES, ROOTS, AND SUFFIXES

How do you like to make sandwiches? Do you put a lot of meat on two slices of bread? Do you add lettuce and tomatoes? Each time you change the ingredients, you make a different kind of sandwich.

Like sandwiches, words are made up of different parts. When you change the parts, you can make new words. There are three different word parts that make up many words in English: prefixes, roots, and suffixes. Many of these came from the ancient Latin and Greek languages. Once you get to know the meanings of some of these word parts, you will be able to figure out the meanings of many new words without a dictionary. The context clues in the sentences will also confirm your understanding of the word. You may already know many of these word parts.

1. **Prefixes** come at the beginning of a root word. They often change the meaning of a word. What's the difference between *correct* and *incorrect*? What does the prefix in- do to the meaning of the word *correct*?
2. The **root**, or **base**, of the word contains its meaning. It can come at the beginning, middle, or end of a word:

   football, barefoot, footstep, footpath

3. The **suffix** comes at the end of a word and often changes the function of the word or the meaning:

   loving, lovable, lovely, lover, lovesick

Tips to Keep in Mind

1. Some words have no prefixes or suffixes, like the word *pass*. But we can add a prefix to make *impasse*. Note how the spelling changed and an *e* was added to the end of the word.
2. Sometimes the spelling of a word may change as prefixes and suffixes are added, but the root of the word still has the same meaning.
   For example:

   Because of the rockslide, the road was *impassable*.

   Adding the suffix *-able* (meaning "a condition of being able") to the word *impasse* (a noun) makes a new word:

   im + pass + able = impassable (an adjective)

   (not) + pass + (able to) = (not able to pass through)

3. Some word parts can have more than one meaning. For example:

   In the word *incapable*, the prefix *in-* means "not."

   In the word *inborn*, the prefix *in-* means "into."

Tables of Prefixes, Roots, and Suffixes

PREFIXES

PREFIX	MEANING	EXAMPLES
ab-	away from	abnormal, abstain
ad-	to, toward	advance, adjacent
anti-	against	antiwar, antisocial
auto-	self	autobiography, automobile, autograph
bi-	two	bicycle, bimonthly, binoculars
circum-	around	circle, circumference
com-	with, together	common, community
con-	with, together	connect, confide, construct
de-	down, away	descend, deject (cast down)
dia-, di-	through, across	diameter, diagonal
dis-	apart, away from	disinterested, discomfort, disengage
e-	out of, from	elect (choose out of), eject (throw out)
ex-	out of, from	exhaust, expel
hyper-	over	hypertension, hyperactivity
hypo-	under	hypodermic
il-	not	illegal, illegible (not readable)
im-	not	imperfect, impolite, impossible
in-	not	incorrect, invisible
ir-	not	irregular, irrational, irresponsible
un-	not	unfinished, undamaged
im-	into	impress, import
in-	into	incorporate, inscribe, inside, inborn
inter-	between	interview, interstate
intra-	within	intrastate
mal-, male-	bad, wrong	malfunction, malnutrition
micro-	small	microscope, microbiology
mono-	one, single	monologue, monotheism, monorail
peri-	around	perimeter, periscope
poly-	many, several	polygon, polygamy
post-	after	postgraduate, postpone
pre-	before	precede, predict (to tell before)
pro-	for, forward	promote, project, progress (to step forward)
re-	again, back	repeat, recede, regress (step back)

PREFIX	MEANING	EXAMPLES
sub-	under	submarine, subhuman
sur-, super-	over, above	superhuman, superego, surpass
syn-, sym-, syl-,	with, together sys-	symphony, synonym, system, syllable
tele-	distant, far off	telephone, telepathy, television, telegram
trans-	across	transatlantic, transport (carry across)
tri-	three	ticycle, tripod

COMMON ROOTS

ROOTS	MEANING	EXAMPLES
act	act on	actor, action
ann, enni	year	anniversary, annual
aqua, aque	water	aquatic, aquarium
aud	sound	auditorium, audible
bio	life	biography, biology, antibiotic
cent	one hundred	century, centimeter
cess	to stop	cease, recess
cred	believe	incredible, credibility, credit
de	away	depart, deliver, descend
demo	people	democracy, epidemic
derm	skin	dermatitis, dermatology
duct	to bring or take	reduction, deduct, conduct
equ	equal	equal, equity, equality
gam	marriage	monogamy, polygamy
geo	earth	geology, geography
graph	writing, printing	biography, telegraph, geography
ject	throw	inject, reject, subject, project
magn	large	magnify, magnate, magnificent
man	hand	manufacture, manual, manuscript
metri, meter	measure	geometric, thermometer, metric
min	small	minority, minute
mit, miss	send	permit, submission, mission
mor, mort	death	mortal, immortality
neuro	nerve	neurosurgeon, neuron, neurobiology
path	feeling, suffering	sympathy, telepathy, pathology

Continued...

COMMON ROOTS (continued)

ROOTS	MEANING	EXAMPLES
phobia	exaggerated fear	claustrophobia, arachnophobia
phon, phone	sound	symphony, telephone
port	carry	portable, transport, report
psych	soul, spirit, mind	psychology, psychic
scope	to look	telescope, horoscope, midroscope
sec, sect	cut	dissect, section
struct	to build	construct, instruct
terr	earth	territory, terrestrial
therm	heat	thermal, thermos, thermometer
vit	life	vital, revitalize, vitamin
zoo	animal	zoo, zoology

SUFFIXES

SUFFIX	DEFINITION	EXAMPLES
-able	the condition of being able to	flammable, likable, touchable
-ion	a state, a condition, or a quality of	discussion, mission
-ive	a state or quality	festive, instructive
-ment	a state, a condition, or a quality of	engagement, commencement
-y	quality of	sunny, sugary, funny
-ate	an action	operate, calculate, communicate
-cide	kill	patricide, infanticide, herbicide, suicide
-ectomy	cutting	appendectomy, tonsillectomy
-er, -or	one who	actor, teacher, lawyer, doctor
-ist	one who	pianist, vocalist, psychiatrist
-ic, -tic, -ical, -ac	having to do with	surgical, dramatic, biblical
-ism	the belief in	terrorism, communism, Judaism
-ly	in the manner of	quietly, quickly, happily
-less	without	hopeless, careless, sunless
-logy	study of	biology, geology
-ward	in the direction of	toward, forward, backward

MyReadingLab

PRACTICE 4

Using the tables of prefixes, roots, and suffixes, write the meanings of these prefixes and roots. Then, use these word parts to complete the missing word parts in the paragraph that follows. The first one is done for you.

PREFIXES	ROOTS
mono- *one*	gam- *marriage*
poly- ________	cent- ________
bi- ________	
tri- ________	

Polygamy and Monogamy

Before the 11th century, Jewish men practiced *poly-* gamy, which allowed them to have many wives at once. After the 11th century, most Jewish men practiced ________ gamy, which only permitted marriage to one wife. Even today, some countries, such as Sudan in Africa, still practice poly ________ , and have numerous wives. In most Western countries, it is illegal to have two wives or husbands; therefore, ________ gamy is considered a crime in the United States. In England between the 17th and 19th ________ uries, the term ________ gamy referred to someone who had three wives or husbands at the same time.

MyReadingLab

PRACTICE 5

Use the tables of prefixes, roots, and suffixes to complete the following story with the correct word parts from the box. Some answers will be used more than once.

de-	sub-	trans-	-ward	sur-
in-	port	-er	-ly	

The Florida bank robber had a(n) ________ genious plan. He walked to ________ the front of the bank carrying a(n) ________ folio and looked around. He cautious ________ approached the tell ________ 's window and ________ mitted a withdrawal slip. On it, he had written, "I want a cashier's check for $100,000. This is a stick up, and I have a gun!" The teller looked ________ prised, and said, "Yes, sir. I understand. I will be happy to make this ________ action for you. First, I'll need to see your driver's license, and then I'll write the check." The robb ________ reached into his wallet and gave it to her. She copied down his name, address, and license number, then wrote out the check and handed it to him. He ________ parted the building and raced off in his car. Minutes later, the police ________ tained and arrested him from the information he gave to the teller!

For more practice using word parts, complete the Building Vocabulary section at the end of this chapter.

U-REVIEW 2

For each of the following sentences, write "T" if the statement is true or "F" if the statement is false. As you go over the answers with your team, discuss why the false statements were false.

1. f The part of the word that carries the meaning is the root.
2. T All words have a prefix, a root, and a suffix.
3. T Some prefixes may have more than one meaning.
4. T The spelling of a word part sometimes changes.
5. F A word never has more than one prefix or suffix.

READING SELECTIONS

MyReadingLab

Reading 1
VOCABULARY PREVIEW

"Dangerous Duty" by Corinne Fennessy

The following vocabulary words are from the article "Dangerous Duty." With a partner or in a team, choose the correct meanings of the underlined words in the following sentences. Use context clues (LEADS), word part clues, and parts of speech to help you figure out the meanings.

1. The felon (FELL-un) finally collapsed when Deputy Martin managed to shoot him in the leg.
- **a.** a major crime
- **b.** a person who commits a major crime
- **c.** an injured person
- **d.** someone having a prison record

2. The three gunmen were alone in the house, with easy access to the adjoining (add-JOIN-ing) garage.
- **a.** newly built
- **b.** unfinished
- **c.** attached to the house
- **d.** distant from

3. "Bullets were ricocheting (rik-o-SHAY-ing) everywhere off the concrete floor," she recalls.
- **a.** shooting
- **b.** falling
- **c.** bouncing
- **d.** falling

4. "When you go through something like that," she says, reflecting on her ordeal (or-DEEL), "mindset is really important. I was not going to die in that garage."
- **a.** effort
- **b.** an idea
- **c.** orders
- **d.** a difficult experience

5. "When you go through something like that," she says, reflecting on her ordeal, "mindset (MIND-set) is really important. I was not going to die in that garage."
   a. a state of mind or thought
   b. stubbornness
   c. refusal
   d. agreement
6. The suspects had planned to steal the contraband (KON-tra-band) from Isola's husband, Clinton, who had hidden marijuana and cash in the house.
   a. money
   b. something illegal
   c. something helpful
   d. large
7. The president of the United States awarded the officer a medal of valor (VAL-or) for her bravery in protecting the children.
   a. bravery
   b. distinction
   c. award
   d. reward
8. The officer recuperated (ree-KOOP-er-ate-ed) from her gunshot wounds and is now a detective in the sheriff's department.
   a. was relieved
   b. was injured
   c. was healed
   d. was promoted
9. She bought a bridal gown for her forthcoming (forth-COM-ing) wedding in September.
   a. honest
   b. fourth in a row
   c. late
   d. coming soon
10. "In retrospect (RET-ro-spekt), I wish I had majored in nursing instead of business."
    a. looking down
    b. looking back
    c. looking ahead
    d. looking inside

MyReadingLab

Reading 1 PREVIEW

1. Have you ever experienced or heard of a situation in which a member of the police department, fire department, or EMT services rescued you or someone you know? Describe the situation.
2. If you saw some children in danger, would you be willing to take a risk to save them? Why or why not?

Directions: As you read this article, practice the four-step reading process. Preview the article, and then write on the following lines one or two questions that you would hope to have answered.

MyReadingLab

Reading 1

As you read, answer the questions in the margins to check your comprehension.

"Dangerous Duty"

by Corinne Fennessy

1 The early May morning was pleasantly warm. Isola Marino secured the seat belt straps on her two-year-old twins, seated in the back of her mini-van. She called for her eight-year-old son, Dustin, from the garage adjoining her house.

2 "Hurry or you'll be late for school," she warned.

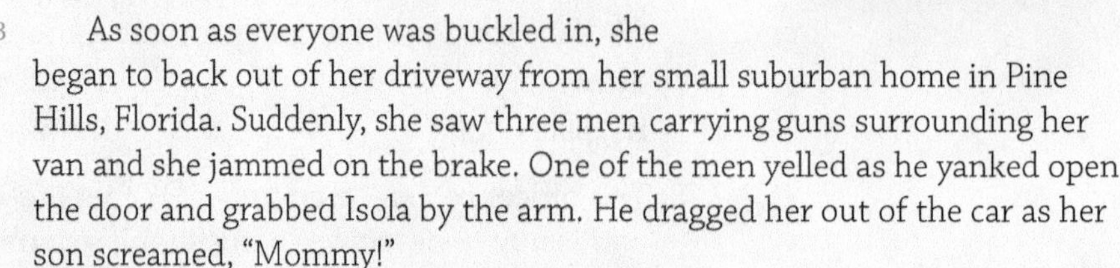

3 As soon as everyone was buckled in, she began to back out of her driveway from her small suburban home in Pine Hills, Florida. Suddenly, she saw three men carrying guns surrounding her van and she jammed on the brake. One of the men yelled as he yanked open the door and grabbed Isola by the arm. He dragged her out of the car as her son screamed, "Mommy!"

4 The third man got into the van and drove it back into the garage. After locking the children inside, he went into the house. The other two men demanded that Isola tell them where all her cash was hidden, and she begged them not to harm her children.

5 Dustin was terrified by these strange men who had dragged his mother away and locked him and his sisters in the car. But the eight-year-old noticed that his mother's purse was still sitting on the front seat. He found her cell phone and dialed 911.

6 A patient operator on the 911 line got the information she needed from Dustin and told him to keep calm and stay in the van until the police arrived.

7 Two Orange County Sheriff's deputies arrived on the scene, followed by Deputy Jennifer Fulford and a trainee. When the police arrived, the men inside the house sent Isola to answer their knock and tell them that everything was fine. Isola knew this would be her only chance to save her children, even if she were killed for alerting the police.

8 "Is everything all right, ma'am?" asked the deputy.

9 "No!" she cried, "Please, save my children!" She pointed to the garage just before she was yanked back and the door was slammed shut.

10 The deputy heard shouting from inside and ran back to the other deputies. Deputy Jennifer Fulford looked back at the van parked in the open garage.

Why did the deputies go into the garage?

11 "I'm going to try to get those kids," Deputy Fulford declared, as she drew her weapon and hurried to the garage. Deputy Martin followed her.

12 Just then, three shots were fired from inside the house into the garage. Both deputies dropped down behind the van. The door to the house opened and one of the gunman named Jenkins fired at Deputy Fulford. She returned fire with her Glock .45, striking Jenkins, but he kept on firing as he went down.

13 Deputy Fulford was worried that someone would hit the kids inside the van. If there were only some way to get them out—but it was too dangerous. Dustin was flattened face down on the front seat in terror as the twins screamed from the back.

14 Another gunman suddenly emerged from the house and fired across the hood, hitting Deputy Fulford four times. Bullets ricocheting off the concrete floor struck her again and again. Glass exploded. Fulford went down and Jenkins, who was still alive, shot her in the shoulder of her shooting arm.

What happened to Deputy Fulford and Deputy Martin?

15 The gun dropped from her hand onto the floor, but she grabbed it with her left hand and saw the second gunman coming. She fired off two rounds, hitting him twice in the head. But even that didn't stop him. He stumbled into the driveway and shot at Deputy Martin, hitting him in the shoulder. He grabbed his shoulder in pain and squeezed off one more round, hitting the felon in the leg and bringing the man down with a thud.

16 The shooting stopped, and Deputy Fulford lay bleeding on the floor of the garage. She felt light-headed and lost consciousness momentarily.

17 She was thinking about her beautiful bridal gown, the one that she would wear to her forthcoming wedding with firefighter Tom Salvano. She wondered if she'd ever get the chance to wear that elegant dress, or walk down the aisle on her father's arm at her wedding.

18 "Hey, Fulford! Are you OK?" her partner, Kevin Curry, called to her.

19 "No! Please help me get out of here!" she cried. She knew she had been hit several times and she was losing blood fast. She knew she could die. But she had a mindset that she wasn't going to die in this garage. Not today.

20 The other deputies got the children safely out of the van and gave Deputy Fulford assistance while Isola was rescued from inside the house.

21 Deputy Fulford and Deputy Martin were rushed to the nearest hospital. Fulford underwent surgery for seven gunshot wounds and recuperated within four months. Two of the felons died from their injuries; the third one was convicted and sentenced. At the house, police had found over 340 pounds of the husband's marijuana and $54,000 in cash. Isola was charged with trafficking contraband and sent to jail for committing a felony. Her children went to live with relatives.

What happened to Isola and her children?

22 Jennifer Fulford is now Detective Jennifer Salvano. She and Tom were married and she was promoted to detective. She now investigates cases of child abuse. For her bravery, she received the Presidential Public Safety Officer Medal of Valor and the American Deputy Sheriff's Association named her Deputy of the Year for the United States. She was also named Deputy Sheriff of the Year in Florida.

23 In retrospect, someone else may have questioned the decision to go inside the garage that day, but not Deputy Fulford. After the ordeal, she was asked if she is a hero, and she replied, "No, just doing my job!"

920 words divided by .... minutes = ... words per minute

MyReadingLab
Reading 1
REVIEW

It is a good habit to summarize everything you read to strengthen your comprehension.

Directions: Begin by filling in the details for "Dangerous Duty" on the lines below, using the information from the article.

Deputy Sheriff Jennifer Fulford rescued Deputy martin from three men with guns. She and her partner were shot but managed to fire back.

MyReadingLab
Reading 1
COMPREHENSION QUESTIONS

The following questions will help you to recall the main idea and the details of "Dangerous Duty." Review any parts of the article that you need to in order to find the correct answers.

1. What is the topic (subject) of this article? (Who or what is it about?)
  a. a rescue
  b. Deputy Jennifer Fulford's rescue of three children
  c. three children trapped in a car during a gunfight
  d. a woman who was taken hostage

MAIN IDEA

2. What is the main idea of the story? (What is the most general statement that tells the most important point?)
  a. Deputy Fulford risked her own life to protect the lives of three children.
  b. Three men took a woman hostage.
  c. The police stopped three men from harming a family.
  d. An eight-year-old boy called 911 to save his family.

SUPPORTING DETAILS

3. When one of the men, Jenkins, started firing at her, Deputy Fulford:
  a. ran back to her patrol car and called for backup.
  b. returned fire and shot him.
  c. got into the van.
  d. got hit in the right shoulder and lost her weapon.

4. After she was shot, Deputy Fulford:
  a. was thinking about her retirement.
  b. was thinking about a promotion.
  c. tried to climb into the van to get the kids.
  d. was thinking about her forthcoming wedding.

DRAWING CONCLUSIONS

5. The three suspects had attacked the family because:
  a. they knew that Isola's husband had cash and marijuana in the house.
  b. they wanted to take the family hostage and demand money.
  c. they were running from the police.
  d. they were terrorists.

6. **Deputy Fulford made the decision to go into the garage because:**
   a. she planned to go into the house through the garage.
   b. she wanted to protect the children in the van.
   c. she was told to go in by Deputy Martin.
   d. she tried to stay out of the line of fire.

7. **How did the children end up alone in the van inside the garage?**
   a. The gunmen took them out to the garage.
   b. The mother put the children in the van for safety when she saw the gunmen.
   c. After the mother was taken, one gunman drove it into the garage.
   d. The children ran into the garage and locked themselves inside the van.

8. **With which statement would the author probably agree?**
   a. The criminals were planning to kill the entire family.
   b. The criminals didn't know there was money and marijuana in the house.
   c. The eight-year-old boy was a hero for calling 911.
   d. The mother of the children didn't know there was 341 pounds of marijuana in the house.

VOCABULARY IN CONTEXT

Using context clues and word part clues, determine the best meaning for the underlined words in the following sentences. If necessary, use a dictionary.

9. **"She called for her eight-year-old son, Dustin, from the garage <u>adjoining</u> her house." (paragraph 1).**
   a. two-car
   b. attached
   c. spacious
   d. separate

10. **"Bullets <u>ricocheting</u> off the concrete floor struck her again and again" (paragraph 14).**
    a. sliding
    b. coming from
    c. bouncing off
    d. sinking in

POLICE LINE DO NOT CROSS
POLICE DEPT

MyReadingLab

Reading 1 VOCABULARY PRACTICE

Use the vocabulary words from the Word Bank to complete the following sentences. Write the words into the blanks provided.

WORD BANK

felon	adjoining	ricochet	ordeal	valor
contraband	mindset	forthcoming	recuperated	retrospect

1. Rita and her best friend had .... rooms at the dormitory.

2. As a convicted ...., Mr. Smith was serving a lengthy jail sentence.

3. Firefighters who rescue people in dangerous situations must have .... and strength.

4. After surviving the hurricane that destroyed her home, Mrs. Lopez didn't want to talk about her ....

5. To succeed in college, you must have the .... that you can and will succeed.

6. In ...., I wish now that I had met with my academic advisor so that I would have taken the right courses for my major.

7. The man injured in Tuesday's fire has .... and has been sent home from the hospital.

8. Thinking about her .... graduation from college, Shanika decided to throw a big party.

9. Hidden inside the truck's seats, the officers discovered the .... that was being smuggled across the border.

10. A speeding bullet can .... off a hard surface and strike someone nearby.

MyReadingLab

Reading 1 QUESTIONS FOR WRITING AND DISCUSSION

Review any parts of the article you need to answer the following questions.

1. Think about the actions that Deputy Fulford took to protect the lives of the children in the car. Describe how she showed courage and a sense of responsibility to protect and serve.

2. Describe how teamwork was important to Deputy Fulford's success in protecting the children inside the car.

3. In your opinion, do you think that the mother, Isola, should have been sentenced? Why or why not?

4. What qualities are needed in a good police officer, firefighter, or rescue worker?

5. What do the actions of the eight-year-old boy who called 911 tell you about this child?

Reading 1 VOCABULARY PRACTICE

Together with your team, use the clues in the first column to unscramble the jumbled words in the second column. Then, use the letters in the circles to unscramble a phrase.

WORD BANK

RICOCHET VALOR ORDEAL ADJOINING FORTHCOMING
MINDSET RETROSPECT FELONY CONTRABAND RECUPERATED

CLUES (Note: Clues are not definitions, just "clues")	**SCRAMBLED WORDS**	**WORD**
1. Reconsidering	TCERROPSET	R ◯ T R O S P Ⓔ C T
2. Connected	NINIGOADJ	_ _ _ _ ◯ _ _ _ _
3. Attitude	SEIMNTD	_ _ _ _ ◯ _ _
4. Suffering	LARDOE	_ _ _ ◯ ◯ _
5. Heroes	ROLVA	_ _ _ _ ◯
6. Illegal	RACADBOTNN	◯ _ _ _ ◯ _ _ _ _ _
7. Future	HOMONRCGIFT	Ⓕ _ _ ◯ _ _ _ _ ◯ _ _
8. Healthy	RAUPETCEDER	_ _ ◯ _ ◯ _ _ ◯ _ _ _
9. Bullets	TECHIRCO	_ _ _ _ ◯ _ _ ◯
10. Kidnap	ENLOFY	_ ◯ _ _ _ _

Write the letters from inside the circles on the following lines. Use them to unscramble the phrase. (The picture is a clue.)

_ _   _   _   _ _   _   _ _   _ _ _   _ _ _   _ _ _

P _ _ _ _ _ _ _ _   _ _ K _ _

_ _ _ _ _ _ _

MyReadingLab

Reading 2 VOCABULARY PREVIEW

"Leap of Faith" by Mike Santangelo, Mara Bovsun, and Allan Zullo

The following vocabulary words are from "Leap of Faith." With a partner or with your team, try to figure out the meanings of the underlined words in the following sentences. Use context clues ("LEADS"), word part clues, and parts of speech. Choose the correct meaning for each underlined word as it is used in the sentence.

1. When Ricki's parents told him he couldn't afford to own a car, he conjured (CON-jurd) up a plan to show them that he could.
a. tricked
b. convinced
c. separated
d. created

2. The team's strategy to score the winning goal was so audacious (aw-DAY-shus) that no one believed that it would work.
a. simple
b. daring
c. fearful
d. rejected

3. The fireman used his pike to break a hole through the wall of the smoke-filled room.
a. dagger
b. pole-like tool
c. fish
d. courage

4. Her plan for getting into college hinged on (hinj'd on) getting good grades and participating in high school government to qualify for scholarships.
a. waited upon
b. planned
c. was dependent upon
d. attached to

5. When Mrs. Bumford found the snake in her desk drawer, she gave out shrill cry.
a. sad
b. painfully loud
c. muted
d. musical

6. The humidity in the South during the summer is almost intolerable (in-TOL-er-a-bul).
a. unbearable
b. unwelcome
c. incomplete
d. offensive

Continued...

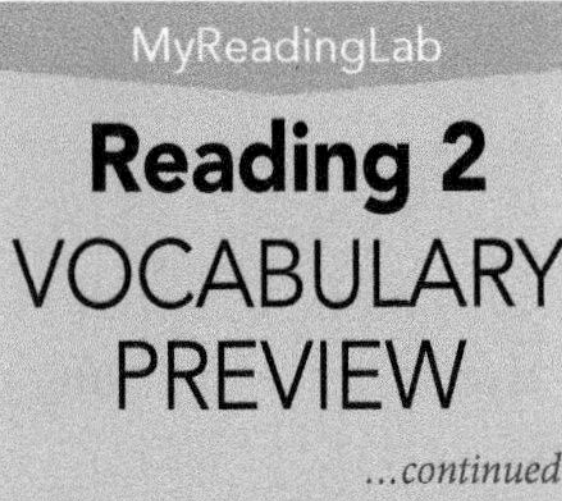

7. As a result of his accident, Sam suffered numerous <u>lacerations</u> (lass-sir-RAY-shuns) and needed over 100 stitches.
   a. bruises
   b. broken bones
   c. deep cuts
   d. bloody
8. He was awarded a Medal of Honor for his <u>gritty</u> (GRIT-ee) rescue of three other soldiers under enemy fire.
   a. sandy
   b. ingenious
   c. courageous
   d. oblivious
9. After parachuting from the plane, Martha lay on the ground in a <u>fear-induced paralysis</u>, unable to respond to our questions.
   a. frozen with fear
   b. frightened
   c. grim
   d. morose
10. Chen <u>maneuvered</u> (man-OO-verd) his way through the crowd, holding a drink high in each hand to avoid spilling them.
   a. outraged
   b. departed
   c. recuperated
   d. weaved

MyReadingLab

Reading 2
PREVIEW

1. Share what you know about how firefighters work together to put out fires.
2. Do you know anyone who has had a fire emergency and had to call the fire department? Describe what happened.

Directions: As you read this story, practice the four-step reading process. Preview the article, and then write on the following lines one or two questions that you would hope to have answered.

....

....

....

....

MyReadingLab

Reading 2

As you read, answer the questions in the margins to check your comprehension.

From: *The Greatest Firefighter Stories Never Told*

"Leap of Faith"

by Mike Santangelo, Mara Bovsun, and Allan Zullo

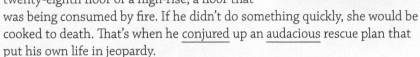

1 Lieutenant John Traphagen (TRAP-hay-gan) faced a daunting challenge: He needed to rescue a woman trapped in an elevator on the twenty-eighth floor of a high-rise, a floor that was being consumed by fire. If he didn't do something quickly, she would be cooked to death. That's when he conjured up an audacious rescue plan that put his own life in jeopardy.

2 Because it was a Saturday, most offices were empty, but there were some employees working that day, including elevator operator Joy Buckbee.

3 Buckbee had been in an elevator on a low floor when the fire broke out on the twenty-eighth floor. The heat of the flames summoned all the elevators to the burning floor, including the one she was in. When the elevator door opened, she faced a wall of flames. She couldn't get the elevator to go up or down because by now all the elevators had ceased to function. Buckbee was trapped in what was now an oven with an uncontrollable, rising thermostat, and there was nothing she could do.

What problem did Lt. Traphagan have to solve?

4 When Traphagen arrived on the scene, he was briefed on the deadly situation. He and his firemen couldn't use the elevators. They would have to climb the stairs.

5 Traphagen and his group joined a procession of firefighters, some carrying hoses and others armed with axes, steel bars, or pikes, who were working their way up toward the fire floor.

6 Meanwhile, Buckbee was suffering in a metal oven heated by a fire that had fully engulfed the twenty-eighth floor. The only reason she was still alive was that the elevator shaft was acting like a chimney. Fresh air was being sucked up from the bottom of the building by an updraft with hurricane-force winds. The upward rush of air not only was giving the trapped woman just enough oxygen to survive but it was keeping the elevator car from bursting into flames.

7 After Traphagen and his panting firefighters reached the twenty-eighth floor, stubborn flames filled the hallway.

8 There was only one option that he figured could possibly work: He would come in from above the flames through the elevator shaft, get down to the elevator roof, pry open the escape hatch on top, and lift Buckbee out. Then, both would be pulled out to an upper floor elevator door and to safety by his men.

Scott Pack: cylinders of compressed air for breathing.

9 Traphagen gulped some fresh air from his **Scott Pack** and started to climb the stairs to the next floor. The air was thick with smoke because the

Continued...

MyReadingLab

Reading 2

...continued

fire had now spread to the twenty-ninth floor. "Let's try the next floor," he yelled to his men as he scrambled up to the next landing. On the thirtieth floor, just below the top floor, the air seemed clear enough to take a chance.

10 Using pry bars and axes, the firefighters forced open the metal doors to the elevator shaft. A blast of hot, smoky air slapped him in the face. A shrieking, violent updraft in the shaft was driving pitch black smoke from the twenty-eighth floor to the top of the shaft. The air was hot enough to roast wieners.

11 The lieutenant hesitated, but for only a split second. "Go back down to the twenty-ninth," he ordered his men. "And get the door to the elevator shaft open as quickly as you can."

12 In answer to the puzzled look on their faces, Traphagen explained, "I'm going down the cable and I'll need you to pull me out."

What plan did Lt. Traphagan have to rescue Joy Buckbee?

13 He told them that once he got Buckbee out onto the roof of the elevator car, he would pass her up to them through the pried-open elevator door on the twenty-ninth floor. This plan hinged on the fire-fighters from the other companies extinguishing the flames on that floor so that his men could reach the elevator door. Otherwise he'd have to find a way to get up to the thirtieth floor with Buckbee in tow. No one-including Traphagen-thought he could ever climb back up the cable while holding onto the woman.

14 While his men hustled off to the floor below, he took a flying leap into the shaft and latched onto the metal elevator cable. He was immediately assaulted by a shrill roar, the stove-hot updraft, and biting smoke. It felt like he was in a tunnel that led straight to hell. Traphagen buried his face in the collar of his turnout coat to shelter his skin from the intolerable heat and smoke. *This is no time to have second thoughts or doubts*, he told himself.

15 He eased his way down the cable, which was growing hotter by the second. Adding to his woes, the cable was so ragged it was ripping his gloves, heavy turnout coat, trousers, and boots with every move.

16 All the way down Traphagen talked to himself to keep his mind off what he might find inside the elevator car. By now, the sharp metal strands of the cable had sliced deep into his hands, legs, and feet. Despite the pain from his lacerations, he continued his gritty descent, which was becoming increasingly difficult because his blood was trickling down the cable, making it slippery for him to grab.

17 The thickening, choking smoke hid the elevator car. *How much further,* he wondered. Just then his boot touched the top of the car.

18 Another blast of hot, smoky air hit him in the face as he fumbled for the escape hatch, his bloody hands cramping from his struggle down the rope. Using a small metal pry bar, he wrenched the hatch off. His heart sank as he peered inside. Buckbee was curled in the corner on the floor of the smoke-filled chamber. She looked dead.

19 He had to find out for sure if she had died. Just as he was getting ready to jump down into the elevator, Buckbee twitched and slowly turned her head. Two big eyes, filled with terror, gazed up at him.

What obstacles did Lt. Traphagan face in trying to rescue Buckbee?

20 "Put your hands up and reach for me! Traphagen shouted above the wail of the fire-driven wind rushing up the elevator shaft. Buckbee didn't respond. She just stared at him.

21 Traphagen was ready to jump into the chamber when Buckbee suddenly snapped out of her fear-induced paralysis. Without a word, she gradually stood up and raised her hands above her head, reaching for him. The look of terror was still etched on her face.

22 He leaned over and clamped his gloveless, bloody hands around her wrists. "One yank and I can get you out of there," he told her as he began to haul her out of the baking elevator.

23 When he maneuvered her head and shoulders through the hatch, he heard the screech and thunk of metal being pried apart above him. He looked up and through the smoke, he saw two of his firefighters grinning at him from the open elevator door.

24 "Are you going to stay in there all day, Lieutenant?" one of his men yelled down.

25 Maybe some other time Traphagen would have laughed, but not this time. He could see that Buckbee was losing consciousness and needed oxygen immediately. "Cut the jokes and let's go!" he snapped to his men. He lifted Buckbee high enough for the firefighters from the floor above to snatch her to safety. Then the men helped him out of the shaft.

How did Lt. Traphagan rescue Joy Buckbee?

26 Wiped out from the ordeal and coughing from the heavy smoke he inhaled in the elevator shaft, Traphagen sucked in oxygen and rolled over in his mind what had just happened. His coat was shredded beyond repair, as were his boots. His gloves were so torn they had fallen off his hands down the shaft. A few feet from where Buckbee was receiving oxygen, the medic turned to Traphagen and said,

"She's going to be fine. She was right on the edge of being dead, but she's recovering nicely."

27 It was a spectacular rescue in an otherwise ordinary fire. Buckbee recovered quickly in the hospital from smoke inhalation and the effects of heat. The hero firefighter became the first man to receive his department's Medal of Valor. It was pinned on him in a full-dress ceremony by a very grateful Joy Buckbee.

1,352 words divided by .... minutes = ... words per minute

MyReadingLab

Reading 2 REVIEW

It's a good habit to summarize everything you read to strengthen your comprehension.

Summarizing after you read will help you to understand the author's purpose and main idea. Complete the summary of "Leap of Faith" by filling in the blanks below.

A woman named ________ was trapped in ________ on the ________ floor during a fire. Lieutenant ________ devised a plan to rescue her. He ________ and got her out of the ________ through the ceiling, and then handed her to ________ who came through the ________ on the floor above them. They lifted the woman out and the Lieutenant was later awarded a ________.

MyReadingLab

Reading 2 COMPREHENSION QUESTIONS

The following questions will help you to recall the main idea and the details of the story. Review any parts of the story that you need to in order to find the correct answers.

1. What is the topic (subject) of this article? (Who or what was it about?)
   - **a.** firefighting
   - **b.** a firefighter's rescue of a woman
   - **c.** rescuing a person from an elevator
   - **d.** A firefighter's duty

MAIN IDEA

2. What is the central point of the story? (What is the most general, broad statement that tells the most important point of the story?)
   - **a.** Firefighters have a very dangerous job.
   - **b.** The elevators in a high-rise building will not work during fires.
   - **c.** It is dangerous to stay in a building once it catches on fire.
   - **d.** Firefighter Lt. Traphagan rescued a woman from an elevator during a high-rise fire.

SUPPORTING DETAILS

3. According to the article, when the firefighters first opened the elevator doors on the thirtieth floor:
   - **a.** the elevator car was visible directly below them in clear air.
   - **b.** there were flames reaching all the way up the elevator shaft.
   - **c.** the firefighters faced hot, pitch-black smoke.
   - **d.** the cable holding the elevator car was melting in the heat.

4. After Lt. Traphagan got onto the elevator cable, he noticed that:
- **a.** the cable was so hot it melted his gloves and burned his hands.
- **b.** the cable was so shredded that it cut through his gloves, hands, and suit.
- **c.** the cable was unraveling and may not hold him long enough to rescue the woman.
- **d.** the elevator car was sliding down the shaft towards the flames below.

5. When Lt. Traphagan first opened the elevator car escape hatch he found that:
- **a.** the woman looked as if she were already dead.
- **b.** the woman was terrified and refused to come to him.
- **c.** the woman was too large to fit through the escape hatch.
- **d.** the elevator car was so filled with smoke that he couldn't see the woman.

DRAWING CONCLUSIONS

6. Based on the facts in the article, which statement would most likely be true?
- **a.** Firefighters are not paid enough for what they do.
- **b.** Lt. Traphagan did not give up even when he faced several obstacles to making a rescue.
- **c.** The fire was probably caused by someone who was careless with matches.
- **d.** Firefighters shouldn't make jokes when they are dealing with life or death situations.

VOCABULARY IN CONTEXT

Use context clues, word part clues and parts of speech to determine the meanings of the underlined words in these sentences:

7. Lieutenant John Traphagen faced a <u>daunting</u> challenge: He needed to rescue a woman trapped in an elevator on the twenty-eighth floor of a high-rise, a floor that was being consumed by fire. (par. 1)
- **a.** impossible
- **b.** powerful
- **c.** overwhelming
- **d.** undetermined

8. The heat of the flames <u>summoned</u> all the elevators to the burning floor, including the one she was in. (par. 3)
- **a.** to arise
- **b.** called
- **c.** drove
- **d.** surrounded

9. Buckbee was trapped in what was now an oven with an uncontrollable, rising <u>thermostat</u>. (par. 3)
- **a.** temperature
- **b.** temperature controller
- **c.** heat conductor
- **d.** cooker

10. Traphagen and his group joined a <u>procession</u> of firefighters, some carrying hoses and others armed with axes, steel bars, or pikes, who were working their way up toward the fire floor. (par. 5)
- **a.** a moving line
- **b.** a parade
- **c.** a ceremony or event
- **d.** a poor economy

Reading 2 VOCABULARY PRACTICE

Fill in the missing information in the table below using the vocabulary words from Reading 2: "Leap of Faith."

WORDS	DEFINITIONS	SENTENCES
1.	1. deep cuts in the skin	1. The EMT's quickly applied first aid to stop the bleeding of several .... on the man's arm.
2. hinged on	2.	2. Buying the new house .... the sale of their old house first.
3.	3.	3. The boy hiding under his bed suffered from .... and could not come out.
4. maneuvered	4.	4. The quarterback skillfully .... his way through the opposing team to make a touchdown.
5.	5. bold; daring	5. Frank Lloyd Wright's .... idea to build a house over a waterfall had never been done before.
6. conjured	6.	6. Tanya cleverly .... up a scheme to get back her bike after it was stolen.
7.	7. a pole-like tool	7. The firefighter used his .... to knock burning limbs from trees in the wildfire.
8.	8. courageous	8. It takes a .... character to parachute into a blazing wildfire.
9.	9.	9. Her screams were so .... that they woke the entire neighborhood.
10.	10.	10. The heat from the blazing inferno was almost ....

MyReadingLab

Reading 2 QUESTIONS FOR WRITING AND DISCUSSION

Fill in the missing information in each row of the following table using the vocabulary words from "Leap of Faith."

1. Why do you think firefighters like Lt. Traphagan and his men risk their lives to save other people?

2. In what ways did the firefighters who rescued Joy Buckbee work as a team?

3. At what point did Lt. Traphagan have second thoughts of wanting to back out of his plan? What do you think made him go ahead despite the obstacles he faced?

4. What qualities would a person need to be a good firefighter?

5. Do you think that Lieutenant Traphagan should have received the Medal of Valor? Why or why not?

MyReadingLab

Reading 2 VOCABULARY PRACTICE

First, complete the following sentences using the vocabulary words in the Word Bank. Then, find and circle the words on the puzzle grid. The words may be horizontal, vertical, diagonal, or backwards. If you need a hint, look in the row number shown after each sentence.

WORD BANK

conjured	audacious	pike	hinged on
shrill	intolerable	lacerations	gritty
fear-induced paralysis	maneuvered		

1. The boy lay upon the ledge of the cliff, in a fear-................................ and could not reach up to grab the rope that his friends had sent down to save him (row 1).

2. The rescue workers made a .... rescue by climbing down the cliff and carrying the boy back up to safety (row 13).

3. Saving the boy from a deadly fall .... getting him off the ledge and tied securely to the rescue worker (row 2).

4. The rescue workers used a .... to break off loose pieces of rock from the cliff that could cause injuries (row 14).

5. When Candice was told she probably wouldn't get hired at the shoe store, she .... up a plan to convince the manager that she was the best person for the job (row 5).

6. Her plan to show up at the shoe store and convince customers to buy shoes was ...., but it worked. The manager hired her on the spot (row 8).

7. The baby's cries were so .... that she awoke all the residents in the apartment building (row 2).

8. Talking on a cell phone during class is considered .... by most college professors (row 1).

9. After the fight at the hockey game, several people were taken to the hospital due to severe .... (row 6).

10. During the race, Jason .... his bike between his competitors until he was in first place (row11).

Reading 2
VOCABULARY PRACTICE—PUZZLE GRID

	A	B	C	D	E	F	G	H	I	J	K	L	M
1	I	N	S	E	C	U	R	I	T	I	E	S	Z
2	N	N	D	O	S	H	R	I	L	L	A	R	T
3	D	O	T	I	M	I	X	E	D	N	U	T	S
4	U	N	D	O	V	N	W	D	A	N	C	E	R
5	C	A	L	L	L	G	R	I	P	L	C	I	S
6	E	X	L	A	C	E	R	A	T	I	O	N	S
7	D	E	C	I	X	D	R	U	E	A	N	O	P
8	P	L	A	A	N	O	P	A	R	T	J	E	M
9	A	R	T	U	I	N	O	E	B	X	U	Z	P
10	R	Q	E	D	R	E	A	D	Y	L	R	I	P
11	A	F	M	A	N	E	U	V	E	R	E	D	O
12	L	E	A	C	K	R	D	W	O	R	D	Y	S
13	Y	G	R	I	T	T	Y	X	E	A	M	L	A
14	S	I	P	O	S	P	R	Y	Q	E	O	H	J
15	I	H	M	U	G	B	C	X	K	L	E	A	F
16	S	H	U	S	A	L	N	C	J	F	D	S	I

MyReadingLab

REAL-LIFE READING

DRUG TESTING CONSENT FORM

Read the following Drug Testing Consent Form, which is a form some job applicants are required to fill out. Use the four-step reading process as you read, and then answer the questions that follow to check your comprehension.

consent: to give permission

initial: first one

metabolites: chemical substances

JOB APPLICANT FINALIST
DRUG TESTING **CONSENT** FORM

I, ..., as a job applicant finalist for a full-time position at the Acme Painting Company, do hereby agree to submit to the physical examination of my person in conjunction with my employment with the company.

I further agree to an **initial** test and a confirmation test as required in accordance with the provisions of the company, a copy of which I have received prior to the execution of this drug testing consent form, and more particularly described as follows:

Initial Test. The following cutoff levels shall be used when first screening specimens to determine whether they are positive or negative for these drugs or **metabolites**. All levels equal to or exceeding the following shall be reported as positive:

Amphetamines 1,000 ng/ml
Cannabinoids 100 ng/ml
Cocaine 300 ng/ml
Opiates 300 ng/ml
Barbiturates 300 ng/ml
Methadone 300 ng/ml

Confirmation Test. The following confirmation cutoff levels shall be used when analyzing specimens to determine whether they are positive or negative for these drugs or metabolites. All levels equal to or exceeding the following shall be reported as positive:

Amphetamines 500 ng/ml
Cannabinoids 15 ng/ml
Cocaine 150 ng/ml
Opiates 300 ng/ml
Barbiturates 150 ng/ml
Methadone 150 ng/ml

I understand that consent to the tests described above in accordance with the above described policy of the company is a condition of my initial employment with the company, and I further understand that a confirmed test result that is positive may result in denial of my employment.

I further release and hold harmless the company from and against any claims, losses, liability, judgments, costs or expenses of any nature which I may have with regard to or which may arise out of any drug testing I undergo in compliance with the company's policy.

I hereby authorize any physician or drug testing laboratory to release to the company all information concerning the results of my initial or confirmation tests together with all relevant reports, data, and medical records pertaining to any such test. I further authorize the company to discuss all test results with the personnel of the testing facility and with the consulting physician.

Witness Signature .... Applicant's Signature .... Date ....

1. **What is the topic of this form?**
   a. a consent form for drug testing only
   b. a consent form for a physical examination only
   c. a consent to have a physical examination and a drug test
   d. none of the above
2. **What happens if your first test result is above the limits shown for any of the chemicals being tested?**
   a. You will be required to take another test (a confirmation test).
   b. You will be reported to the police.
   c. You will be denied employment.
   d. You will be sent for drug counseling.
3. **What does the form state about who is responsible for any costs or expenses?**
   a. The company will pay for all costs and expenses.
   b. The drug testing center will pay for the expenses.
   c. The applicant must pay for the test.
   d. If there are any costs, the company is not responsible for paying them.
4. **True or false: The results of the test are sent to you and no one else.**
   a. true
   b. false
5. **True or False: Your results may be discussed with a consulting physician and the personnel of the testing facility.**
   a. true
   b. false

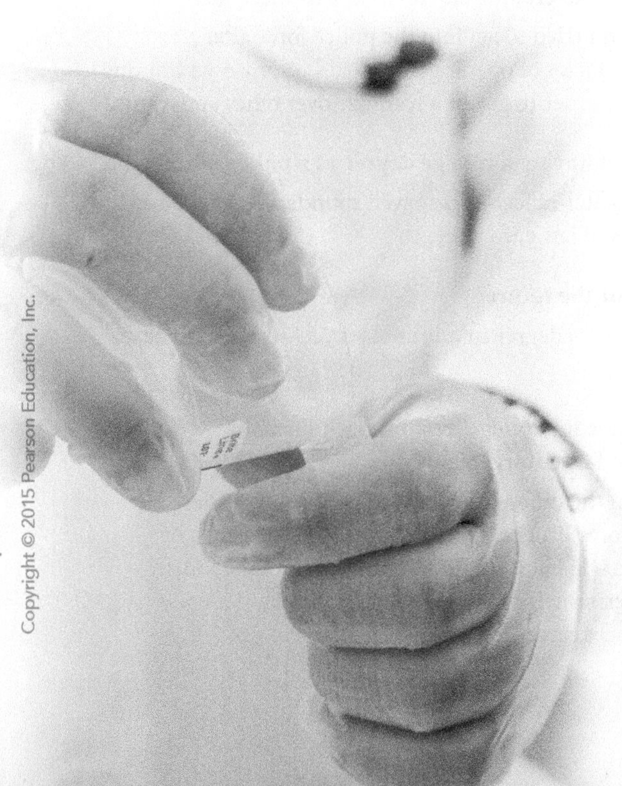

ON THE JOB INTERVIEW

LIEUTENANT DAVID SCOTT

PEPPERELL (MASSACHUSETTS) POLICE DEPARTMENT

How did you become interested in becoming a police officer?

My father was in the police force, and I spent a lot of time around police officers when I was growing up.

What training or education have you had?

When I was younger, I joined the auxiliary police force to get experience. I received training and got to ride in the squad car with a professional police officer to get some experience in the job. After I graduated from college, I went into the police academy and completed my training there.

What do you like about your job?

I most like being able to help people at some of their worst times in life. In my job, you get involved in other people's lives, including family problems, drugs, and other criminal activity. In a community like Pepperell, Massachusetts, you get to know a lot of people and become involved with them on a more personal level than in big cities. I liked doing the D.A.R.E. program with kids. It enabled me to get to know more kids, who later became teenagers. That kind of contact can make a difference for some kids. It's also gratifying when people you have helped through a tough time come back and say thank you.

What do you dislike about your job?

Now, the hours sometimes conflict with family plans. When I first started, I volunteered for nights and overtime because there were more opportunities to get involved during those times.

What about the danger police officers face?

Yes, the danger is always there, but if you stay alert and keep up with training, you can stay relatively safe. It's a part of the job that we all accept.

When you were in college, did you have to overcome any obstacles to succeed?

Not in college, but when I tried to get into the police force after graduation, there weren't a lot of openings. So I paid for my own training at the police academy in order to get an advantage over other applicants.

What's the advantage of having a college degree as a police officer?

I think it makes you a better officer—more well rounded—and it gives you more opportunities in law enforcement.

What are your plans for the future?

I am working on a master' s degree in criminal justice, so I plan to have that completed soon.

What advice do you have for college freshmen who may be considering a career in law enforcement?

Get involved in some of the different aspects of police work. There are programs like the Explorer Program, the Junior Police Academy, or Citizens Academy. This will help you find out more about the job. In school, take classes in criminal justice, and do an internship if your college offers it. It's a great career for the right people.

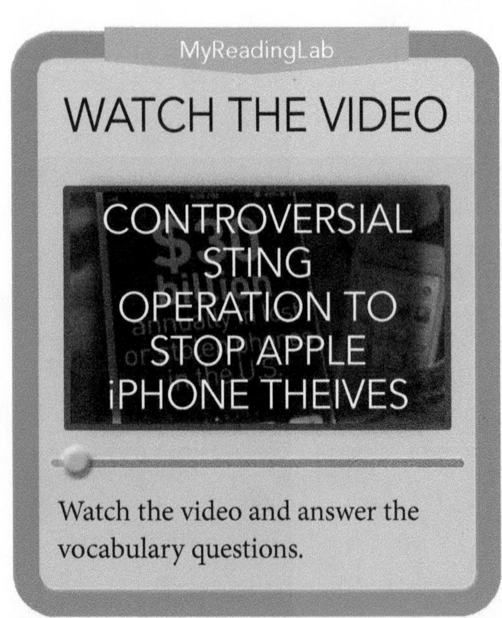

MyReadingLab
WATCH THE VIDEO
CONTROVERSIAL STING OPERATION TO STOP APPLE iPHONE THEIVES
Watch the video and answer the vocabulary questions.

MyReadingLab

TEXTBOOK GRAPHIC AIDS

Study the following graph, and then answer the questions that follow.

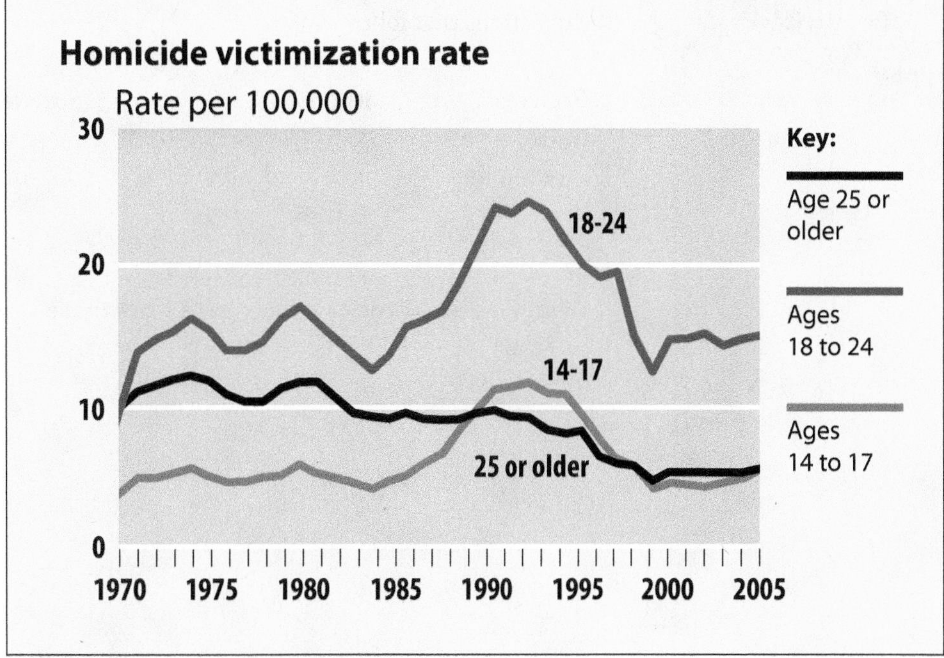

(Based on U.S. Bureau of Justice Statistics.)

1. What does this graph show?

2. Which age group had the highest homicide victim rate per 100,000 for all years represented in the chart?

3. Which age group had the lowest homicide victim rate per 100,000 in the year 1985?

4. During what years did the homicide victim rate peak at its highest number?

5. About how many homicide victims per 100,000 were there in 2005 for the 18–24 group?

MyReadingLab

BUILDING VOCABULARY

Throughout this course, you will be introduced to word parts that make up many words in the English language. Study the following word parts, and then answer the questions that follow.

Prefixes	Roots	Suffixes
trans- *across*	-port- *to carry*	-able *a condition of being able to*
e-, ex- *out*	-act- *to act on*	-er, -or *one who*
re- *again*		

What English words can you create from these word parts?

Using a dictionary, look up the meanings of any of the words you wrote that you can't define. Use one of the words you wrote in a sentence that reveals its meaning with a context clue:

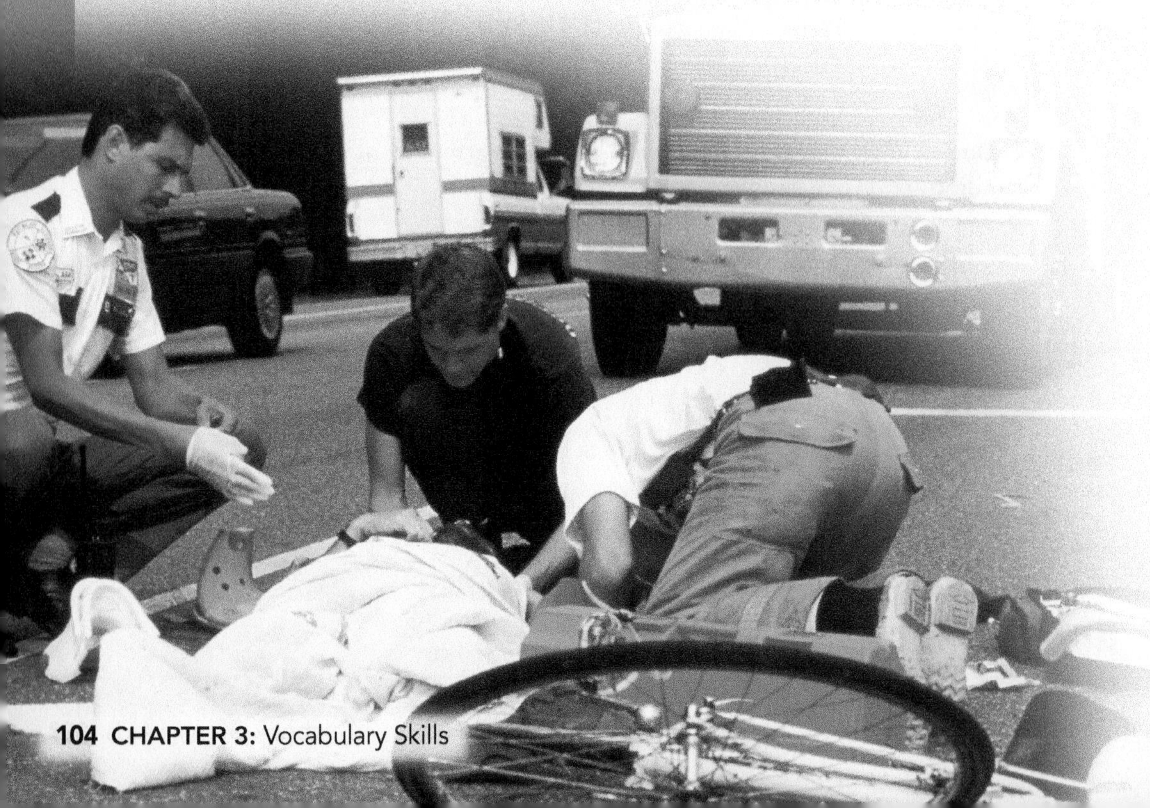

MyReadingLab

CHAPTER PRACTICE 1

Use word part clues to choose the correct meanings of the underlined words in the following sentences. If necessary, refer back to the tables of prefixes, roots, and suffixes from earlier in this chapter to help you determine the meanings of the words.

1. Ryan wanted to become a dermatologist (der-ma-TOL-uh-jist).
   a. belonging to a political party
   b. one who studies people
   c. one who studies the skin
   d. dentist
2. He took a circuitous (sir-KYOU-it-us) route to the fair.
   a. direct
   b. long way around
   c. short
   d. fast
3. The woman showed antipathy (an-TIP-path-ee) toward her neighbor.
   a. kindness
   b. dislike
   c. not interested
   d. interest
4. Steve reverted (re-VERT-ed) to his bad behavior as soon as he came home from rehab.
   a. went back to again
   b. went forward
   c. came to
   d. went against
5. The captain was awarded a posthumous (POSS-tyoo-mus) award.
   a. before his death
   b. after his death
   c. famous
   d. costly

MyReadingLab

CHAPTER PRACTICE 2

Read the following passage, and then choose the best meaning for each underlined word as it is used in the sentence. Use context clues (LEADS), word part clues, and parts of speech to help you determine the best meaning.

SAR dogs are "search and rescue" dogs, trained to assist police and rescue workers in an emergency and respond immediately to commands given by hand signals. If a dog passes the obedience test, it must then go through intensive training. Dogs must complete the agility course by jumping from various heights, out of windows, and by walking on balance beams. Next, the dogs are trained to follow a scent. Their sense of smell is hundreds of times more acute than a human's. When tracking scented items, the dogs must disregard all distractions that are placed in their way. The training is done in a large rural area outside of town where the dogs are trained to locate the items in a specific amount of time and then sit down at their handler's side.

1. If a dog passes the obedience test, it must then go through intensive training.
   - **a.** something done on purpose
   - **b.** something intended to be done
   - **c.** very difficult
   - **d.** easily done

2. Dogs must complete the agility course by jumping from various heights, out of windows, and by walking on balance beams.
   - **a.** ability
   - **b.** the ability to move quickly and accurately
   - **c.** intelligence
   - **d.** obedience

3. Their sense of smell is hundreds of times more acute than a human's.
   - **a.** accurate
   - **b.** serious
   - **c.** deadly
   - **d.** attractive

4. When tracking a scent, the dogs must disregard all distractions that are placed in their way.
   - **a.** dislike
   - **b.** having no feelings for
   - **c.** disobey
   - **d.** ignore

5. The training is done in a large rural area outside of town...
   - **a.** open
   - **b.** city
   - **c.** countryside
   - **d.** housing tracts

MyReadingLab

CHAPTER PRACTICE 3

Read the following passage, and then choose the best meaning for each underlined word as it is used in the sentence. Use context clues (LEADS), word part clues, and parts of speech to help you determine the best meaning.

Correctional officers in state and federal prisons watch over roughly 1.5 million offenders who are incarcerated at any given time. Correctional officers maintain security to prevent disturbances, assaults, and escapes. To make sure that inmates are orderly and obey rules, correctional officers watch the activities of inmates. They also settle disputes between inmates and enforce discipline. Correctional officers sometimes inspect the facilities. They check cells and other areas of the institution for unsanitary conditions, fire hazards, and any evidence of infractions of rules. In addition, they routinely inspect locks, window bars, grilles, doors, and gates for signs of tampering.

1. Correctional officers in state and federal prisons watch over roughly 1.5 million offenders who are incarcerated (in-CAR-sir-ate-ed) at any given time.
   a. not honest
   b. put into
   c. imprisoned
   d. called to

2. They also settle disputes (dis-PYOOTS) between inmates and enforce discipline.
   a. arguments
   b. lawsuits
   c. matches
   d. displays

3. They check cells and other areas of the institution for unsanitary (un-SAN-i-tar-y) conditions, fire hazards, and any evidence of infractions of rules.
   a. unusual
   b. not clean
   c. not busy
   d. perfect

4. They check cells and other areas of the institution for unsanitary conditions, fire hazards, and any evidence of infractions (in-FRAK-shuns) of rules.
   a. sections
   b. parts of something
   c. correcting
   d. violations

5. In addition, they routinely inspect locks, window bars, grilles, doors, and gates for signs of tampering (TAM-per-ing).
   a. opening
   b. harmful changes
   c. illegally using
   d. leaving

MyReadingLab

TEXTBOOK PRACTICE

Read the following passage, and then choose the best meaning for each underlined word as it is used in the sentence. Use context clues (LEADS), word part clues, and parts of speech to help you determine the best meaning. To check your answers, substitute your answer for the underlined word to see if the sentence makes sense and does not change the meaning.

The Hunt for Eric Rudolph

With shattering glass, splitting brick, and shredding human flesh, the explosion engulfed the New Woman All Women Health Care clinic in Birmingham, Alabama, on January 20, 1996. In an instant, an off-duty city police officer lay dead and a nurse severely injured. With a crude-but-lethal mix of dynamite and nails, the mysterious antiabortion clinic terrorist had struck again. But this time, witnesses spotted a truck near the clinic and had the presence of mind to get the license number. Police quickly identified the vehicle owner—a 32-year-old former U.S. Army demolitions man who lived in a remote area at the western end of North Carolina. The chase would wind across some of the country's most rugged and foreboding terrain as well as back in time. Rudolph's bombs had a signature in the nails they used. That signature and other clues allowed authorities to tie Rudolph to several bombings in the Atlanta area, including the knapsack bomb detonated in the midst of the 1996 Olympics in Atlanta's Centennial Park.

1. With shattering glass, splitting brick, and shredding human flesh, the explosion engulfed (en-GULF'd) the New Woman All Women Health Care clinic in Birmingham, Alabama, on January 20, 1996.
   a. split
   b. completely overcame
   c. heard
   d. within

2. With a crude-but-lethal mix of dynamite and nails, the mysterious antiabortion (ant-eye-a-BOR-shun) clinic terrorist had struck again.
   a. insane
   b. for abortion
   c. against abortion
   d. doing abortions

3. The chase would wind across some of the country's most rugged and foreboding (for-BODE-ing) terrain as well as back in time.
   a. threatening
   b. interesting
   c. beautiful
   d. peaceful
4. Rudolph's bombs had a signature (SIG-na-chur) in the nails they used.
   a. where someone signs his or her name
   b. permission
   c. brand name
   d. a clue as to who committed the crime
5. That signature and other clues allowed authorities to tie Rudolph to several bombings in the Atlanta area, including the knapsack bomb detonated (DET-oh-nate-ed) in the midst of the 1996 Olympics in Atlanta's Centennial Park.
   a. dangerously
   b. container
   c. practiced
   d. exploded

Adapted from "*The Hunt for Eric Rudolph*"

STUDY SKILL REVIEW

A good way to review material for a test is to make note cards. Complete the following note cards for Chapter 3.

Context Clues

Context clues: look at the information in the sentence or paragraph to help you figure out the meaning of the word

Types of Context Clues

1. Logic of the passage: use logic and reasoning skills to figure out the meaning of the unknown word

Ex: The precipice was dangerously steep and unsafe to climb.

2. Examples: Examples illistrate what the word means

Ex: Marsupials include kangaroos and opossums.

3. antonym *The sentence gives a word that means the opposite of the unfamiliar word. Ex: My health insurance was comprehensive, but Marco's* ***didn't cover everything****.*

4. .... *The sentence gives the meaning of the word or term, using* ....

Ex: Smoking is my one vice (bad habit).

5. .... *The sentence gives a word that means the same as the unfamiliar word.*

Ex: Although she gave her testimony in court, most of her statements were untrue.

Word Parts

.... *Part added to the beginning of a word that often changes the meaning of the word.*

Ex: true, untrue

Roots: Part that has the ....

Ex: barefoot, football, footing

Suffixes: ....

....

Ex: act, action, activate, activity

READING LAB ASSIGNMENTS

SKILL REVIEW

1. Login to **MyReadingLab** and in the menu click on **Reading Skills** and **Learning Path**. On the main screen, click **Vocabulary**. Complete the review and practice activities recommended by your instructor.

COMPREHENSION IMPROVEMENT

2. From the menu in **MyReadingLab** click on **Reading Level** and **Next Reading**. Choose two reading selections from the list on the main screen. Read the articles and answer the diagnostic and exercise questions.

CAREER EXPLORATION

3. Go to the Live Career Web site and take the Career Inventory test to find out what careers are best for you.

4. Go to **MyReadingLab** and in the menu click on **My Search Lab**. In the section in the main screen titled **Research My Topic**, type in a topic you would like to know more about, such as "auto theft" or "Internet crime." Print out an article. Underline unfamiliar words, and then use context clues and word part clues to write your own definitions for the underlined words. Check your definitions with a dictionary.

5. Go online to the Occupational Outlook Handbook at the Bureau of Labor Statistics and search for a career that you would like to learn more about. Print out the information you find. Present the ideas in the article to your team or your class.

MyReadingLab

LEARNING REFLECTION

Think about the skills and concepts presented in this chapter. What have you learned that will help your reading comprehension and enable you to do well in college? Which learning strategy helped you the most in your learning?

MyReadingLab

STAYING ON TRACK

Write your thoughts about the following questions on the lines provided.

1. Go back to Chapter 1 and read your short-term goals. Are you still on track to meet your short-term goals? If not, how do you plan to get back on track to meet those goals?

2. Are you sticking to the study schedule you created in Chapter 1? Are you finding that you have enough time to study and do homework? If not, what changes will you do to make the time?

MyReadingLab

SELF-EVALUATION CHECKLIST

Rate yourself on the following items, using the following scale:

1 = strongly disagree

2 = disagree

3 = neither agree nor disagree

4 = agree

5 = strongly agree

1. I completed all of the assigned work on time. ....
2. I understand all the concepts in this chapter. ....
3. I contributed to teamwork and class discussions. ....
4. I completed all of the assigned lab work on time. ....
5. I came to class on time. ....
6. I attended class every day. ....
7. I studied for any quizzes or tests we had for this chapter. ....
8. I asked questions when I didn't understand something. ....
9. I checked my comprehension during reading. ....
10. I know what is expected of me in the coming week. ....

4 TOPICS AND STATED MAIN IDEAS

LEARNING STRATEGIES

How to Find the Topic 115

Stated Main Ideas 120

Where to Find the Topic Sentence 124

READING SELECTIONS

READING 1: "Escaping the Debt Trap" 132

READING 2: "Getting the Job of Your Dreams" 142

READING FOR LIFE

On the Job Interview 151

Real-Life Reading 152

Building Vocabulary 154

Textbook Graphic Aids 155

CHAPTER REVIEW

Chapter Practice 156

Textbook Practice 159

Study Skill Review 160

Reading Lab Assignments 162

Learning Reflection 162

Self-Evaluation Checklist 163

FOCUS ON: Business and Personal Finance

Throughout the readings in this chapter, you will learn about building wealth and managing money. You will also learn about careers in business and finance and read about real people who have started their own successful businesses. Perhaps you can turn your passion into a profitable business, making money doing what you love. This chapter will help you understand the skills that are needed to be successful in business and with your personal finances.

Clearly stating a topic and main idea will be valuable to you in business and personal finance. A good marketing campaign requires a clearly stated main idea, and a plan for a new business will benefit from clear and distinct goals. When evaluating agreements and contracts, being able to identify the major topics will help you make sense of complex documents.

In this chapter you will:

LEARNING OBJECTIVES

1 identify the topic of a reading selection.

2 identify the stated main idea.

TOPICS, STATED MAIN IDEAS, AND TOPIC SENTENCES

Topic: the subject of a reading selection.

Knowing who or what a selection is about is the first step in understanding what you are reading. Knowing the general **topic** can help you better understand the points that are being made.

It's important to identify the topic of the selection you are reading because knowing the topic will put you on the right track to finding the main idea. The topic is usually mentioned or referred to in the sentence containing the main idea.

OBJECTIVE **1**

Identify the topic of a reading selection.

How to Find the Topic

Begin by asking, "Who or what is this selection about?" Next, look for the subject that is most frequently mentioned in the reading, usually a word or phrase that is repeated often in the subjects of the sentences. A topic is a subject, like surfing, Egypt, classic cars, or 19th century poets. Topics are not complete sentences. Paragraphs may have the topic as a title, but not always. For example, a paragraph on the best seafood restaurants in town may have a catchy title that does not state the topic plainly, like "Fishing for Great Dining."

Directions: As you read the following paragraph, ask yourself, "Who or what is this about?" Underline any words or phrases that give you a clue.

There are several key elements that make a great leader in business. First, you must have good leadership skills. Good leaders are good listeners and have excellent communication skills. They know how to read people and inspire them. Also, they must be dedicated to learning their business. The best business leaders constantly look for new ways of doing things to gain new customers while continuing to maintain their present ones. Third, good leaders in business have goals. They know what they want to accomplish and how they are going to do it within a specific time frame. Having these key elements can make anyone a good business leader.

1. Which of the following topics is the best "fit" for this passage?
   a. business
   b. leaders
   c. good business leaders
   d. leadership

Getting the Specific Topic

Finding the right topic to fit the passage is like finding a pair of shoes that fit. Some topics are too broad; some are too narrow. One that is just right will fit the passage perfectly. Read the following passage, and as you read, try to find the topic of this passage. Ask yourself, "Who or what is this passage about?"

Underline any words or phrases that give you a clue to the topic.

An IRA, or individual retirement account, is a savings and investment program for your personal finances so that you will have income after you retire. There are several different types of IRAs. One type is known as the traditional IRA. This IRA will allow you to contribute up to $3,000 of your annual salary to a retirement fund before the salary is taxed. For example, if you made a salary of $50,000 a year, you would be able to save $3,000 into a traditional IRA and only be taxed on the remaining $47,000. This lowers your income tax and allows you to invest the money until you reach the age of 59½, the age when you may begin to withdraw the money.

1. Which of the following topics is the best "fit" for this passage?
   - **a.** IRAs
   - **b.** retirement accounts
   - **c.** investing money
   - **d.** saving money

Answers (b), (c), and (d) are too broad because they include other ways to save not described here. Answer (a), IRAs, is the perfect fit for this passage because most of the sentences in the paragraph describe the traditional IRA.

Specific versus General Topics

As you have seen in the example above, some topics are broader than others. When a passage has a wide variety of details and can be broken down into subtopics, it will have a broad topic. But if a passage discusses only one thing, it will have a narrower (more specific) topic.

Look at the following groups of words, and circle the broadest topic in each row:

1.	2.	3.
notebook	New York	sports equipment
pens	Texas	basketball
school supplies	California	tennis racket
highlighter	United States	basketball hoop

Now look at the following groups of topics. Number them in order from the most general (1) to the most specific (4). The first set is done for you.

EXAMPLE:

- 1 books (This is the broadest term; all of the subtopics below could fall into this category.)
- 2 novels (Novels are a type of book, and they contain both items listed below.)
- 3 paragraphs (Paragraphs are in novels and include sentences.)
- 4 sentences (Sentences make up a paragraph.)

1.

- ☐ team sports
- ☐ pitchers
- ☐ baseball
- ☐ sports

2.

- ☐ Ford Motor Co.
- ☐ U.S. auto manufacturers
- ☐ manufacturers
- ☐ American manufacturers

3.

- ☐ bushes with flowers
- ☐ bushes
- ☐ red roses
- ☐ roses

4.

- ☐ actors
- ☐ entertainers
- ☐ film actors
- ☐ Brad Pitt

5.

- ☐ iPhone
- ☐ cell phone companies
- ☐ technology companies
- ☐ Apple

LEARNING STRATEGIES

MyReadingLab

PRACTICE 1

Read the following paragraphs, and underline any clues that help you determine the topics. Then, write the topic that best fits each paragraph on the line below.

If you apply for a credit card or a loan and you're turned down, it may be because of your credit history. In some cases, if you have never borrowed money before, you may not have a credit history. In other cases, you may have borrowed money but have been late on your payments, or you may have a poor credit history due to fraud—specifically, identity theft. One way to find out about your credit history is to get a credit report. Your bank can direct you where to get one, or you can look online for credit reports. It is recommended that consumers check their credit history once every two or three years.

The topic of this passage is:

Money/Payments

MyReadingLab

PRACTICE 2

Read the following paragraphs, and underline any clues that help you determine the topics. Then, write the topic that best fits each paragraph on the line below.

Stocks, also known as *equity shares*, are units of ownership in a company. If a company wants to raise money to develop new products or services, it may sell shares of the company. The price of a stock is determined by its demand. The demand to buy the stock may go up when investors feel the stock may make them a good profit. Typically, investors buy stocks at a lower price and hold onto them until the price of the stock goes up. Then they sell the stocks and keep the profit. The stock market is constantly changing due to many factors. However, like all products, the price of stocks will increase when the demand to buy increases, and it will decrease when the demand to buy decreases.

The topic of this passage is:

MyReadingLab

PRACTICE 3

Read the following paragraphs, and underline any clues that help you determine the topics. Then, write the topic that best fits each paragraph on the line below.

When a company needs money to make the business grow, it may go to a bank and ask for a loan, but this means the company will have to begin making monthly payments in addition to paying an interest charge. Another way to raise the money is to sell bonds. A bond is just a loan from investors. Bonds have the principal (the amount borrowed) and interest (the lending fee) due at a much later date, called the "maturity date."

Companies can sell bonds to raise money without having to pay them back immediately in monthly payments. Unlike stockholders, bondholders do not own any share of the company. Also, bonds have a maturity date when they must be paid back with interest, whereas stocks can be held indefinitely.

The topic of this passage is:

....

MyReadingLab

TEXTBOOK SELECTION 1

Read the following paragraph, and underline any clues that help you determine the topic. Then, write the topic that best fits the paragraph on the line below.

If you are a first-time borrower and have no credit history, it may be difficult to get a bank loan. You may want to think about joining a credit union. A credit union is like a bank, but it is owned by its members. The board of directors and loan committee are elected by the members of the credit union. In the United States, credit unions typically charge lower interest rates on loans and pay higher interest dividends on savings accounts than most banks. Credit unions offer many of the same services as banks. Some credit unions are small and run by a few members, while others are huge with several billion dollars in resources and more than a hundred thousand members.

The topic of this passage is:

....

U-REVIEW 1

For each of the following sentences, write "T" if the statement is true or "F" if the statement is false. As you go over the answers with your team, discuss why the false statements were false.

1. .... Topics tell us who or what the reading passage is about
2. .... Topics are complete sentences.
3. .... Topics are often found in the sentence that states the main idea.
4. .... Topics are usually not found in titles or bold print.
5. .... Knowing the topic will help you find the main idea.

OBJECTIVE 2

Identify the stated main idea.

Stated Main Ideas

A main idea is the most important point that the author is making about the topic of the paragraph. When determining the main idea, here are some points to keep in mind:

- The main idea is always a complete sentence, never a question or a phrase.
- The main idea can be found anywhere in the paragraph; it is not always found in the first sentence.
- The main idea is broad enough to include all the ideas discussed in the paragraph.
- There are several styles of main ideas.

A **topic sentence** is the sentence that states the main idea, the author's most important point.

When a main idea is stated in a paragraph, the sentence that expresses the main idea is called a **topic sentence**. Remember that the main idea is an idea (concept) which can be either stated or implied (suggested). When it's stated, the sentence that gives us the main idea is the topic sentence. Don't confuse this term with the *topic*, which is the general subject of the passage. The most common mistake students make when determining the *topic sentence* is choosing one of the supporting details. To make sure you have the right topic sentence, you must always check by asking, "Do most of the sentences in the paragraph tell me more about this idea?" If they do, then you have chosen the correct topic sentence.

Read the following paragraph and note the main idea in bold print.

> Jennae leaves her textbooks in the back seat of her car and forgets to put them into her book bag before she goes to class. When she gets her papers back, she shoves them into her book bag where they get mixed in with her other papers that have been accumulating all semester. When Jennae tries to find an assignment, it's never in her notebook. She scoops through the mass of wrinkled papers in her bag, but never finds it. **Jannae doesn't have organizational skills that will enable her to succeed in college.**

Topic: Jannae's lack of organization

Main Idea: Jannae doesn't have organizational skills that will enable her to succeed in college.

Notice how the other sentences in the paragraph explain and prove that Jennae is disorganized by giving specific examples. These are called supporting details, and you'll learn more about them in the next chapter.

The Main Idea Is a Key

Finding the main idea of a reading passage is the most important part of reading comprehension. Knowing the key message that the author is trying to get across will unlock many other supporting roles.

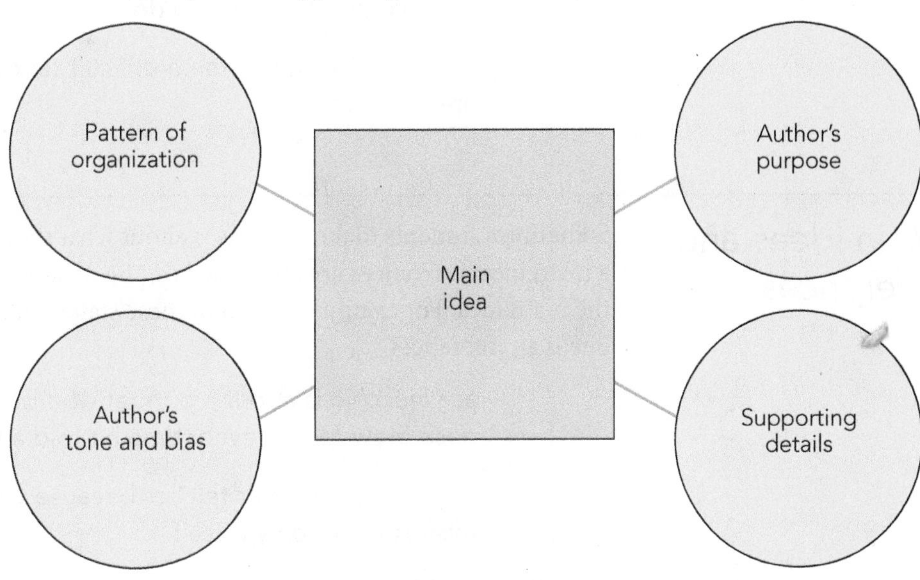

Main Idea Styles

1. Some main ideas will introduce the major points that the paragraph will discuss.

   There are *several types* of marketing methods which would be appropriate for this product. (The several types would be the major details.)

   Three main factors are important to consider when deciding upon the correct way to solve a crime. (The three factors would be the major details.)

2. Some main ideas are a summary of the main point of the paragraph.

   Mozart was one of the most influential composers of all time. (The major details would explain why he was one of the most influential composers.)

   Thomas Edison worked tirelessly to create new inventions and processes. (The major details would explain how he worked to create new inventions and processes.)

3. In definition pattern paragraphs, the definition of the term is the main idea. It is usually followed by an explanation and may include examples in the supporting details

   Immediate memory is the temporary memory where information is processed briefly (in seconds) and subconsciously, then either blocked or passed on to working memory.

   Self-concept: The image or perception someone has about oneself.

4. Other main ideas may be a conclusion of a study, experiment, or discussion.

> The results of the study show that, over the period of a lifetime, students who do not get a college degree will earn less than half the income of those who do.
>
> In conclusion, it is often a difficult task to establish the cause of a fire as arson.

Main Ideas and Inferences

Sometimes students make inferences about what they have read, thinking that it is a main idea. Inferences are also based on the details, but are not the same thing as the main idea. For example, which of these statements is the main idea, and which one is an inference?

> a. *Pinocchio* is about a puppet who became a real boy whose nose grew longer every time he told a lie.
>
> b. You should never tell lies because you will only bring misfortune upon yourself.

The main idea tells what the story was about, an inference is a conclusion that you make based on the details in the story. Answer a. is the main idea and b. is a conclusion based on the story.

Knowing the main idea is the key to good comprehension, and will help you in many other aspects of your learning: in writing good paragraphs and essays, in highlighting, and in note-taking.

Mark which of the following statements would be considered stated main ideas.

1. .... There are several benefits to having a college degree.
2. .... Ways to save money for college.
3. .... How to get financial assistance in college
4. .... Finding money to pay for college can be a challenge.
5. .... What are the best ways to save for college?

Stated Main Idea: Checking Your Answer

Once you have found the topic sentence, you should check to see if the other sentences tell you more about it. If they don't, then look again for a sentence that might better state the author's most important point. Always choose a statement that is general enough to relate to the details discussed in the paragraph. In the following paragraph, the topic and the topic sentence are underlined. Most of the other sentences help to prove the topic sentence.

> Have you ever been to a restaurant and stood there next to an empty desk waiting to be seated? Or once you were seated, did you have to wait more than five minutes for a waiter to approach your table? Even after the meal, did you become frustrated trying to get the waiter's attention so you could get your check? If you've experienced any of these things, then you know how important it is to have good customer service. Customers who have a poor experience at a restaurant or any other business are not likely to come back and may even tell their friends about it. Customer service is one of the most important factors in a business.

MyReadingLab

PRACTICE 4

Read the following paragraph. Find the topic by underlining the subject that is most often mentioned. Then, decide which sentence states the main point that the author is trying to make about the topic. This will be the topic sentence. When you think you have found it, ask yourself, "Do most of the other sentences tell me more about this idea?" If the answer is yes, you have the correct topic sentence.

> When trying to save money, you need to know about your options. Most people save their money in a savings account at a bank. They are paid interest from the bank for allowing the bank to hold and use their money. If you save money in a money market account, your interest rate will be determined by how well the stock market is doing. Although you won't lose any of your original investment, you won't be making much interest when interest rates are low. Another way to save money is to buy a certificate of deposit, or CD. You cannot cash in the certificate until it reaches a certain age, but CDs are a good investment if you don't need the money right away.

1. What is the topic of this passage?
   - a. savings accounts
   - b. money market accounts
   - c. banking
   - d. ways to save money
2. What is the topic sentence?
   - a. Most people save their money in a savings account at a bank.
   - b. When trying to save money, you need to know about your options.
   - c. If you save money in a money market account, your interest rate will be determined by how well the stock market is doing.
   - d. Saving money today will keep you from financial trouble in the future.

Where to Find the Topic Sentence

Topic sentences can be found anywhere in a paragraph, but there are some places where they are more likely to appear.

Topic Sentence at the Beginning

Topic sentences are often the first sentence of the paragraph, as in the following paragraph. Notice that the topic is in bold print, and it is mentioned in the topic sentence.

One way of investing money is to purchase **real estate**. Most people want to buy **real estate** not only as an investment but for a place to live. Others may want to lease out the property to renters so they can make money. But investing in **real estate** is like any other investment—there are no guarantees of making money. In fact, buying the wrong property or buying when real estate prices are going down can result in losing money. When there are not enough buyers or renters to match the flood of properties on the market, **real estate** won't sell. Many people can get behind in their taxes and mortgage payments and lose their property to the banks who lent them the money to buy it.

Topic Sentence at the End

Sometimes the topic sentence comes at the end of a paragraph, as in the following passage.

A **loan** is an amount of money borrowed from a lender. Most **loans** are paid back in regular monthly payments, plus an interest charge. The interest charged on a **loan** can be high or low, depending upon the terms of the **loan** contract. If the interest rate is high, the cost of the **loan** will be high. A borrower must also look at the terms of the **loan** contract. Questions like, "Can I pay off the loan at any time?" and "What happens if I am late on my payment?" should be answered in the contract. Some lenders have high fees or increase the interest rate of your loan for being late on payments. There are many factors to consider when taking out a **loan.**

Topic Sentence in the Middle

In some cases, the topic sentences appears in the middle of the paragraph, as is shown here.

When a company or bank loans money to a borrower, it will often ask for something as "**collateral.**" This is usually some type of property such as a car or real estate that can be held until the loan is paid off. The lender will hold the title (ownership papers) of the car, or place a "lien" (a claim) on the real estate. **Collateral** is used to secure a loan to make sure that the lender receives some sort of repayment if a loan is not paid back. This means that the lender must be paid back first when the **collateral** is sold. If the borrower does not pay back the loan, or is late on payments for a certain number of months, the lender can keep the **collateral**.

Topic Sentences in the First and Last Sentences

Often an author will want to emphasize an important point. To do this, the author may present the topic sentence first and then restate the same idea again at the end. Usually, a repeated topic sentence is stated in different words but has the same key idea. Notice how the topic sentences in this paragraph are similar but not identical:

> Beware of borrowing money from **loan sharks**, because you may end up in serious trouble. People who loan money with extremely harsh terms are known as "**loan sharks.**" Their customers are usually people who are desperate, poor, and not well informed about borrowing money safely. **Loan sharks** sometimes commit criminal acts if the payments are late. Some **loan sharks** threaten or even assault borrowers for missing payments. They charge very high interest rates, which make it impossible for the loans to ever be paid back. Or they may have hidden terms in their contracts that allow them to charge extra fees or take away personal property as collateral. Borrowing from **loan sharks** is a dangerous way to get money, no matter how badly it's needed.

TIPS ON TOPIC SENTENCES

Here are some things to keep in mind about topic sentences:

- They are always complete sentences, never a phrase or a question.
- They state the author's most important point about the topic.
- They are explained or proved by most of the other sentences in the paragraph.
- They are broad statements that are general enough to include all the details in the paragraph.
- They are not the same as inferences or conclusions.
- Topic sentences usually mention the topic or make a reference to the topic.

MyReadingLab

PRACTICE 5

Read the following groups of sentences. One item is the topic, one is the topic sentence, and the others are sentences that explain or prove the topic sentence. These are known as supporting details. Label each item T = topic, TS = topic sentence, or SD = supporting detail.

EXAMPLE:

TS Using the Internet is one way to conduct business online.

SD Pop-up ads can appear on Web sites to advertise new products or services.

T Internet Business

SD A "shopping cart" is a feature that allows people to buy products online.

Continued...

MyReadingLab

PRACTICE 5

...continued

Group 1

__________ A business plan is a written plan that shows how a business will be conducted.

__________ It includes details about how much it will cost to start and run the business.

__________ Business plans predict about how much money the business will make in the next few years.

__________ Business plans

Group 2

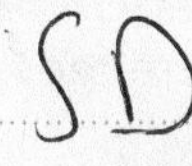

__________ Examples of small businesses are hair salons, restaurants, newsstands, or locksmiths.

__________ Small businesses

__________ There are many different kinds of small businesses.

__________ The term "small business" means businesses with less than 100 employees.

Group 3

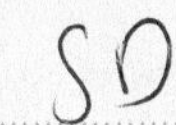

__________ Franchises

__________ Some popular franchises include fast-food restaurant chains, convenience stores, and gas stations.

__________ Franchises are branches of a large corporation that own a chain of small businesses with the same brand name and same products or services.

__________ Franchise owners enjoy the benefits of a large corporation, but must pay a percentage of their profits to the corporation.

Group 4

__________ There are several reasons why more than half of all new businesses go bankrupt within the first five years.

__________ Many new businesses do not have enough money to keep them going during the years when they are trying to get established.

TS Some new businesses fail because the managers do not have enough experience in management.

SD New Business Failures

Group 5

SD Start-up capital

SD One source of start-up capital is to sell shares of stock in the company.

T Sometimes private investors will give money to a new business in return for a percentage of the business.

T New businesses need money to get started, known as "start-up capital."

MyReadingLab

PRACTICE 6

In each of the following paragraphs, underline the topic and locate the topic sentence.

APR means the annual percentage rate that you will pay as interest on your loan. The APR is determined by the lender and the general economy. Some lenders charge much higher APRs than others. If you have a credit card, your APR for charging purchases may be less than the APR for transferring balances to other credit cards or for cash advances. Sometimes the APR changes depending on how much money you owe or your credit score. Often credit card companies will advertise a low introductory APR for anywhere from 3 to 6 months, and then it will increase. When taking out a loan, you need to know not only your APR, but also the terms under which it may change, so read the loan or credit card application carefully.

1. What is the topic of this paragraph?

a. loans
b. APRs
c. credit cards
d. applying for a loan

2. What is the topic sentence of this paragraph?

a. APR means the annual percentage rate that you will pay as interest on your loan.
b. The APR is determined by the lender and by the general economy.
c. Sometimes the APR changes depending on how much money you owe or your credit score.
d. When taking out a loan, you not only have to know your APR, but the terms under which it may change, so read the loan or credit card application carefully.

Continued...

MyReadingLab

PRACTICE 6

...continued

Oprah Winfrey was born in Mississippi to a poor, single mother. They moved to the inner city of Milwaukee, where life was hard. She earned a scholarship to Tennessee State University, where she majored in communications. After a series of successful jobs as a news anchor, she moved to Chicago to host a morning talk show. Her popularity gave her so much success that she soon had her own show and moved into film acting. Oprah Winfrey is a role model for women everywhere because she overcame poverty and hardship to achieve great success. Oprah always found new ways to stay challenged. She started her own magazines and her own television and film production company, which were huge successes. For three years in a row, she was the world's leading African American billionaire, worth more than $2.5 billion. But Oprah's success is more than financial. She has raised millions of dollars for charities and donated millions of dollars of her own money. She has won many awards for her humanitarian efforts, making her one of the most influential and generous women in the world.

1. What is the topic?
   - a. Oprah's TV show success
   - b. the world's richest woman
   - c. Oprah Winfrey
   - d. rich women
2. What is the topic sentence?
   - a. Oprah Winfrey was born in Mississippi to a poor, single mother.
   - b. Oprah Winfrey is a role model for women everywhere because she overcame poverty and hardship to achieve great success.
   - c. For three years in a row, she was the world's leading African American billionaire, worth more than $2.5 billion.
   - d. She has won many awards for her humanitarian efforts, making her one of the most influential and generous women in the world.

If you purchase an item with your credit card, you may withhold payment if the product is damaged or of poor quality. First, you must try to resolve the problem with the company that sold you the goods. Under the Fair Credit Billing Act (a federal law), you can have payment withheld if the sale took place within 100 miles of your home address and it is worth $50 or more. If you can't get a refund, write to your credit card company or call its customer service number. Otherwise, you will lose your rights to stop payment. Your credit card company will investigate the claim, and if it is approved, you will not have to pay for the item.

1. What is the topic of this paragraph?
   - a. withholding a credit card payment
   - b. returning damaged goods
   - c. credit cards
   - d. the Fair Credit Billing Act

2. Which of the following is the topic sentence for this paragraph?
   - a. First, you must try to resolve the problem with the company that sold you the goods.
   - b. If you can't get a refund, write to your credit card company or call its customer service number.
   - c. Your credit card company will investigate the claim, and if it is approved, you will not have to pay for the item.
   - d. If you purchase an item with your credit card, you may withhold payment if the product is damaged or of poor quality.

When Larry Page was a student at the University of Michigan, he loved turning his creative ideas into useful technology. After he graduated with his bachelor's and master's degrees in computer science, he enrolled in the PhD program at Stanford University. There he met another student who was also interested in the Internet, Sergey Brim. Together, they created a computer program to find data more easily and tried it on the Stanford University Web site. It worked so well that they decided to create their own company and named it Google. Today, both young men are listed in Forbes magazine's richest people in the world. Each of them has a net worth close to $20 billion. Larry Page and Sergey Brim created one of the most successful Internet companies in history—Google.

1. What is the topic? (Who or what are most of the details about?)
   - a. Larry Page
   - b. Sergey Brim
   - c. Google
   - d. Larry Page and Sergey Brim
2. What is the topic sentence?
   - a. When Larry Page was a student at the University of Michigan, he loved turning his creative ideas into useful technology.
   - b. Together, they created a computer program to find data more easily and tried it on the Stanford University Web site.
   - c. It worked so well that they decided to create their own company and named it Google.
   - d. Larry Page and Sergey Brim created one of the most successful Internet companies in history—Google.

MyReadingLab

TEXTBOOK SELECTION 2

Read the following textbook selections, underline the topics, and then answer the questions that follow.

The field of marketing is extensive—and so are the opportunities for someone graduating with a marketing degree. While one person may seek out the excitement of an advertising agency that serves multiple clients, another might prefer to focus on brand management at a single organization. For someone else interested in marketing, working as a buyer for a retail chain is appealing. A few people might want to get into marketing research. Others might have an aptitude for supply chain management or *logistics management*, the aspect of supply chain management that focuses on the flow of products between suppliers and customers. A lot of people are attracted to sales positions because of the potential financial rewards.

QUESTIONS

1. What is the topic?
   - **a.** logistics management
   - **b.** management
   - **c.** sales
   - **d.** marketing
2. Which of the following is the topic sentence for this paragraph?
   - **a.** The field of marketing is extensive—and so are the opportunities for someone graduating with a marketing degree.
   - **b.** A few people might want to get into marketing research.
   - **c.** For someone else interested in marketing, working as a buyer for a retail chain is appealing.
   - **d.** Others might have an aptitude for supply chain management or logistics management, the aspect of supply chain management that focuses on the flow of products between suppliers and customers.

To see the PowerSki JetBoard in action, visit the PowerSki Web site. Watch the streaming videos that demonstrate what the JetBoard can do. (Rider in photo is Chad Montgomery, son of Robert E. Montgomery, Inventor of the PowerSki JetBoard and Flat Engine Technology.)

Have you ever wanted to go surfing but couldn't find a body of water with decent waves? You no longer have a problem: the newly invented PowerSki JetBoard makes its own waves. This innovative product combines the ease of waterskiing with the excitement of surfing. A high-tech surfboard with a 40-horsepower, 40-pound watercraft engine, the PowerSki JetBoard has the power of a small motorcycle.

Continued...

Where do product ideas like the PowerSki JetBoard come from? How do people create products that meet customer needs? How are ideas developed and turned into actual products? How do you forecast demand for a product? How do you protect your product ideas? In this chapter, you'll learn the answers to many questions about products.

QUESTIONS

1. What is the topic?
   a. PowerSki JetBoard
   b. surfing
   c. products
   d. selling products
2. Which of the following is the topic sentence for this paragraph?
   a. Have you ever wanted to go surfing but couldn't find a body of water with decent waves?
   b. This innovative product combines the ease of waterskiing with the excitement of surfing.
   c. You no longer have a problem: the newly invented PowerSki JetBoard makes its own waves.
   d. In this chapter, you'll learn the answers to many questions about products.

U-REVIEW 2

List six ways you can identify a topic sentence of a paragraph. Then, check your answers with your team to see if there are any you forgot. (Hint: If you need help getting started, go back and reread "Tips on Topic Sentences.")

1. ....
2. ....
3. ....
4. ....
   ....
5. ....
6. ....

Bonus Question: What question should you ask to check if you have the correct topic sentence?

....

MyReadingLab

Reading 1
VOCABULARY
PREVIEW

"Escaping the Debt Trap"

by Corinne Fennessy

The following vocabulary words are from the article "Escaping the Debt Trap." With a partner or in a team, choose the correct meanings of the underlined words in the following sentences. Use context clues (LEADS), word part clues, and parts of speech to help you figure out the meanings.

1. If you look at money from the wrong perspective (per-SPEK-tiv), it can cause a lot of unhappiness. (Hint: The root is "spect," meaning "to see or view.")
   a. proportion
   b. viewpoint
   c. amount
   d. idea
2. Rather than trying to break down words into their parts, some people prefer to read them with a holistic (hole-IS-tik) approach.
   a. in sections
   b. the whole thing
   c. solid
   d. unusual
3. Patients with terminal (TER-min-ul) diseases are not expected to live. (Hint: The root, "term," is from the Latin root "terminus," meaning "to end.")
   a. serious
   b. unexpected
   c. fatal
   d. watchful
4. It was so sweltering (SWELL-ter-ing) on the day of the parade that many of the marchers fainted from the heat.
   a. extremely hot
   b. mild
   c. chilly
   d. important
5. He invited me to open a charge account at his store, but I declined (dee-KLINE 'D) his offer.
   a. accepted
   b. listened to
   c. didn't accept
   d. questioned
6. The forlorn (for-LORN) look on Jim's face told me that his team had lost the basketball game.
   a. sad
   b. puzzled
   c. happy
   d. long

7. Even though Jamika finds math difficult, her <u>perseverance</u> (per-sa-VEER-ence) has enabled her to pass Algebra with a B.
   a. presence
   b. hardness
   c. determination
   d. frustration

8. If you trust me with your apartment while you are gone, I promise to be a good <u>steward</u> (STOO-ard) and make sure everything is kept safe until you return.
   a. caretaker
   b. babysitter
   c. waiter
   d. cook

9. The lessons I learned about hard work were <u>imprinted</u> (im-PRINT-ed) upon me by my mother, who was always busy working.
   a. written on
   b. impressed upon
   c. given to
   d. taken from

10. After her car accident, Jaya got into a <u>funk</u>, and nothing seemed to cheer her up.
   a. junk car
   b. dance
   c. situation
   d. depressed mood

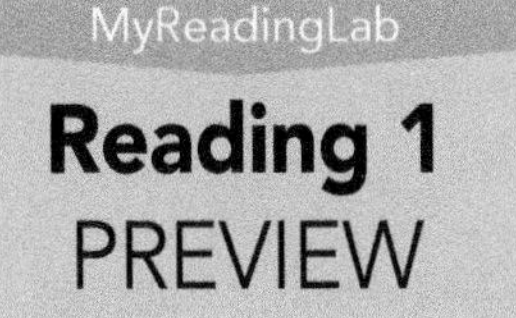

1. Do you owe money on credit cards or student loans?
2. What kinds of things do you buy with credit cards?

Directions: As you read this article, practice the four-step reading process. Preview the article, and then write on the following lines one or two questions that you would hope to have answered.

MyReadingLab

Reading 1

As you read, answer the questions in the margins to check your comprehension.

"Escaping the Debt Trap"

by Corinne Fennessy

Many students rely heavily on credit cards to get through college. Some graduates owe thousands of dollars on credit cards in addition to their college loans, digging themselves into a financial hole so deep that they see no escape. Here's how one couple found a way out of the debt trap.

1 Dana was afraid to open her mailbox. She dreaded seeing the envelopes with red warnings stamped "Final Notice" and "Overdue" stabbing at her. Dana took a few deep breaths before opening bills. Upon opening each one she sunk deeper into depression until she was feeling forlorn and crying.

2 She sank into a funk and pushed the bills aside, thinking, "How can I ever pay all these bills?" She and her boyfriend, Kyle, barely made enough at their part-time jobs to cover their living and college expenses. She hated the unpaid bills, the calls from collection companies, and the threats from the car leasing company. She felt as if she had a terminal disease with no cure.

3 One bill from a credit card company showed that Kyle had purchased a new phone for himself. She became so enraged that when he came home, she started yelling at him about the bill. He accused her of spending money at her salon every month.

4 Like many couples, Dana and her boyfriend, Kyle, were always fighting about money. They fought over how much the other one spent and what was purchased. Each blamed the other for the desperate financial situation they faced. Dana reasoned that their debt problem was ruining their relationship. Before they had become so deeply in debt, they had been a happy couple. But now, their financial problems were the source of every argument. Dana knew she couldn't go on like this. She loved Kyle, but hated what was happening to their relationship. One day, Dana's girlfriend suggested that she and Kyle go for some counseling—financial counseling.

Why were Dana and Kyle arguing?

5 What they learned from the financial counselor surprised them. The counselor offered a new perspective about money. Instead of focusing on the negative aspect of their debt, he suggested that they should take a holistic approach and learn to manage their money more efficiently. It would mean making sacrifices for a while until they could get back on their feet. They discovered that even though they owed more than their combined income, there was a way for them to climb out of debt and start to save money. Both Dana and Kyle had to learn to become better stewards of their financial resources. The counselor asked if they would be willing to give it a try. Neither of them declined the challenge.

6 First, they had to write down the amounts they owed and all of their expenses, along with the annual percentage rate (APR) on their credit cards. One of their credit cards had an APR of 24% and the other only 15%.Their counselor told them to pay off the high interest credit card by transferring the balance onto their lower interest card, and then closing the high interest credit card account.

7 Next, they looked at how much of their budget was used to pay rent. It was over 36% of their total budget—way too high. Dana and Kyle agreed to look for a cheaper place to live that wouldn't cost more than 25% of

What advice did the financial counselor give Dana and Kyle?

their budget but wouldn't leave them sweltering in the summer without air conditioning. It took some shopping, but they finally found a smaller place they liked that was almost half of the rent they were currently paying.

8 Dana had a car loan payment and Kyle had a car lease payment due each month. They decided to keep one car and sell the other. If both of them needed transportation at the same time, they would ask friends or relatives for a ride or take the bus, the subway, or ride a bike. This would save money on car payments, insurance, gas, and repairs.

9 "The first rule of finance is to pay yourself first," the counselor told them. Saving money had always seemed impossible to Dana and Kyle, so the counselor suggested that they let their bank do their saving for them. Each month, their bank would transfer a small amount out of their checking and put it into a savings account. This would help them establish an emergency fund and to save for a down payment on a house. Eventually they would have enough in the fund to cover the cost of a car repair or a dentist's bill so they wouldn't have to keep using their credit card and getting deeper into debt.

What was the "no spending spree" that Dana and Kyle agreed to do?

10 Their financial counselor suggested that they try going on a "no spending spree" for two weeks. Neither of them would spend any money, except to pay bills, pay rent, or buy food. They were put on a strict budget for food expenses, which meant no eating out or buying prepared foods. They would have to eat dinner at home and make their own lunches and drinks to take to school. To help them spend less at the supermarket, the counselor told them about several websites where they could download coupons, and he suggested buying store brands or buying bulk foods at the local farmers' markets.

11 Both Kyle and Dana had expensive cell phone contracts. To reduce their phone charges, they started using the Internet for free long distance calls. They also shopped around and found phone plans with low prepaid monthly fees for unlimited text messages and email, and enough talk minutes each month, saving them over $100 each month.

12 Both of them also agreed to give up spending money on themselves. Dana conceded to do her own hair and nails instead of going to a salon, and Kyle agreed to give up his daily coffee at Starbucks and drink homemade brew from a thermal mug. They couldn't buy any new clothes, so they dug through their closets to find clothes they hadn't worn in a while and traded some clothes with friends and siblings.

13 Their financial counselor also suggested that they try to find additional income. Dana and Kyle went through all of their possessions to find items they no longer used and they held a yard sale at a friend's house. They also asked friends and family if they had any clothes or items they would like to donate. Not only did the yard sale bring them $257, they had a lot of fun interacting with people who came to buy, and they were able to donate the goods that weren't sold to a local charity. After putting that money into their savings account, they both looked for additional part-time work. Dana began babysitting for neighbors and Kyle started washing and waxing cars for his friends. The extra money helped pay for groceries, gas, and school supplies.

14 Learning to live within their means was not easy. It took a lot of perseverance to stick to a budget. They soon realized that they had been spending money to get immediate gratification instead of waiting until they could really afford the things they wanted. "Buying something new made us feel good for a while," Dana said, "until the bill came in."

15 "It was really hard at first," Kyle admitted. "I wasn't used to saying 'no' to

Continued...

MyReadingLab
Reading 1
...continued

myself for things I really felt I deserved to have. Now I know that much of the stuff I wanted I can actually live without and feel okay about it."

16 For three months, Kyle and Dana didn't go out to movies, restaurants, or clubs. They went to the library to borrow movies to watch at home while sharing a bowl of popcorn. They enjoyed the local parks and joined a campus club to volunteer at a soup kitchen. Instead of going out on weekends, they invited friends over and asked everyone to bring something to eat or drink. They soon found they had more fun and more friends than ever before.

How did Dana and Kyle change their money management style?

17 After three months of staying on their "no spending spree" and paying down their debt, Kyle and Dana found they actually had some money left over at the end of the month. This was split up into four parts: one part for savings, one part for making additional payments on their credit card, another part for donating to charity, and the fourth part for spending on themselves. Now they can go out once a month to an inexpensive restaurant and not feel guilty.

18 "Getting a special treat at the end of the month means more now because we've had to work hard to earn it," says Dana. "As soon as we pay off our credit card, we're going to start putting those monthly payments into our savings account. We have learned how to manage our money by spending less and saving more. Now that we're saving money, I don't worry about it anymore. We just try to limit our spending to the things we need and not the things we want. I've also learned that there are some things more important than money. I was so focused on our debt that I didn't see what a great guy Kyle is, or how important it is to have friends who care about you. And no matter how poor you think you are, you can always spare something for somebody who has less than you. I know that someday we will be able to afford the things we want once we are both working full-time. The lessons we learned have been imprinted on us forever. We'll never be into more debt than we can handle ever again."

1,601 words divided by ________ minutes = ________ words per minute

MyReadingLab
Reading 1
REVIEW

It is a good habit to summarize everything you read to strengthen your comprehension.

Directions: Briefly answer the following five questions, and then use this information to write a summary of the article "Escaping the Debt Trap."

1. What is the topic (who or what is this about)?

____

____

2. Action (what happened)?

____

____

3. How?

4. When?

5. Why?

Use your summary notes to write a two- or three-sentence summary of the article on the lines below. In your own words, describe what the article was about and why the author wrote it.

MyReadingLab

Reading 1 COMPREHENSION QUESTIONS

The following questions will help you to recall the main idea and the details of "Escaping the Debt Trap." Review any parts of the article that you need to find the correct answers.

MAIN IDEAS

1. What is the topic (subject) of this article?
   - a. money
   - b. saving money
   - c. Kyle and Dana's debt
   - d. Kyle and Dana's relationship
2. What is the main idea of the article? (What is the most general statement that tells the most important point of the article?)
   - a. After meeting with a financial counselor, Kyle and Dana learned how to manage their finances and get out of debt.
   - b. Dana and Kyle went to see a financial counselor.
   - c. Getting out of debt requires perseverance.
   - d. You should never go into debt because it can ruin your life.
3. What is the main idea of paragraph 9?
   - a. The first rule of finance is to pay yourself first.
   - b. Saving money had always seemed impossible to Dana and Kyle, so the counselor suggested that they let their bank do their saving for them.
   - c. Each month, their bank would transfer a small amount out of their checking and put it into a savings account.
   - d. Eventually they would have enough in the fund to cover the cost of a car repair or a dentist's bill so they wouldn't have to keep using their credit card and getting deeper into debt.

Continued...

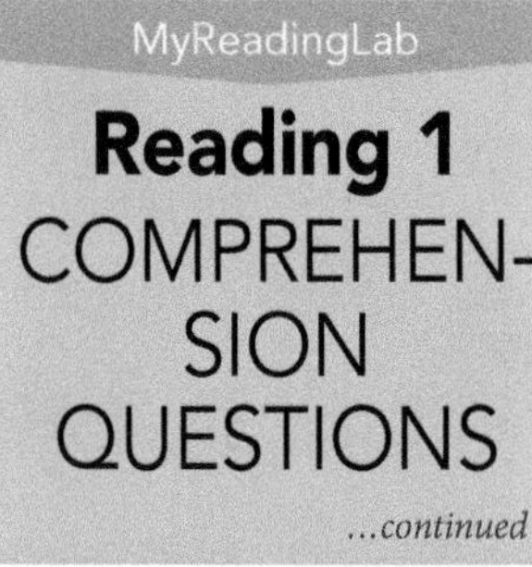

4. **What is the main idea of paragraph 13?**
   a. Their financial counselor also suggested that they try to find additional income.
   b. Dana and Kyle went through all of their possessions to find items they no longer used and they held a yard sale at a friend's house.
   c. Not only did the yard sale bring them $257, they had a lot of fun interacting with people who came to buy, and they were able to donate the goods that weren't sold to a local charity.
   d. After putting that money into their savings account, they both looked for additional part-time work.
5. **According to the article, Kyle and Dana saved money all the following ways except**
   a. transferring their credit card balance to a lower interest card
   b. reducing the cost of their phone plans
   c. moving into a cheaper place to live
   d. buying all their clothes at a thrift store
6. **What did Dana and Kyle discover after living for three months on a "no spending spree"?**
   a. They realized they didn't need to buy things.
   b. They were glad to get their credit cards back.
   c. They had some money left over to spend.
   d. They were no longer in debt.
7. **What did the financial counselor mean when he said, "The first rule of finance is to pay yourself first"?**
   a. You should save some money first and use the rest for expenses and debt reduction.
   b. You should pay your debts first.
   c. You should keep your paycheck and spend it on yourself.
   d. You should save your paycheck for yourself.
8. **From reading the article, you can conclude that (choose all that apply):**
   a. Dana and Kyle no longer spend money on restaurants and movies.
   b. To become debt-free, both partners must be willing to change their attitudes about spending and agree on how to manage their money.
   c. People often spend money as a way to satisfy an emotional need.
   d. People should not use credit cards.

Using context clues and word part clues, determine the best meaning for the underlined words in each of these sentences. If necessary, use a dictionary.

9. **They realized that they had been spending money to get immediate <u>gratification</u> instead of waiting until they could really afford the things they wanted.**
   a. satisfaction
   b. response
   c. recognition
   d. investment
10. **Instead of focusing on the negative <u>aspect</u> of their debt, he suggested that they should take a holistic approach and learn to manage their money more efficiently.**
   a. respect
   b. side
   c. discouraging
   d. reward

MyReadingLab

Reading 1 VOCABULARY PRACTICE

Use the vocabulary words from the Word Bank to complete the following sentences. Write the words into the blanks provided.

WORD BANK

holistic	terminal	sweltering	declined	forlorn
perseverance	funk	perspective	steward	imprinted

1. If you apply for a loan and you are ______________, you can apply for one at another bank or credit union.
2. If you have the right ______________ about money, you will have a healthy financial outlook.
3. Instead of trying to write every little detail about the book in your report, just write a more ______________ summary of the entire novel.
4. The day my team won the championship will be ______________ in my memory forever.
5. Mrs. Jones was diagnosed with a ______________ disease, but the treatment was so successful that she is now expected to live a long life.
6. On a(n) ______________ day like today, the best thing to do is to stay in a cool, air-conditioned room, or go swimming.
7. No one thought Ming would be able to finish college and become an artist, but her hard work and ______________ paid off, and now she works as an illustrator.
8. A small boy who looked very ______________ asked me if I had seen his lost puppy.
9. Dave got into a serious ______________ after his girlfriend left him for another guy.
10. Because Tina is too young to manage her inheritance, her uncle is her financial ______________ until she reaches the age of 18.

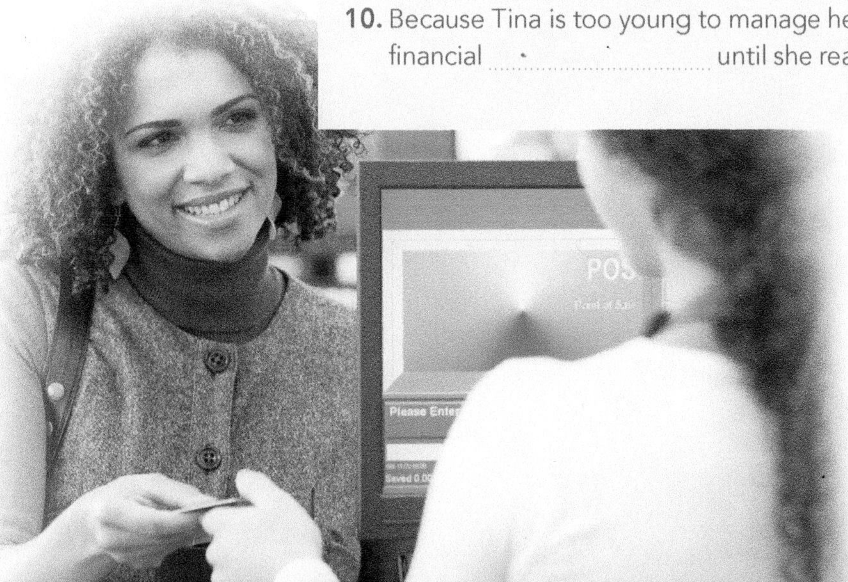

MyReadingLab

Reading 1 QUESTIONS FOR WRITING AND DISCUSSION

Review any parts of the article you need to answer the following questions.

1. What are some things Dana and Kyle learned from their experience?

2. How was Dana's attitude about money different at the end of the story from the beginning, and why do you think she changed?

3. What new perspectives about money did the financial counselor bring to Dana and Kyle?

4. Dana says she learned that some things are more important than money. What do you think some of those things are?

5. Kyle and Dana used to buy things because it was enjoyable. What other ways did they discover to enjoy themselves that didn't cost money?

Reading 1
VOCABULARY PRACTICE—MATCHING

DIRECTIONS: *The object of the game is to be the team with the most matched sets of cards.*

1.

Using an index card or 1/4 sheet of paper, copy **one** of the numbered items from the lists below. Your instructor will inform you about which item(s) to copy onto the card(s). (Some students may have to make more than one card to get all 30 cards made.) Label the word cards with a "W" and the definition cards with a "D" as illustrated.

2.

There are three matching cards for each set: the vocabulary word card, the definition card, and the sentence card. When your instructor tells you to begin, in your teams, match as many sets of 3 cards as you can, matching the word with its definition and the sentence it completes. With the remaining cards that do not match any of your sets, trade cards with other teams.

3.

Lay out the cards into rows as illustrated on the right.

4.

When time is called, the team with the most correctly matched sets of cards wins.

W sweltering	D very hot	It was such a _____ day, our ice cream cones quickly melted
W Cards (Words)	**D Cards (Definitions)**	**Sentence Cards**

W Cards (Words)	D Cards (Definitions)	Sentence Cards
1. holistic	11. turned down	21. It is such a(n) _____ day that I think I would rather swim than go running.
2. terminal	12. determination	22. The _____-looking dog poked his nose through the fence and whined for attention.
3. sweltering	13. referring to the whole thing	23. If you have enough _____, you can succeed at just about anything.
4. declined	14. viewpoint	24. A hospice is a care center for patients with _____ illnesses.
5. forlorn	15. caretaker	25. In ____ medicine, they treat the whole body instead of just one part.
6. perseverance	16. sad, pitiful	26. Serving in the military during a war gave Juan a new _____ on life.
7. perspective	17. final, ending, or fatal	27. I offered to buy James a new basketball, but he _____ my offer.
8. steward	18. impressed upon	28. I promised my brother that I would be a good _____ of his new car if he let me borrow it for a few days.
9. imprinted	19. depressed mood	29. Keisha fell into a(n) _____ after she lost her dream job.
10. funk	20. very hot	30. The memory of 9-11 will be _____ on me as long as I live.

MyReadingLab

Reading 2
VOCABULARY PREVIEW

"Getting the Job of Your Dreams"

by Corinne Fennessy

The following vocabulary words are from "Getting the Job of Your Dreams."

With a partner or in a team, choose the best meaning of the underlined words in the following sentences. Use context clues ("LEADS"), word part clues, and parts of speech to help you figure out the meanings.

1. Every spring, Dimetri laments (la-MENTS) about not getting the grades he wants, but he never improves his study habits to earn them.
   a. celebrates
   b. unhappy
   c. complains
   d. fails

2. If you continue to endeavor (en-DEV-er) despite the challenges you face, you will achieve success eventually.
   a. try
   b. an effort
   c. improve
   d. keep up with

3. LaShonda is in college to get a degree and to find a prospective (pro-SPEK-tiv) partner.
   a. looking for
   b. future
   c. compatible
   d. agree

4. Shawn showed so much initiative (in-NISH-ee-a-tiv) during his internship that the hospital he was working for offered him a full-time job upon graduation.
   a. sense
   b. unwillingness
   c. readiness to work or lead
   d. encouragement

5. The store manager gave me such a daunting (DAWNT-ing) look when I told him about the shortage in my cash register that I thought he might fire me on the spot.
   a. puzzled
   b. surprised
   c. expected
   d. intimidating

6. When my mother relates an incident that happened to her, she always tries to embellish (em-BELL-ish) the facts with a little fantasy.
   a. eliminate
   b. add additional ideas
   c. to implant
   d. humiliate

7. Good writing is concise (kon-SICE) because it leaves out unimportant details and gets to the point.
   a. brief and to the point
   b. understanding
   c. complete
   d. instructive

8. Always wear proper attire (a-TIRE) for a formal occasion; it's better to be overly formal than too informal.
   a. attitude
   b. shoes
   c. confidence
   d. clothing

9. My room mate talks on the phone incessantly (in-SESS-ant-lee) and it's very annoying when I'm trying to study.
   a. appropriately
   b. happily
   c. bothersome
   d. constantly

10. Dr. Johnson is a very competent (KOM-pet-ant) professor, so I would highly recommend her.
    a. competitive
    b. capable
    c. difficult
    d. uninteresting

MyReadingLab

Reading 2 PREVIEW

1. Have you ever applied for a part-time or full-time job? Were you successful in getting the job? Why or why not?
2. Describe the perfect job of your dreams. What preparation would you need to get it?

Directions: As you read this story, practice the four-step reading process. Preview the article, and then write on the following lines one or two questions that you would hope to have answered.

....

....

....

MyReadingLab

Reading 2

"Getting the Job of Your Dreams"

by Corinne Fennessy

1 You've completed your degree requirements, finished college, and opened all the graduation presents. You're looking forward to landing that first big job of your career so you can move into your own place and enjoy the life you planned. That's the dream you share with every college graduate. But to find your first job, you need to use every trick in the book, and here are a few suggestions to help you.

What are some tips for finding a job?

2 Everyone laments the fact that you don't qualify for most full-time jobs without experience, and you can't get experience without getting a job. But you can gain experience in your field even while still in college by following these tips.

- Be prepared. Employers want candidates who have good communication skills, specifically in reading and writing. Endeavor to improve these skills while in college.
- Join a club or organization at school or in the community where you can develop your interpersonal and leadership skills. Try to find something related to your field. For example, if you intend to go into the health field, find a club related to this. If your college doesn't offer one, find a health organization in the community; for instance, volunteer for the Red Cross. It's a great way to network and meet prospective employers or people who will give you great references.
- Try to work part-time in your related field. For example, if your major is computer science, try getting a job in one of the campus computer labs. You may only be assisting students with basic computer questions, but gaining this experience will help you get your next computer job.
- Look for paid or unpaid internships while still in college. These will give you experience in your field and help you network with future employers and gain references.
- Find a mentor in the field where you want to work and offer your services for free. Every busy professional needs someone to run errands, make photocopies, or even just to make coffee. The goal is to get exposure to the field and to let others know who you are and what you can do. This can also count as experience when you apply for a real job.
- Use social networking Web sites to market your abilities and experience. There are specific Web sites just for people seeking jobs. Create a blog just for this purpose to market yourself.

3 Begin keeping a file of all the things you do that help to show what a great employee you'll make. If you are an officer in a club, or have won an award, or have volunteered, or have worked on a special project for something, all of these tell about the kind of person you are and speak volumes about your initiative and motivation. It also gives you something to discuss when you get to an interview.

4 While you're in college, take advantage of free workshops or tutoring to learn how to use some essential computer programs. Employers need graduates with software skills, and having computer skills will make you a more valuable employee no matter what field you choose.

résumé: A written summary of your skills, education, and experience.

How should you write your résumé?

5 Writing a **résumé** can seem like a daunting task. What should you write? How much should you put in? A really good résumé sells you to the employer. Employers want to know if you are the right person for this job. Your résumé should prove that you have the right qualifications and experience, and are the perfect person to fill the position. The important skills to highlight in your résumé are your communication skills, your management skills (reliability, dependability), your interpersonal skills, and technology skills.

6 It's not necessary to hire a professional résumé writer for your first full-time job application. Most colleges have career centers and workshops to help you write a good résumé. There are also free software programs and templates that you can download. But the most important thing is to show your résumé to several people and have them look it over for you **before** you send it out to potential employers. It should be accurate. Don't embellish the truth because getting caught in a lie will exclude you from all current and future opportunities. Be concise, neat, and represent all of your special abilities and qualities. First write a general résumé and save it to your computer. When you apply for a specific position, tailor your résumé to fit the job you are seeking. Emphasize relevant details that show your experience and skills for this position.

7 Focus on applying only for jobs that are right for you. Employers will know if you're not a good match, and you'll waste time applying for something you're not qualified to do. Suppose you find a job listing that is exactly what you're looking for. Go online and do some research about the company. If it's in your locality, go there and look around. If possible, speak to some employees. Most people are happy to tell you about their workplace. Notice the way people dress at the company to get an idea of their expectations for attire at your interview.

8 Once you've applied and have sent in your résumé tailored specifically for that job, follow up with a phone call. Ask if they received it and if they have any questions. Ask if they will be scheduling interviews, and if so, when you can come in. They may tell you that they will call you if they are interested, but don't let that discourage you from calling again in another week. You need to remind people that you are interested and available for the position. Always use your best manners when speaking on the phone or in person. If they say that the position has been filled, maintain a positive tone and thank them for their time. Anyone who comes across as impatient or frustrated will not be considered for a job.

How should you prepare for an interview?

9 If you are invited to an interview, rehearse for it by creating some typical questions and preparing answers for them to help you be more confident at the interview. Typical interview questions are, "What unique abilities can you bring to our company?", or, "Tell us something interesting about yourself." Also, prepare some questions that you have about the company or the position. It's okay to ask about a salary range for the position, but not about how much you will earn. This implies that your first priority is

Continued...

about money and not the job. Remember to smile, look into the person's eyes, shake hands with everyone on the interview committee, and have confidence. This doesn't mean you should brag incessantly or try to sell yourself like a used car. Your goal is to show the interviewer that you are the perfect person for that particular job. Anything you offer should relate to how your skills and qualities match the job description. Always dress in your best clothes, looking clean and neat. Make sure the style is appropriate for an interview.

10 After the interview, thank everyone for their time and shake hands again. Get the name and contact information of your interviewer. When you get home, send a thank you letter or email to your interviewer, saying how much you appreciated the opportunity to talk about your qualifications for the job. Include your contact information again. If you don't hear anything back within a week, call and leave a message asking if the position has been filled. When you leave a message, repeat your name and phone number *slowly* and *clearly*.

11 Keep a file of the actions you have taken in your job search; when and with whom you spoke or emailed so you can make weekly follow-up calls or emails. Go online and browse all of the employment websites. Read their tips and post your résumé.

12 Finding your first full-time career job doesn't happen in a week, or a month. Sometimes it may take a year or more. In the meantime, you can work part-time in your field and continue networking. You may not get the salary you were hoping for in your first job, but it is a stepping stone that gives you the experience you need to step up to the next level in a few years. Once you have proven yourself to be a competent, reliable, and conscientious employee, you'll have the experience needed to qualify for a better job with better pay. Each new position will take you up the ladder of salary and status, along with more responsibility. We all start at the bottom and work our way up by proving ourselves to our employers. Each new job brings unique challenges and rewards of its own.

1,435 words divided by .... minutes = ... words per minute

MyReadingLab

Reading 2
REVIEW

It is a good habit to summarize everything you read to strengthen your comprehension.

Directions: On the following lines, write a two- or three-sentence summary of the article "Getting the Job of Your Dreams." Using the prompts *who, what, when, where, why*, and *how*, describe what the article was about and why the author wrote it.

....

....

....

MyReadingLab

Reading 2 COMPREHENSION QUESTIONS

The following questions will help you recall the main idea and the details of "Getting the Job of Your Dreams." Review any parts of the article that you need to find the correct answers.

1. **What is the topic of this article?**
   - **a.** jobs
   - **b.** dream jobs
   - **c.** how to get a good job
   - **d.** writing a good résumé

MAIN IDEAS

2. **Which of the following sentences best states the main idea for the entire article?**
   - **a.** You're looking forward to landing that first big job of your career so you can move into your own place and enjoy the life you want.
   - **b.** That's the dream you share with every college graduate.
   - **c.** But to find your first job, you need to use every trick in the book, and here are a few suggestions to help you.
   - **d.** Each new job brings unique challenges and rewards of its own.
3. **What is the topic sentence of paragraph 5?**
   - **a.** Writing a résumé can seem like a daunting task.
   - **b.** What should you write?
   - **c.** How much should you put in?
   - **d.** A really good résumé sells you to the employer.
4. **What is the topic sentence of paragraph 7?**
   - **a.** Focus on applying only for jobs that are right for you.
   - **b.** Go online and do some research about the company.
   - **c.** Most people are happy to tell you about their workplace.
   - **d.** Notice the way people dress at the company.
5. **What is the topic sentence of paragraph 9?**
   - **a.** If you are invited to an interview, rehearse for it by creating some typical questions and preparing answers for them.
   - **b.** Also, prepare some questions that you have about the company or the position.
   - **c.** Your goal is to show the interviewer that you are the perfect person for that particular job.
   - **d.** Always dress in your best clothes, looking clean and neat.

SUPPORTING DETAILS

6. **According to the article, why should you keep records of your achievements while in college?**
   - **a.** to show employers about the kind of person you are and to show your initiative and motivation
   - **b.** It gives you something to brag about in the interview.
   - **c.** These remind you that you were successful in college.
   - **d.** You may want to read about them again sometime in the future.
7. **Which of the following is not a good strategy for finding your dream job?**
   - **a.** sending out résumés to every job that is available
   - **b.** applying only to the jobs that are right for you
   - **c.** improving your communication skills while in college
   - **d.** working part-time in the same field as your dream job

Continued...

DRAWING CONCLUSIONS

8. According to the article, which of the following statement is false?

a. You begin to prepare for your dream job while you are still in college.
b. Finding a dream job takes a great deal of time and effort.
c. You will not get your dream job if you don't graduate from college.
d. Employers want people who have good communication skills.

9. Why is it important to know something about the company to which you are applying?

a. so you will know the company's net worth
b. so you will know if the company is the right place for you
c. so you will know how much salary to expect
d. so you will feel comfortable when you interview

VOCABULARY IN CONTEXT

10. Using context clues and word part clues, determine the best meaning for the underlined word in the following sentence. If necessary, use a dictionary. When you apply for a specific position, tailor your résumé to fit the job you are seeking.

a. a clothes maker
b. describe
c. revise
d. submit

MyReadingLab

Reading 2 VOCABULARY PRACTICE

Use the vocabulary words from the Word Bank to complete the following sentences. Write the words into the blanks provided.

WORD BANK

concise	endeavors	embellish	attire	prospective
lament	initiative	incessantly	competent	daunting

1. Deirdre was told to ________ her creative writing assignment to make it more interesting.

2. Mr. James sends calendars out to ________ new clients to attract some attention and grow his business.

3. Some restaurants have a dress code, so you should always inquire about the proper ________ for the establishment.

4. When Dierdre received her English paper back, her professor told her she needed to be more ________ by editing and revising her work more carefully.

5. Employers seek employees who are responsible and who are ________ in reading, writing, and speaking.

6. Each year I have the ________ task of completing our income tax forms, and it seems to get more complicated every year.

7. Kiera always ________ to do her best in her college courses.

8. Instead of waiting for a job offer, Jamal takes the .... to contact prospective employers and inform them that he is seeking employment.

9. My neighbor's dog barks ...., and it is very annoying.

10. You always .... that you have no dates, but then you turn down every person who asks you out!

MyReadingLab

Reading 2 QUESTIONS FOR WRITING AND DISCUSSION

Review any parts of the article you need to answer the following questions.

1. What are some ways you can gain experience before you find your dream job?

2. What are some skills that employers look for in prospective employees?

3. What are some tips for writing a good résumé?

4. What are some interview questions that employers might ask?

5. What are some tips to follow if you go to an interview?

Reading 2
VOCABULARY PRACTICE—TEAM PASSWORD

Direction: *The object of this game is to correctly guess the vocabulary word in three tries. The word list below may be printed on the board or on a sheet of paper.*

1.
Divide the class into groups with two opposing teams within each group.

2.
Each opposing team will take one list of clues, list A or list B. These can be copied out of the book or printed on cards before class. Each team needs only one list to play.

3.
Each team needs a clue reader, a time keeper, and a score keeper. The word list below may be written on the board or on paper to use during the game.

4.
Decide which team will go first to give the clues. The clue reader will read the first clue for 3 points to the other team. The other team has 15 seconds to guess the word. If they don't answer correctly within 15 seconds, give them the second clue for 15 seconds, and then if necessary, the third clue. If they cannot guess the word after all the clues have been given, no points are awarded. The play then goes to the opposing team who will read their first clue for 3 points.

5.
When the opposing team guesses the correct word, they will next read the clues for their first word to the other team.

6.
Continue playing until all the clues and words are completed. The team with the most points wins.

List A	List B
For 3 pts: unhappy For 2 pts: grieve For 1 pt: complain	For 3 pts: overstatement For 2 pts: exaggeration For 1 pt: additional ideas
For 3 pts: persisting For 2 pts: laboring For 1 pt: trying	For 3 pts: succinct For 2 pts: brief For 1 pt: to the point
For 3 pts: potential For 2 pts: possible For 1 pt: future	For 3 pts: garb For 2 pts: cloak For 1 pt: clothes
For 3 pts: self-starter For 2 pts: motivated For 1 pt: taking the lead	For 3 pts: persistently For 2 pts: continuously For 1 pt: constantly
For 3 pts: unwelcome For 2 pts: intimidating For 1 pt: somewhat frightening	For 3 pts: aptitude For 2 pts: skilled For 1 pt: capable

WORD LIST

lament	endeavor	prospective	initiative
attire	daunting	embellish	concise
incessantly	competent		

ON THE JOB INTERVIEW

ADAM METZINGER,

TRUST ADMINISTRATOR

What is your career, and how did you become interested in it?

I work as a vice president for The Bank of New York Mellon in the Global Trust Department. We handle some of the financial deals for governments or large corporations. For example, if a government or corporation wanted to fund a large project, like building a bridge or a power plant, the financial deal would be handled by our department.

What is your training and education?

I earned my bachelor's degree in sociology and criminal justice, and then my master's in business administration.

Did you ever consider quitting when you were in college?

Not really. Some courses were harder than others. While I was doing an internship for my bachelor's degree, I worked as a salesman for a brokerage firm on Wall Street. I found that I wasn't really interested in being a salesman, so I learned something important from that, plus I gained the experience in business that I needed to get this job.

What do you like about your job?

I enjoy lots of things, especially the variety of work that I do. I move around some very large sums of money, which are used for many different purposes all around the world. Each project is unique, and I get to do business on an international scale.

What do you dislike about your job?

I have no dislikes, but working with huge sums of money carries a lot of responsibility, so I have to read everything very carefully, looking at every detail in the contracts.

If you could give college students one piece of advice, what would it be?

My best advice is, even if you do nothing else, go to class. Your professor will get to know you, and you can learn a lot just by being there.

MyReadingLab
WATCH THE VIDEO
COLLEGE STUDENTS AND CREDIT CARDS
GOOD MONEY
Stopping the "Credit Card Epidemic"
NOW

"College Students and Credit Cards" and answer the questions about topic and main idea.

MyReadingLab

REAL-LIFE READING

CREDIT CARD AGREEMENT

If you apply for a credit card with a bank or other financial institution, you should read the terms of the credit card agreement carefully. The following is an excerpt (part) of a credit card agreement. Use the four-step reading process as you read, and then answer the questions that follow to check your comprehension. Preview the selection first, and then read it and answer the questions that follow with your team.

TERMS AND CONDITIONS

FEES: We may charge your account for the following fees. The application and payment of a fee will not release you from responsibility of the action which caused the fees.

LATE PAYMENT: We may charge a $25.00 late fee to your account if you do not pay at least the minimum payment by the stated due date. In addition to the late fee, we will cancel any temporary low rate offers if your payment is late more than one billing cycle during the promotion. We will charge an additional late fee of 10% of your balance for each billing cycle that your account is past due.

OVER THE LIMIT: If you go over your credit limit or cash advance limit by $50.00 or more, we will add an additional $30.00 Over the Limit fee to your account for each billing cycle that you remain over your credit limit.

RETURNED PAYMENT: If you make a payment on your account with a check from some other financial institution and that check is not honored by the financial institution on which it is drawn, you will be charged a fee of $35.00.

RETURNED CHECK: If you write a check from your account and that check is not honored because your account is in default or over the limit, we will charge you a fee of $35.00.

CASH ADVANCE FEE: An additional finance charge will be added to your account each time you obtain a cash advance. This additional finance charge will be 8% of the amount of the cash advance with a maximum of $30.00. Internet transactions are exempt from the cash advance fee.

ENTIRE BALANCE DUE: If you fail to make a required payment when due or default on any other term in this agreement, we can declare the entire balance of your account due and payable at once without notice. We can also demand complete immediate payment if you make any false or misleading statement on your application or if you die or file for bankruptcy.

COLLECTION COSTS: To the extent permitted by applicable law, you agree to pay all costs and disbursements, including reasonable attorney fees, incurred by us in legal proceedings to collect or enforce your indebtedness.

Directions: Complete each sentence with the correct information from the credit card agreement.

1. If you do not make a minimum payment by the date your payment is due, you will be charged a $ ______ late fee.

2. They will cancel any temporary low rate offers if the payment is late more than ______ during the promotion.

3. They will charge an additional late fee of ______ for each billing cycle that the account is past due.

4. For each billing cycle that you charge an amount of $50 or more over your credit limit, they will charge you an additional ______ fee.

5. If you pay your bill with a check that does not clear due to insufficient funds, you will be charged a fee of ______.

6. Each time you make a cash advance on your credit card, you will be charged an additional finance charge of ______, except for Internet transactions.

7. If you fail to make a payment when due, if you default on any other part of the agreement, provide false information, or file for bankruptcy, the bank has the right to demand ______.

8. If the bank must send your account to a collection agency, or if any legal fees result from legal proceedings to collect your debt, you will ______.

MyReadingLab

BUILDING VOCABULARY

Throughout this course, you will be introduced to word parts that make up many words in the English language. Study the following word parts, and then answer the questions that follow.

Prefixes	**Roots**	**Suffixes**
in- *into*	duct- *to bring, to take*	-tion, -sion *action, state of*
de- *away, reverse*	cis- *to cut*	-ive- *a state or quality*

What English words can you create from these word parts?

Using a dictionary, look up the meanings of any of the words you wrote that you can't define. Use one of the words you wrote in a sentence that reveals its meaning with a context clue:

MyReadingLab

TEXTBOOK GRAPHIC AIDS

In business, operations managers often use program evaluation and review technique (PERT) charts for complex schedules. These charts diagram the activities required to produce a good, specify the time required to perform each activity in the process, and organize activities in the most efficient sequence. The following is a PERT diagram showing the process for producing one "hiker" bear at Vermont Teddy Bear. Study the diagram, and then answer the questions that follow.

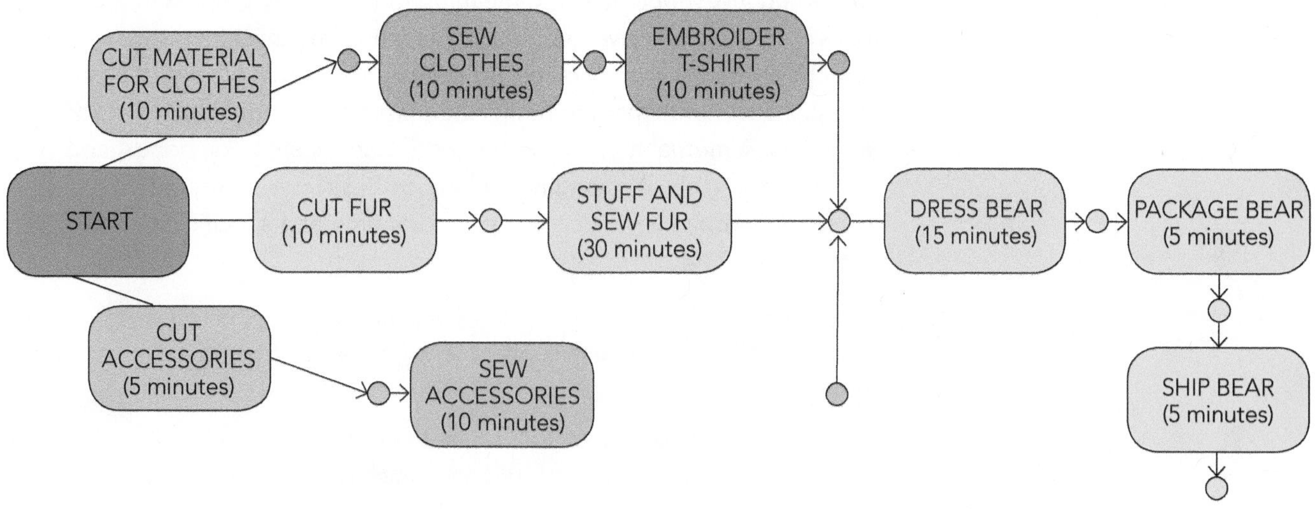

1. What is the topic of this chart?
   a. children's toys
   b. manufacturing stuffed animals
   c. PERT chart for making a Vermont Teddy Bear
   d. sewing
2. What does PERT stand for?
   a. package, export, receive, and transport
   b. program evaluation and review technique
   c. preview examples and revise technology
   d. program explanation and review technique
3. Which stage of the process takes the most time?
   a. cutting material for clothes
   b. cutting accessories
   c. dressing the bear
   d. stuffing and sewing the fur
4. Which three steps can occur all at the same time?
   a. cut material for clothes, cut fur, cut accessories
   b. sew clothes, embroider shirt, stuff and sew fur
   c. cut accessories, sew accessories, dress bear
   d. dress bear, package bear, ship bear
5. For the purple portion of the assembly line, what is the total time needed to complete the operations?
   a. 10 minutes
   b. 45 minutes
   c. 30 minutes
   d. one hour

MyReadingLab

CHAPTER PRACTICE 1

Read the following paragraph. Circle the topic, and underline the topic sentence. Then, complete the exercises that follow.

When you invest your money, you should know which investments are insured and which ones are not. An *insured investment* will guarantee that what you invested will be paid back, plus some interest. An *uninsured investment* is a risk, meaning that you may get less money back than what you invested. Examples of insured investments are savings accounts, money market accounts, and certificates of deposit (CDs). Investments that are not insured are stocks, mutual funds, and annuities. A mutual fund is an account to purchase stocks, bonds, and other investments. An annuity is a long-term savings contract that invests your money for a certain period of time at a specific interest rate.

Label each of the following: T = topic, TS = topic sentence, or SD = supporting detail. One will be a topic, one will be a topic sentence, and two will be supporting details.

1. ________ When you invest your money, you should know which investments are insured and which ones are not.

2. ________ Investments that are not insured are mutual funds and annuities.

3. ________ An annuity is a long-term savings contract that invests your money for a certain period of time at a specific interest rate.

4. ________ Insured and uninsured investments

5. Identify the meaning of the underlined word in the following sentence: An uninsured investment is a risk, meaning that you may get less money back than what you invested.
   a. underinsured
   b. not insured
   c. all insured
   d. not sure

MyReadingLab

CHAPTER PRACTICE 2

Read the following paragraph. Circle the topic, and underline the topic sentence. Then, complete the exercises that follow.

After 25 years of being one of the leading salespeople in her company, Mary Kay Ash found herself passed over for promotion by a man she had trained who made twice her salary. This was a common occurrence in the 1960s because of prejudice against women and minorities. Mary Kay quit her job and started her own company to offer women opportunities to be business owners who sell products from home. Her business was established on the Golden Rule, and on placing faith first, family second, and career third. Today, the Mary Kay Corporation employs 1.8 million people in 35 countries, with more than $2.4 billion in wholesale revenue. Mary Kay Ash showed women how to be independent and successful in business.

Label each of the following: T = topic, TS = topic sentence, or SD = supporting detail. One will be a topic, one will be a topic sentence, and two will be supporting details.

1. .... Mary Kay Ash

2. .... After 25 years of being one of the leading salespeople in her company, Mary Kay Ash found herself passed over for promotion by a man she had trained who made twice her salary.

3. .... Her business was founded on the Golden Rule, and on placing faith first, family second, and career third.

4. .... Mary Kay Ash showed women how to be independent and successful in business.

5. Identify the meaning of the underlined word in the following sentence: Her business was established on the Golden Rule, and on placing faith first, family second, and career third.

a. a place of business
b. increased
c. published
d. founded upon

MyReadingLab

CHAPTER PRACTICE 3

Read the following paragraph. Circle the topic, and underline the topic sentence. Then, complete the exercises that follow.

After your insured property has been damaged or stolen, you may make a claim with your insurance company. The insurance company conducts an investigation, and, if your claim is approved, you will be paid for a repair or complete replacement. Insurance companies hire specialists to conduct these investigations. An insurance investigator is a person who examines all the evidence on a claim and reports his or her findings to the insurance company. Insurance investigators do much of the same work as law enforcement investigators, and may also be called to testify in court during a lawsuit. The salaries of insurance investigators vary depending on the company they work for and the area in which they specialize. Most insurance investigators have some college or technical school education.

Label each of the following: T = topic, TS = topic sentence, or SD = supporting detail. One will be a topic, one will be a topic sentence, and two will be supporting details.

1. .... An insurance investigator is a person who examines all the evidence on a claim and reports his or her findings to the insurance company.

2. .... Insurance investigators

3. .... Insurance investigators do much of the same work as law enforcement investigators and may also be called to testify in court during a lawsuit.

4. .... Most insurance investigators have some college or technical school education.

5. Identify the meaning of the underlined word in the following sentence: The salaries of insurance investigators <u>vary</u> depending on the company they work for and the area in which they are most informed.
   a. are high
   b. are different
   c. are unimportant
   d. individual

MyReadingLab

TEXTBOOK PRACTICE

Preview the following paragraphs, then read actively and answer the questions.

WHY DO BUSINESSES FAIL?

Why do more than half of all new small businesses go out of business within the first five years? And why do one-third of all new businesses go out of business within the first two years? There are many reasons why most new businesses do not make it, and often it is a combination of things that cause them to fail. First, if the business idea was not a good one to begin with, it has a poor chance of success. By doing a little research to find out what people think about your idea first, you can avoid wasting time and money on an idea that won't succeed. The second most common reason is that going into business always takes more start-up capital than people think it will. They underestimate how much they will need to keep going during the first few years. Third, many new business owners have no experience in running a business. The best way to learn is to first take an interim job as a manager in the same business and gain some knowledge of how to avoid mistakes. And fourth, sometimes growing too fast can cause a company to fail. When the sales orders keep coming, and there is not enough stock to fill them or employees to do the job, customers become unhappy.

Label each of the following: T = topic, TS = topic sentence, or SD = supporting detail. One will be a topic, one will be a topic sentence, and two will be supporting details.

1. .... The second most common reason is that going into business always takes more start-up capital than people think it will.

2. .... Reasons why new businesses do not make it

3. .... There are many reasons why most new businesses do not make it, and often it is a combination of things that cause them to fail.

4. .... First, if the business idea was not a good one to begin with, it has a poor chance of success.

5. Identify the meaning of the underlined word in the following sentence: The best way to learn is to first take an <u>interim</u> job as a manager in the same business and gain some knowledge of how to avoid mistakes.
   a. intern's
   b. first
   c. high-paying
   d. temporary

STUDY SKILL REVIEW

You can make an effective study guide using a sheet of notebook paper.

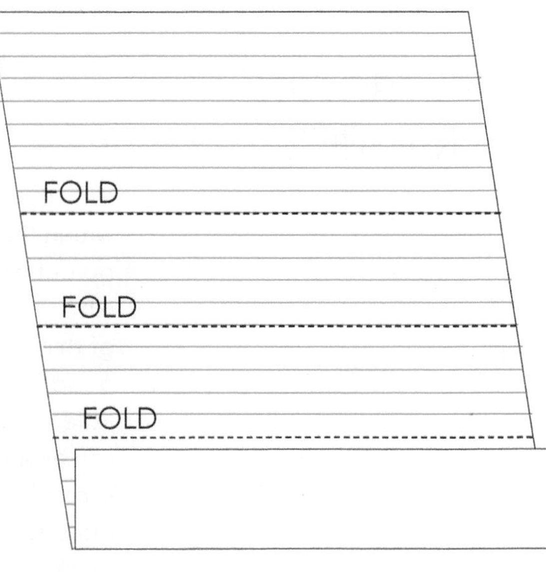

1.

Starting with the bottom, fold up your notebook paper four times, about every five lines, until you have just the top portion of your paper showing.

2.

Write a review question on the top line.

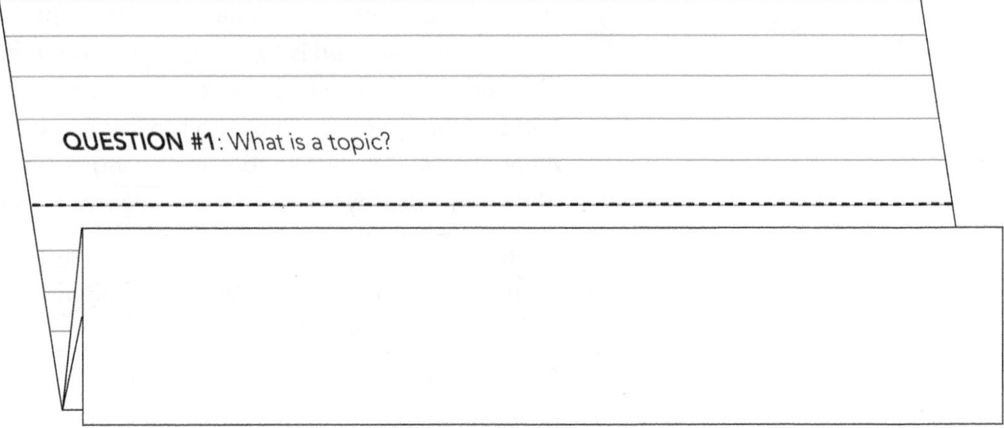

Question 1
Answer 1
Question 2

3.

Unfold the paper once, then write the answer to the question on the lines below the fold. Beneath that, write question #2.

4.

Each time you unfold the paper, write the answer to the question before it and the next question. For example, on the next unfolding, you'd write the answer to question #2 and then write question #3 below it. Continue using both sides of the paper.

5.

After you have created your study guide, read the questions one at a time, giving the answer, and then check your answer by unfolding the paper. Keep the study guide handy, in your purse or pocket, so you can review it often.

Create a study guide for Chapter 4 by copying the following questions on your folded notebook paper and looking up the answers in this chapter.

Question #1: What is a topic?

#1 Answer:

Question #2: What is a main idea?

#2 Answer:

Question #3: What is a topic sentence?

#3 Answer:

Question #4: How do you check to determine if you have found the topic sentence?

#4 Answer:

Question #5: Where are topic sentences found in a paragraph?

#5 Answer:

Make up some of your own questions and answers for the back of the paper.

READING LAB ASSIGNMENTS

STATED MAIN IDEA

1. Login to **MyReadingLab**, and in the menu click on **Reading Skills** and Learning Path. On the main screen, click **Stated Main Ideas**. Complete the review and practice activities recommended by your instructor.

COMPREHENSION IMPROVEMENT

2. From the menu in **MyReadingLab**, click on **Reading Level** and **Next Reading**. Choose two reading selections from the list on the main screen. Read the articles and answer the diagnostic and exercise questions.

SKILL APPLICATION

3. Look at the list of learning objectives at the beginning of the chapter. What applications could these have in your career or in real life? List some ways that you will be able to use the skills taught in this chapter. For example, you can find the topic and main idea in a business report for your job. In what other ways can this skill be used?

CAREER EXPLORATION

4. To find out more about a specific business career, go online to the Occupational Outlook Handbook at the Bureau of Labor Statistics and search for an occupation. This site will tell you what the job is like, what the outlook is for employment, and current salary and educational requirements. Print the article, and then preview, read, highlight, and annotate it.

MyReadingLab

LEARNING REFLECTION

Think about the skills and concepts presented in this chapter. What have you learned in this chapter that will help your reading comprehension and enable you to do well in college? Which learning strategy helped you the most in your learning?

MyReadingLab

SELF-EVALUATION CHECKLIST

Rate yourself on the following items, using the following scale:

1 = strongly disagree

2 = disagree

3 = neither agree nor disagree

4 = agree

5 = strongly agree

1. I completed all of the assigned work on time. ....
2. I understand all the concepts in this chapter. ....
3. I contributed to teamwork and class discussions. ....
4. I completed all of the assigned lab work on time. ....
5. I came to class on time. ....
6. I attended class every day. ....
7. I studied for any quizzes or tests we had for this chapter. ....
8. I asked questions when I didn't understand something. ....
9. I checked my comprehension during reading. ....
10. I know what is expected of me in the coming week. ....

5 SUPPORTING DETAILS

LEARNING STRATEGIES

Major and Minor Details and Transitions 165

Concept Mappaing 177

READING SELECTIONS

READING 1: "Let's Talk About Your Life, Son" 186

READING 2: "Student Travel—See the World!" 198

READING FOR LIFE

On the Job Interview 205

Real-Life Reading 206

Textbook Graphic Aids 208

Building Vocabulary 209

CHAPTER REVIEW

Chapter Practice 210

Textbook Practice 214

Study Skill Review 215

Reading Lab Assignments 216

Learning Reflection 216

Self-Evaluation Checklist 217

FOCUS ON: Hospitality and Tourism

There is an incredible amount of opportunity in the fields of hospitality and tourism because they include so many different occupations. People who love food, entertaining, or travel often find a job they love in one of these areas. One benefit is that you can choose your working environment, such as in a restaurant or a hotel in a national park. If you like to travel, you might become a tour guide in any number of places where you'd like to live. Cruise ships and casinos also offer numerous opportunities for employment, as do theme parks, airlines, and railway companies.

A great travel experience is all about the details. Clients seeking unique travel experiences could be looking for something very different depending on the ages of their children. A "local flavors" menu for guests from abroad might need to avoid meat if the guests are vegetarians or have other dietary restrictions. Being able to dig deeper into clients requests and find out the details of their expectations and requirements will lead to a better client or guest experience.

In this chapter, you will:

LEARNING OBJECTIVES

1 recognize the difference between major and minor details.

2 describe how concept mapping is used to better understand major and minor details.

OBJECTIVE 1

Recognize the difference between major and minor details.

MAJOR AND MINOR DETAILS AND TRANSITIONS

If a friend called you and said, "I just had the most amazing thing happen to me!" you would probably want to know more details. What kinds of details would you expect? You might hear, "I was called into one of my professor's offices and he told me I have been nominated to receive a full scholarship to a four-year college," or, "I was walking down the street and I found two $100 bills lying on the ground." **Supporting details** should explain, prove, or illustrate the main idea. Read the following paragraph and the explanation that follows.

Supporting details provide information that tells us more about the author's main idea.

There are many different fields included in tourism and hospitality. These fields include hotel and restaurant management, theme parks, and gaming management. A person with a degree in hospitality and tourism might also work in event management, including weddings, conventions, or major sporting events like the Super Bowl. The field of tourism includes opportunities in conducting tours and planning travel for foreign and domestic excursions, cruises, ecotourism, and outdoor adventure trips.

Topic: Tourism and hospitality

Main idea: There are many different fields included in tourism and hospitality.

Supporting details:

- Hotel and restaurant management, theme parks, and gaming management
- Event management
- Conducting tours and planning travel

Notice how the main idea is supported with specific examples that illustrate and prove it. Read the example below and fill in the supporting details for the main idea.

There are several reasons why students struggle with academics in college. One reason is that they are under-prepared, meaning they do not have the basic skills needed to read or write at the college level. Another reason is that they do not seek help when they need it, and end up failing their courses. A third reason is that some students do not keep up with homework and studying, which leads to failure and dropping out.

Main idea: There are several reasons why students struggle with academics in college.

Supporting detail #1: They are under-prepared.

Continued...

Supporting detail #2: ....

Supporting detail #3: ....

Try creating a few supporting details for these topic sentences:

- There are several important things to consider when choosing a college.
- There are several factors that make a restaurant a pleasurable dining experience.
- Travelers enjoy visiting many interesting and exciting places during their vacations.

When Details Do Not Support

In college, you will have to write several papers. Good writing is concise. That means that it does not have a lot of *irrelevant* details that do not support the author's main idea. In your team, look at the list of details under each of the following topic sentences, and cross out the ones that do not support the main idea.

EXAMPLE:

Topic sentence: Learning a foreign language has many advantages.

a. Knowing another language can make you more valuable as an employee.

b. ~~Learning another language can be difficult.~~

c. Being able to speak another language enables you to learn more about other people's culture.

d. Speaking a foreign language will make it easier to communicate when you travel.

To find out whether a sentence supports the main idea, ask yourself, "Does this sentence tell me more about the main idea?" If it doesn't, then it is not a supporting detail and should be crossed out.

MyReadingLab

PRACTICE 1

Cross out or circle the detail that does NOT support the topic sentence.

1. **Topic sentence: The hospitality industry is an exciting and challenging field in which to work.**
   a. Some hotels feature luxurious working environments.
   b. Managers often work 10 hours a day.
   c. Many travelers enjoy vacation cruises.
   d. Large hotel and airline companies offer employees free travel and discounts.
2. **Topic sentence: The most famous railway transportation system in Europe is the TVG train system in France.**
   a. The TVG serves more than 150 cities in France and Europe.
   b. The United States does not have a national unified rail system.
   c. The trains in the TVG travel at about 186 mph.
   d. The ride on the TVG is amazingly smooth.
3. **Topic sentence: The rental car business is a large part of the travel industry in the United States.**
   a. Some agencies charge more than others for daily rentals.
   b. More than 5,000 car rental companies operate in the United States.
   c. About 75 percent of the car rental business is situated around airports.
   d. The top four rental agencies maintain about 625,000 rental cars.
4. **Topic sentence: Air travel has become an important factor in the tourism industry.**
   a. Many airlines offer vacation packages that include hotel and rental cars.
   b. During any time of the day, about 4,500 airplanes are flying over the United States.
   c. Jet aircraft have made it possible to visit places that were not accessible before.
   d. Low airfares help to boost hotel occupancy and increase tourism.
5. **Topic sentence: Cruise ships have become a popular vacation choice.**
   a. Many ships feature nonstop entertainment for their passengers.
   b. Some ships offer casinos and live entertainment.
   c. The Diamond Princess is longer than two football fields and carries up to 2,670 passengers.
   d. The market for cruise ship vacations has increased dramatically in recent years.

Major details give us more information about the main idea.

Major and Minor Details

There are two types of details in all writing: **major details** and minor details.

Major Supporting Details

In the following example, the topic is highlighted, the topic sentence is underlined, and the major details are numbered and italicized.

perishability (pair-ish-a-BIL-i-tee): In this context, it means not producing an income.

> [1] *The hospitality industry is one that is open for business 365 days a year. For this reason, it depends heavily on shift work.* [2] *The industry is also dependent upon good customer service that will encourage guests to come back again and again.* [3] *Another characteristic of the hospitality industry is the* ***perishability*** *of its products—hotel rooms, for instance.* Rooms that are vacant for the night are a financial loss to the hotel owner. These are some of the characteristics of the hospitality industry that make it a challenging industry in which to work.

Here is another way to see the information in this paragraph:

Topic: The hospitality industry

Topic sentence: These are some of the characteristics of the hospitality industry that make it a challenging industry in which to work.

Major supporting details:

- The hospitality industry is one that is open for business 365 days a year.
- The industry is also dependent upon good customer service that will encourage guests to come back again and again.
- Another characteristic of the hospitality industry is the perishability of its products—hotel rooms, for instance.

As mentioned earlier, you can make sure that a sentence is a major supporting detail by asking yourself, "Does this sentence tell me more about the main idea or topic sentence?" If it does, then it is a major detail. Another way to find the major details of a paragraph is to turn the main idea into a question. The answers to the question will be the major details.

For example:

> Main idea:
> There are many benefits to getting regular exercise. (What are the benefits of getting regular exercise?)
>
> Main Idea:
> The events that led to the American Revolution can be traced back to more than a decade before it began. (What are the events that led to the American Revolution?)

Minor Supporting Details

Authors also use **minor details** to tell us more information about the major details.

Notice in the earlier example how the first major detail is followed by a minor detail, which explains the first major detail:

Major detail:
The hospitality industry is one that is open for business 365 days a year.

Minor detail:
For this reason, it depends heavily on shift work.

Major detail:
Another characteristic of the hospitality industry is the perishability of its products—hotel rooms, for instance.

Minor detail:
Rooms that are vacant for the night are a financial loss to the hotel owner.

Minor details tell us more information about the major details. They usually follow the major detail they explain.

How Supporting Details Work

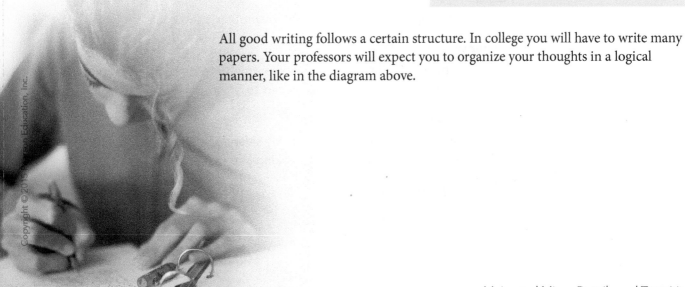

MAIN IDEA
↑
MAJOR DETAIL
supports the main idea
↑
MINOR DETAIL
supports the major detail

All good writing follows a certain structure. In college you will have to write many papers. Your professors will expect you to organize your thoughts in a logical manner, like in the diagram above.

Transitions

Transitions, or "signal words," are words or phrases that help show relationships between ideas.

Transitions, or "signal words," are words or phrases that help show relationships between ideas and can introduce supporting details. There are hundreds of transitions in the English language, and each one of them serves a different function. You will learn more about transitions in future chapters. For this chapter, focus on the transitions that introduce supporting details. Most of these are called "listing transitions" because they list details. Here are some of the most common listing transitions:

first	one	too	for one thing	and
second	another	in addition	moreover	besides
third	also	additionally	furthermore	final(ly)

In the following example, the topic sentence is underlined and the transitions are highlighted and italicized.

> <u>Bianca wants to own her own travel agency for several reasons.</u> *First,* she would like to be independent and not have to worry about relying on an employer for her income. If things slow down in the travel industry, she could be laid off. *Second,* she would like to have the opportunity to make as much money as she wants and not be limited to an hourly wage. Instead of making just a weekly salary, she wants to get commissions from every booking she makes. *Third,* she wants flexible hours that let her decide when she wants to work. With a child at home and another one on the way, she would like to work at her home computer and on the phone.

Notice how the minor details tell us more about each major detail:

Major supporting detail #1:

She would like to be independent and not have to worry about relying on an employer for her income.

<u>Minor</u> supporting detail:

If things slow down in the travel industry, she could be laid off.

Major supporting detail #2:

She would like to have the opportunity to make as much money as she wants and not be limited to an hourly wage.

<u>Minor</u> supporting detail:

Instead of making just a weekly salary, she wants to get commissions from every booking she makes.

Major supporting detail #3:

She wants flexible hours that let her decide when she wants to work.

Minor supporting detail:

With a child at home and another one on the way, she would like to work at her home computer and on the phone.

MyReadingLab

PRACTICE 2

Read each of the following sentences and label them as follows (each set will contain one of each):

T = topic
TS = topic sentence
MA = major supporting detail
MI = minor supporting detail

EXAMPLE:

TS **a.** Technology helps the restaurant business in many ways.

T **b.** Technology in the restaurant business

MA **c.** Palm-sized computers are used by servers to send an order to the kitchen.

MI **d.** The chef can see these orders on a large computer in the kitchen.

Set 1

_______ **a.** Executive chefs

_______ **b.** If they order too much food, it will spoil, but if they order too little, the restaurant cannot meet its clients' needs.

_______ **c.** Executive chefs must estimate how much food to order.

_______ **d.** Among their many tasks, executive chefs are responsible for ordering food.

Set 2

_______ **a.** The training and education of food service managers is important to health and safety.

_______ **b.** Food that is not stored correctly will rot quickly.

_______ **c.** Food service managers must know the correct procedures for storing food and keeping it fresh.

_______ **d.** Food service manager training

Continued...

MyReadingLab

PRACTICE 2

...continued

Set 3

.... **a.** Except for schools, most of these places are open seven days a week and require shift work, sometimes with long hours.

.... **b.** Places where food service managers work

.... **c.** Food service mangers may work in restaurants, cafeterias, schools, factories, casinos, and cruise ships.

.... **d.** There are a variety of places where food service managers can work.

Set 4

.... **a.** Franchising allows a hotel business to use the name brand and financing of a large corporation.

.... **b.** The hotel owner must agree to the terms of the contract with the franchising company.

.... **c.** Franchising

.... **d.** For example, the hotel must agree to use the franchise company's name and meet its standards.

Set 5

.... **a.** Resort hotels

.... **b.** Some resort hotels have package deals for skiers.

.... **c.** A resort hotel offers more than rooms; it offers activities such as golf, swimming, tennis, and skiing.

.... **d.** Guests can get a ski ticket and a hotel room for less than the cost of each one separately.

MyReadingLab

PRACTICE 3

Read the following paragraph. Underline and label the topic sentence with "TS," and underline the major details. Then, answer the questions that follow.

People who enjoy playing games like lotteries, card games, and other games of chance can find employment in the casino industry. Most gaming-service employees work in casinos, and their work can vary from management to surveillance and investigation. *One* career opportunity is as a gaming supervisor. This is someone who oversees the games and the personnel in a specific area. Gaming supervisors make sure that players and workers are following the rules and will explain them clearly if needed. *Another* career opportunity is as a gaming manager. Gaming managers prepare work schedules and are responsible for hiring and training new personnel. *Finally*, gaming dealers are also employed to operate games such as blackjack, roulette, and craps. To become qualified for one of these positions, you will need a degree in hospitality or special training to become licensed by your state's casino control board or commission.

1. What is the topic?

a. gaming supervisors
b. casinos
c. gambling
d. gaming careers

2. What is the topic sentence?

a. People who enjoy playing games like lotteries, card games, and other games of chance can find employment in the casino industry.
b. Most gaming-service employees work in casinos, and their work can vary from management to surveillance and investigation.
c. One career opportunity is as a gaming supervisor.
d. To become qualified for one of these positions, you will need a degree in hospitality or special training to become licensed by your state's casino control board or commission.

3. Which of the following is not a major supporting detail?

a. One career opportunity is as a gaming supervisor.
b. Another career opportunity is as a gaming manager.
c. Gaming supervisors make sure that players and workers are following the rules and will explain them clearly if needed.
d. Finally, gaming dealers are also employed to operate games such as blackjack, roulette, and craps.

4. Identify the minor detail that supports the following major detail: "Another career opportunity is as a gaming manager."

a. To become qualified for one of these positions, you will need a degree in hospitality or special training to become licensed by your state's casino control board or commission.
b. Gaming managers prepare work schedules and are responsible for hiring and training new personnel.
c. Most gaming-service employees work in casinos, and their work can vary from management to surveillance and investigation.
d. This is someone who oversees the games and the personnel in a specific area.

Continued...

MyReadingLab

PRACTICE 3

...continued

5. Which of the following transitions were used to introduce the major details?
   - a. most, one, finally
   - b. one, another, to
   - c. this, to, they
   - d. one, another, finally

MyReadingLab

PRACTICE 4

Read the following paragraph. Underline and label the topic sentence with "TS," and underline the major details. Then, answer the questions that follow.

When you go to a restaurant, do you think about all the different operations that are taking place at the same time? Hosts or hostesses decide where patrons should be seated. Waiters and waitresses take orders, chefs prepare the food, bussers clean the tables, and managers make everything run smoothly. Being a food service manager is a job with many responsibilities. One of the responsibilities is to hire and train good employees. Food service managers must also schedule these employees for various shifts. In addition, they must make sure that groceries are ordered for the kitchen and the quality of the food is good. Food service managers supervise the employees to make sure the restaurant is kept clean and that guests are not kept waiting too long. Also, food service managers must deal with a lot of paperwork to budget expenses and to meet health and safety regulations.

1. What is the topic of this selection?
   - a. food service managers
   - b. hosts and hostesses
   - c. employees in a restaurant
   - d. restaurants
2. What is the topic sentence?
   - a. When you go to a restaurant, do you think about all the different operations that are taking place at the same time?
   - b. Hosts or hostesses decide where patrons should be seated.
   - c. Being a food service manager is a job with many responsibilities.
   - d. Also, food service managers must deal with a lot of paperwork to budget expenses and to meet health and safety regulations.
3. Which of the following is a major detail that supports the topic sentence?
   - a. Hosts or hostesses decide where patrons should be seated.
   - b. Waiters and waitresses take orders, chefs prepare the food, bussers clean the tables, and managers make everything run smoothly.
   - c. When you go to a restaurant, do you think about all the different operations that are taking place at the same time?
   - d. One of the responsibilities is to hire and train good employees.
4. Which of the following transitions were used to introduce the major details?
   - a. there are, being, one
   - b. one, in addition, also
   - c. whenever, being, one
   - d. in addition, is, with

MyReadingLab

TEXTBOOK SELECTION 1

Read the following selection from a textbook. Underline the topic sentence of each paragraph and answer the questions that follow.

1 Many theme restaurants are a combination of a sophisticated specialty and several other types of restaurants. They generally serve a limited menu but aim to wow the guests by the total experience.

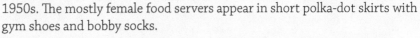

2 Of the many popular theme restaurants, two stand out. The first highlights the nostalgia of the 1950s, as exemplified in the T-Bird and Corvette diners. These restaurants serve all-American food, such as the perennial meatloaf, in a fun atmosphere that is a throwback to the seemingly more carefree 1950s. The mostly female food servers appear in short polka-dot skirts with gym shoes and bobby socks.

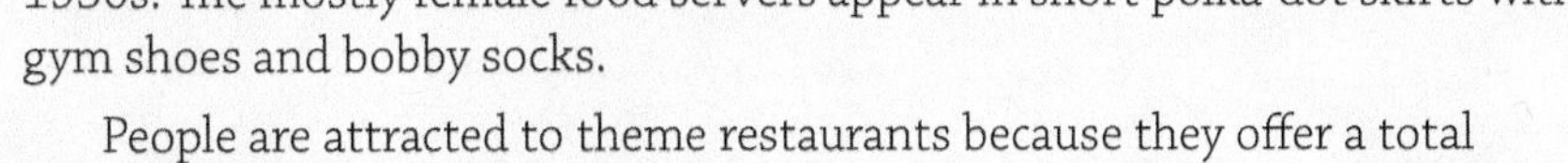

3 People are attracted to theme restaurants because they offer a total experience and a social meeting place. This is achieved through decoration and atmosphere, and allows the restaurant to offer a limited menu that blends with the theme. Throughout the United States and the world, numerous theme restaurants stand out for one reason or another. Among them are decors featuring airplanes, railway dining cars, rock and roll, 1960s nostalgia, and many others.

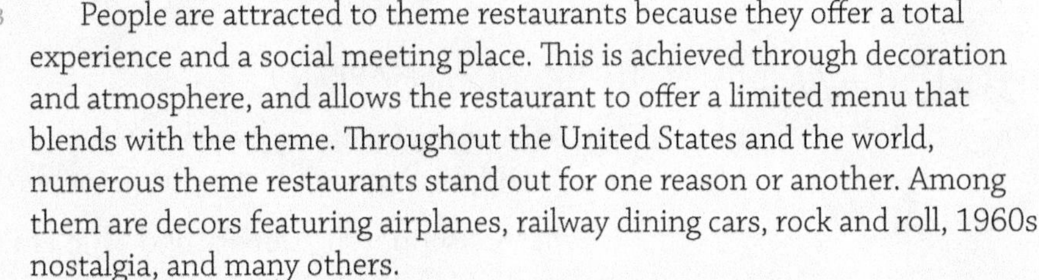

QUESTIONS

1. What is the topic of this selection?
   a. American restaurants
   b. nostalgia restaurants
   c. theme restaurants
   d. dinner houses

2. What is the topic sentence of paragraph 2?
   a. Of the many popular theme restaurants, two stand out.
   b. The first highlights the nostalgia of the 1950s, as exemplified in the T-Bird and Corvette diners.
   c. These restaurants serve all-American food such as the perennial meatloaf in a fun atmosphere that is a throwback to the seemingly more carefree 1950s.
   d. The mostly female food servers appear in short polka-dot skirts with gym shoes and bobby socks.

3. What is the topic sentence of paragraph 3?
   a. People are attracted to theme restaurants because they offer a total experience and a social meeting place.
   b. This is achieved through decoration and atmosphere, and allows the restaurant to offer a limited menu that blends with the theme.
   c. Throughout the United States and the world, numerous theme restaurants stand out for one reason or another.
   d. Among them are decors featuring airplanes, railway dining cars, rock and roll, 1960s nostalgia, and many others.

Continued...

4. Which of the following is a major detail for paragraph 3?

- **a.** People are attracted to theme restaurants because they offer a total experience and a social meeting place.
- **b.** This is achieved through decoration and atmosphere, and allows the restaurant to offer a limited menu that blends with the theme.
- **c.** Throughout the United States and the world, numerous theme restaurants stand out for one reason or another.
- **d.** Among them are decors featuring airplanes, railway, dining cars, rock and roll, 1960s nostalgia, and many others.

5. Identify the following sentence: The mostly female servers appear in short polka-dot shirts with gym shoes and bobby socks.

- **a.** topic
- **b.** topic sentence
- **c.** major detail
- **d.** minor detail

U-REVIEW 1

THINK, PAIR, SHARE

First, answer the following questions to yourself. Then, pair up with a partner and ask each other the questions, taking turns.

1. What are supporting details, and what are their functions?

....

....

2. What does a major detail do?

....

....

3. What does a minor detail do?

....

....

4. What are transitions, and how do they help readers?

....

....

OBJECTIVE 2

Describe how concept mapping is used to better understand major and minor details.

CONCEPT MAPPING

Concept mapping is a way to show relationships among the ideas in a reading selection—for example, among the main idea, the major details, and the minor details. There are many different styles of concept maps, and you have probably seen them in your textbooks.

The following is a concept map of the passage you read earlier about Bianca's travel agency.

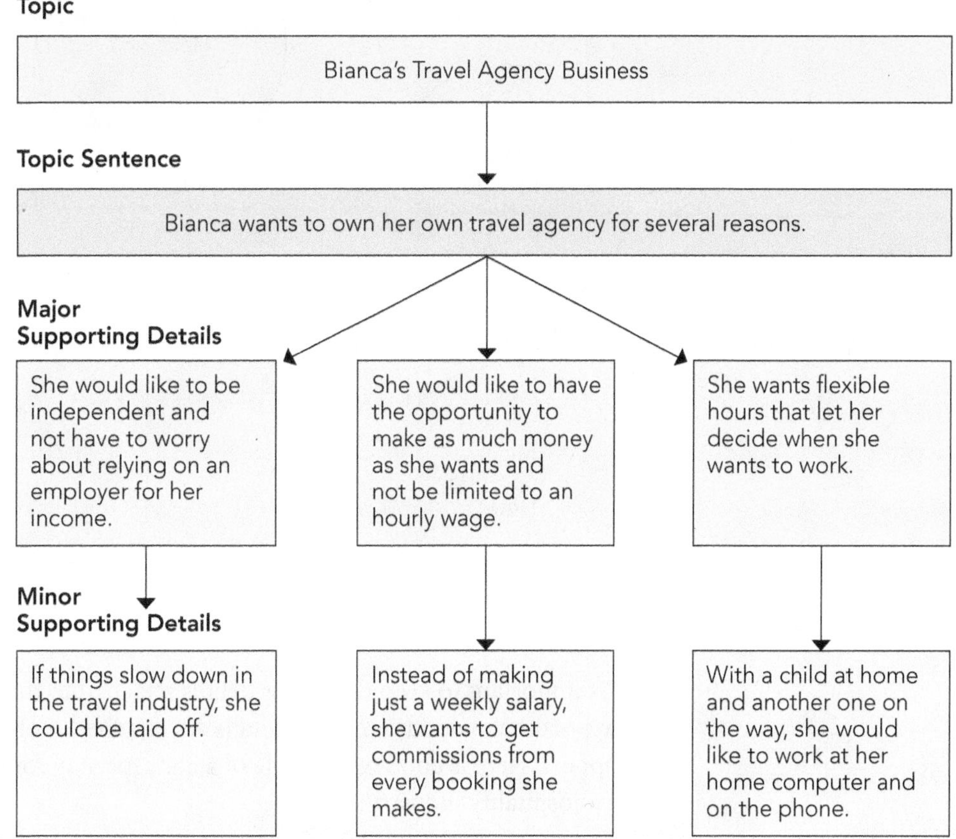

Topic
Bianca's Travel Agency Business
Topic Sentence
Bianca wants to own her own travel agency for several reasons.
Major Supporting Details
She would like to be independent and not have to worry about relying on an employer for her income.
She would like to have the opportunity to make as much money as she wants and not be limited to an hourly wage.
She wants flexible hours that let her decide when she wants to work.
Minor Supporting Details
If things slow down in the travel industry, she could be laid off.
Instead of making just a weekly salary, she wants to get commissions from every booking she makes.
With a child at home and another one on the way, she would like to work at her home computer and on the phone.

Another style of concept mapping is to place the topic and topic sentence in the center of your page, and then add the major details and minor details around it:

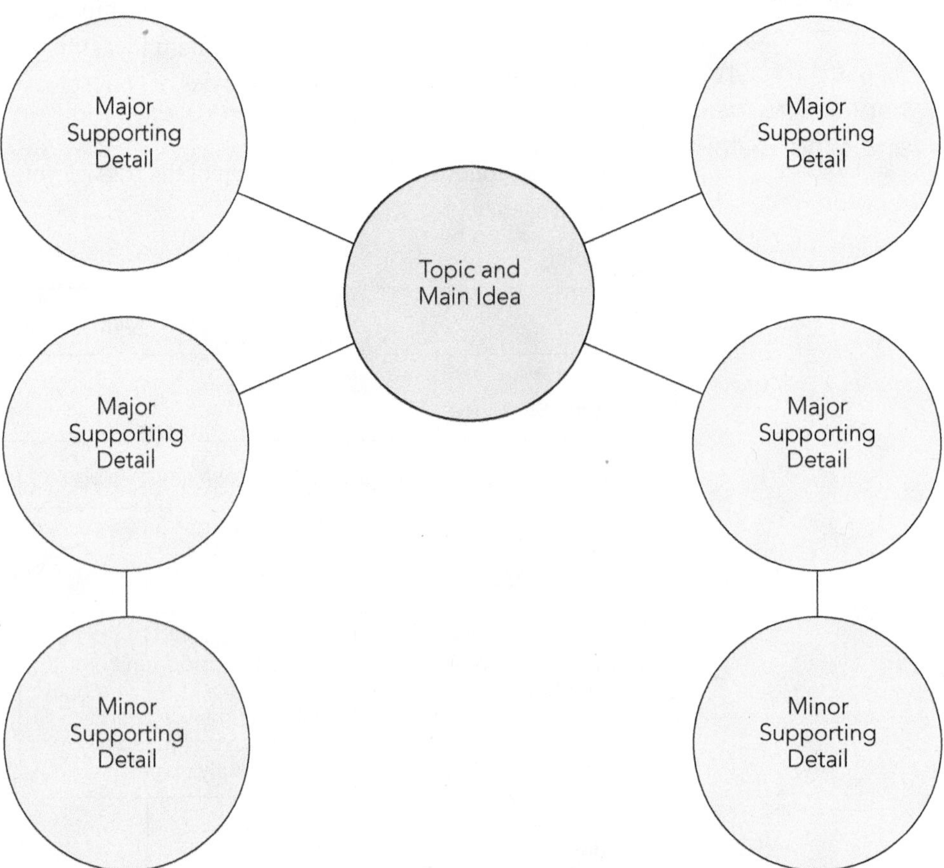

It is important to keep the major details attached to the center circle because they support the main idea. Minor details are attached to the major details that they support. Here is another example of a concept map for the earlier paragraph about the hospitality industry:

Topic: The Hospitality Industry

MAJOR Open for business 365 days a year.	**MAIN IDEA** There are some challenging factors in the hospitality industry.	**MAJOR** Perishability of its products.
MINOR Relies heavily on shift work.	**MAJOR** Dependent on good customer service.	**MINOR** Vacant rooms are a financial loss.

MyReadingLab

PRACTICE 5

Read the following paragraph. Underline the main idea and major details. Then, fill in the missing information in the concept map that follows.

Recreation in the Hospitality Industry

Recreation has become an important segment of the hospitality industry. More hotels and tour companies are expanding their programs for recreation. Golf has long been a popular form of recreation at many resorts and hotels. Resorts also have featured tennis courts and swimming pools. Now hotels are including jogging and biking trails, rock climbing, and boating. The tourist industry also includes ecotourism with trips to observe wildlife in their natural habitats in rainforests, mountains, and waterways.

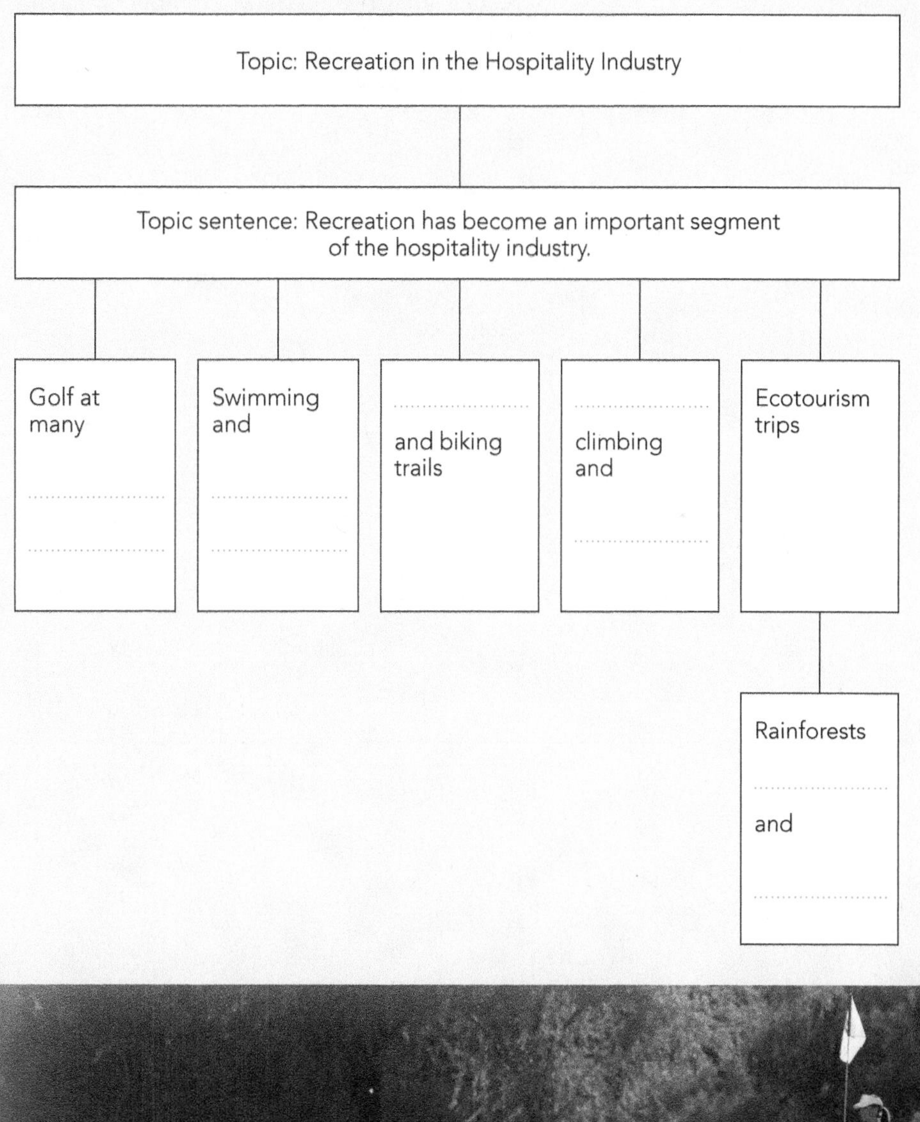

MyReadingLab

PRACTICE 6

Read the following paragraph. Underline the main idea and major details. Then, fill in the missing information in the concept map that follows.

The Theme Park Industry

Some of the most popular tourist destinations around the world are theme parks. They first began with Hershey's Chocolate Company, which opened a leisure park in 1907. Walt Disney opened Disneyland in California in 1955 as a park for children "of all ages." Twenty-eight years later, Walt Disney World, much like Disneyland, opened in Florida. Following Disney's lead, Universal Studios opened its own theme parks in Florida and California. Parks that originally began as animal attractions, such as Sea World, soon expanded to include many theme park features including thrill rides, entertainment, and restaurants. Theme parks are now on all major continents across the world.

Topic: ....

Topic sentence: ....

1907 Hershey's	.... in California	.... in Florida	Florida and California	....

....

MyReadingLab

PRACTICE 7

Read the following paragraph. Underline the main idea and major details. Then, fill in the missing information in the concept map that follows.

According to the International Ecotourism Society, ecotourism is responsible travel to natural areas that conserve the environment and improve the well-being of the local people. Ecotourism is a popular form of tourism where tourists can visit a natural area to help make a difference in the environment and the economy. Tourists who sign up for ecotours are expected to help build environmental awareness and respect. Ecotours also must provide a positive experience for both the traveler and the local people. Another purpose of ecotourism is to provide financial benefits for the conservation of natural resources. Ecotourists visit unusual places and help to make improvements in the areas they visit.

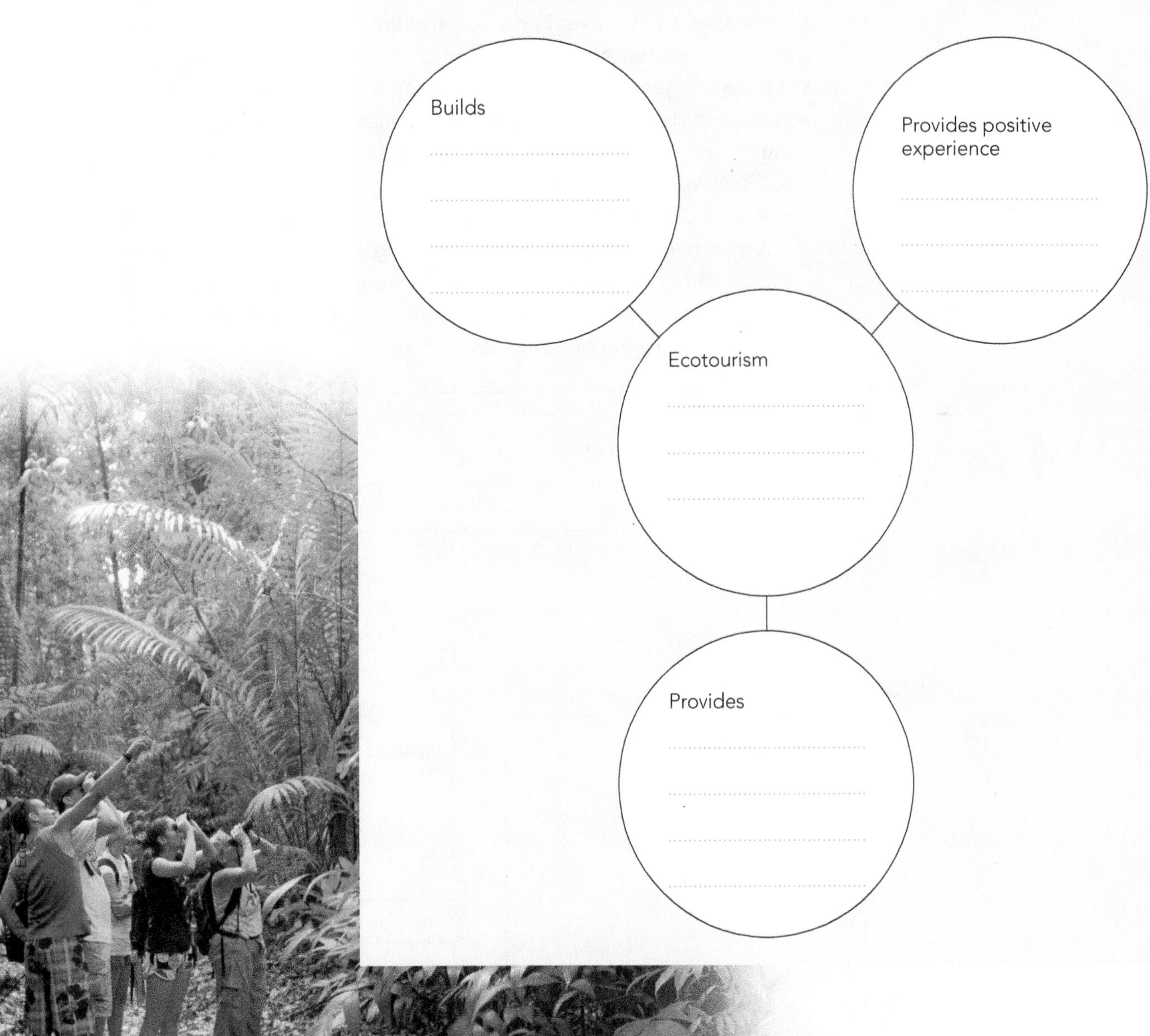

MyReadingLab

TEXTBOOK SELECTION 2

Read the following selection using the four-step reading process. Underline the main idea and major details. Then, fill in the missing items in the concept map that follows.

Social Events

Social function planners and managers work on a broad variety of events. This category of event planning includes weddings, engagement parties, birthday parties, anniversary parties, holiday parties, graduation parties, military events, and all other social gatherings or events. A social event planner is usually responsible for selecting the venue, determining any themes or design schemes, ordering and planning decorations, arranging for catering and entertainment, and having invitations printed and sent out.

Weddings are the most widely recognized social event. Wedding planners are a key player in the social event category. The title seems glamorous and has a certain perception that most of us will hold; yet the management involved in planning a wedding involves strict attention to detail. Don't forget that the planner is responsible for creating what is considered to be the most important day of a couple's life. "Realize this is a business," says Gerard J. Monaghan, president of the Association of Bridal Consultants. "A fun business to be sure, but a business nonetheless." Effective wedding planners will have formed contacts with a variety of services and venues, such as hotels, wedding locations, decorating companies, catering companies, bridal shops, musicians, photographers, florists, and so forth.

Topic: ....

Topic sentence: ....

....

Includes weddings,

....

....

....

....

....

Includes wedding planners,

....

....

Involves strict attention to

....

U-REVIEW 2

Fill in each box below with the correct letter to show the structure of a concept map. Some answers will be used more than once.

A. topic
B. main idea
C. major detail
D. minor detail

....

....

....

....

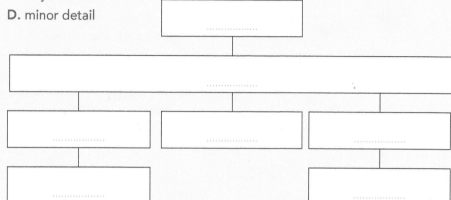

MyReadingLab

Reading 1
VOCABULARY
PREVIEW

"Let's Talk About Your Life, Son"

by Bobby Flay

The following vocabulary words are from the article "Let's Talk About Your Life, Son." With a partner or in a team, choose the correct meanings of the underlined words in the following sentences. Use context clues (LEADS), word part clues, and parts of speech to help you figure out the meanings.

1. Deciding to adopt a child is a serious commitment (kom-MIT-ment) and a huge responsibility.
   a. group
   b. obligation
   c. career
   d. visit
2. Manuel is very unfocused (un-FO-kusd) when he does his homework because he is distracted by the phone and TV.
   a. inattentive
   b. out of focus
   c. unhappy
   d. friendly
3. Even though I was upset by the professor's remark, I acted nonchalantly (non-cho-LONT- lee), as if it didn't bother me.
   a. in an upset manner
   b. carefully
   c. seriously
   d. in a carefree manner
4. Getting a good grade in algebra was gratifying (GRAT-i-fy-ing) after I struggled so hard in that course.
   a. frustrating
   b. unimportant
   c. rewarding
   d. impossible
5. The investigator found tangible (TAN-ji-ble) proof that the crime had occurred in the kitchen. There was blood on the floor, chairs were knocked over, and there was broken glass.
   a. suggested
   b. solid
   c. uncertain
   d. energetic
6. My best friend has such a buoyant (BOY-ant) personality that everyone loves being around her.
   a. depressing
   b. loud
   c. floating
   d. cheerful

7. Even the most mundane (mun-DANE) cooking-school tasks—like "turning" vegetables, or paring them into perfect, uniform shapes—started to seem kind of interesting.
   a. ordinary
   b. exciting
   c. difficult
   d. happy
8. Johnathan was known as one of the most inventive (in-VEN-tiv) chefs around, always creating new dishes and experimenting with unusual combinations of foods.
   a. ideal
   b. creative
   c. best
   d. insane
9. Andy is so passionate (PASH-on-it) about music that he plays four to five hours a day—every day.
   a. having a great love for something
   b. practical
   c. annoying
   d. perfect
10. As a sous-chef (SUE-shef) at the restaurant, Rachael is second in command and only takes orders from the head chef.
   a. cook
   b. waitress
   c. assistant to the head chef
   d. hostess

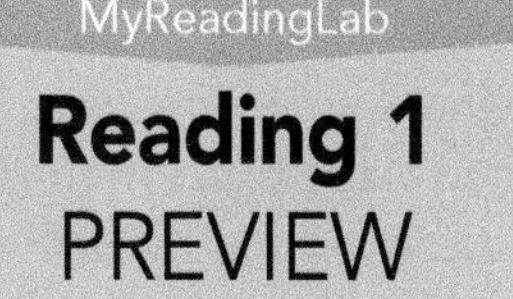

1. What are your favorite places to eat? What are some of your favorite dishes and foods?
2. If you were a chef and wanted to open a restaurant, what kind of restaurant would it be?
3. What do you know about Bobby Flay?

Directions: As you read this article, practice the four-step reading process. Preview the article, and then write on the following lines one or two questions that you would hope to have answered.

MyReadingLab

Reading 1

As you read, answer the questions in the margins to check your comprehension.

"Let's Talk About Your Life, Son"

by Bobby Flay

Bobby Flay is a famous chef, restaurant owner, popular TV show host, author of eight books on cooking, and winner of nine culinary arts awards. In this article, Flay tells about his past, when he had dropped out of high school and had no goals for his life. Read how he turned his life around when he discovered his passion for food.

1 Awhile back I took on a big commitment. I committed to a year volunteering at a public vocational high school in Queens, New York. I went every week to teach a class, and just cooked with the kids. It was a pretty amazing experience. I saw myself in a lot of them. The uncertainty, the insecurities were all there. These kids were a lot like me. Maybe that sounds surprising, coming from someone who's been a success in the restaurant business. Let me tell you more.

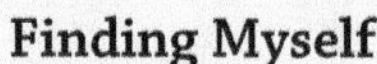

Finding Myself

2 Growing up, I never really thought about becoming a chef—much less owning restaurants or being on TV. The truth is, I didn't really have any goals. I didn't like school. I was unfocused. Most of all, I liked hanging out with my buddies on the corner of Lexington Avenue and 84th Street, on Manhattan's Upper East Side, where I was born and raised, just shooting the breeze. That was the life I imagined for myself when I dropped out of high school. But someone had other plans for me. I was lounging around at home one day, watching TV, when the phone rang. It was my dad. "Come to my office," he said. "We need to talk about your life."

3 My life? I was 17! Was I supposed to have it all figured out? It felt like being called to the principal's office—but worse. My dad is a great guy. He's also very scholarly, so my leaving school must have hit him hard. I didn't want to let him down. But it seemed that was exactly what I was doing. Part of me was scared. Part of me tried to play it cool: just dad being dad. I went down to his office at Joe Alien—a famous restaurant in the theater district that he was a partner in. "Go get a job," he said, "You can't just hang out with your friends on a street corner."

What was Bobby's situation at this point in his life?

4 "Okay," I said nonchalantly, shrugged my shoulders, and headed out to meet my friends. Where was I going to find a job?

5 The next day, Dad called again. He sounded exasperated. I guess he figured out that my hunt hadn't just been a bust, but a complete nonevent.

6 "The busboy had to leave to take care of his grandmother. You're going to fill in." Dad didn't ask me; he told me. "And don't forget; no special treatment. Because you're my son, you better work harder than anyone else. Put your head down, do your job and don't aggravate anybody—including me."

7 I had my marching orders and showed up at the restaurant the next day, and the day after that. I didn't have much interest in the business, but I didn't want to upset Dad. I showed up late sometimes—only to spot Dad waiting for me, eyes on his watch—but I did my job.

Why did Bobby agree to take this job?

Describe in your own words how Bobby's life has changed and how this story might end.

Why did Bobby want to stay, and do you think his father was right in making him go?

8 It wasn't so bad. I was clearing tables and setting tables. Two weeks went by pretty fast. Now what? I wondered. "Do you want a job?" the chef asked me as I was walking out of the kitchen. I think the guy took pity on me. "Sure," I said.

9 He had me start in the pantry. That's when my career really began. I stocked the pantry, washed dishes, and learned how to clean lettuce. I used a knife. I made salad dressing. I didn't think I had any natural skill, but it was gratifying to learn something. And my salads did taste pretty good.

Opportunity Knocks

10 About six months into my job at Joe Alien, something unexpected happened. I remember waking up one morning, staring at the ceiling and saying to myself, "I'm really looking forward to going to work today." Where did that come from? Little things, I think, like learning new cooking techniques and watching my knife skills improve. From that point forward, I looked at work differently. I enjoyed it. I felt I was contributing. Slowly, I was shedding my irresponsible 17-year-old skin. I was prepping in the kitchen one day when my dad and his business partner—and the restaurant's namesake—Joe Alien, sauntered in. "We want to talk to Bobby about something," Joe said to the chef. Uh-oh. What had I done wrong? They took me up to the office.

11 "There's a new school opening," Joe said. "It's called The French Culinary Institute. Do you want to go?"

12 "Nah," I said, "I don't think so." School and I didn't get along so well. In truth, I thought I wasn't good enough to go to cooking school. I had the idea in my head that, as a cook, you either had it or you didn't. It didn't come naturally to me. Cleaning produce was one thing. But if I didn't have "it" at 18, how could I ever possibly be a chef? But they talked me into it. I didn't want to let them down. I studied for my high school equivalency test—a requirement to enter culinary school—and passed. That felt good, like I'd achieved something tangible. To my surprise, I was looking forward to going back to school. It sounded like a great opportunity.

13 It was. The French Culinary Institute had just opened its doors. There were only nine students, but it was a mix of interesting people. I was the youngest by about six years. Our teacher was a great guy—an old-school, formally trained Alsatian chef named Antoine Shaeffers. He was obviously a terrific cook; he also had a wonderful, buoyant personality. Even the most mundane cooking-school tasks—like "turning" vegetables, paring them into perfect, uniform shapes—started to seem kind of interesting. But by then, anything having to do with food had become interesting to me. And since I was still working at the restaurant by night and going to school by day, food really took over my life, 24/7.

14 The culinary program lasted six months. It was intense, and I learned a lot. I went back to Joe Alien, thinking I'd move up the ranks in his restaurant. "Get out of here!" he said. "You're not gonna learn anything else here." *Wait a minute!* I thought. I finally got comfortable doing something I liked, and Joe and my dad were pushing me out? I couldn't believe it. "I want to stay," I pleaded. "I want to be the chef here someday. This is my career."

Continued...

MyReadingLab
Reading 1
...continued

Did I say career? I guess I had grown up, at least a little. They were unmoved. It was time for me to leave Joe Alien.

On My Own

15 I sent out resumés and pounded the pavement. I was hired as a sous-chef at a hot new restaurant on the Upper East Side. It was called Brighton Grill. They had hired a head chef from New Orleans.

16 Two days after the restaurant opened, I showed up at work (on time!) at 8:00 a.m.

17 "We've got a problem," one of the owners said to me. *Uh-oh*, I thought—again. But I knew I hadn't done anything wrong. It was the chef. "We found him passed out on the laundry bag. He apparently hit the tequila last night—and lots of it. He's fired. You're the head chef now." I was in shock. It was like I'd been the understudy in a Broadway show and was about to get my big break. But was I ready to perform? I could cook okay. I didn't have much of a repertoire yet. But somehow I managed. I stayed at the Brighton Grill for a year, learning every day. Then I was itching to move on, to try something new.

18 At The French Culinary Institute, I met a woman named Gail Arnold who was cooking in one of Jonathan Waxman's restaurants. Jonathan was known as one of the most inventive chefs around. I jumped at the chance to work at Bud's—his place on the West Side.

19 That's where I fell in love with the flavors of the southwest. Believe it or not, I'd never been to New Mexico, Arizona, or Texas. But there was something about this food that I just instantly got and instantly loved. We were cooking on a high level at Bud's, with great ingredients. Things that I'd never tasted before—papayas and mangoes, chili peppers and blue corn tortillas. All that stuff was completely new to me. And it was awesome. And the crew was amazing—with energetic cooks eager to experiment. We all learned from each other. It was a rare, special, inspiring place. I wound up working at all three of Jonathan's restaurants. One was a tiny French bistro called Hulot's. But here's how passionate I'd become about cooking: another chef and I would get the keys from the manager and show up there on Sunday afternoons—when the place was closed—just to cook for fun. That's when I knew cooking was my life. I woke up every morning thinking about what I'd cook that day. I still do.

How did Bobby feel about cooking at this point in his life? What changed his attitude?

20 I worked in more kitchens. I kept learning and experimenting. Finally, I was feeling ready to open a place of my own that would feature the bold, southwest flavors I love. I wanted a bigger stage. Of course I talked to my dad about it. If he agreed I was ready to make this move, it would be my green light. By then I knew to trust his judgment better than my own! We started scouring the city for a good location. Then Jerry Kretchmer—who owned a famous restaurant called the Gotham Bar and Grill—came by to talk to me about opening a place. "Do you want to open a southwestern restaurant with me?" he asked. That was a little awkward. I explained to him I'd been looking for a place with my dad. "Well, think about it," he said.

21 I went back to Dad. He actually seemed relieved. "Do it with him," he urged me. "That way you and I can just be father and son." Once again, wise counsel from my most trusted advisor. And soon my first restaurant, Mesa Grill, opened its doors.

At this point in the story, do you think Bobby will be successful? Why or why not?

22 That was more than 17 years ago. I still love every minute of it. I still wake up thinking about flavors, about new dishes to try. I still love the family atmosphere in the kitchen. I'm still amazed I was once that confused kid, without any clear sense of direction—and that there'd been a time when I worried I wasn't good enough to go to culinary school. Do I ever have doubts? You bet.

Giving Back

23 It's hard for me to think of myself as a great chef. I think of myself as someone who's always learning, always wanting to cook better, more delicious food. And that's what I saw in those kids I met at the public high school in Queens—a desire to learn, a commitment to give it their best. At the end of the year, thanks to The French Culinary Institute, I was able to give one of them a scholarship. It was too hard to pick one kid. There was some real talent there. I narrowed it down to five and came up with a plan to secure scholarships for all five of them. Sure, they're a little rough around the edges and have a long way to go, just like I did when I was their age. But in my dad and his partner, Joe, I was blessed with supportive—and demanding—mentors who not only helped turn my life around, but also helped me find my passion. I can't think of a better way to pay them back than to encourage other young people to find their passion too.

What did Bobby do for the high school students in Queens?

2,009 words divided by .... minutes = ... words per minute

MyReadingLab

Reading 1 REVIEW

It's a good habit to summarize everything you read to strengthen your comprehension.

On the following lines, write a two- or three-sentence summary of the article, "Let's Talk About Your Life, Son." In your own words, describe what the article was about and why the author wrote it.

....

....

....

....

MyReadingLab

Reading 1 COMPREHENSION QUESTIONS

The following questions will help you to recall the main idea and the details of "Let's Talk About Your Life, Son." Review any parts of the article that you need to find the correct answers.

1. What is the topic of this article?
   a. learning about cooking
   b. becoming a chef
   c. Bobby Flay
   d. Bobby Flay's restaurant

MAIN IDEAS

2. What is the main idea of the article?
   a. The restaurant business is a fun way to make a living.
   b. Bobby Flay found his passion in cooking and learned how to become a great chef.
   c. Bobby Flay made a big commitment.
   d. It's important to give back to others what you have learned.
3. What is the topic sentence of paragraph 14?
   a. The culinary program lasted six months.
   b. This is my career.
   c. I guess I had grown up, at least a little.
   d. It was time for me to leave Joe Alien.
4. What is the topic of paragraph 19?
   a. Bobby discovers southwest cooking.
   b. Bud's restaurant
   c. cooking in Jonathan's restaurants
   d. Bobby cooks for fun.

SUPPORTING DETAILS

5. According to the article, Bobby was hired at his father's restaurant when:
   a. he applied for a job there as a server.
   b. he was told by his father to take the place of the busboy who couldn't come in to work.
   c. he asked the chef to teach him how to cook.
   d. the chef was found drunk.
6. After Bobby was hired as a sous-chef at the Brighton Grill, he was told that:
   a. he would be working with the servers.
   b. he would be getting a big break on Broadway.
   c. the head chef had been fired for getting drunk on tequila, and now Bobby was head chef.
   d. he would be cooking southwest-style dishes.
7. According to the article, which of these statements is not true?
   a. Bobby opened his own restaurant with Jonathan Waxman and called it Hulot's.
   b. Bobby's father was relieved that he didn't have to be Bobby's partner in a restaurant.
   c. Bobby gave five high school students scholarships to the French Culinary Institute.
   d. Bobby wants to help other young people find their passion.

DRAWING CONCLUSIONS

8. With which of these statements do you think Bobby would disagree?

a. Finding your passion in life sometimes happens when you start out at the bottom in the lowest paying job.

b. We should listen to the advice of someone who has more experience in our chosen careers.

c. When your passion is your job, work seems more like fun than work.

d. If you're not good at something in the beginning, you should probably quit because you have no talent for it.

VOCABULARY IN CONTEXT

Using context clues and word part clues, determine the best meaning for the underlined word in each of these sentences. If necessary, use a dictionary.

9. We started scouring the city for a good location.

a. scrubbing

b. searching

c. arranging

d. finding

10. When Bobby's father learned that his son hadn't even tried to find a job, he was exasperated.

a. frustrated

b. sad

c. amused

d. worried

MyReadingLab

Reading 1 VOCABULARY PRACTICE

Use the vocabulary words from the Word Bank to complete the following sentences. Write the words into the blanks provided.

WORD BANK

commitment	unfocused	nonchalantly	gratifying	tangible
buoyant	mundane	sous-chef	inventive	passionate

1. Danny is such a(n) ________ chef that he keeps coming up with new ideas for recipes.

2. If Sam does a favor for you, don't be surprised if he expects some type of ________ reward, like cash or free tickets to a game!

3. Martina finds that working with handicapped children at the summer camp is very ________.

4. Yun Ling is absolutely ________ about animals. She has three dogs and two cats, and plans on becoming a veterinarian.

5. Heather was hired as a(n) ________, but soon became the head chef at the restaurant.

6. Omar has such a(n) ________ personality that everyone wants to hang out with him.

7. Owning a puppy is a big ________ because you are responsible for feeding it, training it, and taking it to the veterinarian regularly.

8. People who are ________ often do not have any motivation to succeed in life.

9. When Rick asked me if I would like to go out with him, I answered ________, "I guess so."

10. Instead of writing a(n) ________ story for her English Composition class, Maria decided to write about an exciting adventure she had while she was in Puerto Rico.

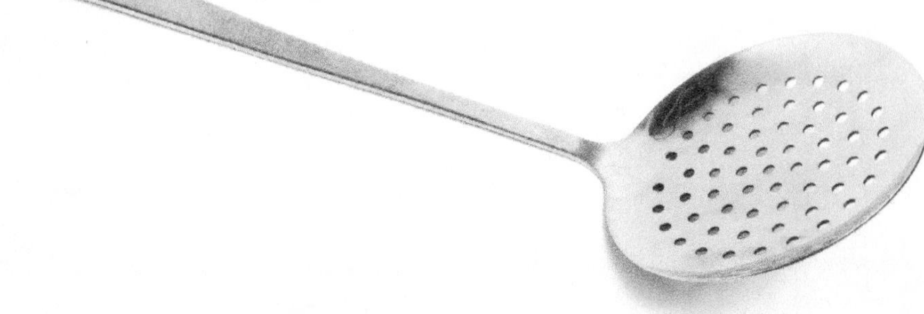

MyReadingLab

Reading 1 QUESTIONS FOR WRITING AND DISCUSSION

Review any parts of the article you need to answer the following questions.

1. What kind of relationship did Bobby Flay have with his father?

2. Why did Bobby's father push him into getting a job at his restaurant? Do you think he should have done that, or do you think he should have let Bobby decide what he wanted to do? Explain your answer.

3. If Bobby had chosen to ignore the advice of his father and Joe Alien, how might his life have been different?

4. Based on what you read in this article, why do you think Bobby Flay achieved so much success?

5. In what ways are Dr. Quiñones (from Chapter 2) and Bobby Flay alike in terms of their attitudes and skills?

Reading 1 VOCABULARY PRACTICE—SPEED QUIZ

Get together in groups of four or five people. Each group should create a set of vocabulary cards according to the following directions.

In this activity, you will be given 60 seconds to give the correct definitions to five vocabulary words. You earn 2 points for each correct answer. Read through all of the directions before you begin.

1.

Fold a sheet of notebook paper into 10 sections. Tear the sections into 10 individual pieces. Give each team member 2 or more pieces to copy some of the words and definitions from the list below onto the squares. Upon completion, all 10 words and definitions will be copied onto the 10 squares.

2.

Put all 10 squares together in a pile and shuffle them face down.

3.

Divide your team into two opposing teams, team A and team B.

4.

Deal out 5 squares to each team, but do not look at your words until it is time to start, and keep them covered.

5.

One person on team A and one person on team B will be the clue givers. When it is time to start, the clue giver on team A will read the words one at a time to team B. Team B has 60 seconds to give the correct definitions to all 5 words. If a team can't remember the definition, they may say, "Pass," and go to the next word. If they complete the remaining words before the 60 seconds are up, they may go back to the ones they passed and try them again. The first answer given by a team is the one that counts–no second attempts are allowed.

6.

One person on team A and one person on team B will be the score keepers. The scorekeeper on team A will keep track of correct responses for team B and give them 2 points per correct answer.

7.

When time is called, both teams must stop. The score for team A is totaled and they are told the answers to any words they couldn't define.

8.

Next the play will be repeated and team B will give the clues to team A, who will have 60 seconds to define the 5 words they are given.

9.

When time is called, the score will be totaled by the scorekeeper on team B.

10.

The team with the highest score wins.

1. commitment: obligation
2. unfocused: inattentive
3. nonchalantly: in a carefree manner
4. gratifying: rewarding
5. tangible: solid
6. buoyant: cheerful
7. mundane: ordinary
8. inventive: creative
9. passionate: having a great love for something
10. sous-chef: assistant to the head chef

Reading 1 SUPPORT-ING DEATILS CHART

With your team, fill in the details for each of the topic sentences from "Let's Talk About Your Life, Son." Only list the details that explain, prove, or illustrate the main idea. There may be only one detail, or there may be two or more details. You may refer back the article to refresh your memory, but try to write the details in your own words. The first one is done for you.

MAIN IDEAS	SUPPORTING DETAILS
1. As a teenager, Bobby Flay had no plan for his future.	• He dropped out of high school and didn't graduate. • He didn't have a job. • He had no goals.
2. Bobby's father and the chef at his restaurant gave him jobs to do.	
3. Bobby got an opportunity to go back to school.	
4. Bobby had to go out on his own to earn a living.	
5. Bobby now gives back to others.	

MyReadingLab

Reading 2
VOCABULARY PREVIEW

"Student Travel—See the World!"

by Corinne Fennessy

The following words are from the article "Student Travel—See the World!" With a partner or in a team, choose the meanings of the underlined words in the following sentences. Use context clues (LEADS), word part clues, and parts of speech to help you figure out the meanings.

1. In history, the medieval (med-dee-EE-val) period is identified with castles, knights, and religious crusades.
   - a. ancient places
   - b. a period in history from the 5th to 15th centuries
   - c. a group of people who lived in the 8th–10th centuries
   - d. a political structure of European countries
2. The ship struck the craggy (KRAG-ee) rocks and sank near the shore.
   - a. hidden
   - b. strong
   - c. sharp and jagged
   - d. chaming
3. The small town on the island is very quaint (kwaint) and picturesque.
   - a. charming
   - b. small
   - c. interesting
   - d. demanding
4. By staying in student hostels (HOS-tels), I was able to save a lot of money on hotel bills.
   - a. medical centers
   - b. student accommodations
   - c. dormitories
   - d. travel agencies
5. Before the industrial revolution, grains were ground into flours in grist mills that were powered by water wheels or wind mills.
   - a. places where grains are ground up
   - b. a time when industry began
   - c. places where flour is made into baked goods
   - d. cereal factories
6. The hand-made furniture in our cabin was rugged (RUG-ed) but comfortable.
   - a. unattractive
   - b. comfortable
   - c. massive
   - d. rough
7. Our dormitory rooms in college were very stark with practically no furniture in them.
   - a. dark
   - b. barren
   - c. uninviting
   - d. unwelcome

8. We can save money on baggage fees if we only take the essentials (ee-SEN-shals) with us when we fly.
   a. smallest things
   b. cheapest items
   c. necessary things
   d. best things

9. We were sojourners (so-JUR-ners) who traveled the world in search of the perfect place to live.
   a. travelers
   b. researchers
   c. adventurers
   d. residents

10. Before exchanging American dollars for foreign currency, always check the exchange rate.
   a. the amount of money you wish to change
   b. the value of the foreign currency
   c. the cost of buying foreign currency
   d. the place where foreign currency is sold

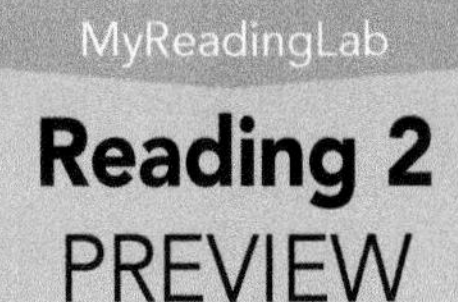

1. Have you ever traveled to another country or to a place far from home? Where did you go? How was it different from your own home town?
2. What places in the world would you like to visit, and why?

Directions: As you read this article, practice the four-step reading process. Preview the article, and then write on the following lines one or two questions that you would hope to have answered.

....

....

....

....

MyReadingLab

Reading 2

As you read, answer the questions in the margins to check your comprehension.

"Student Travel—See the World!"

by Corinne Fennessy

Traveling abroad while in college can be one of the most rewarding and exciting times of your life. Here are some tips for travel from one student's personal experience.

1 All through high school I dreamed of visiting the United Kingdom and read about all the places I'd visit once I got there. London is the iconic British city, with the romantic Thames River flowing lazily past ancient medieval towers and royal palaces. The craggy white cliffs of Dover and the Gothic church cathedrals with classic architecture were all places I yearned to see. As a college freshman I found out about travel abroad programs for students and knew I could make my dream a reality.

2 Coming up with the money to travel took a lot of saving and planning. I saved some of my part-time job pay and took extra jobs whenever I could. After about a year, I had enough money saved to take the trip of my dreams. During that year, I obtained a passport and learned all about the country and travel opportunities for students. I searched for the cheapest airline flights and learned that as a student I could save about 60 percent on airfare flying as a "standby," meaning I had to sit around the airport and wait for an open seat. Luckily, I obtained a seat on the first flight to London that I wanted!

3 It was an experience I will never forget. Years later, I can remember how I walked for miles with a knapsack on my back in the misty rain through castle ruins perched on rocky cliffs or through heavy downpours while visiting Shakespeare's quaint Elizabethan village, Stratford-on -Avon. I crossed the causeway to Holy Island near the Scottish border and toured the ancient monastery that is now a museum. The new hiking shoes I had bought with the sturdy soles were worn into holes before the trip was half over.

Where were some of the places the author stayed?

4 My accommodations were student hostels—places where students can stay a night or two very inexpensively. One hostel, situated on the rugged coast of North Wales, was in an old grist mill with a huge water wheel. Another hostel was on a crooked narrow street a short distance from St. Paul's Cathedral in London. The hostel in Liverpool had once been an old train station. Unfortunately, the trains still ran by all through the night! Each place offered a unique experience at a rock-bottom price. The only requirements were that visitors must arrive on foot (no vehicles), and to help pay the cost of a bed and two meals, visitors were expected to help prepare meals and clean up. The sleeping quarters were stark. Two or three sets of bunk beds with clean sheets and blankets were squeezed into an average-sized bedroom. In the old Welsh grist mill I climbed up a ladder and slept in a loft with the mill wheel shaft right above my head! Bathrooms were shared by all. Dinners and breakfasts were held in a large dining room where I met other students from all over the world. Meeting people from different countries and different cultures was fascinating and exciting.

5 While taking photos of the Tower Bridge in London, I met up with two British students who were in London for the weekend. After chatting,

we grabbed lunch in a pub, where I was introduced to local foods and warm beer (the drinking age in England was 18!). We said our goodbyes after lunch, but it was exciting to make new friends abroad. Similar experiences in other cities allowed me to take photos of my new friends and keep in touch with them after I returned home.

6 Armed with only a few maps, a BritRail pass, and a camera, I followed the route I had carefully planned before my trip. Before departing, I had purchased a new mountaineering backpack and filled it with essentials and a couple changes of clean clothes. I knew I would have to visit laundromats along the way to wash clothes. I kept my money and credit card well hidden and was reasonably cautious about safety. In the evenings, I dined at the hostels with fellow sojourners while listening to their travel stories. The hostels were safe places to hang out, have fun, and be with people my own age.

7 To avoid disappointment, it's vital to research the places you plan to visit. For instance, after spending over an hour on a train, and then walking several miles to visit a palace, I arrived to find out it was closed. Always check the hours of operation before you leave. It's a good idea to email or call before you visit to make sure the place won't be closed due to special circumstances, and to find out if there is an admission fee.

8 Transportation should also be planned before you leave for your destination. My BritRail pass enabled me to hop on and off any train in the U.K. much like using a city bus pass. In London, I used a travel card to pay for urban transportation such as buses and subways (in British, "the Tube"). These passes and travel cards can save a lot of money, but they must be purchased before leaving home because you can't buy them in the country you visit.

What are some advantages of being a student traveler?

9 Being a student traveler has its advantages. First, you can usually find inexpensive student rates on airfares, train travel, or city transportation. Also, student hostels are great places to stay cheaply, and you get to meet other student travelers from many different countries. Most countries have a student hostel organization that can be found online. You should reserve your stays ahead of time because hostels fill up quickly during school breaks. Some student travel organizations and colleges offer college credit for travel abroad. There are hundreds of programs that can be easily found on the Internet. Many colleges offer trips during school breaks or summer. Traveling overseas is a great educational experience because you learn about other cultures first-hand by living among different people, eating regional food and drinks, and enjoying all that their culture has to offer. Whether you visit the French city of Montreal, Canada, or the Aztec ruins in Mexico, you don't have to go far to have a new cultural experience.

10 Because the rates on foreign currency change frequently, it's a good idea to open a credit card account with a bank that doesn't charge fees for overseas transactions. They will also give you the currency exchange rate on the dates that you make your purchases. Shop around for the best credit card deals, and keep your card safely hidden at all times. Having to replace a credit card or passport while traveling can be a huge hassle! Also, remember to obey the local

Continued...

MyReadingLab
Reading 2
...continued

laws and regulations; foreign judicial systems can be much more harsh than in America.

11 Take lots of pictures and keep a diary of your experiences. The memories of special moments when you feel a connection to the places you visit and people you meet will fade over time. Write about them in your journal and make videos. Then someday, when you're older and tied down with a spouse, kids, a mortgage, and a full-time job, you can relive one of the best times of your life—as a student traveling abroad!

1,222 words divided by .... minutes = ... words per minute

MyReadingLab
Reading 2
REVIEW

Directions: On the following lines, write a two- or three-sentence summary of the article "Student Travel—See the World!" In your own words, describe what the article was about and why the author wrote it.

....

....

....

MyReadingLab
Reading 2
COMPREHENSION QUESTIONS

The following questions will help you to recall the main idea and the details of "Student Travel—See the World!" Review any parts of the article that you need to find the correct answers.

MAIN IDEAS

1. What is the topic of this article?

a. the United Kingdom
b. student travel tips
c. how to save money on travel
d. learning about different cultures

2. What is the main idea of the entire article?

a. All through high school I dreamed of visiting the United Kingdom and read about all the places I'd visit once I got there.
b. London is the iconic British city with the romantic Thames River flowing lazily past ancient medieval towers and royal palaces.
c. Being a student traveler has its advantages.
d. A college student offers some tips for student travel.

3. What is the main idea of paragraph 4?

a. My accommodations were student hostels—places where students can stay a night or two very inexpensively.
b. Each place offered a unique experience at a rock-bottom price.
c. The sleeping quarters were stark.
d. Meeting people from different countries and different cultures was fascinating and exciting.

SUPPORTING DETAILS

4. According to the article, in order to help pay for a bed and two meals, visitors must:
- **a.** pay for the room and meals in advance with a credit card.
- **b.** be a member of the country's student hostel organization.
- **c.** help prepare meals and clean up.
- **d.** agree to participate in a fund-raising activity.

5. To avoid disappointment when visiting places such as museums, art galleries, or palaces, it's recommended that you:
- **a.** call ahead to make a reservation.
- **b.** call ahead to make sure the place will be open, and ask if there is an admission fee.
- **c.** bring your camera and a light snack.
- **d.** reserve your transportation to and from the place.

6. The reason you should make purchases with a credit card when traveling abroad is that:
- **a.** foreign banks and stores won't accept American credit cards.
- **b.** you won't have to carry large amounts of cash which could be lost or stolen.
- **c.** you can buy your travel cards and passes with them.
- **d.** you will be given the lowest exchange rate on the date of your purchase.

7. Which of the following minor details supports the following major detail? "Being a student traveler has its advantages."
- **a.** Passes and travel cards must be purchased before you leave home because once you're abroad, you can't buy them in the country you visit.
- **b.** For instance, after spending over an hour on a train, and then walking several miles to visit a palace, I arrived to find out it was closed.
- **c.** My BritRail pass enabled me to hop on and off any train in the U.K. much like using a city bus pass.
- **d.** You can usually find inexpensive student rates on airfares, train travel, or city transportation.

DRAWING CONCLUSIONS

8. By reading the supporting details, you can infer that the author:
- **a.** would recommend that college students consider traveling to another country.
- **b.** would not recommend that college students travel abroad.
- **c.** thinks that traveling abroad can be dangerous and difficult.
- **d.** wants to go on another trip abroad.

VOCABULARY IN CONTEXT

9. Using context clues, word part clues, and parts of speech, determine the meaning of the underlined word in the following sentence: The craggy white cliffs of Dover and the Gothic church cathedrals with classic architecture were all places I yearned to see.
- **a.** expected
- **b.** interested
- **c.** longed
- **d.** determined

Continued...

VOCABULARY IN CONTEXT

10. To avoid disappointment, it's vital to research the places you plan to visit.
   a. urgent
   b. essential
   c. suggesting
   d. gratifying

MyReadingLab

Reading 2 VOCABULARY PRACTICE

Use the vocabulary words from the Word Bank to complete the following sentences. Write the words into the blanks provided.

WORD BANK

medieval	craggy	quaint	hostels	grist mill
rugged	stark	essentials	sojourners	exchange rate

1. The little seaside village with its flower gardens, gas lights, and cottages on winding streets was so .... that we decided to stay for a longer visit.
2. The coastline along northern California, Oregon, and Washington has .... rocks and steep cliffs.
3. Our cabin in the woods was very ...., but we had enough room to sleep and a fireplace to keep us warm on chilly nights.
4. This .... fortress was once a castle, but it has been converted into apartments.
5. The roads going through the mountains are very ...., and so difficult for most vehicles that we often travel by horseback.
6. Staying in .... saved us a lot of money on accommodations, and many of the places were very interesting.
7. If the .... of the foreign currency you are buying goes down, you will get more currency for your dollars.
8. I only bring the .... with me when I go to stay at my sister's house because she has plenty of clothes that we share.
9. In the old days, corn or wheat was taken to a .... to be ground into flour for baking bread or cakes.
10. Be kind to strangers! After all, are we not all just .... together traveling through this journey of life?

MyReadingLab

Reading 2 QUESTIONS FOR WRITING AND DISCUSSION

1. What are some of the advantages of traveling as a student?

2. What were some of the best tips that the author gave for student travel in regard to finding affordable transportation?

3. Why might it be a good idea to obey the laws and regulations when traveling in a foreign country?

4. When traveling abroad, what are some precautions you should take to keep safe?

5. Would you ever consider going abroad while in college? Why or why not?

Reading 2 VOCABULARY PRACTICE—CROSSWORD

How to Play:

One member of the team will be the clue giver and scorekeeper. The other members will be the players.

1.
The clue giver calls on one member to pick a word box number, such as "2 Across."

2.
The clue giver reads the clue to the player; the player has 10 seconds to give the correct answer. Only one answer is allowed.

3.
If the answer is correct, the word is filled in on the player's crossword puzzle, and the player receives points based on the number of letters in the word. If incorrect, the player receives no points, and the next player is called.

4.
The clue giver calls on the next player and asks for a word box number. Play continues until all the words have been completed.

5.
The player with the most points is the winner.

Word Bank

craggy	essentials	exchange rate	
grist mill	hostels	medieval	quaint
rugged	sojourners	stark	

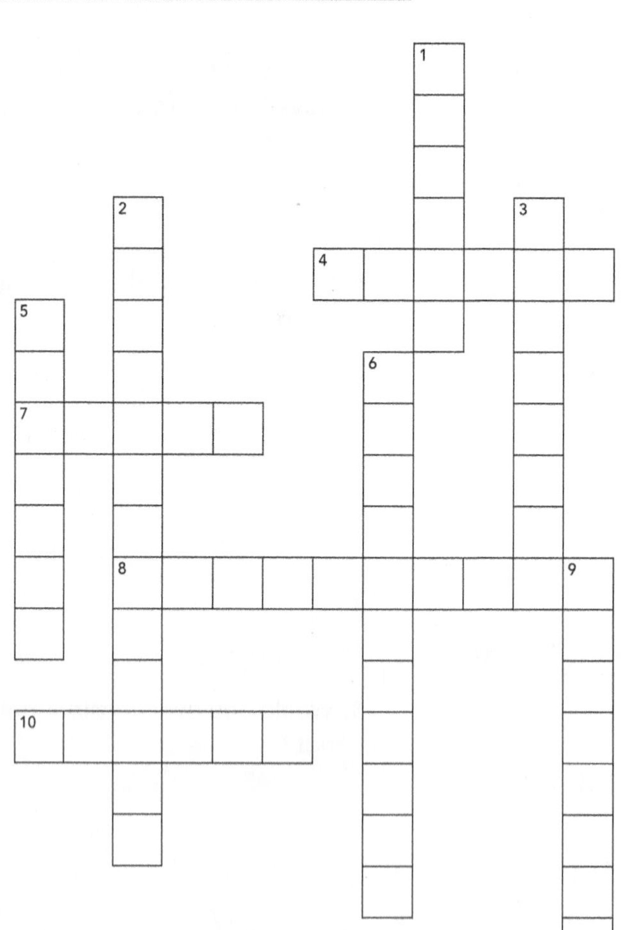

ACROSS

4. rough
7. barren
8. necessities
10. charming

DOWN

1. sharp and jagged
3. value of foreign currency
4. the 5th through 15th centuries
5. student accomodations
6. grind grain into flour
9. traveler

ON THE JOB INTERVIEW

CHEF NORA GALDIANO

How did you get into cooking?

I loved cooking when I was growing up. There were five kids in my family, so I helped my mother in the kitchen a lot. My older brother was a cook in a restaurant. I used to watch him, and I was impressed by his knife skills and wanted to learn how to use a knife like that.

What is your training?

I knew what I wanted to do with my life, and I set goals for myself. I graduated from Kapi'olani Community College in Hawaii, where I grew up, and then attended the Culinary Institute of America in Hyde Park, New York. After graduation, I moved to Florida and worked for the Hyatt Corporation, at the Grand Cypress Resort, and later at the Hyatt Airport Hotel, both in Orlando, Florida. Then four years ago, I started at Isleworth Golf and Country Club as the executive sous-chef. I am also working on my bachelor's degree in hospitality management. I am a Certified Executive Chef (C.E.C.) through the American Culinary Federation. When you are a chef, you have to keep studying and learning. You need to keep up with changes in the industry such as standards, trends, and technology. Learning is a lifelong journey.

What's it like cooking for celebrities and millionaires?

It's similar to cooking for the hotel industry but on a much smaller scale, and more personal. Being in a country club is unique. You are expected to maintain good relationships with the members you are cooking for and know their food preferences. They all have specific wants. We go out into the dining room and talk to the members all the time, and you have frequent personal contact with the members.

What do you like about your job?

I love to cook, of course, and I like being able to get to know the people I'm cooking for. Also, I like creating new dishes and working with a diverse staff. Each person has something to contribute. I have a great relationship with my supervisor, who is a Certified Master Chef (C.M.C.).

What do you dislike about your job?

I don't focus on the negative aspects of the job. I try to always look at the positive aspects and how to improve them. When something negative happens, fix it right away and move on.

What advice do you have for someone who is interested in a career as a chef?

First, get some experience to find out what it's like working in a production kitchen. Do your research, and talk to successful people in the business to get guidance and advice. You have to be in good physical health because you're on your feet all day and the job requires lifting and other strenuous tasks. Really find out what it's like before committing to going to a culinary school. Many culinary students don't realize that you need the hands-on experience to improve your skills and to work your way up the ladder.

MyReadingLab

WATCH THE VIDEO

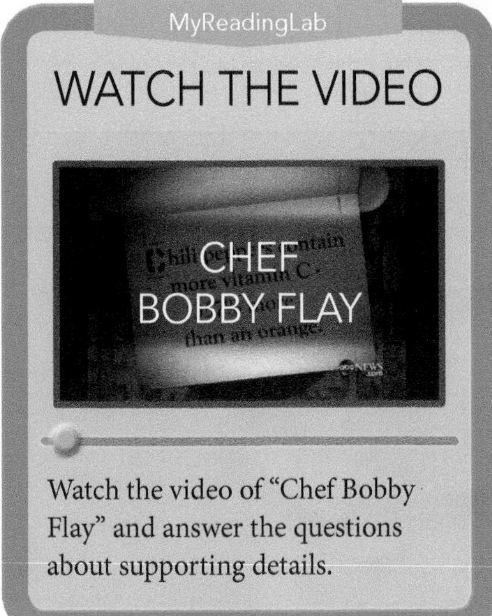

Watch the video of "Chef Bobby Flay" and answer the questions about supporting details.

MyReadingLab

REAL-LIFE READING

HEALTH INSURANCE POLICY

The following is an excerpt from a health insurance policy. Preview the selection first, and then read it and answer the questions that follow.

Calendar Year Deductible[1] Requirement

1. Individual Calendar Year Deductible Requirement

This requirement must be satisfied by each Covered Plan Participant each Calendar Year before any payment will be made for any claim. Only those charges indicated on claims received for Covered Services will be credited toward the Individual Calendar Year [1]Deductible, and only up to the Allowed Amount.

[1] Deductible: an amount deducted from the total medical costs that will first be paid by the insured customer. For example, if you have a $500 deductible listed on your insurance policy and your first medical bill comes to $700, you must pay $500 once, and after that, everything else will be covered for the rest of the year according to the terms of the policy.

2. Family Calendar Year Deductible Requirement Limit

Once the Covered Employee's family has reached such limit, no Covered Plan Participant in that family will have any additional Calendar Year Deductible responsibility for the remainder of that Calendar Year.

3. Prior Coverage Credit for Deductible

a. A Covered Plan Participant shall be given credit for any Deductible met by such Covered Plan Participant under a previous insurance policy maintained by HLP, which is replaced by this Group Health Plan. This provision only applies if the insurance policy was in effect immediately before the Effective Date of the Group Health Plan.

b. Each Covered Plan Participant is responsible for providing any information necessary to apply this previous coverage credit.

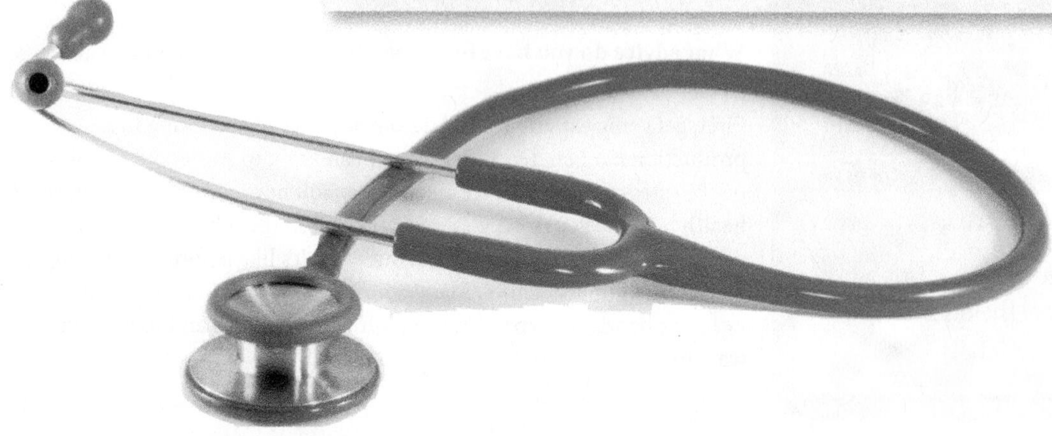

On the lines provided, write whether the following statements are true or false. If the statement is false, correct it on the space provided.

1. Before the insurance company will pay you for medical costs, every individual must first satisfy a Calendar Year Deductible.

2. A deductible is an amount deducted from the total medical costs that will first be paid by the insurance company.

3. Once the Covered Employee's family has reached such limit, no Covered Plan Participant in that family will have any additional Calendar Year Deductible responsibility for the remainder of their lives.

4. Participants in the Group Health Plan will be given credit for any deductibles they have met under a previous health insurance policy maintained by HLP.

5. Each Covered Plan Participant is responsible for providing any information necessary to apply a previous coverage credit.

MyReadingLab

TEXTBOOK GRAPHIC AIDS

Read the following chart, and then answer the questions that follow.

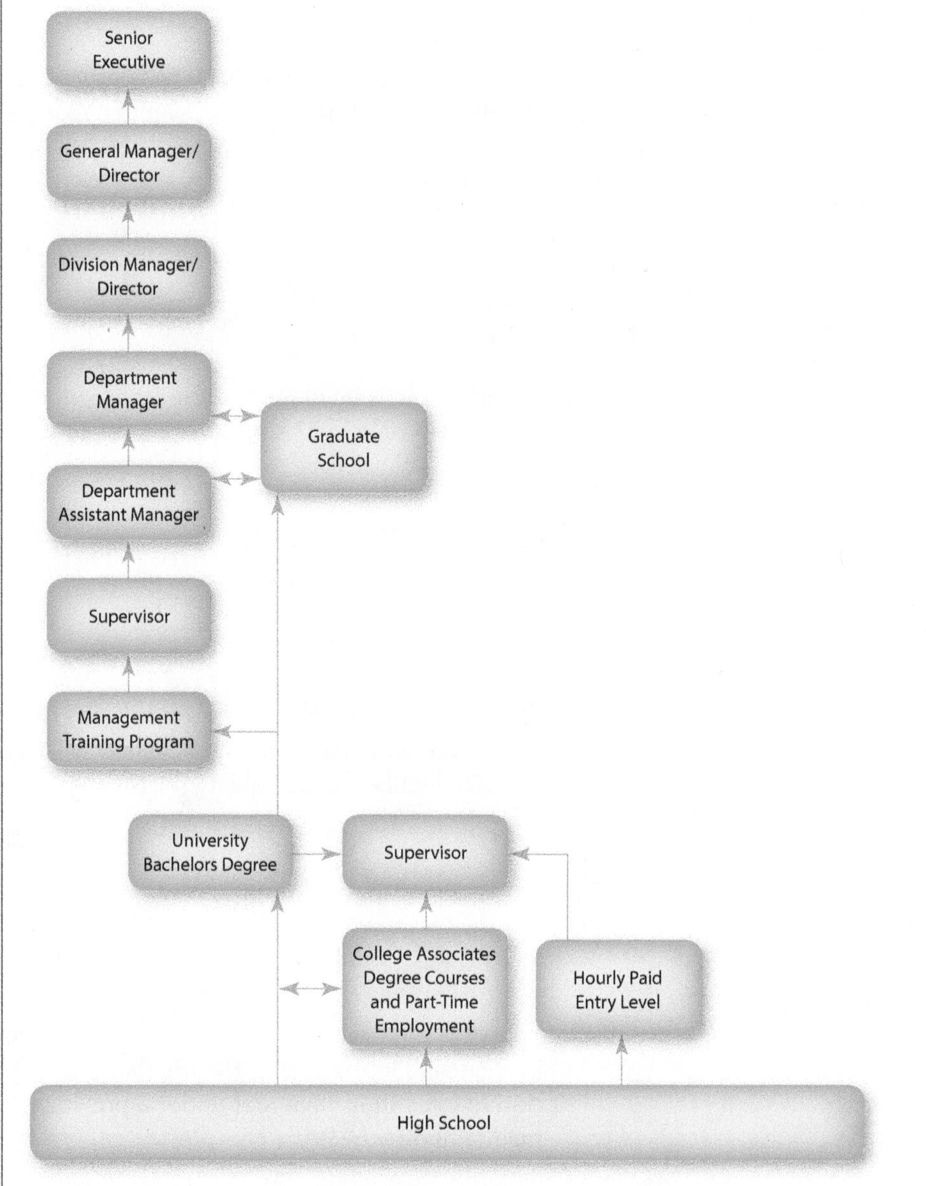

Figure 1.1 A Likely Career Path in the Hospitality Industry. Is Education Worth it? You Bet! Just Think— the Difference in Salary Over a Career Between an Associate's and a Bachelor's Degree is $500,000. Yes, That's Half a Million Bucks! (Source: U.S. Census Bureau Average Lifetime Earnings— Different Level of Education)

1. What is the topic of this chart?
   - **a.** management jobs
   - **b.** a likely career path in the hospitality industry
   - **c.** degrees and jobs
   - **d.** the hospitality industry
2. What type of job is offered to someone with a high school diploma and nothing more?
   - **a.** senior executive
   - **b.** department manager
   - **c.** management training program
   - **d.** hourly paid entry level

3. What type of education would be required for someone to become a division manager?
   a. high school
   b. associates' degree
   c. bachelor's degree
   d. graduate school
4. What type of jobs would be offered to someone with a bachelor's degree? (Circle all that apply.)
   a. general manager/director
   b. supervisor
   c. division manager
   d. department assistant manager
5. Which of these jobs requires a graduate school degree? (Circle all that apply.)
   a. division manager/director
   b. department assistant manager
   c. senior executive
   d. general manager/director

MyReadingLab

BUILDING VOCABULARY

Throughout this course, you will be introduced to word parts that make up many words in the English language. Study the following word parts, and then answer the questions that follow.

Prefixes	Roots	Suffixes
inter- *between*	sect- *part, section*	-ion *action, state of**
bi- *two*	-ject- *to throw*	
re- *again**	-cess- to *stop, cease*	
in- *into**		

*Word parts from previous chapters

1. What English words can you create from these word parts?

....	....	....	....
....	....	....	....
....	....	....	....
....	....	....	....

Using a dictionary, look up the meanings of any of the words you wrote that you can't define. Use one of the words you wrote in a sentence that reveals its meaning with a context clue.

....

....

....

MyReadingLab

CHAPTER PRACTICE 1

Read the following paragraph, and underline the main idea and major details. Then, answer the questions that follow.

When Emeril Lagasse graduated from high school in Fall River, Massachusetts, he was offered a full music scholarship to the New England Conservatory of Music as a percussionist. Instead, he decided to become a professional chef and enrolled at Johnson and Wales University in Providence, Rhode Island. While he was in college, Emeril worked in restaurants. He also studied culinary arts in Paris and Lyon, France. After working in many restaurants, he was offered the job as executive chef at Commander's Palace, a famous restaurant in New Orleans. After achieving success there, he left to open his own restaurant, Emeril's, in New Orleans. A few years later, he began hosting his own TV show, cooking with his own special spice blends that now sell in supermarkets. Emeril has published eight best-seller cookbooks and has opened 10 Emeril's restaurants around the country. Each restaurant has a different style of cuisine, but all of them feature his special blends of bold spices, which he adds with a "Bam!" Emeril has made a successful career as a professional chef and restauranteur.

1. What is the topic?
   a. Emeril's restaurants
   b. Emeril Lagasse
   c. becoming a professional chef
   d. Emeril's cooking
2. What is the topic sentence of this paragraph?
   a. When Emeril Lagasse graduated from high school in Fall River, Massachusetts, he was offered a full music scholarship to the New England Conservatory of Music as a percussionist.
   b. Instead, he decided to become a professional chef and enrolled at Johnson and Wales University in Providence, Rhode Island.
   c. Emeril has made a successful career as a professional chef and restaurateur.
   d. Each restaurant has a different style of cuisine, but all of them feature his special blends of bold spices, which he adds with a "Bam!"
3. Which of the following is not a major detail?
   a. Instead, he decided to become a professional chef and enrolled at Johnson and Wales University in Providence.
   b. After working in many restaurants, he was offered the job as executive chef at Commander's Palace, a famous restaurant in New Orleans.
   c. Emeril has published eight best-seller cookbooks and has opened 10 Emeril's restaurants around the country.
   d. Each restaurant has a different style of cuisine, but all of them feature his special blends of bold spices, which he adds with a "Bam!"

4. Which minor detail tells more about the sentence: "Instead, he decided to become a professional chef and enrolled at Johnson and Wales University in Providence, Rhode Island"?
   a. While he was in college, Emeril worked in restaurants.
   b. After working in many restaurants, he was offered the job as executive chef at Commander's Palace, a famous restaurant in New Orleans.
   c. A few years later he hosted his own TV show, cooking with his own special spice blends that now sell in supermarkets.
   d. Emeril has made a successful career as a professional chef and restauranteur.

5. Identify the best meaning for the underlined word in the following sentence: "Emeril has made a successful career as a professional chef and restauranteur."
   a. someone who goes to restaurants
   b. a restaurant owner
   c. a chef
   d. an investor

MyReadingLab

CHAPTER PRACTICE 2

Read the following paragraph, and underline the main idea and major details. Then, complete the concept map that follows, entering information in the order it is presented in the paragraph.

Mega events are major entertainment productions. Most of these are sporting events that bring in millions of dollars to the production companies and local economies. The biggest sporting event is the Olympic Games, which attracts more than 6 million people to its host city. The competition to host an Olympic Games event is very tough, and countries are willing to spend millions to accommodate this event because of the economic benefits. The World Cup event is the final competition for the best soccer teams in the world. It also draws millions of people during the three years of competition for the championship. The Super Bowl football game is the biggest American sporting event held annually. The halftime entertainment has become as big as the championship itself, featuring spectacular shows. Oddly enough, the commercials produced for this event are as much a part of the event as the entertainment. Other mega events include the World Series baseball championship and the Masters Golf Tournament. One of the most famous sailing races held every year is the America's Cup. Working at any one of these mega events is an exciting and challenging job, and thousands of people are needed to plan, coordinate, and produce these mega events.

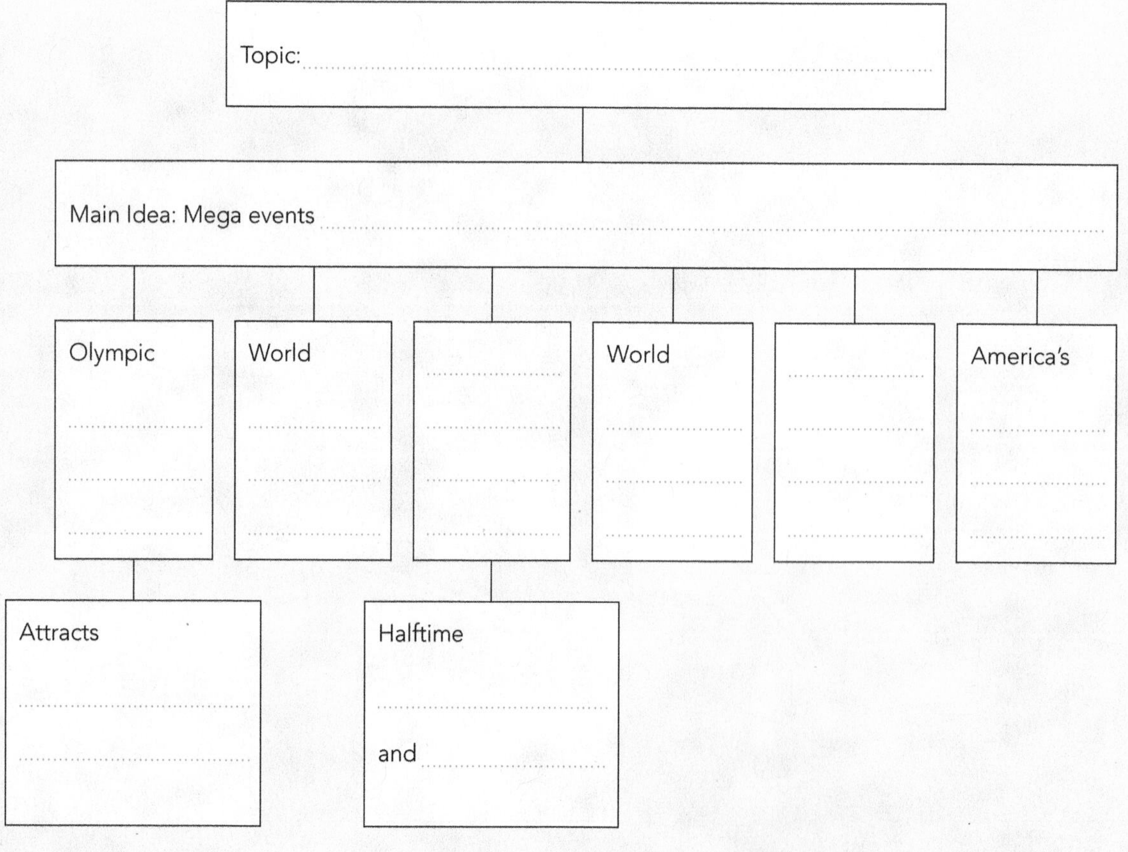

MyReadingLab

CHAPTER PRACTICE 3

Read the following paragraph, and underline the main idea and major details. Then, complete the concept map that follows, entering information in the order it is presented in the paragraph.

A concierge (kon-see-AIRJ) is a hotel employee whose job is to make the guests' stay as enjoyable as possible. The use of the concierge is free and includes a wide variety of services such as obtaining reservations to restaurants in town. They can sometimes get a reservation even when the restaurant tells other guests that there are none available. They also help the guests plan what to do and how to get to the local activities, attractions, and entertainment. They will also make airline reservations or confirm flights and obtain tickets for theater or concert performances. They suggest stores for shopping. They will also sometimes perform unusual services for their guests. One concierge in Madrid helped a guest find a bull to ship home to Japan. Another concierge in London took the place of the best man who was unable to come to a wedding. The job of a concierge is one that is unpredictable and perfect for people who like helping others to enjoy their visit.

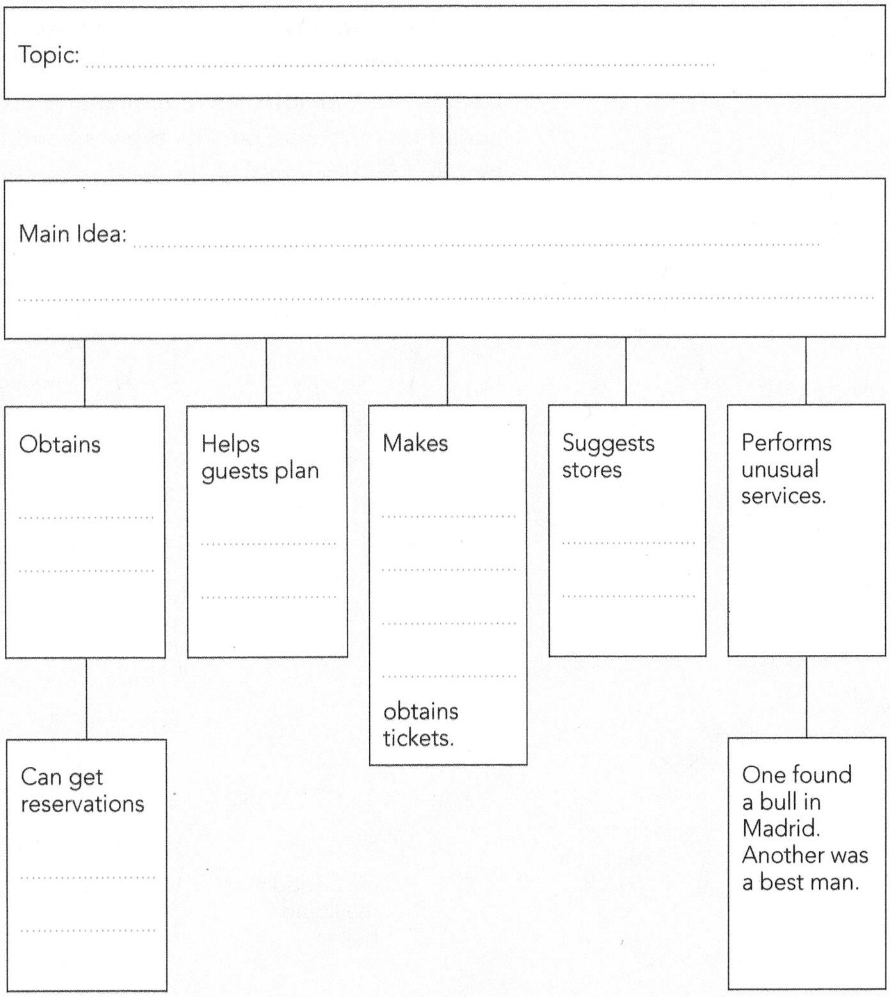

Topic: ....

Main Idea: ....

....

Obtains	Helps guests plan	Makes .... obtains tickets.	Suggests stores	Performs unusual services.
Can get reservations				One found a bull in Madrid. Another was a best man.

MyReadingLab

TEXTBOOK PRACTICE

Read the following textbook selection, and underline the main idea and major details. Then, complete the concept map that follows.

The Brewing Process

Beer is brewed from water, malt, yeast, and hops. The brewing process begins with water, an important ingredient in the making of beer. The mineral content and purity of the water largely determine the quality of the final product. Water accounts for 85 to 89 percent of the finished beer.

Next, grain is added in the form of malt, which is barley that has been ground to a course grit. The grain is germinated, producing an enzyme that converts starch into fermentable sugar. The yeast is the fermenting agent. Breweries typically have their own cultured yeasts, which, to a large extent, determines the type and taste of the beer. Mashing is the term for grinding the malt and screening out any bits of dirt.

The malt then goes through a hopper into a mash tub, which is a large stainless steel or copper container. Here the water and grains are mixed and heated. The liquid is now called wort and is filtered through a mash filter or lauter tub. This liquid then flows into a brewing kettle, where hops are added and the mixture is boiled for several hours. After the brewing operation, the hop wort is filtered through the hop separator or hop jack. The filtered liquid then is pumped through a wort cooler and flows into a fermenting vat where pure-culture yeast is added for fermentation. The brew is aged for a few days prior to being barreled for draught beer or pasteurized for bottled or canned beer.

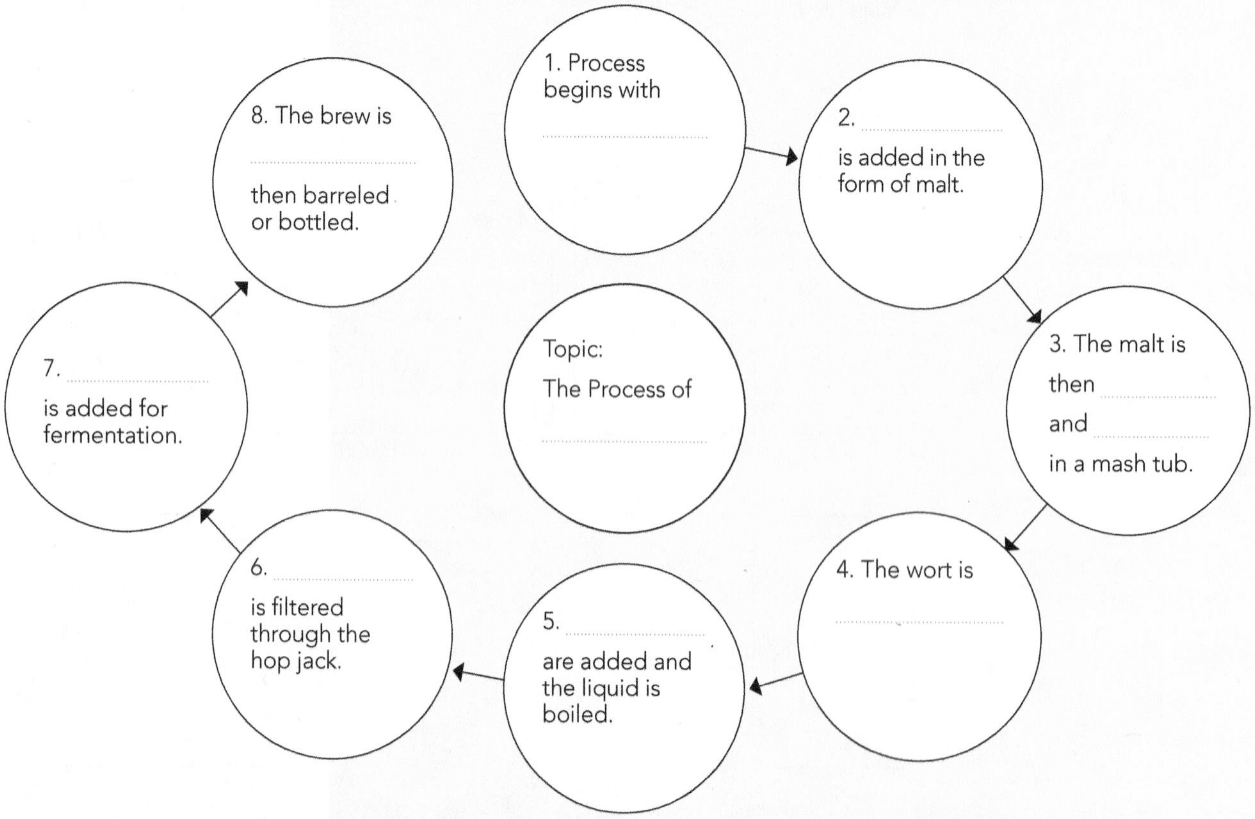

STUDY SKILL REVIEW

Concept maps are a helpful tool for reviewing chapter material, or for planning essays or research papers.

Complete the following concept map for the content covered in this chapter.

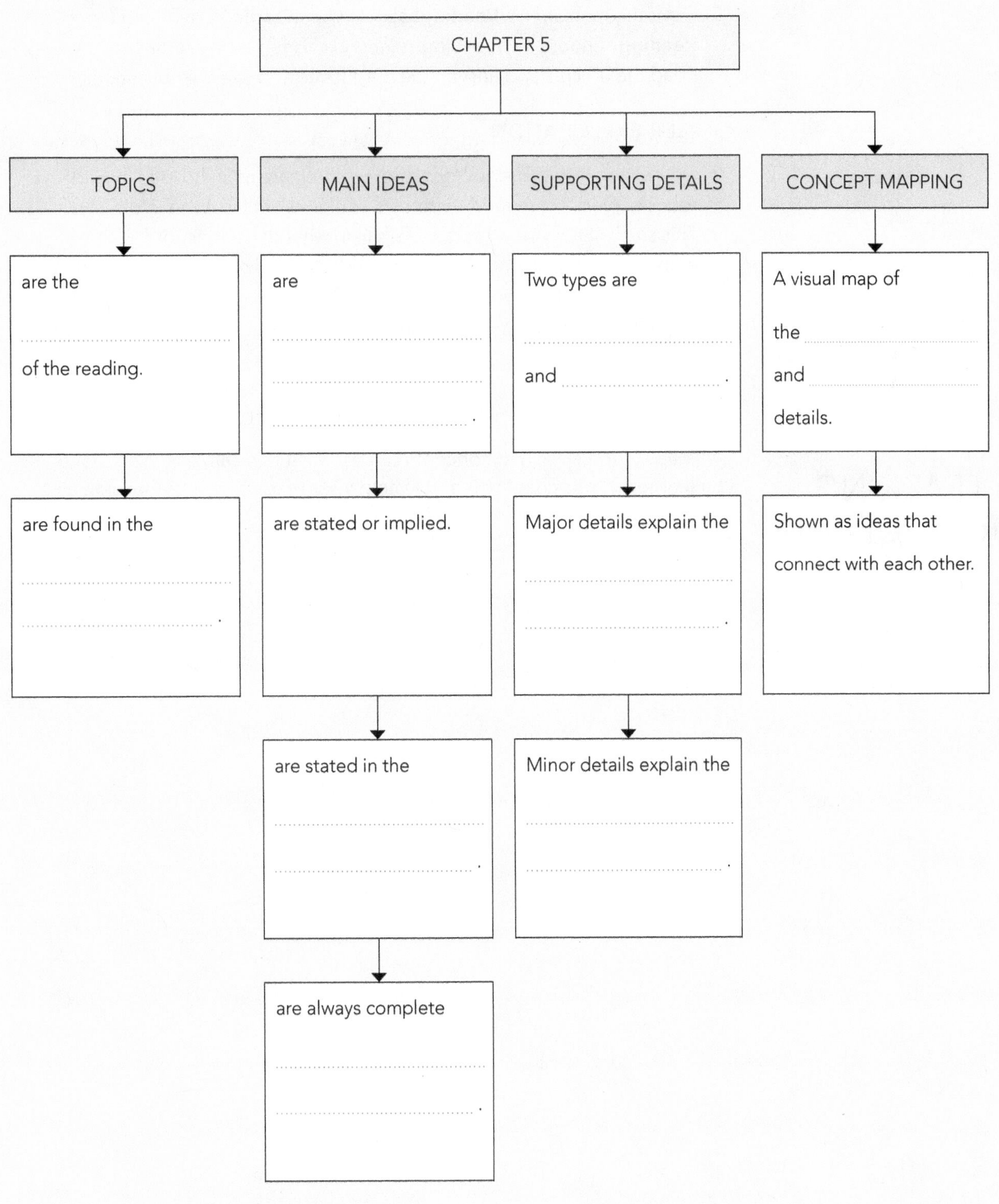
CHAPTER 5
TOPICS
MAIN IDEAS
SUPPORTING DETAILS
CONCEPT MAPPING
are the .... of the reading.
are ....
Two types are .... and ....
A visual map of the .... and .... details.
are found in the ....
are stated or implied.
Major details explain the ....
Shown as ideas that connect with each other.
are stated in the ....
Minor details explain the ....
are always complete ....

READING LAB ASSIGNMENTS

REVIEW PRACTICE

1. Login to **MyReadingLab**, and in the menu click on **Reading Skills** and **Learning Path**. On the main screen, click **Supporting Details**. Complete the review and practice activities recommended by your instructor.

COMPREHENSION IMPROVEMENT

2. From the menu in **MyReadingLab**, click on **Reading Level** and **Next Reading**. Choose two reading selections from the list on the main screen. Read the articles and answer the diagnostic and exercise questions.

CAREER EXPLORATION

3. Go online to www.bls.gov/oco and explore careers in hospitality and tourism. Find a career that interests you, and print out the information. This site will tell you what the job is like, what the outlook is for employment, and current salary and educational requirements. Print the article and then preview, read, highlight, and annotate one or two sections of it. Share what you learned in class.

MyReadingLab

LEARNING REFLECTION

Think about the skills and concepts discussed in this chapter. What have you learned in this chapter that will help your reading comprehension and enable you to do well in college?

MyReadingLab

SELF-EVALUATION CHECKLIST

Rate yourself on the following items, using the following scale:

1 = strongly disagree

2 = disagree

3 = neither agree nor disagree

4 = agree

5 = strongly agree

1. I completed all of the assigned work on time. ....

2. I understand all of the concepts in this chapter. ....

3. I contributed to teamwork and class discussions. ....

4. I completed all of the assigned lab work on time. ....

5. I came to class on time. ....

6. I attended class every day. ....

7. I studied for any quizzes or tests we had for this chapter. ....

8. I asked questions when I didn't understand something. ....

9. I checked my comprehension during reading. ....

10. I know what is expected of me in the coming week. ....

11. Are you still on track with the goals you set in Chapter 1?

....

What changes can you make to improve your performance in this?

....

....

....

....

6 DRAWING CONCLUSIONS

LEARNING STRATEGIES

Drawing Conclusions 219

READING SELECTIONS

READING 1: "College Drinking: Harmless Fun?" 230

READING 2: "Where Wishes Come True" 240

READING FOR LIFE

On the Job Interview 249

Real-Life Reading 250

Building Vocabulary 252

Textbook Graphic Aids 253

CHAPTER REVIEW

Chapter Practice 254

Textbook Practice 257

Study Skill Review 259

Reading Lab Assignments 260

Learning Reflection 260

Self-Evaluation Checklist 261

FOCUS ON: Sociology and Education

People who choose careers in sociology and education often find their greatest satisfaction by helping others improve their lives through better living conditions, improved health, and education. Some opportunities begin with a two-year college degree, and others may require a bachelor's or master's degree. In education, you might enjoy teaching a specific subject, such as sports, technology, or theater. People who work in sociology often help others obtain housing, welfare, health care, and other social services. Some people work directly with clients while others help set up programs and run them.

Drawing conclusions is an invaluable skill in these fields. Social services workers need to be able to evaluate conditions and needs, and come to conclusions about what issues need to be addressed. Teachers need to be able to determine how their class is performing as a whole and as individuals, so that they can tailor their instruction better. To do this, workers in these fields must be able to look at supporting details, use and examine facts, and support their conclusions.

In this chapter, you will:

LEARNING OBJECTIVE

1 learn how to draw logical conclusions.

OBJECTIVE 1

Learn how to draw logical conclusions.

DRAWING CONCLUSIONS

Drawing conclusions is something we all do daily. For example, when a family member gives you a certain look, you know exactly what he or she is thinking. If someone smiles at you, you understand the message being communicated. As a reader, you interpret similar messages. Authors frequently imply an idea by providing you with enough information to draw your own conclusions.

Good readers examine the details and facts and draw logical conclusions. Drawing good, logical conclusions is a skill, like determining the meaning of an unfamiliar word. However, be careful not to assume more than the details tell you. An assumption is something you guess to be true but is not supported by details in the passage. If there is no evidence to prove your conclusion, it is not a valid conclusion.

A **conclusion** is an idea that is based on facts and observations, determined by using inductive reasoning.

Drawing logical **conclusions** is a higher-level thinking skill than finding the stated main idea or recognizing supporting details. It requires *inferential thinking*, which means you have to look beyond the words on the page and think about what is implied. Inferential thinking is a necessary skill in reading comprehension. When you use information to arrive at a conclusion, you are using a method of thinking called *inductive reasoning*.

When you infer something, you are drawing a conclusion from the facts at hand. Making inferences and drawing conclusions both rely on inductive reasoning.

Read the following paragraph and the conclusions:

The newly marketed pain reliever, Drug X, was pulled off the shelf by manufacturers after receiving hundreds of reports from consumers suffering ill effects. Over half of all the consumers reported feeling nauseous within twenty minutes of taking the drug. Nearly twenty percent felt dizzy or disoriented. Another fifteen percent reported ringing in the ears. The pharmaceutical company asserts that Drug X was approved by the Federal Drug Administration and passed all safety tests.

Conclusions:

- Drug X may not be safe for consumers.
- Many consumers felt ill effects after taking Drug X.
- More people experienced nausea than other ill effects.
- Drug X may be related to the effects of nausea, dizziness, or ringing in the ears.

Notice how the conclusions do not say that Drug X actually caused the ill effects. Good conclusions are based on facts, not assumptions, even when the data seems to point to a specific conclusion. The last conclusion says that the ill effects *may be* related to the drug because more testing and scientific evidence would be needed to prove it. For instance, the ill effects suffered by users may be related to the pharmaceutical company's mixing facilities, the process used during the manufacture of the drug, the packaging, or the storage and shipping conditions, rather than the drug itself.

Drawing Conclusions from a Photo

It is said that a picture is worth a thousand words. Look closely at the following photo, and try to draw as many conclusions as you can from the photo. Remember to stick to the facts shown in the photo.

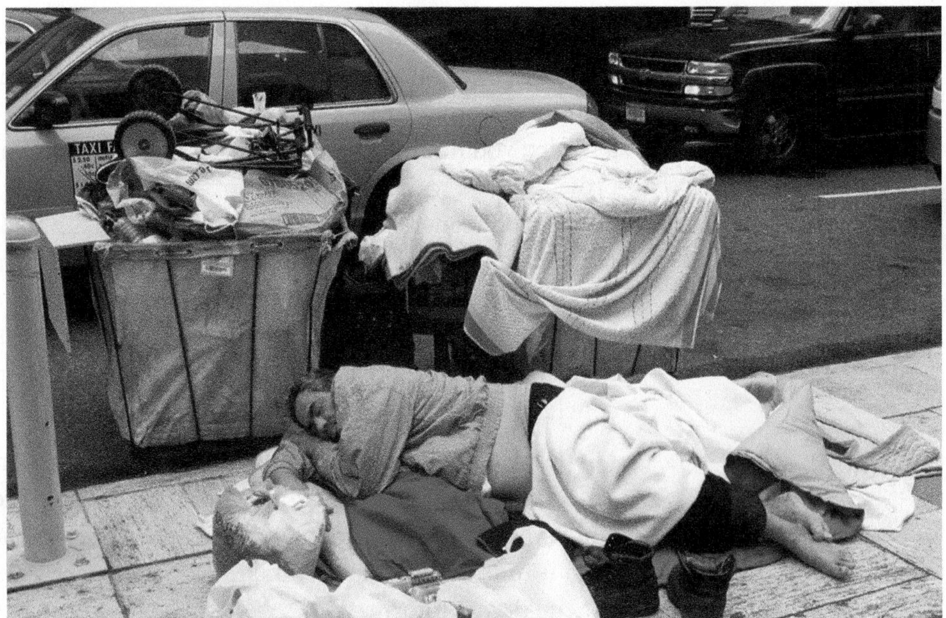

Write your conclusions on the following lines.

How to Draw Logical Conclusions

When drawing logical conclusions, you need to think like a detective. Just as you used LEADS to determine the meanings of unfamiliar words, you can use "CLUES" to reach logical conclusions:

C = **Check your comprehension** of the passage. State the topic and main idea.
L = **Look closely at the supporting details**, both major and minor ones.
U = **Use only the facts** in the details to draw conclusions.
E = **Examine the facts.** When you have made your conclusion, examine the facts to see if they support it. Don't assume more than what is in the passage, even though the conclusion might be something that everyone would agree with.
S = **Support your conclusion** with the facts that prove it.

EXAMPLE #1:
Students who did not complete high school or a certificate program (such as the GED) for the years 1972, 1998, and 2006:

Year	Total % of students who dropped out	Race: Caucasian	Race: African American	Race: Hispanic
1972	14.6%	12.3%	21.3%	34.3%
1998	11.8%	7.7%	13.8%	29.5%
2006	9.3%	5.8%	10.7%	22.1%

(Source: http://nces.ed.gov)

Using the information in this table, identify the following statements as "T" for true or "F" for false.

1. The total percentage of students who dropped out of high school was less in 2006 than in 1972. ....
2. The percentage of African American students who dropped out in 2006 was about half the percentage in 1972. ....
3. High school students were smarter in 2006 than in 1972. ....
4. There were fewer Hispanic students in high school in 1972 than in 2006. ....
5. The percentage of students dropping out of high school has decreased for all races from 1972 to 2006. ....

Some of these statements are false because the table does not provide the facts that you need to decide whether the answer is true or false. For example, for the statement, "There were fewer Hispanic students in high school in 1972 than in 2006," this would be false. Nothing in the table tells you how many students are represented. If something is not represented in a table, or discussed in a passage, do not assume it is true. If there is no supporting information for your conclusion, then it is not a logical conclusion.

Sweeping Generalizations or Absolute Statements

Statements that contain sweeping generalizations or absolute statements are not good, or valid, conclusions. **Sweeping generalizations** apply a condition to all members of a group. A sweeping generalization resembles a stereotype, where all members of a group are included or excluded. For example, saying, "Teenagers are lazy and irresponsible," is a sweeping generalization that implies that all teenagers are lazy and irresponsible. This is stereotyping and not a valid conclusion.

Continued...

Absolute statements include words and phrases such as:

all	everyone	everybody	none
nobody	always	never	no one

Absolute statements also include or exclude all members of a group or condition. For example, saying, "Everyone loves ice cream," or, "Nobody likes getting stuck in traffic," implies that all members love or dislike something. Not only is this unlikely, it is an incorrect, or invalid, conclusion. Unless an idea is directly stated in the passage using one of the absolute phrases listed above, don't assume that it is true.

MyReadingLab

PRACTICE 1

Read the following passage, and then answer the questions that follow. Remember to follow the CLUES.

Teen pregnancy continues to be a serious issue in the United States. Pregnancies among teens between the ages of 15 and 19 are at nearly 1 million per year in the United States. This is the highest rate of all the developed countries in the world and twice the rate of Canada. Teen pregnancies are more common in dysfunctional families and low-income families. Having unplanned pregnancies increases the likelihood that the teen mother will not finish high school and will spend her life in poverty. Although the teens are physically mature enough to conceive, they do not yet have the emotional maturity to understand the difficult consequences of teen pregnancy.

1. What is the topic?

a. pregnancy in the United States
b. teen pregnancies in the United States
c. why teens become pregnant
d. what happens to pregnant teens

2. What is the topic sentence of this paragraph?

a. Teen pregnancy continues to be a serious issue in the United States.
b. Pregnancies among teens between the ages of 15 and 19 are at nearly 1 million per year in the United States.
c. Although the teens are physically mature enough to conceive, they do not yet have the emotional maturity to understand the difficult consequences of teen pregnancy.
d. Teen pregnancies are more common in dysfunctional families and low-income families.

Identify the following statements as "T" for true or "F" for false. Underline the sentences in the passage that provide the support for the true statements.

3. ________ Fewer teens become pregnant in Canada than in the United States.

4. ________ All teens who become pregnant will spend their lives in poverty.

5. ________ Teen girls are more likely to drop out of high school if they have unplanned pregnancies.

MyReadingLab

PRACTICE 2

Read the following passage, and then answer the questions that follow. Remember to follow the CLUES.

Two out of every three crimes committed are drug related. The effects of drug abuse have also increased medical costs nationally, creating a burden on the economy. Because of drug use and drug marketing, the need for more law enforcement both locally and federally continues to increase. Drug users who can no longer work because of their addictions are more dependent upon social services than non-users. This has increased the need for additional social services. Courts are filled with drug-related cases, and the number of cases continues to rise yearly. As a result of drug abuse, the number of prisons and corrections officers has grown significantly, but cannot keep up with the demand. Clearly, the effects of drug abuse have a major impact on our society.

1. What is the topic?
- **a.** drug abuse
- **b.** increased need for law enforcement
- **c.** crimes and drug abuse
- **d.** the effects of drug abuse on society

2. What is the topic sentence of this paragraph?
- **a.** Two out of every three crimes committed are drug related.
- **b.** The effects of drug abuse have also increased medical costs nationally, creating a burden on the economy.
- **c.** Courts are filled with drug-related cases, and the number of cases continues to rise yearly.
- **d.** Clearly, the effects of drug abuse have a major impact on our society.

Identify the following statements as "T" for true or "F" for false. Underline the sentences in the passage that provide the support for the true statements.

3. .... Drug abuse is the fastest growing crime in the nation.

4. .... Drug abuse has resulted in hiring and training more corrections officers.

5. .... Drug abuse had caused an increase in homelessness.

MyReadingLab

PRACTICE 3

Read the following passage, and then answer the questions that follow. Remember to follow the CLUES.

The United States has the highest divorce rate in the world. One of the reasons is that individualism is a trait of many Americans. This means that people are less connected to family members and more concerned with their own individual goals and happiness. Couples who marry young because of an unexpected pregnancy are the most likely to divorce. Another key factor in divorce is addiction to alcohol, drugs, or gambling. If one of the partners has an addiction, the marriage often becomes unstable. Also, if one or both marriage partners have a demanding or highly successful career, they face a higher risk for divorce. People who divorce are more likely to divorce again. For many reasons, divorce has become an acceptable course of action in American society.

1. What is the topic?
   - a. reasons for divorce in the United States
   - b. getting divorced
   - c. society's view of divorce
   - d. the U.S. divorce rate
2. What is the topic sentence of this paragraph?
   - a. The United States has the highest divorce rate in the world.
   - b. One of the reasons is that individualism is a trait of many Americans.
   - c. People who divorce are more likely to divorce again.
   - d. For many reasons, divorce has become an acceptable course of action in American society.

Identify the following statements as "T" for true or "F" for false. Underline the sentences in the passage that provide the support for the true statements.

3. ________ Young couples who marry because of an unplanned pregnancy are at increased risk for divorce.

4. ________ If a marriage partner is addicted to alcohol, the couple is more likely to divorce.

5. ________ Many Americans are individualistic, and focus more on their own happiness than on others'.

MyReadingLab

TEXTBOOK SELECTION

Census 2000: Minorities Now a Majority in the Largest U.S. Cities

The 2000 U.S. census reported that minorities—Hispanics, African Americans, and Asians—are now a majority of the population in 48 of the 100 largest U.S. cities, up from 30 in 1990. What accounts for the change? The reason is that large cities have been losing their non-Hispanic white populations. For example, by 2000, Santa Ana, California, had lost 38 percent of the white population it had in 1990; the drop was 40 percent in Birmingham, Alabama, and a whopping 53 percent in Detroit, Michigan. The white share of the population of the 100 largest cities fell from 52.1 percent in 1990 to 43.8 percent in 2000.

But perhaps the biggest reason for the minority–majority trend is the increase in immigration. Immigration, coupled with higher birth rates among new immigrants, resulted in a 43 percent gain in the Hispanic population (almost 4 million people) of the largest 100 cities between 1990 and 2000. The Asian population also surged by 40 percent (more than 1.1 million people). The African American population remained steady over the course of the 1990s.

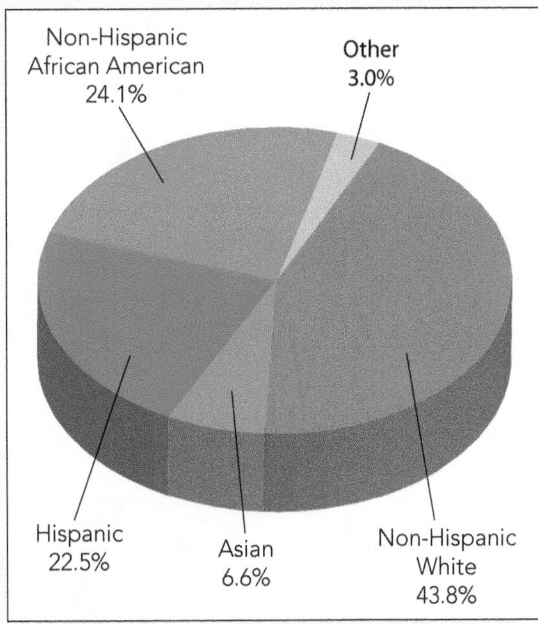

Population Profile for the 100 Largest U.S. Cities, 2000

Racial and ethnic minorities make up a majority of the population of this country's 100 largest cities.

Source: Based on U.S. Census Bureau (2001).

MyReadingLab

TEXTBOOK SELECTION

...continued

QUESTIONS

1. What is the topic?
   a. minorities
   b. racial and ethnic populations
   c. minority populations of U.S. cities
   d. minorities and immigration
2. What is the topic sentence of the first paragraph?
   a. The 2000 U.S. census reported that minorities—Hispanics, African Americans, and Asians—are now a majority of the population in 48 of the 100 largest U.S. cities, up from 30 in 1990.
   b. The reason is that large cities have been losing their non-Hispanic white populations.
   c. For example, by 2000, Santa Ana, California, had lost 38 percent of the white population it had in 1990; the drop was 40 percent in Birmingham, Alabama, and a whopping 53 percent in Detroit, Michigan.
   d. The white share of the population of the 100 largest cities fell from 52.1 percent in 1990 to 43.8 percent in 2000.

Identify the following statements as "T" for true or "F" for false. Underline the sentences in the passage that provide the support for the true statements.

3. ______ The white share of the population is no longer the largest part of the population in 48 of the largest U.S. cities.

4. ______ One reason for the increase in minorities is immigration.

5. ______ Hispanics have a larger share of the population in these cities than non-Hispanic African Americans.

U-REVIEW

With your team, answer the following questions. You may go back to review the information in the chapter if needed.

1. What is a conclusion?

a. a guess about something
b. a guess based on what you think about something
c. an idea that is determined by looking at facts
d. an assumption

2. What does CLUES stand for?

a. comprehend, look at the details, use the facts at hand, explain your main idea, and support your conclusion with facts
b. comprehend, look at the main idea, use the facts at hand, examine the details, and support your conclusion with facts
c. check comprehension, look at the supporting details, use only the facts at hand, examine the facts, and support your conclusion with facts
d. comprehending, logical thinking, understanding, explaining, and simplifying

3. What is an assumption?

a. something you know to be true
b. something you guess is probably true, but there are no facts in the passage to prove it
c. something you do when you use all the facts in the passage
d. making a conclusion based on the facts in the passage

4. What should you do after you make your conclusion?

a. State the main idea.
b. Support your conclusion by looking for the facts in the passage that prove it.
c. Examine the details.
d. Look for absolutes.

5. Which of the following statements is accurate regarding the words *all, none, no one, everyone, always,* and *never*?

a. Never draw a conclusion using one of those terms.
b. You should not assume a conclusion using those terms is true unless the passage specifically states it.
c. Those terms are always acceptable in logical conclusions.
d. Never believe anything that uses these terms.

MyReadingLab

Reading 1
VOCABULARY PREVIEW

"College Drinking: Harmless Fun?"

by Corinne Fennessy

The following vocabulary words are from the article "College Drinking: Harmless Fun?" With a partner or in a team, choose the correct meanings of the underlined words in the following sentences. Use context clues (LEADS), word part clues, and parts of speech to help you figure out the meanings.

1. When Pedro first went to college, he joined a fraternity (fra-TERN-it-ee) during his freshman year.
   a. military group
   b. brotherly
   c. group of college men
   d. sports team
2. To join the fraternity, each pledge (PLEJ) had to dress up like a woman and carry a sign with his phone number on it.
   a. to promise
   b. a person who is trying to become a member of a fraternity
   c. a type of contract
   d. to drench
3. After the big party, the fraternity house was reeking (REEK-ing) of smoke and beer.
   a. stinking
   b. disgusting
   c. distributing
   d. enveloping
4. Because my roommate had stayed out too late, I couldn't arouse (ar-OWS) her to get her to get up for class on time.
   a. interest
   b. awaken
   c. convince
   d. engage
5. Most hotels and restaurants now have portable defibrillators (de-FIB-rill-ate-ors) to shock the hearts of people in cardiac arrest.
   a. pills
   b. medics
   c. oxygen tanks
   d. medical devices that give electrical shocks
6. All of Georgina's efforts to lose weight seemed futile (FYOU-tal) because she never lost more than a pound before putting it back on.
   a. ineffective
   b. ridiculous
   c. ambitious
   d. hard-working

7. During the fire at the club, many people were killed because falling debris created an obstruction (ob-STRUCT-shun) in front of the main exit.
   a. overly large
   b. construction
   c. blockage
   d. opening
8. If a person gets a deep cut that bleeds heavily, you should apply pressure with a clean cloth to stanch (STANCH) the flow of blood.
   a. an odor
   b. hold back
   c. strengthen
   d. not firm
9. Anthony did not receive the scholarship he had wanted because his grades did not meet the required criteria (cry-TEER-ee-ya).
   a. failing
   b. understood
   c. standards
   d. documents
10. The elderly and very young children are more vulnerable (VUL-ner-a-bul) to disease because their immune systems are not as strong as those of healthy adults.
   a. open to
   b. original
   c. inborn
   d. healthy

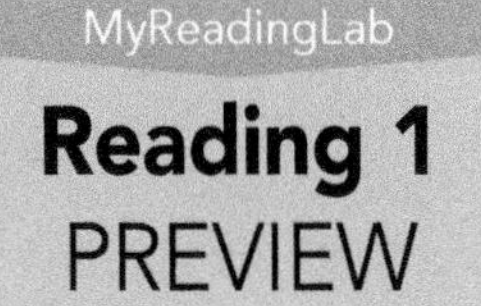

1. Have you ever been to a party where there has been a lot of drinking? Describe the situation.
2. Have you or anyone you know ever been affected by someone else's excessive drinking? Describe the situation.

Directions: As you read this article, practice the four-step reading process. Preview the article, and then write on the following lines one or two questions that you would hope to have answered.

....

....

....

....

....

MyReadingLab

Reading 1

"College Drinking: Harmless Fun?"

by Corinne Fennessy

The most recent studies of college drinking show that it has increased in the past ten years. College drinking may seem like harmless fun to most students, but the truth of its effects is sobering.

1 Fraternities, sororities, spring break, Halloween, or St. Patrick's Day all have something in common at college: drinking. What may seem like harmless fun to most students has a darker side, one that many students ignore.

2 In 2004, a 19-year-old student who had consumed beer and vodka with her college classmates was put into a room to sleep it off and was found dead the next morning. At a fraternity party Adrian Heideman of Palo Alto, California died just by drinking too much blackberry brandy. Scott Krueger, a freshman pledge at M.I.T. with a bright future, also died from drinking. He was just 18. What started as harmless fun ended in tragedy when these students overdosed on alcohol.

3 Approximately 1,400 college students die and over 500,000 are injured each year due to alcohol-related incidents, including car accidents. According to a government study, binge drinking and alcohol-related deaths are on the rise. Binge drinking (4 to 5 drinks at one sitting) has risen to 45 percent of college students, and 29 percent of students drive drunk. It's no surprise that the consequences of such heavy drinking are far-reaching.

4 One night, at Louisiana State University in Baton Rouge, what began as a fraternity keg party ended in disaster. Pledges began drinking at a local bar and continued later at a fraternity house. Donald Hunt Jr. and his best friend and roommate, Benjamin Wynne, were among the group of young men who were partying. By late evening, the pledges were vomiting, and some were taken back to the fraternity house to sleep if off. Around midnight, someone called 911. When the paramedics arrived, they found over a dozen young men lying unconscious and reeking of alcohol. Medics began shaking them, trying to arouse them, shouting, "Can you hear me?" Four of them were unresponsive and one was in cardiac arrest—Benjamin Wynne.

Why were the students hospitalized?

5 Immediately the medics began CPR. They hooked him up to an I.V. and inserted an oxygen tube into his lungs. They shocked him with a defibrillator to restart his heart. He was rushed by ambulance to Baton Rouge General Hospital where tests showed his blood alcohol level was nearly 6 times the legal limit. After doctors' futile efforts to revive him, Benjamin Wynne was finally pronounced dead of acute alcohol poisoning. At the same time, other doctors and nurses worked frantically to save the lives of three other pledges, including Donald Hunt Jr., who also suffered from alcohol poisoning and nearly died.

6 Even though most college drinking may not end like the party at Louisiana State, it does have widespread consequences in terms of assaults, rapes, accidents, unplanned pregnancies, sexually transmitted diseases, and academic failure. College drinking is a contributing factor in 70,000 rapes,

and 70,000 assaults each year. In addition, about 400,000 students engaged in unprotected sex under the influence of alcohol. For example, five of the six college women raped at Daytona Beach, Florida, during spring break in 2010, were drunk or unconscious at the time.

7 A common occurrence resulting in death is that students will leave drunken friends to "sleep it off." "Alcohol kills when the person is too intoxicated to maintain his own airway. He then suffocates on his own vomit or an otherwise harmless obstruction, such as a pillow," says Robert Davis of *USA Today*.

8 Colleges nationwide have conducted alcohol abuse awareness programs and have imposed rigid zero tolerance policies on drinking on campus, but most of these efforts have been unable to stanch the problem. Some college administrators reason that lowering the drinking age from 21 to 18 might help reduce the amount of secret drinking that goes on, but others argue that it will only increase the problem.

What's the most common effect of college drinking?

9 College students drink to have fun, to relieve stress, or to make socializing easier. "What you've got here are people who think they are having fun," Harvard's Henry Wechsler says, "You can't change their behavior by preaching at them or telling them they'll get hurt."

10 For regular college drinkers, the most common effects of frequent drinking are poor grades and dropping out. According to a recent study, one-fourth of the college students who fail courses is a result of excessive drinking. The study also found that nearly a third of all college students met the criteria for alcohol abuse.

11 Recent studies show that drinking among college women is more serious than ever. Wendy Garcia, the director for the Drug and Alcohol Information Center at Florida State reports, "We're seeing more women participating in the drinking games and being competitive with men in the drinking games." One such drinking game involves rolling dice. When your number is rolled, others drink. Other games, like Quarters, require players to bounce quarters into beer glasses. If you succeed, others drink, but if you miss, you drink. Among the most popular drinking games today is Beer Pong. Players try to throw a ping-pong ball across a table and land it into a cup of beer and then must drink it.

12 A study at Columbia University showed that 90 percent of all reported campus rapes happened when either one or both partners were using alcohol. In addition, 60 percent of college women who became infected with sexually transmitted diseases, including AIDS, were drunk at the time.

13 Leslie Baltz, a senior at the University of Virginia, was killed when she drank too much and fell down a flight of stairs. A freshman at Indiana University, Lorraine Hanna, was found dead by her own twin sister after a college New Year's Eve party. Lorraine's blood alcohol level was four times the legal limit. Women tend to get drunk more easily due to a higher level of body fat than men, and their bodies process alcohol more slowly than men's, which makes them more vulnerable to its effects.

Why are women more vulnerable to alcohol?

14 Mindy Sommers was an 18-year-old freshman at Virginia Tech. Her dorm room on the 8th floor had a wide window that was level with her bed. One Friday night, it was Halloween and there were parties all over campus.

Continued...

MyReadingLab

Reading 1

...continued

What programs have been tried on campuses to stop alcohol abuse?

Mindy decided to check out a few, but not go overboard because her parents were coming to visit that weekend for her 19th birthday on Sunday.

15 After partying, she got back to her dorm at 3:00 AM and fell into bed, fully clothed and drunk. The window next to her bed was open, and somehow during the night she fell out of it. Mindy's body was discovered on the grass the next morning by a paperboy. At first he thought it was some kind of Halloween prank. But police and EMT's confirmed that Mindy had died of massive internal injuries from the fall. She had a blood alcohol level only twice that of the legal limit.

16 Efforts to fight alcohol abuse on campus are largely ineffective. Educational programs and scare tactics don't work. "If parents speak with their college students about alcohol, students are less likely to have problems with drinking," says Scott Walters, associate professor of the University of Texas.

17 In the meantime, many colleges will continue to prohibit drinking on campus and offer counseling and support for students. But in the end, if a student really wants to get drunk, there is very little that any college can do to prevent it.

1,240 words divided by .... minutes = ... words per minute

MyReadingLab

Reading 1 REVIEW

It is a good habit to summarize everything you read to strengthen your comprehension.

Directions: On the following lines, write a two- or three-sentence summary of the article "College Drinking: Harmless Fun?" In your own words, describe what the article was about and why the author wrote it.

....

....

....

....

....

....

MyReadingLab

Reading 1 COMPREHENSION QUESTIONS

The following questions will help you to recall the main idea and the details of "College Drinking: Harmless Fun?" Review any parts of the article that you need to in order to find the correct answers.

1. What is the topic of this article?
- **a.** underage drinking
- **b.** alcohol abuse
- **c.** women's drinking habits
- **d.** college students' alcohol abuse

MAIN IDEAS

2. What is the main idea of the entire article?
- **a.** College students drink to have fun.
- **b.** Fraternities, sororities, spring break, Halloween, or St. Patrick's Day all have something in common at college: drinking.
- **c.** But in the end, if a student really wants to get drunk, there is very little that any college can do to prevent it.
- **d.** Excessive drinking by college students has many negative effects.

3. What is the topic sentence of paragraph 11?
- **a.** Studies show that drinking among college women is more serious than ever.
- **b.** Wendy Garcia, the director for the Drug and Alcohol Information Center at Florida State reports, "We're seeing more women participating in the drinking games and being competitive with men in the drinking games."
- **c.** One such drinking game involves rolling dice.
- **d.** Among the most popular drinking games today is Beer Pong.

SUPPORTING DETAILS

4. According to the story, which of the following statements is not true?
- **a.** Donald Hunt Jr. and Benjamin Wynne were best friends and roommates.
- **b.** Mindy Sommers died after falling eight stories from her dormitory room window.
- **c.** Both Donald Hunt Jr. and Benjamin Wynne died from alcohol poisoning.
- **d.** Most rapes, unwanted pregnancies, and sexually transmitted diseases occurred when one or both partners were under the influence of alcohol.

DRAWING CONCLUSIONS

5. Based on the facts in the story, which of the following statements would be a logical conclusion?
- **a.** Alcohol abuse is not considered as serious as drug abuse.
- **b.** Students who abuse alcohol are more likely to fail and drop out of college.
- **c.** Students who abuse alcohol will also abuse drugs.
- **d.** More educational programs about alcohol abuse should be taught in college.

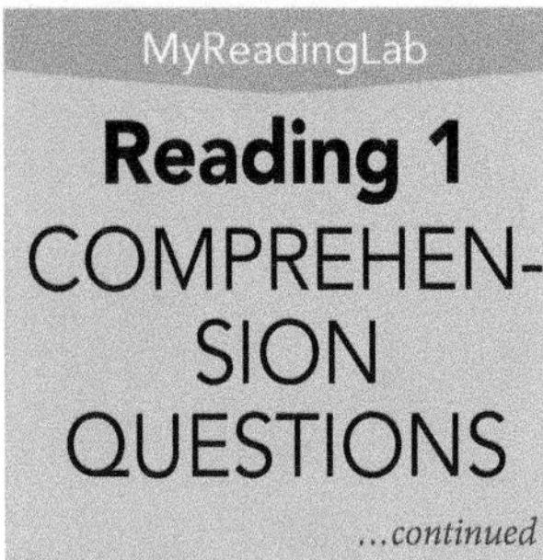
MyReadingLab

Reading 1 COMPREHENSION QUESTIONS

...continued

6. Based on the facts in the story, which of the following statements would be a logical conclusion?
   - **a.** Mindy Sommers was probably a regular drinker.
   - **b.** Students in fraternities tend to drink more than sororities (college women's organizations).
   - **c.** Nearly all students on college campuses have been drunk at one time or another.
   - **d.** Efforts to stop excessive drinking among college students have not been successful.

PATTERNS OF ORGANIZATION

7. What is the overall pattern of organization in paragraphs 14 and 15?
   - **a.** listing
   - **b.** time order
   - **c.** compare and/or contrast
   - **d.** cause and effect

8. Identify the relationship within the following sentence: Women tend to get drunk more easily due to a higher level of body fat than men, and their bodies process alcohol more slowly than men's, which makes them more vulnerable to its effects.
   - **a.** listing
   - **b.** comparison
   - **c.** contrast
   - **d.** cause and effect

9. Identify the relationship between the following sentences: Alcohol kills when the person is too intoxicated to maintain his own airway. He then suffocates on his own vomit or an otherwise harmless obstruction, such as a pillow.
   - **a.** cause and effect
   - **b.** time order
   - **c.** compare and/or contrast
   - **d.** listing

VOCABULARY IN CONTEXT

10. Identify the meaning of the underlined word in the following sentence: Colleges nationwide have conducted alcohol abuse awareness programs and have imposed rigid zero tolerance policies on drinking on campus, but most of these efforts have been unable to stanch the problem.
    - **a.** liking
    - **b.** acceptance
    - **c.** importance
    - **d.** strict

MyReadingLab

Reading 1 VOCABULARY PRACTICE

Use the vocabulary words from the Word Bank to complete the following sentences. Write the words into the blanks provided.

WORD BANK

fraternity	pledge	reeking	arouse	defibrillator
futile	obstruction	stanch	criteria	vulnerable

1. Cathy's husband sleeps so soundly that she can't ______ him even when the baby is screaming.

2. When a person is choking, first check to see if there is a (an) ______ in the airway.

3. My grandmother has poor balance that makes her more ______ to falls and broken bones.

4. The ______ had to wash all his fraternity brothers' cars in one week as a condition of his membership.

5. Despite the company's efforts to ______ the oil leak, it was unable to prevent major ecological damage along the coast.

6. ______ parties often serve a great deal of alcohol, especially beer.

7. The firefighters made a ______ attempt to stop the forest fire, but the high winds spread the fires quickly.

8. The medics tried to revive the man in cardiac arrest with a ______.

9. After the poker game, the hotel room was ______ with smoke.

10. Not all of the candidates for the position of president met the ______ established by the college.

MyReadingLab

Reading 1 QUESTIONS FOR WRITING AND DISCUSSION

Review any part of the article you need to answer the following questions.

1. From the article, describe the example of the effect of drinking that you think is the most powerful.

2. What attempts have been made to curb college drinking and what do you think should be done?

3. Why do you think so many college students drink excessively even when they know the consequences can be serious?

4. If you were with a friend who was drinking more than he or she should, what would you do?

Reading 1 TEAM ACTIVITY — SPEED QUIZ

Get together in groups of four or five people. Each group should create a set of vocabulary cards according to the following directions.

1.

Fold a sheet of notebook paper into 10 squares, and tear into squares. Write the 10 vocabulary words from "College Drinking: Harmless Fun?" and their correct definitions from the "Reading 1 Vocabulary Preview" on the squares—one word and its definition on each square.

FRATERNITY Group of college men	AROUSE Awaken
REEKING Stinking	PLEDGE A person who is trying to become a member of a fraternity
FUTILE Ineffective	DEFIBRILLATORS Medical devices that give electrical shocks
OBSTRUCTION Blockage	STANCH Hold back
CRITERIA Standards	VULNERABLE Open to

2.

Shuffle the squares, and then place them face down on the desk.

3.

Divide your team into two groups so that there are two or three people in each group.

4.

Each group will choose one clue giver and one scorekeeper/timekeeper.

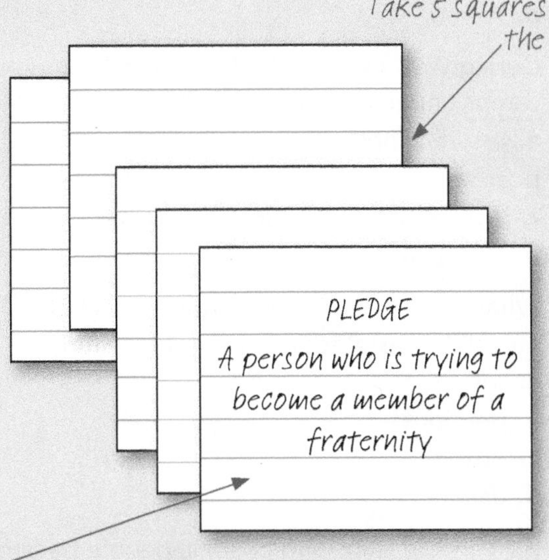
Take 5 squares from the deck.
PLEDGE
A person who is trying to become a member of a fraternity
Read the definition and the other team has to guess the word.

5.

The first group will take five squares from the deck and, when told to start, will read the definitions, one at a time, to the second group. The second group will then have 60 seconds to try to give the word that matches the definition for each of the five words. If they get stuck on an answer, they should say "pass" and go on to the next question. If there is additional time left at the end, they can go back to the words they missed and try again.

6.

The scorekeeper will keep track of how many words the group answered correctly. When 60 seconds are up, the scorekeeper/timekeeper should write down the total number of correct answers given.

7.

Teams will then switch roles. When the cue to start is given, the second team will read the definitions on the remaining five cards to the first team, repeating steps 5 and 6. The team with the most correct answers is the winner.

MyReadingLab

Reading 2
VOCABULARY PREVIEW

"Where Wishes Come True"

by Corinne Fennessy

The following vocabulary words are from "Where Wishes Come True." With a partner or with your team, choose the correct meanings of the underlined words in the following sentences. Use context clues ("LEADS"), word part clues, and parts of speech to help you figure out the meanings.

1. As a successful entrepreneur (on-tra-prah-NOOR), Mr. Lewis owns several businesses that he started himself.
   a. someone who works with a mentor to learn a trade
   b. executive
   c. someone who creates a new business
   d. someone who works for someone else
2. Ever since Robert lost his own parents, he has more empathy (EM-path-ee) for others who have lost theirs too.
   a. space
   b. understanding for the feelings of others
   c. orphan
   d. grief
3. In the courtroom, the defendant looked at her attacker with contempt (kon-TEMPT).
   a. understanding
   b. indifference
   c. carelessly
   d. hatred
4. During World War II, the Nazis imprisoned people in concentration camps under very harsh conditions.
   a. resort camps
   b. prison camps
   c. a place where soldiers live
   d. conservation crew quarters
5. When we returned home after our vacation, we found some moldy, rancid (RAN-sid) food in the refrigerator.
   a. rotten
   b. delicious
   c. frozen
   d. uneaten
6. In many old ships and prisons, people became ill with typhus, (TIE-fus) which was spread by bacteria on rats and lice.
   a. seasickness
   b. homesickness
   c. a disease
   d. food poisoning

7. The bricks in the wall were held together with mortar (MOR-tar).
   a. paste
   b. glue
   c. cement
   d. rockets
8. During his POW imprisonment, Sergeant Morris had to endure (en-DO-ER) terrible conditions and harsh treatment.
   a. bear
   b. enjoy
   c. create
   d. witness
9. Putting the plant in the sun and giving it fertilizer helped it to thrive (THRIVE).
   a. die
   b. become weakened
   c. grow stronger and bigger
   d. wither
10. After the massacre, (MASS-a-ker) the Nazis buried the bodies in a large grave and covered them with earth.
   a. defeat
   b. mass killing
   c. rubbing muscles
   d. loss of soldiers

MyReadingLab
Reading 2
PREVIEW

1. What was your most memorable vacation? Where did you stay?
2. What do you know about Nazi Germany and World War II?

Directions: As you read this story, practice the Four Step Reading Process. Preview the article, and make up one or two questions that you would hope to have answered in this story.

MyReadingLab
Reading 2

As you read, answer the questions in the margins to check your comprehension.

"Where Wishes Come True"

by Corinne Fennessy, based on the book *Gift of Life*, by Henri Landwirth & J.P. Hendricks.

One little girl's dream was the beginning of an incredible journey for one man. Henri Landwirth suffered through the worst inhumanity to humankind, but his pain led him to reach out to others in need and to build "Give Kids the World," a special resort near Orlando, Florida for seriously ill children.

1 Six-year-old Amy, dying of cancer, wanted to meet Mickey Mouse. But while waiting for her dream to come true, she passed away. After learning this, Henri Landwirth, a hospitality entrepreneur, vowed that no child should ever have to die waiting for a last wish to be granted.

2 Henri was born in Belgium, before the Second World War, in a time of peace. He lived with his parents and twin sister in a family strengthened by love. He remembers that his parents loved to dance, and his twin sister and he were very close. They played together and his parents often entertained guests in the evening.

3 Then one day in 1939, a group of Nazis came and arrested their father. His only crime was his religion, and because he was Jewish, they threw him into prison.

4 The family began to suffer without their father's love and support. Food became scarce, and fear filled the city as more arrests were made. Soon, the Nazis came back for the rest of Henri's family. Along with all the other Jewish people they were treated with contempt, herded like cattle into a

ghetto and imprisoned there, with barely enough food to survive. During this time, no one was allowed to worship, to attend school, or do any type of group activity.

5 One day, Henri, his sister Margot, and his mother, were jammed into a crowded boxcar and taken to a concentration camp in Poland. In the camps, they suffered cold, hunger and thirst. Their daily ration of food was two slices of dry bread and one half cup of rancid, watery soup. The men and women were separated, and Henri was taken from his family and put in another section. One day they were all forced to stand in line to receive a tattoo— a number on the forearm for identification. Soon after, Henri contracted typhus and became very sick, like many others in the camp. Death was everywhere, but Henri feared most for his mother and sister. He was alone and afraid, cut off from the people he loved and who loved him.

6 Henri remembers the kindness of some prisoners and he credits his survival to them. But other prisoners thought only of themselves and would do anything to stay alive. Henri and others were beaten for small offenses. His worst beating came when a crust of bread was found hidden in his clothing.

How did Henri's life change after the Nazis took over?

7 One night toward the end of the war, he and a group of other men were taken to the forest to be shot, but by some miracle, he and a few others escaped through the woods. With open wounds, bleeding from his legs and skull, Henri ran and ran, stopping only to rest briefly. In the weeks that followed, he kept going and his wounds became badly infected. One morning as he lay dying in a barn, he was found by an elderly couple who saved his life.

How did Henri escape the concentration camp?

Holocaust: the murder of Jews and others by Nazis in World War II.

8 The Nazis tried to eliminate the Jewish people, but it only gave them strength. Henri says, "Pain and suffering become like mortar to those who have endured it together, and we are all held by it, joined in a common way, one to another, by the burden of having shared the same pain." Millions died in the **Holocaust**. Not just Jews, but also those who suffered a physical disability, were Polish, non-white, or homosexual.

9 In the years after the war, Henri learned that his mother had drowned in a prison ship. His father had been killed in a Nazi massacre, but his sister was still alive. He found her, and they returned to Belgium to try to put their lives back together. Henri became an apprentice diamond cutter and soon learned the trade. But the horrible memories of war would not fade. He needed a fresh start, and decided he would go to America.

10 After the war, America was a beacon of hope for the people of the world. It had not been scarred by war, and it held the promise of a new life. With Henri came millions of others who could not speak English, and were hoping for a new beginning. Life in New York City was very difficult, but he found a job and a place to live. After serving two years in the U.S. Army, he began working in hotels as a bellhop, then at the night desk. Using his veterans' benefits, Henri enrolled in the New York Hotel Technology School, where he learned about the hotel business.

Continued...

MyReadingLab

Reading 2

...continued

11 Two years later, Henri was married and managing a hotel in Miami Beach. There he learned about every aspect of the hotel business, including the restaurant. He later became manager of a new hotel, *The Starlight Motel*. It was built for the growing space industry in Cocoa Beach, Florida. Astronauts and famous news personalities came to stay at the *Starlight*, and became good friends with Henri. Under his management, the *Starlight* was a huge success, and a favorite hangout at Cape Canaveral, in the heart of the space industry.

How did Henri learn the hotel business?

12 Years later, Henri was offered the job as manager of the new *Holiday Inn* in Cocoa Beach. The hotel thrived under Henri's management. His years of experience in the hotel business led to more opportunities and success.

13 Remembering what it was like to suffer hardship, Henri began to use his gifts to help others, and he became involved with helping children with special needs. Henri's childhood experiences gave him empathy and a desire to help others in need. "Find someone who needs a lift up, who needs a little help. Offer him your hand. Once you experience the pleasure of helping others, many of your other problems will go away," Henri says.

14 When little six-year-old Amy wanted to see Mickey Mouse, her parents contacted Henri's foundation and made arrangements to go to Disney World. But it took so long, that Amy died before her wish was granted. When Henri found out, he was devastated. He learned that it took six to eight weeks to grant a sick child's wish. Many children with terminal illnesses didn't have that long to live.

15 Henri decided to do something about it. He contacted Disney World and presented a proposal for the children to come to Disney World before it was too late. He laid out his plans to build a village for sick children and their families. He expected that he would be sent away with the usual, "We'll think it over and get back to you." But instead, the executives agreed to help immediately. Henri was amazed when Disney promised to do more than he asked for.

16 Henri was so excited, he drove straight to Sea World and made the same proposal to them. They too, agreed immediately to be a part of his new plan. Henri needed money for his project, and he turned to his old friends, the NASA Mercury astronauts and friends in the news business, hoping some would help him. They all did—every single one, and *Holiday Inn* donated a million dollars. The ball was rolling on this exciting new project, and Henri's dream of being able to grant wishes to sick children was on its way.

How did *Give Kids the World Village* start?

17 Today, *Give Kids the World Village* is located in Kissimmee, FL, near the theme parks. "The whole village has been built on handshakes. There were no contracts whatsoever," says Henri.

18 This magical place is spread over 70 acres. Accommodations for nearly one hundred and fifty families are home-like villas in a beautifully landscaped park. Families check into the House of Hearts. Guests are welcomed by a six foot rabbit, Mayor Clayton, who holds a birthday party every Saturday night and goes to the villas to tuck the children in at night. There is a wheelchair-accessible pool, a video game arcade, and the Ice Cream Palace serves free ice cream every day. And no one pays for this dream vacation; it is all entirely free.

19 Children from 50 states and 50 countries outside of the U.S have stayed at the Village. Families who stay at the Village are given annual passes to all of the local theme parks, including Disney World, Sea World, Universal Orlando, and others. Over 3000 volunteers provide services, along with a regular paid staff of over 100 employees. Families who have been financially devastated by years of living with a seriously ill child can have a vacation that they would never be able to afford on their own. It is the fulfillment of a dream for every family who comes to the Village.

20 In his book, *Gift of Life*, Henri writes, "I see the connections now. I can draw a link from the past to the present. From the desperation of my own childhood grew the empathy to serve children facing their own desperate circumstances. From survival as a child, to fighting to help other children survive, my life has come full circle." Henri's dream has become his promise, that no child in need will ever be turned away.

1,554 words divided by .... minutes = ... words per minute

MyReadingLab

Reading 2 REVIEW

It's a good habit to summarize everything you read to strengthen your comprehension.

Directions: On the following lines, write a two- or three-sentence summary of the article, "Where Wishes Come True." In your own words, describe what the article was about and why the author wrote it.

....

....

....

....

....

....

MyReadingLab

Reading 2 COMPREHENSION QUESTIONS

The following questions will help you to recall the details of the article and the main idea. Review any parts of the article that you need in order to find the correct answers.

1. What is the topic of this article?
a. World War II
b. Nazi Concentration Camps
c. Henri Landwirth
d. Give Kids the World

MAIN IDEA

2. What is the main idea of the article?
a. Henri Landwirth is a successful hotel manager.
b. Give Kids the World is a village resort for seriously ill children.
c. Although the Nazis tried to kill Henri Landwirth, he survived and came to America.
d. Henri Landwirth's life experiences led him to build *Give Kids the World Village.*

3. What is the stated main idea of paragraph 5?
a. One day, Henri, his sister Margot, and his mother, were jammed into a crowded boxcar and taken to a concentration camp in Poland.
b. In the camps, they suffered cold, hunger and thirst.
c. The men and women were separated, and Henri was taken from his family and put in another section.
d. Soon after, Henri contracted typhus and became very sick, like many others in the camp.

SUPPORTING DETAILS

4. According to the article, Henri's father
a. joined the Nazis and left the family.
b. was killed when the Nazis broke into their home.
c. was taken away by the Nazis and killed in a massacre.
d. went with the family to the concentration camp.

5. According to the article, Henri's mother
a. left the concentration camp and went to Belgium.
b. was drowned in a prison ship.
c. was sent to work in a factory.
d. stayed with Henri during his years at the concentration camp.

6. Henri was able to escape when
a. he dug a tunnel out of the concentration camp.
b. he became sick and was taken to a hospital.
c. the war ended.
d. he was taken to the forest to be shot, but escaped through the woods.

7. According to the story, which of the following is *not* true?
a. Disney World and Sea World were both eager to help build the village.
b. The Mercury astronauts all contributed to the village.
c. The families only have to pay for their meals.
d. The Village was built with handshakes, and not contracts.

8. Label the following sentences from paragraph 7 with "T" for topic, "TS" for topic sentence, "MA" for major details and "MI" for minor detail.

.... Henri Landwirth

.... With open wounds, bleeding from his legs and skull, Henri ran and ran, stopping only to rest briefly.

.... One night toward the end of the war, he and a group of other men were taken to the forest to be shot, but by some miracle, he and a few others escaped through the woods.

.... In the weeks that followed, he kept going and his wounds became badly infected.

DRAWING CONCLUSIONS

9. Henri came to America because

a. he wanted to escape the Nazis.
b. he wanted to forget his past and make a fresh start.
c. he had a dream to build a village for sick children.
d. there were many other people from Europe coming here.

VOCABULARY IN CONTEXT

10. Use context clues, word part clues, and parts of speech to determine the meaning of the underlined word in the following sentence: It is the fulfillment of a dream for every family who comes to the village.

a. idea
b. achievement
c. experience
d. filling

MyReadingLab

Reading 2 VOCABULARY PRACTICE

Use the vocabulary words from the Word Bank to complete the sentences. Write the words in the blanks provided.

WORD BANK

entrepreneur	empathy	contempt	concentration camps
rancid	typhus	mortar	endure
thrive	massacre		

1. The building was so old that much of the .... had fallen out from between the bricks and needed to be replaced.
2. Having had a serious illness herself, Sonia has more .... for other sick people.
3. During World War II, over two million Soviet prisoners of war died in the ....
4. In 2007, the shooting of 32 people at Virginia Tech by a student gunman became known as the Virginia Tech ....
5. As an ...., Bobby Flay has opened his own restaurants, has written 7 successful cook books, and has his own cooking show on TV.
6. It's difficult to .... a boring class in the middle of the afternoon when I always feel tired.
7. When the economy is good and the unemployment rate is low, people have money to spend, and many businesses ....
8. Jessie treats his ex-girlfriend with such .... that it's hard to believe that they once loved each other.
9. After the house was abandoned, the food left in the pantry began to grow ....
10. Antibiotics are used to treat people who have been infected with ....

MyReadingLab

Reading 2 QUESTIONS FOR WRITING AND DISCUSSION

Review any parts of the article you need to answer the following questions.

1. If Henri had not decided to "do something" when he found out that Amy had died, what might have been the outcome?

2. Sometimes bad experiences in life can teach us important lessons. What lessons do you think that Henri learned from other people, both good and bad, in his life?

3. There is an old expression that says, "It takes a village to raise a child." Explain how you think this relates to Henri's life and the creation of *Give Kids the World Village*.

4. Explain what you think Henri means by saying, "Pain and suffering become like mortar to those who have endured it together, and we are all held by it, joined in a common way, one to another, by the burden of having shared the same pain."

5. Anti-Semitism (ant-eye-SEM-it-ism) means prejudice against Jews. The Nazis had tried to eliminate the entire race. Yet, anti-Semitism still exists today. Why do you think some people have this prejudice and what do you think can be done to eliminate it?

Reading 2
VOCABULARY PRACTICE — CROSSWORD

The following words are from the article, "Where Wishes Come True." Crossword Game
How to Play:
One member of the team will be the clue giver and scorekeeper. The other members will be the players.

1.
The clue giver calls on one member to pick a word box number, such as "1 Across."

2.
The clue giver reads the clue to the player and gives the player 10 seconds to give the correct answer. Only one answer is allowed.

3.
If the answer is correct, the word is filled in on the player's crossword puzzle and the player receives points based on the number of letters in the word. If incorrect, the player receives no points and the next player is called.

4.
The clue giver calls on the next player and asks for a word box number. Play continues until all the words have been completed.

5.
The player with the most points is the winner.

Word Bank			
endured	contempt	rancid	entrepreneur
thrive	massacre	mortar	concentration camps
empathy	typhus		

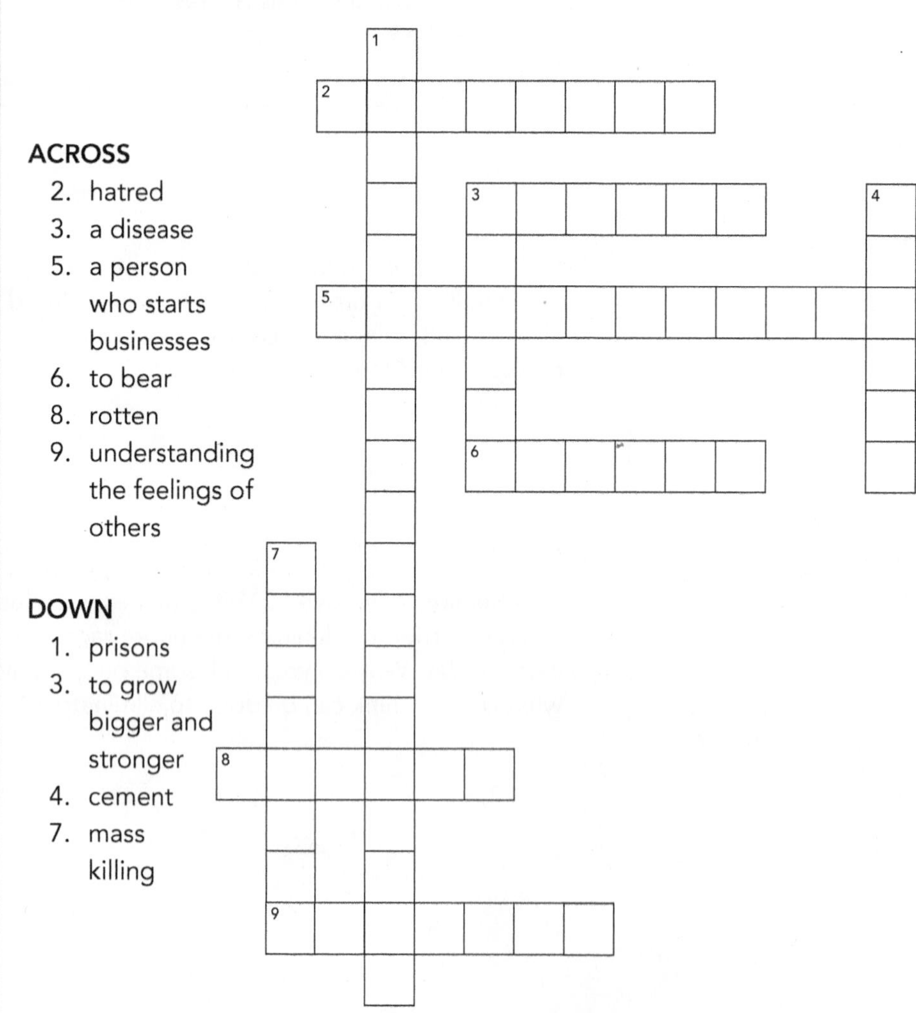

ACROSS
2. hatred
3. a disease
5. a person who starts businesses
6. to bear
8. rotten
9. understanding the feelings of others

DOWN
1. prisons
3. to grow bigger and stronger
4. cement
7. mass killing

ON THE JOB INTERVIEW

KIM WALTER,

HIGH SCHOOL CHEMISTRY TEACHER

How did you become interested in teaching?

When I was young, I used to teach swimming lessons. I really enjoyed helping others learn how to swim. I also had wonderful elementary and high school teachers, so I decided I would go into teaching when I got older. I first wanted to be a physical education teacher; therefore, I had to take courses in anatomy and physiology. I discovered my love for science and decided to change my major to biology.

What is your training and background?

I graduated from State University of New York at Brockport with a bachelor of science degree in science. I achieved a major concentration in biology and minors in chemistry and secondary education. I went on to earn a master of science in education and a master of science in science education.

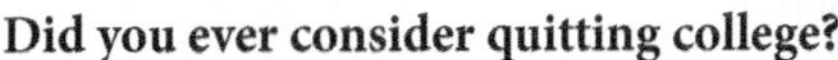

Did you ever consider quitting college?

No, because I knew I had to have a college education to have a successful future. I never thought about quitting.

Where do you work now?

I teach Regents chemistry at Churchville-Chili High School in upstate New York. It was a great honor to be recognized by my students when the National Honor Society chose me as Teacher of the Year. It reinforced the reason I am in this profession.

What do you like best about your job?

I love working with high school kids, and I learn new things every day working with them. Besides teaching them chemistry, I try to teach them things they need to be successful in life, like problem solving, staying organized, establishing good study habits, and working with others.

MyReadingLab
WATCH THE VIDEO
HIGH FASHION, DEADLY FACTORIES
Watch the Video "High Fashion, Deadly Factories" and answer the questions about drawing conclusions.

What do you dislike about your job?

I don't think any teacher likes having to discipline students. Some students don't have respect for education and take their opportunities to learn for granted. And there is a certain amount of politics in any school district that educators have to deal with.

What advice would you give to college students?

I think the best advice I would give them is to choose a career that allows them to do what they love to do. If you do what you love to do, you will always find enjoyment in your work.

What are your plans for the future?

My plans are to keep on teaching for another 10 to 15 years. I still feel enthusiastic about teaching and about my students. I hope to inspire them to become lifelong learners and to help them find joy in learning.

MyReadingLab

REAL-LIFE READING

APPLYING FOR STUDENT FINANCIAL AID

Use the following information from the U.S. Department of Education Web site to answer the questions that follow.

WHY FILL OUT A FAFSA?

The (*Free Application for Federal Student Aid*), or FAFSA, is the first step in the financial aid process. Use it to apply for federal student financial aid, such as the Pell Grant, student loans, and college work-study.

We enter your **FAFSA** responses into a formula (known as the Federal Methodology), which is regulated by the Higher Education Act of 1965, as amended. The result is your Expected Family Contribution, or EFC. The EFC is a preliminary estimate that measures your family's financial strength. It is subtracted from the Cost of Attendance at the school(s) you plan to attend to determine your eligibility for federal student aid.

HOW DO I FIND OUT WHAT MY EFC IS?

We will send you a report, called a ***Student Aid Report*** **(SAR)**, by e-mail or by postal mail, depending on the addresses that we have on file for you. The **SAR** lists the information you reported on your **FAFSA**. At the upper right of the front page of the **SAR**, you'll find a figure called the **EFC**.

HOW MUCH AID DO I GET?

Schools use your **EFC** to prepare a financial aid package (grants, loans, and/or work-study) to help you meet your financial need. Financial need is the difference between your **EFC** and your school's cost of attendance (which can include living expenses).

WHEN DO I GET THE AID?

Your financial aid will be paid to you through your school. Typically, your school will first use the aid to pay tuition, fees, and room and board (if provided by the school). Any remaining aid is given to you for your other expenses.

WHERE CAN I GET MORE INFORMATION ABOUT STUDENT AID?

The financial aid office at the school you plan to attend is the best place to get information about federal, state, school, and other sources of student financial aid.

Information about other nonfederal assistance may be available from foundations, religious organizations, community organizations, and civic groups, as well as organizations related to your field of interest, such as the American Medical Association or American Bar Association. Check with your parents' employers or unions to see if they award scholarships or have tuition payment plans.

WARNING!

Be wary of organizations that charge a fee to submit your application, or to find you money for school. Some are legitimate and some are scams. Generally, any help that you pay for can be received free from your school or Federal Student Aid.

1. Why do you need to answer so many questions in order to get financial aid?

2. How is your EFC used to determine your financial aid?

3. If an organization asks you for money to apply for financial aid or a scholarship, what should you do?

4. Where is the financial aid sent, and what, specifically, can the financial aid be used for?

5. What are some other sources of financial aid for students?

MyReadingLab

BUILDING VOCABULARY

Study the following word parts, and then answer the questions that follow.

Prefixes	**Roots**	**Suffixes**
dis- *apart, away from*	-able- *able to*	-ity *quality of*
in- *not*	-tend- *to move*	-tion, -sion *action, state of**
ex- *out**	-tinct- *to incite or to quench*	-ive *a state or quality**
	-tort- *to twist*	

* Word parts from previous chapters

What English words can you create from these word parts?

Using a dictionary, look up the meanings of any of the words you wrote that you can't define. Use one of the words you wrote in a sentence that reveals its meaning with a context clue:

MyReadingLab

TEXTBOOK GRAPHIC AIDS

Use the following chart to identify the statements that follow as true or false.

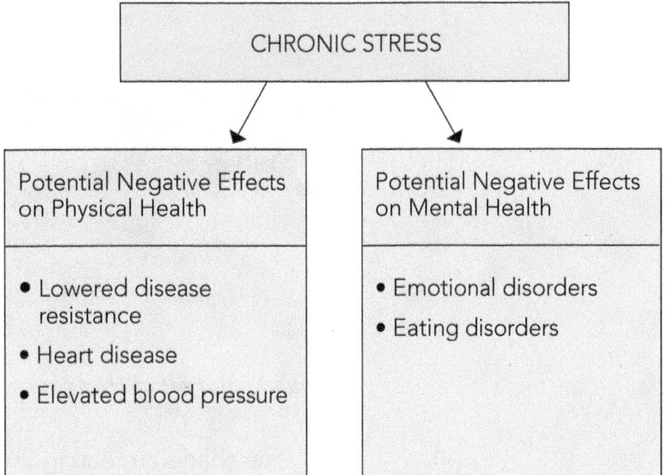

1. .... Heart disease causes mental disorders.

2. .... There are potentially more negative effects of stress on physical health than on mental health.

3. .... Eating disorders may be caused by chronic stress.

4. .... Chronic stress can have an effect on your body's ability to fight off illness.

5. .... People who deal with chronic stress on a daily basis will have heart attacks.

MyReadingLab

CHAPTER PRACTICE 1

Study the following cartoons, and then identify the statements that follow as true or false.

"You've got a bit of thong caught between your front teeth."

1. .... The sharks are eating thongs.

2. .... One shark has eaten a swimmer who wore a thong.

3. .... The artist implies that like people, sharks care about their appearance.

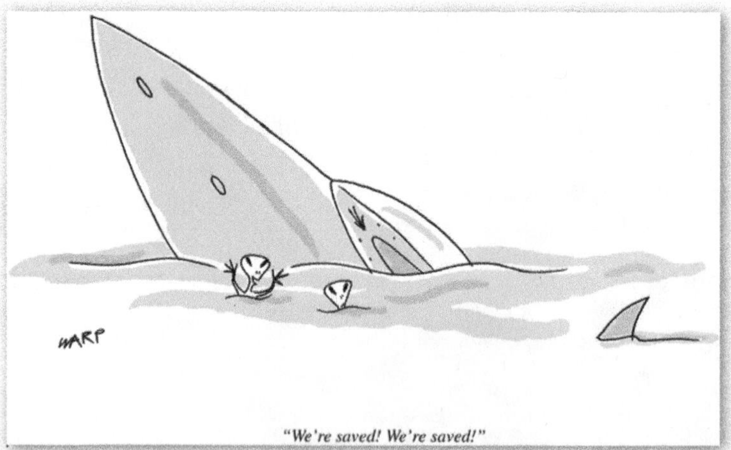

"We're saved! We're saved!"

1. .... The aliens from the space ship think that the shark has come to help them.

2. .... The aliens have been to Earth before and know about sharks.

MyReadingLab

CHAPTER PRACTICE 2

Study the following cartoons, and then identify the statements that follow as true or false.

"Poor old Stanley. He was only 3 months away from paying off his student loan."

1. ________ The man in the grave had been a college student at one time.

2. ________ According to the cartoon, college loans are not difficult to pay back.

"I take it you didn't like my meatballs."

1. ________ The man in the cartoon thinks his wife is a good cook.

2. ________ The cartoonist is implying that all meatballs are terrible.

3. ________ The meatballs the man had on his plate resembled golf balls.

MyReadingLab

CHAPTER PRACTICE 3

Read the following paragraph, and then answer the questions that follow. Remember to use CLUES to help you make logical conclusions.

In the days of ancient Egypt, preserving the body after death was a religious practice that honored the dead. The wealthiest and most important Egyptians were cut open, and their internal organs were placed in clay jars. The brain was removed either through the nostrils or through an incision in the back of the skull. The body was then packed in natron, a natural salt. The mummy was then cleansed and bandaged, while priests recited prayers and applied oils and perfumes. A gold or silver mask was sometimes placed over the face. The mummy was placed into a wooden coffin, which was put into a larger, rectangular stone "sarcophagus" (sar-KOFF-a-gus). The priests performed a formal ceremony for last rites, and the sarcophagus was laid to rest in its own tomb, which was sometimes a giant pyramid.

1. What is the topic of the passage?
   a. mummies
   b. how ancient Egyptians preserved their dead
   c. ancient priests
   d. ceremonies for the dead

2. What is the topic sentence of the passage?
   a. In the days of ancient Egypt, preserving the body after death was a religious practice that honored the dead.
   b. The wealthiest and most important Egyptians were cut open, and their internal organs were placed in clay jars.
   c. The brain was removed either through the nostrils or through an incision in the back of the skull.
   d. The priests performed a formal ceremony for last rites, and the sarcophagus was laid to rest in its own tomb, which was sometimes a giant pyramid.

Identify the following statements as "T" for true or "F" for false.

3. .... The ancient Egyptians showed great respect for their dead.

4. .... The ancient Egyptians were religious.

5. .... Ancient Egyptians believed they needed their entire bodies after death.

MyReadingLab

TEXTBOOK PRACTICE

Read the following textbook selection, and then answer the questions that follow. Remember to use CLUES to help you make logical conclusions.

There may be no way to rid the world of dishonesty, but researchers have learned a great deal about how to tell when someone is lying. According to Paul Ekman, a specialist in analyzing social interaction, clues to deception can be found in four elements of a performance: words, voice, body language, and facial expressions.

1. Words. People who are good liars mentally go over their lines, but they may say something that is inconsistent, thereby suggesting deception.
2. Voice. Tone and patterns of speech contain clues to deception because they are hard to control. Especially when hiding a powerful emotion, a person cannot easily prevent the voice from trembling or breaking.
3. Body language. A "leak" conveyed through body language, which is also difficult to control, may tip off an observer to deception. Subtle body movements, sudden swallowing, or rapid breathing may show that the person is nervous.
4. Facial expressions. Because there are 43 different muscles in the face, facial expressions are more difficult to control than other body language.

Look at the two faces in the photos. Can you tell which is the lying face? It's the one on the left. A real smile is usually accompanied by a relaxed expression and lots of "laugh lines" around the eyes; a phony smile seems forced and unnatural, with fewer wrinkles around the mouth and eyes.

Continued...

MyReadingLab

TEXTBOOK PRACTICE

...continued

1. What is the topic of this selection?

a. clues to deception
b. lying
c. how lying harms society
d. deception

2. What is the main idea of the entire selection?

a. There may be no way to rid the world of dishonesty, but researchers have learned a great deal about how to tell when someone is lying.
b. According to Paul Ekman, a specialist in analyzing social interaction, clues to deception can be found in four elements of a performance: words, voice, body language, and facial expressions.
c. People who are good liars mentally go over their lines, but they may say something that is inconsistent, thereby suggesting deception.
d. Especially when hiding a powerful emotion, a person cannot easily prevent the voice from trembling or breaking.

3. According to the article, what is a "leak"?

a. A leak is something someone does that leads the observer to believe that a person is lying.
b. A leak is when the liar gives out false information.
c. A leak is saying something that is inconsistent with something said earlier.
d. A leak is a phony smile.

4. According to the article, if someone's voice is trembling, what does it mean?

a. It indicates that the person is lying.
b. It indicates that the person is nervous.
c. It indicates that the person is hiding a powerful emotion.
d. It indicates that the person is upset.

5. How can a person tell if someone is probably lying?

a. if the person is smiling a lot
b. if the person is revealing clues through words, voice, body language, and facial expressions
c. when the person smiling is thinking the opposite of what the person is saying
d. if the person smiling is actually sad or angry

STUDY SKILL REVIEW

Creating flow charts is an easy way to remember the steps in a process. Fill in the following flow chart for the steps you learned in this chapter that help you draw logical and valid conclusions.

C: ________________________________.

L: ________________________________.

U: ________________________________.

E: ________________________________.

S: ________________________________.

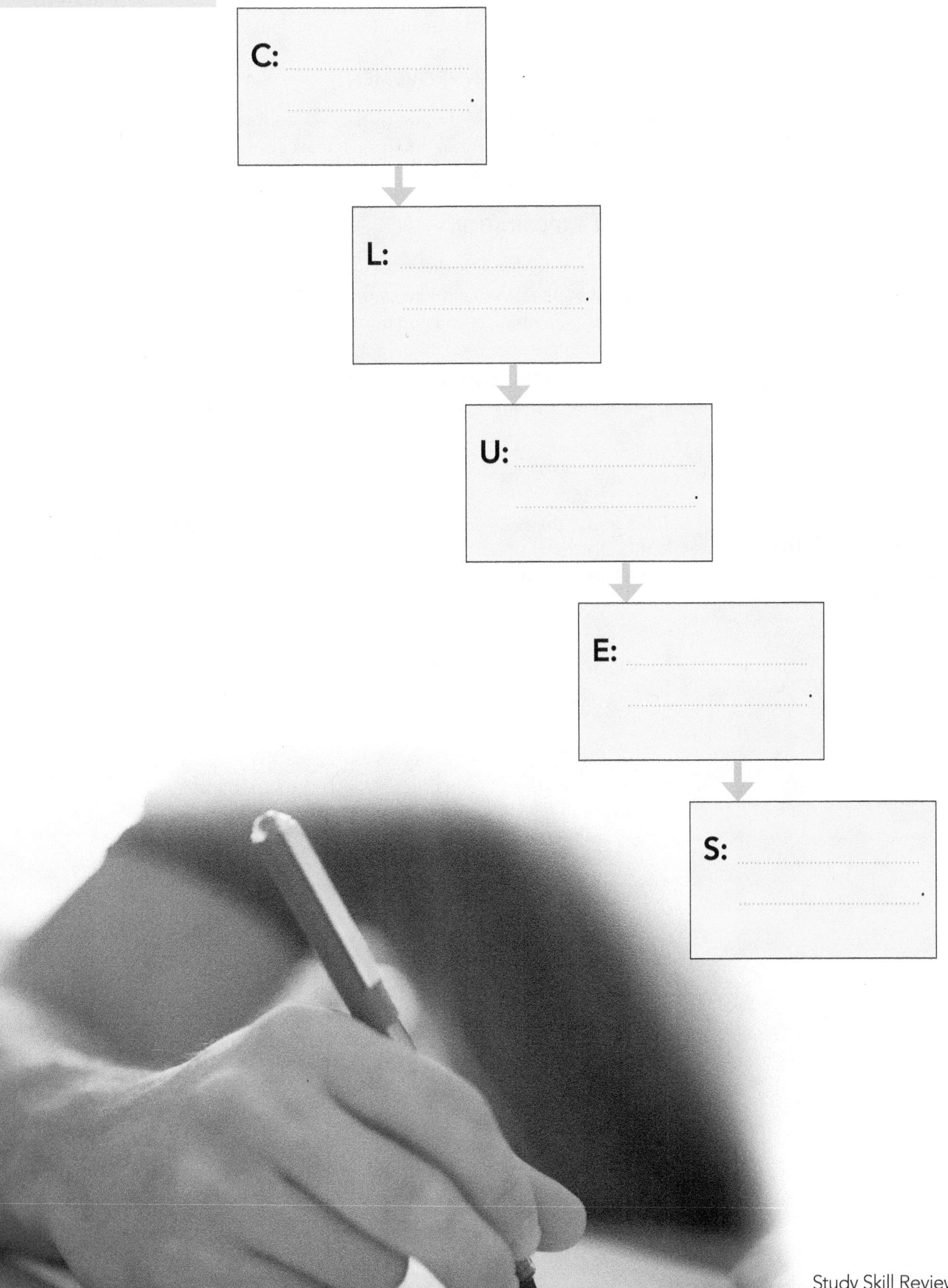

READING LAB ASSIGNMENTS

SKILL PRACTICES

1. Login to **MyReadingLab,** and in the menu click on **Reading Skills** and **Learning Path**. On the main screen, click Inference. Complete the review and practice activities recommended by your instructor.

COMPREHENSION IMPROVEMENT

2. From the menu in **MyReadingLab,** click on **Reading Level** and **Next Reading**. Choose two reading selections from the list on the main screen. Read the articles and answer the diagnostic and exercise questions

CAREER EXPLORATION

3. Go online to the Occupational Outlook Handbook at the Bureau of Labor Statistics and explore careers in sociology or education. Find a career that interests you and print out the information. Print the article, and then preview, read, highlight, and annotate one or two sections of it. Write two conclusions you can draw about the job (for example, whether it would be a good job for you and why you think this job is important).

MyReadingLab

LEARNING REFLECTION

Think about the skills and concepts in this chapter. What have you learned in this chapter that will help your reading comprehension and enable you to do well in college?

MyReadingLab

SELF-EVALUATION CHECKLIST

Rate yourself on the following items, using the following scale:

1 = strongly disagree

2 = disagree

3 = neither agree nor disagree

4 = agree

5 = strongly agree

1. I completed all of the assigned work on time. ....

2. I understand all the concepts in this chapter. ....

3. I contributed to teamwork and class discussions. ....

4. I completed all of the assigned lab work on time. ....

5. I came to class on time. ....

6. I attended class every day. ....

7. I studied for any quizzes or tests we had for this chapter. ....

8. I asked questions when I didn't understand something. ....

9. I checked my comprehension during reading. ....

10. I know what is expected of me in the coming week. ....

11. Are you still on track with the goals you set in Chapter 1?

....

What changes can you make to improve your performance in this?

....

....

....

7 IMPLIED MAIN IDEAS AND CENTRAL POINT

LEARNING STRATEGIES

Implied Main Ideas 263

Recognizing Stated Main Ideas and Implied Main Ideas 268

The Central Point 274

READING SELECTIONS

READING 1: "My Best Role Ever" 281

READING 2: "From Sketch to Screen: Tim Burton" 290

READING FOR LIFE

On the Job Interview 300

Building Vocabulary 301

Real-Life Reading 302

Textbook Graphic Aids 304

CHAPTER REVIEW

Chapter Practice 306

Textbook Practice 309

Study Skill Review 311

Reading Lab Assignments 312

Learning Reflection 312

Self-Evaluation Checklist 313

FOCUS ON: The Arts and Related Fields

Many people have special talents and interests in art, music, filmmaking, theater, photography, digital media, and dance. Although job opportunities and the competition in these fields can be very stiff, anyone who is well prepared and committed to the craft can make a living in the arts—and perhaps a very good one. Jobs are found in theater, television, on cruise ships, resorts, theme parks, schools, private businesses, and studios. Many creative people are self-employed. There are unlimited opportunities to use your talents in these fields if you have good ideas and are dedicated.

Identifying the main idea of an artistic work is a skill you will find valuable whether you are creating art or simply enjoying it. Movies, paintings, and media do not often state what their main idea is—it is something that audiences can find for themselves in the works. Though they may not state it, artists generally do have a central idea they are trying to convey. Your ability to identify the main idea will make your enjoyment of the arts more meaningful, whether you are watching a movie or filming one.

In this chapter, you will:

LEARNING OBJECTIVES

1 identify an implied main idea.

2 identify the central point or thesis.

OBJECTIVE 1

Identify an implied main idea.

IMPLIED MAIN IDEAS

An **implied main idea** is a main idea that is not stated, but is suggested by the details. Using the details, you draw a logical conclusion about the author's most important point. As an active reader, you can figure out the author's main point by following three simple steps:

implied main idea: a main idea that is not stated, but suggested by the details.

1. First, begin with the topic. Who or what is the passage about?
2. Second, find the major details.
3. Third, summarize what the author is saying about the topic in the major details. Be sure to use very broad, general terms to describe the author's point. Ask yourself, "What are the major details telling me about the topic?" When you have formed your implied main idea, ask yourself, "Do the major details tell me more about this idea?" If they do, then you have an implied main idea that is general enough to include all the major points.

Read the following paragraph and the explanation that follows.

> In 2010, there was an estimated 77 percent decrease in the sales of new albums internationally. Fewer new artists are breaking the charts globally than a decade ago. Music sales in Spain fell approximately 22 percent in 2010, with no new artists featured in their top 50 album chart, and other countries experienced similar drops. Experts are predicting that by 2015, about 1.2 million jobs could be lost in Europe's music industry if **digital piracy** is not deterred. Several of the biggest illegal sources of infringing downloads in the US have been shut down, but sources in other countries continue to steal digital music and offer it freely or sell it cheaply to consumers worldwide.

digital piracy: stealing or illegally copying music or other media files.

Topic: Digital music piracy

Supporting Details:

- Fewer new artists are breaking the charts globally than a decade ago.
- Music sales in Spain fell approximately 22 percent in 2010, with no new artists featured in their top 50 album chart, and other countries experienced similar drops.
- By 2015, about 1.2 million jobs could be lost in Europe's music industry.
- Several of the biggest illegal sources of infringing downloads in the US have been shut down, but sources in other countries continue to steal digital music.

Implied Main Idea:

- Digital music piracy is causing a decline in the music industry worldwide.

Notice how the implied main idea summarizes the major details in very general terms. The main idea must be broad enough to include all the supporting details as proof, examples, or illustrations of the main point.

IMPLIED MAIN IDEAS

Read the following example paragraphs, and then answer the questions that follow. The major details have been underlined.

<u>A film director works with other creative members on the production team, such as the cinematographer, screenwriters, the visual effects supervisor, and others.</u> He or she makes the decisions about how the film will be made to create a specific experience for viewers. <u>Directors can have many different styles.</u> Some directors welcome suggestions from production team members, while others prefer to make most of the decisions alone. Many directors also like to be involved with the film's editing, while others work more closely with the screenwriters. Directors work under producers, who set the budget and time limit for creating a movie.

1. What is the topic?
   - a. directors and producers
   - b. directing
   - c. film directors
   - d. styles of directing
2. What do the major details describe?
   - a. how directors have many responsibilities
   - b. how film directors have many different styles and work with various members of the production team
   - c. why film directors are important
   - d. why people want to be film directors

Complete the following implied main idea.

Film directors have many different .... of working with ....

MyReadingLab

PRACTICE 1

Read the following paragraph, and underline the major details. Then, answer the questions that follow.

Walt Disney was born in 1901, and began taking night courses at the Chicago Art Institute when he was a freshman in high school. He was the cartoonist for his school newspaper until World War I broke out, when he was 16. He served three years in the war and then returned home and worked as an advertising artist with his brother. After an unsuccessful attempt with their own company, Walt went back into advertising where he met Fred Harman and began making animated cartoons in Kansas City. Although his animated cartoons were popular, this company also failed due to poor management. Next, Walt and Roy Disney moved to Hollywood to start the Disney Brothers Studio, where he began producing animated cartoons with characters. When they lost the rights to one of his most popular characters, Oswald the Rabbit, the Disney brothers found themselves once more at the bottom. But Walt put his pen to paper and, with the help of another animator, created Mortimer Mouse—later renamed Mickey Mouse. The rest is history.

1. **What is the topic?**
   a. Walt Disney's career beginnings
   b. Walt and Roy Disney
   c. Disney Brothers Studio
   d. animated cartoons

2. **What do the major details describe?**
   a. reasons why Walt Disney is successful
   b. the early influences on Walt Disney's art
   c. Walt Disney's background experience
   d. Disney's most memorable characters

3. **What is the author's implied main idea? (What do the major details describe?)**
   a. Never give up on your dreams.
   b. Walt Disney experienced failures before becoming successful.
   c. Walt Disney went to art school and started his own business.
   d. The Disney Brothers Studio created Mickey Mouse.

MyReadingLab

PRACTICE 2

Read the following paragraph, and underline the major details. Then, answer the questions that follow.

After World War II, a Japanese artist named Tezuka Osamu was influenced by American cartoons, particularly those of Walt Disney. He brought his own artistic style to create *manga*, illustrated stories similar to American comic books. But Osamu created stories for all ages with themes of sorrow, anger, and hatred. In 1958, Osamu founded his own animation company and created the Mighty Atom character. When this character came to the United States in the 1960s, he became Astroboy, and the animé industry was born. Osamu's animé style remains popular today, featuring characters with big eyes and rounded features. The success of animé sparked international interest, which soon brought more characters such as Pokemon, Speed Racer, and Akira to a worldwide stage. Animé is now one of the most popular forms of graphic novels in the world.

1. **What is the topic?**
   a. animé
   b. manga
   c. the history of animé
   d. the comic industry

Continued...

MyReadingLab

PRACTICE 2

...continued

2. What do the major details describe?
   a. a list of animé characters
   b. how animé became popular internationally
   c. who started animé
   d. why animé is so popular
3. What is the author's implied main idea? (What do the major details describe?)
   a. The success of the Mighty Atom helped Tezuka Osamu to succeed in animé.
   b. Tezuka Osamu was the father of modern manga and animé.
   c. Animé is now one of the most popular forms of graphic novels in the world.
   d. Internationally popular animé originated in Japan, with an artist named Tezuka Osamu.

MyReadingLab

PRACTICE 3

Read the following paragraph, and underline the major details. Then, answer the questions that follow.

In the late 1800s, New Orleans was a thriving seaport that drew people from all around the world. Everywhere in the city was filled with many different styles of music from various cultures. Bands were very popular, and almost everyone played an instrument, even those who couldn't read music. Band music was one of the first musical influences on early jazz. Another popular style of music was "ragging." This means playing a melody in an off-beat style. Ragging had its roots in Africa and developed into "ragtime," another influence on early jazz. A third influence on jazz was the blues. The blues came from early African-American spiritual music and followed a simple four-chord pattern. Jazz developed from these three styles of music, using the off-beat rhythms of ragtime, the melodies and instruments of band music, and the feel of the blues.

1. What is the topic?
   a. music
   b. the blues
   c. influences on jazz
   d. jazz
2. What do the major details describe?
   a. the history of jazz
   b. why New Orleans is known for jazz
   c. music in New Orleans
   d. the styles of music that influenced jazz
3. What is the author's implied main idea? (What do the major details describe?)
   a. There are many styles of music in New Orleans.
   b. Jazz is a form of the blues.
   c. The history of jazz is interesting.
   d. The history of jazz shows that it developed from three styles of music.

MyReadingLab

TEXTBOOK SELECTION 1

genre (ZSHAN-rah): a type or variety of something.

Read the following textbook selection, and underline the major details. Then, answer the questions that follow.

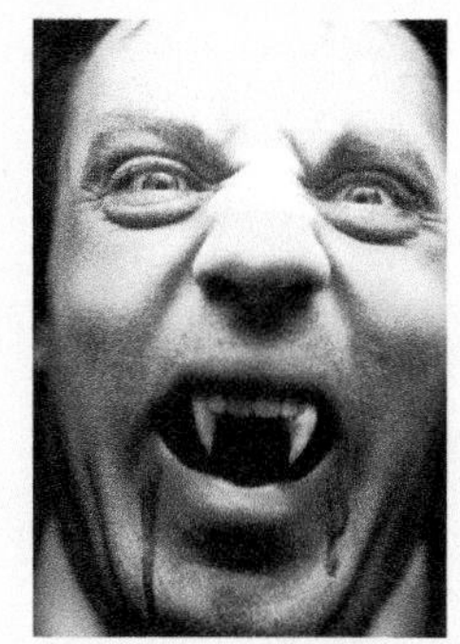

The evolution of the horror film demonstrates how **genre** conventions change. Old conventions become exhausted, and filmmakers search for new ones in their never-ending challenge to retain the interest of the audience. Horror films of the 1930s and 1940s portrayed the monster using an actor in (often brilliant) makeup, whereas contemporary films often use computer-based special effects to visualize the creatures. Moreover, horror films during their golden age tended to end on a very comforting note. The monster was destroyed, and the romantic couple reached safety unharmed. Horror often was left to the viewer's imagination in contrast with the graphic gore of modern films, which use contemporary effects technology to visualize the elaborate violence that is now basic in the genre. (In this respect, *The Blair Witch Project* [1999], *The Sixth Sense* [1999], and *The Others* [2001], all of which work through suggestion rather than graphic violence, are a return to the golden age of horror.)

By the 1970s and 1980s, in such films as *Halloween* and the never-ending *Nightmare on Elm Street* and *Friday the 13th series*, the monster became indestructible and undefeatable. These monsters—Freddy, Jason, Michael Myers of the *Halloween* films, and the aliens in the *Alien* series—remain alive at the end of each episode, and viewers know they will come back again to haunt and terrify. Contemporary horror films, therefore, are more disturbing and unsettling than horror was in previous decades, when narrative traditions insisted that normality be restored and secure at film's end. The monsters today are everywhere, and they cannot be defeated, a perception that the narrative design of contemporary horror emphasizes.

QUESTIONS

1. What is the topic?
   - **a.** horror films
   - **b.** why horror films are popular
   - **c.** the evolution of horror films
   - **d.** famous horror films
2. What do the major details describe?
   - **a.** a history of horror films
   - **b.** the differences between horror films of the past and present
   - **c.** famous monsters
   - **d.** the best horror movies ever made
3. What is the author's implied main idea? (What do the major details describe?)
   - **a.** Monsters in horror films are more frightening than ever before.
   - **b.** The evolution of horror films has changed these movies into something more disturbing and uncertain.
   - **c.** People want horror films to be scarier than they used to be.
   - **d.** The evolution of the horror film demonstrates how genre conventions change.

U-REVIEW 1

For each of the following sentences, write "T" if the statement is true or "F" if the statement is false. As you go over the answers with your team, discuss why the false statements are false.

1. ________ Implied main ideas are usually found at the beginning of a paragraph.

2. ________ Implied main ideas are found by looking for the idea most often repeated.

3. ________ An implied main idea is not stated and must be formed by the reader.

4. ________ To find the implied main idea, focus on the topic and major supporting details.

5. ________ A question to ask when finding the implied main idea is, "What are the major details telling me about the topic?"

RECOGNIZING STATED MAIN IDEAS AND IMPLIED MAIN IDEAS

How do you know when an author has stated the main idea or implied it? To help you become more adept at knowing the difference, study the following examples.

Read the following paragraph, and then answer the questions that follow. The major details have been underlined.

abstract (AB-strakt): art that does not show objects as they appear in reality; it emphasizes emotions and impressions.

> Cubism is a form of modern art that is **abstract** and uses geometric shapes and forms. This form of art was introduced by Pablo Picasso and Georges Braque in Paris between 1907 and 1914. Picasso was influenced by the African art that he viewed in the Palais de Trocadero in Paris. The "cubes" in his paintings often represent figures, suggest a scene, or emphasize an emotion. The construction of a cubist painting is something like cutting up a traditional painting into geometric sections, and then reassembling it onto a canvas. Many other artists also adopted this style of modern art, which had a significant influence on 20th century art and sculpture.

Topic: Cubism

Main idea: Cubism is a form of modern art that is abstract and uses geometric shapes and forms.

Notice that the first sentence introduces the topic and defines the term cubism. All of the other sentences tell you more about the topic, so it is the topic sentence. It is broad and general enough to include all of the details that follow. In paragraphs where the details describe a term, the definition is often the topic sentence. As you read the next paragraph, look for a general statement that summarizes or makes a point about the topic (the major details have been underlined).

> In New York City, Latino Americans and African Americans created a new style of music and dance that grew out of deejaying, called "hip hop." DJs created strong rhythms by moving a vinyl record back and forth on a turntable in a rhythmical beat. They also used microphones to accompany the beat with rhythmic rhymes, which became known as rapping. Rap developed in the street parties of the Bronx, and, by the late 1970s, rap gained media attention. It was popularized by rappers such as Kool Herc and The Furious Five. By the mid-1980s, rap music artists made social statements about poverty, violence, drugs, and sex. Hip hop is now a global culture, giving youth a voice to express their ideas and to challenge traditions and old ideas.

What is the topic?

....

Notice that the paragraph lacks a general statement that summarizes the details about the topic, hip hop. It begins with a major detail about how hip hop originated and moves to other details about how it grew to be a worldwide music style. Because no broad statement summarizes the topic or states an important general point about it, you must infer the main idea.

Which of these statements expresses the implied main idea?

a. Hip hop became a famous cultural style of music in the 1970s.
b. Hip hop was made popular by rappers.
c. Hip hop music grew out of deejaying techniques.
d. Hip hop began as a music and dance style that became a worldwide-culture.

To determine if a sentence is a major detail or a topic sentence, ask yourself, "Does this provide a specific fact or detail, or is it a general description of the major details?" If the sentence provides a specific fact or detail about the topic, it is either a major or a minor detail. A general description or a general point about most of the major details is the topic sentence, or stated main idea.

MyReadingLab

PRACTICE 4

Read the following paragraph, and underline the major details. Then, answer the questions that follow.

One of the world's most **prestigious** film festivals is the Cannes Film Festival, which is held every year in Cannes (pronounced "kan"), France. Each year, filmmakers from around the world submit their works to the judges at the festival, hoping to win a "golden palm" for the best film. Like the Oscars, the Cannes festival bestows awards in many different categories, such as Best Short Film, Best Director, and Best Student Film. For 13 days in May of each year, hundreds of films are shown. Many movie stars attend this famous event, taking time out to pose for photographers and reporters. Filmmakers hope that their films will not only win awards, but be sold to distributors who will market their films all over the world.

prestigious (pres-TEEJ-us): highly respected; honored

1. What is the topic?
   a. Cannes
   b. Cannes Film Festival
   c. filmmakers hoping to win awards
   d. filmmakers
2. What do most of the major details describe?
   a. how filmmakers win awards at Cannes
   b. what kinds of awards are given at Cannes
   c. why filmmakers go to Cannes
   d. what the Cannes Film Festival is
3. Is the main idea stated or implied?
   a. stated
   b. implied
4. Which of the following sentences best states the main idea (either stated in the paragraph or implied)?
   a. One of the world's most prestigious film festivals is the Cannes Film Festival, which is held every year in Cannes, France.
   b. Each year, filmmakers from around the world submit their works to the judges at the festival, hoping to win a "golden palm" for the best film.
   c. Filmmakers hope that their films will not only win awards, but be sold to distributors who will market their films all over the world.
   d. The Cannes Film Festival is attended by filmmakers and entertainers from all over the world.

MyReadingLab

PRACTICE 5

documentary: a film that attempts to document, or record, a real event or subject

Read the following paragraph, and underline the major details. Then, answer the questions that follow.

Two University of Central Florida film school students decided to make a horror movie in a **documentary** style. Daniel Myrick and Eduardo Sanchez used their credit cards to finance the $22,000 project. Three unknown actors played college students who became lost in a Maryland woods while seeking the legendary Blair Witch. The murderous Blair Witch, which the audience never does get to see, lurks in the woods at night. The suspense and terror that the film created made this an amazingly compelling movie. *The Blair Witch Project* captured much attention at the Sundance Film Festival in Utah. Later, it was bought for $1.1 million. It soon became an international blockbuster, racking up $250 million in sales, making it the most profitable independent film in American history.

1. What is the topic?
- **a.** the legend of the Blair Witch
- **b.** *The Blair Witch Project* movie
- **c.** Daniel Myrick and Eduardo Sanchez
- **d.** the most profitable independent film in American history

2. What do most of the major details describe?
- **a.** how frightening the movie was
- **b.** why the movie was so successful
- **c.** how two film school students made a successful movie
- **d.** who made the movie

3. Is the main idea stated or implied?
- **a.** stated
- **b.** implied

4. Which of the following sentences best states the main idea (either stated in the paragraph or implied)?
- **a.** Two University of Central Florida film school students decided to make a horror movie in a documentary style.
- **b.** Three unknown actors played college students who become lost in a Maryland woods while seeking the legendary Blair Witch.
- **c.** It soon became an international blockbuster, racking up $250 million in sales, making it the most profitable independent film in American history.
- **d.** Two college film school students made a very successful horror movie, *The Blair Witch Project*, on a small budget.

MyReadingLab

PRACTICE 6

Read the following paragraph, and underline the major details. Then, answer the questions that follow.

Vincent van Gogh (1853–1890)

At the age of 16, Vincent van Gogh (van-GO) worked for an art dealer and did sketching and watercolors as a hobby. Because he suffered from depression, he couldn't hold a job, so his brother Theo suggested that he take up a career in art. Van Gogh studied art and began painting in oils. Over the years, van Gogh fell deeper into mental illness and had hallucinations. During an argument with painter Paul Gauguin (go-GAN), he cut off part of his own ear. Van Gogh went into a mental hospital for treatment, and there he painted *The Starry Night.* Van Gogh began to receive recognition as a painter, but his success did not improve his mental condition. He committed suicide at the age of 37, leaving behind some of the most celebrated paintings in art history.

1. What is the topic?
   - **a.** Vincent van Gogh's art
   - **b.** how van Gogh lost his ear
   - **c.** van Gogh's mental illness
   - **d.** how van Gogh became an artist
2. What do most of the major details describe?
   - **a.** the life of van Gogh
   - **b.** the art of van Gogh
   - **c.** van Gogh's mental illness
   - **d.** why van Gogh was famous
3. Is the main idea stated or implied?
   - **a.** stated
   - **b.** implied
4. Which of the following sentences best states the main idea (either stated in the paragraph or implied)?
   - **a.** Throughout his life, painter Vincent van Gogh struggled with mental illness.
   - **b.** Because he suffered from depression, he couldn't hold a job, so his brother Theo suggested that he take up a career in art.
   - **c.** Van Gogh was the painter who created *The Starry Night.*
   - **d.** He committed suicide at the age of 37, leaving behind some of the most celebrated paintings in art history.

MyReadingLab

TEXTBOOK SELECTION 2

Read the following textbook selection, and underline the major details. Then, answer the questions that follow.

Frank Lloyd Wright remains one of the greatest American artists in any medium. His primary message stressed the relationship of architecture to its setting, a lesson that some modern architects seem to have forgotten. Wright's buildings appear to grow out of their environment.

One of his most inventive designs—the Kaufmann House, also known as "Falling Water," at Bear Run, Pennsylvania, built in 1936–1937—projects out over a waterfall with exciting, dramatic imagery. "Falling Water" erupts out of its natural rock site, and its beige concrete terraces blend tastefully with the colors of the surrounding stone. Wright has successfully blended two seemingly contrasting styles: the house stays a part of its environment, yet it has the rectangular design, which Wright usually opposed. He has taken those geometric boxes and made them harmonize with their natural surroundings. Wright's great asset and greatest fault was his insistence on using his own ideas. This meant he could work only with clients who would bend to his wishes. So, unlike many architects whose designs are influenced by the client, what Wright built remained Wright's, and Wright's only.

QUESTIONS

1. What is the topic?
   a. Falling Water
   b. Frank Lloyd Wright
   c. Frank Lloyd Wright's architectural designs
   d. architecture
2. What do most of the major details describe?
   a. Frank Lloyd Wright's life
   b. Frank Lloyd Wright's architectural style
   c. Falling Water
   d. how Frank Lloyd Wright became a famous architect
3. Is the main idea stated or implied?
   a. stated
   b. implied
4. Which of the following sentences best states the main idea (either stated in the paragraph or implied)?
   a. Frank Lloyd Wright remains one of the greatest American architects in any medium.
   b. Wright's buildings appear to grow out of their environment.
   c. One of his most inventive designs—the Kaufmann House, also known as "Falling Water," at Bear Run, Pennsylvania, built in 1936–1937—projects out over a waterfall with exciting, dramatic imagery.
   d. Wright has successfully blended two seemingly contrasting styles: the house stays a part of its context, yet it has the rectangular design, which Wright usually opposed.

OBJECTIVE 2

Identify the central point or thesis.

A **central point** is the main idea of a reading selection that is longer than one paragraph.

THE CENTRAL POINT

A **central point** is the main idea of a reading selection that is longer than one paragraph. A central point may also be called a **thesis statement** or a **central idea**. It's the most important point that the author makes about the topic. Like a main idea, the central point may be stated or implied. It is always a complete sentence and never a question. It usually names or refers to the topic and makes a broad, general point about it. To find the central point, first find the main idea of each paragraph. These will provide the main points the author is making in the essay as a whole. Sometimes the topic sentence of the first paragraph will also act as the central point of the entire reading selection. Read the following example paragraphs, and then see how they are broken down into their main ideas and central point.

> Reggae ("REG-gay") music started in Jamaica in the 1960s, and is characterized by its off-beat rhythms. It has its origins in rhythm and blues, jazz, blues, calypso, and other styles of music. Because of its themes of love, sexuality, social issues, and political issues, reggae soon became popular in other countries around the world. The word "reggae" comes from *regerege*, which means "rags" or "tattered clothing."
>
> The first reggae hit in America was American artist Johnny Nash's "Hold Me Tight" in 1968. The ever-popular British band the Beatles picked up on the reggae style and recorded their own song, "Ob-La-Di, Ob-La-Da." The most famous reggae band was The Wailers, featuring Bob Marley. Bob Marley became the most well-known reggae musician, earning 11 different awards, including a Grammy Lifetime Achievement Award, his name in the Rock and Roll Hall of Fame, and a star on the Hollywood Walk of Fame. In the United Kingdom, British rocker Eric Clapton recorded Bob Marley's song, "I Shot the Sheriff," which helped to bring reggae into popular music around the world.

Main idea of the first paragraph:
(implied) Reggae music started in Jamaica in the 1960s and soon became popular around the world.

Main idea of the second paragraph:
(implied) Notable musicians made reggae music popular worldwide.

Central point:
Jamaican reggae music owes its popularity to the musicians who made it famous worldwide.

MyReadingLab

PRACTICE 7

Read the following paragraphs, underline the major details, and then answer the questions that follow.

Creative individuals who enjoy art may become graphic designers. Using art materials or computers, they illustrate ideas or objects. Graphic designers create visual images for publications or Web sites. Their goal is to make an idea or product look appealing and interesting to their audience.

Industrial designers make cars, tools, appliances, entertainment systems, and other devices more beautiful and practical to use. They choose the shape, style, and feel of objects to make them look as good as they work. Industrial designers work with engineers to create products that will function well and attract buyers.

Interior designers bring the elements of furniture, lighting, décor, and space together in a pleasing and functional way. Interior designers create not only home environments but also public spaces such as stores, airports, restaurants, hotels, and office buildings. Interior designers usually specialize in one type of environment, such as residential or commercial space. Good design has a powerful impact on humans, affecting the way they think and feel in an environment.

1. What is the topic?
   - a. artists
   - b. designers
   - c. graphic designers
   - d. creative individuals
2. What is the main idea of the first paragraph?
   - a. Creative individuals who enjoy art may become graphic designers.
   - b. Using art materials or computers, they illustrate ideas or objects.
   - c. Graphic designers create visual images for publications or Web sites.
   - d. Their goal is to make an idea or product look appealing and interesting to their audience.
3. What is the main idea of the third paragraph?
   - a. Interior designers bring the elements of furniture, lighting, décor, and space together in a pleasing and functional way.
   - b. Interior designers create not only home environments but also public spaces such as stores, airports, restaurants, hotels, and office buildings.
   - c. Interior designers usually specialize in one type of environment, such as residential or commercial space.
   - d. Good design has a powerful impact on humans, affecting the way they think and feel in an environment.
4. What is the central point of the selection (either stated in the reading or implied)?
   - a. Creative individuals who enjoy art may become graphic designers.
   - b. Industrial designers make cars, tools, appliances, entertainment systems, and other devices more beautiful and practical to use.
   - c. Designers make images, objects, and living spaces more beautiful and functional.
   - d. Good design has a powerful impact on humans, affecting the way they think and feel in an environment.

MyReadingLab

PRACTICE 8

Read the following paragraphs, underline the major details, and then answer the questions that follow.

Each year, the members of the National Academy of Recording Arts and Sciences, also known as the Recording Academy, recognize individuals with an award known as "the Grammy." Throughout the year, record companies and members of the Recording Academy suggest names of people who they think should be considered for an award. There are more than 100 categories of awards given to musicians, producers, engineers, and recording professionals. The members of the academy select the winners based on their artistic achievement and excellence in the recording industry. The winners are not based on record sales or chart position in the top 100 songs of the year.

The Recording Academy originated in 1957 for the purpose of improving culture through music. There are now 12 chapters throughout the United States with thousands of members. To be considered for membership in the academy, an applicant must be credited on at least six tracks of any album. Applicants must also be recommended by two other voting members of the academy.

1. **What is the topic of the first paragraph?**
- **a.** the National Academy of Recording Arts and Sciences
- **b.** how to win a Grammy award
- **c.** the Grammy award
- **d.** the Recording Academy

2. **What do most of the major details in the first paragraph describe?**
- **a.** why Grammy awards are given
- **b.** who wins the Grammy awards
- **c.** what the Grammy award is
- **d.** where the Grammy award is given

3. **Is the central point of the entire reading stated or implied?**
- **a.** stated
- **b.** implied

4. **What is the central point of the selection (either stated in the reading or implied)?**
- **a.** The National Academy of Recording Arts monitors the quality of music.
- **b.** To be considered for membership in the academy, an applicant must be credited on at least six tracks of any album.
- **c.** Throughout the year, record companies and members of the Recording Academy suggest names of people who they think should be considered for an award.
- **d.** Each year, the members of the National Academy of Recording Arts and Sciences, also known as the Recording Academy, recognize individuals who have achieved the admiration of their peers and give them a very special award known as "the Grammy."

MyReadingLab

PRACTICE 9

Read the following paragraphs, underline the major details, and then answer the questions that follow.

In the valley of the Vezere River in France, just outside of a small town, a group of children played among the caves. No one knew about the amazing treasures hidden in the Lascaux (lahs-KOE) caves until the children explored them in 1940 and discovered cave paintings on the walls. Archaeologists determined the ancient paintings were made in 14,000–16,000 B.C. The caves were sealed in 1963 to prevent damage to the paintings from the atmosphere. Visitors to the caves today are shown exact copies in a nearby quarry.

The images in the original paintings show running herds of bulls, horses, and deer. The paintings are up to 12 feet high, and the artists who made them demonstrate their artistic ability to show the animals in motion. The paintings were done in a 30- by 100-foot mural over a long period of time by many artists. It is interesting to imagine how these artists painted them with simple materials, working under the light of a flickering torch.

The paintings tell us more about these artists than their admiration for the power and beauty of animals. The magnificent cave paintings at Lascaux reveal the mind and soul of these people, who not only possessed artistic skill but the desire to create an image that would communicate the sights and sounds of the thundering herds.

1. What is the topic?

- **a.** the cave paintings at Lascaux
- **b.** ancient artists
- **c.** Lascaux, France
- **d.** animal paintings

2. What is the topic sentence of the first paragraph?

- **a.** In the valley of the Vezere River in France, just outside of a small town, a group of children played among the caves.
- **b.** No one knew about the amazing treasures hidden in the Lascaux (lahs-KOE) caves until the children explored them in 1940 and discovered cave paintings on the walls.
- **c.** Archaeologists determined the ancient paintings were made in 14,000–16,000 B.C.
- **d.** The caves were sealed in 1963 to prevent damage to the paintings from the atmosphere.

3. What is the topic sentence of the second paragraph?

- **a.** The images in the original paintings show running herds of bulls, horses, and deer.
- **b.** The paintings are up to 12 feet high, and the artists who made them demonstrate their artistic ability to show the animals in motion.
- **c.** The paintings were done in a 30- by 100-foot mural over a long period of time by many artists.
- **d.** It is interesting to imagine how these artists painted them with simple materials, working under the light of a flickering torch.

Continued...

MyReadingLab

PRACTICE 9

...continued

4. What is the central point of the selection?

a. In 1940, some children discovered ancient paintings on the walls of the caves of Lascaux, France.

b. The paintings on the walls of the caves in Lascaux, France, were done by many artists more than 16,000 to 18,000 years ago.

c. The magnificent cave paintings at Lascaux reveal the mind and soul of these people, who not only possessed artistic skill but the desire to create an image that would communicate the sights and sounds of the thundering herds.

d. The paintings in the caves at Lascaux, France, are still on the walls and sealed from the damaging atmosphere.

MyReadingLab

TEXTBOOK SELECTION 3

Read the following selection, underline the topic sentences and major details, and then answer the questions that follow.

Pyramid building (circa 2,700 B.C.) produced the most remarkable structures of Egyptian civilization. Egypt's pyramids, the oldest existing buildings in the world, also rank among the world's largest structures. The largest stands taller than a 40-story building and covers an area greater than that of 10 football fields. More than 80 pyramids still exist, and their once smooth limestone surfaces hide secret passageways and rooms. The pyramids of ancient Egypt served a vital purpose: to protect the pharaohs' bodies after death. Each pyramid originally held not only a pharaoh's preserved body but also all the goods he would need in his life after death.

complex (KOM-plex): a group of structures that have a common purpose

Egyptian pyramids typically contained a temple that was constructed a short distance from the pyramid and connected by a causeway. The most elaborate example of the temple appears at Giza (GEE-za), with the pyramids of three kings built close together. Beginning in the 10th century, the entire Giza **complex** served as a source of building materials for the construction of Cairo. As a result, all three pyramids were stripped of their original smooth outer facing of limestone.

The three pyramids at Giza have a carefully planned layout. Each stands along the north–south line of longitude, with the faces of the pyramids pointing directly north, south, east, and west. The larger two rise neatly along a southwest diagonal, with the third slightly offset and smaller. Scholars assume that this peculiar layout was a deliberate choice made by the architects, but the reasons for such a choice (if one existed) remain mysterious.

QUESTIONS

1. What is the topic?
   - **a.** pyramids
   - **b.** the pyramids of Giza
   - **c.** Egyptian pyramids
   - **d.** Egyptian architecture
2. What is the topic sentence of the second paragraph?
   - **a.** Egyptian pyramids typically contained a temple that was constructed a short distance from the pyramid and connected by a causeway.
   - **b.** The most elaborate example of the temple appears at Giza (GEE-za), with the pyramids of three kings built close together.
   - **c.** Beginning in the 10th century, the entire Giza complex served as a source of building materials for the construction of Cairo.
   - **d.** As a result, all three pyramids were stripped of their original smooth outer facing of limestone.

Continued...

MyReadingLab

TEXTBOOK SELECTION 3

...continued

3. What is the topic sentence of the third paragraph?

a. The three pyramids at Giza have a carefully planned layout.

b. Each stands along the north–south line of longitude, with the faces of the pyramids pointing directly north, south, east, and west.

c. The larger two rise neatly along a southwest diagonal, with the third slightly offset and smaller.

d. Scholars assume that this peculiar layout was a deliberate choice made by the architects, but the reasons for such a choice (if one existed) remain mysterious.

4. What is the central point of the selection?

a. Pyramid building (circa 2,700 B.C.) produced the most remarkable structures of Egyptian civilization.

b. Egypt's pyramids, the oldest existing buildings in the world, also rank among the world's largest structures.

c. The three pyramids at Giza have a carefully planned layout.

d. Egyptian pyramids typically contained a temple that was constructed a short distance from the pyramid and connected by a causeway.

U-REVIEW 2

Answer the following questions, and then check your answers with another student.

1. What is an implied main idea?

....

....

2. What do you focus on when trying to figure out the implied main idea?

....

....

3. What question should you ask yourself to find the implied main idea?

....

....

4. What is a central point?

....

....

5. What should you do first to find the central point?

....

....

MyReadingLab

Reading 1
VOCABULARY PRACTICE

"My Best Role Ever!" by Marcia Gay Harden

The following vocabulary words are from the article "My Best Role Ever!" With a partner or in a team, choose the correct meanings of the underlined words in the following sentences. Use context clues (LEADS), word part clues, and parts of speech to help you figure out the meanings.

1. While waiting for the nurse to insert the IV into my arm, I steeled (STEEL'd) myself for the pain.
a. rededicated
b. encouraged
c. resisted
d. braced

2. Our high school history teacher would say it is irony (EYE-ron-ee) that Juan graduated from college with a degree in history since he always skipped his high school history class.
a. a bad situation
b. the opposite of what you expect
c. an incomplete sentence
d. good advice

3. The date of the historic home that had just been renovated was listed as "circa (SIR-ka) 1750."
a. around
b. over
c. since
d. late

4. When Juan saw how upset his wife was over denting the car, his anger dissipated (DIS-i-pay-ted).
a. increased
b. enraged
c. disappeared
d. tentative

5. When she stays at her brother's house, Julia sleeps on a small pallet (PAL-et) on the floor.
a. chair
b. pillow
c. mattress
d. footstool

6. I was dumbfounded (dum-FOUND-ed) when I discovered that I had the winning lottery ticket to the $100,000 jackpot.
a. knocked down
b. speechless
c. distressed
d. devastated

7. Knowing there were few prospects (PRAH-spekts) for acting jobs in a small town like Garland, Nebraska, Giovanni decided to move to Los Angeles.
a. ideas
b. restitution
c. agents who hire actors
d. opportunities

8. To soothe the frightened, injured rabbit, Jenny spoke to it in dulcet (DULL-sit) tones and stroked its fur.
a. soft and gentle
b. careful
c. sad
d. loud

Continued...

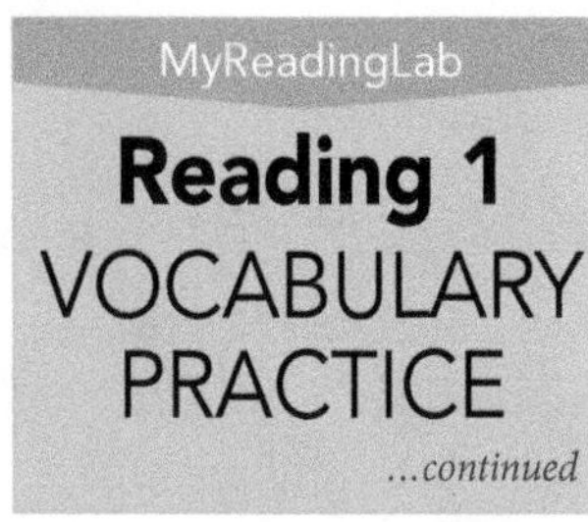

9. Sandra took some medicine and laid down on the sofa for an hour to <u>alleviate</u> (a-LEEV-ee-ate) her migraine headache.
   - a. to strengthen
   - b. undermine
   - c. radiate
   - d. to lessen the severity of

10. Even though she was tired, Heather <u>reluctantly</u> (re-LUCK-tant-lee) agreed to work an extra shift at the restaurant to cover for her friend.
    - a. happily
    - b. eagerly
    - c. unwillingly
    - d. realistically

MyReadingLab

Reading 1 PREVIEW

1. Have you ever performed on stage before an audience? What did you do? How did you feel about the experience?
2. Would you ever consider acting as a career? Why or why not?

Directions: As you read this article, practice the four-step reading process. Preview the article, and then write on the following lines one or two questions that you would hope to have answered.

MyReadingLab

Reading 1

As you read, answer the questions in the margins to check your comprehension.

"My Best Role Ever!"

by Marcia Gay Harden

Academy Award winner Marcia Gay Harden says that acting is really about connecting with people and making the right choices. In her story, she describes the time when her big chance finally came along, and she had to make a difficult choice. Should she turn down the biggest break in her career or break her promise to a child?

1 Look up "struggling young actress" in the dictionary, and you might see a picture of me, <u>circa</u> 1982. I rushed to open casting calls in between waiting tables and always worried about how to pay the rent. I was based in Washington, D.C., where I was waiting to get my Screen Actors Guild Union card. When I did, then I'd make the big move to New York City.

2 It was an uncertain time in my life, but one thing I was certain of: acting meant everything to me. From the first part I'd played in high school, there was a quality about acting that made me feel in touch with something big and mysterious and meaningful. It may sound funny, but when I was playing a role I connected with, I got the feeling that God was using me for something good. I felt like I was doing something I was truly meant to do. Of course, most days found me hustling through a pair of swinging restaurant doors with a stack of hot plates on my arm. And that was fine too. I was paying my dues, doing what all young actors did.

3 One day, as I was finishing up a long hard lunch shift, I found myself in a particularly upbeat mood. The famous director, Oliver Stone, was coming to town to do a casting call for his upcoming movie *Born on the Fourth of July*, the story of paralyzed Vietnam War veteran Ron Kovic. The call was just for crowd-scene extras, but I didn't care. The way I figured, Oliver Stone would notice me, pull me out of the lineup, and, lo and behold, I'd have my big break.

What was Marcia looking forward to doing?

4 Two women came in, sat down at a table in my section and smiled like they knew me when I came up to take their order. And they did. "We saw your performance in a play last week. You were wonderful! We'd like to offer you a job." I asked what the part was.

5 "Probably not what you think," the other woman said. "Snow White."

6 "Snow White? Where's the production?" I asked.

7 "Georgetown University Hospital," the first woman said. "We're from the Make-A-Wish Foundation. A seven-year-old girl named Bonnie is dying of pediatric cancer. She doesn't have much more than a month to live. Our foundation grants wishes to terminally ill children, and Bonnie's wish is to meet Snow White." I promised them I'd be available the day they needed me. I'm not a big fan of irony. So you can imagine how I felt two days later when one of the Make-A-Wish ladies called to give me the date for my appearance at the hospital. You guessed it. The same date as my big casting call.

8 "Couldn't you make it another day?" I asked, panicked.

9 "I'm sorry," she said. "Bonnie's running out of time."

10 I hung up and called the casting agency in charge of Oliver Stone's visit, asking if I could audition on another day.

What problem is Marcia facing at this point?

11 "Oliver's only in town for that day," the casting director told me. "Marcia, this is a great opportunity. Whatever conflicts you have on that date, I'd advise you to find a way to reschedule them."

12 I didn't sleep a wink that night. I had to make a decision. What was right for me? Success had to be priority number one. It was as simple as that. They could get another Snow White. I might not get another prospect like this. I'd call first thing in the morning and cancel the hospital job. Yet it just didn't feel right. I'd promised to make a sick little girl's wish come true. How could I put ambition above that?

13 The next day I called the agency and told them I couldn't make the casting call. "I have another engagement I can't back out of," I said reluctantly.

14 By the day of my performance as Snow White, I was as ready as I'd ever

Continued...

MyReadingLab

Reading 1

...continued

been for any role I'd played in my life. The only problem was I kept bursting into tears. I was positive the casting call would've been my big break—my one chance to make it. And I was letting it go.

How was Marcia feeling about her situation?

15 I must have been a curious sight as I made my way to Georgetown University Hospital. How many times do you see a weeping Snow White at the wheel of a yellow convertible VW Bug? On top of everything else, traffic was horrible. I got to the hospital late and flew in—stopping only to make one last call to the casting director to beg once more for a chance to reschedule. "No, Marcia," the agent said. "This is it."

16 I hung up, asked for directions at the information desk, and went running for the elevator. Down at the end of a long hallway, a woman and a girl were standing outside the hospital room: Bonnie's mother and 12-year-old sister. Bonnie's mom recognized me and greeted me with a big hug. Then she handed me a bag with some toys in it. "If you don't mind, I thought it would be nice if Snow White gave Bonnie some presents. She's having a bad day, but she's looking forward to this so much."

17 "Sure," I said, taking the bag of toys. Then I took a deep breath and steeled myself—the way I do before every performance—and walked into the room. What I found stopped me cold. All my qualms about whether this was the right thing to do dissipated. I'd been prepared to meet a sick girl. But the girl sitting on a pallet on the floor was so small and thin. I knew Bonnie was seven, but she barely looked five. Bonnie raised her eyes and stared at me. Her pale face lit up like a candy store. "Snow White!" she cried.

Why was Marcia shocked when she entered Bonnie's room?

18 I stood there dumbfounded. *Come on*, something inside me said, *pull it together. You know what you're here for.* Then something clicked. I wasn't just a struggling actress playing Snow White. I ***was*** Snow White.

19 "Hello, Bonnie!" I said in dulcet tones, "I'm so glad to see you! I'm so sorry that Grumpy and Sneezy and Doc (I named all seven) weren't able to make it!" We talked for a while. I told her all about the handsome prince and gave her the gifts.

20 "Snow White?" Bonnie said, grabbing my hand.

21 "Yes, Bonnie?"

22 "When I die, will the prince kiss me and then I'll wake up again?"

23 The room fell silent. How do you answer a child's question like that? It had never struck me that Bonnie wanted to meet Snow White to answer a life-after-death question. What could I say to this brave, beautiful, honest girl? I closed my eyes for a second and tried to imagine what Bonnie must be feeling. How lonely it must be to be this young and this sick.

24 "No, Bonnie," I said, "it's even better. When you go to heaven, God will kiss you and then you'll wake up again."

25 You remember what I was saying earlier about how the real mystery of acting came when I was playing a role I knew I was meant to play? Well, at that moment in that hospital room with Bonnie, I got that feeling. I got it like I had never gotten it before in my life. I knew that I was exactly where I was meant to be, playing exactly the role I was meant to play.

What did Marcia learn from Bonnie?

26 Bonnie died just a week later. Was I able to alleviate her passing? Hopefully, I was part of that plan. And Bonnie was definitely part of the plan for me. She taught me that acting is about connecting, not about

union cards and red carpets and ambition. Eventually I got my SAG card and moved up to New York City. After a couple more years of acting classes, waitressing, living in shoddy apartments, and all the rest of that stuff, I got my big break. Two directors, Joel and Ethan Coen, cast me in their movie *Miller's Crossing*. I was on my way.

27 Later, I received an Academy Award for my work as the painter Jackson Pollock's wife, Lee Krasner, in Ed Harris's film *Pollock*. I also played the mother of Chris McCandless in the film *Into the Wild*. I had wonderful roles in wonderful movies. Roles that, while I was playing them, made me *know* I was where I was meant to be, and that all the struggle and uncertainty was for a reason. It's a wonderful feeling.

1,485 words divided by .... minutes = ... words per minute

MyReadingLab

Reading 1
REVIEW

It is a good habit to summarize everything you read to strengthen your comprehension.

Directions: On the following lines, write a two- or three-sentence summary of the article "My Best Role Ever!" In your own words, describe what the article was about and why the author wrote it.

....

....

....

MyReadingLab

Reading 1
COMPREHENSION QUESTIONS

The following questions will help you to recall the main idea and the details of "My Best Role Ever!" Review any parts of the article that you need to find the correct answers.

1. What is the topic of this article?
   a. the best role an actress ever played
   b. Bonnie
   c. a tough decision actress Marcia Gay Harden had to make
   d. an actress's career

MAIN IDEA

2. What is the central point (main idea) of the entire article?
   a. An actress played Snow White for a dying girl.
   b. Marcia Gay Harden gave up an opportunity for a role in a movie to play Snow White to a dying girl.
   c. Marcia Gay Harden worked hard to become an actress and finally got her chance.
   d. Marcia Gay Harden worked her way up to become an Academy Award–winning actress.

Continued...

MyReadingLab

Reading 1 COMPREHENSION QUESTIONS

...continued

3. **At the time of the story, why was Marcia waiting to move from Washington, D.C., to New York City?**
   a. because there were no acting jobs available in New York City
   b. because she had family in Washington, D.C.
   c. because she was waiting to get her Screen Actors Guild Union card
   d. because she didn't have enough money to move to New York City

4. **Why was Marcia crying when she drove to the hospital to see Bonnie?**
   a. because she wished that she had not agreed to play the part of Snow-White
   b. because she feared that she would disappoint Bonnie
   c. because she felt she had given up her only chance to get a part in a movie with a famous director
   d. because she had lied to Bonnie's mother about wanting to play Snow-White

DRAWING CONCLUSIONS

5. **Why did Marcia believe that she was meant to be an actress?**
   a. After she performed in a high school play, her teacher and director told her she was meant to be on the stage.
   b. She always studied her part and was well prepared for her roles.
   c. Her parents had encouraged her to become an actress.
   d. She felt something special when she was playing a part that she knew she was meant to play.

6. **What did Marcia mean when she said, "Then something clicked. I wasn't just a struggling actress playing Snow White. I was Snow White"?**
   a. She believed that she was the real Snow White.
   b. To Bonnie, she was the real Snow White and knew she had to become that person for her.
   c. She wanted to be like the Snow White in the fairy tale.
   d. She turned into Snow White.

IMPLIED MAIN IDEAS

7. **The implied main idea of paragraph 3 is:**
   a. Marcia was finishing up her shift as a waitress.
   b. Director Oliver Stone was coming to town for a casting call for a new movie.
   c. Marcia was excited because she believed she would get her big break at a casting call with director Oliver Stone.
   d. Marcia intended to be a crowd scene extra in a movie.

8. **The implied main idea of paragraph 23 is:**
   a. Bonnie had a serious question for Snow White.
   b. Marcia realized that Bonnie wanted to know what would happen if she died.
   c. Marcia tried to imagine what Bonnie was going through.
   d. Bonnie proved herself a brave and honest girl.

VOCABULARY IN CONTEXT

9. **Identify the meaning of the underlined word in the following sentence: After a couple more years of acting classes, waitressing, living in <u>shoddy</u> apartments, and all the rest of that stuff, I got my big break.**
   a. deluxe
   b. shabby
   c. drafty
   d. expensive

10. Identify the meaning of the underlined word in the following sentence: All my qualms about whether this was the right thing to do dissipated.
   a. doubts
   b. potential
   c. suspicions
   d. intentions

MyReadingLab

Reading 1 VOCABULARY PRACTICE

Use the vocabulary words from the Word Bank to complete the following sentences. Write the words into the blanks provided.

WORD BANK

irony	circa	steeled	dissipated	pallet
dumbfounded	prospect	dulcet	alleviate	reluctantly

1. By finishing his degree, Sean felt he would have a better .... for getting the job he wanted.
2. Darla's hopes for getting a full scholarship .... when she saw her failing grade in algebra.
3. When my best friend confessed that she had secretly been dating my boyfriend, I was totally ....
4. The new mother held her baby snugly and, singing in a(n) .... voice, rocked him to sleep.
5. It was just .... that Wanda, who never really liked high school, became a high school teacher.
6. The ancient ruins were so old that no one had an exact date of their construction, but archaeologists believe they were built .... 100 B.C.
7. I .... agreed to babysit for my older sister's kids because I knew they could be difficult to handle.
8. Whenever we go to the mountains to camp, I usually sleep on a(n) .... made from a pillowcase stuffed with pine needles.
9. Sonia tried to .... her aunt's loneliness by visiting her at least once every week.
10. Jenny .... herself to face the possibility that she might not have gotten a part in the play.

MyReadingLab

Reading 1 QUESTIONS FOR WRITING AND DISCUSSION

Review any parts of the article you need to answer the following questions.

1. What had led Marcia to believe that she was meant to be an actress?

2. Why do you think Marcia decided to go through with her decision to play Snow White?

3. Describe a time when you had to give up something you wanted to do in order to do something for someone else. How did you feel about it afterward?

4. Like many successful people, Marcia had "paid her dues" by working as a waitress for more than two years while trying to achieve success. Do you feel there is such a thing as an "overnight sensation" (meaning someone becomes instantly famous without first having to suffer disappointment and failure)? Why or why not?

5. Describe a time when you had to speak or perform in front of a crowd. What did you do? Were you nervous? Describe what happened.

Reading 1 VOCABULARY PRACTICE—DRAWING WORD GAME

Get together in groups of four or five people.

1.

Each group should write the following vocabulary words on 10 slips of paper. Fold them in half, and put them into an envelope or container. Mix them well.

irony	**circa**
steeled	**dissipated**
pallet	**dumbfounded**
prospect	**dulcet**
alleviate	**reluctantly**

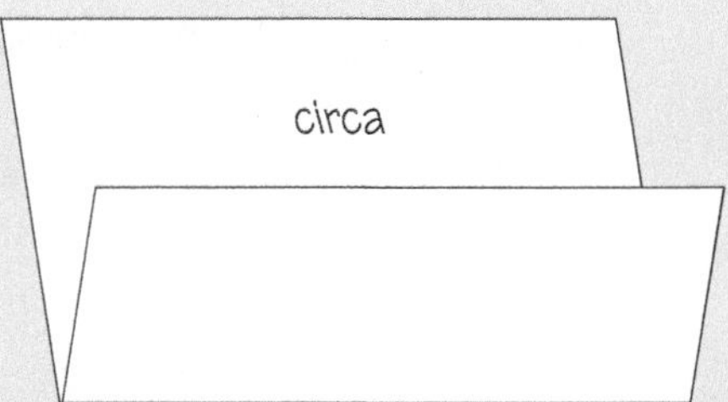

2.

Form two teams of partners. Decide which team will go first.

3.

One partner on the first team will take one of the slips (do not show it to anyone) and draw a picture on a piece of paper to represent the idea or a clue for the word. The artist may include words on the drawing, but no form of the word, definitions, or word clues to the definition may be used.

4.

The artist will then show the drawing to his or her partner, who will have one minute to guess the word. The other team will keep time and keep score.

5.

If the partner correctly names the word, the team receives one point. If the answer is incorrect or time runs out, no points are given. Only three guesses are allowed. Players are allowed to look at the word list when answering.

6.

When all the words have been drawn, the team with the most points wins.

7.

The play goes to the second team and one partner will draw the word while the first team keeps time and score. Each member of each team will take turns drawing.

MyReadingLab

Reading 2
VOCABULARY PREVIEW

"From Sketch to Screen: Tim Burton"

The following vocabulary words are from the article "From Sketch to Screen: Tim Burton." With a partner or in a team, choose the correct meanings of the underlined words in the following sentences. Use context clues (LEADS), word part clues, and parts of speech to help you figure out the meanings.

1. One of Tasha's best attributes (AT-trib-yoots) is that she always thinks positively in every situation.
   a. reasons
   b. causes
   c. characteristics
   d. goals
2. Most parents have unconditional (un-con-DISH-on-al) love for their children. They will love them no matter what offenses their children commit.
   a. without pity
   b. guaranteed
   c. unable to measure
   d. understanding
3. Animators will often use maquettes (ma-KETS) to draw from when creating images for a movie.
   a. live models
   b. storyboards
   c. life-sized sculptures
   d. small models
4. Julia uses an economy (ee-CON-nom-ee) of lines when she draws, but you can still tell what the image represents.
   a. a great deal
   b. thickened
   c. unimportant
   d. less of something
5. Crystal likes to create her own animation (an-i-MAY-shun) videos featuring funny characters.
   a. photos
   b. moving characters
   c. slides with sound
   d. picture
6. The students in my multi-media class all collaborated (ko-LAB-or-ated) on an animated film about penguins.
   a. consulted
   b. contributed
   c. worked together
   d. studied

7. Artists must be willing to do some painstaking (PAINS-take-ing) work when producing an animated film.
   a. painful
   b. carefully detailed
   c. capturing
   d. unavoidable

8. Artists' sketches translate (TRANS-late) to realistic, three-dimensional characters in the animation.
   a. transform
   b. change language
   c. improve
   d. regulate

9. The 1933 movie *King Kong* was filmed using stop-motion animation (stop motion an-i-MAY-shun) by photographing the ape's figure one frame at a time.
   a. a video recording
   b. a film technique for animating figures
   c. a photograph
   d. a story board

10. This technique has never been replicated (REP-li-cay-ted) by any other artist because it is too difficult to copy.
    a. attempted
    b. reproduced
    c. stimulated
    d. characterized

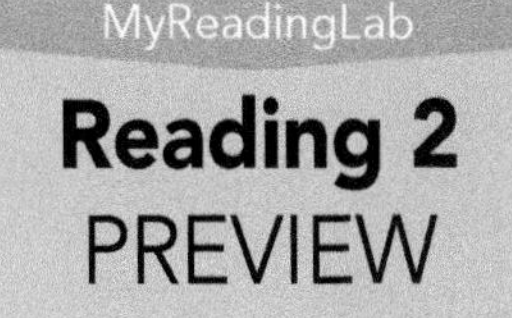

1. What were some of your favorite cartoons or animated films as a child?
2. What creative activities do you enjoy doing?

Directions: As you read this story, practice the four-step reading process. Preview the article, and then write on the following lines one or two questions that you would hope to have answered.

MyReadingLab

Reading 2

As you read, answer the questions in the margins to check your comprehension.

"From Sketch to Screen: Tim Burton"

Tim Burton's fantastical films start with his own drawings. He is an artist, filmmaker, and director of many award-winning movies, such as *Frankenweenie, The Nightmare Before Christmas*, the *Batman movies, Sleepy Hollow, Planet of the Apes, Charlie and the Chocolate Factory, Alice in Wonderland*, and many others.

1 Drawing has always been an important part of Burton's life, even in high school. He grew up in Burbank, California, not far from the movie studios that would eventually launch his career. A shy teenager, young Tim spent his time reading the horror stories of Edgar Allan Poe, watching classic horror films, and drawing. He didn't think he was a particularly good artist, but his art teacher encouraged him to keep sketching.

From Dorms to Disney

2 Burton attended the California Institute of the Arts, where he studied animation. He learned all aspects of making a film, from designing characters to setting up the perfect shot. These skills landed him a dream job as an animator and storyboard artist at Walt Disney Studios. At Disney, Burton met fellow animator Rick Heinrichs. They decided to work together.

3 "I'd always been a fan of Tim's own work," Rick Heinrichs told Scholastic Art. "I liked how his characters were drawn with an economy of line. I wanted to see them three-dimensional. I took it upon myself to make sculptures of his work." In 1982, an executive at Disney gave them $60,000 to make a short stop-motion animation film called *Vincent*. The two artists have since collaborated on Burton's feature films, *The Nightmare Before Christmas* (1993) and *Frankenweenie* (2012).

How did Tim Burton learn to make animated movies?

4 On a movie set, the director never works alone. An entire team of art directors, production designers, costumers, and artists collaborate to bring the director's vision to life. And, in the case of Tim Burton's new movie, *Frankenweenie*, it took nearly 30 years to get it right!

It Starts with an Idea

5 In the early 1980s, Burton was thinking about two things—his childhood dog and his love of classic horror movies like the *Frankenstein* movies. Based on the novel by Mary Shelley, *Frankenstein* is about a scientist who brings a man back from the dead. Burton thought of combining the two ideas—casting the family dog in the role of the creature that is brought back to life.

6 "The relationship you have with a pet is unconditional," Burton told *Scholastic Art*. "And because animals usually don't live as long, it's the first death that you...that I experienced. That is very powerful." He sketched a series of drawings of a boy named Victor and his dog, Sparky, who is

brought back to life. In the sketches, Sparky's squat, round body and long snout are exaggerated. He shares many of the scary attributes of his horror-movie inspiration, such as neck bolts and stitches, but he still has a comical look.

Sparky: Take One

7 In 1984, Burton created a live-action short film about Victor and Sparky. In the original *Frankenweenie*, the production team cast a real dog in the role of Sparky. The newest version of the film uses puppets and stop-motion animation.

Puppet Building 101

What was Tim Burton's inspiration for the movie *Frankenweenie*?

8 Though Burton doesn't make the puppets himself, he oversees their production. Designers create maquettes, or small sculptures, of the characters based on Burton's drawings. Constructing these miniatures is painstaking work. They serve as a reference to the artists who create and maintain the puppets.

It's Alive!

9 The puppet Sparky shares many characteristics with Burton's drawings, such as the small forelegs and droopy nose. The line work and textures on the drawing, including the dark scribbles around the eyes and stitches on the body, also translate to the puppet.

10 Even the drawing style of the original sketches is replicated in the finished movie still from *Frankenweenie*. The dark tone and shadows in the film are a reflection of Burton's use of shading in his drawings. In addition, the movie is in black and white, in keeping with the color scheme of his original art.

11 How does Burton feel about seeing his drawings come to life? "You're seeing not just me, but the hands of many artists," he says. "That's the cool thing about it—you feel the original drawing and all the other steps of the artists along the way.

Q&A with Tim Burton

How are Tim Burton's characters brought to life in movies?

12 *Scholastic Art* asked Tim Burton about his drawings, his movies, and what life was like for him in high school.

13 **Scholastic Art: Can you talk about the art teachers who inspired you?**

Tim Burton: I had a great teacher in junior high. There was another in high school who recognized each individual for who they were. She'd look at what kids liked to do and let them explore. If I hadn't had that, I would've thought: "I can't draw. I'm not good at this." It's important to have teachers who inspire you to keep at it.

14 **SA: Have you always drawn in the same style, with loose, expressive lines?**

TB: No, I tried everything. One day I was sketching at a farmer's market. I was very frustrated about my inability to draw accurately. Then I remembered one of my teachers saying, "Don't worry about how you *should* draw it. Just draw it the way you see it." And in that moment, I thought,

Continued...

MyReadingLab
Reading 2
...continued

"Well, that's it. I don't care how good or bad I am. This is how I do it, and that's it."

15 **SA: Many of your characters are outsiders. Is that how you see yourself?**

TB: Yeah. That's where *Edward Scissorhands* came from. I think most kids experience it. In my new movie, *Frankenweenie*, all the kids are weird. That's the truth of the matter. You feel like you're the only weirdo in class, when in fact that's pretty much how everybody feels.

16 **SA: Which artists influenced you the most?**

TB: It's like movies—there are so many inspirations. I remember the first time I saw **Van Gogh's** paintings in person, the landscapes. They blew me away. And **Matisse**. When you see the work of certain artists for real, it's mind-blowing. My studio is where [British book illustrator] **Arthur Rackham** once lived and worked. I'm lucky to have certain key things that inspire me.

17 **SA: Have you faced any setbacks?**

TB: Oh, yeah. For many years, I thought, "I'm not that good at animation. Maybe I'll try illustrating children's books." But that door closed. It's never a smooth path. Many of my projects are 10 years in the making.

18 **SA:** Do you have advice for aspiring young artists or filmmakers?

TB: It's best just to have passion. If your passion turns into something that somebody else likes and wants, great. But if it doesn't, at least you have it. Go with your instincts. If you're sitting in class and you want to be a filmmaker, go make a film. You can do it. The tools are there.

999 words divided by ________ minutes = ________ words per minute

MyReadingLab

Reading 2
REVIEW

Summarizing after you read will help you to understand the author's purpose and the main idea.

Directions: On the following lines, write a two- or three-sentence summary of the article, "From Sketch to Screen: Tim Burton." In your own words, describe what the article was about and why the author wrote it.

MyReadingLab

Reading 2
COMPREHEN-SION QUESTIONS

The following questions will help you recall the main idea and details of "From Sketch to Screen: Tim Burton." Read any parts of the article that you need to find the correct answers.

MAIN IDEA

1. What is the central point of this article?
   a. Drawing has always been an important part of Burton's life, even in high school.
   b. Because of Tim Burton's artistic passion and creativity, he has a successful career as an artist, animator, and filmmaker.
   c. A whole team of artists, animators, and filmmakers must collaborate to produce one animated feature movie.
   d. You should follow your passion and be true to your individual, unique style instead of copying others.
2. What is the stated main idea of paragraph 2?
   a. Burton attended the California Institute of the Arts, where he studied animation.
   b. He learned all aspects of making a film, from designing characters to setting up the perfect shot.
   c. These skills landed him a dream job as an animator and storyboard artist at Walt Disney Studios.
   d. At Disney, Burton met fellow animator Rick Heinrichs.
3. What is the implied main idea of paragraph 5?
   a. In the early 1980s, Burton was thinking about two things—his child-hood dog and his love of classic horror movies like the *Frankenstein* movies.
   b. *Frankenstein* is about a scientist who brings a man back from the dead.
   c. Burton recreated *Frankenstein* by casting his dog in the role of the creature that is brought back to life.
   d. *Frankenweenie* is an animated feature about a dog that is brought back to life.

Continued...

MyReadingLab

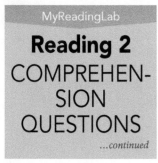

Reading 2
COMPREHEN-SION QUESTIONS
...continued

4. How was Tim Burton able to get hired as an animator for Walt Disney Studios?
- **a.** He was highly recommended by his high school art teachers.
- **b.** He had an impressive portfolio of his artistic work.
- **c.** One of his parents worked for Disney and got him the job.
- **d.** He studied animation at the California Institute of the Arts.

SUPPORTING DETAILS

5. How was Rick Heinrichs involved in Tim Burton's career?
- **a.** He drew all the sketches for several of Burton's movies.
- **b.** He began by making sculptures from Burton's drawings and collaborated on several of his films.
- **c.** He was the producer and director for many of Tim Burton's films.
- **d.** As an animator at Walt Disney Studios, he convinced Disney to produce Burton's movies.

DRAWING CONCLUSIONS

6. From the article, you can conclude that Tim Burton would agree that
- **a.** he is the sole creator, director, and producer of many popular movies.
- **b.** it's important to draw accurately from life.
- **c.** you should develop your own unique style and follow your passion in life.
- **d.** everyone should go to college and learn a skill that will bring the highest possible income.

7. From the article you can conclude that Tim Burton feels his success is due to
- **a.** his teachers, famous artists, and other creative people who work with him.
- **b.** his own artistic talent and unique creativity.
- **c.** his good luck and numerous fortunate opportunities.
- **d.** learning from his failures.

VOCABULARY IN CONTEXT

8. Determine the correct meaning of the underlined word in the following sentence. In the sketches, Sparky's squat, round body and long snout are exaggerated.
- **a.** short
- **b.** thick
- **c.** round
- **d.** squiggly

9. Determine the correct meaning of the underlined word in the following sentence. Even the drawing style of the original sketches is replicated in the finished movie still from *Frankenweenie*.
- **a.** a final cut of a movie
- **b.** an excerpt from a movie
- **c.** filmmaking process
- **d.** a photo taken from the movie

MyReadingLab

Reading 2 VOCABULARY PRACTICE

Use the vocabulary words from the Word Bank to complete the following sentences. Write the words into the blanks provided.

WORD BANK

animation	stop-motion animation	economy	attributes
maquettes	collaborated	translate	unconditional
painstaking	replicated		

1. Belinda felt that Omar's creative character sketches would .... well into three-dimensional action figures.

2. Pet owners often have such .... love for their pets that they willingly tolerate their pets' bad behavior more than other people.

3. One of the techniques filmmakers use is called .... because only one photo is taken at a time to produce a motion picture.

4. Creating detailed art sometimes requires a lot of .... work.

5. Tim Burton sketches with an .... of line, sketching only enough lines to suggest an image.

6. One of the most important .... of an artist is creativity.

7. Mario makes his own .... films and uploads them to the Internet.

8. Brianna, Destiny, and Latasha .... on painting the campus cafeteria mural.

9. Jason and Margarita were hired to create .... from clay and wire that would be used as models for the animation artists.

10. An image can easily be .... by scanning it into a computer.

MyReadingLab

Reading 2 QUESTIONS FOR WRITING AND DISCUSSION

Review any parts of the article you need to answer the following questions.

1. Who were some of the most influential people in Tim Burton's career?

2. How important is teamwork in making animated movies?

3. How does Tim Burton's artistic styling of his characters differ from other popular cartoon characters?

4. Why do you think so many successful people advise others to follow their passion in life?

5. What things inspire you to create new ideas?

Reading 2 VOCABULARY PRACTICE—CROSSWORD

Practice the vocabulary words from "From Sketch to Screen: Tim Burton" with a partner or team in the following crossword building game.

1.
Make two teams, each with one to three people.

2.
One team will complete all of the odd numbered clue questions. The other team will do the even numbered questions. Answer the questions in the order they appear, taking turns.

3.
First, answer the question by writing the correct answer from the Word Bank. Then, write the word anywhere on the grid, using one letter per square. Try to use letters that are already on the grid, including the letters in "Word Search."

4.
Teams get five points for each word they correctly answer. Each time you cross over another letter, you get one extra point. You may cross over as many other words as you can to earn points for each word you write, but the letters must match what is already there. You can go across, down, diagonally, or backwards.

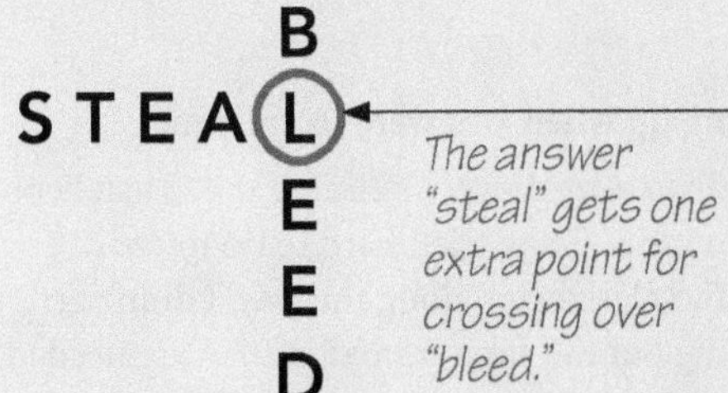
B
STEAL
E
E
D
The answer "steal" gets one extra point for crossing over "bleed."

5.
One person on each team should keep time. Each team has one minute to write a correct answer or lose their turn.

6.
All words must be spelled correctly. The team with the most points at the end is the winner.

WORD BANK

animation, collaborated, stop-motion animation, economy, attributes, maquettes, translate, unconditional, painstaking, replicated

	W	O	R	D		S	E	A	R	C	H		

CLUE QUESTIONS

1. Belinda felt that Omar's creative character sketches would .... well into three-dimensional action figures.

2. Pet owners often have such .... love for their pets that they willingly tolerate their pets' bad behavior more than other people.

3. One of the techniques filmmakers use is called .... because only one photo is taken at a time to produce a motion picture.

4. Creating detailed art sometimes requires a lot of .... work.

5. Tim Burton sketches with an .... of line, sketching only enough lines to suggest an image.

6. One of the most important .... of an artist is creativity.

7. Mario makes his own .... films and uploads them to the Internet.

8. Brianna, Destiny, and Latasha .... on painting the campus cafeteria mural.

9. Jason and Margarita were hired to create .... from clay and wire that would be used as models for the animation artists.

10. An image can easily be .... by scanning it into a computer.

ON THE JOB INTERVIEW

MEAGHAN GIROUARD

GRAPHIC ARTIST

What kind of work do you do?

I work for a national trade show contractor company that designs trade shows. I work with 3D modeling programs, animation programs, and other graphics programs. I design the layout of the shows, the overall look of the shows, the decorating, and anything related to the show including logos, and graphic design.

What kind of training did you have for this job?

I graduated from art school with a bachelor's in fine arts in visual communication and a minor in business, and I worked as a freelance designer before taking this job.

What do you like best about this job?

I enjoy collaborating with other people on projects. I like the variety of projects that we do, and the creativity that's involved. I love my job because it's a constant challenge, and there are always new projects to work on, and each one is different.

What do you dislike about your job?

Sometimes there isn't enough time to do all that I would like to do on a project. I sometimes must put in late hours to meet deadlines. And some people can be difficult to work with.

How did you become interested in this career?

I loved art in school and didn't want to become a painter, so graphic design was the perfect area for me.

When you were in college, did you have to overcome any obstacles to succeed?

I certainly did! I have dyslexia, which is a learning disability, so it was a real challenge for me to succeed. I had to work a lot harder than other students, but I knew my strength was in art, so I kept going even though many courses were difficult for me.

Did you ever think about giving up when you were in college?

There were times when everything seemed overwhelming. But I just kept my head down and worked through it. I just tried hard to do my best. I got a lot of help from teachers and classmates along the way. I didn't get where I am today without seeking out the support and guidance I needed to get through my schooling.

If you had any advice for college freshmen interested in graphic art, what would it be?

I would strongly suggest that they do whatever they can to get as much experience as possible. By that I mean do volunteer work, internships, or freelance work. Try to network with people in the business so that you can make the transition from college to the real world. Graphic design is a good career with plenty of opportunity and variety. But getting your foot in the door isn't always easy, so that's why networking and experience are helpful.

MyReadingLab

WATCH THE VIDEO

AFRICAN ORPHAN
NOW BALLERINA

Watch the Video "African Orphan Now Ballerina" and answer the questions about implied main idea and central point.

MyReadingLab

BUILDING VOCABULARY

Throughout this course, you will be introduced to word parts that make up many words in the English language. Study the following word parts, and then answer the questions that follow.

Prefixes	Roots	Suffixes
extra-, extro- *outside*	-vert-, -vers- *to turn**	-tion, -sion *action, state of**
in- *into**	-tract- *to draw, to drag*	-er, -or *one who*
con-, com- *with, together**		
ex- *out**		

* Word parts from previous chapters

What English words can you create from these word parts?

Using a dictionary, look up the meanings of any of the words you wrote that you can't define. Use one of the words you wrote in a sentence that reveals its meaning with a context clue:

MyReadingLab

REAL-LIFE READING

CAR LEASING AGREEMENTS

Leasing a car is like renting it long term. When you lease a car, you are renting it from a leasing company that owns the vehicle. You should be aware of some unfair deals that can happen with a lease. Use the four-step reading process as you read the following excerpt from a car leasing agreement, and then answer the questions that follow to check your comprehension.

Vocabulary Terms:

lessor: the person or company who leases the car to you

default: if you fail to do anything that is required in the agreement

Terms of Lease Agreement
VEHICLE MAINTENANCE You must maintain and service the Vehicle at your own expense, using materials that meet the manufacturer's specifications. This includes following the owner's manual and maintenance schedule, keeping records of maintenance performed, and making all needed repairs.
DAMAGE REPAIR You are responsible for repairs of all damage that is not a result of normal wear and use. Repairs must be made with original equipment manufacturer parts. Failure to do so will result in damage charges.
TERMINATION This lease will terminate (end) upon (a) the end of the term of this lease, (b) the return of the Vehicle to Lessor, and (c) the payment by you of all amounts owed under this lease. The Lessor may cancel this lease if you default. If you default, you may be required to pay damages to the Lessor.
RETURN OF VEHICLE If you do not buy the Vehicle at lease end, you must return it to the Lessor. If you fail to return the Vehicle, you must continue to pay the monthly payments plus other damages to the Lessor, including amounts payable under default, which can be up to 40% of the monthly payment. Payment of these amounts will not allow you to keep the Vehicle.
EXCESS WEAR AND USE You are responsible for all repairs to the Vehicle that are not the result of normal wear and use. If any such damage is found on the vehicle when it is returned, you will be charged for the repairs to such damage.

1. **Which of the following is included in the required vehicle maintenance?**
   a. following the owner's manual
   b. following the maintenance schedule
   c. keeping a record of maintenance performed
   d. all of the above

2. **What happens if you repair a damaged part with one that is not an original manufacturer part?**
   a. You will not be allowed to return the car.
   b. You will be charged extra in damage charges.
   c. You will have to buy the vehicle.
   d. It doesn't matter which kind of parts you use, so nothing happens.

3. **What happens if you default?**
   a. You must pay more money each month.
   b. You are given the option to buy the car.
   c. You may have to pay damages to the company, and you could lose the car.
   d. You are given a warning and a second chance to catch up on payments.

4. **What happens if you don't return the vehicle at the end of the lease?**
   a. You must continue to pay the monthly payments plus other damages, including amounts up to 40% of the monthly payment.
   b. You keep on paying for the car until it's paid for and you keep it.
   c. You will be charged with grand theft auto.
   d. Nothing will happen because the car dealers won't know about it.

5. **What happens if you return the car with a large dent in the hood?**
   a. The vehicle will be accepted.
   b. The repairs will be done by the dealership at no cost to you.
   c. You must pay for the repairs.
   d. You are charged a small Excess Wear and Use fee.

MyReadingLab

TEXTBOOK GRAPHIC AIDS

Study the following graph, and then answer the questions that follow.

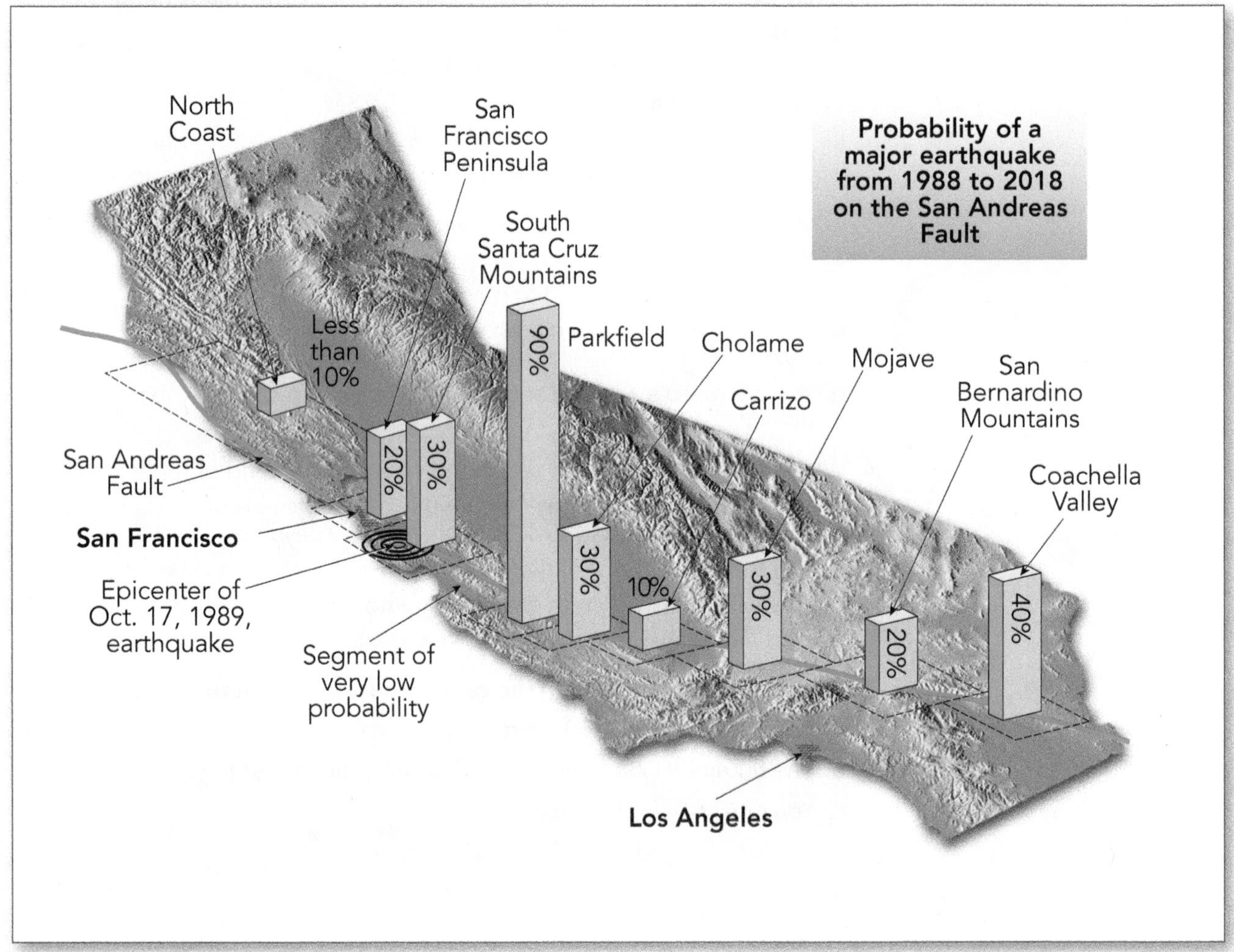

1. What does the graph show?
   a. cities in California where earthquakes have occurred (1988–2018)
   b. locations in California that have had the most earthquakes
   c. the probability of major earthquakes along the San Andreas Fault (1988–2018)
   d. the percentage of earthquakes in various areas of California (1988–2018)
2. Which city has the highest probability of a major earthquake by 2018?
   a. Parkfield
   b. San Francisco
   c. San Andreas Fault
   d. Los Angeles

3. Which area has the lowest probability of a major earthquake before 2018?
   a. the area north of San Francisco
   b. San Francisco
   c. Carrizo
   d. Los Angeles
4. Which of the following conclusions can you draw from the graph?
   a. The probability of a major earthquake is high anywhere on the San Andreas Fault.
   b. The probability of a major earthquake is lower north of San Francisco.
   c. A major earthquake will destroy all the cities on the San Andreas Fault.
   d. The probability of a major earthquake along the San Andreas Fault is higher than in other parts of California.
5. According to the graph, the two largest cities shown, San Francisco and Los Angeles, have an equal probability of a major earthquake before 2018.
   a. true
   b. false

MyReadingLab

CHAPTER PRACTICE 1

Read the following paragraph, underline the major details, and then answer the questions that follow

Fashion designers are artists who create "art" to wear. They begin by studying art and design at a college, university, or private art and design school. Their training includes fashion history, design, drawing, pattern making, and using computer-aided design (CAD) programs. Besides having a foundation in art and design, designers must have a good sense of what is pleasing to the eye. They must understand how color, texture, and proportion play important roles in the overall look of a style. In addition to being creative, fashion designers must be able to communicate their ideas to others. Most fashion designers start out as sketching assistants or pattern makers for a professional designer or clothing label. After gaining experience and proving their talent, they can work their way up into higher positions as fashion designers. Teamwork skills are important since designers must work with many other people to achieve the final product.

1. What is the topic?
- **a.** fashion design
- **b.** fashion designers
- **c.** designing fashions for others
- **d.** art as fashion

2. What do most of the major details describe?
- **a.** how a person becomes a fashion designer
- **b.** how fashions are designed
- **c.** what is needed to be a fashion designer
- **d.** why fashion designers create designs

3. Is the main idea stated or implied?
- **a.** stated
- **b.** implied

4. Which of the following sentences best states the main idea (either stated in the paragraph or implied)?
- **a.** Fashion designers are artists who create "art" to wear.
- **b.** Besides having a foundation in art and design, designers must have a good sense of what is pleasing to the eye.
- **c.** Most fashion designers start out as sketching assistants or pattern makers for a professional designer or clothing label.
- **d.** Teamwork skills are important since designers must work with many other people to achieve the final product.

MyReadingLab

CHAPTER PRACTICE 2

Read the following paragraphs, underline the major details, and then answer the questions that follow.

On October 28, 1886, the Statue of Liberty was dedicated to celebrate the signing of the Declaration of Independence 100 years prior. The statue was a gift from France to celebrate the friendship that had been established between the two countries during the American Revolution.

The famous statue is of a robed woman, wearing a crown and holding a torch, which is coated in gold leaf—a thin layer of gold. The statue is over 150 feet tall. The design of the statue is based on ancient Roman statues, and its features are symbols of freedom. By the statue's feet are broken chains, symbolizing America's freedom from Great Britain. The torch she holds represents wisdom and truth. The seven spikes on the crown she wears represent the seven seas and continents of the world. July 4, 1776, the date of America's Declaration of Independence, is written on the tablet she holds. Her location on Liberty Island in the New York Harbor welcomed visitors and immigrants to the United States who arrived by ships in earlier times.

1. What is the topic?
   a. construction of the Statue of Liberty
   b. the meaning of the Statue of Liberty
   c. the Statue of Liberty
   d. the location of the Statue of Liberty
2. What do most of the major details describe?
   a. why the statue was given to the United States and what it represents
   b. who designed the statue
   c. how the statue was constructed
   d. where the statue is located
3. Is the main idea stated or implied?
   a. stated
   b. implied
4. Which of the following sentences best states the main idea (either stated in the reading or implied)?
   a. On October 28, 1886, the Statue of Liberty was dedicated to celebrate the signing of the Declaration of Independence 100 years prior.
   b. The statue was a gift from France to celebrate the friendship that had been established between the two countries during the American Revolution.
   c. The Statue of Liberty, a gift from France, represents independence, truth, and freedom.
   d. The design of the statue is based on ancient Roman statues, and its features are symbols of freedom.

MyReadingLab

CHAPTER PRACTICE 3

Read the following paragraphs, underline the major details, and then answer the questions that follow.

When Michaela DePrince leaps weightlessly across the stage, landing gracefully upon her toes, she's not thinking of her past struggles, she's focused on her dance. Michaela was born in war-torn Sierra Leone, Africa, in 1995. When she was three years old, her father was killed by rebels, and her mother died of starvation soon after. Michaela was taken to an orphanage where she witnessed the brutal murder of her teacher. While at the orphanage she found a torn picture of a ballerina and hoped that some day she might dance the ballet. A year later, she was adopted and taken to the United States. Her new parents took her to ballet lessons. In 2012, Michaela graduated from the Jacqueline Kennedy Onassis School in New York, and then joined the Dance Theatre of Harlem. Her first professional premiere was in *Le Corsaire* in 2012. Since then, Michaela has performed in theaters around the world, and she has been featured in magazines and newspapers in the U.S. and abroad. Her journey is an inspiration for all who seek to live their dreams.

1. What is the topic?
   - **a.** ballet dancing
   - **b.** ballerinas
   - **c.** dancing
   - **d.** Michaela DePrince

2. What do most of the major details describe?
   - **a.** how Michaela became a ballerina
   - **b.** how Michaela performs her dances
   - **c.** what ballet dancing is
   - **d.** why Michaela loves to dance

3. Is the main idea stated or implied?
   - **a.** stated
   - **b.** implied

4. Which of the following sentences best states the main idea (stated or implied)?
   - **a.** When Michaela DePrince leaps weightlessly across the stage, landing gracefully upon her toes, she's not thinking of her past struggles, she is focused on her dance.
   - **b.** Michaela lost her parents at the age of 3 and became a dancer.
   - **c.** Although Michaela DePrince had a tragic childhood, she has become one of the world's most admired ballet dancers.
   - **d.** Michaela achieved her dream of becoming a ballerina because she worked hard and persisted.

MyReadingLab

TEXTBOOK PRACTICE

Preview the following paragraphs, then read actively and answer the questions. Read the following textbook selection, underline the major details, and then answer the questions that follow.

American painter Georgia O'Keeffe (oh-KEEF), born near Sun Prairie, Wisconsin, grew up on her family's farm in Wisconsin. She spent 1904–1905 at the Art Institute of Chicago and 1907–1908 at the Art Students League of New York, and then supported herself by doing commercial art and teaching at various schools and colleges in Texas and the South. Her break came in 1916, when her drawings were discovered and exhibited by the famous American photographer Alfred Stieglitz, who praised and promoted her work vigorously. They maintained a lifelong relationship, marrying in 1924, and O'Keeffe became the subject of hundreds of Stieglitz's photographs.

Her early pictures lack originality, but by the 1920s she had developed a uniquely individualistic style. Many of her subjects include enlarged views of skulls and other animal bones, flowers, plants, shells, rocks, mountains, and other natural forms. Her images have a mysterious quality about them, with clear color washes and a suggestive, psychological symbolism that often implies eroticism. She created her best-known work in the 1920s, 1930s, and 1940s, but remained active as a painter almost until her death in 1986. Her later paintings exalt the New Mexico landscape, which she loved.

1. What is the topic?
   a. Georgia O'Keeffe's art
   b. Georgia O'Keeffe
   c. the art of the 1920s to 1940s
   d. a famous woman painter

2. What is the main idea of the first paragraph (either stated or implied)?
   a. American painter Georgia O'Keeffe (oh-KEEF), born near Sun Prairie, Wisconsin, grew up on her family's farm in Wisconsin.
   b. Georgia O'Keeffe studied and taught art before her marriage to photographer Alfred Stieglitz, who praised her work vigorously.
   c. They maintained a lifelong relationship, marrying in 1924, and O'Keeffe became the subject of hundreds of Stieglitz's photographs.
   d. Her break came in 1916, when her drawings were discovered and exhibited by the famous American photographer Alfred Stieglitz, who praised and promoted her work vigorously.

3. What is the main idea of the second paragraph (either stated or implied)?
   a. Her early pictures lack originality, but by the 1920s she had developed a uniquely individualistic style.
   b. Many of her subjects include enlarged views of skulls and other animal bones, flowers, plants, shells, rocks, mountains, and other natural forms.
   c. O'Keeffe's early style of painting was not considered very good.
   d. She created her best-known work in the 1920s, 1930s, and 1940s, but remained active as a painter almost until her death in 1986.

Continued...

MyReadingLab
TEXTBOOK PRACTICE
...continued

4. What is the central point of the selection (either stated or implied)?

a. American painter Georgia O'Keeffe (oh-KEEF), born near Sun Prairie, Wisconsin, grew up on her family's farm in Wisconsin.

b. After meeting Stieglitz, O'Keeffe spent most of her time in New York, with occasional periods in New Mexico, but she moved permanently to New Mexico after her husband's death in 1946.

c. Her early pictures lack originality, but by the 1920s she had developed a uniquely individualistic style.

d. Georgia O'Keeffe was an American painter who painted enlarged views of natural subjects in a unique, original style.

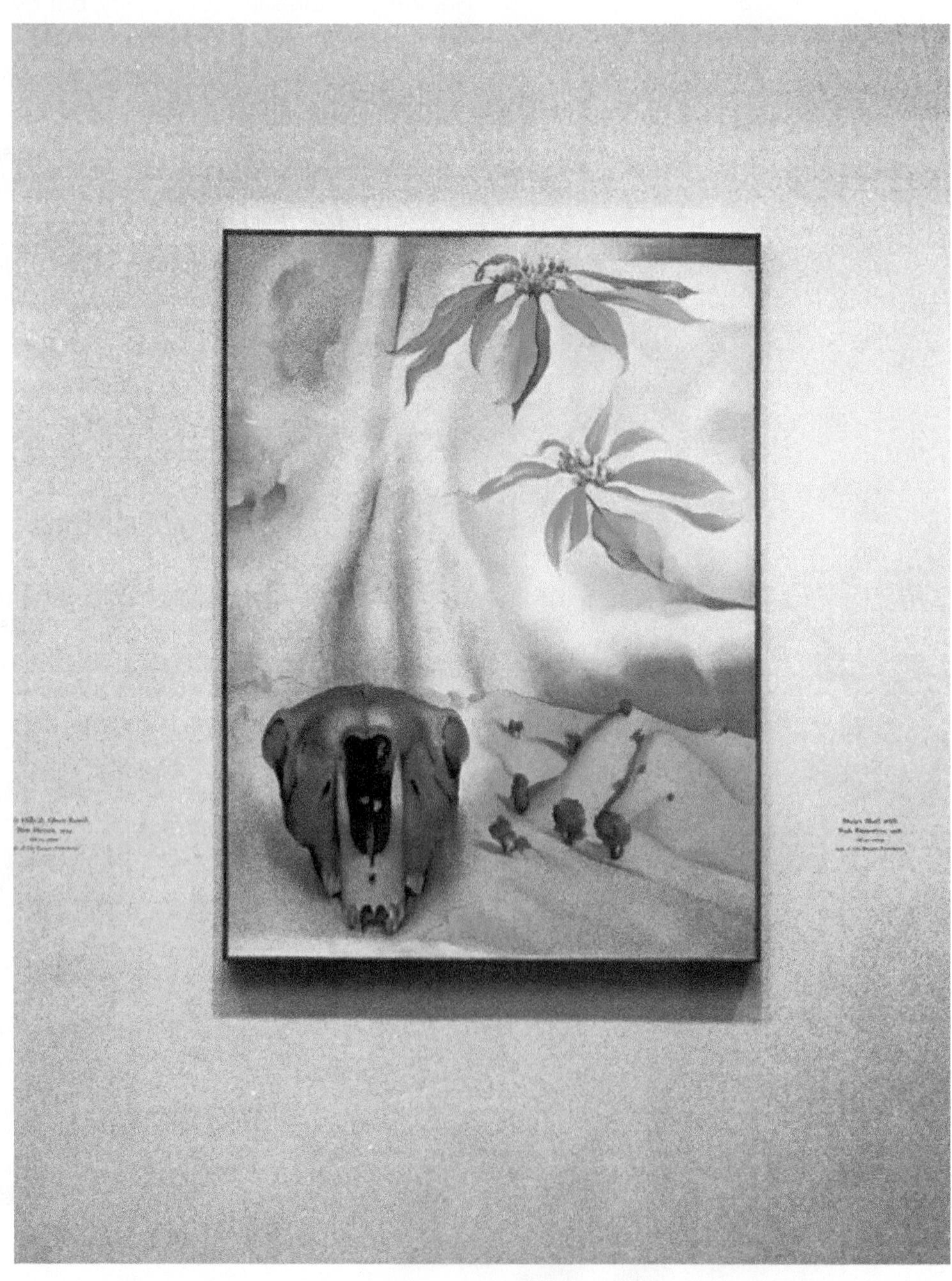

STUDY SKILL REVIEW

Cornell Notes are a style of note taking shown in the following example. Complete the Cornell Notes to review the concepts you learned in Chapter 8.

Cue/Question Column	Notes
What is the first step to finding an implied main idea?	First, ...
What is the second step to finding the implied main idea?	Second, ...
What is the third step to finding the implied main idea?	Third, ...
What question should you ask yourself to find the implied main idea?	Ask yourself, ...
What should you do to check your implied main idea?	When you have formed your implied main idea, check your answer by asking yourself, ...
What is a central point or thesis statement?	It is ....

READING LAB ASSIGNMENTS

SKILL PRACTICES

1. Login to MyReadingLab, and in the menu click on **Reading Skills** and **Learning Path**. On the main screen, click **Implied Main Idea**. Complete the review and practice activities recommended by your instructor.

COMPREHENSION IMPROVEMENT

2. From the menu in **MyReadingLab,** click on **Reading Level** and **Next Reading**. Choose two reading selections from the list on the main screen. Read the articles and answer the diagnostic and exercise questions.

CAREER EXPLORATION

3. Go online to the Occupational Outlook Handbook at the Bureau of Labor Statistics and explore careers in the arts. Find a career that interests you and print out the information. Preview, read, highlight, and annotate the article. Find one paragraph with an implied main idea and write the implied main idea in a margin.

SKILL APPLICATION

4. Using your textbooks for other classes or newspaper articles, read a section and then state the implied main idea in your own words. Remember to focus on the major supporting details and summarize what the details are telling you in a general statement. Read an entire section under a heading and determine the central point by focusing on the main ideas for each paragraph. Then, state the author's central point in your own words.

MyReadingLab

LEARNING REFLECTION

Think about the skills and concepts in this chapter. What have you learned in this chapter that will help your reading comprehension and enable you to do well in college?

....

....

....

....

....

....

....

....

MyReadingLab

SELF-EVALUATION CHECKLIST

Rate yourself on the following items, using the following scale:

1 = strongly disagree

2 = disagree

3 = neither agree nor disagree

4 = agree

5 = strongly agree

1. I completed all of the assigned work on time. ....

2. I understand all of the concepts in this chapter. ....

3. I contributed to teamwork and class discussions. ....

4. I completed all of the assigned lab work on time. ....

5. I came to class on time. ....

6. I attended class every day. ....

7. I studied for any quizzes or tests we had for this chapter. ....

8. I asked questions when I didn't understand something. ....

9. I checked my comprehension during reading. ....

10. I know what is expected of me in the coming week. ....

11. Are you still on track with the goals you set in Chapter 1?

....

What changes can you make to improve your performance in this?

....

....

....

....

8 PATTERNS OF ORGANIZATION

LEARNING STRATEGIES

Patterns of Organization 315

Relationships Within and Between Sentences 316

Recognizing Overall Patterns of Organization 328

READING SELECTIONS

READING 1: Dangerously Strong 335

READING 2: True Grit: Bethany Hamilton's Story 347

READING FOR LIFE

On the Job Interview 355

Real-Life Reading 356

Building Vocabulary 358

Textbook Graphic Aids 359

CHAPTER REVIEW

Chapter Practice 360

Textbook Practice 364

Study Skill Review 366

Reading Lab Assignments 368

Learning Reflection 368

Self-Evaluation Checklist 369

FOCUS ON: Sports and Fitness

While there are many talented athletes who enter college with scholarships and establish themselves on college sports teams, only a small percentage of these hundreds of thousands of students will go on to play in professional sports. But there are many exciting and rewarding careers in fitness and sports, even if you are not an athlete. Many of these careers offer the opportunity to work with professional athletic teams. There is also a great deal of variety in the environments in which you may work: high schools, colleges, universities, cruise ships, exclusive vacation resorts, or health clubs, to name a few. Sports-related job opportunities are also available in the retail business selling sporting equipment. Outdoor sports are becoming increasingly popular, and you can enjoy activities like mountain climbing or skiing as an instructor or guide.

Athletes use different strategies for training and performance, routines that they can follow and modify to meet their individual needs. These patterns provide structure and familiarity to athletes in training. But training and exercise patterns are not one size fits all. Some patterns and routines work better for certain sports or certain athletes. The best athletes know what patterns and routines are available to them, and how to select the best one for their purpose.

In this chapter, you will:

LEARNING OBJECTIVES

1 recognize relationships within and between sentences.

2 identify different patterns of organization and indicate why they are important to comprehension.

PATTERNS OF ORGANIZATION

Look at the following lists, and try to memorize the numbers in 60 seconds:

LIST 1	LIST 2
2, 4, 6, 8, 10, 12, 14	1, 5, 13, 90, 515, 267, 301

After the minute is up, turn the page so you're not looking at the numbers, wait one minute, and then try to recite or write the lists by memory. When you are ready, turn back to see how well you did. Which list was the most difficult to remember? You probably thought List 2 was the most difficult, because it consisted of random numbers, and you probably were able to repeat List 1 without any trouble.

The reason you probably had all of the numbers in List 1 right is because you recognized a familiar pattern. You could probably also predict what numbers would come next in the sequence because, once the brain recognizes a pattern, it starts to look for other pieces that fit the pattern. Our brains seek to find organization in what we observe or do. We are wired to understand information better when it is presented in an orderly way. We can also recall it more easily, as we saw with List 1. Similarly, knowing the common patterns of organization in writing and reading will not only improve your comprehension, but it will also improve your thinking and writing skills.

Patterns of organization, or thought patterns, are the ways that writers arrange the details in a sentence, a paragraph, or an essay.

Patterns of organization, or thought patterns, are the way that writers arrange details in a sentence, a paragraph, or an essay. We will be looking at patterns at all three levels.

Relationships: Organizational patterns within and between sentences

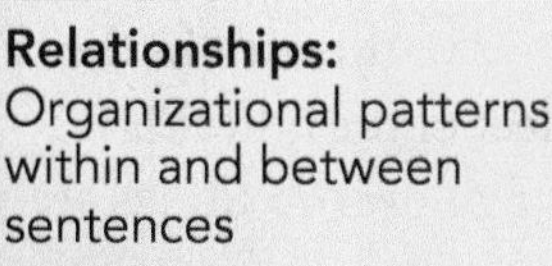

Patterns of organization are found within sentences, between sentences, and in the overall structure of a reading selection. Once you learn the various types of patterns in this chapter, you will be able to recognize and identify them. When we look at patterns within and between sentences, they are usually referred to as relationships. Here are some examples of **relationships** within and between sentences:

> Jim wanted to take microbiology this semester, *but* he found out that biology was a prerequisite for the course.

Notice how the second half of the sentence after the first comma shows a contrast between what Jim wanted to do and what he had to do (take biology first). This is called a **contrast** relationship because it is showing an opposite. The transition word, *but*, indicates that an opposite idea is to follow.

Shareen's check that she wrote to pay for her college classes was returned for insufficient funds. *As a result*, she was dropped from all of her classes.

In these two sentences, the second sentence shows a result of what happened in the first sentence. This is called a **cause and effect** relationship. The *cause* was the bad check and the *result* was she was dropped from her classes. The transitional phrase, "as a result," indicates that an effect is being described.

Transition Words and Phrases

One way to figure out the relationship within a sentence is to look for clues, such as transition words. As you may recall from Chapter 5, **transitions** are words or phrases that signal an author's train of thought. Learning the transitions for each pattern can help you determine the relationship of ideas being shown in the sentence. There is a chart of patterns and their transitions in the Appendix of this text book. Also, be aware of sentence punctuation. A comma or semi-colon is often used to separate two or more ideas in a sentence. Try to figure out how the first idea relates to the second idea in the same sentence. For example:

First, we went to the dining hall to have lunch, and then we went to the Physical Education center to play basketball.

Notice how the comma separates the two parts of the sentence, and the relationship between the two ideas shows when the two events occurred. *First,* they had lunch, and *then* they played basketball. This is called a *time order* relationship.

Because some sentences do not have any transitions, or the transitions you see may not signal the actual relationship, you need to figure out the relationships by noticing the details in the sentences. For example:

Eating too many carbohydrates can increase body fat.

This sentence has no transitions, but the relationship being shown is one of cause and effect. Eating too many carbohydrates is the cause, and increasing body fat is the effect. Because transitions may or may not always be helpful, always **ask yourself how the idea in the first half of the sentence relates to the idea in the second half**. Does it show how one thing causes or is an effect of the other? Is it adding on more information about the topic? Or is it showing how two things are alike or different?

OBJECTIVE **1**

Recognize relationships within and between sentences.

RELATIONSHIPS WITHIN AND BETWEEN SENTENCES

As you learn the following patterns of organization, determine which patterns are used within or between the sentences that you are reading.

Definition Pattern

A definition pattern is easy to spot because it defines a word or term. The term may be shown in bold or italics, though not always. Definitions are often set off by commas, dashes, brackets, or parentheses. Here is an example showing a definition relationship:

> Kinesthetic sense **means** an awareness of body movement and action.

Notice the transition *means,* which indicates a definition of a term. Being aware of transition words associated with the definition pattern will help you recognize a definition when you see one. Use the definition transitions in the next box to complete the sentences that follow. There may be more than one transition that can complete a sentence correctly.

DEFINITION TRANSITIONS

are	are known as	defined	definition	describes
is	is known as	means	refers to	is (are)
called	that is			

1. Meditation .... a state of complete mental and physical relaxation.

2. Abnormally high blood pressure .... hypertension.

3. Carbohydrates .... sugars that are a source of energy for the body.

4. The basic substances found in foods that your body needs to maintain health .... nutrients.

5. LBP .... low back pain, a condition associated with a lack of exercise.

LEARNING STRATEGIES

Listing Pattern

The listing pattern, also known as *simple listing*, presents a random list of ideas. The order of the ideas is not important. Here is an example of a listing relationship:

> Sports and fitness trainers work in health clubs, schools, resorts, **and** in professional sports team training centers.

Notice the transition *and* at the end of the sentence which indicates another idea is being listed in the series. Also notice the commas separating the list of items. These are both clues to the listing pattern. Use the listing transitions in the next box to complete the sentences that follow. There may be more than one transition that can complete a sentence correctly.

LISTING TRANSITIONS

one	final	furthermore	third	in addition
last	then	also	and	first
moreover	besides	another	next	second
for one thing	finally			

1. Three joints found in the human body are the ball and socket, the hinge joint, ... the pivot joint.

2. To maintain a healthy body weight, first, you should exercise; ...., eat healthy foods that are low in fat; and ...., drink plenty of water.

3. .... exercising, it is .... important to provide the body with enough rest.

4. Smoking can increase the risk of stroke, ... it can increase heart rate and blood pressure.

5. When training for her marathons, Karen runs eight kilometers, rides 20 kilometers on her bike, ... swims 10 kilometers at least twice a week.

Cause-and-Effect Pattern

The cause-and-effect pattern shows the causes and/or the effects of one or more actions. It can also show how one effect can have several causes or how several causes can have several effects.

Here is an example of a cause and effect relationship:

> **Because** Kevin has added swimming to his weekly workouts, he has increased his muscle mass and decreased his body fat.

Notice the transition *because* at the beginning of the sentence, which indicates a cause of something (Kevin added swimming to his workouts), and in the second half of the sentence after the comma, we see the effect (increased muscle mass and decreased body fat). Use the cause-and-effect transitions in the next box to complete the sentences that follow. There may be more than one transition that can complete a sentence correctly.

The word **affect** is a verb, meaning "to cause or influence." The word **effect** is a noun, meaning "a result."

CAUSE-AND-EFFECT TRANSITIONS

Cause Transitions			Effect Transitions		
affect	due to	lead to	as a result	consequently	**effect**
cause	because	reason	result	consequence	thus
since	if...then	explanation	so	therefore	

1. A lack of exercise can .... obesity.

2. If weight-bearing exercise is increased, ... the muscle fibers will increase in size.

3. Another .... of regular exercise is improved mental health because the brain releases chemicals during exercise that cause a sense of well-being.

4. Anabolic steroids, substances taken to increase muscle mass, can .... serious physical and mental health risks.

5. One .... of strength training is that it can reduce or eliminate lower back pain.

Compare-and-Contrast Pattern

The compare and/or contrast pattern shows how things are alike or different. When you compare things, you examine their similarities. When you contrast things, you examine their differences. Authors sometimes use only one of these patterns or both together, so this pattern is referred to as "compare and/or contrast." Here is an example of a compare and/or contrast relationship:

> The leading NFL Hall of Fame rusher was Walter Payton, but in 2011, Emmitt Smith became the lead rusher with 18,355 yards, culminating his 15-year career.

Notice the transition *but* after the comma in this sentence. It indicates that a contrast, or difference, is being shown between the idea in the first half of the sentence and the idea in the second half after the comma. The first half of the sentence shows who the leading rusher was, and the second half shows who became the new leading rusher. Use the compare-and-contrast transitions in the next two boxes to complete the sentences that follow. There may be more than one transition that can complete a sentence correctly.

Comparison shows similarities. **Contrast** shows differences.

COMPARISON TRANSITIONS (show similarities)

alike	as	both	in the same way	same
in a similar way	like	likewise	similar	

1. When beginning a weight-training program, women achieve strength .... quickly as men do.

2. The human brain stores information .... a computer.

3. The brain works .... as a shipping company, carrying loads of information to long-term storage.

4. American soccer and British football are ....

5. .... aerobic exercises and swimming can improve heart function and fitness.

Than is used for comparison. **Then** signifies time order.

CONTRAST TRANSITIONS (show differences)

although	as opposed to	but	contrast
contrary to	differ	different	even
though	however	instead	in spite of
less than	more than	nevertheless	rather than
than	unlike	while	yet
on the other hand	on the contrary		

1. People at their recommended body weight are likely to live longer .... those who are overweight and obese.

2. .... overweight individuals, people who maintain a healthy weight have fewer health, skeletal, and joint problems.

3. .... too much stored fat is not healthy, you would never want to eliminate it from your diet.

4. Salt is a necessary nutrient for the body; ...., most people eat much more salt than they should, which increases their blood pressure.

5. Controlling your weight means permanently changing the way you eat by choosing low-fat and low-calorie foods .... high-fat and high-calorie foods.

Time Order (Chronological Order) Pattern

The time order pattern shows the supporting details in the order in which they happened in a chain of events. The transitions for this pattern answer the question "when?" In addition to the transitions below, dates that are listed in chronological order are also considered signals of the time order pattern. Here is an example of the time order pattern:

> To avoid injury, it is important to gently stretch muscles **before** beginning an exercise workout.

Notice the transition word *before* in the sentence. It indicates when something should occur. First, you should stretch your muscles, and then exercise next. Be aware of transitions for time order which tell readers the order in which things happened or should happen.Using the transitions in the box below to complete the following sentences will help you learn some transitions for the time order pattern. There may be more than one transition which can complete a sentence correctly.

TIME ORDER TRANSITIONS

first	second	third	next
finally	later	meanwhile	during
then	after(ward)	before	until
current(ly)	last	often	now
while	previous(ly)	over time	when
as	begin	beginning	start
started, starts, starting			

1. .... you load new hardware on your computer, you must .... restart the computer.

2. To create a basic web page, you must .... choose a template with the format you would like to use.

Continued...

3. .... Mr. Simon's lecture, he went online to show us several examples of well designed websites.

4. To access recently used websites on your computer, ... click on "File," .... , click on "Recent webs" and .... , click on the name of the website you want.

5. .... Abdul turned in his final project he saved a copy of it on his flash drive.

MyReadingLab

PRACTICE 1

In the following sentences, choose the correct type of relationship that is being shown within or between the sentences.

1. **To stay healthy, you should *include* vegetables, fruits, and whole grains in your daily diet.**
   a. definition
   b. listing
   c. cause and effect
   d. compare and/or contrast

2. **Don't drink soda with your meals because it's high in calories and sodium. *Instead*, have a glass of milk, soy milk, or water.**
   a. definition
   b. listing
   c. cause and effect
   d. compare and/or contrast

3. **As people age, they become weaker and can develop osteoporosis. Osteoporosis is *defined* as a bone disease in which the mineral content of the bone is reduced and the bone is weakened.**
   a. definition
   b. listing
   c. cause and effect
   d. compare and/or contrast

4. **Some fruits and vegetables can lose some of their vitamins during cooking. *Therefore*, it is best to eat them raw or only slightly cooked.**
   a. definition
   b. listing
   c. cause and effect
   d. compare and/or contrast

5. **He started playing football in high school and *later* became a leading rusher for his college team.**
   a. compare and/or contrast
   b. cause and effect
   c. time order
   d. listing

MyReadingLab

PRACTICE 2

Read the following paragraph, and underline the main idea and major details. Then, identify the relationships in the questions that follow.

THE PARALYMPICS

Talented athletes who have physical disabilities are able to compete internationally like non-disabled athletes in the International Paralympic Games. The word "paralympic" means "with the Olympics." Disabled athletes compete in many of the same events as the regular Olympics. They compete in swimming, skiing, basketball, and many other sports. Because of the athletes' disabilities, many of the games have been modified. Ice hockey is played on small sledges, and many games, such as curling and basketball, are played in wheelchairs. Like the regular Olympics, the athletes are awarded bronze, silver, and gold medals. The idea of having athletic competitions for disabled athletes started in England in 1948 with wheelchair races. In 1952, games for the disabled were held along with the Olympics. The first official Paralympics started in 1960 when 400 athletes represented 23 countries. Now they are held every four years in the same city as the regular Olympic Games.

1. Talented athletes who have physical disabilities are able to compete internationally *like* non-disabled athletes in the International Paralympic Games.
   a. definition
   b. listing
   c. cause and effect
   d. compare and/or contrast

2. The word "paralympic" *means* "with the Olympics."
   a. definition
   b. listing
   c. cause and effect
   d. compare and/or contrast

3. They compete in swimming, skiing, basketball, and many other sports.
   a. definition
   b. listing
   c. cause and effect
   d. compare and/or contrast

4. *Like* the regular Olympics, the athletes are awarded bronze, silver, and gold medals.
   a. definition
   b. listing
   c. cause and effect
   d. compare and/or contrast

5. *Because of* the athletes' disabilities, many of the games have been modified.
   a. time order
   b. listing
   c. cause and effect
   d. compare and contrast

MyReadingLab

PRACTICE 3

Read the following paragraphs, and underline the main idea and major details. Then, answer the questions that follow.

WIND SPRINTS

Wind sprints are short bursts of high-intensity exercise that increase your fitness level by forcing your body to adapt to a higher level of intensity. During the lower-intensity phase, your body builds fat-burning enzymes (substances your body makes). These enzymes help you handle the stress of the high-intensity sprint. This also increases your fat-burning ability. A person of average fitness who is not an athlete can do this during a 30-minute walk. Begin with a 5- to 10-minute warm-up. Next, sprint (run) for 30 seconds. Then, walk as you normally would for 1 minute. Repeat the sprint-and-walk pattern 3 times. In the second phase, walk for 5 minutes at normal speed. In the third phase, sprint for 1 full minute, and then walk for 1 minute. Repeat this pattern 3 times. In the last phase, return to your regular walking pace to warm down for the remaining time.

It is not necessary to go extremely fast when you run, but just fast enough to feel winded. There are other ways to do wind sprints, and they are described in various fitness articles found on the Internet. Just search for "wind sprints" to find the one that is right for you.

1. What is the topic sentence of this selection?
   - **a.** Wind sprints are short bursts of high-intensity exercise that increase your fitness level by forcing your body to adapt to a higher level of intensity.
   - **b.** During the lower-intensity phase, your body builds fat-burning enzymes (substances your body makes).
   - **c.** It is not necessary to go extremely fast when you run, but just fast enough to feel winded.
   - **d.** Just search for "wind sprints" to find the one that is right for you.
2. What is the meaning of the word "enzyme" as it is used in the second sentence?
   - **a.** a type of exercise
   - **b.** a level of exercise
   - **c.** a substance that is produced by the body
   - **d.** a drug
3. Identify the relationship within the following sentence: Wind sprints are short bursts of high-intensity exercise that increase your fitness level by forcing your body to adapt to a higher level of intensity.
   - **a.** definition
   - **b.** listing
   - **c.** cause and effect
   - **d.** compare and/or contrast

4. Identify the relationship between the following sentences: During the lower-intensity phase, your body builds fat-burning enzymes (substances your body makes). These enzymes help you handle the stress of the high-intensity sprint.
   a. definition
   b. time order
   c. cause and effect
   d. compare and/or contrast

5. Identify the relationship within the following sentence: It is not necessary to go extremely fast when you run, *but* just fast enough to feel winded.
   a. definition
   b. listing
   c. cause and effect
   d. compare and/or contrast

MyReadingLab

TEXTBOOK SELECTION 1

Read the following selection, and underline the main idea and major details. Then, answer the questions that follow.

Selecting Activities

Every exercise prescription includes at least one mode of exercise—that is, a specific type of exercise to be performed. For example, to improve cardiorespiratory—heart and respiration—fitness, you could select from a wide variety of activities, such as running, swimming, or cycling. To ensure that you'll engage in the exercise regularly, you should choose activities that you will enjoy doing, that are available to you, and that carry little risk of injury.

Physical activities can be classified as being either high impact or low impact, based on the amount of stress placed on joints during the activity. Low-impact activities put less stress on the joints than high-impact activities. Because of the strong correlation between high-impact activities and injuries, many fitness experts recommend low-impact activities for fitness beginners or for people susceptible to injury (such as people who are older or overweight). Examples of low-impact activities include walking, cycling, swimming, and low-impact aerobic dance. High-impact activities include running, basketball, and high-impact aerobic dance.

Swimming and volleyball are both excellent for the cardiovascular system. Swimming puts less stress on the joints and is considered a low-impact activity, whereas volleyball puts more stress on the joints and is considered a high-impact activity.

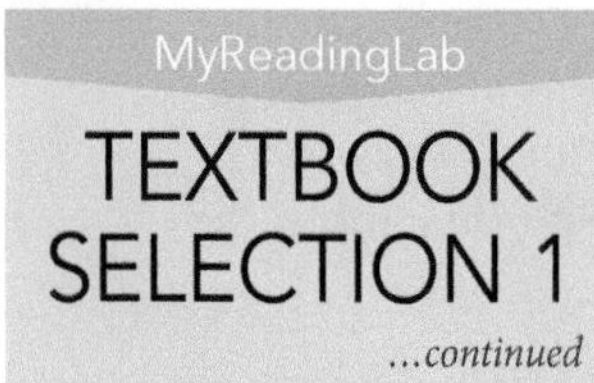

QUESTIONS

1. What is the topic of this selection?
   a. high- and low-impact activities
   b. modes of exercise
   c. cardiorespiratory fitness
   d. selecting activities

Identify the relationships within the following sentences.

2. Every exercise prescription includes at least one mode of exercise—that is, a specific type of exercise to be performed.
   a. definition
   b. listing
   c. cause and effect
   d. compare and/or contrast
3. To ensure that you'll engage in the exercise regularly, you should choose activities that you will enjoy doing, that are available to you, and that carry little risk of injury.
   a. definition
   b. listing
   c. cause and effect
   d. time order
4. Low-impact activities put less stress on the joints than high-impact activities.
   a. definition
   b. listing
   c. cause and effect
   d. compare and/or contrast
5. Because of the strong correlation between high-impact activities and injuries, many fitness experts recommend low-impact activities for fitness beginners or for people susceptible to injury (such as people who are older or overweight).
   a. definition
   b. listing
   c. cause and effect
   d. compare and/or contrast

U-REVIEW 1

Use the patterns listed below to answer the following questions. When you have finished, pair up with another person to check your answers.

definition
listing
cause and effect
compare and/or contrast
time order

1. If you were trying to explain the outcome of an experiment you performed in a science lab, what pattern would you choose, and why?

2. If you were taking notes at a lecture on the characteristics of a democracy, which pattern would you use, and why?

3. If you wanted to buy a car but hadn't yet decided which one to buy, which pattern would you use to help you decide, and why?

4. If you were trying to explain to your study group what marsupials are, which pattern would you use, and why?

5. If you were giving a report on the history of the Civil War, which pattern would you use, and why?

OBJECTIVE 2

Identify different patterns of organization and indicate why they are important to comprehension.

RECOGNIZING OVERALL PATTERNS OF ORGANIZATION

Recognizing overall patterns means looking at the whole paragraph instead of just a sentence or two to determine the pattern. As you are reading, look specifically at the major supporting details and ask yourself, "How are the supporting details organized?" The topic sentence can often give you a clue as to the paragraph's overall pattern of organization. For example, if the topic sentence contrasts two items, then it is likely the rest of the paragraph will give details about how the two items differ from one another. Note that the overall pattern of organization may differ from the patterns shown within or between sentences.

As you read the following paragraph, think about the topic, the main idea, and the major details.

The Benefits of Rest

Exercise causes muscle tissue breakdown, energy loss, and fluid loss. Getting enough rest after exercising or training is very beneficial to the body. One benefit of rest is that it allows the body to renew its energy, like a rechargeable battery renews its charge. Another effect is that it allows the body to repair damaged tissues. Resting also allows time for the body to remove chemicals that build up in the body during exercise.

Topic: The benefits of rest

Main idea: Getting enough rest after exercising or training is very beneficial to the body. (To find the major details, ask, "What are the benefits of getting enough rest?")

Major detail #1: One benefit of rest is that it allows the body to renew its energy.

Major detail #2: Another effect is that it allows the body to repair damaged tissues.

Major detail #3: Resting also allows time for the body to remove chemicals that build up in the body during exercise.

How are the major details organized?

a. a definition of a term
b. a list of ideas in no particular order
c. showing the effects of an action
d. comparing things that are alike or contrasting things that are different

In a paragraph that lists the effects of something, you may think that it is a listing pattern—answer (b). But remember that the main idea is "Getting enough rest after exercising or training is very beneficial to the body." In this case, the author intends to show the *effects* of resting after exercise, so the correct answer would be (c). You should always go back to the main idea to look for clues as to what the author intended to show with the supporting details.

MyReadingLab

PRACTICE 4

Read the following paragraph, and determine the overall pattern of organization. Underline the main idea and major supporting details, and then answer the questions that follow.

WARM-UPS

[1] It's always tempting to begin a game or an exercise and skip over the warm-up, such as stretching. [2] But warm-ups are an important part of training and exercise with several advantageous effects. [3] First, after doing a warm-up routine, muscles that are warmed will perform better and increase strength and speed. [4] Second, a warm-up will raise the body's temperature and improve the flexibility of the muscles, reducing the risk of injury. [5] Third, the blood vessels will grow larger, increasing blood flow and reducing the stress on the heart. [6] Also, your body will increase its production of hormones for energy, which will increase your endurance. [7] Finally, a good warm-up will help you to focus mentally on the exercise or the game.

1. What is the main idea?
   a. It's always tempting to begin a game or an exercise and skip over the warm-up, such as stretching.
   b. First, after doing a warm-up routine, muscles that are warmed will perform better and increase strength and speed.
   c. But warm-ups are an important part of training and exercise with several advantageous effects.
   d. Finally, a good warm-up will help you to focus mentally on the exercise or game.

2. Which sentences give the major details?
   a. sentences 1, 4, 5, and 6
   b. sentences 1, 2, and 3
   c. sentences 5, 6, and 7
   d. sentences 3, 4, 5, 6, and 7

3. Which of the following transitions are found in the major supporting details?
   a. another, also, additionally, and
   b. first, second, third, also, finally
   c. but, is, means, always
   d. but, however, in contrast, differently

4. How are the major details organized?
   a. They define what a warm-up is.
   b. They compare different types of warm-ups.
   c. They explain the causes of warm-ups.
   d. They describe the beneficial effects of warm-ups.

5. What is the overall pattern of organization?
   a. definition
   b. listing
   c. cause and effect
   d. compare and/or contrast

MyReadingLab

PRACTICE 5

Read the following paragraph, and determine the overall pattern of organization. Underline the main idea and major supporting details, and then answer the questions that follow.

ERGOGENIC AIDS

1 Ergogenic (er-go-JEN-ik) aids are substances, drugs, procedures, or devices that improve athletic performance. 2 These can be legal or illegal and are used by many athletes both amateur and professional. 3 Some of these ergogenic aids have been banned by sporting authorities because they are unsafe and give players an unfair advantage. 4 One is ephedrine (eff-FED-drin), which is a stimulant, meaning it increases the heart rate, raises blood pressure, and can cause death if too much is taken. 5 Others are anabolic (an-a-BOLL-ik) steroids (STAIR-oids), which are various chemicals made in a laboratory to increase muscle mass. 6 They delay fatigue and give players a false feeling of well-being. 7 But the side effects of these drugs are often severe and cause serious damage to the body and mind with long-term use.

1. What is the main idea?
   - a. Ergogenic (er-go-JEN-ik) aids are substances, drugs, procedures, or devices that improve athletic performance.
   - b. These can be legal or illegal and are used by many athletes both amateur and professional.
   - c. Some of these ergogenic aids have been banned by sporting authorities because they are unsafe.
   - d. But the side effects of these drugs are often severe and causes erious damage to the body and mind with long-term use.
2. Which sentences give the major details?
   - a. sentences 1, 2, and 3
   - b. sentences 3, 4, 5, and 6
   - c. sentences 2, 4, and 6
   - d. sentences 4 and 5
3. Which of the following transitions are found in the major supporting details?
   - a. is, are
   - b. also, but
   - c. both, because
   - d. another, but
4. How are the major details organized?
   - a. They provide a list of ergogenic aids.
   - b. They define two ergogenic aids.
   - c. They compare ergogenic aids.
   - d. They contrast ergogenic aids.
5. What is the overall pattern of organization?
   - a. definition
   - b. listing
   - c. cause and effect
   - d. time order

MyReadingLab

PRACTICE 6

Read the following paragraph, and determine the overall pattern of organization. Underline the main idea and major supporting details, and then answer the questions that follow.

NUTRITION

[1] Good nutrition is following a diet that supplies all of the body's needs for good health. [2] Not eating enough of the right foods can lead to poor nutrition and health problems. [3] For example, not getting enough vitamin C can lead to scurvy, a disease that causes swelling and bleeding. [4] An iron deficiency will lead to anemia, causing fatigue. [5] Diets that are high in fat or sugar can cause many different types of health problems, including diabetes, obesity, cardiovascular disease, and certain types of cancer. [6] Therefore, to maintain good health, it is important to have good nutrition by following the dietary guidelines given by the Food and Drug Administration.

1. What is the main idea?

- **a.** Good nutrition is following a diet that supplies all of the body's needs for good health.
- **b.** Not eating enough of the right foods can lead to poor nutrition and health problems.
- **c.** Diets that are high in fat or sugar can cause many different types of health problems, including diabetes, obesity, cardiovascular disease, and certain types of cancer.
- **d.** Therefore, to maintain good health, it is important to have good nutrition by following the dietary guidelines given by the Food and Drug Administration.

2. Which sentences give the major details?

- **a.** sentences 2 and 6
- **b.** sentences 1, 2, and 3
- **c.** sentences 1 and 6
- **d.** sentences 3, 4, and 5

3. Which of the following transitions are found in the major supporting details?

- **a.** for example, lead to
- **b.** is, therefore,
- **c.** lead to, therefore
- **d.** lead to, types

4. How are the minor details organized?

- **a.** They explain the definition of good nutrition.
- **b.** They list examples of good nutrition.
- **c.** They show the effects of poor nutrition.
- **d.** They compare foods that are nutritious to poor foods.

5. What is the overall pattern of organization?

- **a.** definition
- **b.** listing
- **c.** cause and effect
- **d.** compare and/or contrast

MyReadingLab

TEXTBOOK SELECTION 2

Read the following textbook selection, and determine the overall pattern of organization. Underline the main idea and major supporting details, and then answer the questions that follow.

Personality Behavior Patterns

[1] People's different reactions to the same stressful situation can be due to personality differences and how they have learned to respond. [2] There are many different ways to describe personalities and behavior patterns.

[3] People who exhibit Type A behavior pattern (TABP) are highly motivated, time conscious, hard driving, impatient, and sometimes hostile, cynical, and angry. [4] They have a heightened response to stress, and their hostility and anger, especially if repressed, place them at a greater risk for heart disease. [5] Individuals with Type B behavior pattern are easygoing, non-aggressive, and patient, and they are not prone to hostile episodes like their TABP counterparts. [6] People with Type B behavior pattern are less likely to perceive everyday annoyances as significant stressors and are at low risk for heart disease from stress. [7] People with Type C behavior pattern have many of the positive qualities of TABP; they are confident, highly motivated, and competitive. [8] However, individuals with Type C behavior pattern typically do not express the hostility and anger seen with TABP, and they use their personality characteristics to maintain a constant level of emotional control and to channel their ambition into creative directions. [9] As a result, individuals with Type C behavior pattern experience the same low risk for stress-related heart disease as do those with Type B behavior pattern. [10] Similar to those with Type A behavior pattern, individuals with Type D behavior pattern are also considered to be at greater risk for stress-related disease. [11] These individuals are prone to anxiety and worry, and also tend to be socially inhibited and uneasy when interacting with others.

QUESTIONS

1. What is the main idea?
   - **a.** People's different reactions to the same stressful situation can be due to personality differences and how they have learned to respond.
   - **b.** There are many different ways to describe personalities and behavior patterns.
   - **c.** People who exhibit Type A behavior pattern (TABP) are highly motivated, time conscious, hard driving, impatient, and sometimes hostile, cynical, and angry.
   - **d.** These individuals are prone to anxiety and worry, and also tend to be socially inhibited and uneasy when interacting with others.

2. Which sentences give the major details?
   - **a.** sentences 3, 4, 5, and 6
   - **b.** sentences 3, 5, 7, and 10
   - **c.** sentences 3, 7, 9, and 10
   - **d.** sentences 3, 5, 10, and 11

3. Identify the relationship within the following sentence: As a result, individuals with Type C behavior pattern experience the same low risk for stress-related heart disease as do those with Type B behavior pattern.
   a. definition
   b. listing
   c. cause and effect
   d. compare and/or contrast

4. Identify the relationship between sentences 8 and 9.
   a. definition
   b. time order
   c. cause and effect
   d. compare and/or contrast

5. How are the major details organized?
   a. They define the different types of behavior patterns while at the same time comparing and contrasting the different types.
   b. They show the causes of different behavior patterns.
   c. They show the effects of different behavior patterns.
   d. They give examples of different behavior patterns.

U-REVIEW 2

On the following lines, write whether the statements are true or false. If the statement is false, correct it to make it true on the lines provided.

1. When looking for a paragraph's overall pattern, you should look at the minor supporting details.

2. The main idea will often give a clue to the paragraph's pattern of organization.

3. Sometimes the transitions in the sentences do not match the overall relationship being shown in a paragraph.

4. To determine the pattern of organization, you should ask yourself, "How are the major supporting details organized?"

5. Every sentence in the paragraph will have the same pattern of organization as the whole paragraph.

MyReadingLab

Reading 1
VOCABULARY PREVIEW

"Dangerously Strong" by Elizabeth Foy Larsen

The following vocabulary words are from the article "Dangerously Strong." With a partner or in a team, choose the correct meanings of the underlined words in the following sentences. Use context clues (LEADS), word part clues, and parts of speech to help you figure out the meanings.

1. What compelled (kom-PELL'd) you to quit your job and join the Peace Corps?
   a. to accept
   b. incredibly
   c. drove
   d. insisted
2. Many medicines that were made from plants are now made in synthetic (sin-THET-ik) forms using chemistry in laboratories.
   a. organic
   b. man-made
   c. official
   d. natural
3. Jason began weight training and he has bulked up (BULK'd up) his muscle mass.
   a. created
   b. inflated
   c. disguised
   d. increased
4. The doctor recommended that Jerod take supplemental (sup-le-MEN-tal) vitamins to increase his resistance to illness.
   a. antibiotic
   b. healing
   c. additional
   d. nutritious
5. When Julia was a little girl, she used to prance around in her ballerina costume and pretend she was a dancer.
   a. to strut
   b. to ignore
   c. graceful
   d. strongly built
6. Some forms of arthritis can be treated through diet and exercise instead of a more radical (RAD-i-kal) treatment such as surgery.
   a. current
   b. extreme
   c. undesirable
   d. dangerous
7. Getting stronger became such an obsession (ob-SESS-shun) for Jack that he spent all of his time and money on it.
   a. habit
   b. idea
   c. addiction
   d. endurance
8. Some athletes set unattainable (un-a-TAIN_able) goals for themselves and spend their entire lives trying to achieve them.
   a. not achievable
   b. not likable
   c. harmful
   d. high
9. The water from our tap was filled with so many contaminants (kon-TAM-i-nants) that it was unsafe to drink.
   a. unhealthy
   b. bad-tasting
   c. pollutants
   d. poisonous
10. By increasing the amount of exercise a little more during each workout, you can increase your endurance (en-DUR-ance) to do more.
    a. strength
    b. stamina
    c. distance
    d. time

MyReadingLab

Reading 1 PREVIEW

1. How do you feel about famous sports celebrities who admit to using drugs or other aids to improve their physical abilities?
2. Why do you think Americans idolize sports celebrities?

Directions: As you read this article, practice the four-step reading process. Preview the article, and then write on the following lines one or two questions that you would hope to have answered.

MyReadingLab

Reading 1

As you read, answer the questions in the margins to check your comprehension.

"Dangerously Strong"

by Elizabeth Foy Larsen

1 It seemed like Taylor Hooton had everything going for him. Popular, with a 3.8 GPA, the 17-year-old loved relaxing with friends and cruising around in his black Dodge truck with his girlfriend. He was a talented baseball pitcher who dreamed of going pro.

2 The summer before his senior year, Taylor stormed upstairs to his bedroom and hanged himself. In the tortured days that followed, his family members wondered what could have compelled such a healthy and successful teen to take his own life. Their answer came after the police searched Taylor's bedroom and found a stash of **anabolic steroids**. These powerful drugs are prescribed by doctors to treat serious health issues.

anabolic steroids: synthetic drugs used by athletes to build muscle and improve performance.

3 They are also used illegally by athletes to quickly build muscle and improve performance. These synthetic forms of testosterone, along with the pure, human-derived form, are banned in professional sports. Still, hundreds of professional and Olympic athletes, most recently cyclist Lance Armstrong, have been disgraced—some even stripped of their awards and medals—after admitting to steroid use.

Continued...

MyReadingLab

Reading 1

...continued

4 But even as steroid scandals in professional sports make headlines, thousands of teens are risking their health—and their lives—by using these powerful drugs.

Fits of Anger

5 In the months before Taylor's death, his parents noticed that he had bulked up. They simply believed he'd been training hard, and that his new muscles were a result of his more intense weight-lifting program. The real story: When Taylor was 16, a coach in his hometown of Plano, Texas, told him that if he wanted to make varsity, he'd need to bulk up. This advice still shocks his father, Don Hooton. "Taylor was already 5'11" and 180 pounds," he says.

6 Experts estimate that hundreds of thousands of teens currently use anabolic steroids in their quest to bulk up. Few understand that they risk permanent injury to their bodies—or worse.

What did doctors believe caused Taylor's suicide?

7 One serious side effect of steroid use is that users can become mentally unbalanced, with uncontrolled fits of anger and irrational thinking. This, doctors explained to Taylor's parents, is what likely had happened to their son, and what led him to take his own life.

8 Of course being fit is an important part of being healthy. For older teens, lifting weights can improve strength and athletic performance, as it did for Lucas Atwood, a high school rugby player from Denver, Colorado. Following a knee injury during his freshman year, Lucas lifted weights to keep in shape and regain strength in his knee. Today, he is an all-state rugby player, and he plans to study physical education in college. "For me, lifting weights has helped my confidence," he says.

9 But for some boys, weight lifting isn't about fitness—it's about appearance: getting bigger and more ripped.

10 In a recent University of Minnesota study of middle and high school students in the Minneapolis-St. Paul area, 91 percent of guys said they had exercised in the past year to increase their muscle mass. Thirty-five percent reported using supplemental protein powders or shakes to bulk up and get toned.

11 Just a few decades ago, ultra-muscled bodies were mainly seen on circus performers and professional weight lifters. Today, actors like Channing Tatum flaunt their bare chests on magazine covers. Chris Brown and Justin Bieber prance shirtless as they sing and dance.

12 In forums on websites such as bodybuilding.com, teens chart their workout goals and share photos of themselves. Photo galleries show boys who undergo seemingly miraculous transformations—from skinny guys to Incredible Hulks. Are these pictures even real? It's unclear, since many of the faces are blocked out. But the sites are popular with teens, and users post messages urging others to become as big as possible. "[Freshman year] I was such a **beta**, let girls walk all over me and let bigger boys bully me," writes an 18-year-old who goes by the name "Maverickcrash." "[Now] I'm motivating the guys that were at my stage to get big and become real men."

beta: (BAY-ta) (slang usage) unimportant; secondary; unproven

False Advertising.

Why are so many young teens taking anabolic steroids and supplements?

13 Are such radical transformations even possible for most teens? Experts

genetics: the physical and mental characteristics that are handed down to offspring from parents.

say no. Almost anyone can build their muscles and make them more defined through exercise and diet. But how big a person's muscles can grow (naturally) is determined by **genetics**.

14 What about those guys you see in advertisements for most bodybuilding supplements—with massive muscles, carved abs, and turkey-drumstick calves? "The message in these ads is that if you work hard and buy the right supplements, you'll look this way," says Dr. Harrison Pope, an author and professor at Harvard Medical School. "But the vast majority of the people in these images are taking steroids."

15 Pope has studied and written about what he calls "body obsession" in men and boys. He says that the black market availability of anabolic steroids has created a new breed of bodies that set an unrealistically high bar for attractiveness.

How are boys being "brainwashed" about body image?

16 These unattainable standards can cause a mental illness called body *dysmorphic disorder* in some teens—no matter how much they work out, they never feel like they're "big enough." In other words, boys are being brainwashed by images of bodies that are unnatural.

Supplements 101

17 And what about those nutritional supplements and protein powders sold at fitness centers and health food stores? Most doctors dismiss the idea that they can help build muscle. They also point out that though these supplements are legal, they are not regulated by the U.S. Food and Drug Administration. Unlike food and drug companies, supplement manufacturers don't have to prove that their health claims are accurate.

How effective are nutritional supplements for increasing muscle mass?

18 "These products make it look like they'll give you more power," says Dr. Linn Goldberg, a professor of sports medicine at Oregon Health & Science University and the co-director of the ATLAS and ATHENA programs, which promote healthy, drug-free training and nutrition for high school athletes. "But you have no idea what is actually in a supplement." In fact, the experts at *Consumer Reports* caution that some nutritional supplements can contain dangerous substances, such as synthetic steroids, pesticides and heavy metals that can be damaging to the body. They found similar contaminants in several brands of protein powders.

19 More important, for kids like Taylor Hooton, using supplements can easily become a bridge to using anabolic steroids.

20 So how can you tell if you or someone you know is taking muscle-making too far? If persistent thoughts about being too heavy or too wimpy make you feel the need to work out every day for hours, that's a red flag, says Annie Fox, the author of *Too Stressed to Think?* So is constantly monitoring your calories, weight, or body fat. This goes for boys and girls.

21 To combat this obsessing, Fox recommends not looking at magazines and websites that show super-built men and women (or at least looking at them with a grain of salt). Otherwise, you'll feel inferior—when, actually, you're

Continued...

MyReadingLab

Reading 1

...continued

How can teens avoid obsessing about their bodies?

not. "If it's a print image, it's been airbrushed, but we don't think about that. People on the red carpet have had a lot of enhancements and help," says Fox.

22 If taking a media break doesn't turn off the voice inside your head that tells you that your body isn't good enough, talk to an adult you trust about getting professional help.

Balanced Approach

23 Excessive weight lifting—even without supplements or steroids—can also be dangerous. Doctors don't recommend weight lifting to boys younger than 14. For those old enough to weight lift, it's important to work out under the supervision of a qualified trainer. If you try too hard to get killer **abs** or bulging **biceps**, you might cause an overuse injury—damage to the tendons or joints that can cause ongoing pain and problems.

abs: abdominal muscles
biceps: upper arm muscles

24 The best fitness approach is a well-rounded one. "Do as many kinds of activities as possible," advises Craig Helmer, a trainer who works with teens at Balance Fitness Studio in Minnesota. Shoot baskets at your local park. Bike. Swim. Walk. Dance. Do push-ups and crunches. Go to the weight room at your school (for strength training, not to make your biceps bigger). Join a team.

25 That balanced approach worked for Kallie Harper, a senior at North Hills Senior High School in Pennsylvania. A basketball and softball player, Kallie exercises throughout the year and mixes conditioning with endurance and skills training. "When you work hard, it makes you feel good—like you've accomplished something," she says.

26 That's a message that Don Hooton wishes Taylor had heard—and one that he hopes more teens take to heart. "Taylor didn't understand that there are permanent decisions," he says, "and he lost his life."

1,409 words divided by .... minutes = ... words per minute

MyReadingLab

Reading 1 REVIEW

Summarizing after you read will help you to understand the author's purpose and the main idea.

Directions: On the lines below, write a two or three sentence summary of the article, "Dangerously Strong." In your own words, describe what the article was about, and why the author wrote it.

MyReadingLab

Reading 1 COMPREHENSION QUESTIONS

The following questions will help you to recall the details of the article and the main idea. Review any parts of the article that you need in order to find the correct answers.

1. What is the central point of the entire article?

a. Taylor Hooton had been taking anabolic steroids before he hanged himself.
b. Young teen boys are becoming obsessed about having large muscles.
c. Some teens use anabolic steroids and supplements to increase their muscle mass, but these supplements have harmful side effects.
d. Many athletes use anabolic steroids to win competitions.

2. What is the stated main idea of paragraph 12?

a. In forums on websites such as bodybuilding.com, teens chart their workout goals and share photos of themselves.
b. Photo galleries show boys who undergo seemingly miraculous transformations—from skinny guys to Incredible Hulks.
c. But the sites are popular with teens, and users post messages urging others to become as big as possible.
d. "[Now] I'm motivating the guys that were at my stage to get big and become real men."

3. What is the implied main idea of paragraph 18?

a. Drugs and health supplements are never good for anyone.
b. Drug and health supplements can provide users with more powerful muscles.
c. All drug and health supplements are dangerous.
d. Consumers have no idea what is actually in some drug and health supplements.

SUPPORTING DETAILS

4. According to the article, what led Taylor Hooton to take his own life?

a. He had lost an important baseball game.
b. He had broken up with his girlfriend.
c. His use of anabolic steroids made him angry and irrational.
d. He felt guilty for using anabolic steroids to increase his muscle mass.

5. According to the article, what determines how big a person's muscles can grow naturally?

a. how many different drugs and supplements are used
b. the genes that a person inherits from his or her parents
c. the amount of exercise that muscles are given
d. the types of exercise that a person does

6. One reason why nutritional supplements are not regulated by the U.S. Food and Drug Administration is that:

a. dietary supplement manufacturers don't have to prove that their products actually do what they claim.
b. supplement manufacturers already enforce their own safety and reliability standards.
c. the FDA does not want to do inspections on supplement manufacturing facilities.
d. all dietary supplements are harmless.

DRAWING CONCLUSIONS

7. From the article you can conclude that:
- **a.** teen boys who view photos on the Internet of other teens with big muscles believe that they should look like those teens.
- **b.** if you take the right supplements you will have larger muscles.
- **c.** teen boys with big muscles are more popular than those without them.
- **d.** dietary supplements are good for your health.

8. From the article you can conclude that:
- **a.** some people are never as strong as they could be.
- **b.** some people are obsessed about the physical appearance of their bodies.
- **c.** the Internet is causing teens to seek bigger muscles.
- **d.** weight lifting is the best way to keep fit.

VOCABULARY IN CONTEXT

9. Identify the correct meaning of the underlined word in the sentence: Most doctors <u>dismiss</u> the idea that they can help build muscle.
- **a.** to release
- **b.** to take away
- **c.** to exclude
- **d.** to disbelieve

10. Identify the correct meaning of the underlined word in the sentence: Today, actors like Channing Tatum <u>flaunt</u> their bare chests on magazine covers.
- **a.** to beat
- **b.** to show off
- **c.** to hide
- **d.** to prove

Reading 1
VOCABULARY PRACTICE

Use the vocabulary words from the Word Bank to complete the following sentences. Write the words into the blanks provided.

WORD BANK

compelled	prance	contaminants	synthetic	radical
endurance	bulked up	obsession	supplemental	unattainable

1. Cigarettes contain so many .... that they cause serious illnesses like cancer.
2. Joshua thinks that if he lifts weights four hours a day and takes a .... product, he can greatly increase his muscle mass.
3. Some athletes feel so .... to win that they will do anything, short of killing themselves, to achieve their goals.
4. My little niece likes to .... around the living room in her pajamas and pretend she is a pony.
5. Parents should be suspicious of substance abuse when their teens have a .... change in their bodies or personality.
6. Taylor Hooton wanted to be .... so he could perform better as an athlete.
7. Doing regular exercise over a long period of time can help to build ....
8. Scientists are able to reproduce many natural substances in the lab by creating .... copies of them.
9. Some teens try to achieve a body build that is .... because of the genes that they have inherited.
10. Jonathan has such a(an) .... about his physical appearance that he spends all of his spare time in the gym lifting weights.

MyReadingLab

Reading 1 QUESTIONS FOR WRITING AND DISCUSSION

Review any parts of the article you need to answer the following questions.

1. Why do some teens like Taylor Hooton feel they must use drugs or supplements?

2. What are some of the physical and mental dangers of "bulking up"?

3. What are some signs that someone may be using drugs or supplements to increase muscle mass?

4. How has the Internet influenced teen boys about their physical appearance?

5. Why do you think many Americans, such as the teens in this article, obsess over their appearance? Do you think this is good or bad? Why?

Reading 1
VOCABULARY PRACTICE—CONCENTRATION GAME

The object of the game is to memorize the positions of the cards and to match up as many correct words with definitions as you can. The player with the most matching cards wins.

1. Write the 10 vocabulary words and 10 definitions from the Vocabulary Preview word bank on 20 small cards or pieces of paper so there is one word card and a matching definition card for each word. Shuffle them and place them face down in four rows.

2. The first player turns over two cards but doesn't pick them up. If the two cards are a word and its matching definition, the player picks up both cards and keeps them, and the player gets another turn. If the two cards do not match, the cards are turned face down in the exact same spots and the play goes to the next person

3. The next player turns over any two cards, and the game continues in the same way as described above.

Word and Definition Cards

compelled	synthetic	bulled-up	supplemental
prance	radical	obsession	unattainable
contaminants	endurance	stamina; long-lasting	extreme
additional nutrients	to strut	large muscle mass	not achievable
driven	compulsion, addiction	pollutants	man-made

	SYNTHETIC		
			MAN-MADE

MyReadingLab

Reading 2
VOCABULARY PREVIEW

"True Grit: Bethany Hamilton's Story"

The following vocabulary words are from the article "True Grit: Bethany Hamilton's Story." With a partner or in a team, choose the correct meanings of the underlined words in the following sentences. Use context clues (LEADS), word part clues, and parts of speech to help you figure out the meanings.

1. Bethany recounts (re-COUNTS) the day of her accident as we listen intently.
   a. to count again
   b. to retell a story
   c. an amount of something
   d. regrets
2. To stop the bleeding from his wrist, Marco used his belt for a tourniquet (TUR-ni-kit).
   a. an emergency kit
   b. a shoulder strap
   c. a leash
   d. a cord to stop blood flow
3. The English instructor had to retrain (re-TRAIN) her students on the correct way to cite a source for a paper.
   a. to train again
   b. to over train
   c. to instruct
   d. to write
4. To increase your heart rate, you need to do some vigorous (VIG-or-us) exercises.
   a. healthy
   b. low-impact
   c. energetic
   d. calming
5. When Elisha told us her side of the story, she left out some minor, but nevertheless (nev-er-the-LESS) important details.
   a. however
   b. strangely
   c. untrue
   d. small
6. Brad wanted Anika to hike up the mountain with him, but because of storm clouds on the horizon, she had some reservations (res-er-VAY-shuns).
   a. appointments
   b. doubts
   c. considerations
   d. evaluations

Continued...

7. After Lia returned from active duty in Afghanistan, she suffered from post-traumatic stress (post-tra-MAT-ik-stress) from a roadside bombing.
   a. stress caused by overwork
   b. a condition caused by life-threatening events
   c. substance abuse
   d. a condition caused by excessive physical stress

8. Nothing gets my adrenaline (a-DREN-a-lin) flowing faster than a loud, unexpected crack of thunder.
   a. a type of medicine
   b. a chemical that brings out anger
   c. a chemical causing stress
   d. a hormone causing bodily changes

9. Lamont's appetite diminished (dim-MIN-ish'd) after eating so much popcorn during the movie.
   a. increased
   b. decreased
   c. inflated
   d. awakened

10. Monica's enthusiasm for organic foods is so infectious (in-FEK-shus) that she has everyone in her dorm eating them now.
   a. causing infection
   b. extreme
   c. causing to spread
   d. germ-free

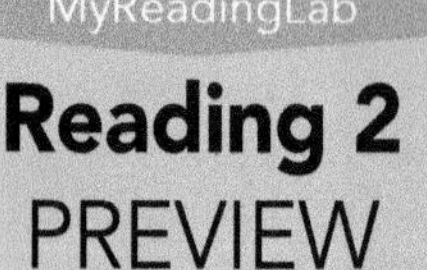

1. What sports do you enjoy playing? Have you ever played in competitions? Describe your experiences.
2. Have you ever tried surfing, snowboarding, or skateboarding? Describe your experience.

Directions: As you read this article, practice the four-step reading process. Preview the article, and then write on the following lines one or two questions that you would hope to have answered.

MyReadingLab

Reading 2

"True Grit: Bethany Hamilton's Story"

by Margy Rochlin

At age 13, Bethany Hamilton lost her arm in a tragic accident. Today she's a world-class surfer—and the inspiration for a new movie

1 Cheri Hamilton had no doubt that her only daughter would grow up to become a professional surfer. At age 4, Bethany was riding waves off the beaches of her home in Kauai. By the time she was 8 she was competing in surfing contests. Taking on gigantic waves was Bethany's specialty, and her parents, both surfers, would encourage her. "We'd tell her, 'You can win this because you're strong. The other kids are going to run away from the big surf,' " recalls Cheri. And sure enough, Bethany, who squealed with delight when she caught a wave, would take home the trophy.

2 But eight years ago Bethany's dream of surfing greatness nearly came to an end after she was attacked by a 14-foot tiger shark that tore off her left arm. That headline-making tragedy, and her astonishing path to recovery, is the subject of a new movie, *Soul Surfer*, starring Anna Sophia Robb (as Bethany) and Helen Hunt (as Cheri).

3 Today, sitting with her mother in a Santa Monica hotel lounge, Bethany, 21, looks every bit the Hawaiian beach girl, dressed in cutoffs, a Rip Curl jean jacket and bare feet. She smiles and laughs easily but becomes soft-spoken when she recounts the events of that horrible day

What happened to Bethany when she was 13 that changed her life?

4 Bethany and some friends had gone to Tunnels Beach, one of her favorite surfing spots off Kauai's North Shore. She was lying on her surfboard when she suddenly felt pressure on her arm and then a back-and-forth tugging—"you know, like how you eat a piece of steak," she says—before noticing that the turquoise water around her was quickly turning red from her own blood. "I just had a sense of peace throughout it all," says Bethany, whose friends fashioned a tourniquet from a surfboard leash once they paddled her to shore. "I think that was one of the key factors that helped me—if I had panicked I would have lost more blood."

5 When Cheri finally saw her daughter at the local hospital, "I was just thankful she was alive," she says. "That was my whole focus—we'll deal with whatever we have to deal with, but at least she's alive." Bethany's left arm was now a small knob of skin held together with stitches. As the wound healed, her focus returned to the water. Not only would she continue to ride waves, but she also decided she would retrain herself. "To me it was like never getting in a car again because you're afraid of having another collision," Bethany says. "Not surfing just didn't work for me." About a month after the attack, around the time her doctor gave her the go-ahead to surf, Bethany stood up on a board as her mother, her father, Tom, and her two older brothers, Noah and Timmy, cheered her on.

Continued...

MyReadingLab

Reading 2

...continued

6 In *Soul Surfer*, it's clear how much Bethany's family played a part in her comeback success. One scene shows her brothers helping her rebuild her strength through vigorous weight training and long runs on the beach. Another has her father (played by Dennis Quaid) installing a handle on the upper end of her board so she could catch her balance. "Our goal was to help her be at the top of her game," says Cheri, who nevertheless had reservations about her daughter's return to competitive surfing. Cheri knew surfing is traditionally a two-armed sport: You need both arms to paddle, grab the sides of the board and raise yourself from a prone position. Instead of cheering her on, she wondered, should they be encouraging her to slow down? "I wasn't sure she should do contests. At one point I told her, 'Just go and support your friends,'" says Cheri. "I didn't want to set her up for failure."

Why didn't Bethany's mother want her to return to competitive surfing?

7 Cheri couldn't bring herself to go with Bethany to her first comeback competition on Hawaii's Big Island two months after the attack ("too painful," she says, wincing). But when her daughter returned home with fifth place, she shifted gears. "If you can get fifth place, you can get fourth place," Cheri told her. Six months later Bethany won her division in a bigger contest in Waikiki. At the time of her attack she was considered an amateur with signs of promise. Today she is ranked among the top 25 female surfers in the world.

8 There have been moments when Bethany and her mother are haunted by that October 2003 morning. Out on the water, Bethany might think, *was that a shark in the distance? Will it happen again*? But "I hardly ever get worried," she says, and she has ways of calming herself down. "I'll pray," she says, "or I'll sing a song, like, 'Ain't No Mountain High Enough' or 'Somewhere Over the Rainbow.'"

What after-effects has Bethany suffered from her experience?

9 Cheri struggles with post-traumatic stress. "If I'm sleeping and I hear a noise, I'll wake up and feel adrenaline running through my body," she says. "It's diminished over the years, but it still happens."

10 Mostly, though, Bethany uses her story to inspire people. She gives motivational talks and, through her nonprofit foundation, Friends of Bethany, she works with other amputees and shark-attack survivors. "I met one boy in Australia who was born with no limbs and I took him surfing with me," she says. "We all have different challenges, but his attitude was so positive it was infectious." The rest of the time she's traveling around the world, catching waves—and trophies—on the competitive surfing circuit. "People ask me if I'm excited about the movie," says Bethany, who was on the Oahu set with her family and did most of the one-armed surfing scenes in the film. "I am. It's a once-in-a-lifetime opportunity. But I'm way more excited about surfing. Surfing is what I do."

How has Bethany used her experience to help others?

981 words divided by ________ minutes = ________ words per minute

MyReadingLab

Reading 2 REVIEW

It's a good habit to summarize everything you read to strengthen your comprehension.

Directions: On the following lines, write a two- or three-sentence summary of the article, "True Grit: Bethany Hamilton's Story." In your own words, describe what the article was about and why the author wrote it.

MyReadingLab

Reading 2 COMPREHENSION QUESTIONS

The following questions will help you recall the main idea and the details of "True Grit: Bethany Hamilton's Story." Review any parts of the article that you need to find the correct answers

1. What is the central point of this article?
   - a. Bethany Hamilton was attacked by a shark at age 13 and lost her arm.
   - b. You should never let obstacles get in the way of achieving your dreams.
   - c. Bethany Hamilton remained strong despite the loss of her arm.
   - d. Bethany Hamilton achieved her dream as a professional surfer despite the loss of her arm from a shark attack.
2. What is the implied main idea of paragraph 5?
   - a. Despite having lost her arm, Bethany was determined to return to surfing after her shark attack.
   - b. After the shark attack, Bethany's mother was grateful that her daughter was still alive.
   - c. Bethany's family cheered her on as she went back to surfing a month after the shark attack.
   - d. Bethany had to retrain herself to surf in a new way because of the loss of her arm.
3. What is the implied main idea of paragraph 4?
   - a. Bethany and some friends had gone to Tunnels Beach, one of her favorite surfing spots off Kauai's North Shore.
   - b. Bethany was lying on a surfboard when she felt the shark tugging on her arm and saw her own blood in the water.
   - c. After Bethany was bitten by a shark, her friends paddled her to shore and gave her first aid.
   - d. Bethany remained calm during the shark attack.

SUPPORTING DETAILS

4. According to the story, Bethany's family
   - a. didn't want her to return to surfing because they knew she wouldn't be successful without both arms.
   - b. helped to train her, added a handle to her board, and cheered her on.
   - c. made a board just for her and entered her in the Special Olympics.
   - d. moved from Hawaii to the mainland so Bethany could compete in more surfing competitions.

DRAWING CONCLUSIONS

5. From the article, you can conclude that Bethany
   - a. will never be a first place winner in any surfing competition.
   - b. will probably win the world surfing championship someday.
   - c. uses her experiences to help others with disabilities.
   - d. will become a famous movie star when her movie is released.

PATTERNS OF ORGANIZATION

6. What is the relationship within the following sentence? But eight years ago Bethany's dream of surfing greatness nearly came to an end after she was attacked by a 14-foot tiger shark that tore off her left arm.
   - a. cause and effect
   - b. compare and contrast
   - c. listing
   - d. time order

7. What is the relationship between the following sentences? You need both arms to paddle, grab the sides of the board and raise yourself from a prone position. Instead of cheering her on, she wondered, should they be encouraging her to slow down?
   a. definition
   b. cause and effect
   c. compare and contrast
   d. listing

8. What is the overall pattern of organization for this article?
   a. listing
   b. time order
   c. compare and contrast
   d. cause and effect

9. What is the overall pattern of organization for paragraph 2?
   a. definition
   b. listing
   c. cause and effect
   d. compare and contrast

VOCABULARY IN CONTEXT

10. What is the meaning of the underlined word in the following sentence? You need both arms to paddle, grab the sides of the board and raise yourself from a <u>prone</u> position.
   a. likely to
   b. having a habit for something
   c. lying face down
   d. squatting

MyReadingLab

Reading 2 VOCABULARY PRACTICE

Use the vocabulary words from the Word Bank to complete the following sentences. Write the words into the blanks provided.

WORD BANK

recounts	tourniquet	retrain	vigorous
nevertheless	reservations	post-traumatic stress	infectious
adrenaline	diminished		

1. After hearing about the wildfires in California, I had .... about going there on vacation.

2. Artists who have lost the use of a hand must .... themselves to paint with the opposite hand.

3. The coach always gives his team an energetic pep talk before each game to get their .... flowing.

4. As soon as we got our sailboat out onto the lake, the wind .... and we had to row back to shore.

5. Selina's laughter and light-hearted manner is so .... that she soon has everyone around her in a happy mood.

6. Jeremy needed counseling after he was in the Boston Marathon bombing because he suffered from ....

7. We start every day with .... exercises to get our blood flowing and build energy.

8. Each time Harry .... the story of how he caught that fish, the fish gets bigger and bigger.

9. The Scouts learned how to give first aid and how to apply a .... to stop bleeding.

10. The best months in London for good weather are in the summer; ...., take an umbrella with you when you go.

MyReadingLab

Reading 2 QUESTIONS FOR WRITING AND DISCUSSION

Review any parts of the article you need to answer the following questions.

1. What role did Bethany's family play in helping her to overcome her disability and achieve her dream?

2. If Bethany had not returned to surfing right after her accident, how might her life have changed?

3. What factors do you think have contributed to Bethany's success?

4. Bethany admits to still having fears when she hears a sudden noise or sees something that looks like a shark. How does she handle her fear?

5. What is one example of someone who has overcome difficult obstacles to achieve success?

MyReadingLab

Reading 2 VOCABULARY PRACTICE

Together with your team, use the clues in the first column to unscramble the jumbled words in the second column. Then, use the letters in the circles to unscramble a phrase.

WORD BANK

RECOUNTS, NEVERTHELESS, ADRENALINE, TOURNIQUET, RESERVATIONS, DIMINISHED, RETRAIN, POST-TRAUMATIC STRESS, INFECTIOUS, VIGOROUS

CLUES (Note: Clues are not definitions, just "clues")	**SCRAMBLED WORDS**	**WORD**
1. Like a disease	SINTEFUCIO	I N F E C T (I) O U S
2. Jumping rope is	ROGUSIVO	◯ _ ◯ _ _ _ _ _
3. On the other hand…	LEVESENSTERSH	_ _ _ _ _ _ ◯ _ _ _ _ _
4. Made smaller	NISMIDHIED	◯ _ _ _ _ _ _ _ _ _
5. Having second thoughts	VORSITRESEAN	_ _ _ _ _ _ _ _ ◯ _ _ _
6. Terror attacks can cause…	MARSTAUPESCITROSTST	_ _ _ ◯ _ _ _ _ ◯ _ _ _ _ _ _ _ ◯ _ _
7. Increases heart rate	READANNILE	_ _ _ _ ◯ _ _ _ _ _
8. Telling a narrative	SCOUNTER	◯ _ _ _ _ _ _ _
9. Medical emergency aid	QUIETONTUR	_ _ _ _ _ _ _ _ ◯ _
10. Teach over	NIRTERA	_ _ _ _ ◯ _ _

Write the letters from inside the circles on the following lines. Use them to unscramble the phrase describing something we would all love to do.

_ _ _ _ _ _ _ _ _ _ _ _ _ I

Phrase: L _ _ I _ _   _ _ _   _ _ _ _ _

ON THE JOB INTERVIEW

RICK MUHR

COACH AND CONSULTANT

What is your career, and how did you become interested in coaching?

For 12 years I was head coach for Team in Training, sponsored by the Leukemia and Lymphoma Society, to help prepare people for running marathons. During those years, I was able to help others and raise money for an important cause. I also coached track and cross country at Worcester State College in Massachusetts. I am now an independent consultant and coach for many organizations and individuals. I've always been a runner, and I carried the Olympic Torch in St. Louis in 2004. A life-changing event occurred when my mother died of leukemia, and I made a promise to her that I would do something significant with my life to make her proud and to help others.

What is your training and education?

I graduated from college with a degree in business, and this has enabled me to work with a variety of businesses and organizations and to run my own business as a consultant and coach. I became certified in the areas of exercise and physiology, but most of my knowledge has been acquired through my own study.

Did you ever consider quitting?

I am not a quitter, so that wasn't something I would consider. Even when I ran a marathon of 117 miles in 24 hours, I never considered giving up. Once you have experienced running in a marathon like that, when you cross the finish line, you realize what you are capable of, and you appreciate the small things in life more. I have learned more from failure and disappointment than anything else in life. So quitting is not an option.

Where do you work now, and what do you like about your job?

I am now an independent coach and consultant. What I love most about my job is helping all kinds of people and inspiring them to become whole in body, mind, and spirit. I love connecting to people on a personal level and being able to help others achieve a sense of being whole.

What do you dislike about your job?

There is nothing I really dislike about my job. It's my passion, and I love what I do.

If you could give college students one piece of advice, what would it be?

Believe in yourself. Be open minded to different ideas and possibilities. Get comfortable being uncomfortable—meaning, go outside of your comfort zone to discover your capabilities. Work hard, learn from your failures, and give praise and credit to others. Take a challenging class, or get a college degree, or a better job. Think about your legacy early in life, and do whatever it takes to achieve it. Follow your passion!

MyReadingLab

WATCH THE VIDEO

FIVE POWER FOODS

Watch the Video "Five Power Foods" and answer the questions about patterns of organization.

MyReadingLab

REAL-LIFE READING

REFUND AND REPAYMENT POLICY

Read the following "Refund and Repayment Policies," taken from a university catalog. Then, working with your team, answer the questions that follow.

REFUND AND REPAYMENT POLICIES

Students should be aware that if they withdraw from the University after having received financial assistance, they may have to repay a portion of that assistance. Students who received Federal Stafford Loans should also know that the Student Financial Assistance Office is required to notify lenders of student withdrawals.

REFUNDS

Financial assistance recipients planning to withdraw from the University should first consult the University's Withdrawal Policy published under Academic Policies and Procedures in the University Catalog.

If the student is due a refund according to this policy, the financial assistance program(s) from which the student received assistance will first be reimbursed. Any remaining balance after refunding all appropriate assistance programs will be refunded to the student.

In no case will the amount refunded to the assistance program exceed the amount paid to the student.

REPAYMENT

If a student withdraws on or before the midterm point in the time of the period of enrollment, calculated using calendar days, a portion of the total Title IV funds awarded a student must be returned according to the provisions of the Higher Education Amendments of 1998.

The calculation of the return of these funds may result in the student owing a balance to the University and/or the federal government. This calculated amount will be returned to the Title IV programs in the following order:

1) Unsubsidized Federal Stafford loans
2) Subsidized Federal Stafford loans
3) Federal Perkins loans
4) Federal PLUS loans
5) Federal Pell Grants
6) Federal SEOG
7) Other grant or loan assistance authorized by Title IV of the HEA
8) State aid
9) Institutional aid
10) Other

Students should schedule an appointment with or come to the Student Financial Assistance Office prior to withdrawing from classes to confirm the consequences of that withdrawal.

On the lines provided, write whether the following statements are true or false. If the statement is false, change it to make it true.

1. If a student who receives financial assistance withdraws from a course, he or she may have to repay a part of that loan.

2. If a student withdraws, he or she will receive a refund, and then the lender will be refunded.

3. All of the lenders who gave the student financial aid will be refunded in a specific order before the student is refunded.

4. Federal PLUS loans will be refunded before institutional aid.

5. If a student withdraws on or before the midterm point, the student will not have to pay back any of the money that he or she was loaned.

MyReadingLab

BUILDING VOCABULARY

Study the following word parts, and then answer the questions that follow.

Prefixes	Roots	Suffixes
con-, com- *with, together*	-struct- *to build*	-er, -or *one who**
im- *into*	-pose- *to place, to put*	-ive- *a state or quality**
in- *into**		

* Word parts from previous chapters

What English words can you create from these word parts?

Using a dictionary, look up the meanings of any of the words you wrote that you can't define. Use one of the words you wrote in a sentence that reveals its meaning with a context clue.

MyReadingLab

TEXTBOOK GRAPHIC AIDS

Examine the following maps, and then answer the questions that follow.

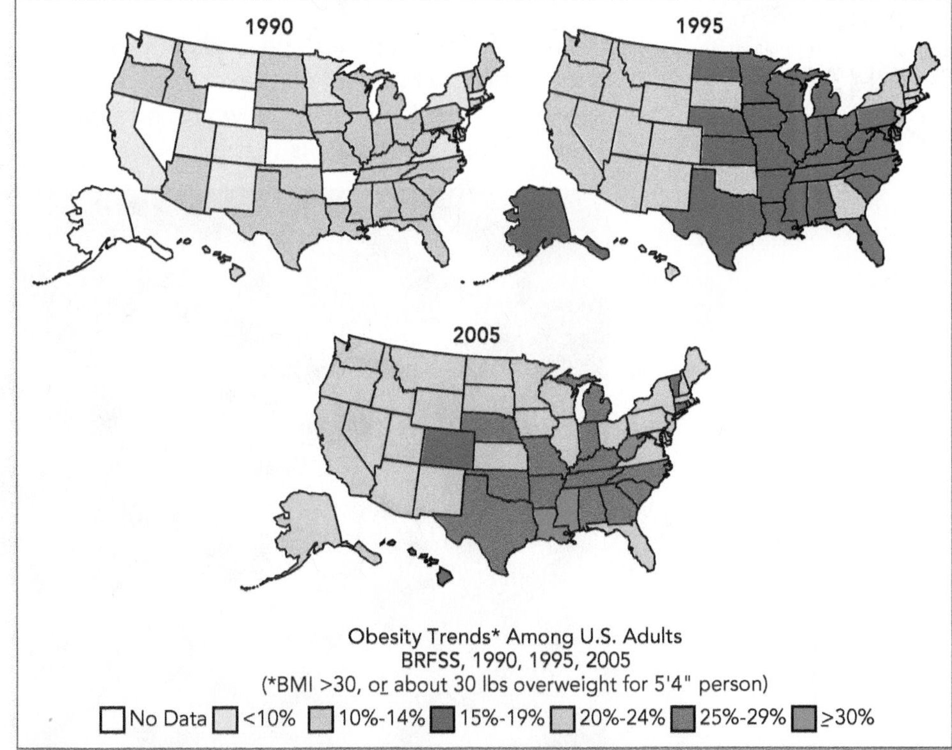

1. According to the Obesity Trends maps, in 1990, how many states had less than 10% of their population as obese adults?
   - a. no states
   - b. 1–5 states
   - c. 6–11 states
   - d. 12 or more states

2. In 1995, what was the obesity rate of most of the western states?
   - a. less than 10% of the population
   - b. 10%–14% of the population
   - c. 15%–19% of the population
   - d. more than 30% of the population

3. By 2005, which region of the country had the highest obesity rates?
   - a. Northwest
   - b. Southwest
   - c. Northeast
   - d. Southeast

4. By 2005, how many states had an obesity rate of more than 30% of the population?
   - a. 28 states
   - b. 3 states
   - c. 16 states
   - d. 30 states

5. By how much did the obese population change in the state of Alaska between 1995 and 2005?
   - a. It increased by 25–29%.
   - b. It decreased by 20–24%.
   - c. It increased by 15–19%.
   - d. It increased by 5–9%.

MyReadingLab

CHAPTER PRACTICE 1

Read the following paragraph, and determine the overall pattern of organization by focusing on the main idea and major supporting details. Remember to ask yourself, "How are the supporting details organized?" Then, answer the questions that follow.

In soccer, each player has a specific role in helping the team score goals. First, there are **forwards**, also known as **attackers** and **strikers**. They play nearest to the other team's goal and are responsible for making the most goals. Most teams have one to three forwards. The center forward is the principal goal-scorer of the team. The **wingers** are stationed near the touchlines. Wingers must try to beat defenders from the other team. **Defenders**, or **backs**, are the players responsible for providing support to the goalkeeper and keeping the other team from scoring. The **center backs**, or **central defenders**, have the job of stopping the opposing team's strikers. One of these center backs is the **sweeper**, who sweeps up the ball if the opponent breaks through the team's defense. The **fullbacks** prevent the opposing players from getting the ball into the penalty area, and they support other positions. There are also various types of **midfielders**, who play between the strikers and defenders. Their main job is to keep possession of the ball from the opposing team's players.

1. What is the topic of this selection?
   a. soccer
   b. how to play soccer
   c. soccer positions
   d. scoring goals

2. **Which sentence states the main idea?**
   a. In soccer, each player has a specific role in helping the team score goals.
   b. First, there are forwards, also known as attackers and strikers.
   c. Most teams have one to three forwards.
   d. Their main job is to keep possession of the ball from the opposing team's players.
3. **According to the passage, what are "backs"?**
   a. They are responsible for making the most goals.
   b. They have the job of stopping the opposing team's strikers.
   c. They are the principal goal-scorers of the team.
   d. They are responsible for providing support to the goalkeeper and keeping the other team from scoring.
4. **Identify the relationship within the following sentence: Defenders, or backs, are the players responsible for providing support to the goalkeeper and keeping the other team from scoring.**
   a. definition
   b. listing
   c. cause and effect
   d. time order
5. **What is the overall pattern of organization used in this paragraph?**
   a. definition
   b. listing
   c. cause and effect
   d. compare and/or contrast

MyReadingLab

CHAPTER PRACTICE 2

Read the following paragraph, and determine the overall pattern of organization by focusing on the main idea and major supporting details. Remember to ask yourself, "How are the supporting details organized?" Then, answer the questions that follow.

Recreational therapists are trained therapists who help people with disabilities or illnesses by using games or other techniques to improve their physical and mental health. They help patients to recover basic motor skills and flexibility. They also help people to improve their social skills. Recreational therapists work in hospitals, nursing homes, schools, or patients' homes. They assess the patient's needs and plan programs to help the individual or group, and then they work on the specific skills. Some recreational therapists specialize in art therapy or aquatic therapy. Most recreational therapists have an associate's or a bachelor's degree in recreational therapy. However, a few hold master's or doctoral degrees. Some require certification by the National Council for Therapeutic Recreation. A good recreational therapist is one who enjoys working with other people, likes to play, has good communication skills, and is patient.

1. What is the topic of this passage?

a. recreational therapy
b. recreational therapists
c. helping people with disabilities
d. therapists

2. What is the main idea of this passage?

a. Recreational therapists are trained therapists who help people with disabilities or illnesses by using games or other techniques to improve their physical and mental health.
b. Recreational therapists work in hospitals, nursing homes, schools, or patients' homes.
c. They assess the patient's needs and plan programs to help the individual or group, and then work on specific skills.
d. A good recreational therapist is one who enjoys working with other people, likes to play, has good communication skills, and is patient.

3. Identify the relationship within the following sentence: Recreational therapists work in hospitals, nursing homes, schools, or patients' homes.

a. definition
b. listing
c. cause and effect
d. compare and/or contrast

4. Identify the relationship between the following sentences: Most recreational therapists have an associate's or a bachelor's degree in recreational therapy. However, a few hold master's or doctoral degrees.

a. definition
b. listing
c. cause and effect
d. compare and/or contrast

5. What is the overall pattern of organization used in this passage?

a. definition
b. listing
c. cause and effect
d. compare and/or contrast

MyReadingLab

CHAPTER PRACTICE 3

Read the following paragraph, and determine the overall pattern of organization by focusing on the main idea and major supporting details. Remember to ask yourself, "How are the supporting details organized?" Then, answer the questions that follow.

[1] There are two different forms of exercise that can improve muscular strength. [2] Isotonic (eye-so-TON-ik) exercise involves contracting the muscles against a moving load, such as a weight machine. [3] Different muscles are used when lifting the weight than when lowering the weight. [4] To increase muscle mass, a person would increase the amount of weight and the number of lifts. [5] In contrast, isometric (eye-so-MET-trik) exercises involve moving muscles against a nonmoving load at a fixed angle. [6] An example would be to get into a push-up position and hold it for 10 seconds. [7] Increasing the amount of time would lead to improved strength over a period of time. [8] There are two important differences between isotonic and isometric exercise. [9] First, in isometric training, the range of motion is limited. [10] Second, during isometric exercises, people have a tendency to hold their breath, which can reduce blood flow to the brain and cause dizziness or fainting. [11] During both types of exercise, it is necessary to continue breathing.

1. What sentence states the main idea of this passage?

a. There are two different forms of exercise that can improve muscular strength.

b. Isotonic (eye-so-TON-ik) exercise involves contracting the muscles against a moving load, such as a weight machine.

c. In contrast, isometric (eye-so-MET-trik) exercises involve moving muscles against a nonmoving load at a fixed angle.

d. During both types of exercise, it is necessary to continue breathing.

2. Which sentences provide the major details?

a. sentences 2 and 3 **c.** sentences 9 and 10

b. sentences 2, 3, 4, and 5 **d.** sentences 2, 5 and 8

3. Identify the relationship within the following sentence: Second, during isometric exercises, people have a tendency to hold their breath, which can reduce blood flow to the brain and cause dizziness or fainting.

a. definition **c.** cause and effect

b. listing **d.** compare and/or contrast

4. Identify the relationship between sentences 9 and 10.

a. definition **c.** cause and effect

b. listing **d.** compare and/or contrast

5. What is the overall pattern of organization used in this passage?

a. definition **c.** cause and effect

b. listing **d.** compare and/or contrast

MyReadingLab

TEXTBOOK PRACTICE

Read the following selection, and determine the overall pattern of organization by focusing on the main idea and major supporting details. Remember to ask yourself, "How are the supporting details organized?" Then, answer the questions that follow.

WHAT ARE THE GUIDELINES FOR A HEALTHY DIET?

Nutrition may seem like a complex subject, but the basics of consuming a healthy diet are fairly simple: balance the calories, eat a variety of foods, and consume unhealthy foods only in moderation. Additionally, everyone should strive to be physically active.

To make these points more clear, and to provide specific guidance in these areas, several national health agencies have suggested guidelines for healthy diets. For instance, the United States Department of Agriculture (USDA) released its latest version of the Dietary Guidelines for Americans in 2005.

Among its key points of advice:

- Consume adequate nutrients within energy needs: choose foods that limit the intake of saturated and trans fats, cholesterol, added sugars, salt, and alcohol.
- Balance energy intake with energy expended.
- Engage in regular physical activity.
- Consume sufficient amounts of fruits, vegetables, and whole grains while staying within energy needs.
- Consume less than 10% of energy intake from saturated fats and less than 300 mg per day of cholesterol; consume as little trans fat as possible.
- Choose fiber-rich fruits, vegetables, and whole grains often; choose and prepare foods and beverages with little added sugars or caloric sweeteners.
- Consume less than 1 tsp of salt per day.
- If you choose to drink alcohol, do so only in moderation.
- Take proper food safety precautions.

1. What sentence states the main idea of this passage?

a. Nutrition may seem like a complex subject, but the basics of consuming a healthy diet are fairly simple: balance the calories, eat a variety of foods, and consume unhealthy foods only in moderation.

b. Additionally, everyone should strive to be physically active.

c. To make these points more clear, and to provide specific guidance in these areas, several national health agencies have suggested guidelines for healthy diets.

d. For instance, the United States Department of Agriculture (USDA) released its latest version of the Dietary Guidelines for Americans in 2005.

2. Identify the relationship within the following sentence: To make these points more clear, and to provide specific guidance in these areas, several national health agencies have suggested guidelines for healthy diets.
   a. definition
   b. listing
   c. cause and effect
   d. compare and/or contrast

3. Identify the relationship between the following sentences:
   - Consume adequate nutrients within energy needs: choose foods that limit the intake of saturated and trans fats, cholesterol, added sugars, salt, and alcohol.
   - Balance energy intake with energy expended.
   - Engage in regular physical activity.

   a. definition
   b. listing
   c. cause and effect
   d. compare and/or contrast

4. According to the selection, about how much salt should a person consume in one day?
   a. 1 tablespoon
   b. 1 teaspoon
   c. 300 mg
   d. less than 1 teaspoon

5. What is the overall pattern of organization used in this passage?
   a. definition
   b. listing
   c. cause and effect
   d. compare and/or contrast

STUDY SKILL REVIEW

Fill in the missing information in the following concept map about the four patterns of organization that you have learned in this chapter. Then, complete the summary that follows about the patterns of organization.

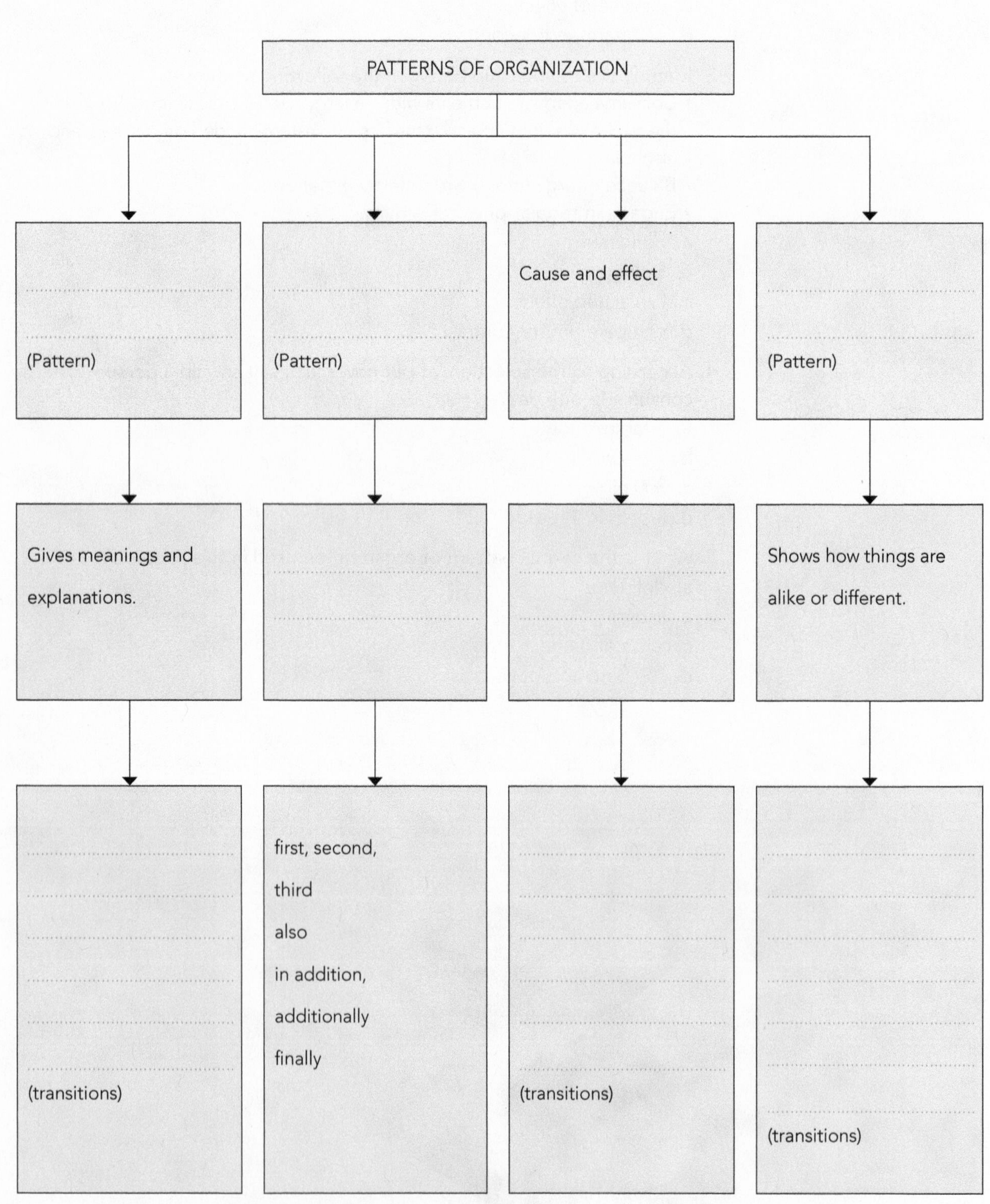

Summary: Patterns of Organization

Patterns of organization are:

....

....

....

Some patterns studied so far are:

....

....

....

Transitions are:

....

....

....

PATTERN	CHARACTERISTICS	TRANSITIONS
Definition	Explains the meaning of a word or phrase.	is, refers to, can be defined as, means, consists of, involves, is a term that, is called, is known as
Time Order	Describes events in the order they occurred. Transitions describe **when** something happens.	first, second, later, before, next, as soon as, after, then, finally, meanwhile, following, last, during, in, on, when, until
Listing	Indicates that additional information will follow.	Furthermore, in addition, moreover, again, first, second, next, finally
Cause-Effect	Describes how one or more things cause an action, and the effect(s) of the action	*Cause*: because, because of, since, stems from, cause, reason, leads to, creates, yields, produces, due to, breeds *Effect*: consequently, result, therefore, thus, as a result, effect, product of
Comparison-Contrast	Shows similarities and/or differences among ideas, concepts, objects, or persons	*Similarities*: both, also, similarly, like likewise, too, as well as, resembles, correspondingly, in the same way, to compare, in comparison. *Differences*: unlike, differs from, in contrast, on the other hand, instead, despite, nevertheless, however, in spite of, whereas, as opposed to, yet, but

READING LAB ASSIGNMENTS

SKILL REVIEW

1. Login to **MyReadingLab,** and in the menu click on **Reading Skills** and **Learning Path**. On the main screen, click **Ten Patterns of Organization** (Combined). Complete the review and practice activities recommended by your instructor.

COMPREHENSION IMPROVEMENT

2. From the menu in **MyReadingLab,** click on **Reading Level** and **Next Reading**. Choose two reading selections from the list on the main screen. Read the articles and answer the diagnostic and exercise questions.

CAREER EXPLORATION

3. Go online to the Occupational Outlook Handbook at the Bureau of Labor Statistics and explore careers in sports, fitness, and recreation. Find a career that interests you, and print out the information. This site will tell you what the job is like, what the outlook is for employment, educational requirements, and current salary. Print the article, and then preview, read, highlight, and annotate one or two sections of it. Find three examples of relationships within and between sentences using the patterns you have learned so far. Underline and label the sentences with the correct type of relationships shown.

SKILL APPLICATION

4. Using your textbooks for other classes or articles in newspapers or magazines, look for examples of the patterns of organization that you have learned so far. Explain how knowing the pattern helps your comprehension of the material.

MyReadingLab

LEARNING REFLECTION

Think about the skills and concepts in this chapter. What have you learned in this chapter that will help your reading comprehension and enable you to do well in college?

MyReadingLab

SELF-EVALUATION CHECKLIST

Rate yourself on the following items, using the following scale:

1 = strongly disagree

2 = disagree

3 = neither agree nor disagree

4 = agree

5 = strongly agree

1. I completed all of the assigned work on time. ....

2. I understand all of the concepts in this chapter. ....

3. I contributed to teamwork and class discussions. ....

4. I completed all of the assigned lab work on time. ....

5. I came to class on time. ....

6. I attended class every day. ....

7. I studied for any quizzes or tests we had for this chapter. ....

8. I asked questions when I didn't understand something. ....

9. I checked my comprehension during reading. ....

10. I know what is expected of me in the coming week. ....

11. Are you still on track with the goals you set in Chapter 1?

....

What changes can you make to improve your performance in this?

....

....

9 CRITICAL READING AND THINKING

LEARNING STRATEGIES

Critical Reading and Thinking	371
Fact and Opinion	371
Author's Purpose	376
Author's Tone	378
Author's Intended Audience	379

READING SELECTIONS

READING 1: "Operation Seal Rescue"	386
READING 2: "A Greener Earth: Energy Alternatives"	396

READING FOR LIFE

On the Job Interview	406
Building Vocabulary	407
Real-Life Reading	408
Textbook Graphic Aids	410

CHAPTER REVIEW

Chapter Practice	412
Textbook Practice	415
Study Skill Review	417
Reading Lab Assignments	418
Learning Reflection	418
Self-Evaluation Checklist	419

FOCUS ON: Science

Are you a person who likes to know how things work, or why something happens? Do you like to explore new ideas and create? All of these are characteristics of a scientific mind. Crime scene investigators, medical researchers, and environmental biologists all strive to find answers to important questions. Some scientists work in laboratories at least part of the time, but many of them work outdoors observing, collecting samples, measuring, and conducting experiments. Some work in zero gravity in outer space while others explore our solar system from powerful telescopes on land. Some technicians' jobs may require only an associate's degree while others require higher degrees. For curious individuals, science can offer a world of exploration and discovery in many different areas.

Being able to read and think critically will be valuable to your career as a scientist. You'll need to evaluate the research of others and analyze and interpret information. You'll find it helpful to be able to distinguish between fact and opinion, understand an author's purpose and tone, and to apply those skills to your own research and writing.

In this chapter, you will:

LEARNING OBJECTIVES

1 distinguish the difference between fact and opinion.
2 identify the author's purpose.
3 identify the author's tone.
4 identify the intended audience.

CRITICAL READING AND THINKING

Being a critical reader and thinker means that you look beyond the words printed on the page and that you use what you know to make new connections and draw logical conclusions. Critical readers use facts and reasoning skills to evaluate an author's point. Also, they ask many questions, such as, "Why did the author write this?" They analyze facts and interpret what they read. They recognize techniques that authors may use to persuade readers, and they detect any personal bias that an author may have. Critical readers and thinkers apply what they have learned to new situations to solve problems or create new ideas.

OBJECTIVE 1

Distinguish the difference between fact and opinion.

FACT AND OPINION

One of the most basic critical reading and thinking skills is being able to distinguish a fact from an opinion. Facts are provable, but opinions are not.

Examples of facts:

> The Earth is approximately 4.5 billion years old.
>
> The diameter of the Earth is about 8,000 miles (12,800 km).
>
> This college has 10,000 students.

Examples of opinions:

> Dr. Johnson is the best physiology instructor at the college.
>
> He probably wishes that he had fewer classes to teach.
>
> Dr. Johnson's students are lucky to be in his class.

Because facts are statements that can be proved as either true or false, a fact does not have to be true to remain a fact. It may be referred to as a "false fact." For example, the college mentioned in the third fact may only have 9,999 students, but it remains a fact because we can prove it as true or false. Facts can be proved by some observable or measurable means.

Incorrect statements that can be proved true or false are still facts. Through the centuries, our understanding of the world has evolved and changed. For instance, we recently considered it a fact that Pluto was a planet; now we know that Pluto is not a true planet but a dwarf planet. Future discoveries will continue to change our understanding of what is true and what is false. Facts will change, but they will remain facts—true or false—as long as they can be proved.

On the other hand, opinions are not provable and use words or phrases that imply judgment, such as "best" or "worst." Some opinions are very popular, and most people may agree with them, but they're still opinions. For example, many people agree that we should not pollute, but it is still an opinion.

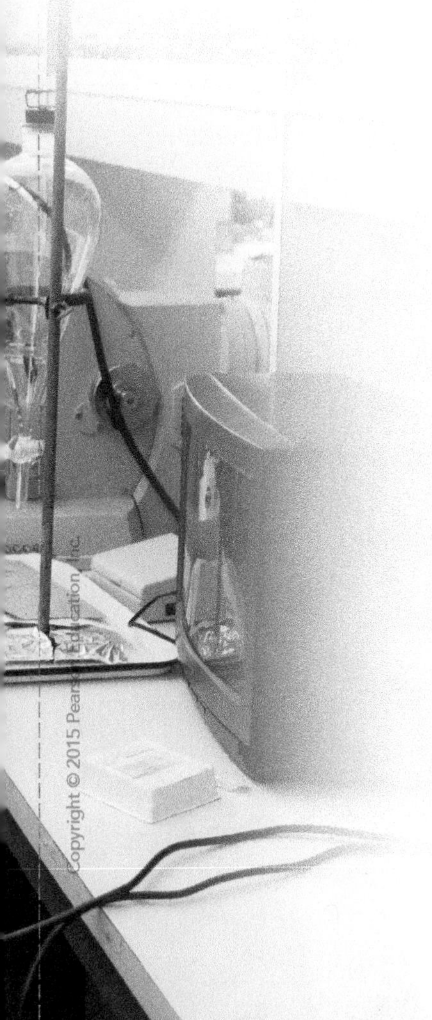

FACTS	OPINIONS
Facts can be proved true or false by observable or measurable means.	Opinions cannot be proved as either true or false.
Quotations can be proved. Think of it this way: Can you prove that this person said this? Yes, so the quotation is a fact, even if what the quotation asserted is an opinion.	Opinions include feelings, attitudes, beliefs, and guesses.
	All future events, including predictions, are opinions (because they cannot be proved true or false with the information currently available to us).

Words That Signal Opinion

You can recognize opinions by words or phrases that suggest guesses or attitudes. Here are some examples:

it appears that	apparently	it seems that	believe
guess	surmise	presumably	in my opinion
in my view	it's likely that	possibly	this suggests
should	ought to	may	could

Keep in mind that the context of the word in the sentence is important to consider when deciding if a sentence is a fact or an opinion. Although the word "may" appears in both of the following sentences, one is a fact and one is an opinion. In such situations, ask yourself, "Can this be proved true or false?"

EXAMPLE:

1. Scientists may discover life on other planets in the universe. (Opinion: future event)
2. This rock cycle may occur either beneath the Earth's surface or on the Earth's surface. (Fact: The rock cycle can happen in two places—beneath the Earth's surface or on the Earth's surface.)

Judgment Words in Opinions

You can also identify opinions by looking for words that make judgments about something, such as:

worst	best	horrible	amazing
wonderful	awful	weird	troublesome

EXAMPLES:

> Allowing our planet to become polluted is a *terrible* legacy to leave for the next generation.
>
> The octopus is *amazingly* intelligent, and during experiments it performs many tasks that require thinking.

Sentences with Both Fact and Opinion

Occasionally you will see a sentence that has both fact and opinion. If you are offered the option of choosing "fact and opinion" on a test, that is the best description. But often, you are only offered two answer choices: fact or opinion. In this case, consider the entire sentence to be opinion if any portion of it is opinion.

EXAMPLE:

> The production of carbon dioxide from human activities includes burning coal, gas, and oil, which *may* cause *serious* climate change on Earth. (The first half of this sentence is a fact, but the ending is an opinion because of the words "may" and "serious.")

Is It Wrong to Use Opinions in Writing?

expert opinions: opinions provided by one or more experts in a field.

Expect to find opinions in just about everything you read, including newspapers, textbooks, and reference materials. Opinions form a valuable part of our understanding of a subject, and they should not be excluded from writing. We cannot make important predictions about the future without stating opinions. We rely on experts who have knowledge and experience to give us their *expert opinions*, which give us insight to problems and solutions. For instance, meteorologists predict the weather every day, and most of the time they are correct.

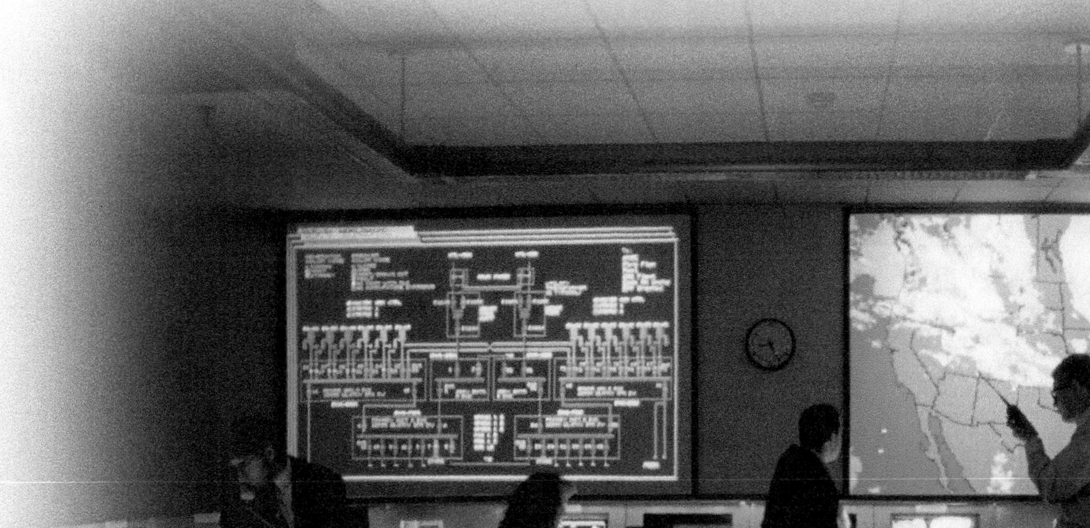

Can It Be Proved?

Read the following statements, and decide if they can be proved. Ask yourself, "Can this be proved by some measurable means?" Write "Y" for yes or "N" for no on the lines provided. Underline any clues that helped you decide.

EXAMPLES:

......Y...... Jellyfish are meat eaters and feed on anything from small worms to large fish.

......N...... Bats are the worst mammals to encounter in the wild.

1. .... When volcanoes erupt, hot lava spreads down the sides.
2. .... Entire cities have been destroyed by volcanoes.
3. .... Volcanoes are the most dangerous natural disaster on Earth.
4. .... The seas cover about 72 percent of the Earth's surface.
5. .... There will be less land as the ocean levels rise higher in the next decades.

Read the following paragraph. Turn the sentences into facts by crossing out the words that make them opinions.

> One of the most fascinating sharks in the sea is the goblin shark. It is the ugliest shark because it has a long pointed snout that sticks up above its mouth. Its strange pink and grey body is covered in soft, flabby flesh. It lives in the darkest and deepest level of the ocean, which is a good place for a goblin to stay.

MyReadingLab

PRACTICE 1

Label each of the following sentences as fact (F) or opinion (O), and underline any words or phrases that signal an opinion.

1. .... The most beautiful sunsets can be seen in the Caribbean Sea.
2. .... The changing of the seasons is caused by the Earth's 23-degree tilt on its axis.
3. .... The color of the sky is determined by the number of particles in the atmosphere.
4. .... The Northeast has the worst weather in the country.
5. .... In the coming decade, automobiles will use less energy and will cause less pollution.

MyReadingLab

PRACTICE 2

Label each of the following sentences as fact (F) or opinion (O), and underline any words or phrases that signal an opinion.

1. .... It appears that global surface temperatures may have increased more rapidly over the past 10 years than in the past.

2. .... Global temperatures have increased more rapidly over the past 10 years than in the past.

3. .... Climate change has not been equal across all parts of the globe.

4. .... The most increasingly warming trend has occurred over North America and Eurasia.

5. .... Scientists have been keeping excellent records of the temperatures around the globe over the past century.

MyReadingLab

PRACTICE 3

Read the following paragraph, and then label each sentence as fact (F) or opinion (O). Underline any words or phrases that signal an opinion.

[1] Scientists get their information about the Earth's climate from many natural sources. [2] Some data is found in tree rings, which can be seen when the trunk is cut in half and the rings are examined. [3] The difference in the size of some tree rings is interesting because it shows years of larger amounts of precipitation (rain or snow) and years of drought. [4] Wider rings mean that there was more growth during the season due to additional precipitation. [5] Using the data from tree rings and other natural sources, scientists are able to form some remarkable conclusions about the history of our planet's climate.

Sentence 1: .... Sentence 4: ....

Sentence 2: .... Sentence 5: ....

Sentence 3: ....

MyReadingLab

TEXTBOOK SELECTION 1

Read the following textbook selection, and then label each sentence as fact (F), opinion (O), or fact and opinion (F & O). Underline any words or phrases that signal an opinion.

Sea-Level Rise

[1]An important effect of human-caused global warming is a rise in sea level. How is a warmer atmosphere related to a global rise in sea level? [2]The most obvious connection is the melting of glaciers. [3]Also important is that a warmer atmosphere causes an increase in ocean volume of water due to expansion. [4]Higher air temperatures warm the upper layers of the ocean, which in turn causes the water to expand and sea level to rise. [5]Research indicates that sea level has risen between 10 and 25 centimeters (4 and 8 inches) over the past century, and that the trend will continue at an accelerated rate.

Sentence 1: ....

Sentence 2: ....

Sentence 3: ....

Sentence 4: ....

Sentence 4: ....

U-REVIEW 1

On a sheet of paper, make two columns. Label one column "facts" and the other column "opinions." Working with a partner or a team, you will be given a few minutes to write down everything you have learned about facts and opinions without looking in the text. When the paper is passed to each person, he or she must write and read one point about facts or opinions. When time is called, compare your team's list to others in the class. For each idea that you wrote that is not on another team's list, you earn one point. The team with the most points wins.

OBJECTIVE 2

Identify the author's purpose.

AUTHOR'S PURPOSE

When authors write something, they always have a purpose in mind. Three basic reasons why authors write are to inform, persuade, and entertain. To learn the author's purpose, ask yourself, "Why did the author write this?" Consider the main idea or central point. An author's purpose is closely related to the author's main idea. Notice how the main idea gives a clue to the author's purpose in the following examples.

To inform: Here the author's purpose is to give information.

The ocean tides are a result of the gravitational pull of the sun and moon.

To persuade or convince: An author uses persuasion to try to convince readers to accept his or her ideas or opinions. Look for phrases and judgment words that signal an opinion (see the lists of words under "Words That Signal Opinion," on page 372.)

EXAMPLE:

> You *should not* swim in areas inhabited by sea lions and seals.

To entertain: This is when an author tries to convey a feeling or an emotion.

EXAMPLE:

> Women will never be equal to men until they can walk down the street with a bald head and a beer gut and still think they are sexy.

MyReadingLab

AUTHOR'S PURPOSE

Read the following paragraphs to determine the author's purpose, and then answer the questions that follow.

Paragraph 1

Two students walked in late to a physics lecture, and, as they whispered to each other to find seats, several students told them to be quiet. One of the late students asked the other one, "Why do we have to be so quiet?" The other replied, "So we won't wake up the other students!"

What is the author's purpose? (Why did the author write this?)

a. The author is trying to inform the reader.
b. The author is trying to persuade the reader.
c. The author is trying to entertain the reader.

Paragraph 2

A typical lightning bolt contains 1 billion volts of electrical current. A household electrical outlet typically carries 120 volts. The average lightning flash can light a 100-watt light bulb for 3 months.

What is the author's purpose? (Why did the author write this?)

a. The author is trying to inform the reader about lightning.
b. The author is trying to persuade the reader that lightning is dangerous.
c. The author is trying to entertain the reader with a story about lightning.

Paragraph 3

Drinking alcohol can increase the risk of certain types of cancer. People who drink and smoke can double their risk of getting cancer. Reducing your risk of cancer can be as simple as following healthful eating habits. You should eat a low-fat, balanced diet that includes fruits and vegetables every day to reduce your risk factor.

What is the author's purpose? (Why did the author write this?)

a. The author is trying to inform the reader about cancer.
b. The author is trying to persuade the reader that healthful eating habits can reduce risk of cancer.
c. The author is trying to entertain the reader with a story.

OBJECTIVE 3

Identify the author's tone.

AUTHOR'S TONE

Tone refers to the author's feelings about the topic. When trying to determine the author's tone, also consider the author's purpose and intended audience. Ask yourself, "What are the author's feelings or attitude about this topic?" Do not be influenced by your own attitude about the topic. Always begin by stating the topic and the main idea, and then consider the author's intended audience, the author's purpose, and the author's point of view about the topic. Look for words or phrases with positive or negative tones.

EXAMPLE:

The Town Council members have done it again. They've voted to approve the building of shopping malls, car dealers, and small businesses on what is now prime farmland. These people have no respect for agriculture. Their foolish decision will affect the future of this town and change its traditions and character forever. There will be more traffic, more pollution, and more crime as shoplifters and thieves are drawn to this area. We need to reverse this decision and stop further development of farmland before there is no land left for growing crops.

Topic: developing farmland

Main idea: The town's farmland should be used for growing crops and not for development.

Intended audience: the people who live in the town

Author's purpose: to persuade readers that developing farmland is unwise

Author's tone: The author's tone is critical. Note the underlined words and phrases that reveal the author's concern about the topic.

MyReadingLab

AUTHOR'S TONE

Directions: Use the paragraphs on page 380 to answer the following questions.

1. What is the author's tone in paragraph 1 about the Great White shark?
   a. happy
   b. worried
   c. factual
   d. angry
2. What is the author's tone in paragraph 2 about shark fishing on the Great Barrier Reef?
   a. concerned
   b. excited
   c. sad
   d. careless
3. What is the author's tone in paragraph 3 about the features of the Great Barrier Reef?
   a. frightened
   b. serious
   c. funny
   d. positive

Tone Words

Following is a list of common tone words. There are many more words used to describe tone, but in this text, you will only use some of them. Neutral tone words state facts objectively, without opinion.

LIST OF COMMON TONE WORDS

POSITIVE TONE WORDS	NEGATIVE TONE WORDS	NEUTRAL TONES WORDS
amused	angry	informative
cheerful	discouraging	factual
funny	critical	objective
excited	frustrated	neutral
joyful	hateful	straightforward
happy	harsh	unbiased
approving	disapproving	indifferent

OBJECTIVE 4

Identify the intended audience.

AUTHOR'S INTENDED AUDIENCE

Critical thinkers ask not only why an author wrote something but also for whom the selection was written. Knowing the intended audience can help you determine the author's purpose and tone. When trying to decide who the intended audience is, think about the source of the material. For example, the intended audience for a textbook is students. The intended audience for a medical journal is medical professionals.

MyReadingLab

AUTHOR'S INTEDENED AUDIENCE

As you read the following paragraphs, try to determine for whom these paragraphs were written. Then, answer the questions that follow.

Paragraph 1

The Great White shark is a powerful fish that can kill a person with a single bite. It eats other fish, sea turtles, birds, porpoises, seals, other sharks, and sometimes humans. When it charges to attack, its eyeballs roll back into its head for protection. Great White sharks are found throughout the world's seas and sometimes migrate over long distances.

The intended audience is:

a. newspaper reporters
b. biology students
c. wildlife artists
d. television producers

Paragraph 2

We must stop shark fishing on the Great Barrier Reef of Australia. The Australian government is allowing more than 70,000 sharks to be killed each year in this reef. This will contribute to the global decline of shark populations. Killing these sharks could have a terrible impact on the ecosystem of the reef. Protecting these sharks is necessary for protecting all marine wildlife living on the Great Barrier Reef.

The intended audience is:

a. students
b. tourists
c. people who want to preserve nature
d. news reporters

Paragraph 3

The Great Barrier Reef is one of Australia's most beautiful natural environments. The reef is made up of more than 3,000 reef systems and hundreds of tropical islands with sun-drenched, white sandy beaches and turquoise water. You can explore the exotic islands in a boat, snorkeling, or scuba diving among the coral reefs, or simply lie on the beach enjoying the balmy, soft ocean breeze.

The intended audience is:

a. tourists
b. environmentalists
c. biology students
d. writers

Notice how the first paragraph contains many facts about Great White sharks, whereas the second paragraph tries to convince the reader to stop shark fishing on the Great Barrier Reef. The third paragraph points out the most enjoyable features of the Reef.

MyReadingLab

PRACTICE 4

Read the following paragraph, and underline the main idea (if stated) and the major details. Then, answer the questions that follow.

A black hole in space is a region where the gravity is so strong that nothing can escape its pull. The entrance to the black hole is called an *event horizon*. Objects, such as asteroids, can get pulled into the hole but never come out. They are called black holes because even light is pulled into the massive dark center. *Escape velocity*—the speed at which something must travel to escape being pulled into the black hole—exceeds the speed of light. There are different types of black holes according to their size. Some are as massive as a solar system. Once a black hole is formed, it can continue to grow in size by absorbing more matter. Astronomers believe that hundreds of massive black holes wander the galaxy. Fortunately, the nearest black hole to Earth is thousands of **light years** away.

light year: About 6 trillion miles; the distance light travels in one year.

1. What is the main idea?
   a. Black holes wander the galaxy.
   b. A black hole in space is a region where the gravity is so strong that nothing can escape its pull.
   c. They are called black holes because even light is pulled into the massive dark center.
   d. Fortunately, the nearest black hole to Earth is thousands of light years away.
2. What is the author's purpose?
   a. to inform readers about black holes
   b. to entertain readers with a story about black holes
   c. to persuade readers that black holes are dangerous
   d. to inform readers why black holes exist
3. Who is the intended audience?
   a. astronomers who study the universe
   b. people who want to know about black holes
   c. astronomy magazine advertisers
   d. newspaper reporters
4. What is the author's tone?
   a. humorous
   b. disapproving
   c. concerned
   d. informative
5. Determine whether the following sentence is a fact, an opinion, or both. Underline any words or phrases that signal an opinion. "Objects, such as asteroids, can get pulled into the hole but never come out."
   a. fact
   b. opinion
   c. fact and opinion

MyReadingLab

PRACTICE 5

Read the following paragraph, and underline the main idea (if stated) and the major details. Then, answer the questions that follow.

On April 20, 2010, an explosion on an oil rig in the Gulf of Mexico killed 11 people and caused several pipe leaks about 50 miles off the coast of Louisiana. Oil poured out at a rate of up to 60,000 barrels a day, making it one of the worst environmental disasters in recent history. Oil drilling in the Gulf of Mexico was a disaster waiting to happen. A fragile marsh environment along Louisiana's coast serves as a buffer in storms. Damage to the salt marshes from an oil spill can cause major erosion from storm surge and impact wildlife all along the southern coast. Offshore oil drilling is too dangerous. Instead of drilling for oil, our resources should be directed to developing cleaner and safer energy resources.

1. What is the main idea?

a. There was a major oil spill in 2010 in the Gulf of Mexico.
b. Louisiana will lose coastal land due to erosion and loss of marshes.
c. Instead of drilling for oil, our resources should be directed to developing cleaner and safer energy resources.
d. Oil drilling in the Gulf of Mexico was a disaster waiting to happen.

2. What is the author's purpose?

a. to inform readers about the 2010 oil spill
b. to persuade readers that offshore oil drilling is dangerous
c. to persuade readers that instead of offshore oil drilling, our resources should be directed to developing cleaner and safer energy resources
d. to entertain readers about offshore oil drilling

3. Who is the intended audience?

a. people who work for the oil company
b. people who care about the environment
c. people who want lower gas prices
d. people who own gas stations

4. What is the author's tone?

a. critical
b. straightforward
c. objective
d. approving

5. Determine whether the following sentence is a fact, an opinion, or both. Underline any words or phrases that signal an opinion. "Oil drilling in the Gulf of Mexico was a disaster waiting to happen."

a. fact
b. opinion
c. fact and opinion

MyReadingLab

PRACTICE 6

Read the following paragraphs, and underline the main idea (if stated) and the major details. Then, answer the questions that follow.

Birds fly from one place to another during their seasonal migrations to find food and breeding grounds. Some birds travel thousands of miles. For instance, the arctic tern flies about 18,600 miles each way—an incredible journey for any bird. Today scientists are able to track migrating birds with geo-locators similar to the GPS systems in cars. They were surprised to discover that songbirds fly more than 300 miles a day. In addition, more than half of the bird species they tracked show a shift in their migration patterns due to climate change. Another alarming trend is that nearly half of the migrating water birds are decreasing in number. Because of climate change, some birds must also fly farther than ever before to find certain types of habitats. This requires more energy and food sources than before and, unfortunately, may be a reason why some populations of birds are decreasing. Biologists are concerned about the negative effects of climate change on birds and will continue to study them closely.

1. What is the main idea of the selection?
   - **a.** Because of geo-locators, scientists are learning about the trends in bird migration and population.
   - **b.** Birds fly from one place to another during their seasonal migrations to find food and breeding grounds.
   - **c.** Today scientists are able to track migrating birds with geo-locators similar to the GPS systems in cars.
   - **d.** Biologists are concerned about the negative effects of climate change on birds and will continue to study them closely.
2. What is the author's purpose?
   - **a.** to persuade readers to study birds
   - **b.** to entertain readers about birds
   - **c.** to describe different kinds of birds
   - **d.** to inform readers about bird migrations and population trends
3. Who is the intended audience?
   - **a.** anyone interested in birds
   - **b.** retail managers
   - **c.** biologists
   - **d.** artists
4. What is the author's tone?
   - **a.** objective
   - **b.** upset
   - **c.** critical
   - **d.** concerned
5. Determine whether the following sentence is a fact, an opinion, or both. Underline any words or phrases that signal an opinion. "They were surprised to discover that songbirds fly more than 300 miles a day."
   - **a.** fact
   - **b.** opinion
   - **c.** fact and opinion

MyReadingLab

TEXTBOOK SELECTION 2

As you read the following textbook selection, circle the topic and underline the main idea (if stated) and the major details. Then, answer the questions that follow. Consider the source of the selection and the topic when answering the questions.

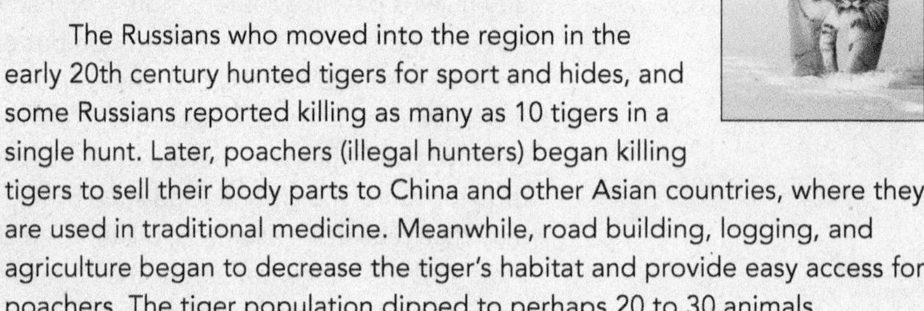

Historically, tigers roamed widely across Asia from Turkey to northeast Russia to Indonesia. Within the past 200 years, however, people have driven the majestic striped cats from most of their historic range. Today, tigers are exceedingly rare and are creeping toward extinction.

The Russians who moved into the region in the early 20th century hunted tigers for sport and hides, and some Russians reported killing as many as 10 tigers in a single hunt. Later, poachers (illegal hunters) began killing tigers to sell their body parts to China and other Asian countries, where they are used in traditional medicine. Meanwhile, road building, logging, and agriculture began to decrease the tiger's habitat and provide easy access for poachers. The tiger population dipped to perhaps 20 to 30 animals.

International conservation groups began to get involved, working with Russian biologists to try to save the decreasing tiger population. One such group was the Hornocker Wildlife Institute, now part of the Wildlife Conservation Society (WCS). In 1992, the group helped launch the Siberian Tiger Project, devoted to studying the tiger and its habitat.

Today, WCS biologists track tigers with radio collars, monitor their movements and health, determine causes of death when they die, and provide funding for local wildlife officials to stop and capture poachers. Thanks to such efforts, today, Siberian tigers in the wild number roughly 330 to 370, and about 1,500 more survive in zoos and captive breeding programs around the world.

QUESTIONS

1. What is the central point of the entire selection?
   - **a.** Historically, tigers roamed widely across Asia from Turkey to northeast Russia to Indonesia.
   - **b.** Within the past 200 years, however, people have driven the majestic striped cats from most of their historic range.
   - **c.** Although tigers were nearly hunted to extinction, due to conservation efforts, the number of tigers in the world has increased.
   - **d.** The Russians who moved into the region in the early 20th century hunted the tigers until they were nearly extinct.
2. What is the author's purpose?
   - **a.** to entertain readers with a story about tigers
   - **b.** to persuade readers to contribute to tiger conservation groups
   - **c.** to inform readers about how conservation helps tigers to avoid extinction
   - **d.** to inform readers about the history of tigers

3. Who is the intended audience?
- **a.** biologists who work with tigers
- **b.** business managers
- **c.** biology students
- **d.** advertisers

4. What is the author's tone?
- **a.** straightforward
- **b.** frustrated
- **c.** upset
- **d.** discouraged

5. Determine whether the following sentence is a fact, an opinion, or both. Underline any words or phrases that signal an opinion. "Meanwhile, road building, logging, and agriculture began to decrease the tiger's habitat and provide easy access for poachers."
- **a.** fact
- **b.** opinion
- **c.** fact and opinion

U-REVIEW 2

Complete the following sentences with a word or phrase from the list below.

author's purpose	author's tone	intended audience
fact	opinion	

1. When thinking about whom something was written for, you are thinking about the ________________.

2. To find the ________________, you should ask, "What is the author's attitude toward this topic?"

3. Something that cannot be proved true or false is a(n) ________________.

4. To find the ________________, you should ask, "Why did the author write this?"

5. Something is a(n) ________________ if you can answer yes to the question, "Can this be proved true or false?"

MyReadingLab

Reading 1
VOCABULARY PREVIEW

"Operation Seal Rescue"

The following words are from the article, "Operation Seal Rescue." With a partner or in a team, choose the meanings of the underlined words in the following sentences. Use context clues (LEADS), word part clues, and parts of speech to help you figure out the meanings.

1. After his surgery, Marco had to go to a nursing home for several weeks to recuperate (re-COO-per-ate) before he could go home.
   a. get treatment
   b. go back on medication
   c. pay the bills
   d. recover from illness
2. As part of his rehabilitation (re-ha-bil-i-TAY-shun), Marco had to exercise for two hours a day with a physical therapist.
   a. therapy to regain health
   b. exercises
   c. getting off medications
   d. prescriptions
3. Parasites (PAIR-a-sites), including ticks and fleas, cannot survive without a host to live on.
   a. organisms that feed off others
   b. marine mammals
   c. germs
   d. viruses
4. Many rescued seals suffered from lungworm (LUNG-worm), and did not survive.
   a. a breathing condition
   b. a parasite that attacks animals' lungs
   c. a type of insect
   d. a type of sea animal
5. In any rescue operation, logistics (lo-JIS-tics) are important to keep the operation running smoothly.
   a. mathematics
   b. time management
   c. efficient management of resources
   d. money management
6. Eating healthy foods and exercising can strengthen your immune system (im-YOON sis-tem), and prevent illness.
   a. nutritional system
   b. the system that regulates oxygen
   c. physician network
   d. defense system against disease

7. Some elderly people are vulnerable (VUL-ner-a-ble) to infections because their immune systems are not strong.
   a. capturing
   b. unlikely to have
   c. at risk for
   d. resistant
8. Some of the rescued animals were emaciated (eh-MAY-see-ate-ed) because they had not been fed or given water in several days.
   a. extremely thin
   b. thirsty
   c. rejected
   d. saved
9. Emma liked to fly kites, but her kite string always got entangled (en-TANG-l'd) in nearby tree branches.
   a. cut
   b. knotted
   c. brushed by
   d. broken
10. The baby seal was so exhausted from searching for food that his strength was waning (WAY-ning)
    a. growing
    b. weakening
    c. remaining
    d. surviving

MyReadingLab

Reading 1
PREVIEW

1. Describe an animal rescue that you have seen or heard about.
2. If an animal is injured and needs first aid, what would you do?

After you preview the article, write one or two preview questions on the lines below:

MyReadingLab

Reading 1

As you read, answer the questions in the margins to check your comprehension.

"Operation Seal Rescue"

by Monica Rozenfeld

Volunteers from around the world team up to save hundreds of baby seals stranded during a storm.

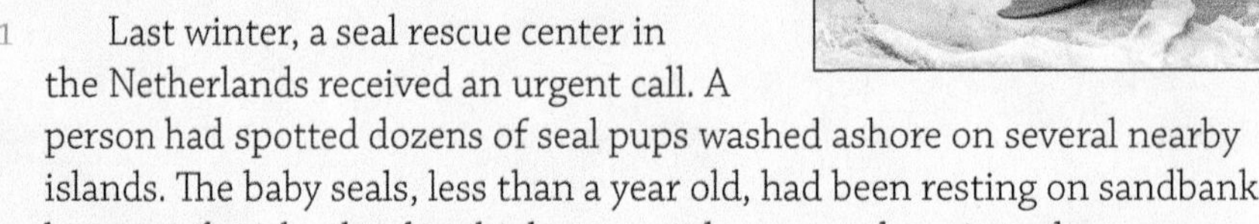

1 Last winter, a seal rescue center in the Netherlands received an urgent call. A person had spotted dozens of seal pups washed ashore on several nearby islands. The baby seals, less than a year old, had been resting on sandbanks between the islands when high storm tides swept them into the water.

2 Many of the pups drowned in the high tides. Others were stranded on local beaches and didn't have the energy to hunt for fish. With their strength waning, they were vulnerable to deadly illness and starvation.

3 A rescue squad from the Seal Rehabilitation and Research Centre in Pieterburen, Netherlands, sprang into action. In the next few weeks, the squad rounded up 385 stranded grey and harbor seals.

4 The center usually takes in about 300 to 400 seals a year, nursing them back to health and returning them to the wild. But the numbers have been growing recently. Last year, the facility rescued more than 800 seals. Why? One reason is climate change, which can lead to more intense storms. In addition, pollution, disease, and fewer fish to eat have left pups fighting harder than ever before to survive.

Why have seal pup rescues been increasing over recent years?

Pup Rescue

5 Pulling off a rescue effort as large as the one last winter was a challenge. About 70 volunteers from the Netherlands and around the world lent a hand to save the seals. People everywhere donated necessities like towels, bowls, and even small backyard pools for the pups to rest in. "When you have a rescue station, you have to be very creative," says Lenie 't Hart, the center's founder.

6 Getting the pups to the center was another issue. They had to be transported by ferries, rescue boats, and vans. One van held 20 seals at once! The logistics were very complex. "It was like a military operation," says 't Hart.

7 Once the pups were on the mainland, they were driven to the rehabilitation center, where they could get medical treatment, food, and some much-needed rest.

Health Checkup

8 At the center, the first thing on the agenda was to weigh and measure the seals. Workers drew blood samples to check for diseases, and gave them vaccinations to ward off infections.

9 One of the biggest threats to stranded seal pups is the disease lungworm. This respiratory infection is caused by worm-like parasites from the fish the seals eat. The parasites grow inside the seal's lungs, making it difficult for the animal to breathe.

10 Healthy seals can usually fight off lungworm infections. But 't Hart has noticed more seals dying from it in recent years. Infected seals that are too exhausted to hunt stay onshore instead of returning to the water. If they're not rescued, they become emaciated and die in a matter of days or weeks.

11 Pollution and overfishing may be partly to blame for seals becoming more vulnerable to infections like lungworm. Pollution can weaken a seal's disease-fighting immune system. The same is true for overfishing. If there aren't enough fish for the pups to eat, they will be underweight and have a harder time fighting off illness.

What medical attention must the seal pups get, and why?

Road to Recovery

12 The goal of the rescue is to help the seals recover so they can return to the ocean and survive on their own. At the center, the seal pups are put on a diet consisting of a soupy mixture of ground-up **herring** and water. Then they're moved to an isolated area so they can rest undisturbed in pools until they're healthy.

herring: a type of fish eaten by seals

13 After the pups have had time to recuperate, the rescue team begins to train the young animals to catch their own food. Once the pups reach a healthy weight—roughly 50 kilograms (110 pounds) for grey seals and 35 to 40 kg (77 to 88 lbs) for harbor seals—the rescue center releases them into the wild.

14 About 60 to 70 percent of the seals that come to the Seal Rehabilitation and Research Centre survive. None of them spends longer than six months and the center. "These are independent animals," says 't Hart. "They do not belong in captivity."

What happens to the seal pups after six months in the rehabilitation center?

Continued...

MyReadingLab

Reading 1

...continued

What other marine mammal rescues have been made, and why?

Helping Hands

15 The Netherlands isn't the only place in the world that's equipped to rescue seals. The Marine Mammal Center in Sausalito, California, rescues 600 to 800 sick and injured marine mammals each year. It was one of the many organizations that sent volunteers to help during the large rescue operation in the Netherlands.

16 "The need for seal rescues is growing around the world," says Shelbi Stroudt, who works at the Marine Mammal Center. Sometimes, rescuers are called to help seals that have been stranded by storms or injured during shark attacks. But more often, people are to blame for the seals' troubles. In many instances, the animals are entangled in fishing gear or discarded litter in the water. "No two rescues are alike," says Stoudt.

17 "The human pressures put on wild animals are an important issue," says 't Hart. Since the rescue center opened in the Netherlands 40 years ago, it has saved thousands of seals. "People need to understand the effect their lifestyles have on animals and the environment," she says, "and take steps to prevent further harm."

859 words divided by ______ minutes = ______ words per minute

MyReadingLab

Reading 1 REVIEW

It is a good habit to summarize everything you read to strengthen your comprehension.

Directions: On the following lines, write a two- or three-sentence summary of the article "Operation Seal Rescue." In your own words, describe what the article was about and why the author wrote it.

MyReadingLab

Reading 1 COMPREHENSION QUESTIONS

The following questions will help you recall the main idea and details of "Operation Seal Rescue." Read any parts of the article that you need to find the correct answers.

MAIN IDEAS

1. What is the central point of this article?

- **a.** Scientists are concerned over the decrease in seal populations.
- **b.** Seals are vulnerable to diseases if their immune systems are weakened by lack of food.
- **c.** Humans have an obligation to help animals in distress.
- **d.** Hundreds of seal pups were rescued in the Netherlands after high storm tides swept them into the water.

2. What is the main idea of paragraph 11?

- **a.** Pollution and overfishing may be partly to blame for seals becoming more vulnerable to infections like lungworm.
- **b.** Pollution can weaken a seal's disease-fighting immune system.
- **c.** The same is true for overfishing.
- **d.** If there aren't enough fish for the pups to eat, they will be underweight and have a harder time fighting off illness.

3. What is the implied main idea for paragraph 16?

- **a.** Seal rescuers are increasing at the Marine Mammal Center.
- **b.** People are to blame for the seals' troubles.
- **c.** The need for seal rescues is growing around the world for several reasons.
- **d.** Pollution from discarded litter and fishing gear entangle marine mammals.

SUPPORTING DETAILS

4. According to the article, seals are harmed by all of the following except

- **a.** overfishing
- **b.** boat propellers
- **c.** discarded litter
- **d.** shark attacks

Continued...

MyReadingLab

Reading 1 COMPREHENSION QUESTIONS

...continued

DRAWING CONCLUSIONS

5. From the article, you can conclude that
- **a.** Humans shouldn't discard litter into the ocean.
- **b.** Sick and injured marine mammals cannot survive.
- **c.** The fish that seals need to survive have nearly disappeared from the ocean.
- **d.** Marine mammals who are rehabilitated in rescue centers will always be dependent upon humans for food.

PATTERNS OF ORGANIZATION

6. The overall pattern of organization for this article is
- **a.** compare and contrast
- **b.** definition
- **c.** listing
- **d.** cause-and-effect

7. What is the relationship within the following sentence? Infected seals that are too exhausted to hunt stay onshore instead of returning to the water.
- **a.** time order
- **b.** definition
- **c.** compare and contrast
- **d.** listing

CRITICAL THINKING

8. Correctly identify the following sentence from paragraph 2. With their strength waning, they were vulnerable to deadly illnesses and starvation.
- **a.** fact
- **b.** opinion

9. What is the author's purpose for this article?
- **a.** to inform readers about a seal rescue operation
- **b.** to entertain readers with a story about rescued seals
- **c.** to persuade readers that humans should take steps to prevent further harm to animals and the environment.
- **d.** to explain how wild animals are rescued and treated

10. What is the author's tone in this article?
- **a.** excited
- **b.** frustrated
- **c.** concerned
- **d.** angry

MyReadingLab

Reading 1 VOCABULARY PRACTICE

Use the vocabulary words from the Word Bank to complete the following sentences. Write the words into the blanks provided.

WORD BANK				
recuperate	rehabilitation	parasites	lungworm	logistics
vulnerable	immune system	emaciated	entangled	waning

1. Roberto found his strength ________ while running the last mile of the marathon.

2. An animal's ________ provides defense against illnesses and parasites.

3. The seals were brought to the rehabilitation center to ________ from their illnesses.

4. A parasite known as ________ causes respiratory infections in seal pups.

5. Some of the animals rescued after Hurricane Sandy were very weak and ________ from lack of food.

6. Because electrical cables became ________ in tree branches during the storm, some neighborhoods lost power.

7. After her knee surgery, Brittni needed ________ with a physical therapist.

8. The ________ of an animal rescue operation after a major storm can be very complex.

9. Since the city was unprotected on three sides, it was ________ to attack by enemies.

10. ________ can cause illnesses in animals and people.

MyReadingLab

Reading 1 QUESTIONS FOR WRITING AND DISCUSSION

Review any parts of the article you need to answer the following questions.

1. Why were hundreds of seal pups stranded on local beaches near the Netherlands?

2. Why are volunteers so vital to an animal rescue operation?

3. What are some examples of other animal rescue operations that have taken place around the world?

4. What impact do human activities have on marine mammals?

5. What can be done to improve the environment for marine life and other animals?

Reading 1 VOCABULARY PRACTICE—CONCENTRATION GAME

recuperate	waning	organisms that feed off of others	rehabilitation	lungworm
logistics	extremely thin	a type of parasite	entangled	at risk for
vulnerable	to recover from illness	treatment to regain health	managing resources efficiently	a defense system against diseases
emaciated	weakening	immune system	knotted	parasites

Object: to remember where the matching words and definition cards are located in order to make the most correct matches

Two players

Vocabulary Practice

1.

Copy the ten vocabulary words and ten definitions below onto 20 squares of paper or index cards.

2.

Shuffle the cards, and lay them face down in four rows of five cards.

3.

The first player turns over two cards to find a word and matching definition. If they don't match, they are both turned face down in the same place.

4.

The next player takes a turn turning over two cards. If no match is made, the play goes back to the first player. As soon as a match is found, the player keeps the matching cards, and takes additional turns until no match is made.

5.

The player with the most correct matches wins.

extremely thin

emaciated

MyReadingLab

Reading 2
VOCABULARY PREVIEW

"A Greener Earth: Energy Alternatives" by Corinne Fennessy

The following words are from the article "A Greener Earth: Energy Alternatives." With a partner or in a team, choose the correct meanings of the underlined words in the following sentences. Use context clues (LEADS), word part clues, and parts of speech to help you figure out the meanings.

1. Smoking and overeating are two common factors that are very detrimental (det-ri-MENT-al) to our health.
   a. helpful
   b. harmful
   c. health-conscious
   d. determined
2. Trees and plants take in carbon dioxide during their respiration process, and emit (ee-MIT) oxygen.
   a. reproduce
   b. take in
   c. replace
   d. give out
3. Because of heavy deforestation (de-for-est-AY-shun) by natural and human activity, many geographical areas have turned into deserts.
   a. burning
   b. cutting down
   c. erasing
   d. removal of forests
4. The ecosystem (EE-ko-sis-tem) along the Gulf Coast was damaged by the oil rig explosion which destroyed some of the wildlife in that area.
   a. a system for studying biology
   b. beaches
   c. plants and animals in an area
   d. region
5. The new dishwashing liquid left a filmy residue (REZ-a-doo) on the drinking glasses.
   a. smudge
   b. substance remaining
   c. sticky
   d. residing within
6. During solar energy, the sun's energy is harnessed (HAR-ness'd) and stored for later use.
   a. captured for use
   b. stored
   c. strapped to
   d. eliminated

7. When a strange phenomenon (fen-NOM-in-non) is witnessed in the sky, it's named a UFO, or Unidentified Flying Object.
   a. objects
   b. saucers
   c. an observable event or object
   d. unexplained

8. During exercise, you should replenish (re-PLEN-ish) your body's water loss by drinking water.
   a. use up
   b. measure
   c. shift
   d. refill

9. The student's continued tardiness annoyed his professor because his late arrival would disrupt (dis-RUPT) the professor's lecture.
   a. disturb
   b. intrude
   c. display
   d. detain

10. The party's most popular candidate garnered (GAR-nerd) strong support from the Hispanic community.
   a. accepted
   b. collected
   c. promised
   d. produced

MyReadingLab

Reading 2
PREVIEW

1. What kinds of energy do you use every day to live? Which of these are renewable and which are non-renewable?
2. What would be some of the consequences if the price of gasoline doubled over the next few months?

Directions: As you read this article, practice the four-step reading process. Preview the article, and then write on the following lines one or two questions that you would hope to have answered.

MyReadingLab

Reading 2

As you read, answer the questions in the margins to check your comprehension.

"A Greener Earth: Energy Alternatives"

by Corinne Fennessy

What would happen if humans continued to use non-renewable fuel sources that pollute the environment? This article explores some alternative ways to meet our energy needs and save the planet.

Why Alternative Energy is Needed

1 Over the past two centuries, our planet has come to depend on non-renewable sources of energy such as coal, oil, and natural gas to produce electricity. Energy conservation will help slow down the use of these fuels, but they will run out eventually. Their limited supply drives prices steadily upward to the advantage of oil-producing countries. Besides the fact that these fuel sources will run out, they also are expensive to produce and have detrimental environmental effects.

2 The combustion of fossil fuels produces carbon dioxide. When carbon dioxide enters the atmosphere, it traps heat that is absorbed from the sun, which is why it is called a "greenhouse gas." A greenhouse is a house made of glass or other transparent material to allow sunlight in to help plants grow. The heat from the sun becomes trapped under the glass and the air inside the greenhouse is warmed significantly. The same thing happens when greenhouse gases from burning fossil fuels enter the atmosphere. They trap heat and cause the air to become warmer. As a result, our planet is

experiencing faster than normal changes in climate.

Why must we develop new energy sources?

3 According to scientists, the temperature of the Earth will rise 0.4 degrees C (0.7 degrees F) over the next 20 years. Since 1980, glaciers have lost an average of 9.6 m (31.5 ft) in vertical thickness, and glaciers are melting rapidly world wide. This affects the habitats of animals who live in cold climates and who depend upon wildlife in the coldest climates for survival. In addition to melting glaciers, the warming trend of Earth is causing sea levels to rise. This also affects coral reefs, mangrove forests, and salt marshes, where an abundance of fish, birds, and other marine life live. As the warming trend continues, it will continue to have a greater impact on wildlife, forcing many species to extinction.

Energy Alternatives

What are some disadvantages to nuclear power?

4 Knowing that our fossil fuel energy sources are limited, what are some alternative sources for our growing energy needs? One of the most debated sources is nuclear power—a clean source of power that doesn't emit greenhouse gases, but it has a downside. Several catastrophic events at nuclear power plants including Three Mile Island, Pennsylvania in 1979, Chernobyl, Russia in 1986, and Fukushima, Japan in 2011, have proved that nuclear power can be dangerous if the **reactors** melt down. If radioactive material escapes, it can cause sickness, cancer, and death. Another concern arises from the radioactive waste produced by these plants. Currently, the radioactive waste is stored in facilities all across the country. Transporting and safe-guarding the waste is dangerous and expensive. Moreover, the cost of building safe nuclear power plants and nuclear waste disposal facilities is high.

reactor: a facility to create and control nuclear reactions.

5 Other energy sources are biomass fuels. Biomass fuels are produced by organic matter such as plants and animals, including wood and combustible animal waste. The disadvantage of using biomass fuels is deforestation. Forests are an essential part of our ecosystem, and a significant loss of trees would have a major impact on the Earth's ecosystem. Besides wood, biomass energy sources include corn, sugarcane, soybeans, crop residues (such as cornstalks), manure from farm animals, and other organic materials to make ethanol (a combustible fuel). Biomass fuels can be used to power automobiles and produce electricity without increasing carbon dioxide in the atmosphere.

How does hydroelectric power work?

6 Hydroelectric power uses the force of water to turn turbines to produce electricity. When water passes through a dam, it turns the blades of turbines (large wheels that are moved by the force of wind or water). Examples of turbines include windmills and water wheels. Hydroelectric power is clean and **renewable**, but most of the world's largest rivers that have enough water to produce electricity have already been dammed and the future expansion of hydroelectric power is limited.

renewable: a source which will not run out

7 Solar power takes advantage of the sun's energy to produce electricity and to heat and light homes and commercial buildings. The two forms of solar energy are passive solar energy and active solar energy. In passive solar energy, the sun's energy is harnessed through the use of materials that absorb the sun's light and heat; for instance, placing windows on the south side of a building. Active solar energy uses technology to store the sun's energy; for example, solar panels. Solar panels or solar collectors absorb

Continued...

MyReadingLab
Reading 2
...continued

the sun's heat and transfer it to storage tanks. It is then transported to a steam powered generator to produce electricity. Sunlight can also be directly converted to electricity with photovoltaic cells (PV cells) to power small devices, or homes and buildings.

8 Wind power is produced much like water power. Instead of using the force of water to turn the electricity-producing turbines, wind does the same job. Because some regions do not receive enough sun to produce electricity using solar power, wind power has grown more popular in recent years. In many countries, wind farms are springing up on mountains, plains, and along the ocean shores where the wind speeds average 20% higher than on land. Like solar power, wind power does not pollute or produce hazardous waste. The disadvantage of wind power is that the wind turbines pose some danger for birds and bats, and they spoil the natural beauty of the scenery.

Why must groundwater be replenished?

9 Geothermal energy uses the heat energy of the Earth's hot center core to produce electricity. This phenomenon is seen in places like Yellowstone National Park's geyser, Old Faithful, which erupts when heated groundwater blasts out like steam from a tea kettle. The steam from geothermal heat is used to drive turbines to generate electricity. A downside of using geothermal heat is that when the groundwater runs out, steam is no longer produced. In Napa Valley, California, waste water is pumped back into the ground to replenish the groundwater supply for its geothermal power plant. But the heat inside the Earth shifts slowly over the years, and this can affect steam production. In addition, geothermal energy is restricted to areas that have geothermal resources.

10 Kinetic Energy is energy that is produced by motion. Scientists and engineers are developing ways to use the motion of waves to produce tidal energy. In narrow bays, dams have been constructed which use the force of tidal waves to turn turbines and produce electricity. Although tidal energy doesn't pollute and is a renewable resource, the dams disrupt the marine life in the areas where they are used. Another possible source of kinetic energy is wave energy to harness the energy of ocean waves and ocean currents.

What are some obstacles to using hydrogen as a vehicle fuel?

11 Hydrogen fuel has garnered a great deal of attention recently because it can produce energy cleanly and efficiently, mostly for use in vehicles. In a process known as ***electrolysis***, water atoms are split into their two separate components: oxygen and hydrogen. The hydrogen's electrons provide electricity. Currently this technology is limited because of the lack of facilities to produce, transport, and store hydrogen. Also, concerns about hydrogen escaping and depleting **ozone** in the atmosphere must be considered. Hydrogen is the most plentiful element in the universe, and can be produced in a variety of ways.

ozone: a gas layer in the upper atmosphere that prevents ultraviolet light from reaching the Earth's surface.

12 Each of these alternative energy sources holds great promise for the future. Scientists and engineers are continuing the search for more efficient, renewable, cost-effective, safe, and clean ways to produce energy for our growing energy needs.

741 words divided by .... minutes = ... words per minute

MyReadingLab

Reading 2 REVIEW

It is a good habit to summarize everything you read to strengthen your comprehension.

Directions: On the following lines, write a two- or three-sentence summary of the article "A Greener Earth: Energy Alternatives." In your own words, describe what the article was about and why the author wrote it.

MyReadingLab

Reading 2 COMPREHENSION QUESTIONS

The following questions will help you to recall the main idea and the details of "A Greener Earth: Energy Alternatives." Review any parts of the article that you need to find the correct answers.

1. What is the topic of this article?
   a. energy conservation
   b. climate change
   c. nuclear power
   d. alternative energy sources

CENTRAL POINT

2. What is the central point of the article?
   a. Over the past two centuries, our planet has come to depend on non-renewable sources of energy such as coal, oil, and natural gas to produce electricity.
   b. There are currently many alternative energy sources that can meet our energy needs.
   c. If we don't do something to change the way we use energy, the Earth will become polluted.
   d. Fossil fuels are limited, but wind and sun power are renewable energy sources.

SUPPORTING DETAILS

3. What is geothermal energy?
   a. energy produced by the sun
   b. energy produced by the steam from hot groundwater
   c. energy produced by the wind
   d. any form of energy produced by the Earth

DRAWING CONCLUSIONS

4. From the article, you can conclude that:
   a. nuclear energy poses more risk than solar or wind energy.
   b. alternative energy sources are expensive to construct.
   c. people are not using hydrogen fuel vehicles because they are too costly.
   d. hydrogen fuel cannot be stored for long periods.

Continued...

5. What is the relationship within the following sentence: Because some regions do not receive enough sun to produce electricity using solar power, wind power has grown more popular in recent years.
   a. time order
   b. definition
   c. cause and effect
   d. compare and/or contrast

VOCABULARY IN CONTEXT

6. What is the meaning of the underlined word in the following sentence: Also, concerns about hydrogen escaping and depleting ozone in the atmosphere must be considered.
   a. producing
   b. escaping
   c. shifting
   d. reducing

CRITICAL READING

7. Identify the following sentence as fact, opinion, or both: According to scientists, the temperature of the Earth will rise 0.4 degrees C (0.7 degrees F) over the next 20 years.
   a. fact
   b. opinion
   c. fact and opinion

8. What is the author's purpose in writing this article?
   a. to persuade readers to support alternative energy sources
   b. to inform readers about the various types of alternative energy
   c. to entertain readers about alternative energy
   d. to inform readers about safe forms of nuclear energy

9. What is the author's tone in this article?
   a. approving
   b. critical
   c. persuasive
   d. straightforward

10. Who is the intended audience?
    a. people who want to learn about energy alternatives
    b. people who work in alternative energy industries
    c. magazine editors
    d. scientists who are researching energy alternatives

MyReadingLab

Reading 2 VOCABULARY PRACTICE

Use the vocabulary words from the Word Bank to complete the following sentences. Write the words into the blanks provided.

WORD BANK				
detrimental	disrupt	deforestation	emit	ecosystem
residue	harnessed	phenomenon	replenish	garnered

1. The oil spill in the Gulf of Mexico harmed the fragile .... along the coastal areas.

2. Even a small oil spill will .... the balance of nature in an ecosystem.

3. After the energy of the sun has been ...., it is stored for future use.

4. After washing the dishes, some of my pots and pans still had a greasy ....

5. Wind power has .... support from environmentalists, who feel it is a safer and less polluting form of energy than most fossil fuels.

6. We observed a strange .... in the night sky but later found out it was the aurora borealis (a colorful display of natural glowing light).

7. The combustion of fossil fuels such as gasoline has .... effects on the quality of the air we breathe.

8. Many wooded areas which used to be part of the tropical rain forest have been .... for farmland.

9. It is important to .... trees that are harvested for lumber, paper, and wood products so we will continue to have enough trees to meet future needs.

10. The exhaust system in my car will often .... dark, smelly smoke because the engine is burning oil.

MyReadingLab

Reading 2 QUESTIONS FOR WRITING AND DISCUSSION

Review any parts of the article that you need to answer the following questions.

1. Which of the alternative forms of energy described in the article do you think are the safest and best sources of energy? Why?

2. What are some of the negative effects of using fossil fuels such as coal and oil as energy sources?

3. How would you feel if you learned that a nuclear power plant was going to be constructed next to your neighborhood? What concerns would you have?

4. What are some of the obstacles for hydrogen fueled vehicles, and what are some ways that these obstacles can be overcome?

Continued...

5. What are some ways you can try to conserve energy and reduce air pollution?

Reading 2
VOCABULARY PRACTICE—GUESS THE PHRASE

Preparation: Your instructor will draw blank lines on the board for each letter of a phrase. Divide the class into two to four teams. The object of the game is to be the first team to guess the phrase.

1.
After deciding which team will go first, the instructor will read a question aloud about the vocabulary words from either Reading Assignment 1 and/or 2 to the first team. If the team gives a correct response within 10 seconds, that team can guess one letter of the phrase on the board. If the letter the team guessed is in the phrase, the instructor will write all the instances of that letter on the board where it appears in the phrase. If the team answers incorrectly or doesn't respond in 10 seconds, that team may not guess a letter or try to solve the puzzle.

2.
The play then goes to the next team, which will receive a question. Play will continue until all the questions have been answered or the puzzle has been solved. Teams may only try to solve the puzzle (guess the phrase) when they have correctly answered their question. The team which correctly solves the puzzle wins the game.

ON THE JOB INTERVIEW

DR. SCOTT GEARHART,

VETERINARIAN AT SEA WORLD, ORLANDO, FLORIDA

How did you become interested in veterinary medicine?

As far back as I can remember, I had always dreamed of becoming a veterinarian. I have always been interested in animals and was one of those kids who was always collecting whatever creatures I could get my hands on (much to my mother's chagrin!). Birds, rabbits, squirrels, snakes, toads, insects; you name it, and I likely had those individuals in my possession at some point in my youth. But, as corny as this may sound, what sealed my destiny in becoming a veterinarian was when I was 14, I rushed to the aid of a dog that had just been hit by a car, and it died in my arms. That was when I knew that this was a career that I had to pursue.

What is your training and educational background that prepared you for this job?

I acquired a B.A. degree in zoology before getting into veterinary school. While I was in college, I did some volunteer work at a local nature center, as well as spending some time with the companion animal veterinarian who provided the care for the wildlife that came into the center. Then, during my senior year of veterinary school, I was able to do an externship with a veterinarian in South Florida who worked with many exotic species as well as marine mammals. After I graduated, I worked for a small animal clinic in Las Vegas and then moved on to a mixed animal hospital. After a couple years there, I was hired into my first marine mammal veterinary position with a small park in Fort Lauderdale. After that park was closed, I went into a zoo, wildlife, and exotic animal internship at Kansas State University. From there, I took a job with the San Antonio Zoo, where I remained until I came here to Sea World. So, I have had a wide variety of experiences to get me to this point in my career.

While in school, did you have to overcome any obstacles? Did you ever feel like quitting?

I suppose the biggest obstacle that I had to overcome besides achieving good grades and meeting the veterinary prerequisites was gaining experience in the field, as there are not always a great number of ideal opportunities for students to participate and gain that hands-on experience. As far as feeling like quitting, I do not believe that that had ever crossed my mind, as I was truly driven to achieve my dream.

What do you like best about your job?

I have the greatest job in the world! The diverse collection of species that I get to work with is unmatched, and I also am incredibly fortunate to have ownership, which has the financial resources and desire to provide the very best of care to that collection.

What challenges do you face in your work?

Besides the very nature of my job, which is working with patients that cannot "tell me where it hurts," I face the additional challenge of working with animals who live their entire lives in water; thus, a lot of the more traditional diagnostic and therapeutic options available to other veterinarians working on terrestrial species are not practical for me to

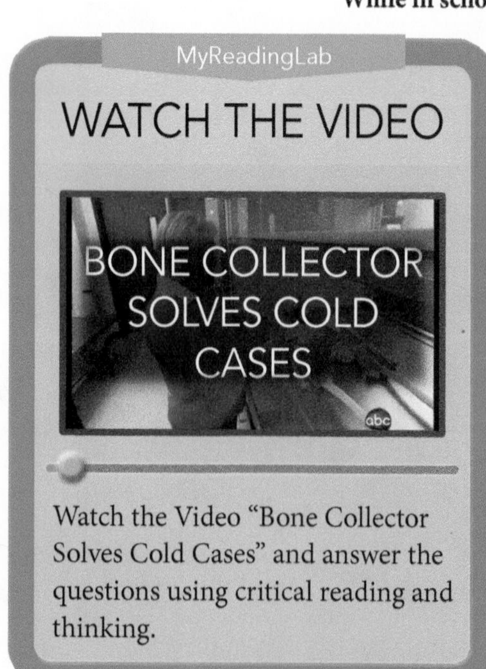

Watch the Video "Bone Collector Solves Cold Cases" and answer the questions using critical reading and thinking.

use. Because my patients are aquatic, they most often need to be removed from the water to be examined, which obviously presents its share of difficulties.

What advice do you have for college freshmen who are considering a career in veterinary medicine?

Obviously, achieving good grades is important, but it's also crucial to look for opportunities to gain experience in the field, even if it means cleaning kennels in a veterinary practice or doing volunteer work with a local wildlife rehabilitation center. It will help set you apart from other veterinary school candidates if you can demonstrate a long-standing interest in the profession.

What are your plans for the future?

I wish to continue working with marine animals, be it as a clinician or perhaps moving into a management position in my field. After that, hopefully a comfortable retirement!

MyReadingLab

BUILDING VOCABULARY

Throughout this course, you will be introduced to word parts that make up many words in the English language. Study the following word parts, and then answer the questions that follow.

Prefixes	Roots	Suffixes
bi- *two*	-angul-, -angle- *angle*	-ar *relating to*
tri- *three*	-ped-, -pod- *foot*	
quad-, quadr- *four*		
pent- *five*		
hexa- *six*		

What English words can you create from these word parts?

Using a dictionary, look up the meanings of any of the words you wrote that you can't define. Use one of the words you wrote in a sentence that reveals its meaning with a context clue:

MyReadingLab

REAL-LIFE READING

g = gram (A current U.S. penny weighs 2.5 grams.)

NUTRITION LABELS

Reading nutrition labels is a good way to make sure you are buying food that is nutritious and good for your health. Foods with high amounts of calories, fat, cholesterol, sugar, and sodium are not good for you. Compare the following labels of two cereals, and then answer the questions that follow.

Here are the suggested amounts for healthy eating with a 2,000-calories-per-day diet:

Recommended Daily Total Amounts

Fat	less than 65 g	Cholesterol	less than 300 mg
Sodium	less than 2400 mg	Total carbohydrates	300 g

Popular Brand Cereal

Nutrition Facts

Serving Size 1 Cup (31g/1.1 oz.) Servings Per Container About 11

	Cereal	Cereal with 1/2 Cup VitaminsA&D Fat Free Milk
Amount Per Serving		
Calories	120	160
	% Daily Value**	
Total Fat 0.5g*	1%	1%
Saturated Fat 0g	0%	0%
Trans Fat 0g		
Cholesterol 0mg	0%	0%
Sodium 220mg	9%	12%
Potassium 50mg	1%	6%
Total Carbohydrate 23g	8%	10%
Dietary Fiber less than 1g	2%	2%
Sugars 4g		
Other Carbohydrate 19g		
Protein 6g		
Vitamin A	15%	20%
Vitamin C	35%	35%
Calcium	0%	15%
Iron	45%	45%
Vitamin E	35%	35%
Thiamin	35%	40%
Riboflavin	35%	45%
Niacin	35%	35%
Vitamin B6	100%	100%
Folic Acid	100%	100%
Vitamin B12	100%	110%
Phosphorus	4%	15%
Zinc	4%	6%
Selenium	10%	10%

* Amount in cereal. One half cup of fat free milk contributes an additional 40 calories, 65mg sodium, 6g total carbohydrates (6g sugars), and 4g protein.

** Percent Daily Values are based on a 2,000 calorie diet. Your daily values may be higher or lower depending on your calorie needs:

Calories	2,000	2,500
Total Fat Less than	65g	80g
Saturated Fat Less than	20g	25g
Cholesterol Less than	300mg	300mg
Sodium Less than	2,400mg	2,400mg
Potassium	3,500mg	3,500mg
Total Carbohydrate	300g	375g
Dietary Fiber	25g	30g

Calories per gram: Fat 9 • Carbohydrate 4 • Protein 4

Store Brand Granola

Nutrition Facts

Serving Size 2/3 Cup (31g/1.1 oz.) Servings Per Container About 9

	Cereal	Cereal with 1/2 Cup Vitamins A&D Fat Free Milk
Amount Per Serving		
Calories	180	220
	% Daily Value**	
Total Fat 4.5g*	1%	1%
Saturated Fat 0g	0%	0%
Trans Fat 0g		
Cholesterol 0mg	0%	0%
Sodium 270mg	12%	15%
Potassium 50mg	1%	6%
Total Carbohydrate 26g	8%	10%
Dietary Fiber less than 4g	4%	4%
Sugars 10g		
Other Carbohydrate 26g		
Protein 8g		
Vitamin A	15%	20%
Vitamin C	35%	35%
Calcium	0%	15%
Iron	40%	40%
Vitamin E	30%	30%
Thiamin	25%	30%
Riboflavin	25%	35%
Niacin	20%	20%
Vitamin B6	35%	35%
Vitamin B12	30%	30%
Phosphorus	1%	12%

* Amount in cereal. One half cup of fat free milk contributes an additional 40 calories, 65mg sodium, 6g total carbohydrates (6g sugars), and 4g protein.

** Percent Daily Values are based on a 2,000 calorie diet. Your daily values may be higher or lower depending on your calorie needs:

Calories	2,000	2,500
Total Fat Less than	90g	100g
Saturated Fat Less than	25g	30g
Cholesterol Less than	300mg	300mg
Sodium Less than	2,400mg	2,400mg
Potassium	3,500mg	3,500 mg
Total Carbohydrate	300g	375g
Dietary Fiber	25g	30g

Calories per gram: Fat 15 • Carbohydrate 8 • Protein 6

1. How much is one serving of cereal for the popular brand?
   a. 1 1/2 cups
   b. 1 cup
   c. 2/3 cups
   d. 2 cups
2. How much is one serving of cereal for Store Brand Granola?
   a. 1 1/2 cups
   b. 1 cup
   c. 2/3 cup
   d. 2 cups
3. How many more calories are in one serving of Store Brand Granola (without the milk) than the popular brand?
   a. 100 calories
   b. 90 calories
   c. 60 calories
   d. 20 calories
4. Which of these nutrients are higher in the popular brand cereal than in the Store Brand Granola (both without milk)?
   a. sodium, vitamin E, and zinc
   b. cholesterol, sodium, and fat
   c. sugars, vitamin A, and selenium
   d. vitamin E, niacin, and iron
5. Which of these nutrients are higher in Store Brand Granola than in the popular brand?
   a. cholesterol, vitamin A, and iron
   b. calcium, sugar, and fat
   c. sugar, cholesterol, and vitamin A
   d. sugar, fat, and sodium

MyReadingLab

TEXTBOOK GRAPHIC AIDS

Study the following diagram, and then answer the questions that follow.

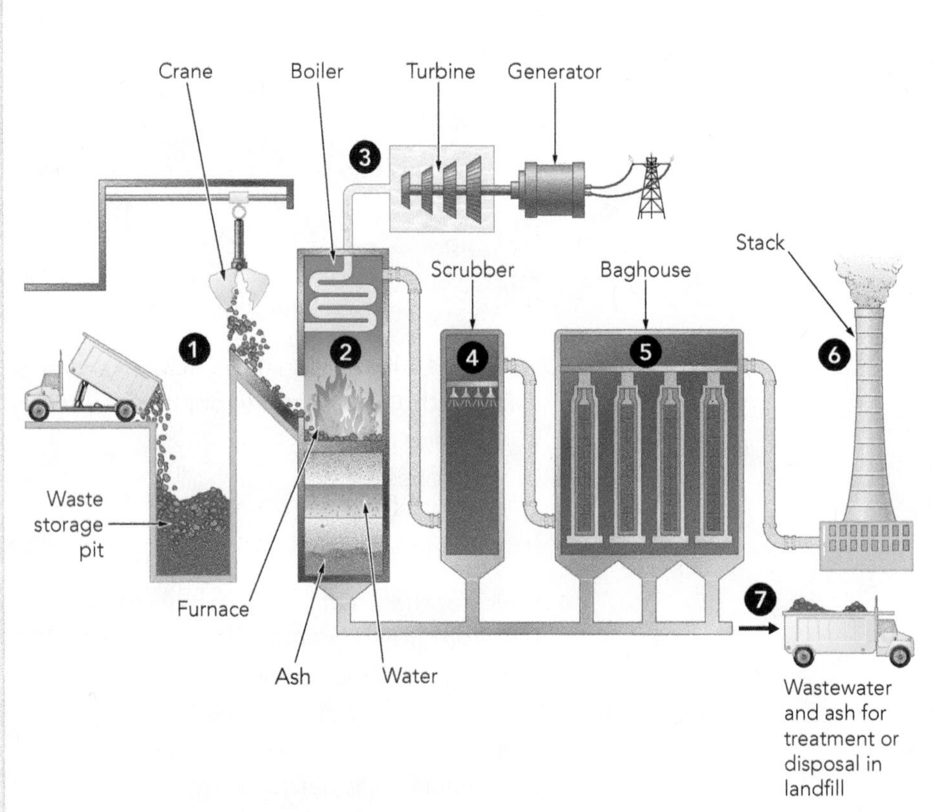

Using Waste to Generate Electricity

Incinerators reduce the volume of solid waste by burning it, but they may emit toxic compounds into the air. Many incinerators are waste-to-energy (WTE) facilities that use the heat of combustion to generate electricity. In a WTE facility, solid waste (**1**) is burned at extremely high temperatures (**2**), heating water, which turns to steam. The steam turns a turbine (**3**), which powers a generator to create electricity. In an incinerator outfitted with pollution-control technology, a scrubber (**4**) chemically mitigates toxic gases produced by combustion, and airborne particulate matter is filtered physically in a baghouse (**5**) before air is emitted from the stack (**6**). Ash remaining from the combustion process is disposed of (**7**) in a landfill.

1. What is WTE?
   a. a method for burning trash
   b. a method for turning trash into energy
   c. waste transfer elimination
   d. a method for turning steam to electricity
2. How is trash converted into steam?
   a. It is burned and then goes into a scrubber.
   b. It is stored in the baghouse.
   c. It goes through a scrubber and comes out of the stack.
   d. It is burned to heat water.
3. Why must steam be created in this process?
   a. Steam is used to filter the impurities out of the trash.
   b. It filters airborne particulate (adjective of particle) matter to prevent air pollution.
   c. It is used to turn the turbines for the generator.
   d. It separates the ash from water molecules.
4. What does the scrubber do?
   a. It filters the ash from the solid waste.
   b. It filters out toxic gases to prevent air pollution.
   c. It turns the trash into solid waste.
   d. It cools the hot air from the boiler.
5. What happens inside the baghouse?
   a. Airborne particulate matter is filtered before it's released in the stack.
   b. The ash is removed from the wastewater before it is disposed in a landfill.
   c. The ash is bagged before it is disposed in a landfill.
   d. The smoke is directed out to the stack.

MyReadingLab

CHAPTER PRACTICE 1

Read the paragraph, and underline the main idea (if stated) and major details. Then, answer the questions that follow.

On May 18, 1980, one of the most tragic natural disasters occurred in Washington State. Mount St. Helens, a volcanic mountain, erupted with incredible force, flattening trees within a 160-mile radius. The eruption killed 59 people, including those who died from the intense heat and the clouds of ash and gases in the air. The gases and ash from the eruption shot more than 11 miles into the atmosphere. This caused crop damage in states as far away as the Midwest. The ash clouds over the city of Yakima, Washington, were so thick that it became as dark as night at noon. Mount St. Helens is one of 15 large volcanoes in the Cascade Mountain Range near the west coast of North America. Several others in this range could erupt in the future.

1. What is the topic?
- **a.** volcanoes
- **b.** volcanic eruptions
- **c.** a volcanic eruption at Mount St. Helens
- **d.** volcanoes in the Cascade Mountain Range

2. What is the main idea?
- **a.** Mount St. Helens is the worst natural disaster in recent history.
- **b.** Several volcanoes in the Cascade Mountain Range could erupt in the future.
- **c.** Volcanoes can cause great damage.
- **d.** On May 18, 1980, Mount St. Helens erupted in Washington State, destroying lives and property.

3. Which of the following statements is an opinion?
- **a.** On May 18, 1980, one of the most tragic natural disasters occurred in Washington State.
- **b.** The eruption killed 59 people, including those who died from the intense heat and the clouds of ash and gases in the air.
- **c.** The gases and ash from the eruption shot more than 11 miles into the atmosphere.
- **d.** The ash clouds over the city of Yakima, Washington, were so thick that it became as dark as night at noon.

4. What is the author's purpose?
- **a.** to entertain readers with a story about a volcano
- **b.** to persuade readers that volcanoes are dangerous
- **c.** to inform readers about the volcanic eruption at Mount St. Helens
- **d.** to explain how volcanoes form

5. What is the author's tone?
- **a.** discouraging
- **b.** serious
- **c.** critical
- **d.** amused

MyReadingLab

CHAPTER PRACTICE 2

Read the following paragraph, and underline the main idea (if stated) and major details. Then, answer the questions that follow. Look for opinions and bias.

Seal hunters kill hundreds of thousands of baby seals each year in Canada, all for the sake of fashion. Baby seal fur is white and very soft, which makes it one of the most beautiful furs for coats and wraps. Trappers may use clubs or hooks to kill seals in horrible ways that cause pain and suffering to these animals just to avoid damaging the fur. Imagine the terrible suffering of the mother seal as she watches her babies being killed and dragged away. Canada has slowed the slaughter of seals, but it has not been completely stopped. We need to stop purchasing products with animal fur. We should demand that the Canadian government enforce laws to permanently stop the hunting of baby seals. Everyone can help by joining protest groups and contacting government officials to demand action to protect these innocent and beautiful animals.

1. What is the topic?
   - a. seal hunting
   - b. seals
   - c. baby seal hunting
   - d. how baby seals are killed
2. What is the implied main idea?
   - a. The seal hunting industry depends on people who buy furs.
   - b. Baby seal fur is white and very soft, which makes it one of the most desirable furs for coats and wraps.
   - c. Seal hunters use painful methods to kill baby seals.
   - d. We should permanently stop the hunting of baby seals in Canada.
3. Which of the following statements is a fact?
   - a. Baby seal fur is white and very soft, which makes it one of the most beautiful furs for coats and wraps.
   - b. Canada has slowed the slaughter of seals, but it has not been completely stopped.
   - c. Imagine the terrible suffering of the mother seal as she watches her babies being killed and dragged away.
   - d. We should demand that the Canadian government enforce laws to permanently stop the hunting of baby seals.
4. What is the author's tone?
   - a. disapproving
   - b. objective
   - c. straightforward
   - d. positive
5. What is the author's purpose?
   - a. to inform readers about baby seal hunting
   - b. to persuade readers to help protect baby seals
   - c. to entertain readers about baby seals
   - d. to persuade readers to stop hunting animals

MyReadingLab

CHAPTER PRACTICE 3

Read the following paragraph, and underline the main idea (if stated) and major details. Then, answer the questions that follow. Look for opinions and bias.

A rainbow is a natural event that is a symbol of hope and has been associated with many legends, such as the one that says there is a pot of gold at the end of every rainbow. Unfortunately, this is not true. Rainbows are created when there are rain clouds in the sky, usually just after a shower, and the sun is shining. When sunlight shines through the raindrops, the light is refracted, or bent. Light is made up of many different-colored light waves. Light is reflected off the inner surface of each raindrop and then bounces back through the side where it entered. As it passes through the raindrop, the light is divided into colorful bands: red, blue, and violet. The result is a colorful rainbow. We can only see part of the rainbow from the Earth's surface, but as you go higher, you can see more of it. From an airplane, the rainbow appears as a complete circle.

1. What is the topic?

a. the colors of a rainbow
b. rainbows
c. how rainbows are formed
d. the colors of light

2. What is the implied main idea?

a. A rainbow is a beautiful natural event that is a symbol of hope and has been associated with many interesting legends, such as the one that says there is a pot of gold at the end of every rainbow.
b. Rainbows occur after a shower when the there are rain clouds and the sun is still shining.
c. Light is made up of many different-colored light waves.
d. A rainbow is the result of light passing through raindrops and refracting into different colors.

3. Which of the following statements is an opinion?

a. A rainbow is a natural event that is a symbol of hope and has been associated with many legends, such as the one that says there is a pot of gold at the end of every rainbow.
b. Unfortunately, this is not true.
c. Rainbows are created when there are rain clouds in the sky, usually just after a shower, and the sun is shining.
d. Light is reflected off the inner surface of each raindrop and then bounces back through the side where it entered.

4. What is the author's purpose?

a. to inform readers about how rainbows are created
b. to entertain readers with a story about rainbows
c. to persuade readers to look for rainbows in the sky
d. to tell legends about rainbows

5. What is the author's tone?

a. approving
b. excited
c. informative
d. cheerful

MyReadingLab

TEXTBOOK PRACTICE

Read the following textbook selection, and underline the main idea (if stated) and major details. Then, answer the questions that follow. Look for opinions and bias.

How Can You Reduce Your Risk of Heart Disease?

Although cardiovascular disease remains the number-one killer in the United States, incidence of the disease has declined over the past 30 years. This drop has occurred primarily because people have reduced their risk factors for coronary heart disease (CHD). Table 9.2 lists the major CHD risk factors. Note that six of the nine major risk factors, and both of the contributing factors, can be modified by behavior. Therefore, you can modify 70 percent of CHD risk factors to reduce your risk of developing cardiovascular disease.

TABLE 9.2
Major and Contributory Risk Factors for Developing Coronary Heart Disease

RISK FACTOR	CLASSIFI-CATION	IS BEHAVIOR MODIFICATION POSSIBLE?	BEHAVIOR MODIFICATION TO REDUCE RISK
Smoking	Major	Yes	Smoking cessation
Hypertension	Major	Yes	Exercise, proper diet, and stress reduction
High blood cholesterol	Major	Yes	Exercise, proper diet, and medication
Diabetes mellitus	Major	Yes	Proper nutrition exercise
Obesity and overweight	Major	Yes	Weight loss, proper nutrition, exercise
Physical inactivity	Major	Yes	Exercise
Heredity	Major	No	
Gender	Major	No	
Increasing age	Major	No	
Stress	Contributes	Yes	Stress management, exercise
Alcohol	Contributes	Yes	Moderate consumption

1. What is the topic?
   a. coronary heart disease (CHD)
   b. bad health habits
   c. Americans at risk
   d. risk factors for CHD

Continued...

MyReadingLab

TEXTBOOK PRACTICE

...continued

2. What is the implied main idea?

a. Many Americans are at risk for CHD.
b. People's risk for CHD depends on their behavior, such as smoking.
c. Although cardiovascular disease remains the number-one killer in the United States, we can often reduce the risk of CHD by modifying our behavior.
d. Many people are in danger because of CHD.

3. What is the author's purpose?

a. to persuade people to eat healthier
b. to inform readers about risk factors for CHD
c. to explain why people shouldn't smoke
d. to entertain readers

4. According to the information in the table, which of these behavior modifications are the most helpful for reducing the risk of CHD? (Choose all that apply.)

a. aging
b. exercise
c. proper diet
d. medication

5. Determine whether the following statement is fact, opinion, or both: Although cardiovascular disease remains the number-one killer in the United States, incidence of the disease has declined over the past 30 years.

a. fact
b. opinion
c. both fact and opinion

STUDY SKILL REVIEW

A study guide is a list of topics with questions and answers. Study guides help you learn the most important information in a unit of study. Begin creating a study guide by listing the topics in the column on the far left. Next, in the middle column, write the most important skills or concepts about each topic in the form of a question. In the far-right column, write the answers to the questions. Complete the following study guide about the concepts you learned in this chapter, and then use it to quiz yourself or your study partners.

TOPIC	QUESTIONS	ANSWERS
Fact and Opinion	What is a fact?	
	What is an opinion?	
Author's Purpose		The reason why an author wrote something.
Intended Audience	What is the intended audience?	
Author's Tone	What is author's tone?	

READING LAB ASSIGNMENTS

SKILL PRACTICES

1. Login to **MyReadingLab,** and in the menu click on **Reading Skills** and **Learning Path**. On the main screen, click **Critical Thinking** and **Purpose and Tone**. Complete the review and practice activities recommended by your instructor.

COMPREHENSION IMPROVEMENT

2. From the menu in **MyReadingLab,** click on **Reading Level** and **Next Reading**. Choose two reading selections from the list on the main screen. Read the articles and answer the diagnostic and exercise questions.

CAREER EXPLORATION

3. Go online to the Occupational Outlook Handbook at the Bureau of Labor Statistics and explore careers in science. Find a career that interests you, and print out the information. Print the article, and then preview, read, highlight and annotate it. Underline and label two facts and one opinion. Write the author's purpose and the tone for the article in the margin.

MyReadingLab

LEARNING REFLECTION

Think about the skills and concepts in this chapter. What have you learned in this chapter that will help your reading comprehension and enable you to do well in college?

MyReadingLab

SELF-EVALUATION CHECKLIST

Rate yourself on the following items, using the following scale:

1 = strongly disagree

2 = disagree

3 = neither agree nor disagree

4 = agree

5 = strongly agree

1. I completed all of the assigned work on time. ....

2. I understand all of the concepts in this chapter. ....

3. I contributed to teamwork and class discussions. ....

4. I completed all of the assigned lab work on time. ....

5. I came to class on time. ....

6. I attended class every day. ....

7. I studied for any quizzes or tests we had for this chapter. ....

8. I asked questions when I didn't understand something. ....

9. I checked my comprehension during reading. ....

10. I know what is expected of me in the coming week. ....

11. Are you still on track with the goals you set in Chapter 1?

....

What changes can you make to improve your performance in this?

....

....

10 STUDY SKILLS

LEARNING STRATEGIES

Paraphrasing and Summarizing 421

Taking Effective Notes 424

Taking Tests 430

Using Metacognition 432

READING SELECTIONS

READING 1: "Bionic Soldiers" 440

READING 2: "Attack of the Cyber-Thieves" 449

READING FOR LIFE

Real-Life Reading 458

On the Job Interview 461

Textbook Graphic Aids 462

Building Vocabulary 464

CHAPTER REVIEW

Chapter Practice 465

Textbook Practice 468

Reading Lab Assignments 469

Study Skill Review 470

Learning Reflection 471

Self-Evaluation Checklist 471

FOCUS ON: Technology

One of the most exciting aspects of technology is its rapid growth, with new applications and devices entering the market on a daily basis. Technology is a large part of most jobs in nearly every industry—even in fields like theater and art. The skills needed for many careers in technology can be achieved with a two year technical degree.

Success in college or in your career is not based as much on your intelligence as your ability to perform. Some of the smartest students you knew in high school have dropped out of college simply because they didn't have the study skills they needed to succeed. Developing good study skills will not only help you in college, but in your personal life and your career. Being an organized, responsible team player with good communication skills can give you the advantage for success. Students with good study skills know how to take notes, study for tests, and monitor their learning. This chapter will help you develop all of these skills so you can achieve the goals you established in Chapter 1.

In this chapter you will:

LEARNING OBJECTIVES

1 learn how to paraphrase and summarize.

2 learn how to take effective notes.

3 learn how to take tests.

4 learn to use metacognition.

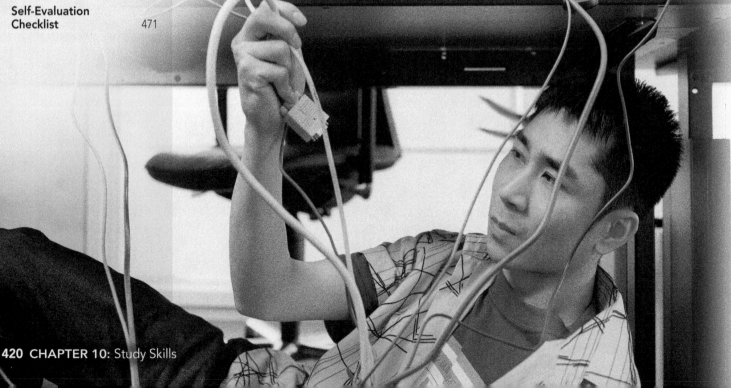

OBJECTIVE 1

Learn how to paraphrase and summarize.

PARAPHRASING AND SUMMARIZING

Paraphrasing and summarizing are not only important skills for note-taking and studying, they are valuable life skills that are used in every career field. You may find yourself having to give a report on something for your job. You may need to keep written records of your patients, your clients, your products, your actions, or your technical operations. For these applications, paraphrasing and summarizing will help you be more concise.

Paraphrasing

Paraphrasing: Restating sentences or quotes to make them shorter and to the point, and saying them in your own words.

Paraphrasing means restating sentences or quotes to make them shorter and to the point, and saying them in your own words. You may paraphrase whenever you want to state an idea clearly by using language that your audience will be able to understand more easily. When paraphrasing, the trick is to say the sentence or paragraph in a more direct way without leaving out important information. It's not necessary to include minor details that are not important for you to remember, however, depending upon the information you need, some details may be included.

Think about the subject of the paragraph or sentence you are paraphrasing and the most important point the author is trying to say about the subject. Instead of copying the language of the paragraph, use your own words to express the idea with language you will understand. Read the following examples of paraphrases.

1. "Due to the overwhelming popularity of weight-loss products, the FDA has cracked down on pharmaceutical companies for producing products with dangerous side effects, such as Fen-phen."

Paraphrase:

The FDA has cracked down on companies producing weight-loss products with dangerous side effects.

2. "The first fully electronic computer was the Colossus Mark 1, constructed between 1941–1943 by Alan Turing, M.H.A. Neuman, Thomas H. Flowers, and others to help the Allies decipher the secret military communication codes of the Axis during World War II." (from *Engineering by Design* 2e, by Gerald Voland, Pearson Prentice Hall, Upper Saddle River. 2004, p. 191.)

Paraphrase:

The first electronic computer was constructed from 1941–1943 to decipher secret military codes of the Axis in World War II.

Paraphrase the following sentences into your own words:

1. The process of freeze-drying coffee is achieved by first percolating the coffee and then partially evaporating the water to make a mixture that is very concentrated. Then the mixture is frozen and made into granules.

2. Although 350,000 supermarket shopping carts are stolen annually at an estimated cost in excess of $30 million, most supermarket chains have not embraced the various designs that have been developed to prevent such theft.

3. When NASA sought bids to build the mirror for the Hubble telescope, the Perkin-Elmer Corporation asked $64.28 million, but Eastman Kodak Company wanted $99.79 million because it intended to test the mirrors before launching them into space. NASA chose the cheaper bid, and later the $1.4 billion Hubble Space telescope failed due to an unsatisfactory mirror built by Perkin-Elmer Corporation.

Summarizing

A **summary** is a brief description that states the main idea and major points in your own words. The length of a summary depends upon the length of the material you are summarizing, your purpose for summarizing, and the requirements of the assignment. It is important to paraphrase the most important points in your own words and write or say them in a form that is shorter than the original text. In general, a summary is usually one-fourth to one-third the length of the original text.

As you read the following paragraph, notice how the main points have been underlined and are included in the summary.

Water

Water makes up approximately 60–70 percent of your body, and it is important for everything from temperature regulation, digestion, absorption, and blood formation to waste elimination. Water is especially important for physically active people. A person engaged in heavy exercise in a hot, humid environment can lose 1 to 3 liters of water per hour through sweating. Losing as little as 5 percent of body water causes fatigue, weakness, and the inability to concentrate; losing more than 15 percent can be fatal. You should consume 8-10 cups of water per day through foods and beverages. Drinking water throughout your day will help you meet this goal, as will eating food with high water content, such as fruits and vegetables. People who experience excessive sweating, diarrhea, or vomiting, or who donate blood, may have higher water requirements.

Read the following summary of "Water":

> Water makes up 60–70 percent of the body and is important for its major functions, including temperature regulation, digestion, absorption, blood formation and waste elimination. Losing water causes fatigue, weakness, and the inability to concentrate; and losing too much can be fatal. Most people require 8–10 cups of water per day.

MAKING A SUMMARY

Read the following paragraph. Underline the information that you think should be included in a summary.

Epidemics

Epidemics are diseases that spread rapidly through a population. Once a person comes in contact with the disease causing germ, he or she may become infected. Infectious diseases are spread in many different ways. First, exposure to body fluids such as saliva, blood, or semen can spread disease. Examples of diseases that are spread this way are sexually transmitted diseases, the common cold, or flu. Another way diseases spread is through an intermediate host, such as an insect. Lyme disease and rabies are spread through intermediate hosts. Third, inhaling a virus from the air after someone coughs or sneezes can spread diseases such as colds or the flu. Finally, ingesting (eating foods containing the germs) also spreads diseases like food poisoning and Mad Cow disease.

Use the information you underlined to help you write a summary of the paragraph above. Try to be as brief as possible but not leave out important points as you paraphrase.

....

....

....

....

....

OBJECTIVE 2

Learn how to take effective notes.

TAKING EFFECTIVE NOTES

One of the most important skills you need to succeed in college and in your career is the ability to take good notes. Students who do poorly in college often do not take effective notes. Some students don't take any notes, assuming they will remember everything they need to know, but even people with extremely good memories cannot remember everything. Note-taking in class is not only a way to remember what you learned, but it also is a way to stay actively involved in your learning. Note-takers are less likely to daydream or feel bored during class. Also, the act of writing something down will actually help you to remember it because you are using an additional learning style known as kinesthetic learning. Many students use laptop computers or electronic tablets to take notes. Some record lectures, and then write their notes afterward from the recording. Whichever way you choose, the important thing is to take notes.

One of the biggest challenges that most students have is deciding what to write. Some students don't write enough information and miss the most important points while others try to write everything and soon realize they can't keep up. The key to taking good notes is to be a good listener and thinker. Listen to what the instructor says and ask yourself, "What are the most important points that I need to remember?" Here are some helpful tips for becoming a good note-taker:

- Be prepared to take notes before class begins. Have your notebook out and your pen or pencil ready. If you're using a laptop or tablet, have the page open to where you will begin typing.
- To improve your listening, make sure you can hear and see the presenter clearly. Sit away from distractions such as windows or talkative students.
- Focus on the lecturer and what is being said. If you think of something that distracts you, write it in a margin to deal with later.
- Notice what is on the screen during a presentation. This is usually the most important information in the lecture.
- Listen for ideas that are emphasized and repeated.
- Think like a professor. What topics would you want your students to know? What questions would you ask them on a test? These are important points to write down.
- Use abbreviations whenever possible. Use some standard abbreviations and make up others.
- Avoid writing in complete sentences. Use words and phrases only.
- Draw diagrams or charts to organize information.
- Listen for phrases that indicate something important will be said, such as "in conclusion" or "to summarize."
- Listen for lists such as "three factors," "several reasons," or "possible effects."
- Mark any information that the instructor tells you will be a test item with a star, or write "test" next to it in the margin.
- If you get behind while taking notes, leave a few blank lines on your paper to fill in later, and pick up where the lecturer is now.

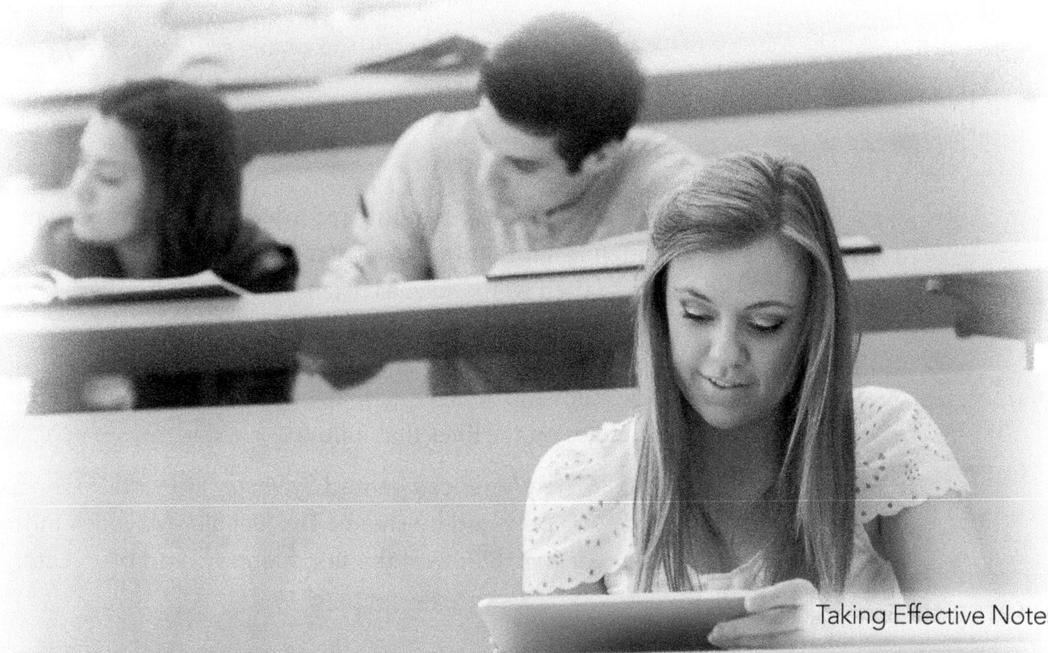

What to Write

Good note-taking depends on knowing what is important and what is not. Your prior knowledge of the topic is helpful, so be sure to come to class prepared by reading the homework assignments. Also, your understanding of the topic, main idea, major details, and minor details is very important. Notes should include the topic, main idea, and major details. Topics and subtopics are key words that should be included in your notes. Also listen for definitions of terms and record those accurately. To keep up with the presentation, paraphrase as much as possible and keep your notes short. You can always go back later and fill in missing details by using your textbook or someone else's notes. Read the following excerpt from a professor's lecture and the student's notes that follow. Notice how key information has been highlighted and included in the notes.

> There are several **types** of satellites which each have a different function. **Astronomical satellites**, like the Hubble, are used by astronomers to study the planets, galaxies, and other heavenly bodies. Another group of satellites are **biosatellites**, which carry living organisms for scientific experiments. **Communication satellites** are used in telecommunications, such as cell phones. **Navigational satellites** use radio time signals for GPS systems. Another kind of satellite is the **reconnaissance satellite**, which is mostly used by governments and militaries for obtaining information. **Weather satellites** are used to monitor Earth's changing weather and climates. With so many categories of satellites orbiting the Earth, it is incredible that there are not more collisions in outer space.

STUDENT'S NOTES:

Types of Satellites

- *astronomical - to study stars, planets, heavenly bodies. Ex- Hubble*
- *biosatellites- carry living organisms for scientific experiments*
- *communication- telecommunications. Ex-cell phones*
- *navigation- use radio time signals for GPS*
- *reconnaissance- used by gov'ts & military for info.*
- *weather- monitor weather and climate*

Notice how the student has only recorded the most important information and has written in short phrases, not sentences. Abbreviations were also used for commonly used words such as "example" and "information," and a longer word such as "governments" was abbreviated to "gov'ts."

Read the following paragraph, marking important information and then fill in the missing notes on the lines that follow.

> In 1867, an American named Sylvester Howard Roper created a bicycle that was powered by steam. The Daimler-Maybach motorcycle, invented in Germany in 1885, was the first fuel-powered bike. Later, more motorcycles

appeared with internal combustion engines, and by World War I, the Indian was the largest motorcycle manufacturer in the world. By 1920, Harley-Davidson took first place with dealers in 67 countries. After World War II, the BSA Group became the largest motorcycle producer. Companies like NSU and Moto-Guzzi began designing more streamlined motorcycles. From the 1950s through the 1990s, small engine motorcycles were popular worldwide. Today there are hundreds of different types of motorcycles manufactured throughout the world. The history of motorcycles is one filled with variety and innovation.

(Topic?) ....

- 1867 - Sylvester Howard Roper- steam bicycle
- ....
- By WWI -Indian largest motorcycle manufacturer in world
- ....
- After WW II BSA Group largest producer
- ....
- Today- 100s of diff. types of motorcycles manufactured in world

Outlining

Outlining is another way to take notes. Like concept maps, outlines provide the major and minor details in a paraphrased form. Formal outlines follow a specific sequence in their format. But for your own notes, you may make up a simpler format that is easy to remember.

When making an outline, use the following guidelines:

1. Use phrases, not sentences.
2. Use paraphrasing to state a general idea.
3. Work from most general to most specific, indenting to show the relationships of more specific ideas.

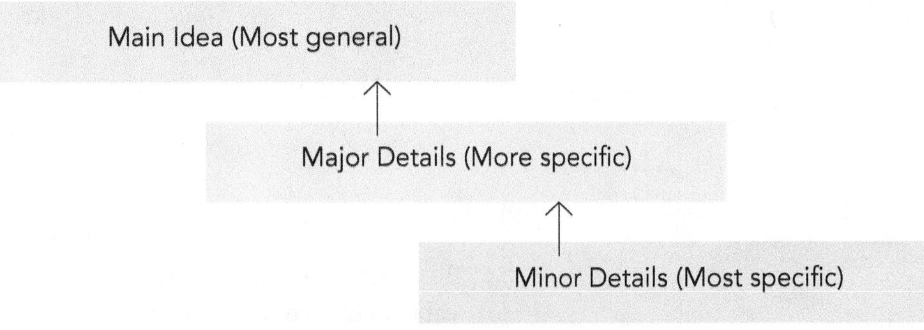

Read the following paragraph and study the outline.

Leonardo da Vinci (1452-1519) is one of the most famous artists in history. He painted the *Mona Lisa* and *The Last Supper*, two of the world's most treasured paintings. But Leonardo also had another talent as an inventor. His notebooks and journals are filled with ideas for inventions, everything from flying machines to weapons. He designed machines to do mechanical work and for military use. Some of his designs included a winch for lifting heavy loads, a lathe for drilling holes, a cutting machine, and a heat-powered rotisserie for roasting meat. His weapon designs included a giant crossbow, a mechanical rapid-firing arrow machine, rapid-firing cannons, and artillery guns that could fire multiple rounds at once. Leonardo Da Vinci is admired not only because he was a talented artist, but also because of his ability to create in so many different fields.

Outline of the Paragraph

Topic: Leonardo daVinci (1452-1519)

Main Idea — I. Da Vinci was a talented artist and inventor.

Major Details — A. Painted *Mona Lisa* and *The Last Supper*

B. Designed machines for mechanical work

Minor Details — 1. Winch for lifting loads

2. Lathe for drilling holes

3. Cutting machine

4. Heat-powered rotisserie

Major Details — C. Designed weapons

Minor Details — 1. Giant crossbow

2. Rapid-firing arrow machine

3. Artillery guns firing multiple rounds

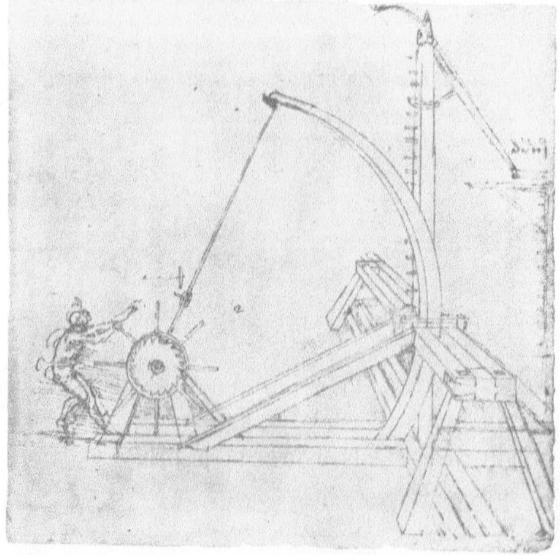

Technical drawing of siege catapult by Leonardo da Vinci, 1470-1520.

Practice Outlining

Read the following selection and complete the outline that follows.

Leonardo Da Vinci was also an inventor of musical instruments. He designed mechanical drums that were attached to wagon wheel axles, and they played automatically as an army marched into battle. He also invented a stringed instrument that could be played with a keyboard, called the "viola organista." He sketched ideas for flutes and keyboards for wind instruments. He invented a pipe instrument which was played with a mechanical **bellows** that provided a continuous movement of air. He even designed a portable organ that could be carried and played. Bells were another of his interests, and he spent considerable time experimenting with casting bronze bells.

bellows: a device for pumping air

Topic: Leonardo Da Vinci

Main Idea I. ....

Major Details A. Mechanical drums

Minor Details 1. ....

....

Major Details B. Viola Organista

Major Details C. Flutes and ....

....

Minor Details 1. ....

....

Major Details D. Organs

Minor Details 1. ....

Major Details E. ....

Minor Details 1. Experimented with casting bronze bells.

OBJECTIVE 3

Learn how to take tests.

TAKING TESTS

The idea of taking a test can cause stress. When you become stressed, your brain produces certain chemicals that actually block your memory. Many students become so stressed that they cannot recall the information they need to answer questions correctly. There are many stress-relieving techniques that can help, such as taking deep breaths, mediating, or visualizing your success on the test. Positive self-talk is an important part of reducing stress. Reminding yourself that you know the material and can answer the questions correctly is much better than thinking that you are doomed to fail even before you start. Using alcohol or other "helpers" will only worsen your brain's ability to think clearly.

Important Tips for Test Taking

Prepare

Being prepared means studying

Maybe in the past you have studied, but did not see results. The reason could be the *way* that you studied. Here are some tips to help you prepare:

- Prepare for the test by having good notes. Keep your notebook up to date, and use any prepared notes from the instructor.
- Use a variety of methods to study. If you know your learning style, you can use specific ideas for your style. Try using flash cards, voice recordings, outlines, question and answer cards, diagrams, maps, Internet resources, and other aids.
- Study every day, even if it's only for 20 minutes. Short study times of 15 to 20 minutes each day for a week are much more effective than one two-hour session.
- Divide the material into sections. Study one section each day and review the previous sections afterward because your brain remembers the *first* thing you learn the best.
- Know when the test will be given. You can't do your best when the test comes as a surprise.
- Know what will be on the test and the format (essay, objective, true-false, etc.).
- Form a study group to ask each other questions. Split up the chapter so each person is responsible for teaching and reviewing one part with the group.
- For application courses such as Math, Reading, or English, make sure you know the rules, formulas, and procedures. *Use what you have been taught to do.*

Study Tips

- If you find yourself getting sleepy while studying, take a five minute break to get a drink of water and walk around. Do some exercises to get your blood circulating and add more oxygen into your blood.
- Take advantage of any free tutoring services available at your school. Many colleges have free tutoring services, and you only need to ask for an appointment. Ask your instructor or go online to your school's website to find tutoring.

Effective Learning

There are two things you need to do before you can learn effectively. First, you must correctly understand the material; it must *make sense to you*. Second, the learning must have *meaning* for you. Think of ways that you can use the information, or how you can apply it to situations in your own life.

The Day Before the Test

Get your materials ready the day before the test. If you need a #2 pencil, a pen, a good eraser, an electronic scanning answer sheet, or a composition booklet, don't wait until the test starts to find out that you don't have them.

The Day of the Test

Testing day begins the night before. ALWAYS get a good night's rest and a nutritious breakfast. Water, protein, and glucose (a type of sugar found in fruit) are all important brain fuel. Avoid caffeine since drinks with excessive amounts of caffeine can cause your thinking to become unfocused. Leave early for the test. Do a brief preview of the material while waiting to start, but don't start studying new information. Concentrate on what you feel you know already.

At the Test

Read through the questions before you begin, paying close attention to the instructions. Underline the verbs which tell you what you must do, such as "explain," "define," "give an example," "tell how," "give reasons," etc. Also note how many parts there are to each question. If there are two parts, you must answer both parts to get full credit. Find out whether you must answer in pencil or in ink and if you can write on both sides of the paper.

Example:

"Explain four causes of the Civil War, and give five effects of the War."

Note the word "explain." That does not mean you just list the causes; it means you must provide specific details about them.

Notice how many items you must answer. Some directions tell you to answer all of the questions, while others allow you to choose a certain number.

Note how many points each section is worth so you can concentrate on the questions worth the most points. Be aware of how much time you have to complete the test, and don't spend excessive time on one question.

- **Never change an answer unless you are sure that the answer you have is wrong.** Usually your first choice is correct. Before you hand in your paper, go over it again to make sure you answered every single question that you were supposed to answer.
- **Leave no blanks.** If you are having a hard time finding the correct answer, eliminate the two least correct answer choices and then make an educated guess based on factual information or logical reasoning. Leaving a question blank will guarantee a wrong answer, but if you guess an answer by choosing between two answers, you have a 50 percent chance of getting it right.
- Be sure you leave no stray marks or smudges on electronic scoring answer sheets.
- When taking tests online, be sure to save and submit your answers.

OBJECTIVE 4

Learn to use metacognition.

USING METACOGNITION

According to researcher David A. Sousa, metacognition (met-ah-cog-NISH-un) is the awareness one has of his or her own thinking processes. It means that as a student, you should know not only what you are learning, but how you are learning it, and if your learning processes are successful or not. If they're not successful, you should think about why they aren't and what you should do to fix the problem. Students who are successful use metacognitive strategies regularly.

Metacognition involves several steps:

1. Look at what you are trying to learn and describe it in your own words by asking, "What is my learning objective?"
2. With your personal learning style in mind, choose an appropriate learning strategy that will help you to learn the objective or material. For example, will you practice something, make note cards, make a recording to listen to, work with a study partner, or watch a video?
3. Use the strategies that you have chosen to study. Practice every day.
4. Monitor your learning by using self-testing or other means. Go back to analyze your errors and figure out why you made them.
5. Decide if you have successfully learned the material, and if you haven't, make changes in your learning strategies to accomplish your goal. Then try again.

Knowing your learning style strengths can be important for deciding what strategies to use to learn something. Here's an example of how one student uses metacognition:

> Keisha, a visual and kinesthetic learner, was trying to learn to solve equations for a math exam. Her learning strategy was to study some examples of equations in her textbook and practice some of these problems. She spent a few hours doing this, and then took the quiz at the end of the chapter and checked her answers. Half of them were wrong, and she wondered why. She looked at the ones she missed and compared them to the ones she had correct. The problems she missed all included division as one of the steps. She looked "division" up in her textbook and read all the references to it. She discovered that multiplication comes before division in the order of operations, not after it as she had thought. She then reworked the problems that she had missed and got them all correct. Keisha learned that in the order of operations, multiplication always comes before division. On her math exam, she earned 95 percent and was pleased with her results.

1. What was Keisha's learning objective?

2. How did Keisha monitor her learning?

3. What did Keisha do that enabled her to be successful on her second try?

4. What changes did Keisha make in learning strategies that enabled her to succeed?

5. If she had been unable to figure out why she missed half of the questions, what could she have done to reach her learning objective?

MyReadingLab

PRACTICE 1

Read the following paragraph and underline the main idea and major details. Then, write a short summary on the lines that follow.

> Nearly everything we do involves technology of some kind, such as phones, television, or computers. Computer support specialists provide technical assistance to workers, customers, and others who have computer or software needs. They may work in an office as a help desk technician or out in the field servicing computer systems in businesses, hospitals, schools, or factories. Network systems analysts are responsible for maintaining local area networks, wide area networks, Internet, and other similar systems. Furthermore, they monitor and adjust these networks to meet future needs. Another computer expert is a Web developer, who creates Web sites and monitors them to make sure they work correctly and achieve the sponsor's goals. Many people employed in these industries work from home.

On the following lines, write a summary of the paragraph by paraphrasing the major details.

MyReadingLab

PRACTICE 2

Read the following paragraph, marking important information, and then fill in the missing notes on the lines that follow.

Robots may change the way we explore the universe. NASA (National Aeronautics and Space Administration) is conducting research into creating robots that will build a space station on the moon. Robotic parts have been used successfully in previous space missions. One example was in 2008, when a robotic arm on the *Mars Lander* scooped soil from the surface for analysis. Two other examples of robots are in the Mars rovers, named *Opportunity and Spirit*. They have robotic parts that help them travel over the *Martian* surface and send data back to Earth. Also, on the International Space Station, a $200 million dollar robot is used to handle maintenance outside of the station, so that fewer human space walks are needed. Robots have successfully demonstrated that they have an important role in future space explorations.

Topic? ....

- NASA is conducting research to create robots for space sta. on moon
- Robotic parts used in space missions - Ex: ....

  ....
- ....

  ....
- ....

  ....

MyReadingLab

PRACTICE 3

Read the following paragraphs and fill in the missing details in the outline below.

Drafters are people who prepare technical drawings and plans for many different **types** of products, big and small. Nearly all drafters today use CADD (Computer Assisted Design and Drafting) software on computers. Drafters are given rough drawings showing the shapes and sizes of the object to be drawn. They use their knowledge and training to construct the final drawing on a computer. For this reason, drafters usually work in one specialty area.

Aeronautical drafters are trained in preparing engineering drawings for aircraft and spacecraft. Another type of drafter is the architectural drafter who specializes in drawings of buildings or other structures. Another kind of drafter produces mechanical drawings for manufactured products, such as cars or motorcycles. Electrical drafters design wiring and layout diagrams for equipment in buildings. Electronic drafters draw wiring diagrams for the circuit boards used in electronic devices, such as computers or entertainment systems. Civil drafters draw plans and maps for the construction of highways, bridges, pipelines, and sewage systems.

Topic? ....

I. Drafters prepare technical drawings for many different types of products or construction.

A. ....

....

B. ....

....

II. Aeronautical drafters

A. ....

....

III. Architectural drafters

A. ....

....

III. Mechanical drafter

A. ....

....

IV. ....

A. ....

....

V. ....

A. ....

....

VI. ....

A. ....

....

MyReadingLab

TEXTBOOK SELECTION 1

Read the following textbook selection and underline the main idea and major details. Then fill in the missing notes and write a summary from the notes.

Spacecraft *Apollo 13* was 205,000 miles from the earth when the crew noticed a sudden drop in the electrical *voltage* of one of their two power generating systems. They also heard a loud banging sound. The voltage then rose to normal. Even as Duty Commander John L. Swigert, Jr. reported these observations to NASA control in Houston, the voltage in the Main B system dropped to zero, and the voltage in Main A began to fall.

The astronauts were in deadly danger. Without power, *Apollo 13* would become their tomb in space. The engineers in Houston, realizing that action would need to be taken immediately in order to prevent a tragedy, began to evaluate what was known (e.g., **voltage** drops, a loud noise) as they collected further information from the crew. Then, only thirteen minutes after the first voltage drop, Commander Swigert reported that their number 2 oxygen tank was reading empty and that the ship appeared to be leaking gas into space. Moreover, the ship's other tank also was losing oxygen.

voltage: VOL-taj: A measurement of electrical power

MyReadingLab

TEXTBOOK SELECTION 1

...continued

The Houston engineers quickly determined that a rupture in the number 2 oxygen tank would explain all of the observed **phenomena**. A loud noise, such as that first heard by the astronauts, would accompany a rupture in the tank. Furthermore, the gas being leaked into space could be the lost oxygen from the tank (as well as that from the damaged number 1 tank). Finally, since *Apollo 13's* power-generating systems depended upon oxygen in order to operate, a decrease in the oxygen supply would explain the observed loss of electrical power. Once the situation was understood, appropriate actions could be taken to preserve the remaining oxygen and conserve electrical power, thereby allowing the crew of *Apollo 13* to return safely to Earth.

phenomena: (fen-NOM-men-ah) odd or unusual things happening

Notes on Apollo 13's Crisis

- Spacecraft *Apollo 13* was 205,000 miles from the Earth, then:
- Thirteen minutes later,
- The ship's other tank
- Houston engineers determined that a rupture in the number 2 oxygen tank would explain everything.
- Once the situation was understood,

Using the notes, write a summary on the lines below.

U-REVIEW 1

Taking turns with a partner, ask each other the following questions and write down the answers. Refer back in the chapter for any information you may need.

1. What is paraphrasing?

2. What does a summary include?

3. What are three important tips for studying for tests?

4. What is metacognition and how can it help your learning?

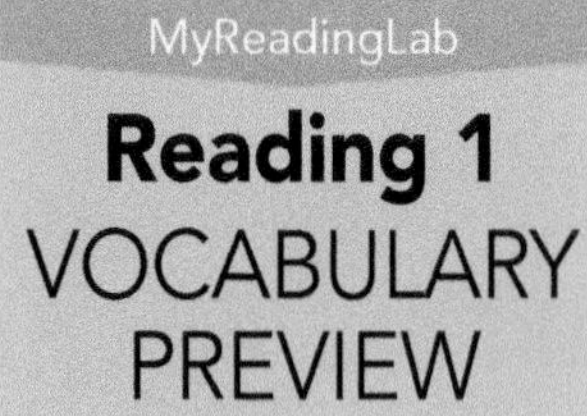

"Bionic Soldiers" by Corinne Fennessy

The following vocabulary words are from "Bionic Soldiers." With a partner or with your team, determine the meanings of the underlined words as they are used in the following sentences. Use context clues (LEADS), word part clues, and parts of speech to help you.

1. After Nadiya lost her leg in a car accident, she soon learned to walk normally with a prosthetic (pros-THET-tic) leg.
   - **a.** a stronger leg
   - **b.** an artificial limb
   - **c.** a brace
   - **d.** a missing leg
2. Dr. Patel works at the army hospital, treating amputees (am-pyoo-TEEZ) who must learn to adjust to a missing limb.
   - **a.** people who work with patients who have lost a limb
   - **b.** people who make prosthetic devices
   - **c.** people who have lost a limb
   - **d.** a prosthetic device
3. The birth of the Ortiz's fourth child necessitated (ness-SESS-it-tated) an additional part-time job for the husband to supplement his income.
   - **a.** made necessary
   - **b.** encouraged
   - **c.** something done for extra money
   - **d.** adjusted
4. Strangely, even though many people survive an amputation (am-pue-TA-shun) for a long while, they still can feel the missing limb.
   - **a.** injury from an accident or war
   - **b.** treatment
   - **c.** surgery
   - **d.** removal of a limb
5. In the laboratory, the prosthetist (pros-THET-ist) first creates a mold for the socket of the missing limb and then adjusts it to fit the amputee's leg.
   - **a.** a person with a missing limb
   - **b.** someone who wears a prosthetic device
   - **c.** someone who creates artificial limbs
   - **d.** someone who helps amputees learn to use prosthetic limbs
6. When a sheet of plastic is heated, it becomes so pliable (PLY-a-ble) that it can be molded into different shapes.
   - **a.** stiff
   - **b.** flexible
   - **c.** small
   - **d.** durable

7. The prosthetic leg must be fitted over the residual (re-ZID-u-al) limb until it fits comfortably and snugly.
   a. the remaining part
   b. the missing part
   c. living in
   d. amputee's
8. Electrical impulses (IM-pul-ses) in the brain signal the muscles to move.
   a. driving forward
   b. on the spur of the moment
   c. acting without thought
   d. short surges in electrical energy
9. In the Army, we often had to drive our Humvee (HUM-vee) off roads and over rough terrain to reach a remote destination.
   a. tractor
   b. motorcycle
   c. a large, heavily secured truck
   d. a tank
10. When George joined the Army, he became a paratrooper (PAIR-a-troop-er) because he loved the idea of flying weightlessly through the air.
   a. an Army soldier
   b. a naval officer
   c. a pilot
   d. someone who jumps from a plane using a parachute

MyReadingLab

Reading 1 PREVIEW

1. Have you ever known anyone with a disability? Describe how this person coped with the disability and any technology he or she used for assistance.
2. Do you know anyone who has served or is serving in the military? What did (does) this person do? Was this person ever involved in a war? Share what you know.

Directions: As you read this story, practice the four-step reading process. Preview the article, and then write on the following lines one or two questions that you would hope to have answered in this story.

MyReadingLab

Reading 1

With advanced technology, amputees who have lost limbs in battle are now able to regain mobility through the use of advanced, highly technical artificial limbs. This article illustrates how amputees are benefiting from this amazing technology.

"Bionic Soldiers"

by Corinne Fennessy

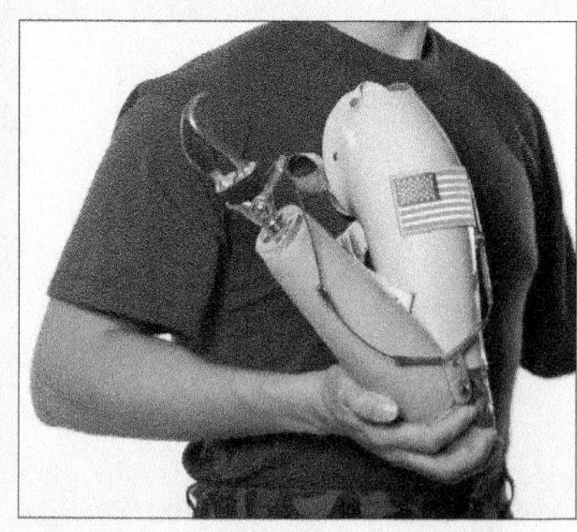

1 George Perez, a Puerto Rican paratrooper from the 82nd Airborne Division, remembers when he was traveling on a road outside of Fallujah, Iraq. When a bomb blasted their Humvee, he flew through the air and hit the ground. Then he tried to get up and saw that his left foot was folded backward onto his knee and his combat boot stood in the road a short distance away—still laced.

2 George Perez is determined to regain the strength and abilities he had before losing his leg to the roadside bomb in Iraq. "I'm not ready to get out of the Army yet," he says. "I'm not going to let this little injury stop me from what I want to do." Perez is one of at least four amputees from the 82nd Airborne Division who decided to re-enlist. With a new carbon-fiber prosthetic leg, Perez intends to show that he can still run, jump out of a plane, and pass all of the other challenging paratrooper tests so he can go back to active duty next year.

How did George Perez lose his leg?

3 Surgeons tried to save part of his leg, but an infection necessitated the amputation of his leg just below the knee joint. After he recuperated and received his prosthetic leg, Perez asked a visiting general if he could stay in the army. "They told me, 'It's all up to you, and how much you want it,'" he says. "If I could do everything like a regular soldier, I could stay in."

4 Perez has worked hard to become accustomed to his prosthetic leg. He began exercising by doing push-ups in bed. Soon he was walking, and then running. Perez gets his inspiration from other paratroopers in the 82nd Division who have lost limbs in combat and have re-enlisted. Staff Sgt. Daniel Metzdorf lost his right leg in combat. After being fitted with a prosthetic leg, he made three appeals to stay in the Army before he was accepted back.

5 Due to advances in prosthetic technology, many soldiers are able to live their lives normally after losing one, two, or more limbs. Some have chosen to return to active duty wearing a prosthetic leg or arm.

orthotics (or-THOT-ix): The branch of medicine dealing with prosthetic aids

CAD/CAM: Computer-aided design/manufacturing

6 The process of creating a prosthetic limb begins at the Walter Reed Hospital's **Orthotics** and Prosthetics laboratory. First, a custom-fit socket is made for the prosthetic. Each one is made to fit the individual amputee. Using **CAD-CAM**, the prosthetist creates a mold for a socket in about 20 minutes. Next, a sheet of plastic is heated until it is pliable, and then it is formed over the foam mold. It is trimmed and sanded, and then the amputee is given a fitting. They continue to make adjustments until it fits snugly and comfortably over the residual limb.

What are three types of prosthetic arms each amputee must learn to use?

7 Next, the amputees move into occupational and physical therapy. Amputees who have lost arms are fitted with three different new arms: a computer-programmed myoelectric (my-oh-e-LEK-trik) arm, a body-powered arm, and a cosmetic arm. The myoelectric arm gives effortless movement, whereas the body-powered is more durable and can get wet without damage. The myoelectric arm uses the electrical impulses from the muscle tissue to control the prosthetic limb. The body-powered limb is controlled by body movements. A cable is attached to a harness system worn on the shoulders or chest, and the cable operates the arm and hand. The cosmetic arm is created to look identical to the other arm and is used when appearance is more important than function.

8 Amputees who have lost legs have a choice of several styles of feet. They can also choose a special style of creative artwork for the socket. Styles have included flags, NASCAR logos, unit patches, or their own design—such as the soldier who has pink Playboy bunnies on a black background.

9 The technology of prosthetic limbs has been making huge strides with the introduction of motorized joints with computer processors. Some prosthetic legs, for example, can determine their resistance with the ground based on the angle of the leg to the floor. This gives the amputee better balance and a steadier, more natural gait. But the newest technology in prosthetic limbs uses Bluetooth wireless technology.

How does Bluetooth technology work in prosthetic limbs?

10 Iraq war veteran Marine Lance Cpl. Joshua Bleil lost both of his legs in a roadside bombing. Bluetooth computer chips located in each artificial leg send signals to the motors in the joints so his ankles and knees move in a coordinated manner. This allows him to walk longer and with less effort. The only disadvantage to Bluetooth prosthetics is that they must be recharged—just like a cell phone.

11 Perez is back in uniform, looking like the same paratrooper he was before his injury. His maroon beret sits at an angle over one eye. His uniform pants have perfectly sharp creases, and his black boot gleams with a mirror shine. Only the running shoe on his other foot sets him apart from other paratroopers. Before he is allowed to jump again, he will have to run two miles in just under 16 minutes, and do 42 push-ups and 53 sit-ups in two-minute stretches. In the meantime, he is working at the armory, maintaining weapons and grenade launchers. He wants to attend the Ranger School, a tough, grueling program at Fort Benning, Georgia. It's a real challenge even for soldiers with two normal legs, but that isn't stopping George Perez. Perez is a determined and strong soldier who works hard to overcome any obstacles.

12 "I've got a lot of things to do," he said. "I want to do as much as I can, and as much as they'll let me."

930 words divided by .... minutes = ... words per minute

MyReadingLab

Reading 1 REVIEW

Summarizing after you read will help you to understand the author's purpose and the main idea.

On the following lines, write a two- or three-sentence summary of the article, "Bionic Soldiers." In your own words, describe what the article was about and why the author wrote it.

MyReadingLab

Reading 1 COMPREHENSION QUESTIONS

The following questions will help you to recall the main idea and the details of the article you just read. Review any parts of the article that you need to in order to find the correct answers.

1. What is the topic of this article?
   - **a.** George Perez
   - **b.** prosthetic devices
   - **c.** bionic soldiers
   - **d.** technology helping amputees
2. What is the main idea of the entire article?
   - **a.** George Perez lost a leg in Iraq, but is now re-enlisting in the 82nd Airborne Division.
   - **b.** Many soldiers have lost limbs in war.
   - **c.** New technology has improved the design and function of prosthetic limbs for soldier amputees.
   - **d.** Perez is a determined and strong soldier who works hard to overcome any obstacles.
3. What is the topic sentence of paragraph 11?
   - **a.** Perez is back in uniform, looking like the same paratrooper he was before his injury.
   - **b.** It's a real challenge even for soldiers with two normal legs, but that isn't stopping George Perez.
   - **c.** He wants to attend the Ranger School, a tough, grueling program at Fort Benning, Georgia.
   - **d.** Perez is a determined and strong soldier who works hard to overcome any obstacles.

SUPPORTING DETAILS

4. After losing his leg, what did George Perez decide to do?

a. Retire from the Army and take a pension.
b. Re-enlist and work hard to do all the same things that other soldiers do.
c. Stay in the Army's Walter Reed Hospital to help other amputees learn to adjust.
d. Become a prosthetist so he could help other amputees.

VOCABULARY IN CONTEXT

5. Identify the meaning of the underlined word in the following sentence: This gives the amputee better balance and a steadier, more natural gait.

a. way of walking
b. an entry
c. appearance
d. amputation

PATTERNS OF ORGANIZATION

6. What is the overall pattern of organization for this article?

a. compare and/or contrast
b. cause and effect
c. definition
d. time order

7. Identify the relationship within the following sentence: Amputees who have lost arms are fitted with three different arms: a computer-programmed myoelectric arm, a body-powered arm, and a cosmetic arm.

a. cause and effect
b. definition
c. listing
d. process

8. Identify the relationship between the following sentences: The prosthetist creates a mold for a socket in about 20 minutes. Next, a sheet of plastic is heated until it is pliable, and then it is formed over the foam mold.

a. process
b. time order
c. listing
d. space order

DRAWING CONCLUSIONS

9. From the article, you can conclude that:

a. There are not many amputee soldiers who have been fitted with prosthetic devices.
b. More soldiers will probably need prosthetic limbs if war continues.
c. Prosthetic devices can be operated easily.
d. Soldiers who wear prosthetic limbs will want to re-enlist in the military.

10. According to the article, some of the amputees have regained their strength so that they could:

a. re-enlist in the Army.
b. become prosthetists.
c. compete in the Paralympics.
d. get jobs outside of the military.

MyReadingLab

Reading 1 VOCABULARY PRACTICE

Use the words from the list to complete the following sentences. Use context clues (LEADS), word part clues, and parts of speech clues to help you.

WORD BANK

prosthetic	amputees	necessitated	amputation	prosthetist
pliable	residual	impulses	Humvee	paratrooper

1. Electrical .... from the brain signal the muscles to move.
2. A wet suit is made of material that is waterproof and .... so the swimmer can move his or her arms freely.
3. Sergeant Bonning was a(n) .... whose parachute didn't open properly, and he broke his leg upon landing.
4. The .... at the military hospital are given artificial limbs as soon as they are well enough to wear them.
5. An artificial limb is known as a(n) .... limb.
6. Losing her leg from a bomb blast .... Amita having to wear an artificial one.
7. The .... made several artificial legs for the amputee until he finally made one that fit comfortably and worked well.
8. The artificial leg is attached to the .... limb.
9. The Army unit was riding in a(n) .... when the bomb exploded under them.
10. When the doctors could not save his leg, Sergeant Munoz was told he would need to have a(n) ....

Reading 1 VOCABULARY PRACTICE— CROSSWORD

Use the words from the list to complete the following sentences. Write the answers in the crossword puzzle. Use context clues (LEADS), word part clues, and parts of speech clues to help you.

ACROSS CLUES

2. Most .... are happy to get a prosthetic limb.
3. Losing my financial aid .... my finding a part-time job while I was in college.
7. She wanted to be a(n) ...., so she joined the Army.
8. The prosthetic arm is fitted over the .... limb.
9. An Army .... transported soldiers to the battlefront.

DOWN CLUES

1. Electrical .... signal the muscle to move the limb.
4. He did not allow the .... of his legs to discourage him from walking again.
5. Learning to walk with a(n) .... leg will take practice.
6. Mr. Hernandez is a(n) .... who treats amputees.
7. This material is so .... that it can be shaped and formed easily.

Word Bank

Humvee	amputation	prosthetic
amputees	pliable	necessitated
residual	prosthetist	paratrooper
impulses		

MyReadingLab

Reading 1 QUESTIONS FOR WRITING AND DISCUSSION

Review any parts of the article you need to answer the following questions.

1. How was George Perez able to re-enlist in the Army?

2. If new technology had not provided prosthetic limbs that could function almost as well as real ones, how would having an amputation be different?

3. What new advances in technology have helped people who are disabled?

4. If you had recently lost a limb in war, would you want to re-enlist? Why or why not?

5. Compare George Perez to one of the other people whom you have read about in previous articles. How are they alike, and how are they different?

MyReadingLab

Reading 2
VOCABULARY PREVIEW

"Attack of the Cyber-Thieves"

by Karen Collins and Jackie Shemko

The following vocabulary words are from "Attack of the Cyber-Thieves." With a partner or with your team, determine the meanings of the underlined words as they are used in the following sentences. Use context clues (LEADS), word part clues, and parts of speech to help you.

1. I was concerned about the confidentiality (kon-fid-en-shee-AL-it-ee) of sharing my personal information with my coworker, Alicia.
   - **a.** sharing
   - **b.** secrecy
   - **c.** collecting
   - **d.** value
2. People who leave their cars unlocked are vulnerable (VUL-ner-a-bul) to theft.
   - **a.** open to
   - **b.** victims
   - **c.** foolish
   - **d.** provoking
3. By charming the ticket seller at the theatre, Marcus was able to finagle (fin-AY-gul) a free ticket to the movie.
   - **a.** send back
   - **b.** steal
   - **c.** authorize
   - **d.** acquire by manipulation
4. For her research paper, Belinda compiled (kom-PIE-LD) a list of resources with the information she needed.
   - **a.** blocked
   - **b.** enriched
   - **c.** gathered
   - **d.** used
5. One company accused its competitors of espionage (ES-pe-on-aj) after its secret formula was stolen.
   - **a.** lying
   - **b.** fraud
   - **c.** spying
   - **d.** copying
6. Because of stiff competition, the company decided not to implement (IM-pla-ment) the new policy to charge customers a transaction fee.
   - **a.** to review
   - **b.** to put into effect
   - **c.** to transmit
   - **d.** to imply

Continued...

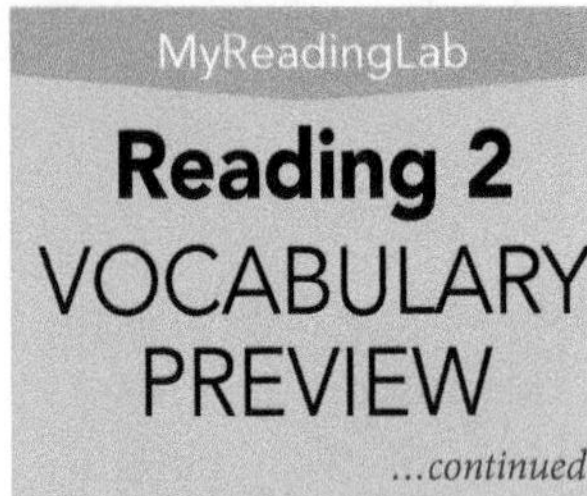

7. During World War II, the Nazis created a machine that was capable of encoding (en-CODE-ing) secret messages, but the British invented a machine to decrypt their messages.
   a. putting into code
   b. writing
   c. proving
   d. responding
8. The buyer asked an antique expert to authenticate (aw-THEN-ti-kate) the artist of the painting by examining the work closely.
   a. to promote
   b. to make an authority
   c. to determine an author
   d. to prove as genuine
9. When I applied for a passport, my signature had to be verified (VER-i-fied) by a notary.
   a. proved as true
   b. witnessed
   c. decoded
   d. informed
10. As consumers, we must be very vigilant (VIJ-a-lent) about how we conduct our online business.
   a. helpful
   b. responsible
   c. watchful
   d. respectful

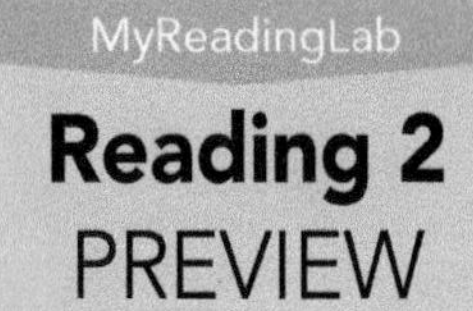

1. Do you shop online for products or services? Which ones?
2. What concerns do you have about someone stealing your identity? Have you ever been robbed via the Internet?

Directions: As you read this article, practice the four-step reading process. Preview the article, and then write on the following lines one or two questions that you would hope to have answered.

MyReadingLab

Reading 2

"Attack of the Cyber-Thieves"

by Karen Collins and Jackie Shemko

1 Many people still regard the Internet as an unsafe place to do business. They worry about the security of credit card information and passwords and the confidentiality of personal data. Are any of these concerns valid? Are you really running risks when you shop electronically? If so, what is being done to make the Internet a safer place to conduct transactions? Let's look a little more closely at the sort of things that tend to bother some Internet users (or, as the case may be, non-users), as well as some of the steps that companies are taking to convince people that e-commerce is safe.

Credit Card Theft

2 One of the most serious barriers to the growth of e-commerce is the perception of many people that credit card numbers can be stolen when they are given out over the Internet. Although virtually every company takes considerable precautions, they are not entirely wrong. Cyber criminals, unfortunately, seem to be tirelessly creative. One popular scheme involves setting up a fraudulent Internet business operation to collect credit card information. The bogus company will take orders to deliver goods— say, Mother's Day flowers— but when the day arrives, it will have disappeared from cyber-space. No flowers will get delivered, but even worse, the perpetrator can sell or use all the collected credit card information.

3 Criminals can also use Internet technology to access credit card data from people who do not shop online. For example, TJX Companies Inc. announced in 2007 that hackers had accessed information from the company's databanks. Millions of customers who had made credit card purchases in the company's stores across Canada were warned that the security of their accounts may have been compromised.

Password Theft

4 Many people also fear that Internet passwords— which can be valuable information to cyber criminals— are vulnerable to theft. Again, they are not altogether wrong. There are schemes dedicated entirely to stealing passwords. In one, the cyber thief sets up a website that you can access only if you register, provide an email address, and select a password. The cyber criminal is betting that the site will attract a certain percentage of people who use the same password for just about everything— ATM accounts, email, employer networks, and so on. Having finagled a password, the thief can try accessing other accounts belonging to the victim. So, one day you have a nice cushion in your checking account, and the next you are dead-broke.

Invasion of Privacy

5 If you apply for a life-insurance policy online, you may be asked to supply information about your health. If you apply for a mortgage online,

Continued...

you may be asked questions about your personal finances. Some people shy away from Internet transactions because they are afraid that such personal information can be stolen or shared with unauthorized parties. Once again, they are right: It does happen.

How Do "Cookies" Work?

6 In addition to data that you supply willingly, information about you can be gathered online without your knowledge or consent. Your online activities, for example, can be captured by something called a cookie. The process is illustrated in the figure below. When you access a certain website, it sends back a unique piece of information to your browser, which proceeds to save it on your hard drive. When you go back to the same site, your browser returns the information, telling the site who you are and confirming that you have been there before. The problem is not that the cookie can identify you in the same way as a name or an address. It is, however, linked to other information about you— such as the goods you have bought or the services you have ordered online. Before long, someone will have compiled a profile of your buying habits. The result? You will soon be bombarded with advertisements targeted to your interests. For example, let's suppose you check out the website for an online diet program. You provide some information, but decide that the program is not for you. The next time you log on, you may be greeted by a pop-up pushing the latest miracle diet. Cookies are not the only form of online espionage. Your own computer, for example, monitors your Internet activities and keeps track of the URLs that you access.

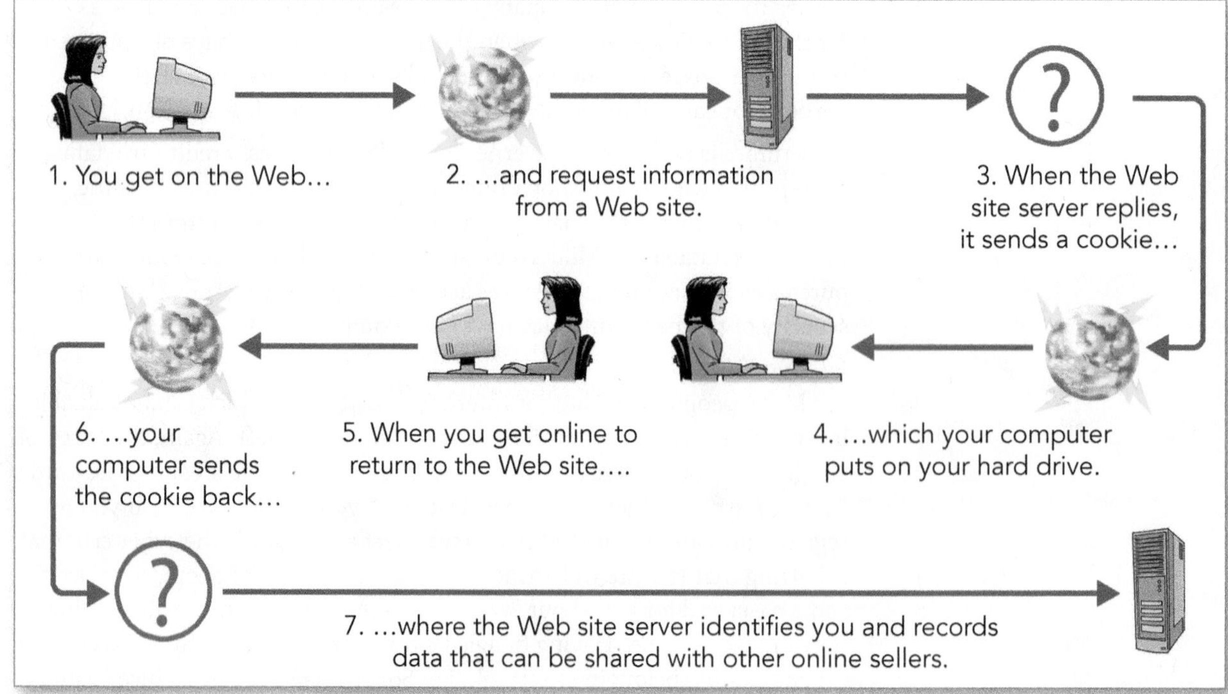

1. You get on the Web...
2. ...and request information from a Web site.
3. When the Web site server replies, it sends a cookie...
4. ...which your computer puts on your hard drive.
5. When you get online to return to the Web site....
6. ...your computer sends the cookie back...
7. ...where the Web site server identifies you and records data that can be shared with other online sellers.

Shoring Up Security and Building Trust

7 So what can companies do to ease concerns about the safety of Internet transactions? First, businesses must implement internal controls for ensuring adequate security and privacy. Then, they must reassure customers that they are competent to safe-guard credit card numbers, passwords, and other personal information. Among the most common controls and assurance techniques, let's look at encryption and seals of assurance.

Encryption

8 The most effective method of ensuring that sensitive computer-stored information cannot be accessed or altered by unauthorized parties is **encryption**— the process of encoding data so that only individuals (or computers) armed with a secret code (or key) can decode it. Here is a simplified example: You want to send a note to a friend on the other side of the classroom, but you do not want anyone else to know what it says. You and your friend could devise a code in which you substitute each letter in the message with the letter that is two places before it in the alphabet. So you write A for C and B for D and so on. Your friend can decode the message, but it will look like nonsense to anyone else. This is an oversimplification of the process. In the real world, it is much more complicated: Data are scrambled using a complex code, the key for unlocking it is an **algorithm**, and you need certain computer hardware to perform the encryption/ decryption process.

algorithm: a set of rules for defining a problem in a certain number of steps.

Certificate Authorities

9 The most commonly used encryption system for transmitting data over the Internet is called secure sockets layer (SSL). You can tell if a website uses SSL if its URL begins with https instead of http. SSL also provides another important security measure: When you connect to a site that uses SSL (for example, your bank's website), your browser will ask the site to authenticate itself— prove that it is who it says it is. You can be confident that the response is correct if it is verified by a certificate authority— a third- party (such as VeriSign) that verifies the identity of the responding computer and sends you a digital certificate of authenticity stating that it trusts the site.

10 Knowing how cyber-thieves attack can help you to become more vigilant about how you use your personal and financial information online. Doing business with companies with recognized brand names is usually the safest way to go, even if you pay more for security. Despite the efforts of Internet security software engineers, hackers who are out to steal from you will always stay one step ahead, so buyer...beware!

1,122 words divided by .... minutes = ... words per minute

MyReadingLab

Reading 2 REVIEW

Summarizing after you read will help you to understand the author's purpose and the main idea. On the following lines, write a two- or three-sentence summary of the article "Attack of the Cyber-Thieves." In your own words, describe what the article was about and why the author wrote it.

MyReadingLab

Reading 2 COMPREHENSION QUESTIONS

The following questions will help you to recall the main idea and the details of the article you just read. Review any parts of the article that you need to in order to find the correct answers.

1. What is the topic of this article?
   - a. credit card theft
   - b. encryption
   - c. invasion of privacy
   - d. Internet security

CENTRAL POINT

2. What is the central point of the entire article?
   - a. Many people still regard the Internet as an unsafe place to do business.
   - b. Knowing how cyber-thieves attack can help you to become more vigilant about how you use your personal and financial information online.
   - c. In addition to data that you supply willingly, information about you can be gathered online without your knowledge or consent.
   - d. Criminals can also use Internet technology to access credit card data from people who do not shop online.

SUPPORTING DETAILS

3. According to the article, what is a cookie?
   - a. a secure, encrypted web site that prevents hacking
   - b. a secure sockets layer that asks the Web site to authenticate itself
   - c. a type of algorithm
   - d. unique information from Web sites you visit that is stored on your computer

DRAWING CONCLUSIONS

4. From reading the article, you can conclude that:
   - a. It is possible to keep your computer's information safe from hackers.
   - b. Cookies are not harmful to your computer's security.
   - c. Some companies are taking steps to increase e-commerce security.
   - d. Passwords are never safe from hackers.

PATTERNS OF ORGANIZATION

5. What is the overall pattern of organization for paragraph 7?
   - a. compare and/or contrast
   - b. cause and effect
   - c. definition
   - d. time order

VOCABULARY IN CONTEXT

6. What is the meaning of the underlined word in the following sentence: Millions of customers who had made credit card purchases in the company's stores across Canada were warned that the security of their accounts may have been compromised.

a. made insecure
b. negotiated
c. given in to
d. made up from

CRITICAL THINKING

7. Identify the following sentence: The most effective method of ensuring that sensitive computer-stored information cannot be accessed or altered by unauthorized parties is encryption—the process of encoding data so that only individuals (or computers) armed with a secret code (or key) can decode it.

a. fact
b. opinion
c. fact and opinion

8. What is the author's purpose for writing this selection?

a. to inform readers about Internet security
b. to convince readers that e-commerce is safe
c. to entertain readers about Internet security
d. to persuade readers not to use e-commerce

STUDY SKILLS

9. Which of the following is the best summary of paragraph 6?

a. When you visit a Web site, it sends back a unique piece of information (a cookie) to your computer. The cookie is stored on your computer until the next time you visit the same site. Then it will tell the site who you are and that you have been there before. It also stores information about your buying habits which can result in pop-up ads sent to your computer.
b. A cookie is a unique piece of information sent to your computer about your buying habits. Cookies come from Web sites on the Internet. You should delete the cookies on your computer that you don't want so they will not send you pop-up ads.
c. In addition to data that you supply willingly, information about you can be gathered online without your knowledge or consent. Your online activities, for example, can be captured by something called a cookie. When you access a certain website, it sends back a unique piece of information to your browser, which proceeds to save it on your hard drive.
d. Cookies give information to other Web sites about who you are and what you buy online. Also your own computer monitors your Internet browsing.

10. Which of the following information would not be included in your notes about this article?

a. A bogus Web site takes your credit card information but doesn't deliver any flowers on Mother's Day.
b. Cyber criminals steal credit card data from people who do not shop online.
c. Thieves set up Web sites that require your personal information through a registration process, and then use your password to access your bank account.
d. A "cookie" is a unique piece of information sent to your computer by a Web site that will identify you the next time you visit that same Web site again.

MyReadingLab

Reading 2 VOCABULARY PRACTICE

Use the vocabulary words from the Word Bank to complete the following sentences. Write the words into the blanks provided.

WORD BANK

espionage	vigilant	verified	implement	finagle
vulnerable	authenticate	encoding	compiled	confidentiality

1. You should be concerned about the ________ of giving out your Social Security number over the Internet.

2. People who do a lot of online shopping are more ________ to Internet fraud than those who do not shop online.

3. A cyber-thief was caught and convicted of Internet ________ for stealing passwords and accessing bank accounts.

4. If you use an online dating service, you should be ________ about the kinds of information you give potential partners.

5. After I registered online, the Web site could not ________ my identity because I had misspelled my college's email address.

6. During the process of ________ data, the information is encrypted by special computer hardware and software.

7. I ________ my identity at the financial aid office by showing them my driver's license.

8. I ________ a list of resources for my research paper.

9. The college will ________ its new policies on class attendance in the fall semester.

10. I tried to ________ some way of getting a biology textbook without buying one, but I was unsuccessful.

MyReadingLab

Reading 2 QUESTIONS FOR WRITING AND DISCUSSION

Review any parts of the article you need to answer the following questions.

1. Has reading this article changed your thinking about how you use the Internet? Why or why not?

2. What are some things you can do to protect yourself against cyber crime?

3. Why are third-party authorities such as VeriSign important for online security?

4. In your opinion, what are the best ways to protect your confidential information online *and* when doing business in person?

5. Have you, or someone you know ever had a bad experience doing business online? If so, describe what happened and how you solved it.

Reading 2 VOCABULARY PRACTICE—GUESS THE PHRASE

Preparation: Your instructor will draw blank lines on the board for each letter of a phrase. Divide the class into two to four teams. The objective of the game is to be the first team to guess the phrase.

1.

After deciding which team will go first by a coin toss, the instructor will read a question about the vocabulary words from either Reading Assignment #1 or #2 to the first team. If the team gives a correct response within 10 seconds, that team can guess one letter of the phrase on the board. If the letter the team guessed is in the phrase, the instructor will write all instances of that letter on the board where they appear in the phrase. If the team answers incorrectly or doesn't respond in 10 seconds, that team may not guess a letter or try to solve the puzzle.

2.

The play then goes to the next team, which will receive a question. Play will continue until all the questions have been answered or the puzzle has been solved. Teams may only try to solve the puzzle (guess the entire phrase) when it is their turn.

READING FOR LIFE

MyReadingLab

REAL-LIFE READING

Following instructions is one of the most important reading skills needed to survive in today's high-tech society. Read the following instructions on how to install memory into a portable computer, and then answer the questions that follow to check your comprehension.

INSTRUCTIONS

Replacing or upgrading the memory in your laptop computer involves removing the battery and putting it back in after installing the memory.

Installing Memory

1. Shut down your computer and disconnect the powercord, Ethernet cable, and any other connected cords to prevent damage to the computer. If your computer was on, wait 10 minutes to let the internal components cool before proceeding.

2. Turn the computer over and remove the battery as shown in Figure 1.

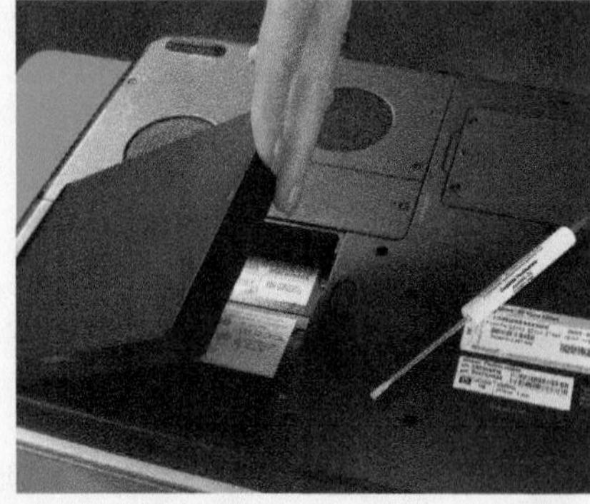

Figure 1

3. Remove the screw(s) for the memory compartment and take off the cover. Note the location of any screws and keep them safe for replacement. To prevent harming the computer, do not touch any other internal components (Figure 2).

4. Touch a metal surface inside the computer to discharge any static electricity from your body. Avoid creating static electricity as you are working, such as standing on carpeted floors.

5. Press the pins on the sides of the memory away from the memory card. The memory card will pop up at an angle. Notice the slot where the memory was seated (Figure 3).

6. Gently unplug the card at the same angle (Figure 4).

7. Align the new memory card with the slot at the same angle as the old one was removed.

8. Push the new card gently into the slot at an angle until it is in place, and then push it down until the pins on each side snap in place to hold it flat securely.

9. Replace the compartment cover and replace the screw(s). Install the battery and other cords before turning the computer back on.

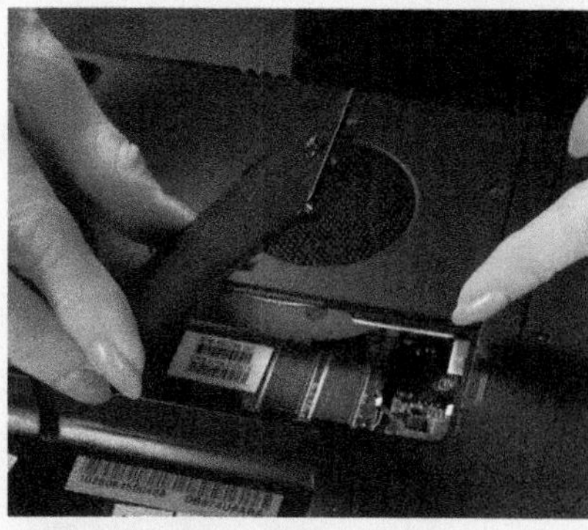

Figure 2

Figure 3

Figure 4

1. What is the first thing you should do before you start to remove the old memory card from your computer?
   - **a.** Take out the battery.
   - **b.** Remove the screws from the memory compartment, and then remove the cover.
   - **c.** Shut down the computer and let the components cool for 10 minutes before starting the installation.
   - **d.** Discharge any static electricity that you may have by touching something metal inside the computer.

Continued...

MyReadingLab

REAL-LIFE READING

...continued

2. When removing the old memory card, what must you do?

a. Press the pins at the sides of the memory card down.
b. Press the pins at the sides away from the memory card.
c. Use a small screwdriver to pry up the old card.
d. Disconnect the Ethernet cable or any USB cables.

3. What should you notice before taking out the old memory card?

a. Notice how many screws were used to secure the compartment cover.
b. Notice the location of all the other screws on the back of the computer.
c. Notice if there are any scorch marks on the old card.
d. Notice the locations and angle of the slot that holds the old memory card.

4. What's the first thing you must do when installing the new memory card?

a. Push the new card into the memory slot.
b. Use two fingers with firm, even pressure to push down on the memory card.
c. Align the new card with the slot at the same angle as the old card, and then push it into place until the pins snap in place to hold it securely.
d. Hold the memory card by its edges without touching the connectors.

5. Once the new memory card has been installed, what should you do?

a. Replace the compartment cover and screw(s) and reinstall the battery.
b. Turn on the computer after plugging it into an AC outlet.
c. Discharge any static electricity that you may have by touching something metal.
d. Bend the pins down over the new memory card with a small screwdriver.

ON THE JOB INTERVIEW

KYLE WILLIAMS

SHOW SYSTEMS INTEGRATORS IN ORLANDO, FLORIDA.

What is your job description?

As a marketing manager, I have a very broad range of things I do at the company. I do marketing, sales, poject management, and represent the company for the technical support systems for various projects. We have completed the Simpsons Ride for Universal theme parks in both Orlando and Los Angeles. For Six Flags theme parks, we developed the audio system for the new roller coaster. We're currently working on Universal's Rip Ride Rocket coaster here in Orlando.

What is your educational background and training?

I graduated from the University of Southern Mississippi with a degree in business administration and then got another degree in audio engineering from Full Sail in Orlando, Florida. I'm also a musician, and I play several instruments, but guitar is my favorite. I have a small home recording studio where I compose and record my own music. I have also played in bands throughout the years. So I have a musical and technical background.

What do you like about your job?

No one else does what I do. It's a unique blend of business and technology, where we get to be technically creative. This job is a perfect fit for my interests and my educational background.

How did you become interested in this job?

While I was attending school in Orlando, I worked at SSI part time and found my niche here. I was able to utilize my business training and my technical and audio interests.

What do you dislike about your job?

It can be stressful at times when there are deadlines and things don't go smoothly, which is to be expected when pushing the envelope and making technology work in new ways. I try to live and work by the Golden Rule, and maintain my values and ethics on the job, which can be challenging in some situations.

MyReadingLab

WATCH THE VIDEO

ROBOT ARM
GIVES HUMANS
STRENGTH

Watch the Video "Robot Arm Gives Humans Strength" and answer the questions using the study skills from this chapter.

Did you have any particular difficulties in college?

I worked while going to school, so it was always a challenge to manage my time carefully. I wanted to be responsible and independent, and to help pay my way through school. The most difficult thing was moving 600 miles from home and family and being on my own.

If you could give college students some advice, what would it be?

Don't underestimate the curriculum that you are studying. Sometimes the things you're learning that may seem irrelevant or unimportant now turn up being extremely beneficial in your career. Also, I would say to treat others with respect, and you'll benefit from learning how to work with others. Teamwork is really important in most careers.

What plans do you have for the future?

I am committed to the company's welfare and would like to see it grow and succeed. I enjoy what I do and want to continue working and expanding into new projects and creating new opportunities for using technology. Otherwise, I'll just take life as it comes.

Use the following graphs to answer the questions.

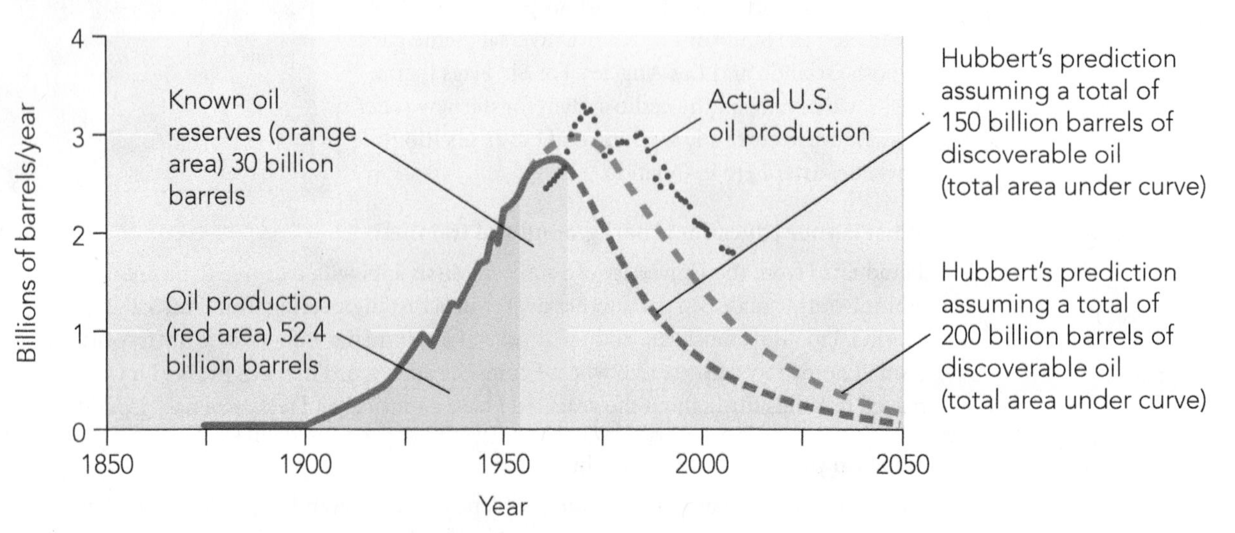

(a) Hubbert's prediction of peak in U.S. oil production, with actual data

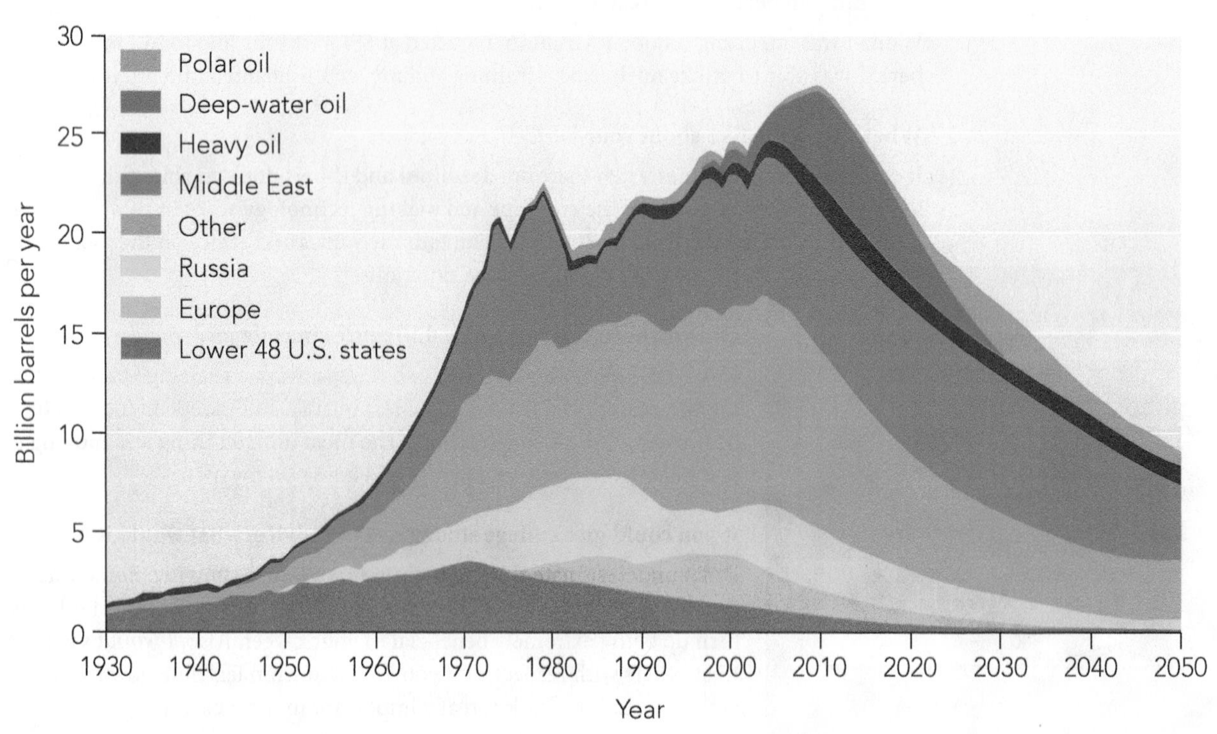

(b) Modern prediction of peak in global oil production

1. **According to the first graph, which of the following is false?**
   a. Geologist M. King Hubbard predicted in the 1950's that the U.S. would reach its peak oil production before 1975.
   b. About 1970, the actual U.S. oil production reached over three billion barrels.
   c. Actual U.S. oil production is less than both of Hubbard's predictions.
   d. Actual U.S. oil production was about two billion barrels in the year 2000.

2. **In the second graph, what is the data being shown?**
   a. How much oil the U.S. produces
   b. Which locations have the most oil
   c. Hubbard's prediction of oil production
   d. A modern prediction of global oil production

3. **In what year did the U.S. lower 48 states reach their peak oil production?**
   a. 1970
   b. 1985
   c. 2005
   d. 2010

4. **Which location has produced the most oil before 1980?**
   a. deep water oil
   b. Middle East
   c. polar oil
   d. other

5. **According to the second graph, what will happen to future oil production for all locations?**
   a. it will increase
   b. it will decrease
   c. it will remain the same
   d. the graph doesn't show this information

MyReadingLab

BUILDING VOCABULARY

Study the following word parts, and then answer the questions that follow.

Prefixes	**Roots**	**Suffixes**
micro- *very small*	-phone- *sound*	-ic *having to do with*
-tele- *distant, far off*	-scope- *to look*	
	-graph- *to write*	

What English words can you create from these word parts?

Using a dictionary, look up the meanings of any of the words you wrote that you can't define. Use one of the words you wrote in a sentence that reveals its meaning with a context clue.

MyReadingLab

CHAPTER PRACTICE 1

As you read the following selection, underline the main idea and the major details. Then answer the questions that follow.

Being an engineer doesn't have to be all work. Kent Seko gets plenty of excitement and thrills as a roller coaster designer. After graduating from the University of Utah, Seko took a job as a drafter at Arrow Dynamics, one of the largest designers and manufacturers of amusement rides. During his years of employment at Arrow, Seko learned more about how to design thrill rides. When he began with the company 15 years ago, the company was designing roller coasters that were over 60 meters tall. Now the company is designing coasters over 90 meters tall. As a designer, Seko must create a ride that is exciting while still maintaining safety and operating within a budget. Numerous other team members help with the layout, structural support design, mechanics, electronics, and construction of the coaster. The most exciting part of his job is when he gets to ride the coaster for the first time.

1. Kent Seko works as a .... for ....

2. He began 15 years ago designing coasters that were over .... tall, but now designs coasters over .... meters tall.

3. He must create a ride that is .... while still maintaining .... and ....

4. The most exciting part of his job is ....

5. **Write a summary of the paragraph using the notes above.**

....

....

....

....

....

....

MyReadingLab

CHAPTER PRACTICE 2

As you read the following selection, underline the main idea and the major details. Then answer the questions that follow.

Yves Rossy flies with his jet-powered wing.

Ten years ago, the idea of wearing a rocket strapped to your back and jetting through the air only happened in animated films and James Bond movies. But today, a Swiss pilot named Yves Rossy has achieved the reality of sustained human flight using a jet-powered wing strapped to his back. Rossy began his career as a fighter pilot in the Swiss Air Force. He later flew Boeing 747s for Swissair and also worked as a pilot for Swiss International Airlines. Rossy developed a carbon-fiber wing and attached four model aircraft engines that he modified. Over the past several years, Rossy has experimented with several models of the jet-powered wing. In 2008, he flew across the English Channel in nine minutes and seven seconds. Later that same year, he flew over the Alps reaching speeds of 189 miles per hour.

Fill in the missing words in the following notes:

1. Rossy began his career as a ...., and later as a pilot for ....
2. Rossy developed a .... and attached ....
3. He flew with the .... strapped to his back.
4. In 2008, he flew across .... and over ...., reaching speeds of .... m.p.h.
5. Write a summary of the paragraph using the notes above.

....

....

....

....

....

....

MyReadingLab

CHAPTER PRACTICE 3

As you read the following selection, underline the main idea and the major details. Then answer the questions that follow.

Shuigeru Miyamoto is one of the world's most influential video game designers. He was born in Kyoto, Japan in 1952. As a child he loved to draw, make wooden puppets, toys, and race cars. Miyamoto went to the Kanazawa College of Art and graduated in 1975. Two years later he became a staff artist for Nintendo, the company that produced some of the first video games, and later produced the Nintendo Entertainment System in 1985. Miyamoto became the driving force of over 70 video popular video games such as Super Mario Galaxy, The Legend of Zelda, and Donkey Kong. Today, he creates games for Wii to bring gaming entertainment to all ages. Among video gamers, Miyamoto is considered the Walt Disney of the gaming world.

Using paraphrasing, write three notes from the paragraph.

....

....

....

....

....

....

Use your notes to write a summary of the article in your own words.

....

....

....

....

....

....

....

....

MyReadingLab

TEXTBOOK PRACTICE

cyanide: (SY-a-nide) a poisonous chemical

Read the textbook selection and answer the questions that follow. Underline the main idea and the major points that you would include in your notes.

Silver can be recovered from used photographic and x-ray plates by soaking these plates in a **cyanide** solution. Workers must wear protective clothing and use respirators in order to prevent contact with deadly cyanide gas.

Film Recovery Systems was one company that was active in this recovery work. Unfortunately, employees were not provided with respirators, but only cloth gloves and paper face masks. Workers frequently became physically ill. Finally, an autopsy revealed that one employee had died of cyanide poisoning, leading the authorities to file murder charges against certain company executives.

The company president, the plant manager, and the plant foreperson were shown to be familiar with the hazards associated with cyanide and its use at their facility. In 1985, each was convicted of industrial murder, fined $10,000 and given a 25-year prison sentence. Although company officials knew the silver recovery process was toxic, they did not provide enough safety precautions, and consequently, they committed industrial murder.

1. What is the topic?
   a. cyanide
   b. Film Recovery Systems
   c. cyanide poisoning
   d. industrial murder
2. What is the topic sentence?
   a. Silver can be recovered from used photographic and x-ray plates by soaking these plates in a cyanide solution.
   b. Film Recovery Systems was one company that was active in this recovery work.
   c. Finally, an autopsy revealed that one employee had died of cyanide poisoning, leading the authorities to file murder charges against certain company executives.
   d. Although company officials knew the silver recovery process was toxic, they did not provide enough safety precautions, and consequently, they committed industrial murder.
3. Which of the following points should be included in your notes? Choose all that apply.
   a. Film Recovery Systems was active in silver recovery work.
   b. Workers must wear protective clothing and use respirators in order to prevent contact with deadly cyanide gas, but were only given cloth gloves and paper masks at Film Recovery Systems.
   c. Silver can be recovered from used photographic and x-ray plates by soaking these plates in a cyanide solution.
   d. An autopsy revealed that one employee had died of cyanide poisoning, and the company officials were convicted of industrial murder.

4. Which of the following points would be the important point to remember for a test?

a. Film Recovery Systems recovered silver from photographic and x-ray plates.

b. The company president, the plant manager, and the plant foreperson were shown to be familiar with the hazards associated with cyanide.

c. In 1985, company officials at Film Recovery Systems were each convicted of industrial murder, fined $10,000 and given a 25-year prison sentence.

d. The company only provided gloves and paper masks to workers using cyanide.

5. What would be the best way to study this material for a test?

a. Memorize it word-for-word.

b. Copy the paragraph exactly as it appears.

c. Take notes on it, and then review the notes frequently.

d. Read it just before the test is given.

READING LAB ASSIGNMENTS

SKILL PRACTICES

1. Login to **MyReadingLab,** and in the menu click on **Reading Skills** and **Learning Path**. On the main screen, click **Note-taking & Highlighting**, **Summarizing & Paraphrasing**, and **Test-taking**. Complete the review and practice activities recommended by your instructor.

COMPREHENSION IMPROVEMENT

2. From the menu in **MyReadingLab,** click on **Reading Level** and **Next Reading**. Choose two reading selections from the list on the main screen. Read the articles and answer the diagnostic and exercise questions.

CAREER EXPLORATION

3. Go online to the Occupational Outlook Handbook at the Bureau of Labor Statistics and explore careers in technology. Find a career that interests you, and print out the information. Print the article, and then preview, read, highlight and annotate it. Underline and label two facts and one opinion. Write the author's purpose and the tone for the article in the margin.

MyReadingLab

LEARNING REFLECTION

Think about the skills and concepts in this chapter. What have you learned in this chapter that will help your reading comprehension and enable you to do well in college?

MyReadingLab

SELF-EVALUATION CHECKLIST

Rate yourself on the following items, using the following scale:

1 = strongly disagree 2 = disagree 3 = neither agree nor disagree

4 = agree 5 = strongly agree

1. I completed all of the assigned work on time.
2. I understand all of the concepts in this chapter.
3. I contributed to teamwork and class discussions.
4. I completed all of the assigned lab work on time.
5. I came to class on time.
6. I attended class every day.
7. I studied for any quizzes or tests we had for this chapter.
8. I asked questions when I didn't understand something.
9. I checked my comprehension during reading.
10. I know what is expected of me in the coming week.
11. Are you still on track with the goals you set in Chapter 1?

What changes can you make to improve your performance in this?

COMBINED SKILLS TESTS

Test 1

Read the next textbook selection, and then answer the questions that follow.

How Can I Prepare for a Classical Music Concert?

1 As often as possible, listen to recordings of the music that will be featured at the concert so you will become familiar with the music. We tend to enjoy the music we know best. Besides preparing for a concert, purchasing the recordings is an excellent way to build your personal music collection.

2 Municipal and university libraries also can be excellent resources. You can listen to recordings at the library or check them out for a few days. Also, pre-set your radio to your local classical music stations (usually FM stations), and you will become familiar with many styles of music. The Web also has satellite radio stations and streaming audio sites dedicated to classical music.

3 Each musical style has its own characteristics. Knowing how to listen to the various styles makes it easier to follow and enjoy the music.

4 Also, become familiar with the composer, the artists, and the background of the music. Sometimes this information is available on an insert accompanying a recording. Many of the greatest geniuses have been as imperfect and vulnerable as any other human being. Their stories are very moving and can give you greater insight into their works.

August, June & Zorn, Jay D. *Listening to Music,* 5th ed. Upper Saddle River: Pearson-Prentice Hall, 2007. p.21

1. What is the topic?
   a. music
   b. concerts
   c. preparing for a classical music concert
   d. musical styles

2. What is the implied main idea?
   a. You should listen to recordings of music before you attend a concert.
   b. You should become familiar with the music, the composers, and background of the music before you go to a concert.
   c. Each musical style has its own characteristics.
   d. There are several things you should do to prepare before going to a classical music concert.

3. Identify the meaning of the underlined word in the following sentence: Their stories are very moving and can give you greater <u>insight</u> into their works.
   a. seeing into
   b. understanding
   c. enjoyment
   d. research

4. According to the selection, why should you become familiar with the music before going to the concert?
   a. so that you will not fall asleep during the concert
   b. so that you will buy the recording and support the artist
   c. so that you will understand and enjoy the music more
   d. to learn more about the composers and how they achieved success

5. Which of these resources was NOT included to prepare for a concert?
   a. your own music collection
   b. libraries
   c. the Internet
   d. classical radio stations

6. What is the overall pattern of organization in this selection?
   a. time order
   b. compare and/or contrast
   c. definition and example
   d. listing

7. Which of the following conclusions can be made from this selection?
   a. Understanding the background stories of the artists and composers can provide insight into their works.
   b. Understanding classical music can be difficult.
   c. Attending concerts can be expensive, but well worth the experience.
   d. You will learn more about composing if you attend more concerts.

8. Which of the following is an opinion?
   a. You can listen to recordings at the library or check them out for a few days.
   b. Municipal and university libraries can be excellent resources.
   c. The Web also has satellite radio stations and streaming audio sites dedicated to classical music.
   d. Each musical style has its own characteristics.

9. What is the author's purpose?
   a. to inform readers about concerts
   b. to explain how to understand music better
   c. to inform readers how to prepare before they attend a concert
   d. to entertain readers by telling them about how to enjoy a concert

10. Who is the intended audience for this selection?
   a. classical musicians
   b. classical music fans
   c. ticket sellers
   d. students in music classes

Test 2

Read the following textbook selection, and then answer the questions that follow.

Larceny-Theft Offenses

1 There are many types of larceny-theft offenses, and their rate of occurrence is considerable. A lack of witnesses or other "concrete" evidence makes larceny a difficult crime to solve. In larceny-theft investigations, the state must show that there was a "taking" at least for a brief time and that the defendant had control over the property "of another." The taking must be deliberate and with the intent to steal.

2 The Uniform Crime Report defines larceny-theft as the unlawful taking, carrying, leading, or riding away of property from the possession or constructive possession of another. It includes crimes such as shoplifting, pocket picking, purse snatching, thefts from motor vehicles, thefts of motor vehicle parts and accessories, and bicycle thefts, in which no use of force, violence, or fraud occurs. In the Uniform Reporting Program, this crime category does not include embezzlement, confidence games, forgery, or worthless checks. Motor vehicle theft is also excluded from this category because it is a separate Crime Index offense.

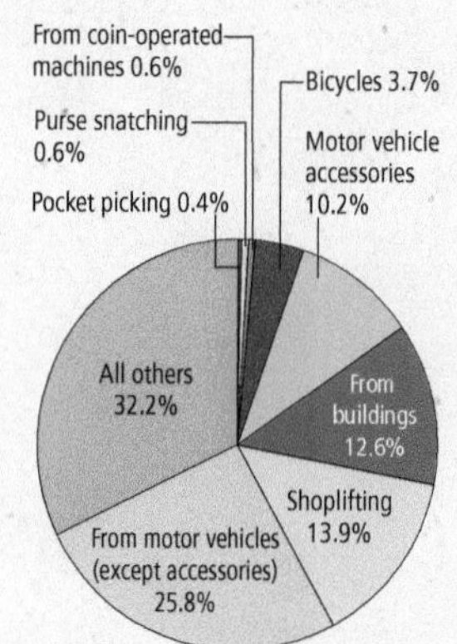

Larceny–Theft Distribution

From: Lyman, Michael D., *Criminal Investigation: The Art and the Science*. Upper Saddle River: Pearson, 2008. pp. 430–432. Graph source: FBI, *Crime in the United States*, 2006

1. What is the topic of this textbook selection?
   - a. theft
   - b. national crime
   - c. investigating crime
   - d. larceny-theft offenses

2. What is the main idea?
   - a. There are many types of criminal offenses.
   - b. There are many types of larceny-theft offenses, and their rate of occurrence is considerable.
   - c. Larceny is defined as the taking of another's property with intent to steal.
   - d. Larceny-theft crimes are difficult to prove.

3. Identify the meaning of the underlined word in the following sentence: Although there are many different types of larceny-theft offenses, in this book we attempt to discuss only a few of the most <u>problematic</u>.
   - a. horrifying
   - b. interesting
   - c. easy to solve
   - d. difficult

4. According to the selection, why is larceny such a difficult crime to solve?
   - a. They are rarely reported.
   - b. The methods to solve such offenses are ineffective.

c. It is difficult to obtain witnesses or other "concrete" evidence.

d. Police are unwilling to solve these crimes.

5. **According to the graph, which of the following conclusions is true?**

a. There is a higher occurrence of theft from buildings than shoplifting.

b. There is a lower occurrence of pocket picking than purse snatching.

c. Bicycle theft is included in "All others."

d. There is less motor vehicle theft than shoplifting.

6. **According to the graph, what is the third largest type of theft committed?**

a. all others

b. motor vehicle accessories

c. shoplifting

d. from motor vehicles

7. **Which patterns of organization are used in paragraph 2?**

a. definition and example

b. compare and/or contrast

c. cause and effect

d. time order and listing

8. **Identify the relationship within the following sentence: Motor vehicle theft is also excluded from this category because it is a separate Crime Index offense.**

a. cause and effect

b. time order

c. definition

d. listing

9. **Which of the following statements is an opinion?**

a. There are many types of larceny-theft offenses, and their rate of occurrence is considerable.

b. The taking must be deliberate and with the intent to steal.

c. The Uniform Crime Report defines larceny-theft as the unlawful taking, carrying, leading, or riding away of property from the possession or constructive possession of another.

d. Motor vehicle theft is also excluded from this category inasmuch as it is a separate Crime Index offense.

10. **Which of the following best describes the author's purpose and tone?**

a. purpose: to warn readers about the dangers of larceny-theft; tone: concerned

b. purpose: to persuade readers to study the types of larceny-theft; tone: serious

c. purpose: to inform readers about the types of larceny-theft; tone: objective

d. purpose: to entertain readers with stories about theft; tone: amusing

Test 3

Read the following textbook selection, and then answer the questions that follow.

terra cotta: a reddish clay used in pottery and sculpture

1 In 1974, two Chinese farmers in Shaanxi Province found broken pieces of **terra cotta** on their land. Shortly thereafter, the tomb of the Chinese emperor Shihuangdi (who ruled 221–210 B.C.) was opened, and excavations began. Shihuangdi unified China and established a code of laws, a writing system, and standardized measurements. He had monumental works of art and architecture made, built roads throughout the country, and defended its borders by extending and completing most of the Great Wall of China.

2 When he died, Shihuangdi decided he would take life with him. So he assembled over 7,000 life-size terra-cotta soldiers and horses to guard him after death. Most were arranged in rows, like military battalions, standing at attention in trenches. Others are shown kneeling and holding the reins of horses. The figures were constructed in sections—torso, limbs, and head—on a base; their remarkably lifelike appearance was achieved by the use of different paint and slight variations in the features. It was not for public viewing, for the emperor had no idea that his soldiers would be excavated, photographed, copied in various sizes for sale, and exhibited throughout the world.

3 Since its discovery, the terra-cotta army has become an international attraction, and visitors to China regularly include this in their travels.

Adapted from: Adams, Laurie Schneider. *Looking at Art.* Upper Saddle River: Prentice Hall, 2002. pp. 128–129

1. What is the topic?
   - **a.** Emperor Shihuangdi's terra-cotta army
   - **b.** Chinese art
   - **c.** Shaanxi Province in China
   - **d.** Chinese emperor Shihuangdi

2. What is the main idea?
   - **a.** Shihuangdi unified China and established a code of laws, a writing system, and standardized measurements.
   - **b.** When he died, Shihuangdi decided he would take life with him.
   - **c.** In 1974, two Chinese farmers in Shaanxi Province found broken pieces of terra cotta on their land.
   - **d.** Chinese Emperor Shihuangdi assembled 7,000 life-size terra-cotta soldiers and horses to guard him after death.

3. Identify the meaning of the underlined word in the following sentence: Shortly thereafter, the tomb of the Chinese emperor Shihuangdi (who ruled 221–210 B.C.) was opened, and excavations began.
   - **a.** construction
   - **b.** digging out
   - **c.** exaggerations
   - **d.** expectations

4. **According to the selection, how was the terra-cotta army discovered?**
   a. Emperor Shihuangdi left it as a monument to his army.
   b. An archaeologist believed there was a burial tomb in the area and began digging.
   c. It was discovered when the Chinese government started construction on the Great Wall of China.
   d. The tomb was discovered in 1974, when two Chinese farmers in Shaanxi Province found broken pieces of terra cotta on their land.

5. **According to the selection, how were the artists able to achieve such a lifelike appearance for the army?**
   a. All the figures were exactly alike.
   b. They used different paint and slight variations in the features.
   c. Actual models posed for the statues.
   d. The figures were of real people that the emperor knew.

6. **Which of the following conclusions can be made from this selection?**
   a. Emperor Shihuangdi believed that he would live on after he died.
   b. Emperor Shihuangdi loved his army and wanted to build a memorial to it.
   c. The Chinese are superstitious people.
   d. Emperor Shihuangdi wanted the people of the world to see his magnificent burial tomb.

7. **Identify the relationship between the following sentences: When he died, Shihuangdi decided he would take life with him. So he assembled more than 7,000 life-size terra-cotta soldiers and horses to guard him after death.**
   a. listing
   b. time order
   c. compare and/or contrast
   d. cause and effect

8. **Which of the following correctly describes this sentence: "The figures were constructed in sections—torso, limbs, and head—on a base; their remarkably lifelike appearance was achieved by the use of different paint and slight variations in the features"?**
   a. fact
   b. opinion
   c. fact and opinion
   d. expert opinion

9. **What is the author's purpose?**
   a. to entertain readers with a story about a Chinese emperor
   b. to persuade readers to visit the site of the terra-cotta army
   c. to inform readers about Emperor Shihuangdi's terra-cotta army
   d. to explain why the Emperor had the terra-cotta army created

10. **What is the author's tone?**
   a. concerned
   b. informative
   c. upset
   d. uninterested

Test 4

Read the following textbook selection, and then answer the questions that follow.

Modern Hydropower

1 Most of our hydroelectric power today comes from holding water in reservoirs behind concrete dams that block the flow of river water, and then letting that water pass through the dam. Because immense amounts of water are stored behind dams, this is called the storage technique. As reservoir water passes through a dam, it turns the blades of turbines, which cause a generator to generate electricity (Figure 16.9). Electricity generated in the powerhouse of a dam is transmitted to the electric grid by transmission lines, while the water flows into the riverbed below the dam to continue downriver. By storing water in reservoirs, dam operators can ensure a steady and predictable supply of electricity, even during times of naturally low river flow.

2 Large dams generate substantial amounts of hydroelectric power. Inside these dams, flowing water is used to turn turbines and generate electricity. Water is funneled from the reservoir through a portion of the dam to rotate turbines, which turn rotors containing magnets. The spinning rotors generate electricity as their magnets pass coils of copper wire. Electrical current is transmitted away through power lines, and the river's water flows out through the base of the dam.

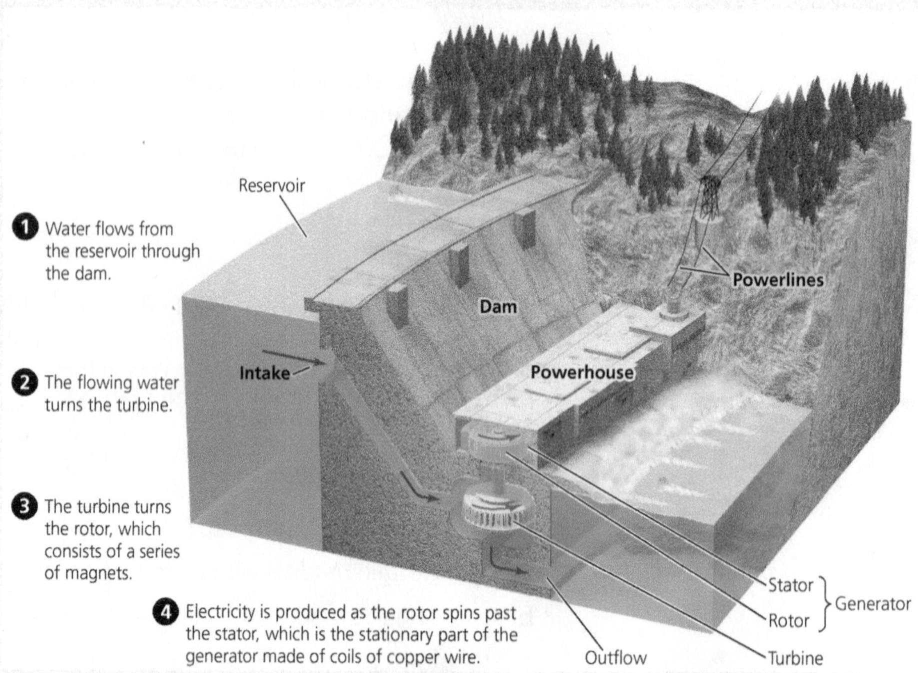

Figure 16.9 Hydroelectric Power

From *Essential Environment: The Science Behind the Stories,* 3e by Jay H. Withgott and Scott R. Brennan.

1. **What is the topic?**
   a. dams
   b. electricity
   c. hydroelectric power
   d. how electricity is made

2. **What is the implied main idea?**
   a. Because immense amounts of water are stored behind dams, this is called the storage technique.
   b. The storage technique is used to generate electricity.
   c. Hydroelectric power is produced by letting water pass through a dam to operate a generator, which makes the electricity.
   d. Electricity generated in the powerhouse of a dam is transmitted to the electric grid by transmission lines.

3. **Identify the meaning of the underlined word in the following sentence: As reservoir water passes through a dam, it turns the blades of <u>turbines</u>, which cause a generator to generate electricity.**
   a. large motors, with blades that turn as air or water pass them
   b. a helicopter rotor
   c. blades of a fan for cooling air
   d. super charged

4. **According to the diagram, what happens after water flows from the reservoir through the dam?**
   a. Electricity is produced as the rotor spins past the stator, which is the stationary part of the generator made of coils of copper wire.
   b. The turbine turns the rotor, which has a series of magnets.
   c. The flowing water turns the turbine.
   d. Electrical current is transmitted away through power lines.

5. **According to the diagram, how is electricity produced?**
   a. Water is funneled from the reservoir through a portion of the dam to rotate turbines, which turn rotors containing magnets.
   b. The spinning rotors generate electrical current as their magnets pass coils of copper wire.
   c. Electrical current is transmitted away through power lines.
   d. The river's water flows out through the base of the dam.

6. **What conclusion can you draw from this selection?**
   a. Electricity is inexpensive to produce.
   b. We should build more hydroelectric plants.
   c. Large bodies of water are possible sources for producing electricity.
   d. Hydroelectric power should be used instead of fossil fuels.

7. **What are the relationships within the following sentence from paragraph 1: Because immense amounts of water are stored behind the dams, this is called the storage technique.**
   - **a.** time order and listing
   - **b.** compare and/or contrast
   - **c.** listing and definition
   - **d.** cause and effect and definition

8. **What is the author's purpose?**
   - **a.** to persuade readers to use hydroelectric power
   - **b.** to inform readers about how hydroelectric power is produced
   - **c.** to entertain readers with a description of hydroelectric power
   - **d.** to explain why hydroelectric power is a cleaner energy source

9. **Identify the relationship within the following sentence: As reservoir water passes through a dam, it turns the blades of turbines, which cause a generator to generate electricity.**
   - **a.** cause and effect
   - **b.** process
   - **c.** time order
   - **d.** listing

10. **Which of the following correctly describes this sentence: "Because immense amounts of water are stored behind dams, this is called the storage technique"?**
    - **a.** opinion
    - **b.** fact
    - **c.** fact and opinion
    - **d.** expert opinion

Test 5

Read the following textbook selection, and then answer the questions that follow.

Contract Manufacturing and Outsourcing

1 Because of high domestic labor costs, many U.S. companies manufacture their products in countries where labor costs are lower. This arrangement is called **international contract manufacturing** or **outsourcing**. A U.S. company might contract with a local company in a foreign country to manufacture one of its products. It will, however, retain control of product design and development and put its own label on the finished product. Thanks to 21st-century information technology, non-manufacturing functions can also be outsourced to nations with lower labor costs. U.S. companies increasingly draw upon a vast supply of relatively inexpensive skilled labor to perform various business services, such as software development, accounting, and claims processing.

2 For years, American insurance companies have processed much of their claims-related paperwork in Ireland. With a large well-educated population, India has become a center for software development and customer call centers for American companies. In the case of India, as you can see in Table 8.1, the attraction is not only a large pool of knowledgeable workers, but significantly lower wages as well.

Table 8.1 Selected Hourly Wages, United States and India

Occupation	U.S. Wage	Indian Wage
Telephone operator	$12.57	Under $1.00
Health-record technical worker/medical transcriber	$13.17	$1.50–$2.00
Payroll clerk	$15.17	$1.50–$2.00
Legal assistant/paralegal	$17.86	$6.00–$8.00
Accountant	$23.35	$6.00–$15.00
Financial researcher/analyst	$33.00–$35.00	$6.00–$15.00

1. What is the topic?
   a. business
   b. wages in the United States and India
   c. contract manufacturing and outsourcing
   d. U.S. business in India and Ireland

2. **What is the main idea?**
   a. To reduce labor costs, many U.S. companies manufacture their products in other countries through international contract manufacturing or outsourcing.
   b. U.S. companies increasingly draw upon a vast supply of relatively inexpensive skilled labor to perform various business services, such as software development, accounting, and claims processing.
   c. A U.S. company might contract with a local company in a foreign country to manufacture one of its products but still keep control of it.
   d. For years, American insurance companies have processed much of their claims-related paperwork in Ireland.

3. **Identify the meaning of the underlined word in the following sentence: It will, however, retain control of product design and development and put its own label on the finished product.**
   a. give up
   b. recall
   c. bring back
   d. keep

4. **According to the selection, what kinds of business services are outsourced?**
   a. machine repairs
   b. drafting
   c. software development
   d. telephone operator

5. **According to the table, which jobs offer higher pay in the United States than in India?**
   a. software developer
   b. machine operator
   c. legal assistant/paralegal
   d. automobile designer

6. **According to the table, what is the difference in wages for a payroll clerk in the United States and India?**
   a. about $17 more in India
   b. about $20 more in the United States
   c. about $17 more in the United States
   d. about $13 more in the United States

7. **Identify the relationship within the following sentence: Because of high domestic labor costs, many U.S. companies manufacture their products in countries where labor costs are lower.**
   a. cause and effect
   b. compare and/or contrast
   c. time order
   d. listing

8. **According to this selection, why do U.S. companies outsource software development and customer call centers to India?**
   a. India has cheaper prices than Ireland.
   b. The U.S. software business doesn't make enough money.
   c. India has a large pool of knowledgeable workers and lower labor costs.
   d. Companies in India do not have their own software developers or customer call centers.

9. **Identify the relationship between the following sentences: A U.S. company might contract with a local company in a foreign country to manufacture one of its products. It will, however, retain control of product design and development and put its own label on the finished product.**
   a. contrast
   b. comparison
   c. cause and effect
   d. listing

10. **Who is the intended audience for this selection?**
    a. manufacturers in the United States
    b. business owners
    c. students
    d. librarians

USING A GLOSSARY OR DICTIONARY

Using a Glossary

If context clues or word parts fail to provide enough information to figure out a word's meaning, check the back of your textbook for a glossary. A glossary is a list of terms used in the textbook that are essential for understanding the subject matter. The words and terms are listed in alphabetical order. Often they are followed by a page number, where you find the term to read more about it and see the context in which it is used. Below is an example of a glossary from a business textbook. The definition for "accounting equation" also includes another term in bold print, "owner's equity." This means that the definition for this term is also included in the glossary, and it would be found under the Os.

A

accounting System for measuring and summarizing business activities, interpreting financial information, and communicating the results to management and other decision makers. [225]
accounting equation Accounting tool showing the resources of a business (assets) and the claims on those resources (liabilities and **owner's equity**). [231]
account payable Record of cash owed to sellers from whom a business has purchased products on credit. [233]

Using a Dictionary

If the glossary doesn't define the word or term you need, or if there is no glossary, a dictionary is another option. Many students access online dictionaries through their cell phones or home computers. Online dictionaries provide most of the information you need, such as the definition, how to break the word into syllables, the parts of speech, how to pronounce the word, and its various meanings. Besides convenience, another advantage of using online dictionaries is that they will provide a list of suggestions if you misspell the word you are looking for. For example, if you were looking for *irresponsible* and spelled it *earesponsable*, the following list appears:

Do you mean:
irresponsible
responsible
responsibly
Click on the correct spelling of the word to see its definitions.

Here is a sample page from an online dictionary:

If you type the word "rhythm" into the search box, the definitions will appear as follows:

rhythm [uncountable and countable]

1 ▶ 🔊 a regular repeated pattern of sounds or movements [metre]

Drums are used to keep the rhythm.

rhythm of
We were dancing to the rhythm of the music.
the steady rhythm of the rain on the roof

2 a pattern of changes or cycles
the natural rhythm of the body

rhythm of
The rhythm of a farmer's life moves with the seasons.

The entry word, "rhythm," is divided into syllables.

Next, the terms "uncountable" and "countable" tell us the type of nouns this word is considered to be. Countable nouns are things that can be counted, such as people or objects. Uncountable ("noncount") nouns are not countable and don't form plurals, such as *strength, confusion, truth,* etc.

The symbol to the left of the definition, ▶ 🔊, is a link to hear the word pronounced.

The word in brackets, [metre] is a synonym for *rhythm.*

The first definition is followed by an example of how the word is used in the first meaning. The phrase "rhythm of" follows the definition, and two examples of this phrase are provided. The second definition is also followed by an example and another example of how the phrase "rhythm of" can be used according to the second definition.

Using a Published Dictionary

The best dictionaries for students in college are college dictionaries. These contain most of the words you will need, and they are printed in paperbacks as well as hardcover editions. Although paperbacks may not have as many words as the larger hardcover editions, they are usually suitable for use in most college courses.

The words listed in bold print in dictionaries are called entries. To find a specific entry such as *jinni,* use the words at the top of the page to locate your word. These are called guide words. The word on the left is the first entry on the page, and the word on the right is the last entry. Like a glossary, all the words are listed in alphabetical order. On the page in this example, you will find all the words that come alphabetically between *jinn* and *jogger.* (The sample shows only the top half of the page.)

jinn	jogger

jinn (jin) n. *pi.* O/JINNI: popularly regarded as a singular, with the pl. **jinns**
jin-ni (ji ne', jin'e) n. [Ar. *jinni*, pl. *jinn*] *Moslem Legend* a supernatural being that can take human or animal form and influence human affairs
jin-rik-i-sha (jin rik'sAS, -sha) n. [Jap, < *jin*, a man +*riki*, power + *sha*, carriage] a small, two-wheeled carriage with a hood, pulled by one or two men, esp. formerly in the Orient; also sp. jin-**rick'sha, jin-rlk'sha**
ji-pt-ja-pa (he'pe ha'pa) n. [Sp. < *Jipijapa*, place in Ecuador] 1. a Central and South
job-ber-y (-ar e, -re) n. [see JOB1 (*vi.* 3)] [Chiefly Brit.] the carrying on of public or official business dishonestly for private gain
Job Corps a U.S. government program for training underprivileged youth for employment
job-hold-er (-hol'der) n. a person who has a steady job; specif., a government employee
job-less (-lis) adj. 1. without a job; unemployed 2. having to do with the unemployed—the **job-less** those who are unemployed—**job'less-ness** n.

The first entry on the page is *jinn*. The word *jinni* appears after it.

The two ways to pronounce the word are in parentheses, (ji-nē', jin' ē). Notice the accent mark (') shows that the accent is on the second syllable in the first pronunciation and on the first syllable in the second pronunciation. Either one is correct. A key to all the symbols and abbreviations can be found in the first few pages of a dictionary.

At the bottom of the page or in the first few pages, you will find a guide for using the pronunciation symbols. Here is the pronunciation guide from the bottom of the sample page:

fat, āpe, cär, ten, ēven (…etc.)

This means that:
a = the *a* sound in fat
ā = the *a* sound in *ape*
ä = the *a* sound in *car*
e = the *e* sound in *ten*
ē = the *e* sound in *even*

The second item in the entry is the part of speech. In this case, *jinni* is a noun, shown by the *n*. Here are some common abbreviations for the parts of speech:

n. = noun
v. = verb
adj. = adjective
adv. = adverb
The symbol *pl* = plural (more than one)

In brackets, we find the origin of the word. The origin of *jinni* is [Ar. *jinni*, pl. *jinn*]. "Ar" means Arabic.

Next is the definition, with a note as to where the word was first used—in a Moslem legend:
"*Moslem Legend* a supernatural being that can take human or animal form and influence human affairs"

FIGURATIVE SPEECH

Authors use many tools to clearly express their ideas. Sometimes they will rely on figurative language to help readers understand their messages. Following are some types of figurative language.

- Comparisons help readers to understand concepts by relating the new idea to something they already know. There are two types of comparisons: literal or figurative. Literal comparisons compare things from the same category. Figurative comparisons use different categories.

Literal comparison example: Like his father, Russ loves taking things apart and putting them back together.

Figurative comparison example: When she walks, she sways as gently as a willow in the wind.

- Any comparison that uses the words *like* or *as* is called a **simile** (SIM-uhl-lee). Notice how the comparisons above use the words *like* and *as*.
- Another type of comparison that does not use *like* or *as* is called a **metaphor** (MET-a-for). It usually states that something *is* or *was* something else. For example:

Metaphor: Life is just a big bag of mixed nuts.
Simile: Life is like a big bag of mixed nuts.

Metaphor: She was a bright star in her father's life.

Simile: She was as bright as a star in her father's life.

- Personification is another way authors try to convey meaning. Personification gives human actions or qualities to a thing or idea. For example:

The angry barren trees clawed at the sky in the bitter wind.

Time was unkind to Grandmother.

- Hyperbole (hi-PER-bo-lee) is deliberate exaggeration. For example:

This purse must weigh a ton!

I've been waiting for my dinner forever.

Denotation and Connotation

Words can have two kinds of meanings. One is the literal meaning—the definition that is found in the dictionary—and this is known as the word's **denotation**. But words also may have an emotional meaning, called **connotation**. For example: the denotative meaning of *skinny* is "thin," but the connotative meaning is more negative than the word *slender* or *thin*. Consider the following words and their connotations.

Words with positive connotations	Words with negative connotations
slender	skinny
crowd	mob
request	demand

IMPROVING READING RATE AND ENDURANCE

Students are often concerned about their reading rate. They want to read faster so they can get through their assignments more quickly. But the real goal of any reading course, first and foremost, is comprehension. When we discuss reading rate, we mean the number of words per minute that you can read with complete comprehension of the material. Here are some tips for improving your reading rate:

Before reading:

- Preview the material before you begin reading to get a general sense of what the passage is about.
- Try to predict what the author will say about the topic. Think of a couple questions that you would like to find the answers to by reading the selection.

During reading:

- Stay focused. Lead your eyes across the page with a pen, pencil, or your finger. Have it pointing one or two words ahead of where you are reading, so that your eyes are trying to "catch up" to the speed of your pencil or finger.
- Stop at the end of a section to recall and summarize what you just read: State the topic and the author's main point about the topic.
- If the material is easy, try to make your pencil or finger go a little faster. When you notice that you cannot summarize what you just read, then slow it down and try again.
- Easy materials that you read for fun, such as a magazine, or a short, easy passage can be read faster than more difficult materials. The level of difficulty for you depends on your vocabulary, your prior knowledge of the subject, and your fluency with language.

After reading:

- Check your comprehension again by summarizing the entire passage or chapter that you just read. Make notes and draw diagrams, charts, or illustrations to help you remember what you read.
- If there are comprehension questions in the book, do them by going back to reread parts of the passage that will help you get the correct answers.

Timed Readings

If you want to improve your reading speed, you can start with the articles in this book. Before you read, follow the steps above under "Before reading." Then, write down the time that you begin reading. When you finish a section without stopping, look at the time, and write it down. Subtract your starting time from your finishing time. Then, count the number of words in the passage. The reading assignment articles in this book have a word count at the end. When you are doing a timed reading, do not stop to answer the comprehension-check questions in the margins until after you have finished the entire article. If you can't answer the questions correctly, it means that you need to read more slowly. Build up your speed gradually. Just racing across a page of print is not reading. Being good at reading is like being good at anything else. It takes time, effort, and practice.

To determine your reading rate, divide the number of words in the passage by the number of minutes that it took you to read them. This will be your "words per minute" score, or your WPM.

$$\text{WPM} = \frac{\text{number of words in passage}}{\text{number of minutes}}$$

Example: If it takes someone 10 minutes to read 1500 words, this person would divide 1500 by 10, as follows:

$$\frac{\text{1500 words in the passage}}{\text{10 minutes}} = \text{150 WPM}$$

By following the techniques listed previously under "Before reading," "During reading," and "After reading," you may see an improvement in your WPM by the end of the semester. But keep in mind that it's better to read a little slower and have good comprehension than it is to read fast and have poor comprehension.

What Influences Your Rate?

You will find that reading about subjects that are familiar to you allows you to read much faster than when reading new material that is complex or contains many new terms. Other factors that slow your rate are habits like going back and rereading the same sentence or phrase. Getting stuck on unfamiliar words—trying to sound them out and figure out what they mean before moving on—can also slow you down. Subvocalizing means that you actually say the words out loud to yourself, although usually not loud enough for other people to hear. Reading aloud, moving your lips, or subvocalizing slows your reading rate. Becoming distracted while reading by things such as television, loud music, or other thoughts will pull you off track and interfere with your rate and your comprehension. For these reasons, it is recommended that you do the following:

- Read in a quiet, comfortable environment, away from noise. Playing soft music may help you relax but not if you're distracted by it.
- Avoid subvocalizing or reading aloud while timing yourself. However, reading aloud is a good strategy when you encounter something difficult.
- Keep your eyes moving forward at a steady pace, resisting the temptation to go back and reread sentences or phrases. You can go back after you have completed the timing to reread the details.
- If you feel tense or nervous, take slow, deep breaths or do some exercises before you start. Being relaxed helps your concentration and your comprehension.
- Try to read in phrases of three to four words instead of individual words. You can increase the number of words in the phrases you read very gradually over time.
- Avoid fixating, or stopping, between words. Try to keep moving ahead at a comfortable rate.
- Keep a notepad handy to write down thoughts that distract you, and then deal with them after you're done reading.
- Gradually increase your reading time period. If you start reading for 45 minutes in one sitting, try to increase it to 50 minutes, and then 55 minutes, and so on.

Post-Test Survey: How Did You Learn?

1. Are you satisfied with your test grade?

2. Did the study methods you used help you to master the concept? Why or why not?

3. What reading or study skills did you use as you took this test?

4. What were the most effective study methods you used? (For example: note cards, charts, pictures; group or study partner; self-testing; repeating things aloud; repeating things in writing; other methods.)

5. What will you do differently for your next test?

CREDITS

TEXT

CHAPTER 2

Page 22: "Getting Down to Business" by Karen Collins from EXPLORING BUSINESS © 2008. Used by permission of Karen Collins; page 23: From HOW THE BRAIN LEARNS by David A. Sousa. Copyright © 2006 by SAGE Publications; page 45: "Excerpt from Illegal Immigrant to Brain Surgeon" by Dr. Alfredo Quinones. Copyright © 2013. Used by permission of C.F. Hopkins; page 56: chart, BELK, COLLEN; BORDEN MAIER, VIRGINIA, BIOLOGY: SCIENCE FOR LIFE, 2nd Ed., © 2007. Printed and Electronically reproduced by permission of Pearson Education, Inc., Upper Saddle River, New Jersey; pages 61–63: "What Is Cancer?", "Genes and Chromosomes", and Figure 6.2, BELK, COLLEN; BORDEN MAIER, VIRGINIA, BIOLOGY: SCIENCE FOR LIFE, 2nd Ed., © 2007. Printed and Electronically reproduced by permission of Pearson Education, Inc., Upper Saddle River, New Jersey.

CHAPTER 3

Page 73: "External Examination of the Crime Scene," SULLIVAN, WILSON T., CRIME SCENE ANALYSIS: PRACTICAL PROCEDURES AND TECHNIQUES, 1st Ed., © 2007. Printed and Electronically reproduced by permission of Pearson Education, Inc., Upper Saddle River, New Jersey; page 91: "Leap of Faith" by Mike Santangelo, Mara Bovsun, Allan Zullo from THE GREATEST FIREFIGHTER STORIES NEVER TOLD, Copyright © 2002 Used by permission of Andrews McMeel Publishing, Inc.; page 108: "The Hunt for Eric Rudolph," LYMAN, MICHAEL D., CRIMINAL INVESTIGATION: THE ART AND THE SCIENCE, 5th Ed., © 2008. Printed and Electronically reproduced by permission of Pearson Education, Inc., Upper Saddle River, New Jersey.

CHAPTER 4

Page 130: "Excerpt on marketing" by Karen Collins from EXPLORING BUSINESS © 2008. Used by permission of Karen Collins; page 130: "Power Speed JetBoard" by Karen Collins from EXPLORING BUSINESS © 2008. Used by permission of Karen Collins; page 155: "PERT diagram of process to produce one Vermont Teddy Bear" by Karen Collins from EXPLORING BUSINESS. Used by permission of Karen Collins; page 159: "Why Do Businesses Fail?" by Karen Collins from EXPLORING BUSINESS © 2008. Used by permission of Karen Collins.

CHAPTER 5

Page 186: "Let's Talk about Your Life, Son" by Flay, Bobby from GUIDEPOSTS, June 2008: Vol. 63 Issue 04. Used by permission of Flay Bobby; page 208: Figure 1.1, WALKER, JOHN R., INTRODUCTION TO HOSPITALITY, 5th Ed., © 2009, pp. 05, 222, 319, 446. Printed and Electronically reproduced by permission of Pearson Education, Inc., Upper Saddle River, New Jersey; page 214: "The Brewing Process," WALKER, JOHN R., INTRODUCTION TO HOSPITALITY, 05th Ed., © 2009, pp. 05, 222, 319, 446. Printed and Electronically reproduced by permission of Pearson Education, Inc., Upper Saddle River, New Jersey.

CHAPTER 6

Page 222: "Teen Pregnancy," MACIONIS, JOHN J., SOCIETY: THE BASICS, 9th Ed., © 2007. Printed and Electronically reproduced by permission of Pearson Education, Inc., Upper Saddle River, New Jersey; page 224: "U.S. Divorce Rate," MACIONIS, JOHN J., SOCIETY: THE BASICS, 9th Ed., © 2007. Printed and Electronically reproduced by permission of Pearson Education, Inc., Upper Saddle River, New Jersey; page 253: POWERS, SCOTT K.; DODD, STEPHEN L.; JACKSON, ERICA M., TOTAL FITNESS & WELLNESS, 3rd Ed., © 2011, pp. 174, 205, 206, 297, 300. Printed and Electronically reproduced by permission of Pearson Education, Inc., Upper Saddle River, New Jersey; page 257: Textbook Practice, MACIONIS, JOHN J., SOCIETY: THE BASICS, 9th Ed., © 2007. Reprinted and Electronically reproduced by permission of Pearson Education, Inc., Upper Saddle River, New Jersey.

CHAPTER 7

Page 273: SPORRE, DENNIS J., CREATIVE IMPULSE: AN INTRODUCTION TO THE ARTS, 8th Ed., © 2009. Printed and Electronically reproduced by permission of Pearson Education, Inc., Upper Saddle River, New Jersey; page 277: SPORRE, DENNIS J., CREATIVE IMPULSE: AN INTRODUCTION TO THE ARTS, 8th Ed., © 2009. Printed and Electronically reproduced by permission of Pearson Education, Inc., Upper Saddle River, New Jersey; page 279: SPORRE, DENNIS J., CREATIVE IMPULSE: AN INTRODUCTION TO THE ARTS, 8th Ed., © 2009. Printed and Electronically reproduced by permission of Pearson Education, Inc., Upper Saddle River, New Jersey; page 282: "My Best Role Ever" by Harden, Marcia Gay from Guideposts. Copyright © 2008. All rights reserved. Used by permission of Marcia Gay Harden; page 292: "Sketch to Screen" by Tim Burton From Scholastic Art, November 2012. Copyright © 2012 by Scholastic Inc. Reprinted by permission of Scholastic Inc.; page 304: Diagram, TARBUCK, EDWARDS J.; LUTGENS, FREDERICK K.; TASA, DENNIS, EARTH SCIENCE, 12th Ed., © 2009. Printed and Electronically reproduced by permission of Pearson Education, Inc., Upper Saddle River, New Jersey; page 309: SPORRE, DENNIS J., CREATIVE IMPULSE: AN INTRODUCTION TO THE ARTS, 8th Ed., © 2009. Printed and Electronically reproduced by permission of Pearson Education, Inc., Upper Saddle River, New Jersey.

CHAPTER 8

Page 325: "Selecting Activities," POWERS, SCOTT K.; DODD, STEPHEN L.; JACKSON, ERICA M., TOTAL FITNESS & WELLNESS, MEDIA UPDATE, 5th Ed., © 2011. Printed and Electronically reproduced by permission of Pearson Education, Inc., Upper Saddle River, New Jersey; page 332: "Personality Behavior Patterns," POWERS, SCOTT K.; DODD, STEPHEN L.; JACKSON, ERICA M., TOTAL FITNESS & WELLNESS, 3rd Ed., © 2011, pp. 174,

205, 206, 297, 300. Printed and Electronically reproduced by permission of Pearson Education, Inc., Upper Saddle River, New Jersey; page 335: Elizabeth Foy Larsen. "Dangerously Strong" from Scholastic Choices, Volume 28 issue 8 (May 2013). Reprinted by permission of Scholastic Inc.; page 359: Map, "Obesity Trends Among U.S. Adults," POWERS, SCOTT K.; DODD, STEPHEN L.; JACKSON, ERICA M., TOTAL FITNESS & WELLNESS, 3rd Ed., © 2011, pp. 174, 205, 206, 297, 300. Printed and Electronically reproduced by permission of Pearson Education, Inc., Upper Saddle River, New Jersey; page 364: "What Are the Guidelines for a Healthy Diet?" POWERS, SCOTT K.; DODD, STEPHEN L.; JACKSON, ERICA M., TOTAL FITNESS & WELLNESS, 03rd Ed., © 2011, pp. 174, 205, 206, 297, 300. Printed and Electronically reproduced by permission of Pearson Education, Inc., Upper Saddle River, New Jersey; page 347: "True Grit: Bethany Hamilton's Story" by Margy Rochlin from Ladies' Home Journal, May 2011 Copyright © 2011. Used by permission of Margy Rochlin.

CHAPTER 9

Page 376: "Sea-Level Rise," TARBUCK, EDWARDS J.; LUTGENS, FREDERICK K.; TASA, DENNIS, EARTH SCIENCE, 12th Ed., © 2009. Printed and Electronically reproduced by permission of Pearson Education, Inc., Upper Saddle River, New Jersey; page 384: Tigers excerpt, WITHGOTT, JAY H.; BRENNAN SCOTT R., ESSENTIAL ENVIRONMENT: THE SCIENCE BEHIND THE STORIES, 3rd Ed., © 2009. Printed and Electronically reproduced by permission of Pearson Education, Inc., Upper Saddle River, New Jersey; page 388: "Operation Seal Rescue" by Monica Rozenfeld From Science World, November 19, 2012. Copyright © 2012 by Scholastic Inc. Reprinted by permission of Scholastic Inc.; page 410: "Using Waste to Generate Electricity," text and chart, WITHGOTT, JAY H.; BRENNAN SCOTT R., ESSENTIAL ENVIRONMENT: THE SCIENCE BEHIND THE STORIES, 3rd Ed., © 2009. Printed and Electronically reproduced by permission of Pearson Education, Inc., Upper Saddle River, New Jersey.

CHAPTER 10

Page 423: "Water," POWERS, SCOTT K.; DODD, STEPHEN L.; JACKSON, ERICA M., TOTAL FITNESS & WELLNESS, 3rd Ed., © 2011, pp. 174, 205, 206, 297, 300. Printed and Electronically reproduced by permission of Pearson Education, Inc., Upper Saddle River, New Jersey; page 437: "Spacecraft *Apollo 13*," VOLAND, GERARD, ENGINEERING BY DESIGN, 2nd Ed., © 2004. Printed and Electronically reproduced by permission of Pearson Education, Inc., Upper Saddle River, New Jersey; page 451: "Attack of the Cyber-Thieves" by Karen Collins from EXPLORING BUSINESS. Used by permission of Karen Collins; page 462: Graphs, WITHGOTT, JAY H., BRENNAN SCOTT R. ESSENTIAL ENVIRONMENT: THE SCIENCE BEHIND THE STORIES, 3rd Ed., © 2009. Printed and Electronically reproduced by permission of Pearson Education, Inc., Upper Saddle River, New Jersey; page 466: Yves Rossy excerpt, From Popular Science Magazine by Eric Hagerman. Published by Popular Science, © 2009; page 468: Silver excerpt, VOLAND, GERARD, ENGINEERING BY DESIGN, 2nd Ed., © 2004. Printed and Electronically reproduced by permission of Pearson Education, Inc., Upper Saddle River, New Jersey.

PHOTOS

FRONT MATTER

Page iii: Eric Audras/ONOKY - Photononstop/Alamy; page iv: Pablo Calvo G/YAY Micro/AGE Fotostock; page v: Corey Hochachka/Design Pics/Corbis; page vi: Robert Nicholas/OJO Images Ltd/Alamy; page vii: Mark Edward Atkinson/Blend Images RM/AGE Fotostock; viii: Huntstock/Disability Images/Alamy; page ix: Julia Grossi/Corbis; page x: Ben Welsh/easyFotostock/AGE Fotostock; page xi: Noel Hendrickson/Blend Images/Corbis; page xii: Image Source/IS147/Alamy; page xiii: image100/Alamy

CHAPTER 1

Page 2: Eric Audras/ONOKY - Photononstop/Alamy; page 5: Praymantis Images/Alamy; page 7: Customimages/Glow Images; page 17: Vincent Leblic/Photononstop/Glow Images

CHAPTER 2

Page 18: Pablo Calvo G/YAY Micro/AGE Fotostock; page 19: S. T. Yiap/easyFotostock/AGE Fotostock; page 25: Ray A. Akey/Alamy; page 27: Christoph von Haussen/doc-stock/Alamy; page 35: David Leahy/Juice Images/Corbis; page 36: ERproductions Ltd/Blend Images/Corbis; page 39: Oleksiy Maksymenko/Alamy; page 45: Lloyd Fox/MCT/Newscom; page 47: Arno Massee/Science Source; page 53: Corinne Fennessy

CHAPTER 3

Page 66: Corey Hochachka/Design Pics/Corbis; page 69: Tetra Images/Glow Images; page 74: TpaBMa/Kalium/AGE Fotostock; page 82: Alan Diaz/AP Images; page 85: iStock/Thinkstock; page 88: Geoff Dann/Dorling Kindersley, Ltd.; page 91: RubberBall/Alamy; page 99: HG Delaney/Alamy; page 101: Custom Medical Stock Photo/Alamy; page 102: Corinne Fennessy; page 104: Kenneth Murray/Science Source; page 109: Dimitri Messinis Agence France Presse/Newscom; page 113: iStock/Thinkstock

CHAPTER 4

Page 114: Robert Nicholas/OJO Images Ltd/Alamy; page 128: Jim Spellman/La Nacion de Costa Rica/Newscom; page 130: PowerSki International (Powerski.com; JetBoard.com); page 134: JGI/Tom Grill/Getty Images; page 139: Noel Hendrickson/Blend Images/Alamy; page 144: Peter Dressel/Blend Images/Alamy; page 151: Corinne Fennessy; pages 152–153: Peter & Georgina Bowater Stock Connection Worldwide/Newscom; page 156: D. Hurst/Alamy; page 163: Harald Eisenberger/LOOK-foto/Glow Images

CHAPTER 5

Page 164: Mark Edward Atkinson/Blend Images RM/AGE Fotostock; page 169: Laurence Mouton/PhotoAlto/AGE Fotostock; page 175: BiR Fotos/Alamy; page 177: Vidler Steve/Prisma/AGE Fotostock; page 179: PNC/Photodisc/Getty Images; page 181: Martin Shields/Alamy; page 183: Gregory Wrona/Alamy; page 186: Walter McBride/Retna Ltd./Corbis; page 192: RF Food Shots/Alamy; page 198: Stephen Oliver/Dorling Kindersley, Ltd.; page 199: Victor

Borg/Rough Guides/Dorling Kindersley, Ltd.; page 200: Pearson Education; page 205: Corinne Fennessy; page 206: Michael Willis/Alamy; page 211: Per Winbladh/Corbis

CHAPTER 6

Page 218: Huntstock/Disability Images/Alamy; page 220: David Grossman/Science Source; page 226: David R. Frazier Photolibrary, Inc./Alamy; page 230: Paul A. Souders/Corbis; page 239: Michael J. Okoniewski/Syracuse University/ AP Images; page 240: Phil Coale/AP Images; page 249: Corinne Fennessy; page 253: Image Source/Corbis; page 254 (top): Nick Downes/The New Yorker Collection/www.cartoonbank.com; page 254 (bottom): Kim Warp/The New Yorker Collection/www.cartoonbank.com; page 255 (top and bottom): www.CartoonStock.com/Thomas Bros; page 257 (left and right): Paul Ekman, Ph.D. Professor of Psychology, University of California, San Francisco; page 259: Laura Doss/Corbis

CHAPTER 7

Page 262: Julia Grossi/Corbis; page 264: Ilene MacDonald/ Alamy; page 265: Everett Kennedy Brown/epa/Corbis; page 267: Bruno Ehrs/Corbis; page 269: Philipus/Alamy; page 273: Mark Burnett/Alamy; page 274: Pictorial Press Ltd/ Alamy; page 278: Ancient Art & Architecture Collection Ltd/ Alamy; page 282: FS2 WENN Photos/Newscom; page 288: Todd Wawrychuk Feature Photo Service/Newscom; page 292: Walt Disney Pictures/Photos 12/Alamy; page 294: Denis Poroy/Invision/AP Images; page 300: Corinne Fennessy; page 301: Ingo Jezierski/Alamy; page 305: Rick E. Martin/ MCT/Newscom; page 308: Jordi Matas/Polaris/Newscom; page 310: Beatriz Terrazas KRT/Newscom

CHAPTER 8

Page 314: Ben Welsh/easyFotostock/AGE Fotostock; page 318: Colin Underhill/Alamy; page 323: Julian Stratenschulte/ dpa/picture-alliance/Newscom; page 325: Koji Aoki/Aflo Foto Agency/AGE Fotostock; page 335: iStock/Thinkstock; page 337: Version One/Alamy; pages 338–339: Daniel Martinez/Fuse/Getty Images; page 347: Kirk Aeder/Icon SMI/Corbis; page 349: Image Source/Getty Images; page 351: Ian McDonnell/E+/Getty Images; page 354: Robert Daly/OJO Images/Getty Images; page 355: Corinne Fennessy; page 358: Andres Rodriguez/Alamy; page 360: Robert Michael/Corbis; page 361: Joe Fox/Radharc Images/ Alamy; page 365: David Cook/blueshiftstudios/Alamy

CHAPTER 9

Page 370: Noel Hendrickson/Blend Images/Corbis; page 373: Kim Steele/Photodisc/Getty Images; page 375: Abdolhamid Ebrahimi/E+/Getty Images; page 377: Keith Levit Photography/Thinkstock; page 379: NASA/Alamy; page 384: Purestock/Thinkstock; page 388: Picturepartners/ Shutterstock; page 390: Fuse/Thinkstock; page 397: Cultura Creative (RF)/Alamy; page 398: Radius Images/Alamy; page 406: Corinne Fennessy; page 411: iStock/Thinkstock; page 413: Dale Wilson/All Canada Photos/Glow Images; page 416: Dennis Welsh/UpperCut Images/Alamy

CHAPTER 10

Page 420: Image Source/IS147/Alamy; page 422: Lillian Feathers/Shutterstock; page 425: Wavebreak Media ltd/ Alamy; page 428: Science Museum/SSPL/The Image Works; page 434: Comstock/Stockbyte/Thinkstock; page 435: NASA; page 438: NASA; page 442: Jupiterimages/Getty Images; page 443: Mark Thiessen/National Geographic Society/Corbis; page 446: Huntstock, Inc./Alamy; page 451: GoGo Images Corporation/Alamy; pages 458–459: Corinne Fennessy; page 460: WoodyStock/Alamy; page 461: Corinne Fennessy; page 466: Unimedia International/ Newscom

END MATTER

Page 473: image100/Alamy

INDEX

A

Absolute statements, 221–222
Active reading. *See also* Critical reading; Reading
  exercises on, 30
  explanation of, 22
  memory and, 23–25
Annotating
  benefits and use of, 23, 25
  example of, 22–23
  explanation of, 22, 23
Antonyms, 68
Assumptions, 219
"Attack of the Cyber-Thieves" (Collins and Shemko), 449–453
Audience, intended, 378, 380
Authors
  intended audience of, 378, 380
  purpose of, 376–377
  tone of, 378
  use of figurative speech by, 490

B

Base. *See* Roots
"Bionic Soldiers" (Fennessy), 440–443
Bovsun, Mara, 91–93
Brackets, 68
Burton, Tim, 290–294

C

Car leasing agreement, 302
Cause-and-effect pattern, 316, 318
Cell phones, used to study vocabulary, 69
Central point, 274
Chronological order pattern, 321
Chunking information, 23–24
CLUES, 220–221
College, readiness for, 9
"College Drinking: Harmless Fun?" (Fennessy), 228–232
Collins, Karen, 449–453
Commas, 67–68
Compare-and-contrast pattern, 320
Comparisons, 320
Computer, installing memory on, 458–460
Concept maps
  explanation of, 177
  types of, 178
  use of, 179–182, 212–215
Concise writing, 166
Conclusions
  absolute statements and, 221–222
  drawn from photos, 220
  explanation of, 219
  main ideas in, 122
  method to draw logical, 220–221
Connotation, 490
Consent form, drug testing, 100–101
Context clues
  to discover meaning of vocabulary, 33, 67
  types of, 67–69
Contrast, 315, 320
Cornell Notes, 311
Credit card agreement, 152–153
Critical reading. *See also* Reading
  distinguishing fact from opinion during, 371–372
  explanation of, 371
  identifying author's intended audience in, 378, 380
  identifying author's purpose in, 376–377
  identifying author's tone in, 378

D

Daily planners, 7–8
"Dangerous Duty" (Fennessy), 82–83
"Dangerously Strong" (Larsen), 334–338
Dashes, 68
Definition pattern
  explanation of, 317
  main ideas in, 121
Definitions
  as context clue, 67–68
  in dictionaries, 487–489
Denotation, 490
Details. *See* Supporting details
Dictionaries
  definitions in, 487–489
  explanation of, 487
  online, 487–488
  use of, 487–489
Digital piracy, 263
Drug Testing Consent Form, 100–101

E

"Escaping the Debt Trap" (Fennessy), 134–136
Examples, 68
Exercise, physical, 430
Expert opinion, 373
Explanations, 68

F

Facts
  distinguishing opinion from, 371–372
  examples of, 371
  explanation of, 371, 372
  sentences containing both opinion and, 373
Fennessy, Corinne, 35–37, 134–136, 144–146, 196–200, 228–232, 238–243, 396–400, 440–443
Figurative speech, 490
Financial aid applications, 250
Flash cards, 69
Flay, Bobby, 184–189
"Flight Nurse Hero" (Fennessy), 35–37
Focus
  on arts and related fields, 262
  on business and personal finance, 114
  on health sciences, 18
  on hospitality and tourism, 164
  on law enforcement, corrections, fire science, and EMT services, 66
  on science, 370
  on sociology and education, 218
  on sports and fitness, 314
  on technology, 420
"From Illegal Immigrant to Brain Surgeon: Dr. Alfredo Quiñones" (Hopkins), 45–48
"From Sketch to Screen: Tim Burton" (Scholastic Art Magazine), 290–294

G

Gearhart, Scott, 406–407
Generalizations, sweeping, 221
"Getting the Job of Your Dreams" (Fennessy), 144–146
Girouard, Meaghan, 300
Glossaries, 487

Goals
identifying your, 4–5
importance of setting, 3–4
sharing your, 5
Graphic aids in textbooks, 56, 155, 208, 253, 304, 359, 462
"A Greener Earth: Energy Alternatives" (Fennessy), 396–400

H

Harden, Marcia Gay, 281–285
Health insurance policy, 206–207
Health sciences, 18
Highlighting
benefits and use of, 23, 25
example of, 22–23
explanation of, 22, 23
Homework assignments, 12, 13. *See also* Reading assignments
Hopkins, C. F., 45–48

I

Immediate memory, 23
Implied main ideas
explanation of, 263–264
identification of, 268–269
Inductive reasoning, 219
Inferential thinking, 219
Information, storage of, 23–24
Installing memory on computer, 458–460

J

Judgment, words that make, 372–373

L

Larsen, Elizabeth Foy, 334–338
LEADS. *See* Context clues
"Leap of Faith" (Santangelo et al.), 91–93
Learning
steps for effective, 431
styles of, 430
Leasing agreement, car, 302
"Let's Talk About Your Life, Son" (Flay), 184–189
Lexile, 10
Listing pattern, 318
Living will, 54–55
Logic, 68–69
Long-term memory, 23–24

M

Main ideas. *See also* Supporting details
central point as, 274
clue to author's purpose in, 376–377
concept mapping and, 177–178
in conclusions, 122
explanation of, 120
identification of, 22, 268–269
implied, 263–264, 268–269
importance of, 121
stated, 268–269
styles to convey, 121–122
support for, 165–166
in topic sentences, 120, 123
topics and, 115
Major details. *See also* Supporting details
concept mapping and, 177–178
explanation of, 165
identification of, 263, 268–269
Memory, 23–25
Metacognition, 432–433
Metaphors, 490
Metzinger, Adam, 151
Millan, Cesar, 4
Minor details. *See also* Supporting details
concept mapping and, 177–178
explanation of, 169
Mistakes, learning from, 3–4
Moise, Arethea, 53
Muhr, Rick, 355
"My Best Role Ever!" (Harden), 281–285
MyReadingLab, 10

N

Note taking
Cornell format for, 311
effective, 424–429
as study aid, 110
tips for, 430
what to write, 426–427
Notebooks, 11–13
Nutrition labels, 408

O

On the Job Interviews
Adam Metzinger, 151
Arethea Moise, 53
David Scott, 102
Kim Walter, 249
Kyle Williams, 461
Meaghan Girouard, 300
Nora Galdiano, 205
Rick Muhr, 355
Scott Gearhart, 406–407
Online dictionaries, 487–488
"Operation Seal Rescue" (Rozenfeld), 386–390
Opinions
distinguishing facts from, 371–372
examples of, 371
expert, 373
explanation of, 371, 372
function of, 372
sentences containing both fact and, 373
words that signal, 372
Order pattern, 321
Organization. *See* Patterns of organization
Outlining, 427–429

P

Paragraphs
main ideas as summary of, 121
outlining, 428
topic sentences in, 120, 123
Paraphrasing, 421–422
Parentheses, 68
Patterns of organization
cause-and-effect, 318
compare-and-contrast, 320
definition, 317
explanation of, 315
listing, 318
recognition of, 328
time order (chronological order), 321
Photos, drawing conclusions from, 220
Phrases, transition, 67, 68, 170–171, 316
Physical exercise, 430
Piracy, digital, 263
Plans, 3, 6
Positive self-talk, 430
Prefixes
examples of, 57
explanation of, 75
table of, 76–77
Preview questions
finding answers to, 22, 26, 28
generation of, 20–21

Previewing
exercises on, 26, 28
explanation of, 20
steps in, 20–21
Pronunciation symbols, in dictionaries, 489
Punctuation, 317
Purpose, of authors, 376–377
Puzzle software, 69

Q

Quotations, paraphrased, 421–422

R

Reading. *See also specific topics*
active, 22–25
distinguishing fact from opinion when, 371–372
identifying author's intended audience when, 378, 380
identifying author's purpose when, 376–377
identifying author's tone when, 378
Reading assignments. *See also* Homework assignments
finding main idea in, 22
making summaries of, 38
recalling information from, 19
Reading comprehension
role of inferential thinking in, 219
vocabulary skills to improve, 67
Reading process
active reading step in, 22–25
highlighting and annotating step in, 22–23
practice activities on, 26–30
preview step in, 20–21, 26
review step in, 25, 32
test taking and, 430
Reading rate
factors that influence, 492
improving your, 491–492
timing your, 491–492
Reading selections
"Attack of the Cyber-Thieves" (Collins and Shemko), 449–453
"Bionic Soldiers" (Fennessy), 440–443
"College Drinking: Harmless Fun?" (Fennessy), 228–232
"Dangerous Duty" (Fennessy), 82–83
"Dangerously Strong" (Larsen), 334–338
"Escaping the Debt Trap" (Fennessy), 134–136
"Flight Nurse Hero" (Fennessy), 35–37
"From Illegal Immigrant to Brain Surgeon: Dr. Alfredo Quiñones" (Hopkins), 45–48
"From Sketch to Screen: Tim Burton" (Scholastic Art Magazine), 290–294
"Getting the Job of Your Dreams" (Fennessy), 144–146
"A Greener Earth: Energy Alternatives" (Fennessy), 396–400
"Leap of Faith" (Santangelo et al.), 91–93
"Let's Talk About Your Life, Son" (Flay), 184–189
"My Best Role Ever!" (Harden), 281–285
"Operation Seal Rescue" (Rozenfeld), 386–390
"Student Travel—See the World!" (Fennessy), 196–200
"True Grit: Bethany Hamilton's Story" (Rochlin), 345–349
"Where Wishes Come True" (Fennessy), 238–243
Real-Life Readings
car leasing agreement, 302
credit card agreement, 152–153
Drug Testing Consent Form, 100–101
health insurance policy, 206–207
installing memory on computer, 458–460
living wills, 54–55
nutrition labels, 408
refund and repayment policies, 356
student financial aid applications, 250
Reasoning, inductive, 219
Refund and repayment policies, 356
Relationships within and between sentences, 315
Review of reading material, 25
Rochlin, Margy, 345–349
Roots
examples of, 57
explanation of, 75
table of, 77–78
Rozenfeld, Monica, 386–390

S

Santangelo, Mike, 91–93
Scott, David, 102
Self-evaluation checklists, 17, 65, 113, 163, 217, 261, 313, 369, 419, 471
Sentences
containing both facts and opinions, 373
paraphrased, 421–422
relationships within and between, 315
Shemko, Jackie, 449–453
Shipley, Stephen, 82–83
Similes, 490
Simple listing, 318
Smith, Larry, 82–83
Sousa, David A., 432
Stress-reduction techniques, 430
Student financial aid applications, 250
"Student Travel—*See* the World!" (Fennessy), 196–200
Study schedules
form for recording, 8
importance of, 25, 430
information for, 6
Study skills
activities to develop, 15, 160–161
guidelines to develop, 430–431
metacognition, 432–433
notes to enhance, 110
outlining, 427–429
paraphrasing, 421–422
summarizing, 421, 423–424
test taking, 430–431
Subjects. *See* Topics
Suffixes
examples of, 57
explanation of, 75
table of, 78
Sullivan, Wilson, III, 73
Summaries
example of, 423–424
explanation of, 423
of reading assignments, 38, 84
Summarizing, 421, 423–424
Supporting details. *See also* Main ideas
concept mapping and, 177–178
explanation of, 165
function of, 169

Supporting details (*Continued*)
  major, 168–171, 263, 268–269
  minor, 169
  organization of, 328
  transitions to introduce, 170–171
Sweeping generalizations, 221
Syllabus, 13
Synonyms, 67

T

Teams
  learning vocabulary in, 74, 88, 237
  skills for working in, 3
  textbook preview by, 30–31
Tests
  note cards to prepare for, 110
  studying for, 430–431
  tips for day of, 431
  tips when taking, 431
Textbooks
  glossaries in, 487
  graphic aids in, 56, 155, 208, 253, 304, 359, 410, 462
  previews of, 30
  sample selections from, 31, 108–109, 119, 130–131, 175, 225, 257, 267, 273, 279, 325, 332, 376, 384, 437–438
than/then, 320
Thesis statement, central point as, 274
Three-ring binders, 11–12
Time management
  daily planners for, 7–8
  importance of, 6
  making choices for, 6–7
Time order pattern, 321
Timed readings, 491–492
Tone
  of authors, 378
  explanation of, 378
Tone words, 379
Topic sentences
  clues for patterns of organization in, 328
  explanation of, 120
  facts about, 125
  main ideas in, 120, 123
  placement of, 124–125
  restatement of, 125
Topics
  explanation of, 115
  method to find, 115, 116, 123
  specific vs. general, 116–117
Transitions
  cause-and-effect, 318
  comparison, 320
  as context clue, 67, 68
  contrast, 320
  definition, 317
  explanation of, 170, 316
  as introduction to supporting details, 170–171
  listing, 318
  time order, 321
"True Grit: Bethany Hamilton's Story" (Rochlin), 345–349
Tutoring services, 430

V

Vocabulary
  context clues to determine, 33, 67–69, 73
  discovering meaning of, 33
  methods to study, 69
  understanding word parts to learn, 57, 75–78
Vocabulary activities
  crosswords, 42, 204, 248
  guess the phrase, 405, 458
  matching game, 344
  puzzle grid, 99
  speed quizzes, 141, 194, 204
  team password, 150
  word drawing game, 289
  word mazes, 52
  word search, 299

W

Walter, Kim, 249
"Where Wishes Come True" (Fennessy), 238–243
Williams, Kyle, 461
Wills, living, 54–55
Word bytes, 22
Word parts, 57, 75–78. *See also* Prefixes; Roots; Suffixes
Words
  denotation and connotation of, 490
  that make judgments, 372–373
  that signal opinion, 371, 372
  tone, 379
  transition, 67, 68, 170–171, 316–321
Working memory, 23
Writing
  concise, 166
  determining purpose of, 376–377

Z

Zullo, Allan, 91–93